Understanding Automotive Electronics

Third Edition

By: William B. Ribbens, Ph.D.
Professor of Electrical Engineering
Director, Vehicular Electronics Library
University of Michigan
Staff Consultant, Texas Instruments Information Publishing Center

Norman P. Mansour, MSEE
Research Associate, Vehicular Electronics Laboratory
University of Michigan
Staff Consultant, Texas Instruments Information Publishing Center

With contributions by: Gerald Luecke, MSEE
Mgr. Technical Products Development
Texas Instruments Information Publishing Center

Charles W. Battle, Editor
Edward C. Jones, Editor
Leslie E. Mansir, Editor
Texas Instruments Information Publishing Center

Revised by: William B. Ribbens, Ph.D.

HOWARD W. SAMS & COMPANY
A Division of Macmillan, Inc.
11711 North College, Suite 141, Carmel, IN 46032 USA

THIRD EDITION
THIRD PRINTING—1990

International Standard Book Number: 0-672-27064-1
Library of Congress Catalog Number: 88-60681

Acquisitions Editor: *Greg Michael*
Development Editor: *James Rounds*
Editor: *Louis Keglovits*
Third Edition Illustrations: *T. R. Emrick*
Word Processor: *Gertrude A. Noble*
Compositor: *Shepard Poorman Communications Corporation*

Printed in the United States of America

Table of Contents

Preface

In the years since the first and second editions of this book were published, there have been significant advances in the application of electronics to the automobile. These advances have rendered the earlier editions of this book somewhat obsolete. Many ideas that were presented in the chapter on future automotive electronic systems have become incorporated in production automobiles. These changes in automotive electronics technology and the obsolescence of the earlier editions have been the motivation for this third edition.

Perhaps the most significant change in automotive electronics since this book was first written is the almost exclusive use of digital rather than analog circuits. Microprocessors and special-purpose computers are now widely used in automotive electronic systems for control and instrumentation applications. In addition, significant changes in sensors and actuators have influenced the implementation of various functions on the automobile and have permitted new functions to be performed.

Although this third edition retains the basic structure of the previous editions, it has been brought up to date with respect to technical developments. There is expanded discussion of digital electronics, particularly with respect to microprocessor and microcomputer applications in the automobile. Similarly, new sensor and actuator technology is explained, as well as the application of these devices in control and instrumentation. Several electronic systems which have reached production since the second edition are explained in detail. An entirely new chapter is devoted to the important function of diagnosing problems in automotive electronic systems.

In its revised form this book explains automotive electronics as of the late 1980s and should prepare the reader for an understanding of future developments in this interesting field.

William B. Ribbens

Automotive Fundamentals

Picture yourself in the not-too-distant future driving your new car along a rural interstate highway on a business trip. The cruise control is maintaining the speed at a steady 100 km/hr (62 mph) and there is relatively little traffic. As you approach a slower moving car, the speed-control system slows your car to match the speed of the slower car and maintain a safe distance of about 165 feet behind the slower car. When oncoming traffic clears, you enter the passing lane and your car automatically increases speed as you pass the slower car.

You press a button on the steering column and an image of a road map appears faintly visible (so as not to obscure the road ahead) on the windshield in front of you. This map shows your present position and the position of the destination city. The distance to your destination and the approximate arrival time are displayed on the digital instrument cluster.

You are talking on your cellular phone to your office about some changes in a contract which you hope to negotiate. After the instructions for the contract changes are completed, a printer in your car generates a copy of the latest contract version.

The onboard entertainment system is playing music for you at a comfortable level relative to the low level wind and road noise in the car. After completing your phone conversation, you press another button on the steering wheel and the music is replaced by a recorded lesson in French verb conjugation which you have been studying. Suddenly, the French lesson is interrupted by a message delivered in natural sounding synthesized speech. "You have fuel remaining for another 50 miles at the present speed. Your destination is 23 miles away. Recommend refueling after exiting the highway. There is a station which accepts your electronic credit near the exit (you know, of course, that the electronic credit is activated by inserting the fuel nozzle into the car). Also, the left rear tire pressure is low and the engine control system reports that the mass air flow sensor is intermittently malfunctioning and should be serviced soon." After this message has been delivered, the French lesson returns.

A short time later, the French lesson is again interrupted by the electronic voice message system: "Replace the disk in the Navigation CD player with disk number 37 for detailed map and instructions to your destination please." Then the French lesson returns.

You insert the correct disk in the Navigation CD player as requested and the map display on the windshield changes. The new display shows a detailed map of your present position and the route to your destination.

As you approach the city limits, the car speed is automatically reduced to the legal limit of 55 mph. The voice message system speaks again: "Leave the highway at exit 203 which is one-half mile away. Proceed along Austin road to the second intersection which is Meyer road. Turn right and proceed 0.1 mile. Your destination is on the righthand side of the road. Don't forget to refuel."

This scenario is not as farfetched as it sounds. All of the events described are technically possible. Some have even been tested experimentally. The electronic technology required to develop a car with the features described exists today. The actual implementation of such electronic features will depend on the cost of the equipment and the market acceptance of the features.

USE OF ELECTRONICS IN THE AUTOMOBILE

Microelectronics will provide many exciting new features for automobiles.

Electronics has been relatively slow in coming to the automobile primarily because of the relationship between the added cost and the benefits. Historically, the first electronics was introduced into the commercial automobile during the decade 1930–1940 in the form of automobile radio receivers. There were a few attempts to introduce electronic ignition and electronically controlled fuel injection during the late 1950s and early 1960s. However, customers did not particularly want these options so they were discontinued from production automobiles.

Environmental regulations and an increased need for economy have resulted in electronics being used within a number of automotive systems.

Two major events occurred during the 1970s which started the trend toward the use of modern electronics in the automobile: (1) the introduction of government regulations for exhaust emissions and fuel economy which required better control of the engine than was possible with the methods being used; and (2) the development of relatively low cost per function solid-state digital electronics which could be used for engine control.

Electronics are being used now in the automobile and probably will be used even more in the future. Some of the present and potential applications for electronics are:

1. electronic engine control for minimizing exhaust emissions and maximizing fuel economy
2. instrumentation for measuring vehicle performance parameters and for diagnosis of on-board system malfunctions
3. driveline control
4. vehicle motion control
5. safety and convenience
6. entertainment/communication/navigation

Many of these applications of electronics will be discussed in this book.

ABOUT THIS CHAPTER

This chapter will give the reader a general overview of the automobile with emphasis on the basic operation of the engine, thus providing the reader with the background to see how electronic controls have been and will be applied. The discussion is simplified to provide the reader with just enough information to understand automotive electronics. Readers who want to know the mechanics of an automobile in more detail are referred to the many books written for that purpose.

THE AUTOMOBILE

The important systems of the automobile are illustrated in *Figure 1-1* and include:

1. engine
2. drivetrain
3. instrumentation
4. suspension
5. steering
6. brakes

In *Figure 1-1*, the frame or chassis upon which the body is mounted is supported by the wheel suspension system. (Some passenger cars are constructed so that the auto body and chassis are not separate.) Moreover, many of the newer cars are being designed with front wheel drive. Nevertheless, this figure provides a convenient reference for discussing automotive fundamentals.

We will see in this book that whenever electronics is used, significant improvements have been achieved in automobile performance.

THE ENGINE

The engine in an automobile provides all the power for moving the automobile, for the hydraulic and pneumatic systems, and for the electrical system. A variety of engine types have been produced, but one class of engine is used most; i.e., the internal combustion, piston type, four stroke/cycle, gasoline fueled, spark ignited, liquid-cooled engine. This engine will be referred to in this book as the spark ignited or SI engine. A typical SI engine is depicted in *Figure 1-2*.

The major components of the engine include:

1. engine block
2. cylinder
3. crankshaft
4. pistons
5. connecting rods
6. camshaft
7. cylinder head
8. valves
9. intake system
10. ignition system
11. exhaust system
12. cooling system

Figure 1-1.
Systems of the Automobile

In most newer cars the engine is mounted transversely for front wheel drive.

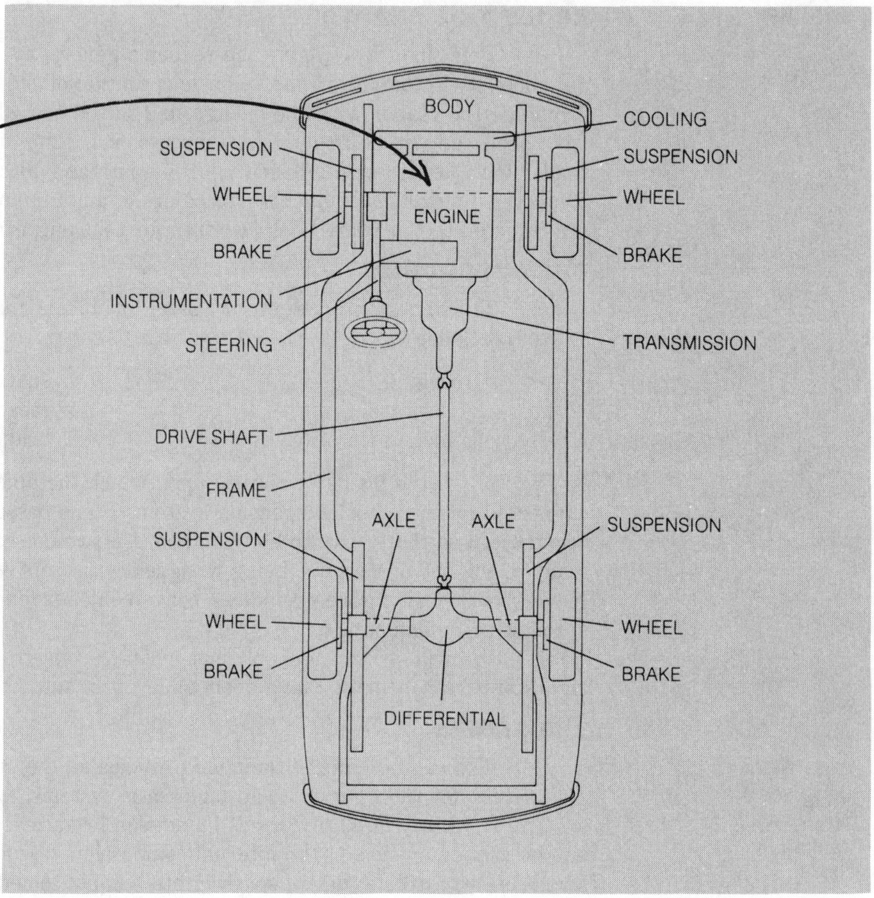

Engine Block

Conventional internal combustion engines convert the movement of pistons to the rotational energy used to drive the wheels.

The cylinders are cast in the engine block and machined to a smooth finish. The pistons have rings which provide a tight sliding seal against the cylinder wall. The pistons are connected to the crankshaft by connecting rods as shown in *Figure 1-3*. The crankshaft converts the up and down motion of the pistons to the rotary motion needed to drive the wheels.

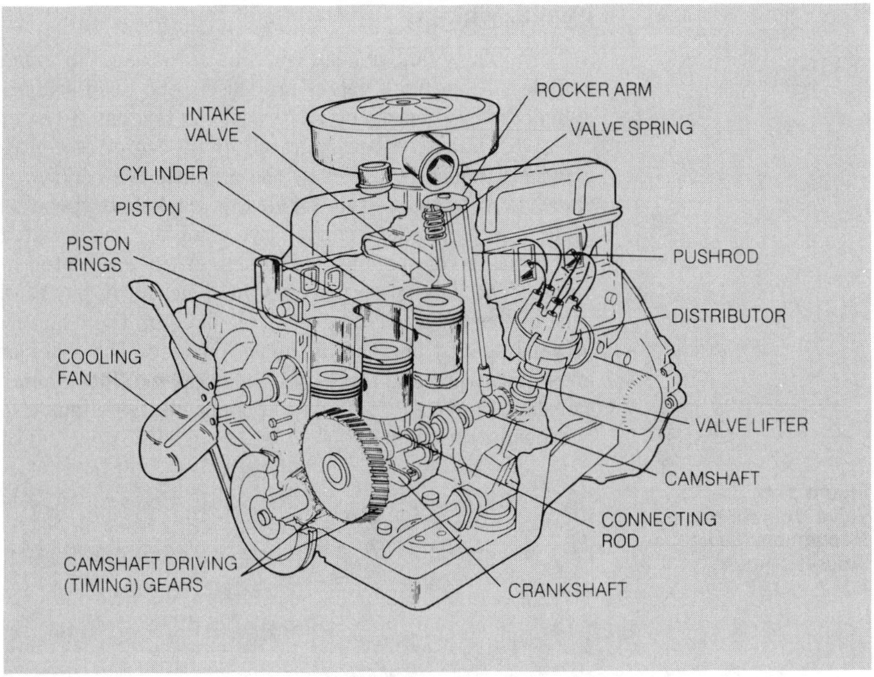

Figure 1-2. Cutaway View of a Six-Cylinder, Overhead-Valve, In-Line Engine *(Source: Crouse)*

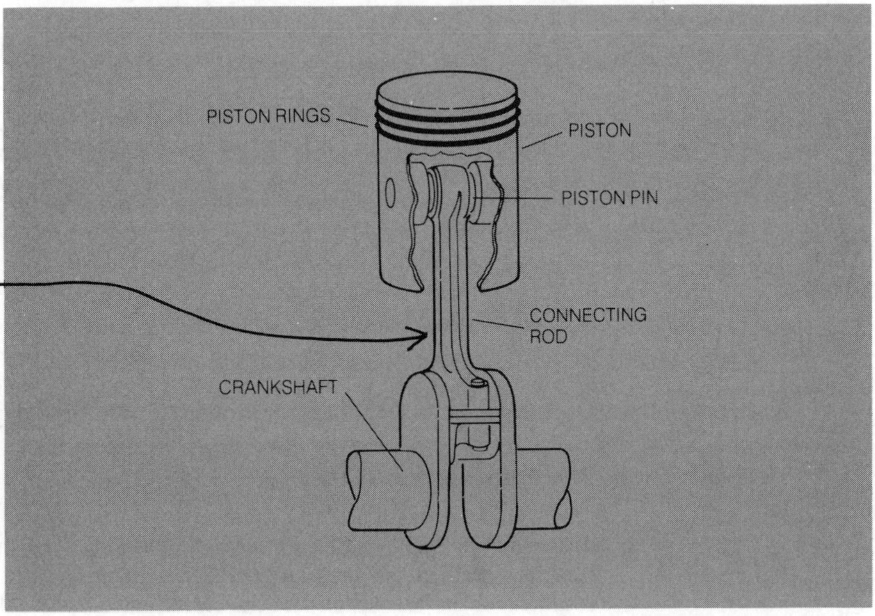

Figure 1-3. Piston Connection to Crankshaft *(Source: Crouse)*

Force due to combustion pressure is applied through the connecting rod to produce torque at the crankshaft.

Cylinder Head

The cylinder head contains an intake and exhaust valve for each cylinder. When both valves are closed, the head seals the top of the cylinder while the piston rings seal the bottom of the cylinder.

The valves are operated by off-center (eccentric) cams on the camshaft, which is driven by the crankshaft as shown in *Figure 1-4.* The camshaft rotates at exactly half the crankshaft speed because a complete cycle of any cylinder involves two complete crankshaft rotations and only one sequence of opening and closing of the associated intake and exhaust valves. The valves are normally held closed by powerful springs. When the time comes for a valve to open, the lobe on the cam forces the pushrod upward against one end of the rocker arm. The other end of the rocker arm goes downward and forces the valve open. (Note: Some engines have the camshaft above the head so the pushrods are eliminated. This is called an overhead cam engine.)

Figure 1-4. Valve Operating Mechanism *(Source: Crouse)*

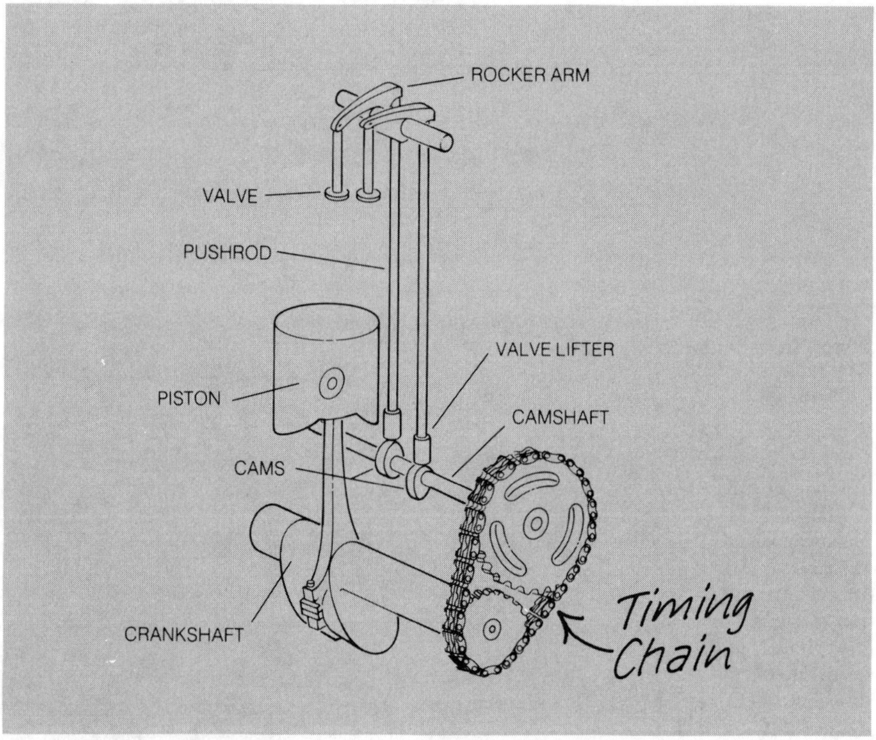

The Four-Stroke Cycle

The operation of the engine can be understood by considering the actions in any one cylinder during a complete cycle of the engine. One complete cycle in the 4-stroke/cycle SI engine requires two complete rotations of the crankshaft. As the crankshaft rotates, the piston moves up

Conventional SI engines operate using four "strokes," with either an up or down movement of each piston. These strokes are named intake, compression, power, and exhaust.

and down in the cylinder. In the two complete revolutions of the crankshaft that make up one cycle, there are 4 separate strokes of the piston from the top of the cylinder to the bottom or from the bottom to the top. *Figure 1–5* illustrates the 4 strokes for a 4-stroke/cycle SI engine which are called:

1. intake
2. compression
3. power
4. exhaust

There are two valves for each cylinder. The left valve in the figure is called the intake valve and the right valve is called the exhaust valve. The intake valve is normally larger than the exhaust valve. Note that the crankshaft is assumed to be rotating in a clockwise direction. The action of the engine during the 4 strokes is described below.

Intake

During the intake stroke (*Figure 1–5a*), the piston is moving from top to bottom and the intake valve is open. As the piston moves down, a partial vacuum is created which draws a mixture of air and vaporized gasoline through the intake valve into the cylinder. The intake valve is closed after the piston reaches the bottom. This position is normally called bottom dead center (BDC).

Compression

The intake stroke draws a combustible mixture of air and gasoline into the cylinder; the compression stroke compresses this mixture in preparation for combustion.

During the compression stroke (*Figure 1–5b*), the piston moves upward and compresses the fuel and air mixture against the cylinder head. When the piston is near the top of this stroke, the ignition system produces an electrical spark at the tip of the spark plug. [The top of the stroke is normally called top dead center (TDC).] The spark ignites the air-fuel mixture and the mixture burns rapidly causing a rapid and extreme rise in the pressure in the cylinder.

Power

The power stroke ignites the mixture and creates a downward force on the surface of the piston. The exhaust stroke forces the exit of burned gases from the cylinder, in preparation for the next intake stroke.

During the power stroke (*Figure 1–5c*), the the high pressure created by the burning mixture forces the piston downward. It is only during this stroke that actual usable power is generated by the engine.

Exhaust

During the exhaust stroke (*Figure 1–5d*), the piston is again moving upward. The exhaust valve is open and the piston forces the burned gases from the cylinder through the exhaust port into the exhaust system and out the tailpipe into the atmosphere.

Figure 1-5. Illustration of the 4 Strokes of a Typical, Modern, Gasoline Fueled *Spark Ignition* Engine.

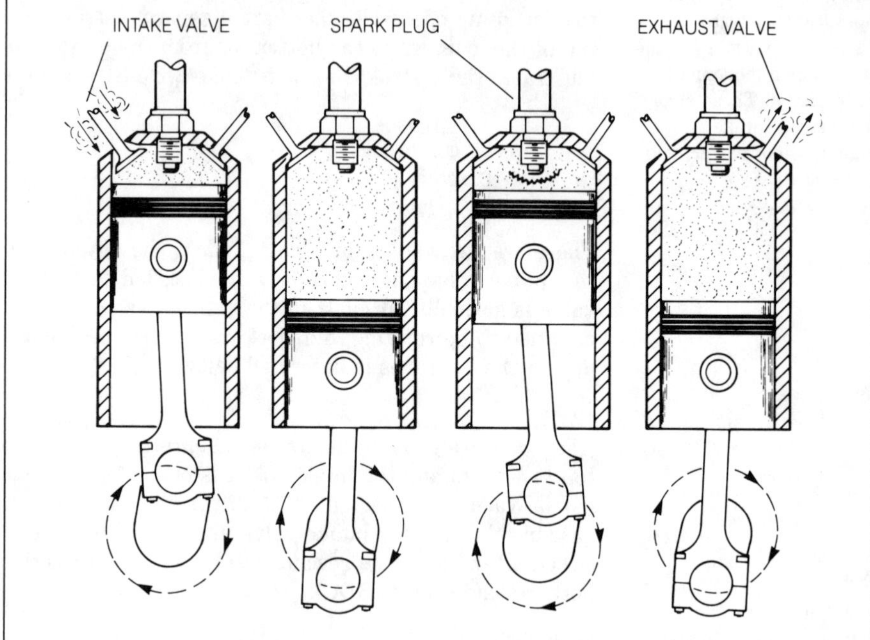

This four-stroke cycle is repeated continuously as the crankshaft rotates. In a single cylinder engine, power is produced only during the power stroke which is only one-quarter of the cycle. In order to maintain crankshaft rotation during the other three-quarters of the cycle, a flywheel is used. The flywheel is a relatively large, heavy, circular, object which is connected to the crankshaft. The primary purpose of the flywheel is to provide inertia to keep the crankshaft rotating during the three nonpower-producing strokes of the piston.

Each piston on a 4-cycle SI engine produces actual power during just one out of four cycles.

In a multicylinder engine, the power strokes are staggered so power is produced during a larger fraction of the cycle than for a single cylinder engine. In a four-cylinder engine, for example, power is produced almost continually by the separate power strokes of the 4 cylinders. The shaded regions of *Figure 1-6* indicate which cylinder is producing power for each 180 degrees of crankshaft rotation. (Remember that one complete engine cycle requires two complete crankshaft rotations of 360 degrees each for a total of 720 degrees.)

Figure 1-6.
Power Pulses from a 4 Cylinder Engine

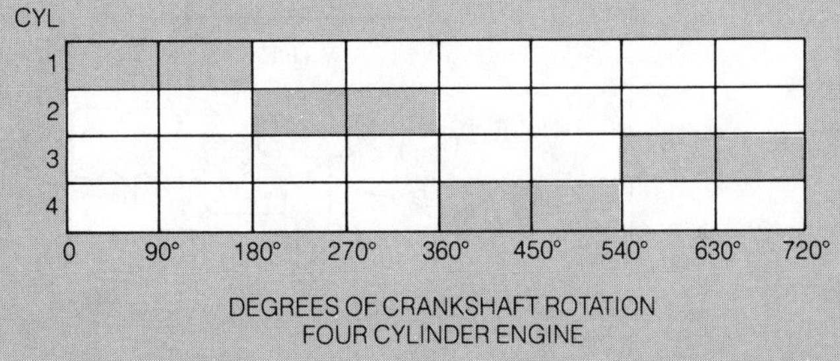

INTAKE SYSTEM

The intake system consists of a carburetor and an assembly of passageways called the intake manifold. The carburetor mixes the air and fuel and the intake manifold routes the mixture to the cylinders, as shown in *Figure 1-7*.

A combination of carburetor and intake manifold is used to route precise amounts of fuel and air to individual cylinders.

The *proportion* of air and fuel in the mixture delivered to the cylinder is basically controlled by the size and shape of the bore of the carburetor, and the size and shape of the metering rods and seats (sometimes called "jets") in the carburetor. The proportion of air and fuel in the mixture is expressed by the ratio of the mass (weight) of air to the mass (weight) of fuel. This ratio is appropriately called the air/fuel ratio. In normal operation, the air/fuel ratio varies in the range of 12:1 to 17:1 (before the advent of emission controls).

The *amount* of the air and fuel mixture delivered to the engine is controlled by the throttle plate. The throttle plate, which acts as an air flow control valve, is controlled by the accelerator pedal.

It is beyond the scope of this book to discuss the details of carburetor operation, but it is important to realize that each carburetor is designed to deliver the correct proportion of air and fuel for a specific engine.

IGNITION SYSTEM

The ignition system provides an electric spark during the compression stroke which ignites the air-fuel mixture. This spark consists of an electric arc across the electrodes of the spark plug. The operation of the ignition system can be explained by describing the operation of a traditional nonelectronic system. (Engine performance has already been greatly improved using electronics in the ignition system. This will be discussed in a later chapter.)

Figure 1-7. Carburetor and Intake Manifold

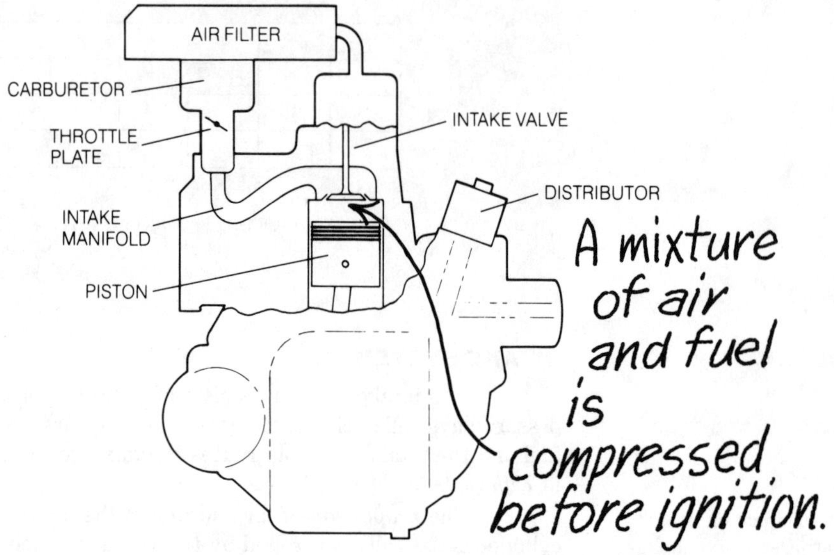

Spark

A typical spark plug configuration is shown in *Figure 1-8.* The spark plug consists of a pair of electrodes, called the center and ground electrodes, separated by a gap. The gap size is important and is specified for each engine. The gap may be 0.025 inch (0.6mm) for one engine and 0.040 inch (1mm) for another engine. The center electrode is insulated from the ground electrode and the metallic shell assembly. The ground electrode is at electrical ground potential because one terminal of the battery is connected to the engine block and frame. This is called the ground connection.

The spark is produced by applying a high-voltage pulse of from 20 kV to 40 kV (1 kV is 1,000 volts) between the center electrode and ground. The actual voltage required to start the arc varies with the size of the gap, the compression ratio, and the air/fuel ratio. Once the arc is started, the voltage required to sustain it is much lower because the gas mixture near the gap becomes highly ionized. (An ionized gas allows current to flow more freely.) The arc is sustained long enough to ignite the air-fuel mixture.

Figure 1-8. Spark Plug Configuration

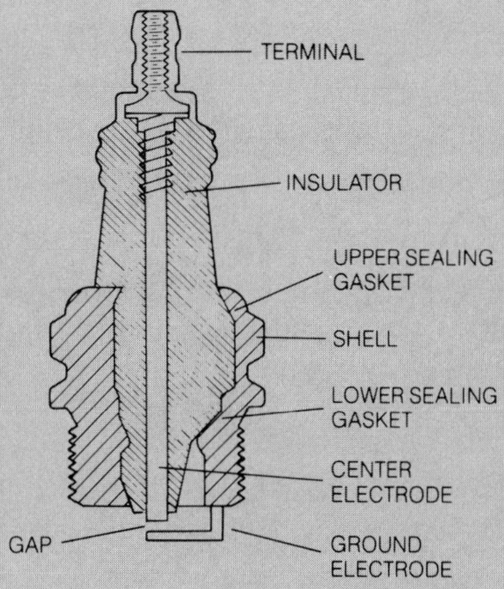

High-Voltage Circuit and Distribution

A special type of electrical transformer, called an ignition coil, is used to create a high-voltage pulse that creates a spark at the spark plug. The distributor transfers this high voltage pulse to the proper spark plug at the correct time.

The ignition system provides the high-voltage pulse which initiates the arc. *Figure 1-9* is a schematic diagram of the electrical circuit for the ignition system. The high-voltage pulse is generated by inductive discharge of a special high-voltage transformer commonly called an ignition coil. The high-voltage pulse is delivered to the appropriate spark plug at the correct time for ignition by a rotary switch which is called a distributor. The rotary switch is driven by the camshaft and the mechanical arrangement ensures that the high voltage is switched to the correct spark plug at the correct time. *Figure 1-10* is an illustration of a distributor.

A set of electrical leads, commonly called spark plug wires, is connected between the various spark plug center terminals and individual terminals in the distributor cap. The center terminal in the distributor cap is connected to the ignition coil secondary.

The rotor on the distributor forms a high voltage switch that distributes the voltage pulse to the selected spark plug.

The rotating part of the high voltage switch, appropriately called the rotor, is driven by the camshaft and distributes the high voltage pulse from the coil to the appropriate spark plug wire. Remember that the camshaft rotates at one-half the crankshaft speed; therefore, one ignition pulse is provided to each cylinder for each two revolutions of the crankshaft.

Figure 1-9. Schematic Diagram of Ignition Circuit

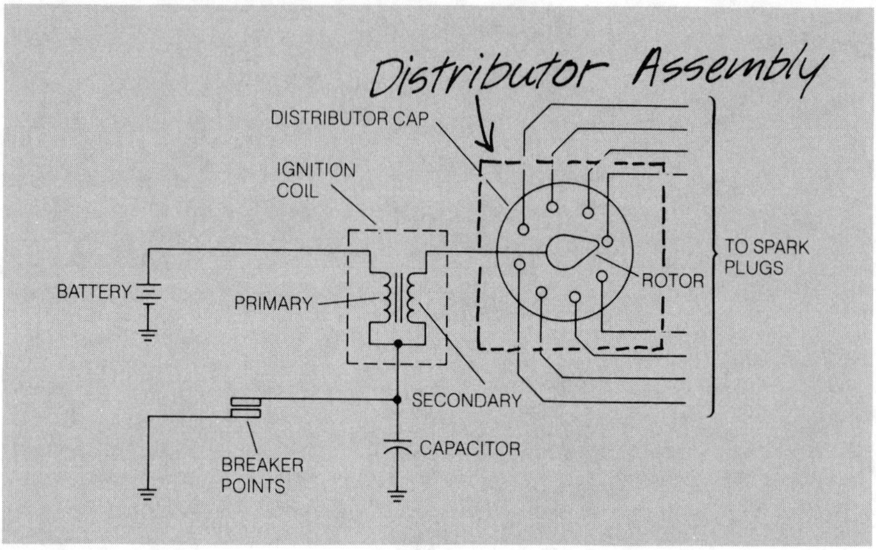

Primary Circuit

A mechanism in the distributor of a conventional ignition system opens and closes the primary circuit of the coil by operating a switch commonly called the breaker points. During the intervals between ignition pulses (i.e., when the rotor is between contacts), the breaker points are closed (known as dwell). Current flows through the primary of the coil and a magnetic field is created which links the primary and secondary of the coil.

The distributor in a conventional ignition system uses a mechanically activated switch called breaker points. The interruption of ignition coil current when the breaker points open produces an HV pulse in the secondary.

At the instant the spark pulse is required, the breaker points are opened. This interrupts the flow of current in the primary of the coil and the magnetic field collapses rapidly. The rapid collapse of the magnetic field induces the high voltage pulse in the secondary of the coil. This pulse is routed through the distributor rotor, the terminal in the distributor cap, and the spark plug wire to the appropriate spark plug. The capacitor absorbs the primary current which continues to flow during the short interval in which the points are opening and prevents arcing at the breaker points.

The waveform of the primary current is illustrated in *Figure 1-11*. The primary current increases with time after the points close (a). At the instant the points open, this current begins to fall rapidly. It is during this rapid drop in primary current that the secondary high voltage pulse occurs (b). The primary current oscillates (the "wavy" portion) (c) because of the resonant circuit formed between the coil and capacitor.

Figure 1-10. Distributor

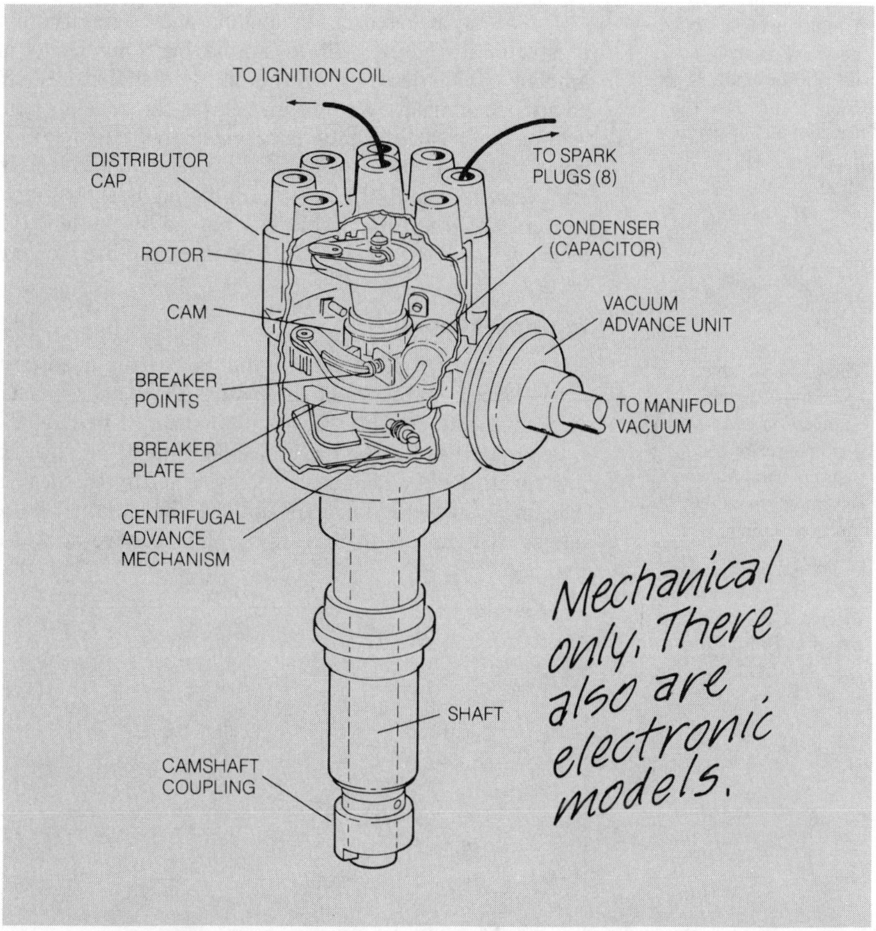

Figure 1-11. Primary Current Waveform

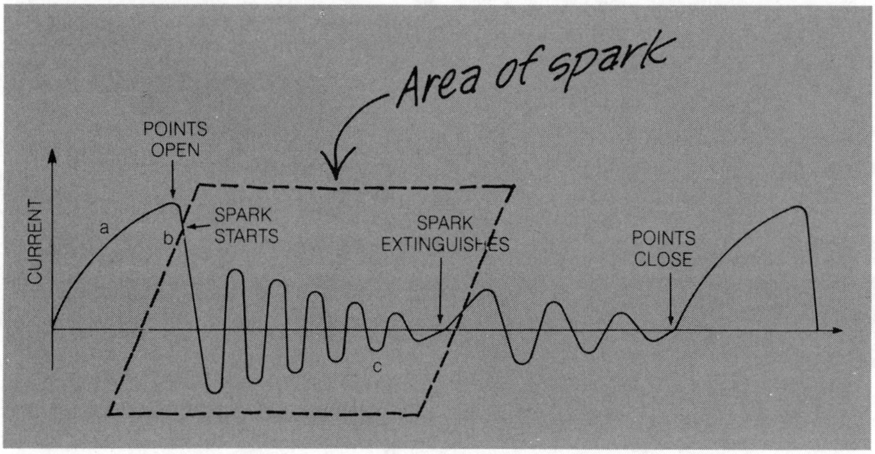

A multisurfaced cam, mounted on the distributor shaft, is used to open and close the breaker points (*Figure 1-12*).

The mechanism for opening and closing the breaker points is illustrated in *Figure 1-12*. A cam having a number of lobes equal to the number of cylinders is mounted on the distributor shaft. As this cam rotates, it alternately opens and closes the breaker points. The movable arm of the breaker points has an insulated rubbing block which is pressed against the cam by a spring. When the rubbing block is aligned with a flat surface on the cam, the points are closed as shown in *Figure 1-12a*. As the cam rotates, the rubbing block is moved by the lobe (high point) on the cam as shown in *Figure 1-12b*. At this time, the breaker points open and spark occurs.

Ignition Timing

The point at which ignition occurs, in comparison to the top dead center of the piston's compression stroke, is known as ignition timing.

Ignition occurs some time before top dead center (BTDC) during the compression stroke of the piston. This time is measured in degrees of crankshaft rotation BTDC. For a modern SI engine, this timing is typically 8 to 10 degrees for the basic mechanical setting with the engine running at low speed (RPM). This basic timing is set by the design of the mechanical coupling between crankshaft and the distributor. The basic timing may be adjusted slightly in many cars by physically rotating the distributor housing.

Figure 1-12. Breaker-Point Operation

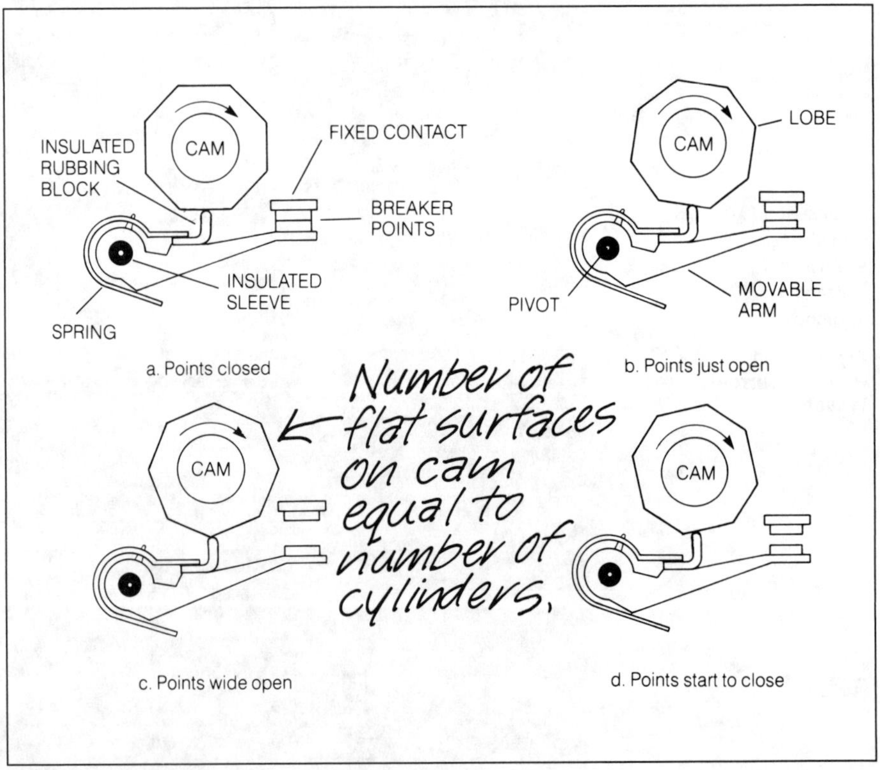

Spark advance changes ignition timing as the speed of an engine increases.

As the engine speed increases, the angle through which the crankshaft rotates in the time required to burn the fuel and air mixture increases. For this reason, the spark must occur at a larger angle BTDC for higher engine speeds. This change in ignition timing is called spark advance. That is, spark advance should increase with increasing engine RPM. In a conventional ignition system, the mechanism for this is called a centrifugal spark advance. It is shown in *Figure 1-10.* As engine speed increases, the distributor shaft rotates faster, and the weights are thrown outward by centrifugal force. The weights operate through a mechanical lever so their movement causes a change in the relative angular position between the rubbing block on the breaker points and the distributor cam, and advances the time when the lobe opens the points.

Ignition timing also varies with pressure within the intake manifold. A vacuum advance mechanism senses the pressure within the intake manifold, and adjusts the timing accordingly.

In addition to speed-dependent spark advance, there is a need to adjust the ignition timing as a function of intake manifold pressure. Whenever the throttle is nearly closed, the manifold pressure is low (i.e., nearly a vacuum). The combustion time for the air-fuel mixture is longer for low manifold pressure conditions than for high manifold pressure conditions (i.e., near atmospheric pressure). As a result, the spark timing must be advanced for low pressure conditions to maintain maximum power and fuel economy. The mechanism to do this is a vacuum operated spark advance. This is also shown in *Figure 1-10.* The vacuum advance mechanism has a flexible diaphragm connected through a rod to the plate on which the breaker points are mounted. One side of the diaphragm is open to atmospheric pressure and the other side is connected through a hose to manifold vacuum. As manifold vacuum increases, the diaphragm is deflected (atmospheric pressure pushes it) and moves the breaker point plate to advance the timing.

Because ignition timing is critical to engine performance, controlling it electronically is a major automotive application.

Ignition timing significantly affects engine performance and exhaust emissions; therefore, it is one of the major factors that is electronically controlled in the modern SI engine. The performance of the ignition system and the spark advance mechanism has been greatly improved by electronic control systems.

DIESEL ENGINE

Clearly the vast majority of automobile engines are SI engines. For many years, alternative engines such as the diesel were simply not able to compete effectively with the SI engine in the United States. Diesel engines were used mostly in heavy duty vehicles such as large trucks, ships, railroad locomotives, earthmoving machinery, etc. The use of diesel engines in passenger cars has been slow in coming to the United States, although now its use is increasing. The motivation for this increased application comes largely from the lower cost of diesel fuel as compared to gasoline and from the better fuel economy of the diesel engine as compared to the gasoline engine.

In many ways, the 4-stroke/cycle diesel engine closely resembles the SI engine. It has a crankshaft, cylinders, pistons, intake and exhaust valves and is usually water cooled. However, there are significant differences between these two classes of engine. For example, the diesel

Diesel engines are similar in basic design to SI engines. However, diesel engines lack an ignition system. Instead, the diesel engine relies on a combination of fuel injection and very high pressure to produce the ignition sequence required for combustion.

engine has no ignition system for normal engine operation. Moreover, the cylinder head, in the best case, contains a fuel injector for each cylinder instead of a spark plug. (A glow plug is used to help heat the air only during starting.) Instead of a high voltage distribution system there is a fuel distribution system. It consists of a fuel pump, fuel filters, a mixture controller, fuel distribution lines, and fuel injectors. *Figure 1-13* shows a cutaway view of a passenger car diesel engine.

The diesel engine has a higher compression ratio and a heavier, stronger construction than the SI engine. The modern SI engine's compression ratio is typically around 8:1 and rarely exceeds 12:1. The diesel engine's compression ratio is typically around 21:1. The cylinder pressure during the power stroke of a diesel has a very rapid rise (almost like an explosion) which places a high stress on the engine's structure. This is the reason for the heavy construction.

The theory of operation of the diesel engine can be explained with reference to *Figure 1-14*. In the diesel engine, the fuel and air are not mixed external to the cylinder as they are in the gasoline engine. After an engine is running and during the intake stroke, the intake valve is open and air alone is drawn into the cylinder. During the compression stroke, this air is compressed by a very large ratio to a very high cylinder pressure of about 500 psi. This high compression heats the air to about 1,000 degrees F. (A simple way to realize the heating effect of compressing air is to feel the bottom of a bicycle air pump after it has been used for a few minutes to inflate tires.) When the fuel is injected near the top of the compression stroke, it is ignited by this high pressure, high temperature compressed air. The cylinder pressure rises rapidly and the tremendous force drives the piston down during the power stroke. Finally, on the exhaust stroke, the exhaust valve opens and the combustion products are forced out of the cylinder. This four-stroke cycle repeats continuously.

One of the important parameters of the diesel engine is the timing of the fuel injection relative to piston position. (This corresponds to the spark timing in the SI engine.) The power produced by the engine is significantly affected by this timing. The control of fuel injection timing is a potential application for an electronic control system.

The timing of the fuel injection is critical to a diesel engine, just as the timing of the spark is critical to an SI engine.

Another parameter affecting diesel engine performance is the speed with which the fuel is injected into the cylinder. The time interval of the combustion process is influenced by this injection speed. There is also a potential for electronically controlling this speed to further optimize engine performance. However, since the majority of automotive engines are the SI engine, the remainder of the book is concerned only with the SI engine.

Figure 1-13.
Four-Cylinder Diesel Engine for Passenger Cars

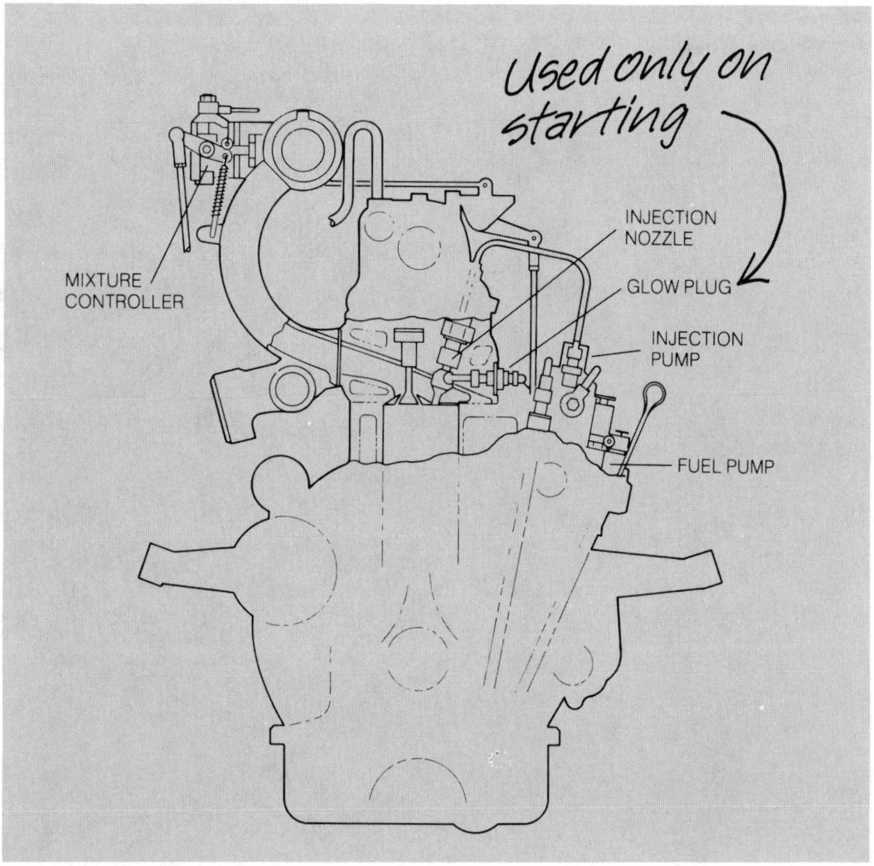

DRIVE TRAIN

The engine drive train system of the automobile consists of the engine, transmission, driveshaft, differential, and driven wheels. We have already discussed the SI engine and we know that it provides the motive power for the automobile. Now let's examine the transmission, driveshaft, and differential in order to understand the role of these devices.

Transmission

The transmission is a gear system which adjusts the ratio of engine speed to wheel speed. Essentially, the transmission enables the engine to operate within its optimum performance range, regardless of the vehicle load or speed. It provides a gear ratio between the engine speed and vehicle speed such that the engine provides adequate power to drive the vehicle at any speed.

Figure 1-14.
Four-Stroke Diesel Cycle

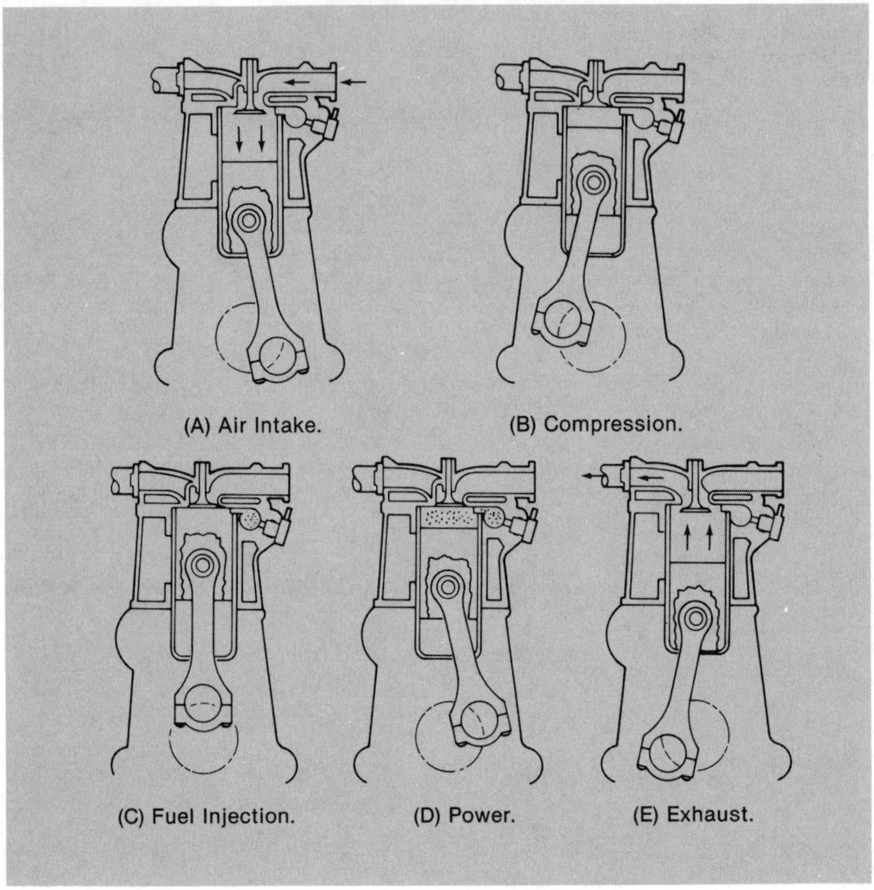

The transmission provides a match between engine speed, and vehicle speed.

To accomplish this with a manual transmission, the driver selects the correct gear ratio from a set of possible gear ratios (usually 3 to 5 for passenger cars). An automatic transmission selects this gear ratio by means of an automatic control system. Most automatic transmissions have three forward gear ratios, although a few have two and some have four. A properly used manual transmission normally has efficiency advantages over an automatic transmission, but the automatic transmission is the most used transmission for passenger automobiles in the United States. In the past automatic transmissions have been controlled by a hydraulic and pneumatic system, but there is a move toward electronic controls in the future. The control system must determine the correct gear ratio by sensing the driver select command, accelerator pedal position, and engine load.

Driveshaft

The driveshaft is used on front engine, rear wheel drive vehicles to couple the transmission output shaft to the differential input shaft. Flexible couplings, called universal joints, allow the rear axle housing and wheels to move up and down while the transmission remains stationary.

Differential

The combination of driveshaft and differential complete the transfer of power from the engine to the rear wheels.

The differential serves three purposes. The most obvious is the right angle transfer of the rotary motion of the driveshaft to the wheels. The second purpose is to allow each driven wheel to turn at a different speed. This is necessary because the "outside"wheel must turn faster than the "inside" wheel when the vehicle is turning a corner. The third purpose is the torque increase provided by the gear ratio. This gear ratio can be changed to allow different torque to be delivered to the wheels while using the same engine and transmission. This gear ratio also affects fuel economy.

Power-assisted steering has become commonplace in recent years and there is a definite trend toward electronic controls and electrically activated power steering. Furthermore, the 4-wheel steering systems will incorporate electronic controls.

SUSPENSION, STEERING, AND BRAKES

Instead of the axles and wheels being directly attached to the frame, they are isolated from the frame by a suspension system to provide a ride inside the car that is much smoother than the road surface over which the car is being driven.

The steering mechanism attached to the front wheels permits the driver to control the direction of vehicle motion by turning the steering wheel. Electronic traction control is advancing rapidly and may become commonplace.

The drum or disk brakes installed on the wheels are the means used to bring the moving automobile to a stop. The most siginficant application of electronics to braking is for antilock braking (discussed later).

Some electronic controls have been applied to braking systems, but thus far electronic control is not commonplace for the suspension and steering of the automobile.

SUMMARY

In this chapter, we have briefly reviewed the major systems of the automobile and discussed the basic engine operation. In addition, we have indicated where electronic technology could be applied to improve performance or reduce cost.

The next few chapters of this book are intended to develop a basic understanding of electronic technology. Then we'll use all this knowledge to examine how electronics has been applied to the major systems. In the last chapter, we'll look at some ideas and methods that may be used in the future.

Quiz for Chapter 1

1. The term TDC refers to
   - a. the engine exhaust system.
   - b. rolling resistance of tires.
   - c. crankshaft position corresponding to a piston at the top of its stroke.
   - d. the distance between headlights.
2. The distributor is
   - a. a rotary switch which connects the ignition coil to the various spark plugs.
   - b. a system for smoothing tire load.
   - c. a system which generates the spark in the cylinders.
   - d. a section of the drivetrain.
3. The air/fuel ratio is
   - a. the rate at which combustible products enter the engine.
   - b. the ratio of the mass of air to the mass of fuel in a cylinder before ignition.
   - c. the ratio of gasoline to air in the exhaust pipe.
   - d. intake air and fuel velocity ratio.
4. Ignition normally occurs
   - a. at BDC.
   - b. at TDC.
   - c. just after TDC.
   - d. just before TDC.
5. Most automobile engines are
   - a. large and heavy.
   - b. gasoline fueled, spark ignited, liquid cooled internal combustion type.
   - c. unable to run at elevations which are below sea level.
   - d. able to operate with any fuel other than gasoline.
6. An exhaust valve is
   - a. a hole in the cylinder head.
   - b. a mechanism for releasing the combustion products from the cylinder.
   - c. the pipe connecting the engine to the muffler.
   - d. a small opening at the bottom of a piston.
7. Power is produced during
   - a. intake stroke.
   - b. compression stroke.
   - c. power stroke.
   - d. exhaust stroke.
8. The transmission
   - a. converts rotary to linear motion.
   - b. optimizes the transfer of engine power to the drivetrain.
   - c. has 4 forward speeds and one reverse.
   - d. automatically selects the highest gear ratio.
9. The suspension system
   - a. partially isolates the body of a car from road vibrations.
   - b. holds the wheels on the axles.
   - c. suspends the driver and passengers.
   - d. consists of 4 springs.
10. The camshaft
   - a. operates the intake and exhaust valves.
   - b. rotates at the same speed as the crankshaft.
   - c. has connecting rods attached to it.
   - d. opens and closes the breaker points.

11. An SI engine is
- **a.** a type of internal combustion engine.
- **b.** a Stirling engine.
- **c.** always fuel injected.
- **d.** none of the above.

12. The intake system refers to
- **a.** the carburetor.
- **b.** a set of tubes.
- **c.** a system of valves, pipes, and throttle plates.
- **d.** the components of an engine through which fuel and air are supplied to the engine.

The Systems Approach to Control and Instrumentation

ABOUT THIS CHAPTER

This chapter is about systems and the systems approach to electronic control and instrumentation. Topics of discussion include what a system is, how to describe what a system does by using diagrams (qualitatively), and how to determine the level of performance of a system through the use of models (quantitatively). The basics of control and instrumentation are discussed, and some specific examples of the systems approach are presented. Most importantly, the material in this chapter lays a foundation for understanding the automotive systems presented in later chapters.

There are many examples of electronic systems in the automobile including:

1. entertainment systems
2. instrumentation (instrument panel) systems
3. engine control systems
4. ride control systems
5. cruise control systems
6. comfort systems

Each of these electronic systems is discussed in this book. However, the present chapter is devoted to explaining the fundamentals of electronic systems for measurement (instrumentation) and for control.

SYSTEMS

A system is a collection of parts that function together to perform a specific task.

A system is a collection of interacting components or parts which function together to perform a specific task. Examples of systems are easy to find. For instance, the bones in the body make up a system called the skeleton which supports the muscles, arteries, veins, and organs that are a part of the cardiovascular and nervous systems. The rules by which we live and conduct ourselves make up our "social system." The exchange of goods and services produces an economic system. We listen to a stereo system and we live within an ecological system. So how can a word (system) be defined that can be applied to such variation? Notice that although each of these systems is unique, they all have at least one thing in common—*each system is a collection of interacting parts.*

This book is concerned primarily with electronic systems that are assemblies of electronic components, interconnected in a way so as to perform a specific task. Each component has an input and an output, and the relationship between these two is determined by the internal configuration.

Systems can often be broken down into a number of subsystems. The subsystems also consist of a number of individual parts.

A stereo system consists of a phonograph, amplifier, and loudspeakers as show in *Figure 2-1a*, but a closer look reveals that the phonograph has a number of parts of its own such as a cartridge and needle, a platter and motor, and a tone arm and switches. The amplifier has even more parts. It is apparent that the stereo system is made up of parts which themselves can be considered a system, while being a subsystem (part) of the stereo system. Each of these subsystems can be further divided into other subsystems, all the way down to the individual nuts, bolts, and electronic devices that make up the lowest level of the system.

It is beneficial to consider an ordinary stereo system as an example of an electronic system. This audio system has features in common with many electronic instrumentation or control systems, and is useful for explaining some of the important issues of this chapter.

Figure 2-1a illustrates the major functional components of the stereo system and its interconnections. Shown in *Figure 2-1b* is another representation known as a block diagram (because the elements are depicted as blocks). Each major functional component is represented by a labeled rectangular block that has an input and an output. The input is shown as an arrow pointing toward the block and the output as an arrow pointing away from the block.

In system science, each component in a system is represented by the functional relationship between its output and input rather than by the details of its internal workings. For example, the amplifier in the stereo system is represented (at least partially) by the relationship

$$v_o = Av_i$$

where

v_o = output voltage
v_i = input voltage
A = voltage gain for the amplifier

Although there are other aspects of the representation of the amplifier, such as input and output impedance or power, that are important in specifying this component, the above equation is adequate for illustrating a functional relationship between output and input.

Figure 2-1. Systems Diagrams

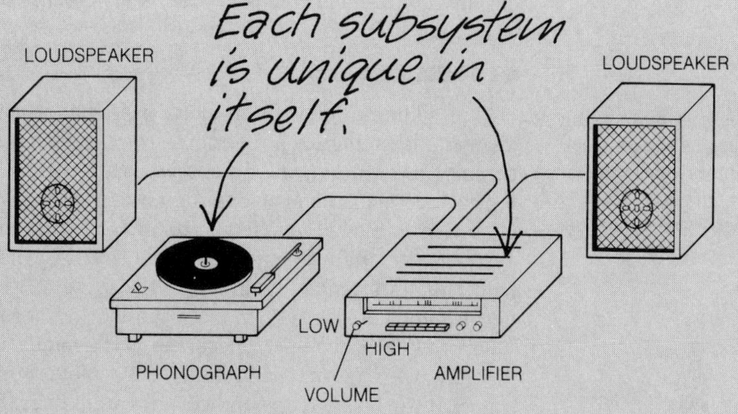

a. Pictorial Diagram of Stereo System

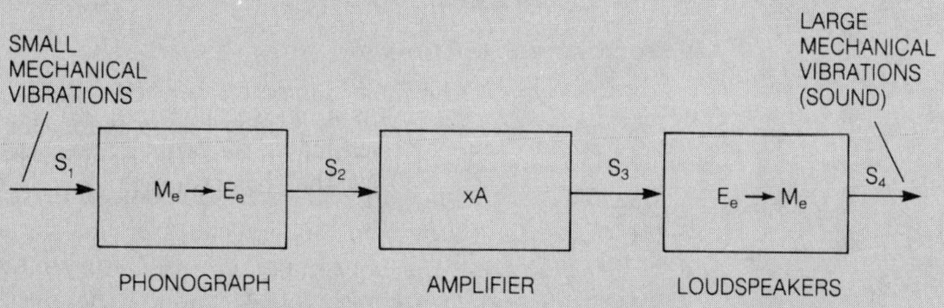

b. System Diagram Showing Major Parts of Stereo System

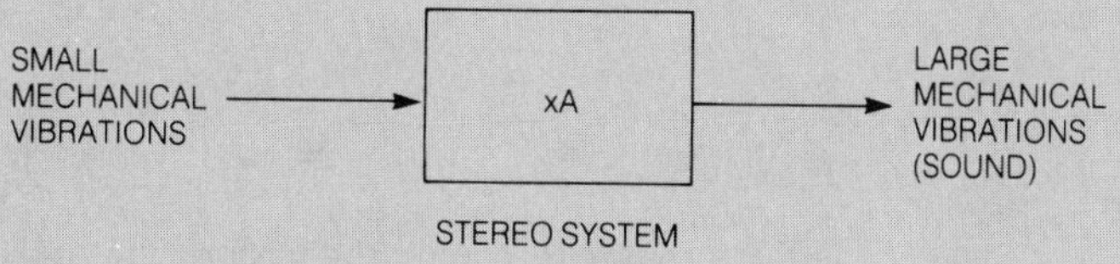

c. Overall System Diagram

It is, of course, possible to assemble a home stereo system without understanding the detailed internal operation of each component. In fact, only a rough understanding of what each stereo system component does is needed to assemble the entire stereo system. For example, the phonograph cartridge produces an output voltage that is a reproduction of the voltage produced during the recording process, but its power level is inadequate to directly drive the loudspeaker. The amplifier boosts the relatively weak phonograph cartridge power level to the level required to meaningfully operate the speaker. In order to assemble the stereo system, it is only necessary to understand (very roughly) the system components input and output requirements. It is not at all necessary to understand the operation of a transistor acting as an amplifier.

SYSTEM DESIGN

The designer of a system often begins with a block diagram in which major components are represented as blocks.

The designer of an electronic system normally begins with a block diagram depicting each functional component and the flow of signals through the system; the functional relationships between input and output for each component provides the basis for thinking about the system operation and whether or not the system will perform as intended. A performance analysis expresses quantitatively how well the system performs its intended task. Often the system designer calculates the performance of the system from the block diagram and from the component functional relationships. This same performance analysis can then be used to refine the system configuration to achieve improved performance. Since this chapter lays the groundwork for understanding the operation of automotive electronic instrumentation, it is instructive to lay the groundwork for performance analysis for such electronic systems.

Performance Analysis

One of the most important *performance analysis methods* is known as the *sinusoidal frequency response* for the system. In determining the sinusoidal frequency response, the system input is assumed to be sinusoidal. The sinusoid is the basis for describing all periodic motion, and the response of a system to a sinusoid provides the most basic description of its performance. For example, the oscillatory motion of a spring and mass combination is sinusoidal. A graph of the motion x as a function of time is shown in *Figure 2-2*, where

$$
\begin{aligned}
x &= X\sin wt \\
X &= \text{amplitude of the motion} \\
w &= 2\pi f \\
f &= \text{frequency of motion} = 1/T \\
T &= \text{period of oscillatory motion}
\end{aligned}
$$

In determining the performance of a system, it is customary to assume that the input to the system varies sinusoidally. The system response will eventually also be sinusoidal at the same frequency.

Figure 2-3 illustrates the input and output for the system. The system output is sinusoidal at the input frequency, and there is a time delay d between the output and input which is expressed as the so-called phase shift. It is common to denote the phase by using the Greek letter phi (ϕ)

$$\phi = (d/T)\ 360°$$

Figure 2-2.
Graph of a Sinusoid

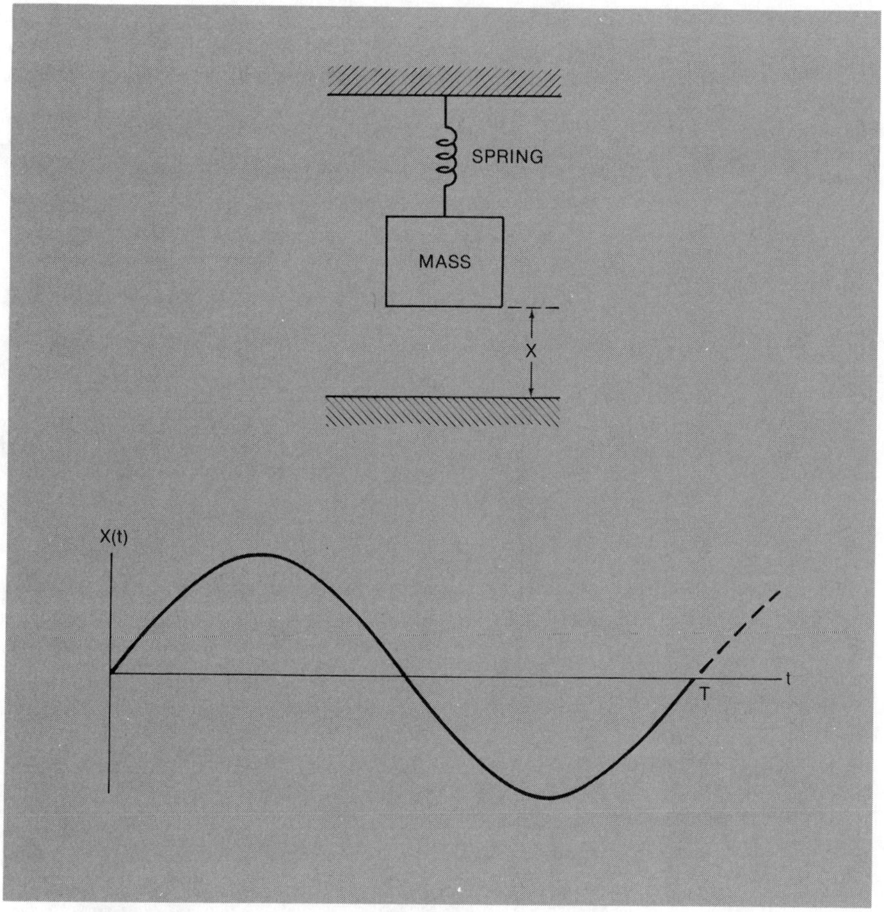

The performance of the parts within a system can be described in terms of mathematical equations.

The performance of the system is expressed by the ratio of output to input

$$H = B/A$$

and by the phase. Both H and the phase vary with frequency. *Figure 2-4* is a graph of H and ϕ vs frequency f for a typical system.

The example system of *Figure 2-4* is known as a first order system.

For the system illustrated here, the amplitude response is nearly constant at low frequencies. The amplitude drops steadily from the low frequency value (i.e., H = 1 in this example) as frequency increases. The frequency at which the response is 71% of its low frequency value is commonly used to represent the bandwidth of this system. In *Figure 2-4*, this frequency is denoted f_o. Also shown in this figure is the variation in phase with frequency. For the example system, this phase decreases with frequency passing through −45° at frequency f_o. The phase then decreases more gradually asymptotically approaching −90°. For other systems, the phase variation with frequency will be different.

Figure 2-3. Input and Output of a System

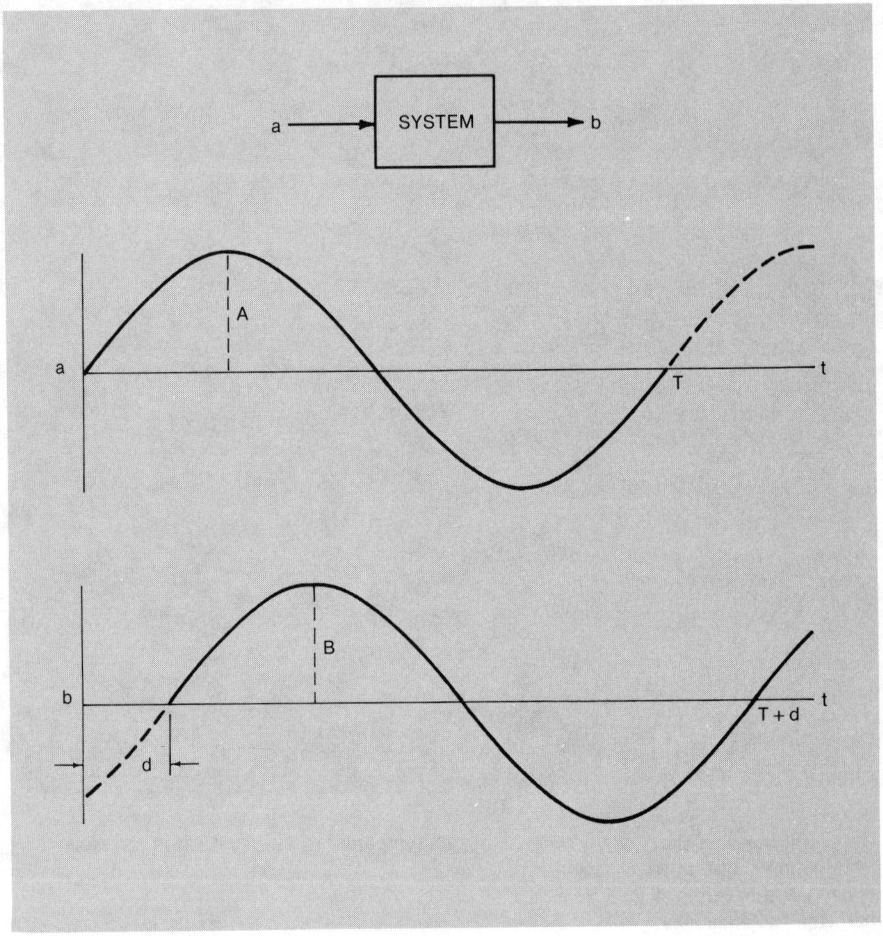

Step Response

The step response also characterizes the performance of a system.

The performance of a system is also represented by its time response which is closely related to its frequency response. Perhaps the most convenient method of assessing the time response of a system is to examine its response to an input step. *Figure 2-5* is a graph of a step input to the example system as well as the system response. The step input is an abrupt change occurring at time t_o. However, the output change is gradual relative to the input. The output asymptotically approaches a steady value HX.

Figure 2-4.
Magnitude and Phase of Frequency Response

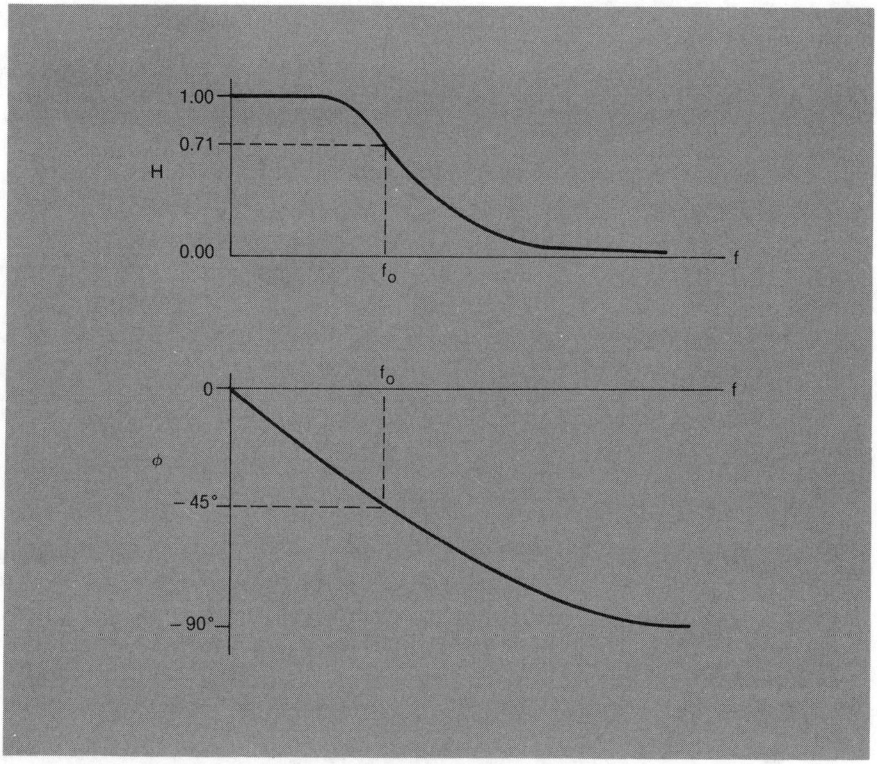

The rate at which the output approaches the final value varies inversely with bandwidth, as illustrated in *Figure 2-5*. Although the actual response of the system depends upon the characteristics of the system, generally speaking, the response time of any system varies inversely with its bandwidth.

INSTRUMENT

Instrumentation systems, whether electrical, mechanical, or a combination of both, measure a physical quantity and provide a report of that measurement.

An instrument (or instrumentation system) is a device for measuring some specific quantity. Automotive instruments have traditionally been mechanical, pneumatic, hydraulic, electrical, or combinations of these. However, modern automotive instrumentation is largely electronic. These electronic instruments or instrumentation systems are used to measure a variety of physical quantities including:

1. vehicle speed
2. total distance traveled
3. engine angular speed (rpm)
4. fuel quantity and/or flow rate
5. oil pressure
6. engine coolant temperature
7. charging current

Figure 2-5.
Illustration of the Step Response of a System

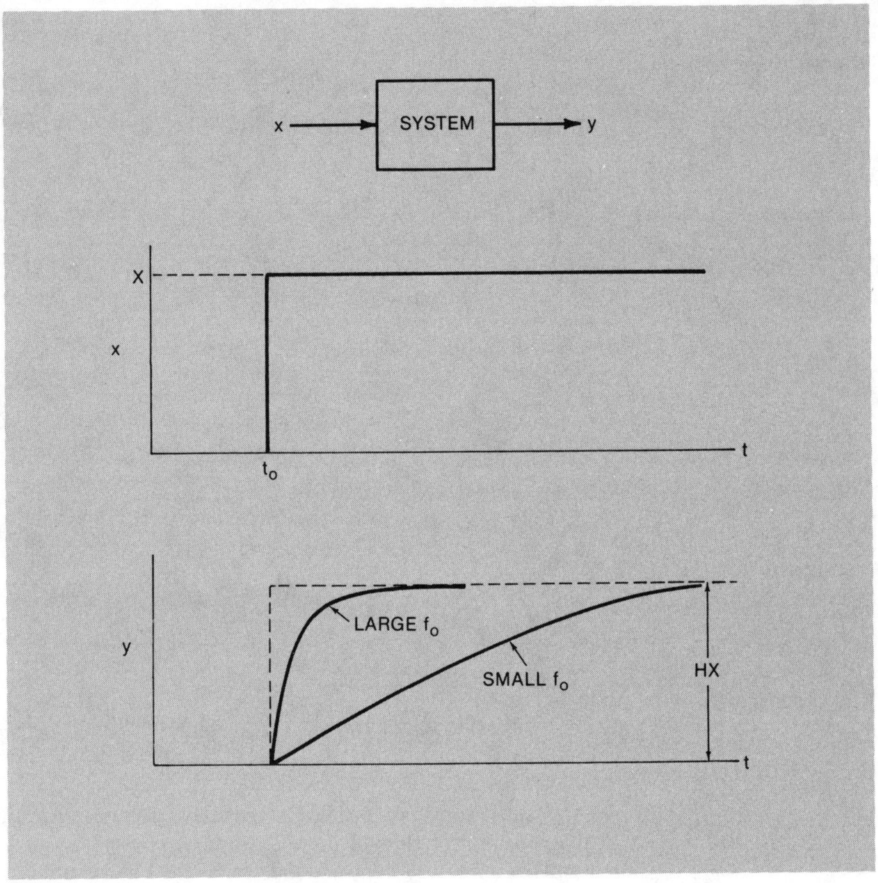

For an understanding of (measurement) instrumentation, it is helpful to review a definition of measurement.

MEASUREMENT

A measurement is defined as a numerical comparison of an unknown magnitude of a given physical quantity to a standard magnitude of the same physical quantity. In this sense, the result of a measurement is normally a numerical value expressing the indicated value of the measurement as a multiple of the appropriate standard. Consequently, an instrument normally has an indicating device capable of displaying numerical values. For example, automotive instrumentation is capable of displaying vehicle speed in the correct units of miles per hour (mph) or kilometers per hour.

On the other hand, automotive instrumentation does not always display measured quantities. Rather, a warning lamp (or buzzer) is activated whenever a given quantity falls outside of allowed limits. For example, it is common practice not to provide a display of measured values for engine oil pressure or coolant temperature. Warning lamps are activated by the electronic instrumentation system whenever oil pressure is too low or coolant temperature is too high.

ISSUES

In any measurement, made with any instrument there are several important issues, including:

1. standards
2. precision
3. accuracy
4. errors
5. calibration
6. reliability

Each of these issues has an important impact on the performance of the instrumentation.

The *precision* of any instrument is related to the number of significant figures that are readable from the display device. The greater the number of significant figures displayed, the greater the precision of the instrument.

The *standard* magnitudes of the physical variables measured by any instrument are maintained by the National Bureau of Standards in the United States. These standard magnitudes and the fundamental relationships between physical variables determine the units for each physical quantity.

Calibration is the act of setting the parameters of an instrument such that the indicated value conforms to the true value of the quantity being measured.

The *accuracy* of any measurement is the conformity of the indicated value to the true value of the quantity being measured. *Error* is defined as the difference between true and indicated values. Hence, accuracy and error vary inversely.

Errors in the accuracy of instruments are due to systematic errors, caused by known imperfections in an instrument; random errors are caused by outside disturbances.

The errors in any measurement are generally classified as either systematic or random. Systematic errors result from known variations in instrument performance for which corrections can be made if desired. There are many sources of systematic error, including temperature variations during calibrating, loading, and dynamic response. Since virtually any component in an instrument is potentially susceptible to temperature variations, great care must be exercised in instrument design to minimize *temperature variations in calibration.* As will be seen later in this book, most automotive instruments have relatively low precision requirements so that temperature variations in calibration are negligible. Random errors are essentially random fluctuations in indicated value for the measurement. Most random measurement errors result from one or another form of noise.

Systematic *loading* errors are due to the energy extracted by an instrument when making a measurement. Whenever the energy extracted from a system under measurement is not negligible, the extracted energy causes a change in the quantity being measured. Wherever possible, an instrument is designed to minimize such "loading effects." The idea of loading error can be illustrated by the simple example of an electrical measurement, as illustrated in *Figure 2-6*. A voltmeter *M* having resistance (R_m) measures the voltage across resistance *R*. The correct voltage (v_c) is given by:

$$v_c = V\left(\frac{R}{R+R_1}\right)$$

However, the measured voltage v_m is given by:

$$v_m = \frac{VR_p}{R_p+R_1}$$

where R_p is the parallel combination of R and R_m:

$$R_p = \frac{RR_m}{R+R_m}$$

Figure 2-6. Illustration of Loading Error

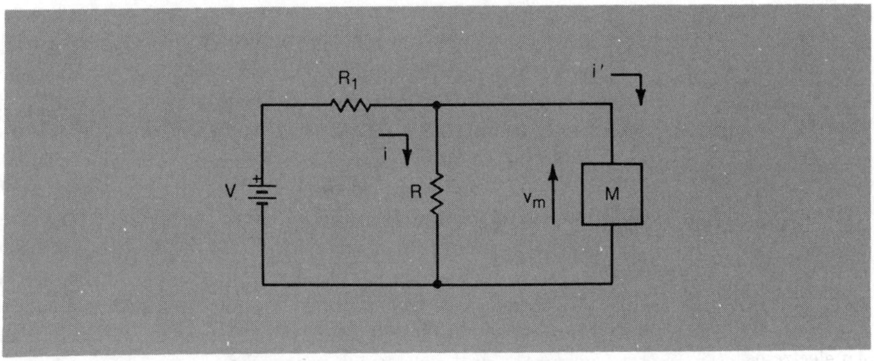

Loading is minimized by increasing the meter resistance to the largest possible value. For conditions where R_m approaches infinite resistance, R_p approaches resistance R, and v_m approaches the correct voltage. Loading is similarly minimized in measurement of any quantity by minimizing extracted energy. Normally, loading is negligible in modern electronic instruments which applies also to most automotive instrumentation.

Another significant systematic error source is the *dynamic response* of the instrument. Any instrument has a limited response rate to the most rapidly changing input, as illustrated in *Figure 2-7*. In this figure, an input quantity to the instrument changes abruptly at some time. The instrument begins responding, but cannot instantaneously change and produce the new value. After a time, the indicated value approaches the correct reading (presuming correct instrument calibration). The greater the bandwidth of an instrument or instrumentation system, the more rapidly it can follow rapid changes in the quantity being measured.

Figure 2-7. Instrument Dynamic Response Error

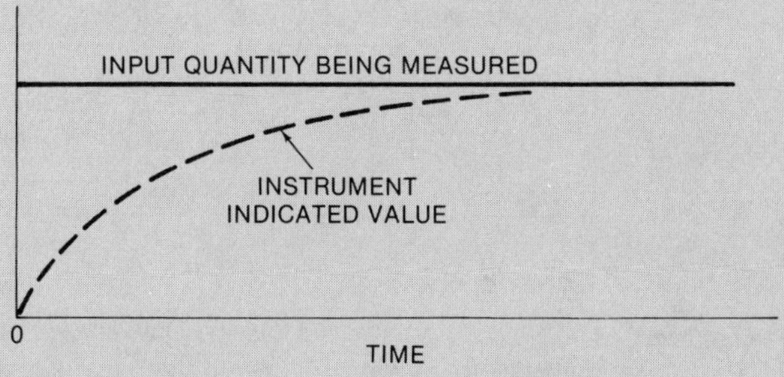

The *reliability* of an instrumentation system refers to its ability to perform its designed function accurately and continuously whenever required, under unfavorable conditions, and for a reasonable amount of time. Reliability must be designed into the system by using adequate design margins, and quality components that operate over the desired temperature range and under the applicable environmental conditions.

BASIC MEASUREMENT SYSTEM

The block diagram for an electronic instrument is depicted in *Figure 2-8*. Although the system itself is electronic, this block diagram is applicable to the measurement of an arbitrary physical variable. Notice that this diagram is similar in form to *Figure 2-1b*.

An electronic instrumentation system consists of three basic parts: a sensor, a signal processing unit, and a form of display device.

An instrumentation system is comprised of three basic parts: (1) a *sensor* that converts the physical quantity, q_o, into an electrical signal, q_1, so that it may be operated on by the signal processor; (2) a *signal processor* that performs some operation on the intermediate signal, q_1, to increase its power level, reliability, and accuracy and to put it into a form so that when displayed, it can be understood by humans; and (3) a *display device* that converts the signal, q_2, from the signal processor into a readable quantity, q_3.

Figure 2-8.
Block Diagram of an Instrument

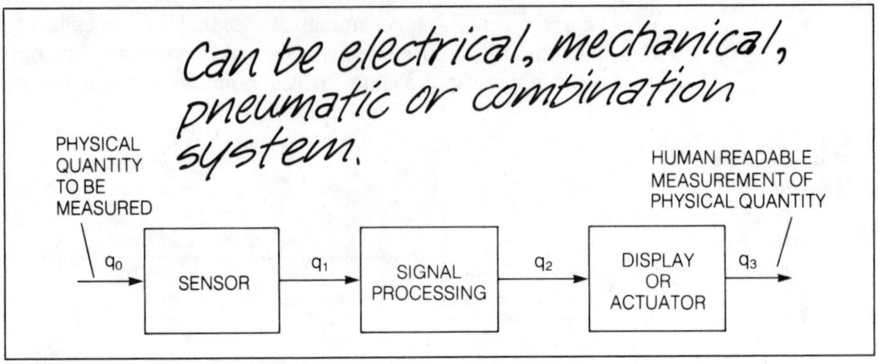

Sensor

Sensors convert one form of energy, such as thermal energy, into electrical energy.

A *sensor* is a device that converts energy from the form of the measurement variable to an electrical signal (*Figure 2-9*). An ideal analog sensor generates an output voltage which is proportional to the quantity being measured:

$$v_o = K_S q_o$$

where K_S is called the sensor calibration constant.

Figure 2-9.
Sensor Illustration

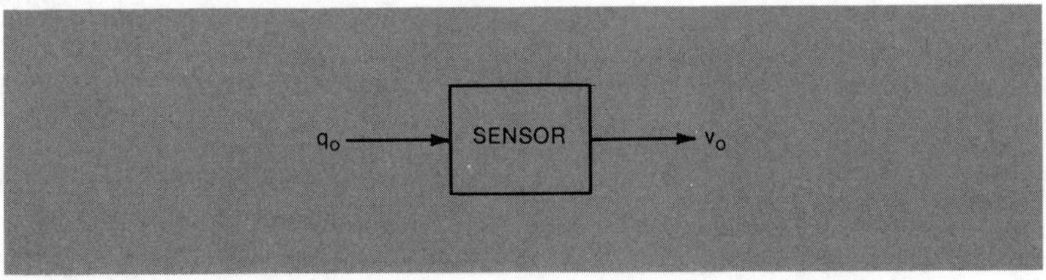

By way of illustration, consider a typical automotive sensor—the throttle-position sensor. The quantity being measured is the angle theta of the throttle plate relative to closed throttle. Assuming for the sake of illustration that the throttle angle varies from 0 to 90 degrees and the voltage varies from 0 to 5 volts, the sensor calibration constant (K_s) is:

$$K_s = (5-0)/(90°-0°) = .056 \text{ volt/degree}$$

Of course, a sensor is susceptible to error just as is any system or system component. Potential error sources include *loading, finite dynamic response, calibration shift,* and *nonlinear behavior*. It is possible to compensate for these and other types of errors in the electronic signal processing unit of the instrument. For example, *loading* results from extracting energy from the system being measured. This phenomenon applies to the sensor and signal processing interface as well as to the typical sensor frequency response. Ideally, this frequency response should be flat over the entire spectral range (i.e., frequency content) for the input quantity. In the example sensor of *Figure 2-10*, the sensor bandwidth is the frequency region depicted up to the frequency f_o, at which the response is 71% of its low frequency value h_o.

Figure 2-10. Sensor Frequency Response

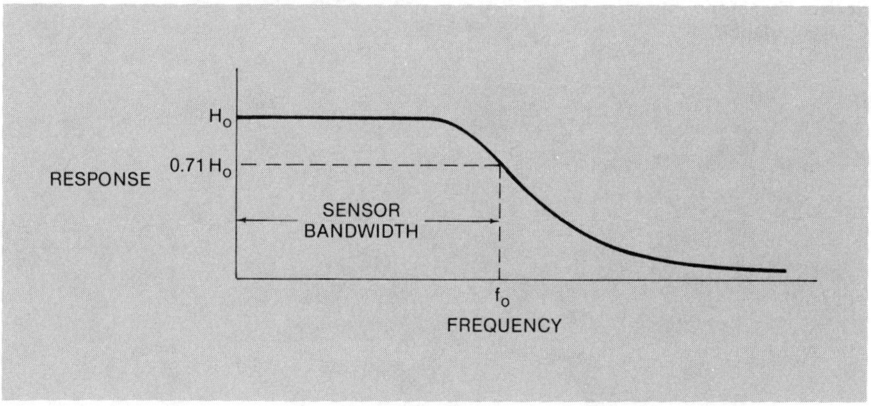

The corresponding time response for the sensor is depicted in *Figure 2-11*. Notice that distortion is present in the sensor output relative to its input owing to the limited bandwidth. Often (as will be explained later), the signal processing component can compensate (at least partially) for the limited bandwidth.

Figure 2-11. Distortion Caused by Limited Dynamic Response of Sensor

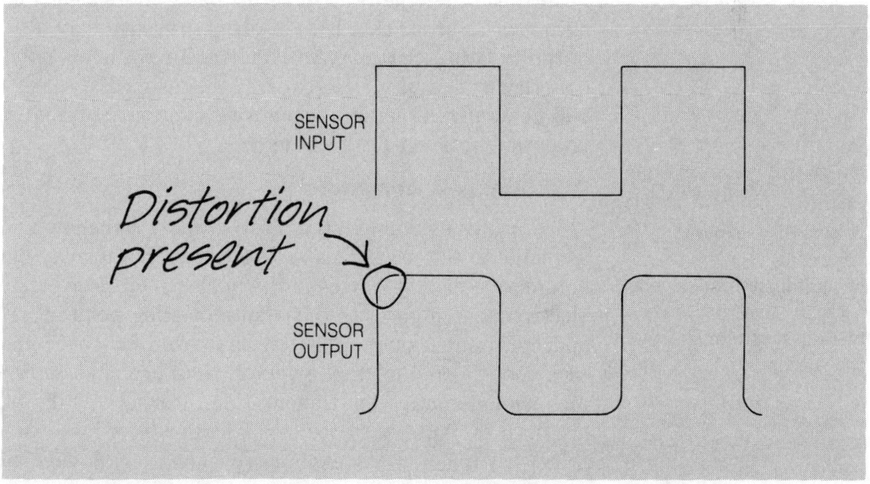

An ideal sensor has a *linear transfer characteristic* (or transfer function) as shown in *Figure 2-12a*. Thus, some signal processing is required to linearize the output signal so that it will appear as if the sensor

Signal processing can be used to compensate for systematic errors of sensors.

has a straight line (linear) transfer characteristic, as shown in the dashed curve of *Figure 2–12b*. Sometimes a nonlinear sensor may provide satisfactory operation without linearization if it is operated in a particular "nearly" linear region of its transfer characteristic (*Figure 2–12b*).

Figure 2-12. Sensor Transfer Characteristics

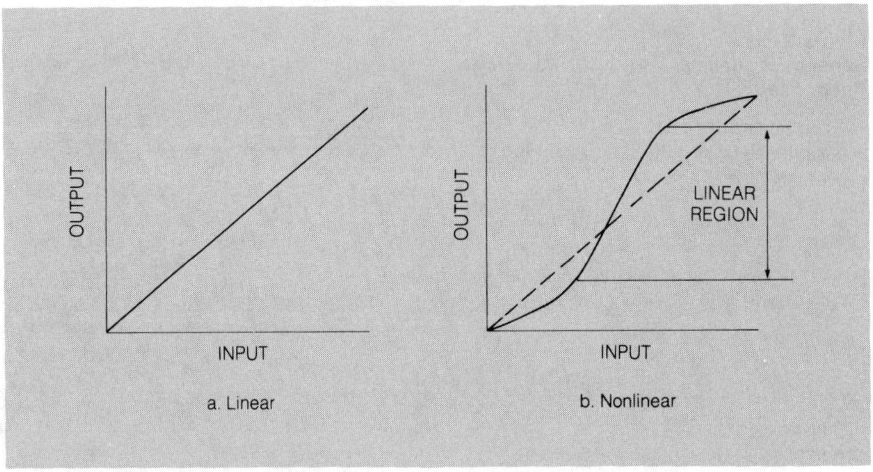

Sensors are subject to random errors such as heat, electrical noise, and vibrations.

Random errors in electronic sensors are caused primarily by internal electrical noise. Internal electrical noise can be caused by molecular vibrations due to heat (thermal noise), or random electron movement in semiconductors (shot noise). In certain cases, a sensor may respond to quantities other than the quantity being measured. For example, the output of a sensor that is measuring pressure may also change as a result of temperature changes. An ideal sensor responds only to one physical quantity or stimulus. However, real sensors are rarely, if ever, perfect and will generally respond in some way to outside stimuli. Signal processing can potentially correct for such defects.

Displays and Actuators

Automotive display devices, typically analog or digital meters, provide a visual indication of the measurements made by the sensors.

An instrumentation system must somehow make its measurements available to the user. This is done through a display device. A traditional automotive display device is the analog meter, or gauge, that uses an electromagnetic force to drive an indicating pointer across a dial that has appropriate markings. This device is used for speedometers and tachometers, and for fuel level, oil pressure, and battery voltage gauges. Modern automotive instrumentation incorporates digital displays such as are used in digital watches (see Chapter 9).

Actuators convert electrical inputs to an action such as a mechanical movement.

An actuator is an energy conversion device having an electrical input signal and an output signal that is mechanical (e.g., force or displacement). Automotive actuators include vacuum controlled diaphragms and switches, and solenoid controlled valves and switches. These are used, for example, in throttle positioners for cruise control, and in spark timing advance mechanisms.

Displays, like sensors, are energy conversion devices. They have bandwidth, dynamic range, and calibration characteristics, and, therefore, have the same types of errors as do sensors. As with sensors, many of the shortcomings of display devices can be reduced or eliminated through the imaginative use of signal processing.

Signal Processing

Any changes performed on the signals between the sensor and the display is considered to be signal processing.

Signal processing, as defined earlier, is any operation that is performed on signals traveling between the sensor and the display. Signal processing converts the sensor signal to an electrical signal which is suitable to drive the display. In addition, it can increase the accuracy, reliability, or readability of the measurement. Signal processing can make a nonlinear sensor appear linear, or it can smooth a sensor's frequency response. Signal processing can be used to perform unit conversions, such as converting from miles per hour to kilometers per hour. It can perform display formatting, such as scaling and shifting a temperature sensor's output so that it can be displayed on the engine temperature gauge from 100 degrees to 300 degrees F instead of from 0° to 200 degrees F; or process signals in a way that reduces the effects of random system errors.

Signal processing can use either analog circuitry or digital circuitry, depending on the application.

Signal processing can be accomplished with analog or digital devices. Analog signal processing uses amplifiers, filters, adders, multipliers, and other analog components. Digital signal processing uses logic gates, counters, binary adders, microcomputers, and other digital components. The difference between analog signals and digital signals is that analog signals are continuously variable and can be any value within a range, while digital signals change in discrete steps and can take only certain values within a range. Chapter 4 has more about digital signal processing, and presents some specific hardware used to convert analog signals to digital and digital to analog.

Traditionally, signal processing has been done with analog circuits, but the trend in signal processing for all electronic instrumentation is digital, particularly that which is accomplished with a digital computer or a microprocessor-based system. However, it is worthwhile to explain certain aspects of analog signal processing as it is still the preferred method for relatively low cost signal processing involving relatively simple functional operations.

The operational amplifier is the predominant analog signal processing building block.

The primary building block of analog signal processing is the operational amplifier, which is depicted symbolically in *Figure 2-13*. An operational amplifier is a very high gain differential amplifier; that is, it amplifies the difference between the two input voltages. These voltages (relative to ground) are denoted v_1 and v_2. The input labeled + in *Figure 2-13* is known as the *noninverting* input, and the one labeled − is called the *inverting* input. The output voltage v_o, relative to ground is given by:

$$v_o = A\,(v_1 - v_2)$$

where A is the so-called open-loop gain. For an ideal operational amplifier, the open-loop gain should be infinite.

Figure 2-13.
Operational Amplifier Diagram

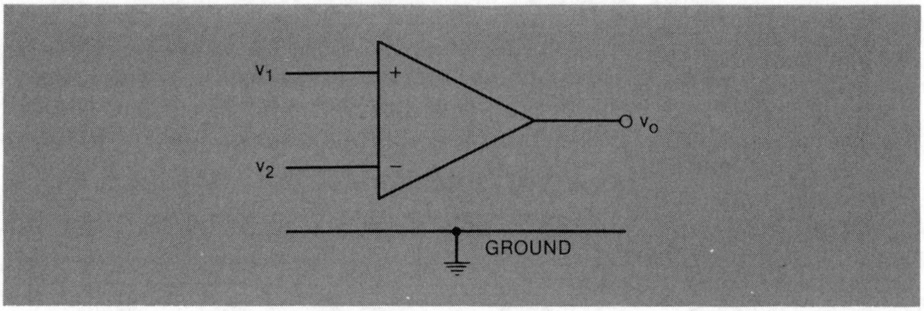

As an example of the signal processing application of the operational amplifier, consider an instrument using a sensor that has an imperfect response. For the purpose of illustration, assume that the frequency response H for the sensor is as shown in *Figure 2-14.* The output voltage for a fixed amplitude input increases linearly with frequency as shown in the graph. Note an example of this type of frequency response is a differentiating sensor.

Figure 2-14.
Example Sensor Frequency Response

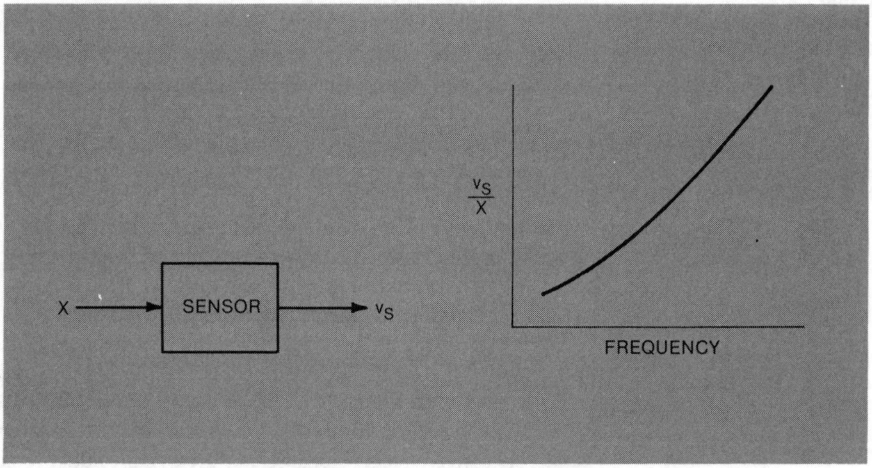

A signal processing circuit that can compensate for the undesirable frequency response is shown in *Figure 2-15.* In this circuit, a parallel resistance-capacitance (R_fC) combination is connected in a so-called "feedback path" from the output to the inverting input. The frequency response for this circuit ($H_{sp}=v_o/v_s$) is shown graphically in *Figure 2-16.* Also shown in this figure is the frequency response for the combination sensor and signal processor. For frequencies above f_1, the frequency response for the combination is flat as is desired. The characteristics and applications of operational amplifiers are discussed in greater detail in Chapter 3.

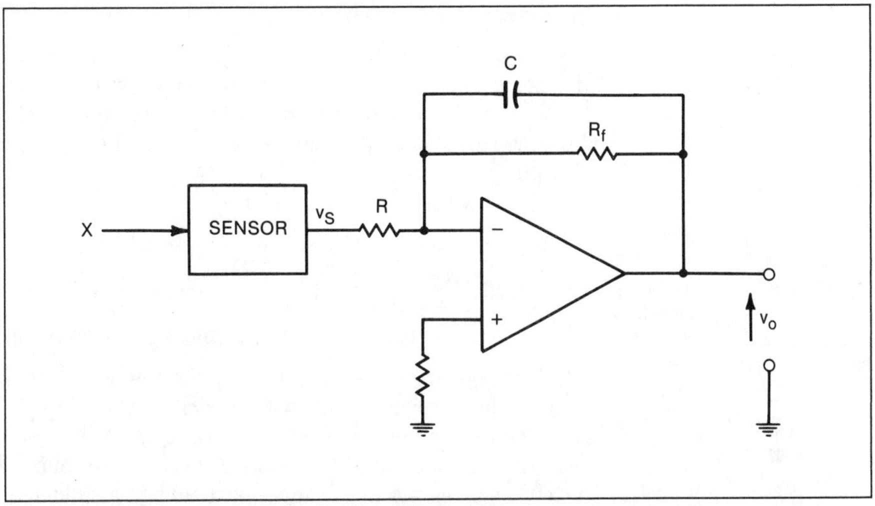

Figure 2-15. Operational Amplifier Circuit Used to Compensate for the Poor Frequency Response of a Sensor

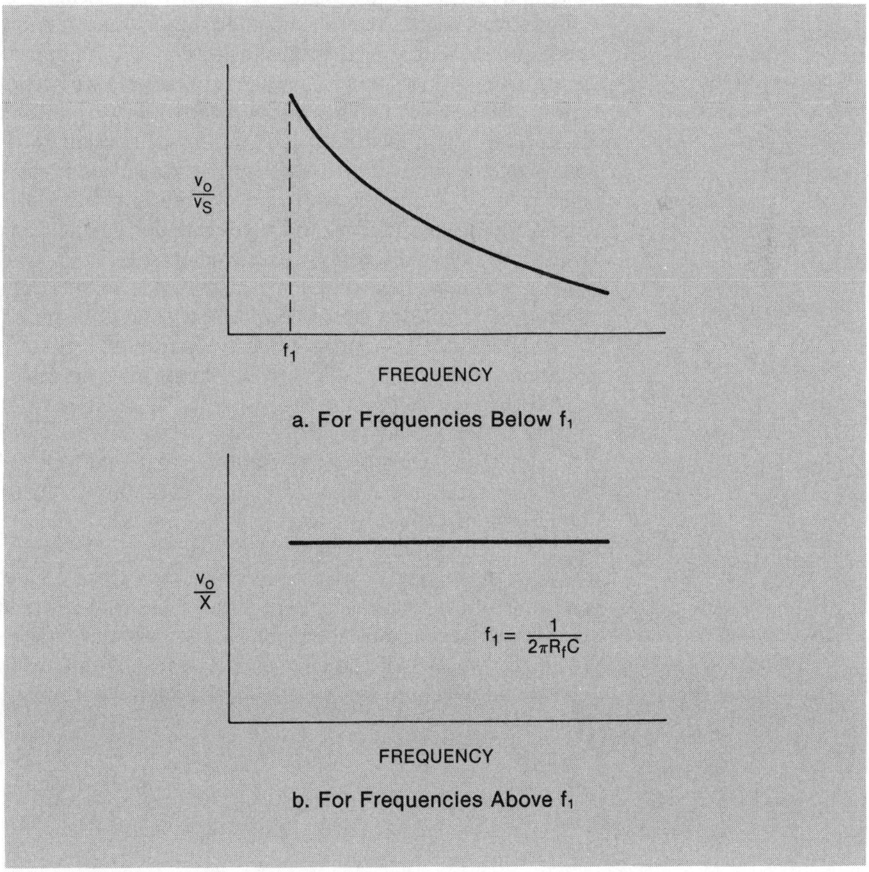

Figure 2-16. Frequency Response for Operational Amplifier Circuit

CONTROL SYSTEMS

Control systems are systems that are used to direct the operation of other systems. For this discussion, the system being controlled is known as the *system plant.* The goal of the control system designer is to improve the performance of the plant by controlling the plant's output in relation to its input.

Control systems, which are used to control the operation of other systems, are measured in terms of accuracy, speed of response, stability, and immunity from external noise.

A control system should:

1. perform its function accurately
2. respond quickly
3. be stable
4. respond only to valid inputs (noise immunity)

A control system's accuracy determines how close the system's output will come to the desired output, with a constant value input command. Quick response determines how closely the output of the system will track or follow a changing input command. A system's stability describes how a system behaves when a change, particularly a sudden change, is made by the input signal. Some unstable systems will oscillate wildly if uncontrolled. Others that are normally controlled may go out of control. Either case is undesirable, and a good controller design will minimize the chance of unstable operation. A system should maintain its accuracy by responding only to valid inputs. When noise or other disturbances threaten to change the system plant's output, good design will eliminate them from system performance as much as possible. The more this invalid response is eliminated, the more noise immunity the control system has. Accuracy, quick response, stability, and noise immunity are all determined by the control system chosen for a particular plant.

The purpose of a control system is to determine the output of the system (plant) being controlled in relationship to the input, and in accordance with the operating characteristics or the controller. The relationship between the controller input and the desired plant output is called the *control law* for the system. The desired value for the plant output is often called the *set point.*

The behavior of the plant is influenced electronically by means of an electromechanical device called an actuator. Looking ahead to our discussion of automotive electronics, a specific actuator will be introduced which is an electrically controlled carburetor. Generally speaking, an actuator has input electrical terminals that receive electrical power from the control electronics. By a process of internal electromechanical energy conversion, a mechanical output is obtained that operates to control the plant. In the case of the electronic carburetor, the air/fuel mixture is controlled which, in turn, controls the engine output.

Open-Loop Control

An open-loop control system never compares actual output with the desired value.

The basic control system block diagram is given in *Figure 2-17.* Here the command input is sent to a system block which performs a control operation on the input to generate an intermediate signal which drives the plant. This type of control is called open-loop control, because the output of the system is never compared with the command input to see if they match.

Figure 2-17. Open-Loop Control System Block Diagram

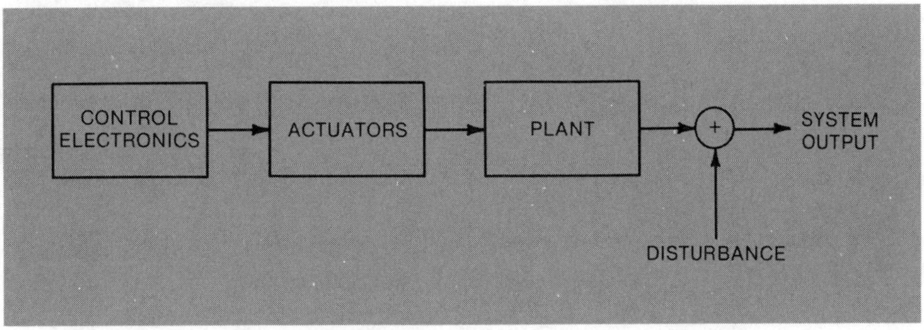

One of the principal drawbacks to the open-loop controller is its inability to compensate for changes that might occur in the controller or the plant. This defect is eliminated in a closed-loop control system in which the actual system output is compared to the desired value in accordance with the input. Of course, a measurement must be made of the plant output in such a system, and this requires measurement instrumentation.

Figure 2-18 is a block diagram of a typical closed-loop control system. This control system has some of the components found in an open-loop system, including the plant to be controlled, actuator(s), and control electronics. In addition, however, this system includes one or more sensors and some signal conditioning electronics. The signal conditioning used in a closed-loop control system plays a role similar to that played by signal processing in measurement instrumentation. That is, it transforms the sensor output as required to accomplish the desired measurement of the plant output. Compensation for certain sensor defects (e.g., limited bandwidth) is possible, and in some cases necessary, to allow for the comparison of the plant output with the desired value.

The component at the left of the block diagram of *Figure 2-18,* called the error amplifier, is the element in which the output is actually compared to the input. An error signal is obtained by electrically subtracting the feedback signal from the command input. The error signal is the input to the control electronic system which, in turn, generates an output called a *control signal.* The control signal is applied to the actuator and the actuator moves in such a direction as to reduce the error between the actual and desired output to zero.

Figure 2-18. Closed-Loop Control System Block Diagram

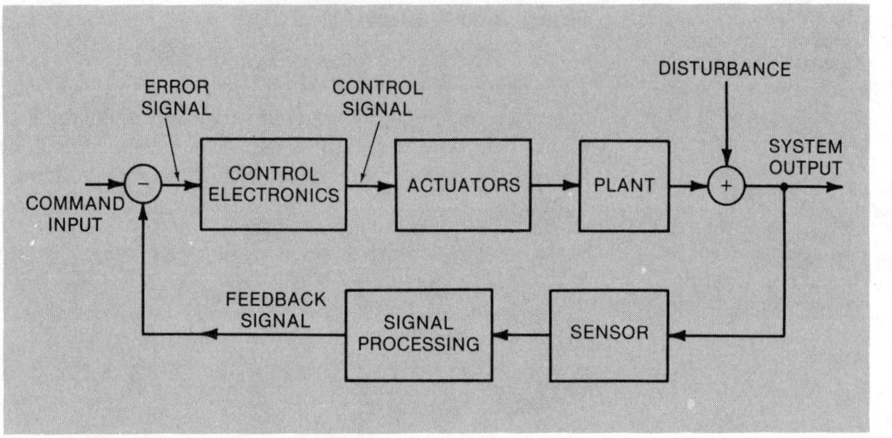

Figure 2-19 is a block diagram for a simple closed-loop control system which is known as a proportional control system. In this figure, the sensor provides a measurement, x_o of the plant output. The error signal e is obtained by subtracting x_o from the desired value x:

$$e = x - x_o$$

and amplified by an amplifier having output v_c which is the control signal:

$$v_c = Ge$$

where

G = amplifier gain.

The actuator causes the plant output y to increase in proportion to v_c. The operation of this control system is as follows. Assume that y_i is larger than desired and corresponds to x_o being greater than x. Consequently, error signal e is negative. The amplified error signal is applied to the actuator, causing the plant output to decrease. Thus, *x_o will decrease until* $x_o = x$, at which point e is zero and the output remains fixed at the desired value.

Closed-Loop Limit-Cycle Control

In a proportional control system the control signal is proportional to the error between desired and actual output.

The control electronics in the previous example provided what is called proportional control because the control signal is proportional to the error signal. Other combinations of control electronics are possible, and it is a challenge to the system designer to develop imaginative types of control electronics to improve the performance of a given plant. Another type of control that is used in automotive applications is limit-cycle control. Limit-cycle control is a type of feedback control that monitors the system's output and responds only when the output goes beyond preset limits. Limit-cycle controllers often are used to control plants with nonlinear or complicated transfer functions.

Figure 2-19. Closed-Loop Control System Block Diagram

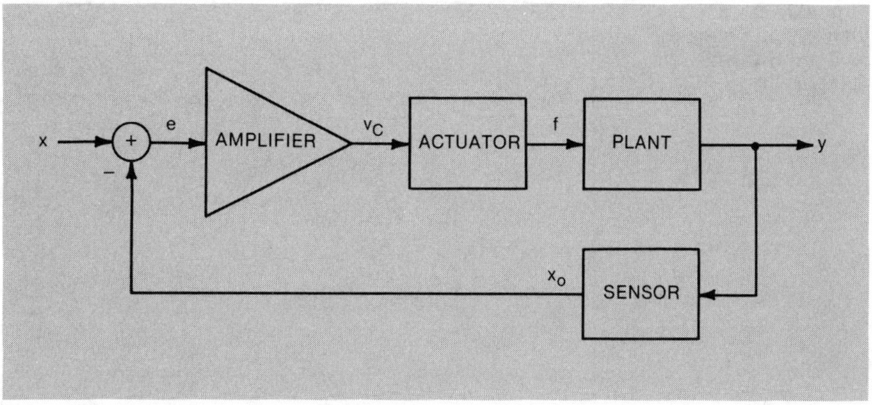

Limit-cycle control responds only when the error is outside of a pair of limits.

An example of a limit-cycle controller is the temperature-controlled oven depicted in *Figure 2-20.* The temperature inside the oven is controlled by the length of time the heating coil is energized. The temperature of the oven is measured with a temperature probe, and the corresponding electrical signal is fed back to the command to obtain an error signal. The control electronics checks the error signal against the temperature control dial to determine if one of the following two conditions exist:

1. oven temperature is below minimum setting of command input
2. oven temperature is above maximum setting of command input

The control electronics responds to error condition 1 by closing the relay contacts to energize the heating element. This causes the temperature in the oven to increase until the temperature rises above a maximum limit, producing error condition 2. In this case, the control electronics opens the relay contracts and the heat is turned off. The oven gradually cools until condition 1 again occurs and the cycle repeats. The oven temperature varies between the upper and lower limit, and the variations can be graphed as a function of time as shown in *Figure 2-21.* The amplitude of the temperature variations, called the differential, can be decreased by reducing the difference between the maximum and minimum temperature limits. As the limits get closer together, the temperature cycles more rapidly (frequency increases) to hold the actual temperature much closer to the desired constant temperature. Thus, the limit-cycle controller controls the system so as to maintain an average value close to the command input. This type of controller has gained popularity due to its simplicity, low cost, and ease of application. Fuel control, one of the most important automotive electronic control systems is, at least partially, a limit-cycle control system (see Chapter 6).

Figure 2-20. Limit-Cycle Controller to Control Oven Temperature

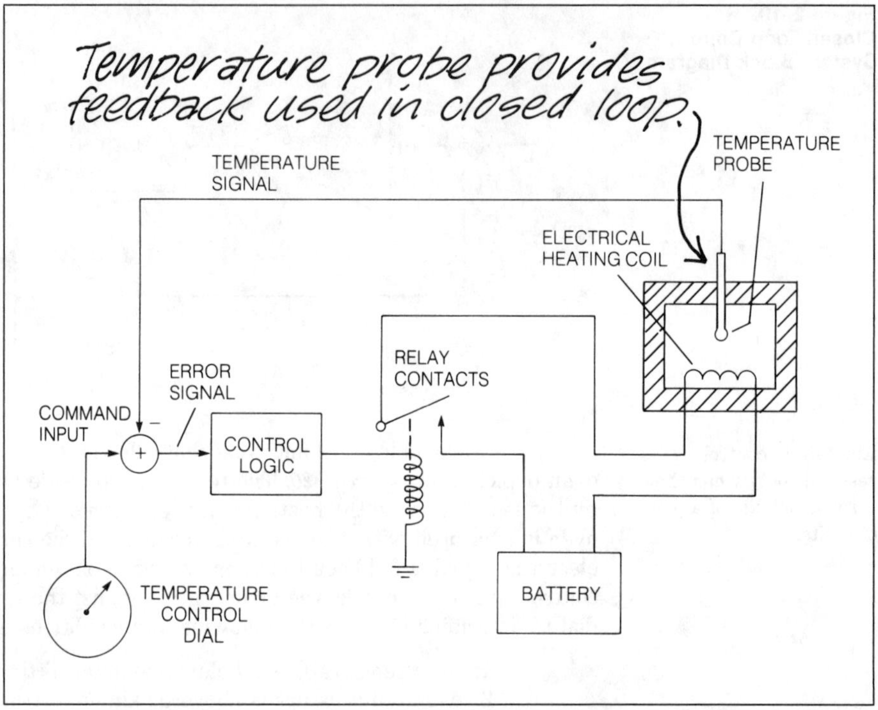

Figure 2-21. Oven Temperature Graph

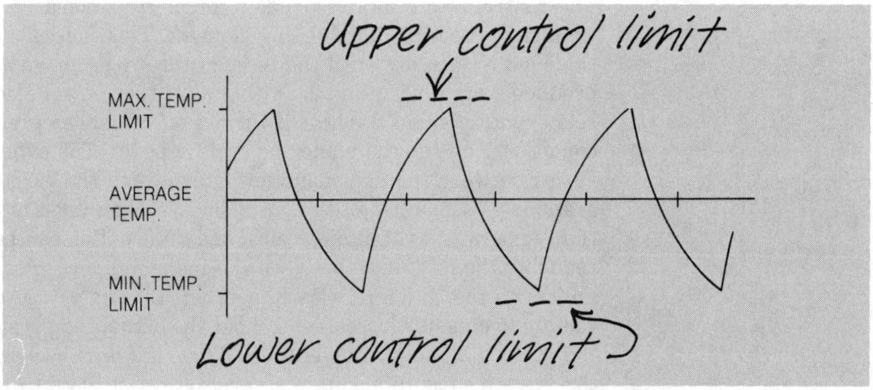

Quiz for Chapter 2

1. Which of the following are examples of systems?
- **a.** clock
- **b.** electric dishwasher
- **c.** communication network
- **d.** society
- **e.** all of the above

2. Block diagrams are developed in what type of analysis?
- **a.** psychiatric
- **b.** quantitative
- **c.** qualitative

3. Specific system parameters are determined in what type of analysis?
- **a.** physical
- **b.** quantitative
- **c.** qualitative

4. What is a sensor used for?
- **a.** converts a nonelectrical input to an electrical output
- **b.** converts an electrical input to a mechanical output
- **c.** reduces the effects of noise and other disturbances on the measured quantity
- **d.** all of the above

5. What does an actuator do?
- **a.** converts a nonelectrical input to an electrical output
- **b.** converts an electrical input to an action
- **c.** reduces the effects of noise and other disturbances on the measured quantity
- **d.** all of the above

6. What does signal processing do?
- **a.** converts a mechanical input to an electrical output
- **b.** converts an electrical input to a mechanical output
- **c.** reduces the effects of noise and other disturbances on the measured quantity
- **d.** all of the above

7. An error amplifier is used to compare which of the following two signals?
- **a.** the output of a sensor and the input to a signal processor
- **b.** the output of a system and the command input of a system
- **c.** the output of a signal processor and the output of an actuator
- **d.** none of the above

8. A basic instrumentation system consists of which of the following components?
- **a.** sensor
- **b.** actuator
- **c.** signal processor
- **d.** all of the above

9. A control system may contain which of the following components?
- **a.** error amplifier
- **b.** control logic
- **c.** plant
- **d.** all of the above

10. Which of the following are examples of a plant?
- **a.** automotive drivetrain
- **b.** high temperature oven
- **c.** an airplane navigation system
- **d.** all of the above

Electronics Fundamentals

ABOUT THIS CHAPTER

This chapter is for the reader who has little knowledge of electronics. It is intended only to provide an overview of the subject so that discussions in later chapters about the operation and use of the automotive electronics control systems will be easier to understand.

The chapter discusses electronic devices and circuits having applications in electronic automotive instrumentation and control systems. Topics include semiconductor devices, analog circuits, digital circuits, and fundamentals of integrated circuits.

SEMICONDUCTOR DEVICES

Semiconductor (or solid-state) devices are basic building blocks for electronic circuits. Semiconductor devices are commonly called solid-state devices because they are made from a solid material. This material in pure form is neither a good conductor nor a good insulator. Therefore, this material is also called semiconductor material, and devices made from semiconductor material are solid-state semiconductor devices.

There are many types of semiconductor devices, but transistors and diodes are two of the most important semiconductor devices in automotive electronics. Furthermore, these devices are the fundamental elements used to construct nearly all modern integrated circuits. Therefore, the discussion of semiconductor devices will be centered on these two.

Semiconductor devices are made from silicon or germanium which is purposely contaminated with impurities that change the conductivity of the material. Transistors are semiconductor devices that are used as active devices in electronic circuits.

The earliest transistors were made from germanium, but silicon is by far the most commonly used semiconductor material for making diodes, transistors, and other semiconductor devices today. Semiconductor material is made to conduct better by diffusing into it in an impurity. Boron and phosphorus often are used as impurity source materials to alter the conductivity of silicon. When boron is used, the semiconductor material becomes a so-called p-type semiconductor. When phosphorus is used, the semiconductor material becomes an n-type semiconductor. It is not necessary for the purposes of this book to understand the differences between p-type and n-type semiconductors. However, the interested reader can consult any of the standard introductory references on the theory of semiconductor devices for further information.

Semiconductor devices such as diodes and transistors are quite different from common linear components such as resistors, capacitors, inductors, and transformers. The following discussion presents an explanation of the operation of these devices.

Diodes

A diode acts much like a one-way "valve" allowing current to flow in only one direction.

A diode is a two-terminal electrical device having one electrode that is called the anode (a p-type semiconductor) and another that is called the cathode (an n-type semiconductor). A solid-state diode is formed by the junction between the anode and the cathode. Diodes can be thought of as one-way resistors or current check valves because they allow current to flow through them in only one direction, depending upon the polarity of voltage (bias) across the anode and cathode. When current flows in the forward (conducting) direction with a plus voltage on the anode, diodes have low resistance (typically a few ohms). This is called the forward biased condition. (The conventional current flow direction of positive to negative is used in this book.) When the current flows in the reverse (nonconducting) direction with a plus voltage on the cathode, diodes have a very high resistance (typically a few million ohms). This is called the reverse biased condition.

Figure 3-1a shows the schematic symbol for a diode, and *Figure 3-1b* shows a graph of the actual and ideal voltage and current transfer characteristics for a typical diode. Notice on the ideal curve that the diode doesn't start conducting until the voltage across it exceeds V_d volts; then, for small increases in voltage, the current increases very rapidly. For silicon diodes, V_d is about 0.7 volt. For germanium diodes, V_d is about 0.3 volt. Even for the actual curve, the change in current is quite steep for 0.1V changes in the voltage across the diode after V_d has been exceeded.

When designing or analyzing circuits, V_d is often ignored in relatively high voltage circuits where $V_d$is very small percentage of the total voltage; however, in low voltage and low level signal circuits, V_d may be a significant factor.

Rectifier Circuit

A diode has low resistance when forward biased and high resistance when reversed biased.

The circuit in *Figure 3-1c*, a very common diode circuit, is called a half-wave rectifier circuit because it effectively cuts the ac (alternating current) waveform in half; consider the circuit first without the dotted-in capacitor. The alternating current voltage source is a sine wave with a peak-to-peak amplitude of 100 volts (50 volt positive swing and 50 volt negative swing). Waveforms of the input voltage and output voltage plotted against time are shown as the solid lines in *Figure 3-1d.* Notice that the output never drops below 0 volts. The diode is reverse biased and blocks current flow when the input voltage is negative, but when the input voltage is positive, the diode is forward biased and permits current flow. Note that if the diode direction is reversed in the circuit, current flow will be permitted when the input voltage is negative and blocked when the input voltage is positive.

The half-wave rectifier is used to convert an ac voltage which goes above and below zero volts into a dc (direct current) voltage which stays either above zero volts or below zero volts, depending on which way the diode is installed. Rectifier circuits are commonly used to convert the ac voltage into a dc voltage for use with automotive alternators to provide dc current for battery charging.

Figure 3-1.
Diode Characteristics

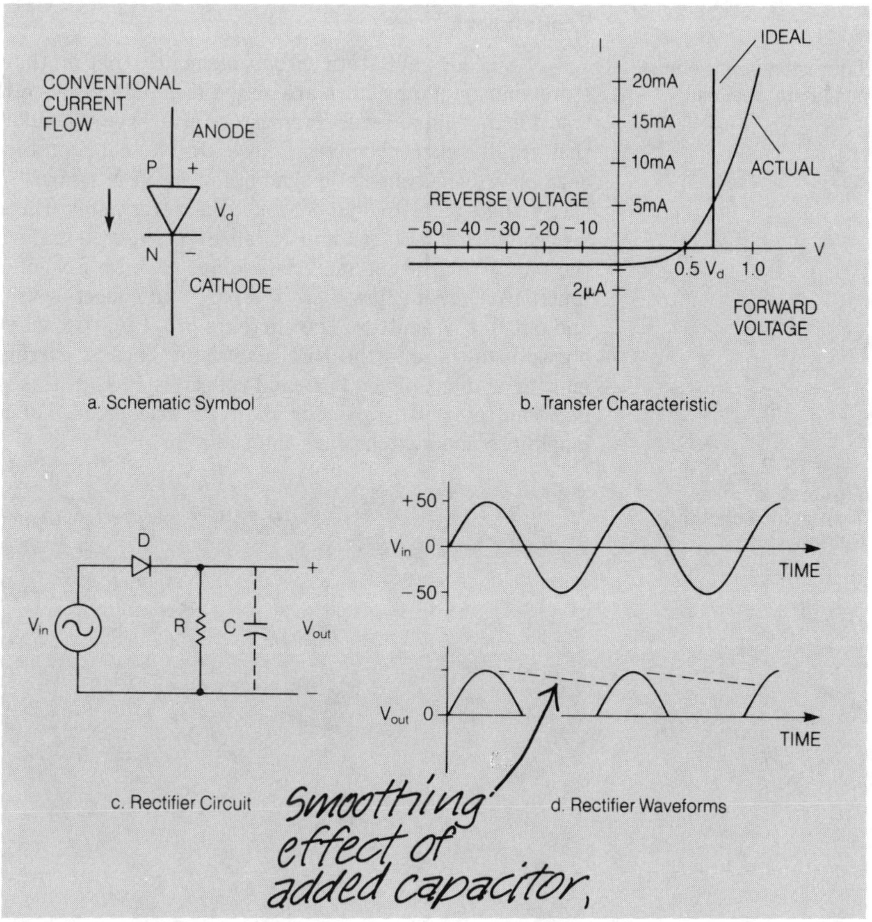

The use of a capacitor to store charges and resist voltage changes smooths the rippling or pulsating output of a half-wave rectifier.

The input voltage V_{in} of *Figure 3-1c* is ac; the output voltage V_{out} has a dc component and a time varying component, as shown in *Figure 3-1d.* The output voltage of the half-wave rectifier can be smoothed by adding a capacitor, which is represented by the dotted lines on *Figure 3-1c.* Since the capacitor stores charge and opposes voltage changes, it discharges (supplies current) to the load resistance (symbolized by R) when V_{in} is going negative from its peak voltage. The capacitor is recharged when V_{in} comes back to its positive peak and current is supplied to the load by the input voltage. The result is an output voltage V_{out} that is more nearly a smooth, steady dc voltage, as shown by the dotted lines between the peaks of *Figure 3-1d.*

Transistors

Transistors are useful as amplifying devices.

Diodes are static circuit elements; that is, they do not have gain or store energy. Transistors are active elements because they can amplify or transform a signal level. Transistors are three terminal circuit elements that act like current valves. There are two common bipolar types. *Figure 3-2a* shows the schematic symbol for an NPN transistor, and *Figure 3-2b* shows the schematic symbol for a PNP transistor. P represents p-type semiconductor material and N represents n-type material. The area where the p-type and n-type materials join is called a PN junction (or simply a junction). Current flows into the base and collector of an NPN transistor and out of the emitter. The currents in a PNP transistor flow exactly opposite to those in the NPN transistor; that is, current flows into the emitter and out of the base and collector. In fact, this is the only difference between the PNP transistor and NPN transistor. Their functions as amplifiers and switches are the same.

Figure 3-2. Transistor Schematic Symbols

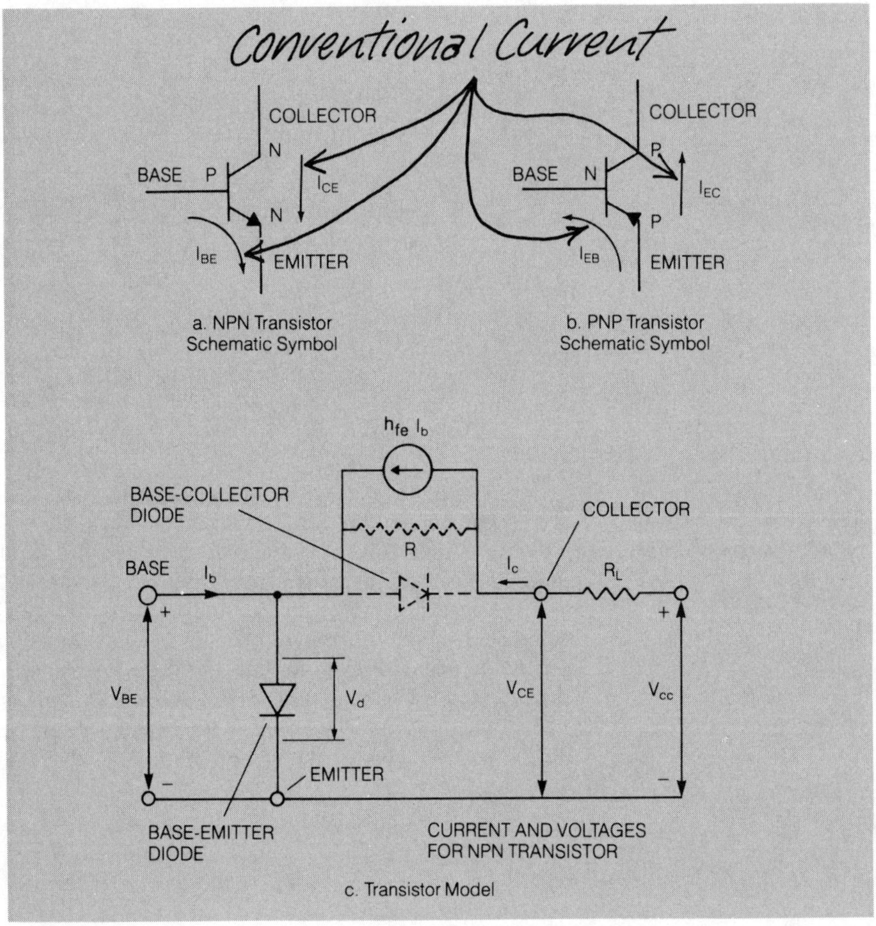

During normal operation, current flows from the base to the emitter in an NPN transistor. The collector-base junction is reverse biased, so that only a very small amount of current flows between the collector and the base when there is no base current flow.

The base-emitter junction of a transistor acts like a diode. Under normal operation for an NPN transistor, current flows forward into the base and out the emitter, but does not flow in the reverse direction from emitter to base. The arrow on the emitter of the transistor schematic symbol indicates the forward direction of current flow. The collector-base junction also acts as a diode, but supply voltage is always applied to it in the reverse direction. This junction does have some reverse current flow, but it is so very small (1×10^{-6} to 1×10^{-12} amperes), that it is ignored except when operated under extreme conditions, particularly temperature extremes. In some automotive applications, the extreme temperatures may significantly affect transistor operation. For such applications, the circuit may include components that automatically compensate for changes in transistor operation.

Under normal linear (analog) circuit operation, the collector-base junction is reverse biased as mentioned above; however, when used as a switch in the ON condition, the collector-base junction can become forward biased. In normal operation, the current which flows through the collector-emitter terminals is controlled by the current flowing through the base terminal. Relatively small base currents control relatively large collector currents through a relatively complicated physical process which is beyond the scope of this book to explain. However, for the purposes of the present discussion, it is correct to think of the transistor as a current amplifying device in which the base current controls the collector current. The current amplification of a typical transistor is on the order of 100. That is, a base current controls a collector current that is about 100 times larger.

Transistor Model

To aid in circuit analysis, *Figure 3-2c* shows the diagram of a commonly used transistor model for an NPN transistor. The base-emitter diode is shown in solid lines in the circuit, while the collector-base diode is shown in dotted lines because generally it can be ignored.

The base-emitter diode does not conduct (there is no transistor base current) until the voltage across it exceeds V_d volts in the forward direction. If the transistor is a silicon transistor, $V_d = 0.7$ volt just as with the silicon diode. The collector current, I_c, also is zero until the base emitter voltage V_{BE} exceeds 0.7 volt. This is called the *cutoff condition* or the *OFF condition* when the transistor is used as a switch.

When V_{BE} rises above 0.7 volt, the diode conducts and allows some base current, I_b, to flow. The collector current, I_c, is equal to the base current, I_b, times the transistor current gain, h_{fe}. h_{fe}, can range from 10 to 200 depending on the transistor type. It is represented by a current generator in the collector circuit of the model. This condition is called the *active region* because the transistor is on and amplifying. It also is called the *linear region* because collector current is (approximately) linearly proportional to base current. The dotted resistance in parallel with the collector-base diode represents the leakage of the reversed biased junction, and it is normally neglected, as discussed previously.

A transistor is saturated when a large increase in the base to emitter current results in only a small increase in the collector current.

A third condition called the *saturation condition* exists under certain conditions of collector-emitter voltage and collector current. In the saturation condition, large increases in the transistor base current produce little increase in collector current. When saturated, the voltage drop across the collector-emitter is very small, usually less than 0.5 volt. This is the ON condition for a transistor switching circuit. This condition occurs in a switching circuit when the collector of the transistor is tied through a resistor, R_L, to a supply voltage, V_{cc} as shown in *Figure 3-2c*. Enough base current is supplied to the transistor to drive the transistor into the saturated condition, where the output voltage (voltage drop from collector to emitter) is very small and the collector-base diode may become forward biased. Having briefly described the behavior of transistors, it is now possible to discuss circuit applications for them.

TRANSISTOR AMPLIFIERS

In a transistor amplifier, a small change in base current results in a corresponding, larger change in collector current.

Figure 3-3 shows a transistor amplifier. The ac voltage source, V_{in}, supplies a signal current to the base-emitter circuit. The transistor is biased to operate in the linear region at some steady state I_b and I_c. The voltage source, V_{cc}, supplies the steady state dc currents, I_b, and I_c, and any signal i_c current change to the collector-emitter circuit. The small signal voltage, V_{in}, varies the base current around the steady dc operating point. This small current change is i_b, and it causes a corresponding but larger change in collector current i_c around the steady-state operating current I_c. The small signal current change causes an output voltage change v_{out} across the load resistor R_c. The small signal voltage gain of the circuit is as shown in *Figure 3-3*:

$$A = \frac{V_{out}}{V_{in}} = h_{fe}\frac{R_c}{R_b}$$

This is found by using the model and the equations, $v_{out} = i_cR_c$; $i_c = h_{fe}i_b$; and $i_b = v_{in}/R_b$, where h_{fe} is the small signal current gain.

Figure 3-3. Transistor Amplifier Circuit

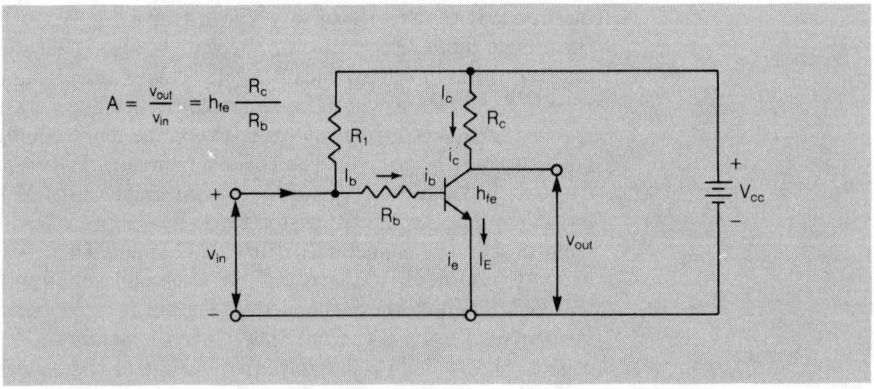

Transistor amplifiers are commonly used in analog circuits, including those in automotive systems.

Circuits such as those depicted in *Figure 3-3* are combined to make many types of amplifiers which are used in a variety of applications. Such circuits, especially when made in one package with integrated circuit technology (to be discussed later), are called linear circuits or analog circuits.

OPERATIONAL AMPLIFIERS

An op amp is a very high gain differential amplifier.

An operational amplifier (op amp) is another standard building block of integrated circuits and has many applications in analog electronic systems. It is normally connected in a circuit with external circuit elements (e.g., resistors and capacitors) that determine its operation. An op amp typically has a very high voltage gain of 10,000 or more, and has two inputs and one output (with respect to ground) as shown in *Figure 3-4a*. A signal applied to the inverting input (−) is amplified and inverted at the output. A signal applied to the noninverting input (+) is amplified but is not inverted at the output.

Figure 3-4. Operational Amplifier Circuit

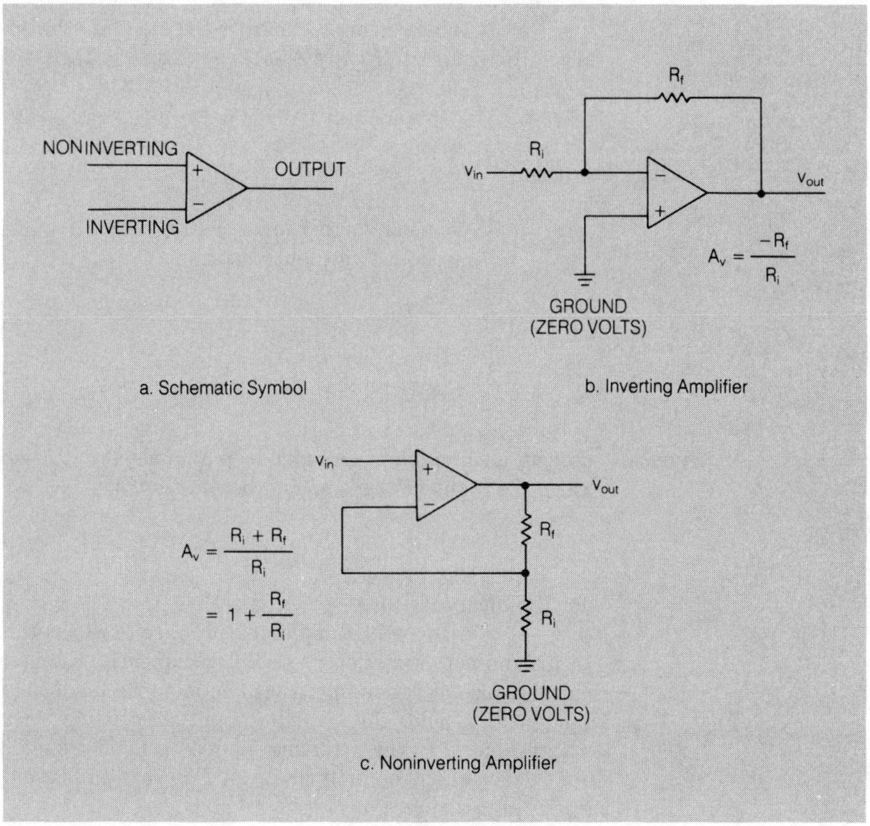

Use of Feedback in Op Amps

The op amp is normally not operated at maximum gain, but feedback techniques can be used to adjust the gain to the value desired as shown in *Figure 3-4b*. Some of the output is connected to the input through circuit elements (e.g., resistors, capacitors, etc.) to oppose the input changes. In the example of *Figure 3-4b*, the feedback path consists of resistor R_f. The gain is adjusted by the ratio of the two resistors and is calculated by:

$$A_v = \frac{-R_f}{R_i} = \frac{v_{out}}{v_{in}}$$

As indicated by applying the signal to the (−) terminal, the minus sign in the equation means signal inversion from input to output; that is, if the input goes positive, the output goes negative.

Since the op amp amplifies the voltage difference between its two inputs, it can be used as a differential amplifier as well as a single input amplifier.

It is interesting to consider the inputs to the op amp in the inverting mode configuration (*Figure 3-4b*). The output voltage v_o is given by:

$$v_o = A(v_1 - v_2)$$

where

V_1 = noninverting input voltage
V_2 = inverting input voltage

or

$$v_1 - v_2 = \frac{v_o}{A}$$

For an ideal op amp, the open-loop gain should approach infinity. In this case, the input voltages should become equal:

$$v_1 - v_2 = 0$$

for the ideal case, or $v_1 = v_2$.

The inverting amplifier of *Figure 3-4b* has the noninverting input at ground potential, i.e., $v_1 = 0$. Consequently, the inverting input is (ideally) also at ground potential. In fact, the feedback path provides a current that holds the inverting input at so-called "virtual ground." Furthermore, as the inverting input is held at ground potential, the input impedance of the op amp circuit of *Figure 3-4b* presented to input voltage v_{in} is the resistance of R_i:

$$\frac{v_{in}}{i_{in}} = R_i$$

By contrast, the input impedance presented to the input voltage v_{in} by the noninverting op amp configuration (*Figure 3-4c*) is ideally infinite. This very high input impedance is one of the primary features of the noninverting op amp configuration.

A noninverting amplifier is also possible, as shown in *Figure 3-4c*. The input signal is connected to the noninverting (+) terminal and the output is connected through a series connection of resistors to the inverting (−) input terminal. The gain, A_v, in this case is:

$$A_v = \frac{v_{out}}{v_{in}} = 1 + \frac{R_f}{R_i}$$

Besides adjusting gain, negative feedback also can help to correct for the amplifier's nonlinear operation and distortion.

Summing Mode Amplifier

One of the important op amp applications is summing of voltages. *Figure 3-5* is a schematic drawing of a summing mode op amp circuit. In this circuit, a pair of voltages v_a and v_b (relative to ground) are connected through resistances R to the inverting input. The output voltage v_o is proportional to the sum of the input voltages:

$$v_o = \frac{-R_f (v_a + v_b)}{R}$$

For example, a compatible stereo broadcast system incorporating a right channel and a left channel characterized by voltages v_R and v_L, respectively, transmits the sum of the channel voltages:

$$v_S = v_R + v_L$$

At the same time, the difference voltage v_D is transmitted on a subcarrier:

$$v_D = v_R - v_L$$

The right channel voltage can be separated from the sum and difference voltages using the circuit of *Figure 3-5*. Replacing voltages v_a and v_b by v_S and v_D, respectively, yields an output:

$$v_o = \frac{-R_f}{R} (v_R + v_L + v_R - v_L)$$

$$= \left(\frac{-2R_f}{R}\right) v_R$$

A simple extension of this circuit permits similar separation of the left channel voltage.

Figure 3-5. Summing Amplifier

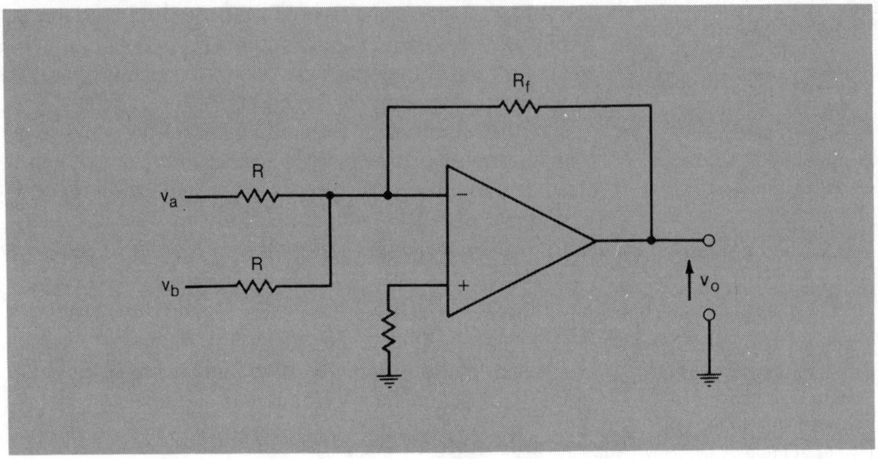

Analog Computers

Analog computers, like those used to simulate the performance of automotive systems, are constructed with operational amplifiers.

The op amp is the basic building block for analog computers. Analog computers are used to simulate the behavior of other systems. Virtually any system that can be described in a block diagram using standard building blocks can be duplicated on an analog computer. If a control system designer is building an automotive speed controller and does not want to waste a lot of time and money testing prototypes on a real car, he/she can program the analog computer to simulate the car's speed electronically. By varying amplifier gains, frequency responses, resistor, capacitor, and inductor values, system parameters can be varied to study their effect on system performance. Such system studies help to determine the parts needed for a system before any hardware is built.

The main problem with analog circuits and analog computers is that their performance changes with changes in temperature, supply voltage, signal levels, and noise levels. While most of these problems are eliminated when digital circuits are used, analog computers are much more cost effective when dealing with relatively simple systems. However, analog computers have effectively been replaced in all practical applications by a corresponding digital computer.

DIGITAL CIRCUITS

Binary circuits can operate in only one of two (binary) states (on or off).

Digital circuits, including digital computers, are formed from binary circuits. Binary digital circuits are circuits whose output can be only one of two different states. Each state is indicated by a particular voltage or current level. An example of a simple binary digital system is a door-open indicator on a car. When your car door is opened, a light comes on. When it is closed, the light goes out. The system's output (the light from the bulk) is either on or off. The on state means the door is open, the off state means it is shut.

Digital circuits also can use transistors. In a digital circuit, a transistor is in either one of two modes of operation: on, conducting at saturation; or off, in the cutoff state.

In electronic digital systems, a transistor is used as a switch. Remember that the transistor has three operating regions; cutoff, active, and saturation. If only the saturation or cutoff regions are used, the transistor acts like a switch. When in saturation, the transistor is ON and has very low resistance; when in cutoff, it is OFF and has very high resistance. In digital circuits, the control input to the transistor switch must be capable of either saturating the transistor or turning it off without allowing operation in the active region. In the model of *Figure 3-2c*, the ON condition is indicated by a very low collector-to-emitter voltage and the OFF condition by a collector-to-emitter voltage equal to the supply voltage.

Binary Number System

Combinations of digital circuits are capable of representing numbers in a binary number system.

Digital circuits function by representing various quantities numerically using a binary number system. In a binary number system, all numbers are represented using only the symbols 1 (one) and 0 (zero) arranged in the form of a place position number system. Electronically, these symbols can be represented by transistors in either saturation or cutoff. Before proceeding with a discussion of digital circuits, it is instructive to review the binary number system briefly.

The binary number system uses only two digits, 0 or 1, and is called a base 2 system. The decimal system uses 10 digits, 0 through 9, and is called a base 10 system. In the decimal system, numbers are grouped from right to left with the first digit representing the one's place (10^0), the second digit the ten's place (10^1), the third digit the hundred's place (10^2), and so on. Each place increases in value by a power of 10.

In the binary system, numbers are also grouped from right to left. The rightmost digit is in the one's place (2^0) and, because only the numbers 0 and 1 can be represented, the second digit must be the two's place (2^1), the third digit the four's place (2^2), the fourth digit the eight's place (2^3), and so on. Each place increases in value by a power of 2. *Table 3-1* shows a comparison of place values. *Table 3-2* shows the binary equivalent for some decimal numbers. For example, the binary number 0010 is read as "zero, zero, one, zero"; not "10."

Table 3-1. Comparison of Place Values

Also called digit position.

	DECIMAL-Base 10				BINARY-Base 2				
PLACE	4	3	2	1	5	4	3	2	1
VALUE	1000	100	10	1	16	8	4	2	1
POWER of BASE	3	2	1	0	4	3	2	1	0

Table 3-2. Comparison of Numbers in Different Bases

DECIMAL Base 10	BINARY Base 2
0	0000
1	0001
2	0010
3	0011
4	0100
5	0101
6	0110
7	0111
8	1000
9	1001
10	1010
11	1011
12	1100
13	1101
14	1110
15	1111
16	10000
255	11111111
256	100000000

To convert from binary to decimal, just multiply each binary digit by its place value and add the products. For instance, the decimal equivalent of the binary number 1010 is given by:

$$\begin{aligned} 1010_2 &= (1 \times 8) + (0 \times 4) + (1 \times 2) + (0 \times 1) \\ &= 8 + 2 \\ &= 10_{10} \end{aligned}$$

1010_2 means that the number is a base 2 or binary number. 10_{10} means the number is a base 10 or decimal number. Normal notation eliminates the subscripts 2 and 10 if the number system is clear from the context.

Converting from decimal to binary can be accomplished by finding the largest number that is a power of 2 (divisor) that will divide into the decimal number (dividend) with a one as a quotient, putting a one in its place, and subtracting the divisor (the number used to divide with) from the decimal number (dividend) to get a remainder. The operation is repeated by dividing with the next lower number that is a power of two until the binary one's place has been tested. Any time the dividend is less than the divisor, a zero is put in that place and the next power of 2 divisor is tried. For instance, to find the binary equivalent for the decimal number 73, the largest number that is a power of two and that will divide into 73 with a quotient of 1 is 64 (2^6):

$$(2^6) \quad \frac{73}{64} = 1 \qquad 73 - 64 = 9$$

$$(2^5) \quad \frac{9}{32} = 0$$

$$(2^4) \quad \frac{9}{16} = 0$$

$$(2^3) \quad \frac{9}{8} = 1 \qquad 9 - 8 = 1$$

$$(2^2) \quad \frac{1}{4} = 0$$

$$(2^1) \quad \frac{1}{2} = 0$$

$$(2^0) \quad \frac{1}{1} = 1 \qquad 1 - 1 = 0$$

therefore:

$$73 = 1001001$$

LOGIC CIRCUITS (COMBINATORIAL)

Digital computers can perform the *b*inary dig*it* (bit) manipulations very easily by using three basic logic circuits or gates. These gates are called the NOT gate, the AND gate, and the OR gate. Digital gates operate on logical variables that can have one of two possible values (e.g., true - false, saturation - cutoff, or 1 - 0). As was previously explained, numerical values are represented by combinations of 0 or 1 in a binary number system.

As mentioned earlier, digital circuits operate with transistors in one of two possible states—saturation or cutoff. Since these two states can be used to represent binary numbers 1 or 0, combinations of transistors that are in one of these two states can be used to represent multiple digit binary numbers. The input and output voltages for such digital circuits will be either "high" or "low," corresponding to 1 or 0. High voltage means that the voltage exceeds a high threshold value that is denoted v_H. Symbolically, the high voltage condition corresponding to logic 1 is written:

$$v > v_H$$

meaning v exceeds v_H. Similarly, low voltage means that voltage v is given by:

$$v < v_L$$

meaning v is less than v_L, where v_L denotes the low threshold value. The actual values for v_H and v_L depend upon the technology for implementing the circuit. Typical values are $v_H = 2.4$ volts, and $v_L = 0.8$ volt.

The representation of digital circuit operation is done in terms of logical variables that are denoted here with capital letters. For example, in the next few sections A, B, and C represent logic variables and can have values 0 and 1.

NOT Gate

A NOT gate inverts input 1 to 0, and input 0 to 1.

The NOT gate is a logic inverter. If the input is a logic 1, the output is a logic 0. If the input is a logic 0, the output is a logic 1. It changes zeros to ones and ones to zeros. The transistor inverting amplifier of *Figure 3-3* performs the same function if operated from cutoff to saturation. A high base voltage (logic 1)[1] produces a low (logic 0) collector voltage and vice versa. *Figure 3-6a* shows the schematic symbol for a NOT gate. Next to the schematic symbol is what is called a "truth table." The truth table lists all of the possible combinations of input A and output B for the circuit. The logic symbol is shown also. The logic symbol is read as "NOT A."

AND Gate

An AND gate requires all input signal levels to be high for the output signal to be high.

The AND gate is slightly more complicated. The AND gate has at least two inputs and one output. The one shown in *Figure 3-6b* has two inputs. The output is high (1) only when both (all) inputs are high (1). If either or both inputs are low (0), the output is low (0). *Figure 3-6b* shows the truth table, schematic, and logic symbol for this gate. The two inputs are labeled A and B. Notice that there are four combinations of A and B, but only one results in a high output.

OR Gate

The output signal of an OR gate is high when any one of its input signal levels is high.

The OR gate, like the AND gate, has at least two inputs and one output. The one shown in *Figure 3-6c* has two inputs. The output is high (1) whenever one or both (any) inputs are high (1). The output is low (0) only when both inputs are low (0). *Figure 3-6c* shows the schematic symbol, logic symbol, and truth table for the OR gate.

NAND and NOR

NAND and NOR gates may be constructed by combining AND, OR, and NOT gates.

Other logic functions can be generated by combining these basic gates. An inverter can be placed after an AND gate to produce a NOT-AND gate. When the inverter is an integral part of the gate, the gate is called a NAND gate. The same can be done with an OR gate and the resultant gate is called a NOR gate. The truth table and schematic symbol for both of these gates are shown in *Figure 3-6d* and *3-6e*. Notice that the

[1]Positive logic defines the most positive voltage as logic 1. Negative logic defines the most positive voltage as logic 0. Positive logic is used throughout this book.

Figure 3-6.
Basic Logic Gates

Provides output conditions for all combinations of inputs.

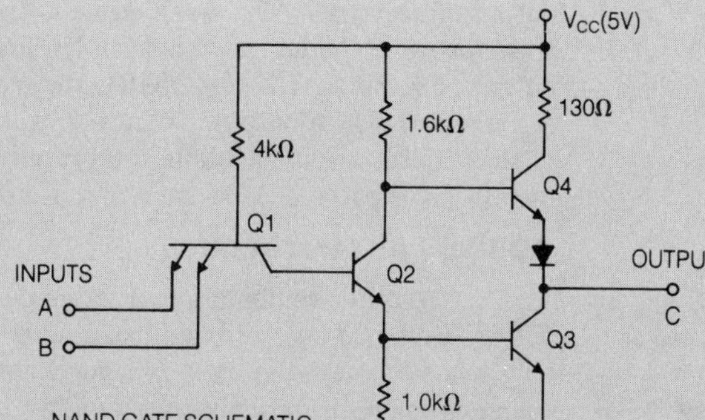

NAND GATE SCHEMATIC

SCHEMATIC SYMBOL	TRUTH TABLE	LOGIC SYMBOL
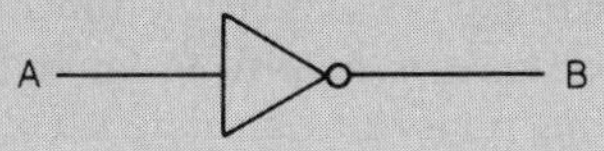 a. NOT	A B 0 1 1 0	$\bar{A}$ (over bar)
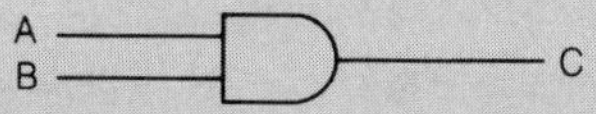 b. AND	A B C 0 0 0 0 1 0 1 0 0 1 1 1	A • B = C (Large dot)
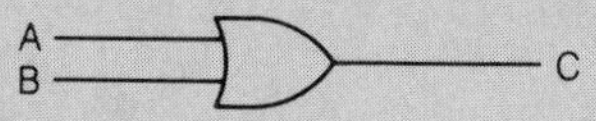 c. OR	A B C 0 0 0 0 1 1 1 0 1 1 1 1	A + B = C (Plus sign)
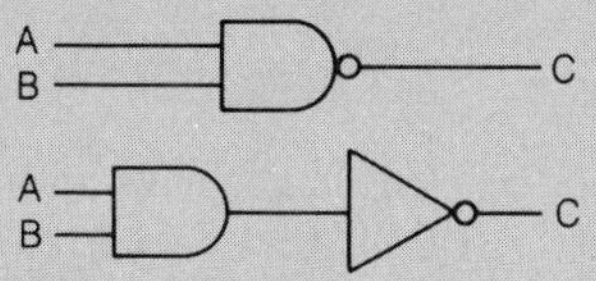 d. NAND	A B C 0 0 1 0 1 1 1 0 1 1 1 0	$\overline{A \bullet B} = C$
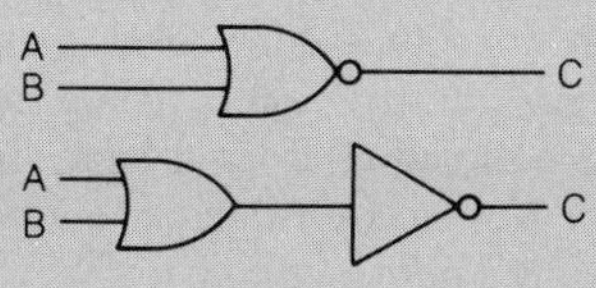 e. NOR	A B C 0 0 1 0 1 0 1 0 0 1 1 0	$\overline{A + B} = C$

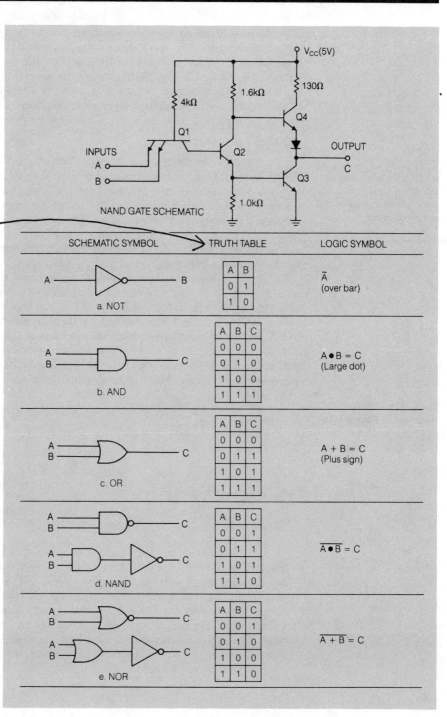

NOT function is indicated on the schematic symbol by a small circle at the output of each gate. The small circle is the schematic symbol for NOT, and the overbar is the logic symbol for NOT. Notice also that the truth table outputs for the NAND and NOR gate are the reverse of those for the AND and OR gate outputs. Where C was 1, it is now 0 and vice versa. All of these gates are available in integrated circuit form with different quantities of gates in a package and a different number of inputs per gate.

XOR and Adder Circuits

XOR gates, which output a high only when one or the other input is high, are commonly used to add binary numbers.

Another combination of gates performs the exclusive OR function, abbreviated as XOR, and is illustrated in *Figure 3–7a*. The output is high only when one input is high, but not when both are high. This gate very commonly is used for comparison of two binary numbers because if both inputs are the same, the output is zero. The equivalent combination of gates that performs this function is shown in *Figure 3–7a*. The XOR gate is also available in an integral package so it is not necessary for the designer to interconnect separate gates to build the function.

All of these gates can be used to build digital circuits that perform all of the arithmetic functions of a calculator. *Table 3–3* shows the addition of two binary bits in all the combinations that can occur. Note that in the case of adding a 1 to a 1, the sum is zero, and a 1, called a carry, is placed in the next place value to be added with any bits in that place value. A digital circuit designed to perform the addition of two binary bits is called a half adder and is shown in *Figure 3–7b*. It produces the sum and any necessary carry, as shown in the truth table.

Table 3-3. Addition of Binary Bits

Bit A	0	0	1	1
Bit B	0	1	0	1
Sum	0	1	1	10

A half adder circuit does not have an input to accept a carry from a previous place value. A circuit that does is called a full adder (*Figure 3–7c*). A series of full adder circuits can be combined to add binary numbers with as many digits as desired. A simple electronic calculator performs all arithmetic operations using full-adder circuits and a few additional logic circuits. In such circuits, subtraction is performed as a modified form of addition by using some of the additional logic circuits. In addition, multiplication is accomplished by repeated addition, and division is accomplished by repeated subtraction.

Figure 3-7.
XOR and Adders

SCHEMATIC SYMBOL	TRUTH TABLE	LOGIC SYMBOL

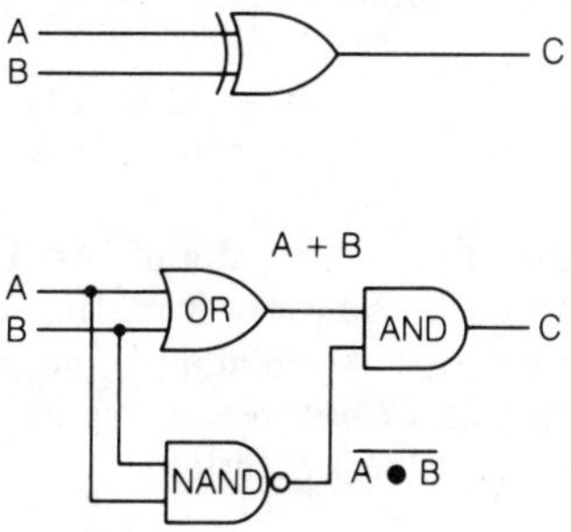

A	B	C
0	0	0
0	1	1
1	0	1
1	1	0

$A \oplus B = C$

$(A + B) \bullet (\overline{A \bullet B}) = C$

a. XOR

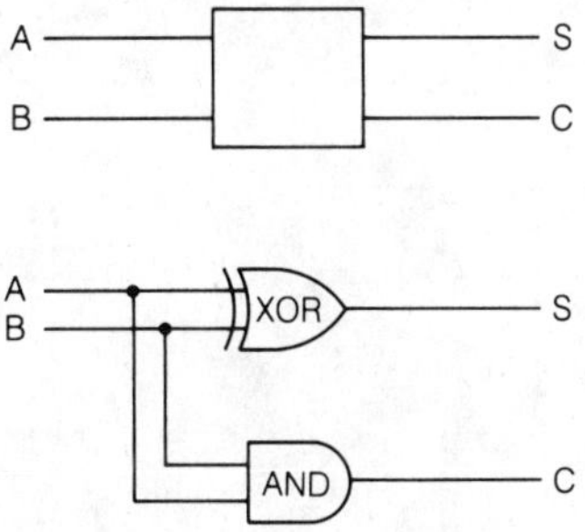

A	B	C	S
0	0	0	0
0	1	0	1
1	0	0	1
1	1	1	0

$S = A\bar{B} + \bar{A}B$

$C = AB$

b. Half-Adder

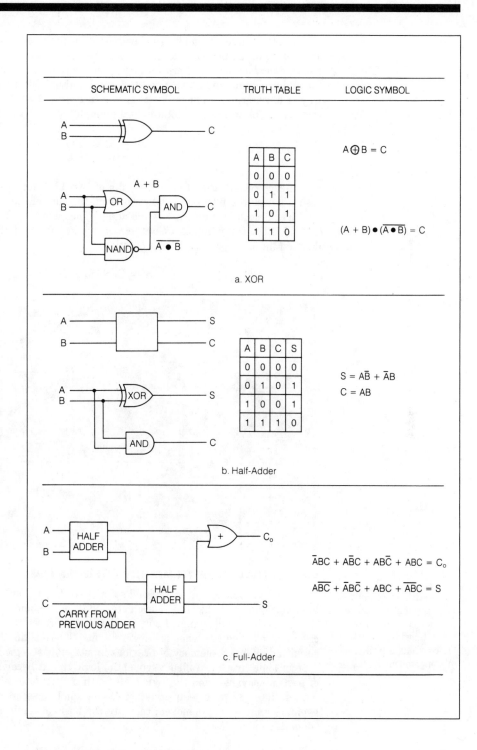

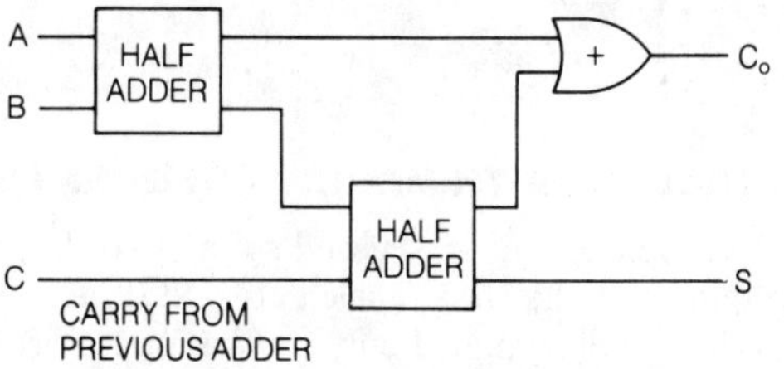

$\bar{A}BC + A\bar{B}C + AB\bar{C} + ABC = C_o$

$A\overline{BC} + \bar{A}B\bar{C} + ABC + \overline{AB}C = S$

c. Full-Adder

Of course, the addition of pairs of 1-bit numbers has no major application in digital computers. On the other hand, the addition of multiple-bit numbers is of crucial importance in digital computers. The 1-bit full adder circuit can be expanded to form a multiple bit adder circuit. By way of illustration, a 4-bit adder is shown in *Figure 3-8*. Here the 4-bit numbers in place position notation are given by:

$$A = a_4\, a_3\, a_2\, a_1$$
$$B = b_4\, b_3\, b_2\, b_1$$

where each bit is either 1 or 0. The sum of two 4-bit numbers has a 5-bit result, where the fifth bit is the carry from the sum of the most significant bits. Each block labeled FA is a full adder. The carry out from a given FA (i.e., C) is the carry in (i.e., C′ of the next highest full adder. The sum S is denoted (in place position binary notation):

$$S = C_4\, S_4\, S_3\, S_2\, S_1$$

Figure 3-8.
A 4-Bit Digital Adder

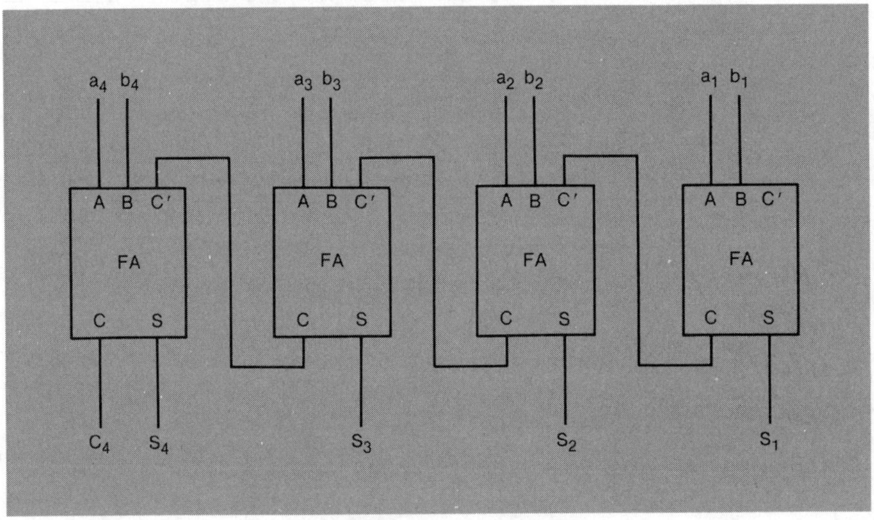

LOGIC CIRCUITS WITH MEMORY (SEQUENTIAL)

Sequential logic circuits have the ability to store, or remember, previous logic states. Sequential logic circuits are the basis of computer memories.

The logic circuits discussed so far have been simple interconnections of the three basic gates NOT, AND, and OR. The output of each system is determined only by the inputs present at that time. These circuits are called combinatorial logic circuits. There is another type of logic circuit and it has a memory of previous inputs or past logic states. This type of logic circuit is called a sequential logic circuit because the sequence of past input values and the logic state at that time determines the present output state. Because sequential logic circuits hold or store information even after inputs are removed, they are the basis of semiconductor computer memories.

R-S Flip-Flop

A sequential logic circuit called an R-S flip-flop can be set into either state. It will remain latched in that state until it set to the opposite state by the presence of opposing logic signals on its two inputs.

A very simple memory circuit can be made by interconnecting two NAND gates, as in *Figure 3–9a*. A careful study of the circuit reveals that when S is high (1) and R is low (0), the output Q is set high and remains high regardless of whether S is high or low at any later time. The high state of S is said to be latched into the state of Q. The only way Q can be unlatched to go low is to let R go high and S go low. This resets the latch. This type of memory device is called a Reset-Set (R-S) flip-flop and is the basic building block of sequential logic circuits. The term "flip-flop" describes the action of the logic level changes at Q. Notice from the truth table that R and S must not be 1 at the same time. Under this condition, the two gates are bucking each other, and the final state of the flip-flop output is uncertain.

Figure 3–9. Flip-Flops

The basic memory building blocks,

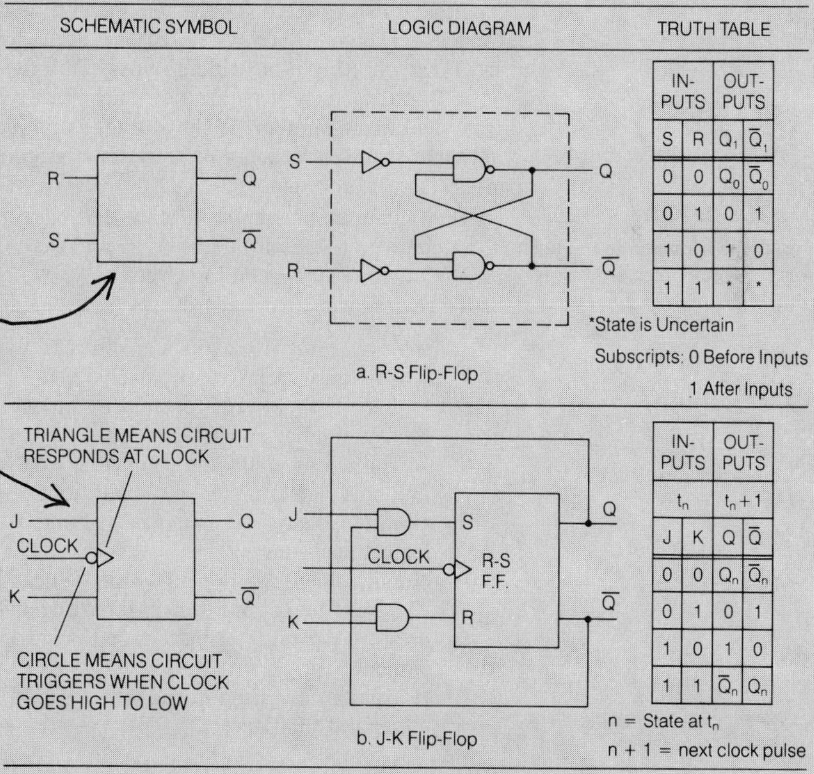

INPUTS		OUTPUTS	
S	R	Q_1	$\overline{Q}_1$
0	0	Q_0	$\overline{Q}_0$
0	1	0	1
1	0	1	0
1	1	*	*

*State is Uncertain

Subscripts: 0 Before Inputs

1 After Inputs

a. R-S Flip-Flop

INPUTS		OUTPUTS	
t_n		t_n+1	
J	K	Q	$\overline{Q}$
0	0	Q_n	$\overline{Q}_n$
0	1	0	1
1	0	1	0
1	1	$\overline{Q}_n$	Q_n

n = State at t_n

n + 1 = next clock pulse

b. J-K Flip-Flop

J-K Flip-Flop

The J-K flip-flop circuit is superior to the R-S flip-flop circuit because it resolves ambiguities resulting from simultaneous inputs.

A flip-flop where the uncertain state of simultaneous inputs on R and S is solved is shown in *Figure 3–9b*. It is called a J-K flip-flop and can be obtained from an R-S flip-flop by adding additional logic gating, as shown in the logic diagram. When both J and K inputs are 1, the flip-flop changes to a state other than the one it was in. The flip-flop shown in this case is a synchronized one. That means it changes state at a particular time determined by a timing pulse, called the clock, being applied to the circuit at the terminal marked by a triangle. The little circle at the clock terminal means the circuit responds when the clock goes from a high level to a low level. If the circle is not present, the circuit responds when the clock goes from a low level to a high level.

Synchronous Counter

Figure 3–10 shows a four-stage synchronous counter. It is synchronous because all stages are triggered at the same time by the same clock pulse. It has 4 stages; therefore, it counts 2^4 or 16 clock pulses before it returns to a starting state. The timed waveforms appearing at each Q output are also shown. It is easy to see how such circuitry can be used for counting, for generating other timing pulses, and for determining timed sequences. One can easily visualize how such stages can be lined up to store the digits of a binary number. If the storage is temporary, then such a combination of stages is called a register. If storage is to be more permanent, it is called memory.

Digital counter circuits can easily be arranged to develop circuits which are used in digital clocks.

Digital clocks, as well as circuits that convert binary numbers to decimal numbers so they can be displayed and read by humans, are made up of many stages of such counting circuits.

To review what has been discussed about digital circuits:

a. they operate with signals at discrete levels rather than with signals whose level varies continuously;
b. high and low voltage levels are commonly used to represent the binary numbers 0 and 1;
c. combinations of 1's and 0's can be used as codes to represent numbers, letters, symbols, conditions, etc.;
d. circuits called gates (*Figures 3–6* and *3–7*) can be combined to make logical decisions;
e. circuits called flip-flops (*Figure 3–9*) can be used to store 1's and 0's. They can be set or reset into particular binary sequences to produce or store digital information, or to count, or to produce timed digital signals;
f. transistors are used in the ON and OFF condition in circuits to form gates and flip-flops.

Figure 3-10. A 4-Stage Synchronous Counter

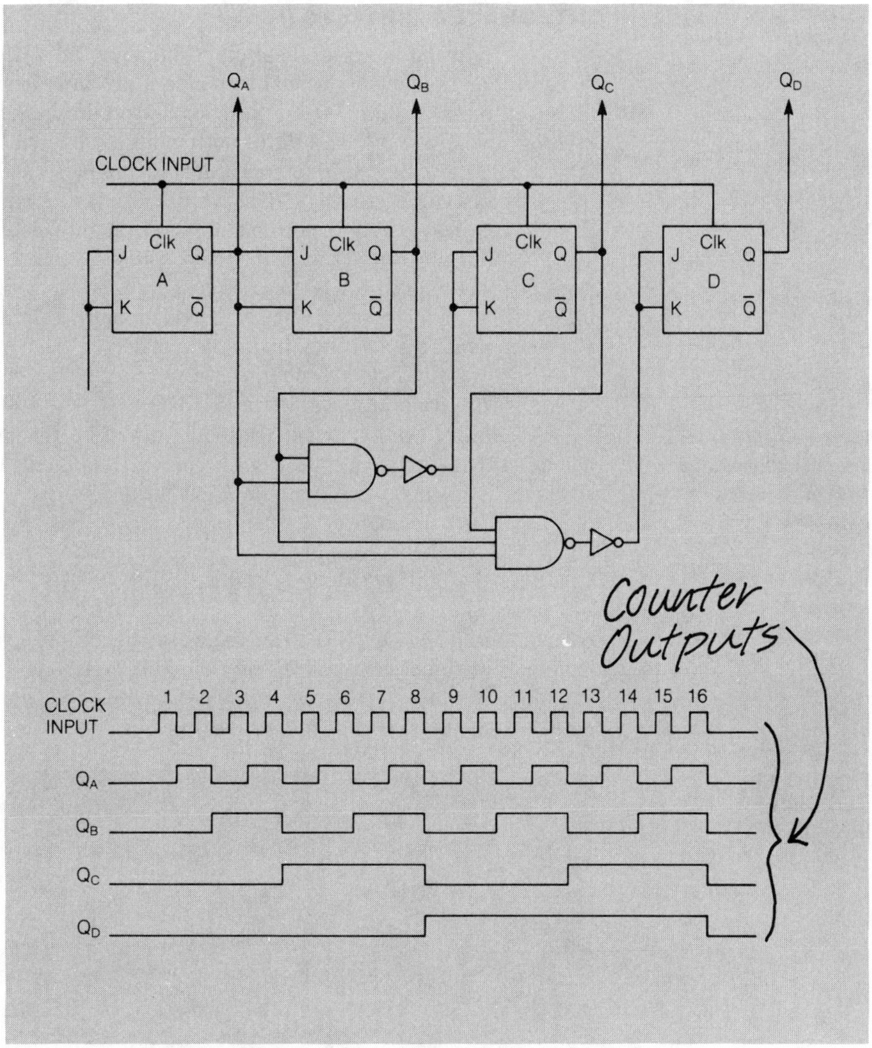

ICs are ideal for digital circuits because the digital circuits consist of many interconnected identical gates.

Digital electronic systems send and receive signals made up of 1's and 0's in the form of codes. The digital codes represent the information that is moved through the digital systems by the digital circuits. Digital systems are made up of many *identical* logic gates and flip-flops interconnected to do the function required of the system. As a result, digital circuits are ideal for implementation in integrated circuits (ICs) because all components can be made at the same time on a small silicon area.

INTEGRATED CIRCUITS (ICs)

By using integrated circuit technology, all of the counters, registers, and binary-to-decimal converters are produced at the same time on a tiny piece of silicon semiconductor material by photolithography (photographic printing) and diffusion (modifying one material by combining it with another using high temperature) techniques. This is the heart of integrated circuit technology. The results are very small, high performance circuits that use very low power and have a high reliability.

The earliest ICs appeared about 1960 and had relatively few gates, typically on the order of 10 to 12. Those devices were known as small scale integration (SSI) circuits (ICs). By 1970, medium scale integration (MSI) ICs were available and they had on the order of 1,000 gates. The evolution of technology continued through phases of large scale integration (LSI) ICs, to very large scale integration (VLSI) ICs that had 5,000 or more gates.

Digital circuits are now available as electronic systems or subsystems packaged as ICs.

One of the important consequences of IC technological progress has been that digital circuits have become available (in IC form) as electronic systems or subsystems. That is, the functional capability of digital circuits in single IC packages or "chips" has spectacularly increased in the past 20 years. One of the important digital systems that is available as an LSI IC is the arithmetic and logic unit (ALU).

Figure 3-11 is a sketch of a typical ALU showing the various connections. This 4-bit ALU has the capability of performing 16 possible logical or arithmetic operations on two 4-bit inputs, A and B. *Table 3-4* is a summary of these various operations expressed by using the logical notation explained earlier in this chapter.

Figure 3-11. ALU Circuit Configuration

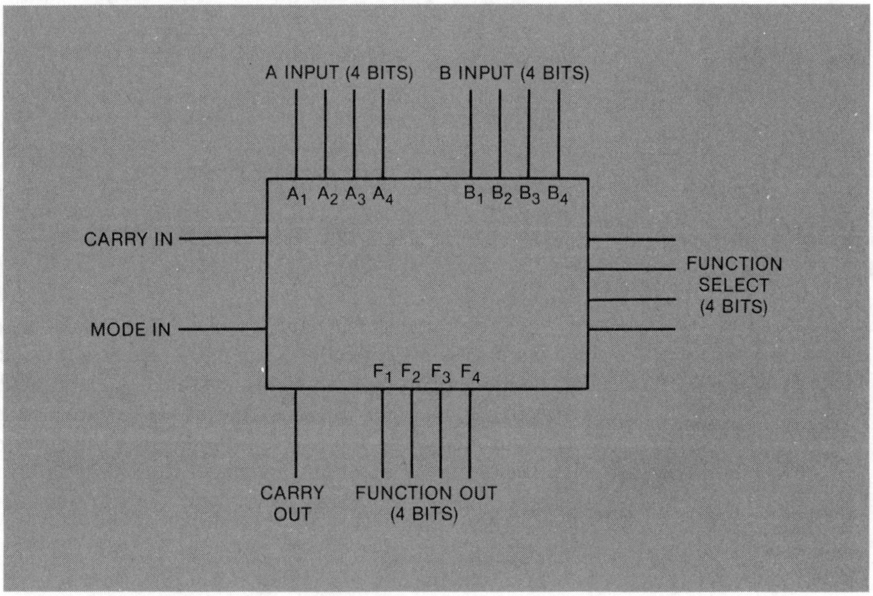

Table 3-4. Arithmetic Logic Functions

Select, S Input	Logic Function, $M = 1$	Arithmetic Function, $M = 0$	
		$c_n = 1$	$C_n = 0$
0000	$F = \overline{A}$ (NOT)	$F = A$	$F = A$ Plus 1
0001	$F = \overline{A + B}$ (NOR)	$F = A + B$	$F = A + B)$ Plus 1
0010	$F = \overline{A}B$	$F = A + \overline{B}$	$F = (A + \overline{B})$ Plus 1
0011	$F = 0$	$F =$ Minus 1 (2's Complement)	$F = 0$
0100	$F = \overline{AB}$ (NAND)	$F = A + A\overline{B}$	$F = (A + A\overline{B})$ Plus 1
0101	$F = \overline{B}$ (NOT)	$F = (A + B)$ Plus $A\overline{B}$	$F = (A + B)$ Plus $A\overline{B} + 1$
0110	$F = AB + B\overline{A}$ (Exclusive OR)	$F = (A - B)$ Minus 1	$F = A$ Minus B
0111	$F = A\overline{B}$	$F = A\overline{B}$ Minus 1	$F = \overline{AB}$
1000	$F = \overline{A} + B$ (Implication)	$F = A + AB$	$F = (A + B)$ Plus 1
1001	$F = \overline{AB} + AB$ (NOT Exclusive OR)	$F = A + B$	$F = (A + B)$ Plus 1
1010	$F = B$	$F = (A + \overline{B})$ Plus AB	$F = (A + \overline{B})$ Plus $A + 1$
1011	$F = AB$ (AND)	$F = AB$ Minus 1	$F = AB$
1100	$F = 1$	$F = A$ Plus A*	$F = (A + A)$ Plus 1
1101	$F = A + \overline{B}$	$F = (A + B)$ Plus A	$F = (A + \underline{B})$ Plus $A + 1$
1110	$F = A + B$ (OR)	$F = (A + B)$ Plus A	$F = (A + \overline{B})$ Plus $A + 1$
1111	$F = A$	$F = A$ Minus 1	$F = A$

**Each bit is shifted to the next more significant position.*

Perhaps the single most important digital integrated circuit to evolve has been the microprocessor (MPU). This important device incorporating about 50,000 gates in an area of about 1/4-inch square has truly revolutionized digital electronic system development. A microprocessor is the operational core of a microcomputer and has broad application in automotive electronics systems.

The MPU incorporates a relatively complicated combination of digital circuits including an ALU, registers, and decoding logic. A typical MPU block diagram is shown in *Figure 3-12*. The double lines labeled "bus" are actually sets of conductors for carrying digital data throughout the MPU. Common IC MPUs use 8, 16, or 32 conductor buses.

Figure 3-12.
MPU Block Diagram

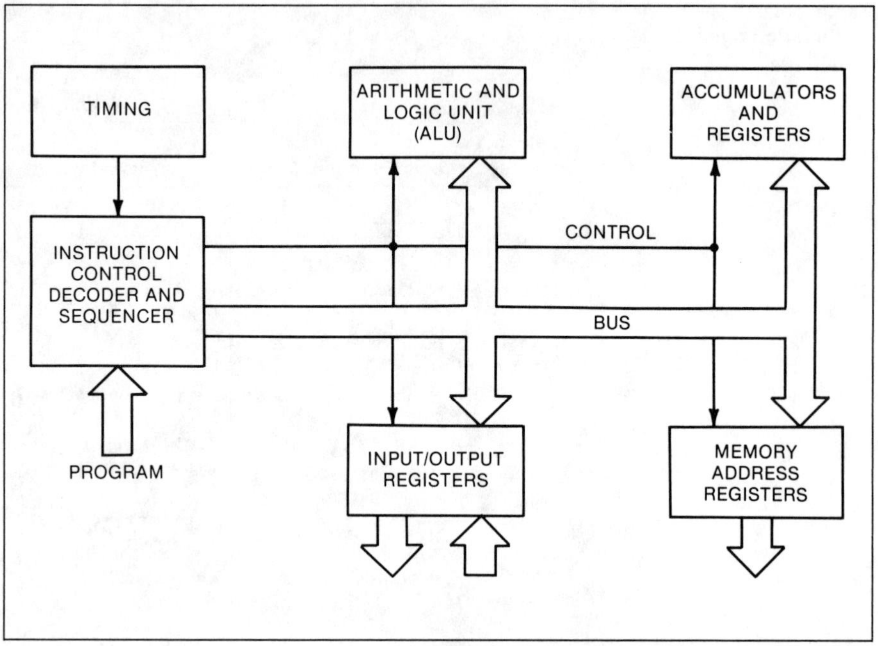

The microprocessor in combination with memory and other circuits under program control can accomplish very complex tasks.

A microprocessor by itself can accomplish nothing. It requires additional, external digital circuitry as explained in the next chapter. One of the tasks performed by the external circuitry is to provide "instructions" in the form of digitally encoded electrical signals. For example, an 8-bit microprocessor operates with 8-bit instructions. There are 2^8 (or 256) possible logical combinations of 8 bits corresponding to 256 possible MPU instructions, each causing a specific operation. A complete summary of these operations and the corresponding instructional called microinstructions is beyond the scope of this book. A few of the more important instructions are explained in the next chapter which further expands the discussion of this important device. The interested reader is directed to other titles in the "Understanding Series" for more detailed discussion of the MPU (e.g., "Understanding Microprocessors").

Quiz for Chapter 3

1. Forward conventional current flows in a diode circuit from
   - **a.** anode to cathode
   - **b.** anode to anode
   - **c.** cathode to anode
   - **d.** cathode to cathode
2. Forward conventional current for a PNP transistor flows from
   - **a.** base to ground
   - **b.** base to emitter
   - **c.** emitter to base
   - **d.** collector to base
3. The op amp is what type of circuit?
   - **a.** digital
   - **b.** analog
   - **c.** logic gate
   - **d.** none of the above
4. The AND gate is what type of circuit?
   - **a.** digital
   - **b.** analog
   - **c.** amplifier
   - **d.** inverter
5. Which conditions cause the output of an XOR gate to be high?
   - **a.** both inputs are low
   - **b.** both inputs are high
   - **c.** either input is high but not both
   - **d.** both inputs a zero
6. An R-S latch is what type of digital logic?
   - **a.** combinational logic
   - **b.** sequential logic
   - **c.** Fortran
   - **d.** J-K
7. Flip-flops are used in what type of logic systems?
   - **a.** memories
   - **b.** counters
   - **c.** data registers
   - **d.** all of the above
8. Integrated circuits are used in automotive electronic systems because they have
   - **a.** excellent functional performance
   - **b.** high reliability
   - **c.** small size
   - **d.** low cost
   - **e.** all of the above
9. Digital circuits operate with voltages representing
   - **a.** an analog of a physical quantity being measured
   - **b.** the electrical equivalent of 1 or 0
   - **c.** proportional currents
   - **d.** none of the above
10. A half adder circuit can be made from
    - **a.** an operational amplifier
    - **b.** three NOT gates
    - **c.** two OR gates
    - **d.** an XOR in combination with AND gate
11. A full adder can be made from
    - **a.** a half adder with carry in
    - **b.** two half adder circuits with carry in
    - **c.** an R-S flip flop
    - **d.** all of the above
12. Which of the following devices require the use of semiconductors?
    - **a.** transistors
    - **b.** diodes
    - **c.** integrated circuits
    - **d.** all of the above

13. In which of the following circuits is a diode used?
a. filter
b. rectifier
c. resistor
d. capacitor

14. What device is used to smooth out the bumpy output of the rectifier circuit?
a. capacitor
b. resistor
c. diode
d. transistor

15. In which type of circuits are transistors used?
a. amplifiers
b. op amps
c. logic gates
d. all of the above

16. Which of the following conditions cause the output of an OR gate to be low?
a. both inputs are high
b. only one input is high
c. both inputs are low

17. Which of the following conditions cause the outputs of an AND gate to be high?
a. both inputs are low
b. both inputs are high
c. one input is low
d. at least one input is low

18. What decimal number does the binary number 0110 represent?
a. 4
b. 3
c. 110
d. 6

19. What binary number does the decimal number 10 represent?
a. 0010
b. 0101
c. 1010
d. 1000

20. The binary addition of 0110 and 10010 produces what binary sum?
a. 1000
b. 0111
c. 1111
d. 1010

Microcomputer Instrumentation and Control

ABOUT THIS CHAPTER

This chapter explains microcomputers and how they are used in instrumentation and control systems. Topics include microcomputer fundamentals, microcomputer equipment, microcomputer inputs and outputs, computerized instrumentation, and computerized control systems. The specific automotive applications of microcomputers are explained in later chapters.

MICROCOMPUTER FUNDAMENTALS

Digital Versus Analog Computers

Analog computers use continuous electrical signals to represent physical quantities so that the performance and functions of physical systems can be simulated. In an analog system, physical variables are represented by proportional voltages that are analogous to corresponding physical variables.

A digital computer represents each variable in terms of binary numbers.

In digital computer-based systems, the physical variables are represented by a numerical equivalent using a form of the binary (i.e., base 2) number system. In the previous chapter it was shown that transistor circuits can be constructed to have one of two stable states—saturation and cutoff. These two states can be used to represent a 0 (zero) or a 1 (one) in a binary number system. To be practically useful, there must be groups of such circuits that are arranged in the form of a place position, binary number system.

By contrast, an analog system has a single lead with a voltage (relative to ground) that is proportional to the relevant physical variable. A digital system will have a group of leads, each one of which can have only two voltage levels representing 0 or 1 (as discussed in Chapter 3). It is common practice for a digital computer to have the number of voltages representing the binary digits (bits) be a multiple of eight. For example, many automotive engine control computers use eight bits to represent data, which means that 256 (2^8) possible levels can be represented. In any application, including automotive, a computer performs various operations on the data. To explain the operation of a digital computer, it is helpful to first explain the operation of its various components.

Parts of a Computer

The parts of a digital computer are shown in *Figure 4-1.* The *central processing unit* (CPU) is the processor, and when made in an integrated circuit, it is called a microprocessor. It is where all of the arithmetic and logic decisions are made. This is the calculator part of the computer.

Figure 4-1. Basic Computer Block Diagram

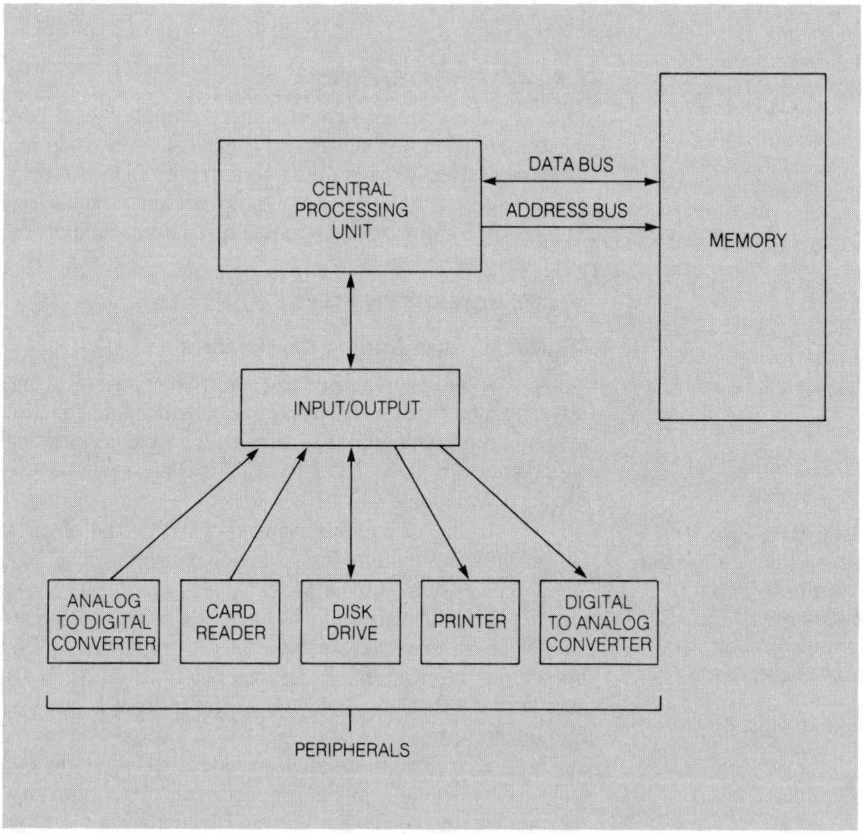

A digital computer consists of a CPU to process information, a memory to store information, and input/output sections to communicate with the user.

Memory holds the program and data. The computer can change the information in memory by writing new information into memory, or it can obtain information in memory by reading the information from memory. Each memory location has a unique address that the CPU uses to find the information it needs.

Information (or data) must be put into the computer in a form that the computer can read, and the computer must present an output in a form that can be read by humans. The input and output devices, called *peripherals*, do these conversions. Peripherals are devices such as paper tape readers and punches, card readers and punches, keyboard/CRT (cathode ray tube) terminals, magnetic tape units, magnetic disk units, and printers. The arrows in *Figure 4-1* on the interconnection lines indicate the flow of data.

Microcomputers Versus Main Frame Computers

Microcomputers cost less and occupy less space than the mainframe computers commonly used by governments and large businesses. However, the microcomputers operate slower and are less accurate in mathematical operations.

With this general idea of what a computer is, it is instructive to compare a general purpose (main frame) computer and a microcomputer. A microcomputer is just a small computer, typically thousands of times smaller than the large, general purpose main frame computers used by banks and large corporations. Microcomputers cost much less than main frames, and their computing power and speed is only a fraction of that of a main frame. A typical main frame computer costs from tens of thousands of dollars to millions of dollars and is capable of hundreds of thousands of arithmetic operations per second (additions, subtractions, multiplications, and divisions). A microcomputer costs from a little less than $1,000 to $15,000 and can perform several thousand operations per second. More important for mathematical calculations than the speed of the operation is the accuracy of the operation. Main frame computers use up to 64 bits to obtain high accuracy when doing arithmetic. The decimal equivalent for the largest number that can be represented using 64 bits is roughly 10 to the 19th power (1 followed by 19 zeros). A typical engine control microcomputer does arithmetic using only 8 bits. The largest decimal number that can be represented in 8 bits is 127, if one of the bits is used as a sign bit to indicate whether the number is positive or negative.

Programs

A program is a set of steps (instructions) in a logical order. The computer follows these steps to perform a given task.

A program is a set of instructions organized into a particular sequence to do a particular task. The first computers were little more than fancy calculators. They did only simple arithmetic and logic decisions. They were programmed (given instructions) by punching special codes into a paper tape that was then read by the machine and interpreted as instructions. A program containing thousands of instructions running on an early model machine might require yards of paper tape. The computer would process the program by reading an instruction from the tape, perform the instruction, read another instruction from the tape, and so on until the end of the program. Reading paper tape is a slow process compared to the speed with which a modern computer can perform the requested functions. In addition, the tape must be fed through the computer each time the program is run which is cumbersome and allows for the possibility of the tape wearing and breaking.

Stored Programs

To minimize the use of paper tape, and to increase computational efficiency, a method was invented several years ago to temporarily store programs inside the computer. The paper tape is read into a large electronic memory made out of thousands of data latches (flip-flops), one for each bit, that provide locations in which to store program instructions and data. Each instruction on the paper tape is converted to binary numbers with a definite number of bits, and stored in a memory location. Each memory location has an address number associated with it like a post office box. In fact, one could think of the computer memory bank as a large bank of post office boxes. The computer reads the binary number (instruction or data) stored in each memory location by going to the address (box number) of the location it wants to read. When the address for a particular location is generated, a *copy* of its information is transferred to the computer. (Note that the original information stays in its location in memory while the memory is being read.) The electronic memory can be read much quicker than paper tape, so after the initial loading of the memory from the tape, the program can be run over and over without wasting the time required for reading paper tape.

All modern electronic computers have the ability to store a program in internal memory. After a program is loaded into the computer's memory from a tape reader, disk drive, etc., the computer can use the program over and over to accomplish tasks.

Storing a computer program inside the computer's memory is what separates a real computer from a fancy calculator. The computer can use some of its memory for storing programs (instructions) and other memory for storing data. The program or data can be easily changed simply by loading in a different program or different data. The *stored program concept* is fundamental to all modern electronic computers.

It should also be noted that paper tape is only one method of loading programs and data and, in fact, isn't used much anymore. The more common ways are entering data directly from keyboard terminals or transferring data from magnetic tape, magnetic disks, or punched cards.

WHAT CAN A MICROCOMPUTER DO?

A microcomputer based engine control system has much greater flexibility than the early systems which were partly analog.

A microcomputer can do the work of many different types of logic circuits. For example, it will be shown in a later chapter that a microcomputer can be configured to control fuel metering and ignition for an engine. The microcomputer-based engine control system has much greater flexibility than the earliest electronic engine control systems which, typically, used elementary logic circuits as well as analog circuits. For these early systems, changes in the performance of the control system required changes in the circuitry. With a microcomputer performing the logic functions, most changes can be made simply by reprogramming the computer. That is, the software (program) is changed rather than the hardware (logic circuits). This makes the microcomputer a very attractive building block in any digital system.

Microcomputers can also be used to replace analog circuitry. Special interface circuits can be used to enable a digital computer to input and output analog signals (this will be discussed later). The important point here is that microcomputers are excellent alternatives to hard wired (dedicated) logic and analog circuitry that is interconnected to satisfy a particular design.

In the subsequent portions of this chapter, both the computer hardware configuration and programs (software) are discussed. Because these two aspects of computers are so strongly interrelated, it is necessary for the following discussion to alternately switch back and forth between the two.

HOW DOES A MICROCOMPUTER WORK?

A microcomputer stores information on a temporary basis within the CPU registers. Information is transferred between the CPU registers and the memory or input/output sections by means of one or more sets of multiple wires; each set is called a bus.

Recall the basic computer block diagram of *Figure 4-1.* The central processing unit (CPU) requests information from memory (or from an input to output device in most kinds of computer design) by generating the address for the data in memory. The address with all its bits is stored in the CPU as a binary number in a temporary data latch type memory called a register. The outputs of the register are sent at the same time over multiple wires to the computer memory and peripherals.

Buses

As shown in *Figure 4-2,* the group of wires that carries the address is called the address bus. (The word bus refers to one or more wires that is a common path to/from various components in the computer.) The address register used in most microcomputers holds 16 bits; these bits enable the CPU to access 65,536 memory locations. In a microcomputer, each memory location usually contains 8 bits of data. A group of 8 bits is called a byte and a group of 16 bits is sometimes called a word.

Figure 4-2.
Buses and Registers

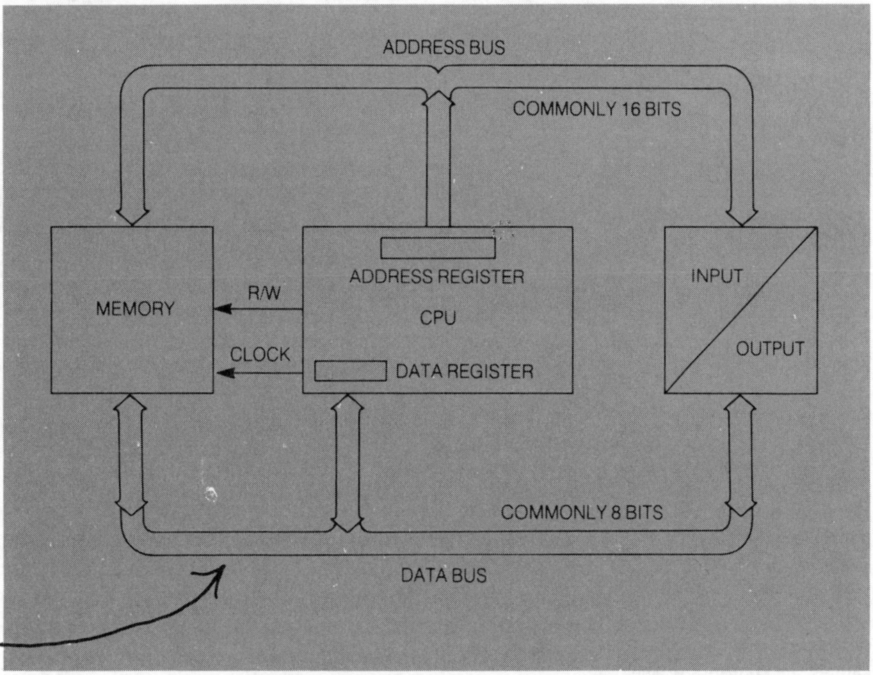

Carries bits of a code in parallel.

Information is sent to or received from memory locations and input/output devices via the bidirectional data bus.

Data is sent to the CPU over a data bus (*Figure 4-2*). The data bus is slightly different from the address bus in that the CPU uses it to *read* information from memory or peripherals, and to *write* information to memory or peripherals. Signals on the address bus originate only at the CPU and are sent to devices attached to the bus. Signals on the data bus can either be inputs to, or outputs from, the CPU that are sent or received at the CPU by the data register. In other words, the data bus is a two-way "street" while the address bus is a one-way "street." Another difference is that the data bus in many microcomputers is only 8 bits wide but as already mentioned, the address bus is typically 16 bits wide.

Memory Read/Write

The CPU always controls the direction of data flow on the data bus because, although it is bidirectional, data can move in only one direction at a time. The CPU provides a special read/write control signal (*Figure 4-2*) that tells the memory in which direction the data should flow. For example, when the read/write (R/W) line is high, the CPU reads information from a memory location. When the R/W line is low, the CPU writes information into a memory location.

Figure 4-3. Timing Diagram for Memory Read

Provides the synchronization for the system.

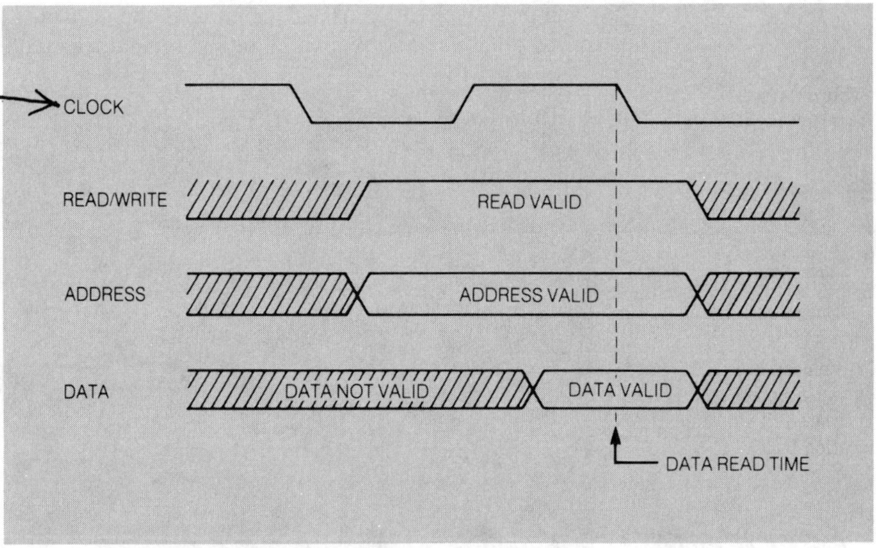

During a memory read operation, the CPU changes the state of the read/write line and puts the appropriate address on the address bus. This causes the contents of the addressed memory location to be placed on the data bus, where it can be read by the CPU.

The timing diagram for a memory read operation is shown in *Figure 4-3*. Suppose the computer has been given the instruction to read data from memory location number 10. To perform the read operation, the CPU raises the R/W line to the high level to tell the memory to prepare for a read operation. Almost simultaneously, the address for location 10 is placed on the address bus (address valid in *Figure 4-3*). The number 10 in binary (0000 0000 0000 1010) is sent to the memory in the address bus. The binary electrical signals corresponding to 10 operate the specific circuits in the memory to cause the binary data at that location to be placed on the data bus. The CPU has an internal register that is activated during this read operation to receive and store the data. The data is then processed by the CPU during the next cycle of operation according to the relevant instruction.

Timing

Microcomputers use a timing signal, called a clock, to determine when data should be written to or read from memory.

A certain amount of time is required (1) for the memory's address decoder to decode which memory location is called for by the address, and (2) for the selected memory location to transfer its information to the data bus. To allow time for this decoding, the processor waits a while before receiving the information requested from the data bus. Then, at the proper time, the CPU opens the logic gating circuitry between the data bus and the CPU data register so that the information on the bus from memory location 10 is latched into the CPU. During the memory read operation, the memory has temporary control of the data bus. Control must be returned to the CPU, but not before the processor has read in the data. The CPU provides a timing control signal, called the clock, that tells the memory when it can take and release control of the data bus.

Refer again to *Figure 4-3*. Notice that the read cycle is terminated when the clock goes from high to low during the time that the read signal is valid. This is the signal the CPU uses to tell the memory that it has read the data and the data bus can be released. The timing for a memory write operation is very similar to the memory read operation except that the R/W line is low instead of high.

The bus timing signals are very important to the reliable operation of the computer. However, they are built into the design of the machine and, therefore, are under machine control. As long as the machine performs the read and write operations correctly, the programmer can completely ignore the logical details of the bus timing signals and concentrate on the logic of the program.

Addressing Peripherals

In memory mapped input-output a peripheral device is treated like a memory location by the CPU.

The reason for distinguishing between memory locations and peripherals is that they perform different functions. Memory is a data storage device, while peripherals are input/output devices. However, many microcomputers address memory and peripherals in the same way because they use a design called memory-mapped I/O (input/output). With this design, peripherals, such as data terminals, are equivalent to memory to the CPU so that sending data to a peripheral is as simple as writing data to a memory location. In systems where this type of microcomputer has replaced some digital logic, the digital inputs enter the computer through a designated memory slot. If outputs are required, they exit the computer through another designated memory slot.

CPU REGISTERS

The programmer (the person that writes the sequences of instructions for a particular task) uses a different model (a programming model) of the microprocessor used in a system than does the hardware designer. This model shows the programmer which registers in the CPU are available for program use, and what function the registers perform. *Figure 4-4* shows a programming model microprocessor for a typical 8-bit microcomputer. The computer has two 8-bit registers and three 16-bit registers. The 16-bit registers are discussed later, but the 8-bit registers are discussed now.

Figure 4-4. Registers Available in a Typical Microcomputer

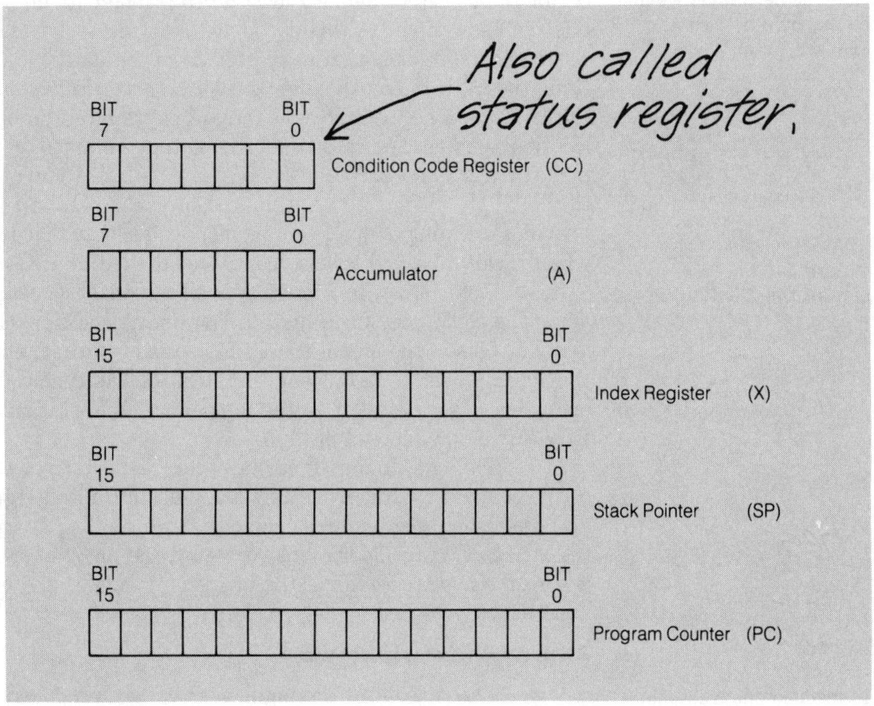

Accumulator Register

The accumulator register, also called the A-register, is used for arithmetic and logical operations.

One of the 8-bit registers is an *accumulator*. An accumulator is a general purpose register that is used for arithmetic and logical operations. The accumulator can be loaded with data from a memory location, or its data can be stored in a memory location. The number held in the accumulator can be added to, subtracted from, or compared with another number from memory. *The accumulator is the basic work register of a computer.* It is commonly called the A register.

Condition Code Register

The condition code register (also called the status register) indicates certain conditions that take place during various accumulator operations.

The other 8-bit register, the condition code (CC) register (also called status register), indicates or flags certain conditions which occur during accumulator operations. Rules are established in the design of the microprocessor so that a 1 or 0 in the bit position of the CC register represents specific conditions that have happened in the last operation of the accumulator. The bit positions and rules are shown in *Figure 4-5a*. One bit of the CC register indicates that the A register is all zeros. Another bit, the carry bit, indicates that the last operation performed on the accumulator caused a carry to occur. The carry bit acts like the ninth bit of the accumulator. Notice what happens when we add one to 255 in binary.

Decimal	**Binary**
255	11111111
+ 1	+ 1
256	100000000

The eight bits in the accumulator are all zeros, but the carry bit being set to a 1 (high) indicates that the result is actually not zero, but 256. Such a condition can be checked by examining the CC register carry bit for a 1.

Figure 4-5.
Use of the CC Register

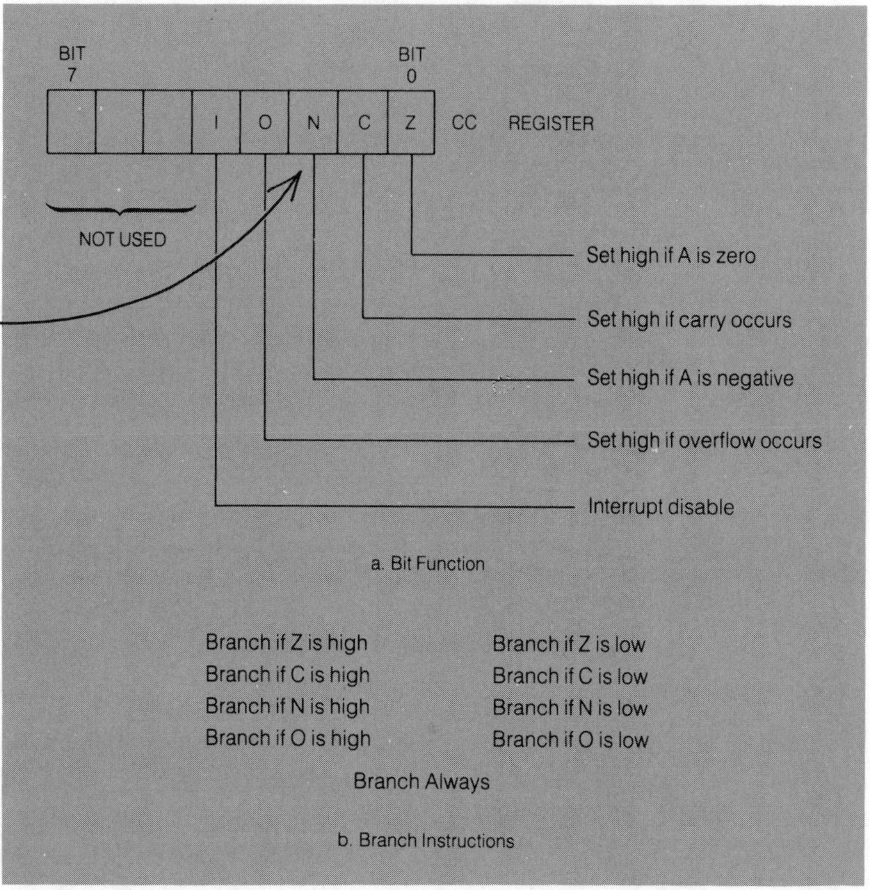

For example, the condition code register can indicate if the value contained in the accumulator is negative. This gives the CPU the ability to represent a much wider range of numbers.

The condition code register also provides a flag which, when set to a 1, indicates that the number in the accumulator is negative. Most microcomputers use a binary format called 2's complement notation for doing arithmetic. In 2's complement notation, the leftmost bit indicates the sign of the number. Since one of the 8 bits is used for the sign, 7 bits (or 15 if 16 bits are used) remain to represent the magnitude of the number. The largest positive number that can be represented in 2's complement with 8 bits is +127 (or +32,767 for 16 bits). The most negative number is −128 (−32,768). Since the accumulator is only 8 bits wide, it can handle only 1 byte at a time. However, by combining bytes and operating on them one after another in time sequence (as is done for 16-bit arithmetic), the computer can handle very large numbers or can obtain increased accuracy in calculations. Handling bits or bytes one after another in time sequence is called serial operation.

Branching

Instructions that direct the microcomputer to other parts of the program are called branches. Branches may be conditional or unconditional.

The CC register provides programmers with status indicators (the flags) that enable them to monitor what happens to the data as the program executes the instructions. The microcomputer has special instructions that allow it to go to a different part of the program. Bits of the CC register are labeled in *Figure 4-5a.* Typical branch type instructions are shown in *Figure 4-5b.*

Program branches are either conditional or unconditional. Eight of the nine branch instructions listed in *Figure 4-5b* are conditional branches. That is to say, the branch is taken only if certain conditions are met. These conditions are indicated by the CC register bit as shown. The branch-always instruction is the only unconditional branch. Such a branch is used to branch around the next instruction to a later instruction, or to return to an earlier instruction. Another type of branch instruction that takes the computer out of its normal program sequence is indicated for the I bit of the CC register. It is associated with an interrupt. An interrupt is a request, usually from an input or output (I/O) peripheral that the CPU stop what it's doing and accept or take care of (service) the special request. There will be more about interrupts later in this chapter.

Microprocessor Architecture

Block diagrams are great aids in explaining microprocessor operation.

Understanding how the microprocessor operates is aided by the block diagram of *Figure 4-6* which is representative of a typical commercial microprocessor. This block diagram is divided into two main portions: (1) a register section, and (2) a control section. The actual operations performed by the microprocessor are accomplished in the register section. The specific operations performed during the execution of a given step in the program are controlled by electrical signals from the instruction decoder.

Figure 4-6. Typical MPU Internal Architecture

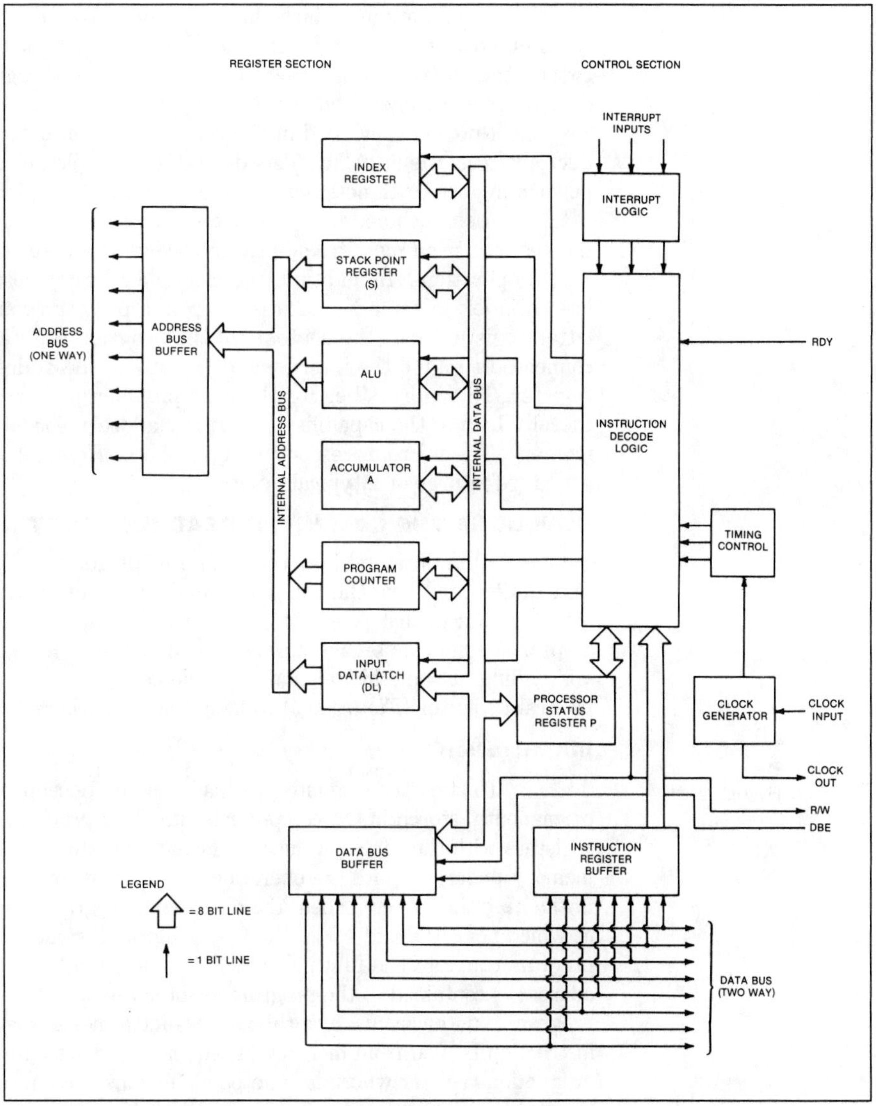

During each program step, an instruction in the form of an 8-bit number is transferred from memory to the instruction register. This instruction is decoded using logic circuits similar to those presented in Chapter 3. The result of this decoding process is a set of electrical control signals which are sent to the specific components of the register section that are involved in the instruction being executed.

The data upon which the operation is performed is similarly transferred from memory to the data bus buffer. From this buffer the data is then transferred to the desired component in the register section for execution of the operation.

Note that included in the register section of this typical microprocessor is an ALU. This device is a complex circuit capable of performing the arithmetic and logic operations as explained in Chapter 3.

Also, included in the register section is the accumulator which is the register used most frequently to receive the results of arithmetic or logical operations. In addition, the example microprocessor register section has an index register X, stack pointer, and program counter, PC. This latter register holds the contents of the program counter. This register is connected through the internal address bus to the address buffer register. The address bus for the example microprocessor has 16 lines, thereby having the capability to directly address 65536 (i.e., 64K) of memory. The microprocessor configuration of *Figure 4–6* illustrates the primary features of a typical device.

HOW DOES THE COMPUTER READ INSTRUCTIONS?

To understand how the computer performs a branch, one must first understand how the computer reads program instructions from memory. Recall that program instructions are stored sequentially (step by step) in memory as binary numbers, starting at a certain binary address and ending at some higher address. The computer uses a register called the program counter (*Figure 4–4*) to keep track of where it is in the program.

Initialization

The first step in starting up a computer is initialization.

To start the computer, a small startup (boot) program that is permanently stored in the computer is run. This program sets all of the CPU registers with the correct values, and clears all information in the computer memory to zeros before the operations program is loaded. This is called *initializing* the system. Then, the operations program is loaded into memory at which point the address of the first program instruction is loaded into the program counter. The first instruction is read from the memory location whose address is contained in the program counter register; that is, the 16 bits in the program counter are used as the address for a memory-read operation. Each instruction is read from memory in sequence and set on the data bus into the instruction register where it is decoded. The instruction register is another temporary storage register inside the CPU. It is connected to the data bus when the information on the bus is an instruction.

Operation Code

The actual instructions in the program are in the form of numeric codes called operation codes (op codes).

Numeric codes contained in the instructions that represent the actual operation to be performed by the CPU are called operation codes (or op codes for short). The block diagram of *Figure 4–7* which illustrates part of the CPU hardware organization should help clarify the flow of instructions through the CPU. The instruction register has a part that contains the numeric op codes. A decoder determines from the op codes the operation to be executed, and a data roster controls the flow of data inside the CPU as a result of the op code instructions.

Figure 4-7. CPU Organization

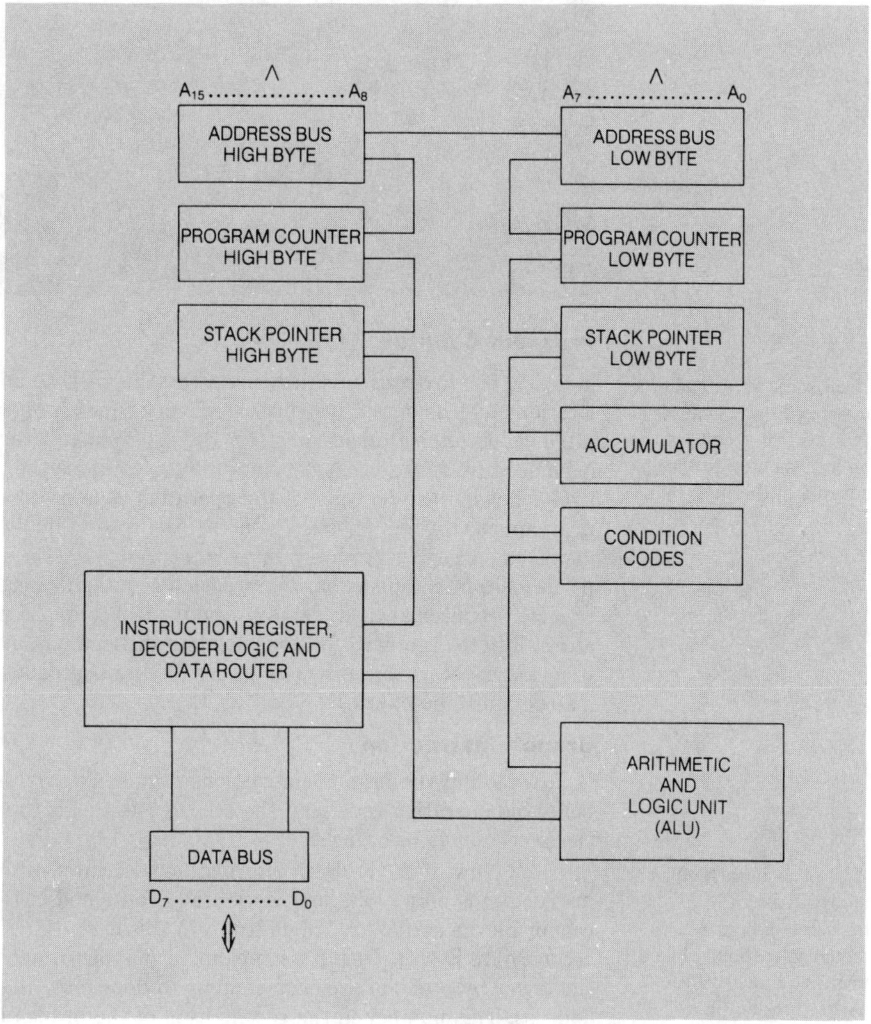

Instructions often are contained in more than one byte. In such cases, the first byte contains the op code, and succeeding bytes contain the address.

One important function of the op-code decoder is to determine how many bytes must be read to execute each instruction. Many instructions require two or three bytes. *Figure 4–8* shows the arrangement of the bytes in an instruction. The first byte contains the op code. The second byte contains address information, usually the low or least significant byte. If there is a third byte, it usually contains the high or most significant byte of the address.

Figure 4-8.
Instruction Byte Arrangement

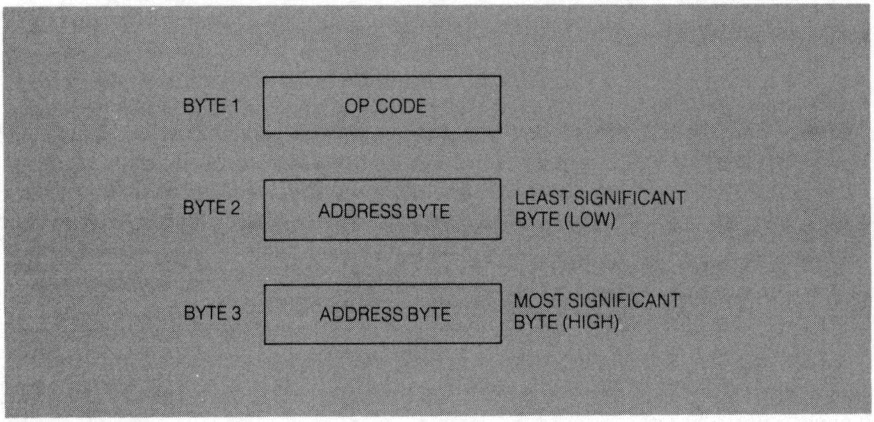

Program Counter

Each successive read of a memory location causes the program counter to be incremented to the address of the next byte.

The program counter is used by the CPU to address memory locations which contain instructions. Every time an op code is read (this is often called fetched) from memory, the program counter is incremented (advanced by one) so that it points to (i.e., contains the address of) the next byte following the op code. If the operation code requires another byte, the program counter supplies the address, the second byte is fetched from memory, and the program counter is incremented. Each time the CPU performs a fetch operation, the program counter is incremented; thus, the program counter always points to the next byte in the program. Therefore, after all bytes required for one complete instruction have been read, the program counter contains the address for the beginning of the next instruction to be executed.

Branch Instruction

All of the branch instructions require two bytes. The first byte holds the operation code, and the second byte holds the location to which the processor is to branch.

A positive branch offset address results in a branch to a higher memory location, while a negative branch offset address results in a branch to a lower memory location.

Now, if the address information associated with a branch instruction is only 8 bits long and totally contained in the second byte, it cannot be the actual branch address. In this case, the code contained in the second byte is actually a 2's complement number which the CPU adds to the lower byte of the program counter to determine the actual new address. This number in the second byte of the branch instruction is called an *address offset* or just offset. Recall that in 2's complement notation, the 8-bit number can be either positive or negative; therefore, the branch address offset can be positive or negative. A positive branch offset causes a branch forward to a higher memory location. A negative branch offset causes a branch to a lower memory location. Since 8 bits are used, the largest forward branch is 127 and the largest backward branch is 128 memory locations.

Offset Example

Suppose the program counter is at address 5,122 and the instruction at this location is a branch instruction. The instruction to which the branch is to be made is located at memory address 5,218. Since the second byte of the branch instruction is only 8 bits wide, the actual address 5,218 cannot be contained. Therefore, the difference or offset (96) between the current program counter value (5,122) and the desired new address (5,218) is contained in the second byte of the branch instruction. The offset value (96) is added to the address in the program counter (5,122) to obtain the new address (5,218), which is then placed on the address bus. The binary computation of the final address from the program counter value and second byte of the branch instruction is shown in *Figure 4-9.*

Figure 4-9. Binary Computation of Branch Address

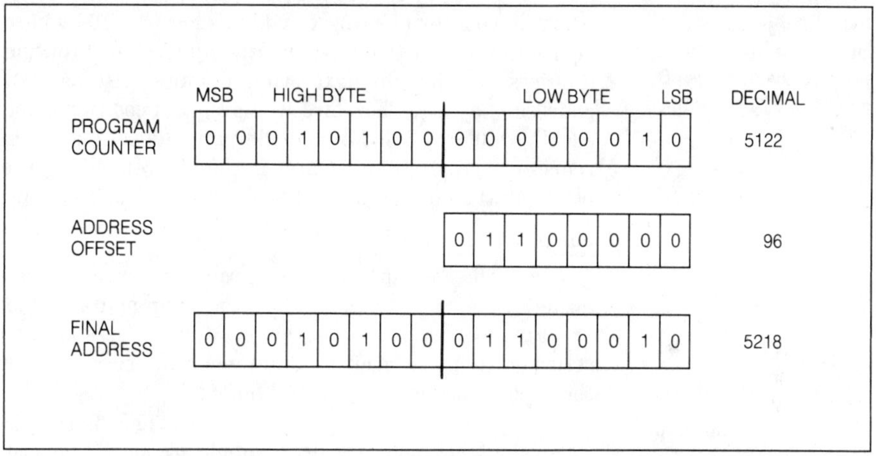

Jump Instruction

Eight-bit branch operations are limited to an offset range of +127 or −128 memory locations. Thus, program branches to locations further away must use jump instructions. These 3-byte instructions contain the entire memory address.

Branch instructions have a range of +127 or −128. If the branch needs to go beyond the range, a jump instruction must be used. The jump instruction is a 3-byte instruction. The first byte is the jump op code and the next two bytes are the actual jump address. The CPU loads the jump address directly into the program counter, and the program counter effectively gets restarted at the new jump location. The CPU continues to fetch and execute instructions in exactly the same way it did before the jump was made.

The jump instruction causes the CPU to jump out of one section of the program into another. The CPU cannot automatically return to the first section because no record was kept of the previous location. However, another instruction, the jump-to-subroutine, does leave a record of the previous instruction address.

Jump-to-Subroutine Instruction

Subroutines are short programs used to perform specific tasks, particularly those tasks that must be performed several times within the same program.

A subroutine is a short program that is used by the main program to perform a specific function. It is located in sequential memory locations separated from the main program sequence. If the main program requires some function such as addition several times at widely separated places within the program, the programmer can write one subroutine to perform the addition, then have the main program jump to the memory locations containing the subroutine each time it is needed. This saves having to rewrite the addition program over and over again. To perform the addition, the programmer simply includes instructions in the main program which first loads the numbers to be added into the data memory locations used by the subroutine, and then jumps to the subroutine.

The second and third bytes of a jump-to-subroutine instruction provide the address of the subroutine to be jumped to.

Refer to *Figure 4-10* to follow the sequence. It begins with the program counter pointing to address location 100 where it gets the jump-to-subroutine instruction (step 1). Each jump-to-subroutine instruction (step 2) requires also that the next two bytes must also be read to obtain the jump address (step 2a). Therefore, the program counter is incremented once for each byte (steps 3 and 4) and the jump address is loaded into the address register. The program counter is then incremented once more so that it points to the op-code byte of the next instruction (step 5).

Saving the Program Counter

The contents of the program counter are saved by storing them in a special memory location before the jump address is loaded into the program counter. This program counter address is saved so that it can be returned to in the main program when the subroutine is finished. This is the record that was mentioned before.

For a jump-to-subroutine, the contents of the program counter (after being incremented) are stored in two memory locations pointed to by the stack pointer. After storing it, the stack pointer value is decreased by one to prepare it for the next store.

Now refer back to *Figure 4-4*. There is a register in *Figure 4-4* called the stack pointer (SP). The address of the special memory location used to store the program counter content is kept in this 16-bit stack pointer register. When a jump-to-subroutine op code is encountered, the CPU uses the number code contained in the stack pointer as a memory address to store the program counter to memory (step 2b). The program counter is a two-byte register, so it must be stored in two memory locations. The current stack pointer is used as an address to store the lower byte of the program counter to memory (step 6). Then the stack pointer is decremented (decreased by 1) and the high byte of the program counter is stored in the next lower memory location (step 7). The stack pointer is then decremented again to point to the next unused byte in the stack to prepare for storing the program counter again when required (step 8).

The special memory locations pointed to by the stack pointer are called stacks; if one considers memory locations as being slots stacked one atop the other, it makes sense to think of the stack pointer stacking data like plates on a shelf.

Figure 4–10.
Jump-to-Subroutine

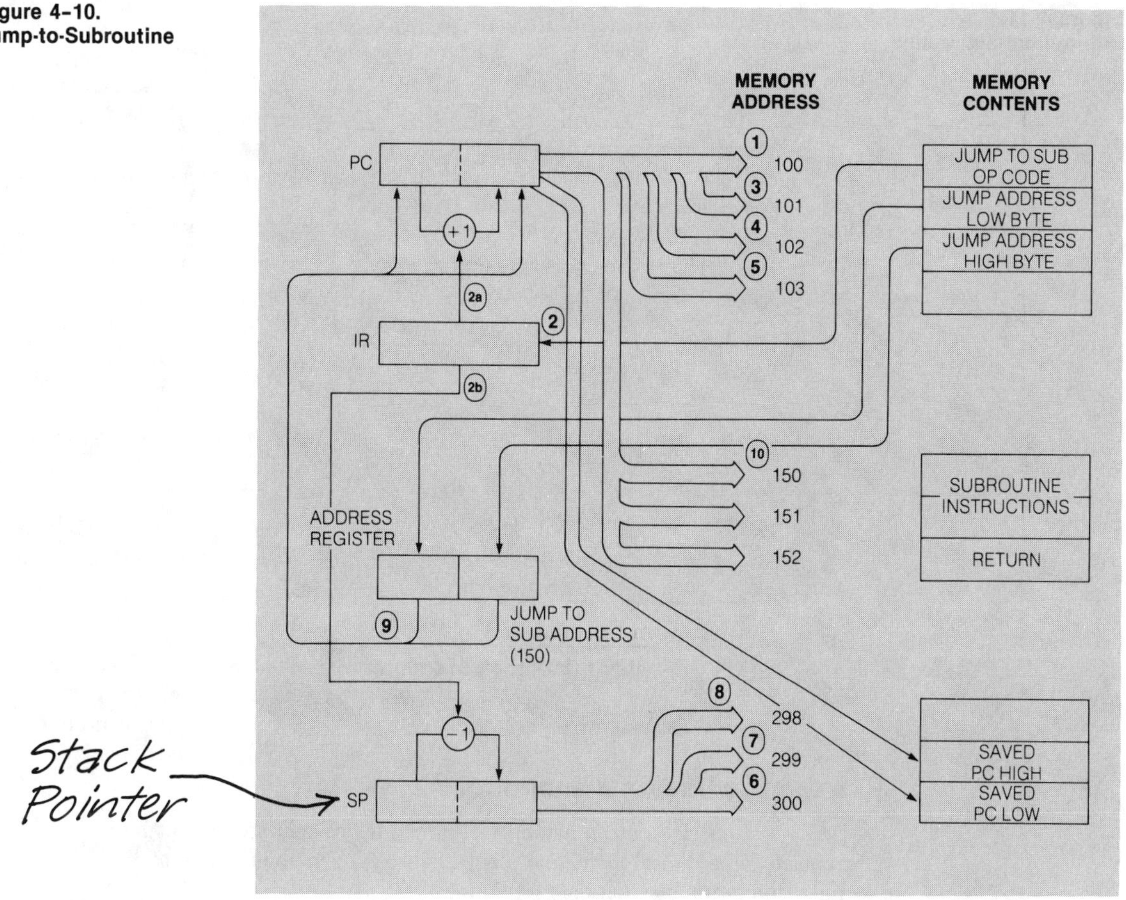

When the subroutine is completed, a return instruction retrieves the saved program counter value from the stack pointer and loads it into the program counter. Execution of the main program then resumes from the point at which the jump occurred.

After the program counter has been incremented and saved, the jump address is loaded into the program counter (step 9). The jump to subroutine is made, and the CPU starts running the subroutine (step 10). The only thing that distinguishes the subroutine from another part of the program is the way in which it ends. When a subroutine has run to completion, it must allow the CPU to return to the point in the main program from which the jump occurred. In this way, the main program can continue without missing a step. The return-from-subroutine instruction is used to accomplish this. It is decoded by the instruction register, and increments the stack pointer as shown in *Figure 4–11*, step 1. It uses the stack pointer to address the stack memory to retrieve the old program counter value from the stack (steps 2 and 4). The old program counter value is loaded into the program counter register (steps 3 and 5), and execution resumes in the main program (step 6). The return-from-subroutine instruction works like the jump-to-subroutine instruction, except in reverse.

Figure 4-11.
Return-from-Subroutine

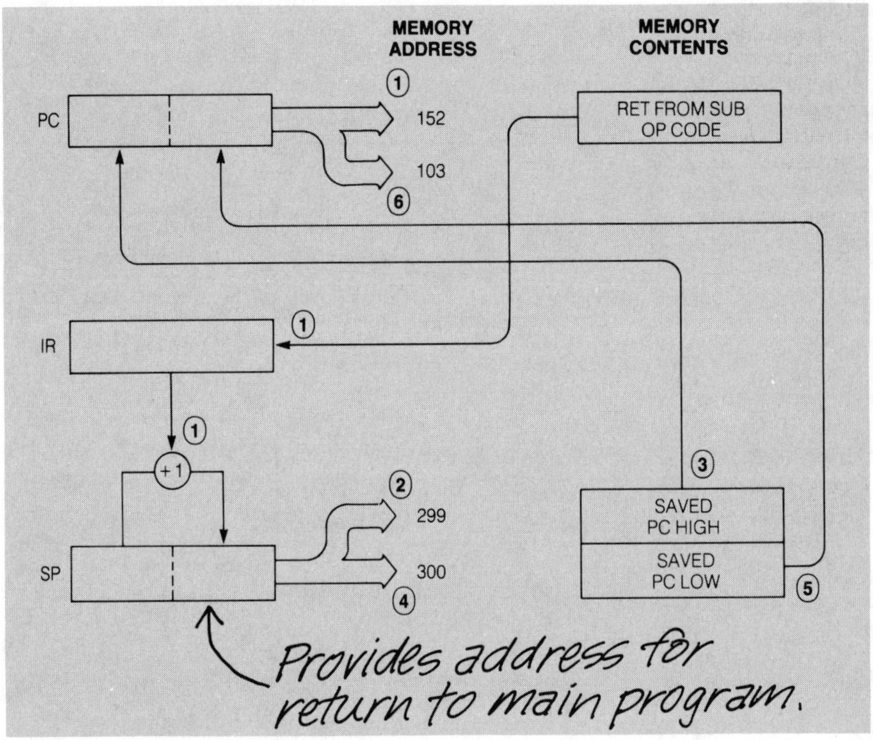

EXAMPLE USE OF A MICROCOMPUTER

Let's look at an example of how a microcomputer might be used to replace some digital logic, and along the way learn about some more microcomputer instructions.

Microcomputers can be used in place of discrete logic circuits such as AND gates.

The digital logic to be replaced in this example is a simple AND gate circuit. Now, no one would use a microcomputer to replace only an AND gate, because an AND gate costs a fraction of what a microcomputer costs. However, if the system already has a microcomputer in it, the cost of the AND gate could be eliminated by performing the logical AND function in the computer rather than with the gate. This is a perfectly legitimate application for a microcomputer and is something that microcomputers do very well. Moreover, this example well illustrates the use of a microcomputer.

Suppose there are two signals that must be ANDed together to produce a third signal. One of the input signals comes from a pressure switch located under the driver's seat of an automobile; its purpose is to indicate whether someone is occupying the seat. This signal will be called A, and it is at logic high when someone is sitting in the seat. Signal B is developed within a circuit contained in the seat belt and is logic high when the driver's seat belt is fastened. The output of the AND gate is signal C. It will be logic high when someone is sitting in the driver's seat AND has the seat belt fastened.

Buffer

Buffers provide temporary storage for peripheral inputs and let the microcomputer treat peripherals, such as sensors, as if they were memory locations.

In order to use a microcomputer to replace the AND gate, the computer must be able to detect the status of each signal. Remember that the computer knows only what is stored in its memory. The microcomputer used here has memory-mapped I/O where peripherals are treated exactly like memory locations. The task is to provide a peripheral that allows the computer to look at the switch signals as if they were bits in a memory location. This can be done easily by using a device called a buffer (*Figure 4-12*). To the microcomputer, a buffer looks just like an 8-bit memory slot at a selected memory location. The 8 bits in the memory slot correspond to 8 digital signal inputs to the buffer. Each digital input controls the state of a single bit in the memory slot. The digital inputs are gated into the buffer under control of the CPU. The microcomputer can detect the state of the digital inputs by examining the bits in the buffer any time after the inputs are gated into the buffer.

Figure 4-12. Buffer

Gates input information into buffer.

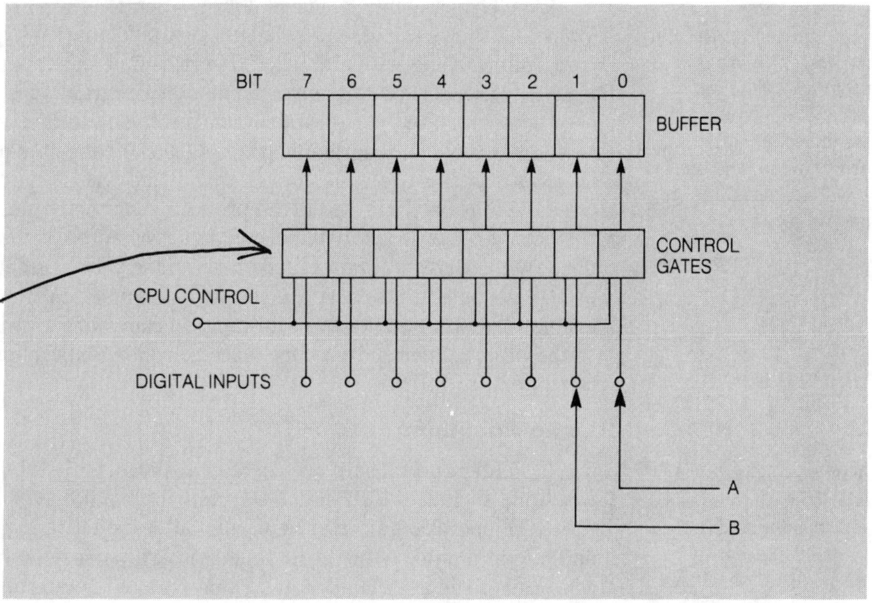

In this application, signal A will be assigned to the rightmost bit (bit 0) and signal B to the next bit (bit 1). It doesn't matter that the other 6 bits are left unconnected,. The computer will gate in and read the state of those lines, but the program will be written to purposely ignore them. With the logic signals interfaced to the microcomputer, a program can be written that will perform the required logic function.

However, before writing a program, one must know the code or "language" in which the program is to be written. Computer languages come in various levels including: (1) high level language such as BASIC, (2) assembly language which is designed for a specific microprocessor, and

(3) machine language which is the actual language in which a program is stored in memory. For the present example, we choose the intermediate level language (assembly language) to illustrate specific CPU operations.

Assembly Language

Microcomputer instructions are written in assembly language, a type of shorthand that uses initials or shortened words to represent microcomputer instructions.

Assembly language is a special type of abbreviated language, each symbol of which pertains to a specific microprocessor operation. Some assembly language instructions such as branch, jump, jump-to-subroutine and return-from-subroutine have already been discussed. Others will be discussed as they are needed to execute an example program. Assembly language instructions have the form of initials or shortened words which represent microcomputer functions. These abbreviations are only for the convenience of the programmer because the program that the microcomputer eventually runs must be in the form of binary numbers. When each instruction is converted to the binary code that the microcomputer recognizes, it is called a machine language program.

Once the program has been written in assembly language, a special kind of program, called an assembler, converts the assembly-language program into the binary code recognized by the microcomputer.

The assembly language abbreviation for the jump instruction is JMP. *Table 4-1* shows the assembly language equivalents for typical microcomputer instructions, along with a detailed description of the operation called for by the instruction. When writing a microcomputer program, it is easier and faster to use the abbreviated name rather than the complete function name. Assembly language simplifies programming tasks for the computer programmer because the abbreviations are easier to remember and write than the binary numbers the computer uses. However, the program eventually must be converted to the binary codes that the microcomputer recognizes as instructions, and this is done by a special program called an assembler. The assembler program is run on the computer to convert the assembly language to the binary codes. This enables the programmer to write the program using words that have meaning to the programmer and produce machine codes that have meaning to the computer.

Logic Functions

A microcomputer can AND the contents of its accumulator with a memory location to perform the logical AND function.

Microprocessors are capable of performing all of the basic logic functions such as AND, OR, NOT, and combinations of these. For instance, the NOT operation affects the accumulator by changing all ones to zeros and zeros to ones. Other logic functions are performed by using the contents of the accumulator and some memory location. All eight bits of the accumulator are affected, and all are changed at the same time. As shown in *Figure 4-13*, the AND operation requires two inputs. One input is the contents of the accumulator and the other input is the contents of a memory location; thus, the eight accumulator bits are ANDed with the eight memory bits. The AND operation is performed on a bit-by-bit basis. For instance, bit 0 of the accumulator (the rightmost bit) is ANDed with bit 0 of the memory location, bit 1 with bit 1, bit 2 with bit 2, and so on. In other words, the AND operation is performed as if eight AND gates were connected with one input to a bit in the accumulator, and the other to a bit (in the same bit position) in the memory location. The resulting AND outputs are stored back into the accumulator in the corresponding bit

Table 4-1. Assembly Language Mnemonics

Mnemonic	Operand	Comment
JMP	(Address)	Jump to new program location
JSR	(Address)	Jump to a subroutine
BRA	(Offset)	Branch using the offset
BEQ	(Offset)	Branch if accumulator is zero
BNE	(Offset)	Branch if accumulator is non-zero
BCC	(Offset)	Branch if carry bit is zero
BCS	(Offset)	Branch if carry bit is non-zero
BPL	(Offset)	Branch if minus bit is zero
BMI	(Offset)	Branch if minus bit is non-zero
RTS		Return from a subroutine

a. Program Transfer Instructions

Mnemonic	Operand	Comment
LDA	(Address)	Load accumulator from memory
STA	(Address)	Store accumulator to memory
LDA	# (Constant)	Load accumulator with constant
LDS	# (Constant)	Load stack pointer with constant
STS	(Address)	Store stack pointer to memory

b. Data Transfer Instructions

Mnemonic	Operand	Comment
COM		Complement accumulator (NOT)
AND	(Address)	AND accumulator with memory
OR	(Address)	OR accumulator with memory
ADD	(Address)	ADD accumulator with memory
SUB	(Address)	SUBtract accumulator with memory
AND	# (Constant)	AND accumulator with constant
OR	# (Constant)	OR accumulator with constant
SLL		Shift accumulator left logical
SRL		Shift accumulator right logical
ROL		Rotate accumulator left
ROR		Rotate accumulator right

c. Arithmetic and Logical Operations

positions. The OR logic function is performed in exactly the same way as the AND except that a 1 would be produced at the output if signal A or signal B were a 1, or both were a 1 (i.e., using OR logic).

Figure 4-13. Microcomputer logic *AND* function

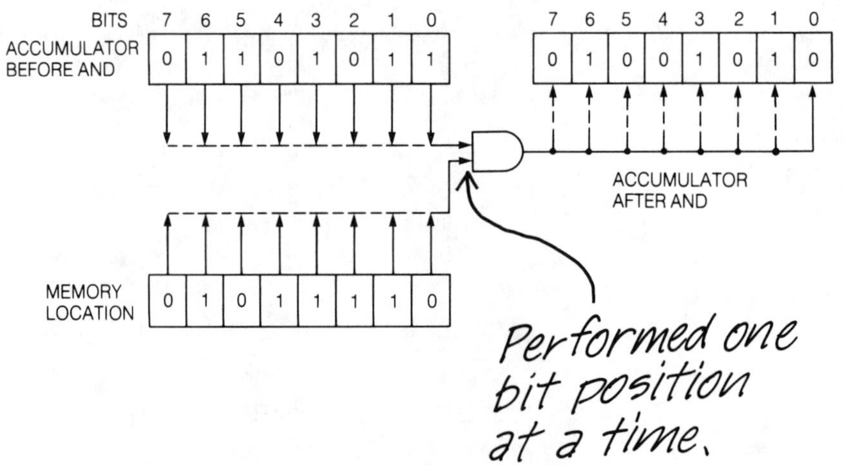

Shift

Using a logical operation known as SHIFT, a microcomputer can shift all the bits present in the accumulator to the left or right.

Instead of the AND gate inputs being switched to each bit position as shown in *Figure 4-13*, the microcomputer uses a special type of sequential logic operation, the shift, to move the bits to the AND gate inputs. A shift operation causes every bit in the accumulator to be shifted one bit position either to the right or to the left. It can be what is called a logical shift or it can be a circulating type shift. *Figure 4-14* shows the four types of shift (logical, circulating, right, left) and their effects on the accumulator. In a left shift, bit 7 (the leftmost bit) is shifted into the carry bit of the CC register, bit 6 is shifted into bit 7, and so on until each bit has been shifted once to the left. Bit 0 (the rightmost bit) can be replaced either by the carry bit or by a zero, depending on the type of shift performed. Depending upon the microprocessor, it is possible to shift other registers as well as the accumulator.

Programming the AND Function

It is the task of the programmer to choose instructions and organize them in such a way that the computer performs the desired tasks. To program the AND function, one of the instructions will be the AND, which stands for "AND accumulator with contents of a specific memory location," as shown in *Table 4-1c*. Since the AND affects the accumulator and memory, values must be put into the accumulator to be ANDed. This requires the load accumulator instruction, LDA.

The programmer often uses special names (labels) to refer to specific memory locations.

The assembly language program of *Figure 4-15* performs the required AND function. The programmer must first know which memory location the digital buffer interface (*Figure 4-12*) occupies. This location is identified, and the programmer writes instructions in the assembler program that the buffer memory location will be referred to by the label or name SEAT. SEAT is easier for the programmer to remember and write than the address of the buffer.

Figure 4-14. Types of Shift Operations

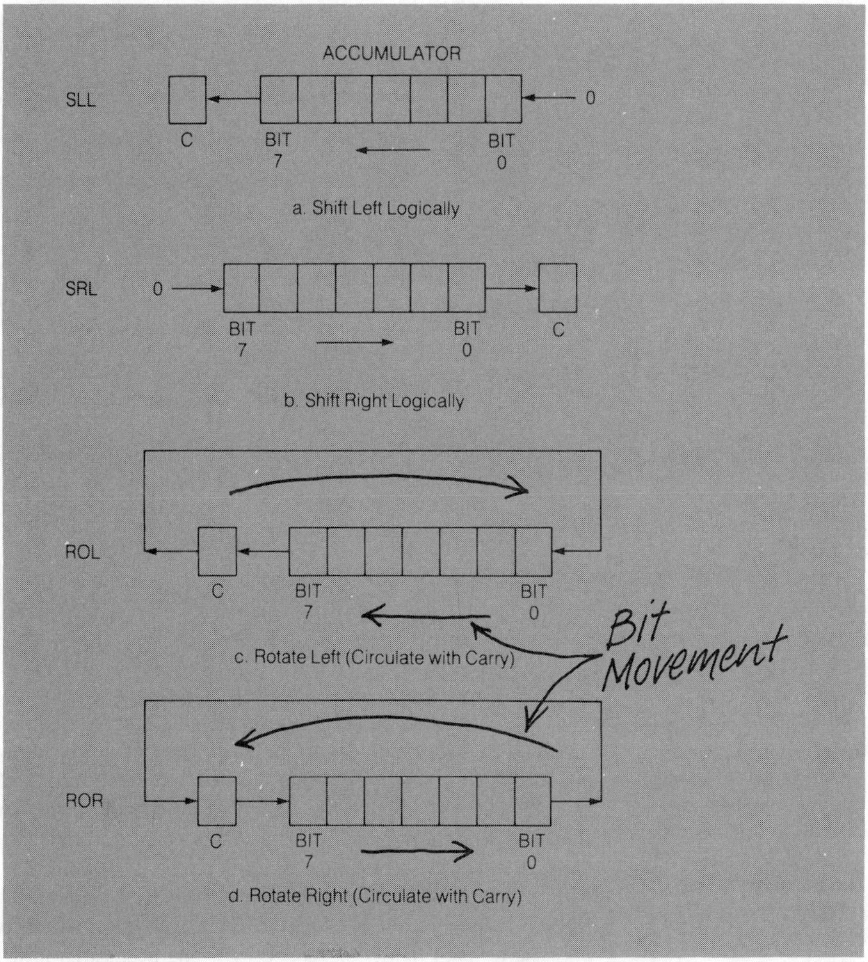

The use of a mask allows the microcomputer to separately examine two or more digital signals (bits) occupying the same 8-bit byte.

The operation of the program is as follows. The accumulator is loaded with the contents of the memory location SEAT. Note in *Figure 4-12* that the two digital logic input signals, A and B, have been gated into bits 0 and 1, respectively, of the buffer that occupies the memory location labeled SEAT. Bit 0 is high when someone is sitting in the driver's seat. Bit 1 is high when the driver's seat belt is fastened. Only these two bits are to be ANDed together; the other six are to be ignored. But there is a problem because both bits are in the same 8-bit byte and there is no single instruction to AND bits in the same byte. However, the two bits can be effectively separated by using a mask.

Figure 4-15. Assembly Language Subroutines

Program Label	Mnemonic	Operand
1 CHECK	LDA	SEAT
2	AND	#00000001 B
3	SLL	
4	AND	SEAT
5	RTS	

a. Subroutine CHECK

Program Label	Mnemonic	Operand
1 WAIT	JRS	CHECK
2	BEQ	WAIT
3	RTS	

b. Subroutine WAIT

Masking

During a mask operation, the accumulator contents is ANDed with the mask value which has a zero in each bit location except for the bit(s) to be saved. The saved, or masked, bit(s) comes through unchanged, but all others are set to zero.

Masking is a technique used to allow only selected bits to be involved in a desired operation. Since the buffer contents have been loaded into the accumulator, only bits 0 and 1 have meaning, and these two bits are the only ones of importance that are to be kept in the accumulator. To do this, the accumulator is ANDed with a constant that has a zero in every bit location except the one that is to be saved. The binary constant in line 2 of *Figure 4-15a* (00000001) is chosen to select bit 0 and set all others to zero as the AND instruction is executed. This ANDing procedure is called *masking* because a mask has been placed over the accumulator which allows only bit 0 to come through unchanged. If bit 0 was a logic 1, it is still a logic one after masking. If bit 0 was a logic 0, it is still a logic 0. All other bits in the accumulator are set to zero by the masking operation. Therefore, the accumulator now contains the correct bit information about bit 0.

During the final part of the AND operation, the Shift Left Logically instruction is used to align the bits of signal A with the correct bits in signal B so the logical AND can be accomplished.

Shift and AND

In our example program, the accumulator is still not ready to perform the final AND operation. Remember that SEAT contains the contents of the buffer and the condition of Signal A and Signal B. The contents of the accumulator must be ANDed with SEAT so that signals A and B are ANDed together. A copy of signal A is held in the accumulator in bit 0, but it is in the *wrong* bit position to be ANDed with signal B in SEAT in the bit 1 position. Therefore, signal A must be shifted into the bit 1 position. To do this the shift left logical instruction is used (*Figure 4-14a*). With signal A in bit 1 of the accumulator and signal B in bit 1 of SEAT, the AND operation can be performed on the two bits. If both A and B are high, the AND operation will leave bit 1 of the accumulator high (1). If either is low, bit 1 of the accumulator will be low (0).

Subroutines Usefulness

The previous example program has been written as a subroutine named CHECK so that it can be used at many different places in a larger program. For instance, if the computer is controlling the speed of the automobile, it might be desirable to be able to detect whether a driver is properly fastened in the seat before it sets the speed at 55 miles per hour.

Since the driver's seat information is very important, the main program must wait until the driver is ready before allowing anything else to happen. A program such as shown in *Figure 4-15b* can be used to do this. The main program calls the subroutine WAIT which in turn immediately calls the subroutine CHECK. CHECK returns to WAIT with the condition codes set as they were after the last AND instruction. The Z bit (*Figure 4-5a*) is set if A and B are not both high (the accumulator is zero). The BEQ instruction (Table 4-1) in line 2 of WAIT branches back because the accumulator is zero and causes the computer to reexecute the JSR instruction in line 1 of WAIT. This effectively holds the computer in a loop rechecking signals A and B until the accumulator has a nonzero value (A and B are high).

Timing Error

The time required for the microcomputer to sample sensor inputs and perform its instructions must be taken into account during program design; otherwise, timing errors may result.

A flaw in the subroutine CHECK could cause it to incorrectly perform the AND function. Notice that the logic state of A and B is sampled at different times. Signal A is first read in and masked off, then signal A and B are ANDed together. There is a possibility that during the interval between the time A is read and the time A and B are ANDed, the state of A could change. A computer is fast, but it still takes a certain amount of time for the microprocessor to execute the program instructions. For the driver's seat application, the signals have a long time between change so the time lag is not critical. However, in systems where the timing of signals is very tight, the program would have to be rewritten to remove the lag. Even after correcting such a lag, there may be applications where variables change more rapidly than the sampling time. Special compromises must be made in such cases, or a new technique found to solve the problem.

MICROCOMPUTER HARDWARE

The microcomputer system electronic components are known as computer hardware. (The programs the computer runs are called software.) The basic microcomputer parts were described as the CPU, memory, and I/O (input and output peripherals). We next expand upon this discussion of important components and the associated operations.

CPU

The central processing unit is a microprocessor. It is an integrated circuit similar to the one shown in *Figure 4-16a.* It contains thousands of transistors and diodes on a chip of silicon small enough to fit on the tip of a finger. It includes some form of arithmetic-logic unit (ALU), as well as registers for data and instruction storage and a control section. The chip is housed in a rectangular, flat package similar to the one shown in *Figure 4-16b.* It is less than 3 inches long and has two rows of small pins that make connections to external circuits. The CPU gets program instructions from a memory device.

Memory ROM

Permanent memory, called ROM, maintains its contents even when power is turned off. ROMs are used for CPU instructions requiring permanent storage.

There are several types of memory devices available, and each has its own special features. Systems such as those found in the automobile that must permanently store their programs use a type of permanent memory called *Read Only Memory* (ROM). This type of memory can be programmed only one time and the program is stored permanently, even when the microcomputer power is turned off. The programs stored in ROM are sometimes called *firmware* rather than software since they are unchangeable. This type of memory enables the microcomputer to immediately begin running its program as soon as it is turned on.

Memory RAM

A form of memory that can be written to and changed, as well as read from, is commonly referred to as RAM.

Another type of memory, one that can be written to as well as read from, is required for the program stack, data storage, and program variables. This type of memory is called *Random Access Memory* (RAM). This is really not a good name to distinguish this type of memory from ROM because ROMs are also random access type memories. Random access means the memory locations can be accessed in any order. They don't have to be accessed in any particular sequence. A better name for the data storage memory would be Read/Write Memory (RWM). However, the term RAM is commonly used to indicate a read/write memory, so that is what will be used here. A typical microcomputer contains both ROM and RAM type memory.

I/O Parallel Interface

Microcomputers require interface devices that enable them to communicate with other systems. The digital buffer interface used in the driver's seat application discussed earlier is one such device. The digital buffer interface is an example of a parallel interface because the eight buffer lines are all sampled at one time or in parallel. The parallel buffer interface in the driver's seat application is an input or readable interface. Output or writeable interfaces allow the microcomputer to affect external logic systems. An output buffer must be implemented using a data latch so that the binary output is retained after the microcomputer has finished writing data into it. This permits the CPU to go on to other tasks while the external system reads and uses the output data. This is different from the parallel input where the states could change between samples.

Figure 4-16. IC Chip Microprocessor

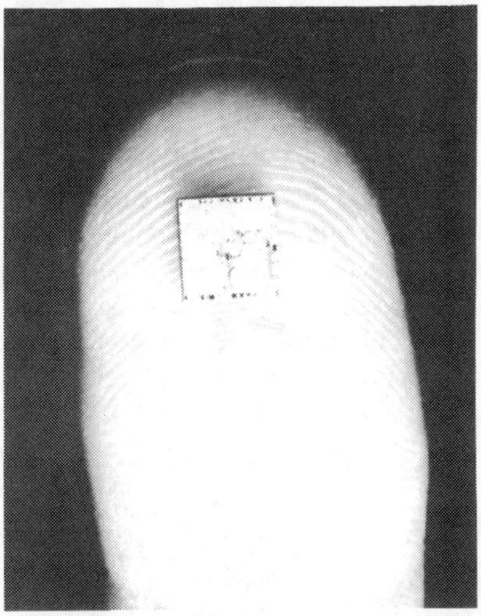

a. IC Chip

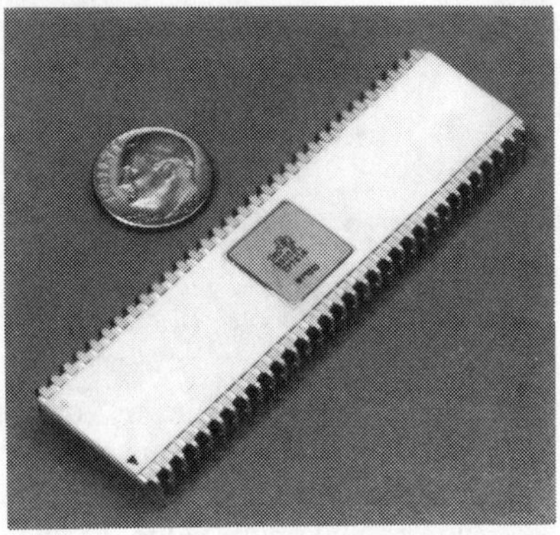

b. IC Package

Digital-to-Analog Converter

A DAC converts binary signals from the microcomputer to analog voltages that are proportional to the number encoded in the input signals.

The parallel input and output interfaces are used to examine and control external digital signals. The microcomputer can also be used to examine and control analog signals through the use of special interfaces. The microcomputer can produce an analog voltage by using a digital-to-analog converter (DAC). A DAC accepts inputs of a certain number of binary bits and produces an output voltage level that is proportional to the input number. DACs come in many different versions with different numbers of input bits and output ranges. A common microcomputer DAC has 8-bit inputs and a 0–5 volt output range.

A simple 8-bit digital-to-analog converter is shown in *Figure 4-17.* This type of DAC uses a parallel input interface and two operational amplifiers. The 8 bits are written into the parallel interface and stored in data latches. The output of each latch is a digital signal that is zero volts if the bit is low and 5 volts if the bit is high. The first op amp is a summing amplifier and has a gain of $-(R_f/R_i)$. The second op amp has a gain of -1; thus, it is only an inverter. The effect of the two amplifiers is to scale each bit of the parallel interface by a specially chosen factor and add the resultant voltages together. For instance, if only bit 0 is high and all the others are low:

$$V_{out} = 5\left[1\left(\frac{1}{256}\right) + 0\left(\frac{1}{128}\right) + 0\left(\frac{1}{64}\right) + \ldots + 0\left(\frac{1}{2}\right)\right]$$

$$= \left(\frac{5}{256}\right)$$

$$= 0.0195\text{V}$$

If only bits 0 and 7 are high:

$$V_{out} = 5\left[1\left(\frac{1}{256}\right) + 0\left(\frac{1}{128}\right) + 0\left(\frac{1}{64}\right) \ldots + 1\left(\frac{1}{12}\right)\right]$$

$$= \left(\frac{645}{256}\right)$$

$$= 2.5195\text{V}$$

The DAC output voltage can only change in discrete steps. This causes the analog output voltage to have a staircase appearance as the binary number at the input is increased one bit at a time from minimum value to maximum value, as shown in *Figure 4-18.* This DAC can have any one of 256 different voltage levels, and for many applications, this is a close enough approximation to a continuous analog signal.

The accuracy of the DAC's representation of the digital input signal varies with circuit design, and with the rate at which the input signal is sampled.

The DAC output voltage can change only when the computer writes a new number into the DAC data latches. The computer must generate each new output often enough to ensure an accurate representation of the changes in the digital signal. The analog output of the digital-to-analog converter can take only a specific number of different values and can change only at specific times determined by the sampling rate. The output of the converter will always have small discrete step changes (resolution). The designer must decide how small the steps must be to produce the desired shape and smoothness in the analog signal so that it is a reasonable duplication of the variations in the digital levels.

Analog-to-Digital Converter

In addition, microcomputers can measure analog voltages by using a special interface component called an analog-to-digital converter (ADC). Analog-to-digital converters convert an analog voltage input into a digital number output that the microcomputer can read.

Figure 4-17. Digital-to-Analog Converter Circuit Block

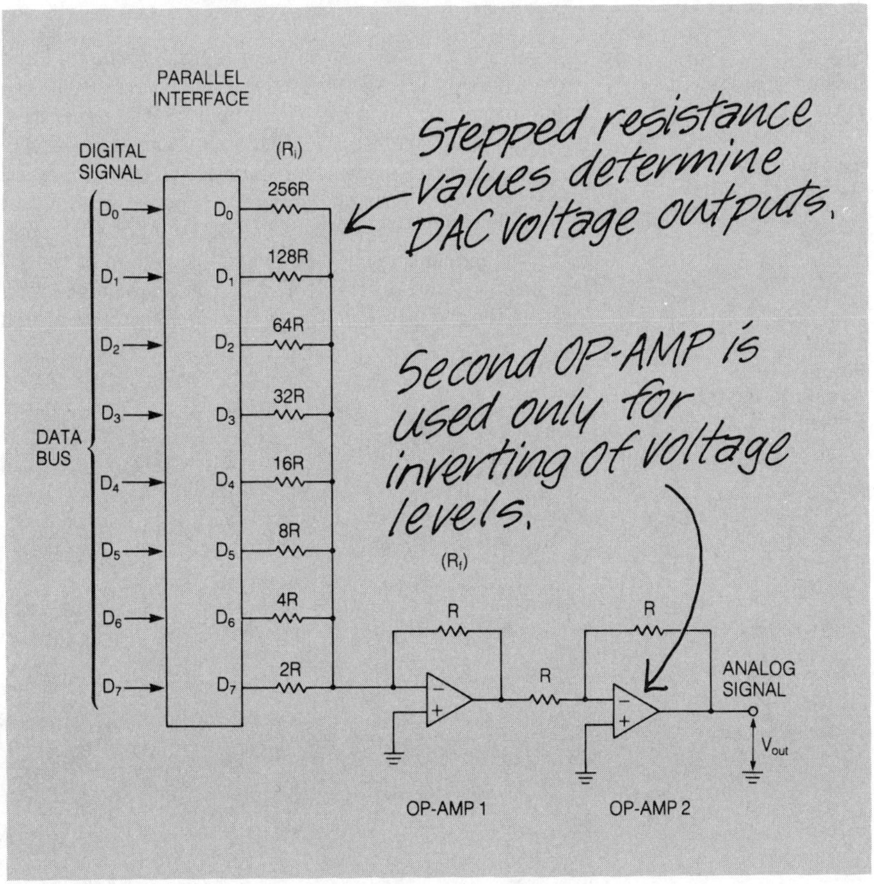

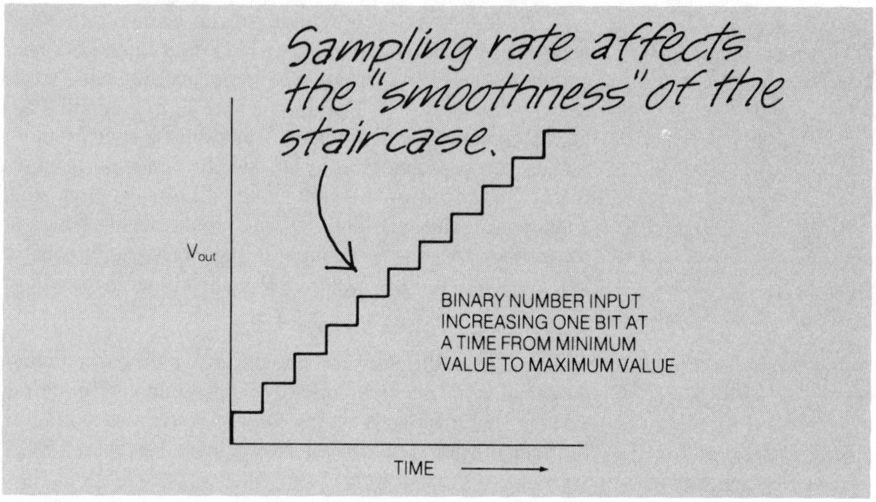

Figure 4-18. Staircase Output Voltage of the DAC in Figure 4-17

The ADC performs a function opposite of the DAC; it converts an analog signal into digital form for processing by the microcomputer.

Figure 4-19 shows a conceptually simple, but not very practical, way of making an ADC by using a DAC and a voltage comparator. The input to the DAC is a binary number that is generated by the microcomputer that starts at the minimum value and increases toward the maximum value, as seen in *Figure 4-18*. This binary number is generated at the parallel output of the microcomputer. The output of the DAC, V_{out}, is one input to the comparator. The other input is the input voltage, V_{in}, that the ADC is measuring. When the V_{out} voltage of the DAC is less than V_{in}, the output of the comparator, V_{comp}, is a low logic level. When V_{out} is greater than V_{in}, the output of the comparator is a high level.

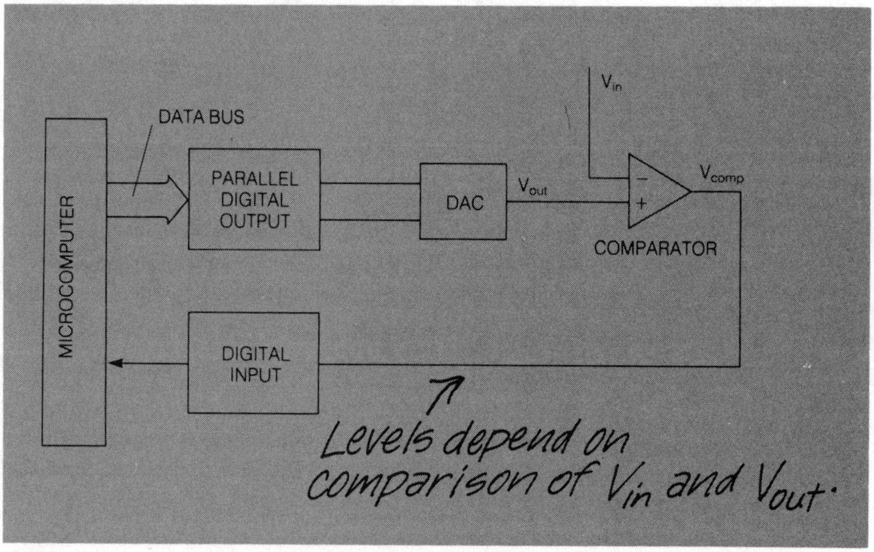

Figure 4-19. Analog-to-Digital Converter

As soon as the binary number generated by the microcomputer causes V_{out} from the DAC to be greater than V_{in}, the comparator output goes high and stops the microcomputer from changing the binary number input further. The binary number is used by the microcomputer as the equivalent of the analog input voltage, V_{in}. The microcomputer then resets and starts the binary number generation again to make another match to the V_{in} voltage. In this manner, a binary number, equivalent to a V_{in} and analog voltage, is produced at a selected sampling rate. The output of the comparator is fed back to the microcomputer through a digital input.

Sampling

The accuracy of the DAC increases as the rate of sampling of the input signal increases.

The designer determines how quickly the microcomputer must change the DAC voltage to accurately follow the analog signal. *Figure 4-20* shows a sine wave analog signal and some digital approximations with various sampling rates. Notice that *Figure 4-20a* with 13 samples per sine wave cycle follows the sinusoid much closer than *Figure 4-20b* which only samples twice in a cycle. When the sampling rate is less than two, as in *Figure 4-20c*, the staircase output doesn't follow well at all. This is because the computer didn't change the DAC input often enough to produce an output signal that closely approximates the desired signal.

Figure 4-20. Analog Output Voltage Versus Sampling Rate

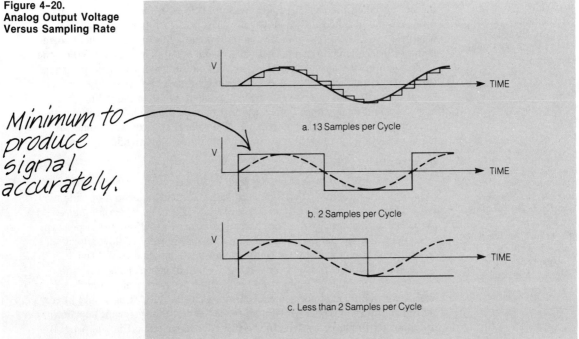

Minimum to produce signal accurately.

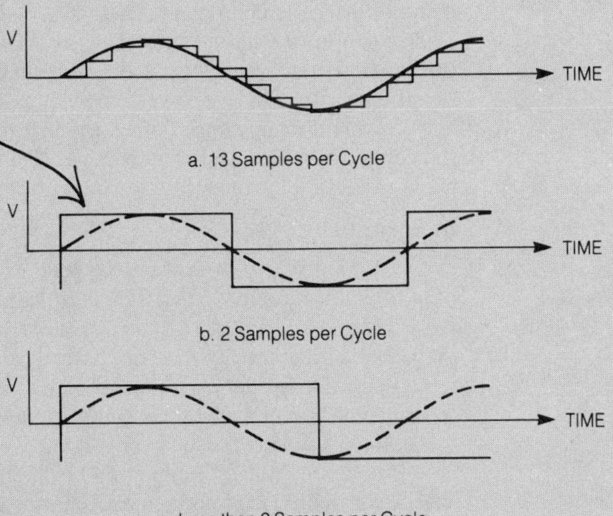

a. 13 Samples per Cycle

b. 2 Samples per Cycle

c. Less than 2 Samples per Cycle

The input sampling theorem states that an input signal must be sampled at least twice per cycle to be minimally accurate.

An engineer named H. Nyquist studied the sampling rate problem and determined that in order to reproduce a sinusoidal signal properly, the *signal must be sampled at least twice per cycle* (the Nyquist sampling theorem). Of course, more samples per cycle is better, but two samples per cycle is the minimum required.

Polling

Analog-to-digital converters are available that perform everything by themselves. The microcomputer simply tells them when to make a conversion and then waits until the conversion is done. ADCs require anywhere from a few millionths of a second to a second to complete the conversion.

Conversion time can be a serious limitation when slow converters are used. The microcomputer cannot afford to waste time waiting while the converter works. This is especially true when the microcomputer is used to control and monitor many systems at the same time. Instead of waiting for the ADC to finish, the computer could be off running another part of the program and come back only when the conversion is done. But how will the computer know when the conversion is finished?

Polling is used in some microcomputers to periodically check the ADC interface rather than waiting in an idle state for the ADC to do the conversion.

One way of doing this is for the microcomputer to periodically check the interface while it is running another part of the program. This method is called *polling*. A program subroutine is included in the main program and is called up whenever an ADC interface is being used. This usually consists of a few lines of assembly language code that checks to see if the interface is done and collects the result when it is finished. When the polling subroutine determines that the ADC is finished, the main program continues without using the polling subroutine until the ADC interface is called up again. The problem with such a scheme is that the polling routine may be called many times before the interface is finished. This can waste the computer's time and slow it down. Therefore, an evaluation must be made in certain systems to determine if polling is worthwhile.

Interrupts

Interrupts cause the CPU to jump to a specific location in the program. By signaling the microprocessor for service only when needed, interrupts are more efficient than polling.

An efficient alternative to polling uses control circuitry called an *interrupt*. An interrupt is an electrical signal that is generated outside of the CPU and is connected to an input on the CPU. The interrupt causes the CPU to temporarily discontinue the program execution and to perform some operation on data coming from an external device. A slow analog-to-digital converter, for instance, could use an interrupt line to tell the processor when it is finished converting. When an interrupt occurs, the processor automatically jumps to a designated program location and executes the interrupt service subroutine. For the ADC, this would be a subroutine to read in the conversion result. When the interrupt subroutine is done, the computer returns to the place where it left off in the program as if nothing had happened. (Recall the previous discussion on the jump-to-subroutine instruction.) Interrupts reduce the amount of time the computer spends dealing with the various peripheral devices.

Another important use for interrupts is in time keeping. Suppose that a system is being used that requires things to be done at particular times; for instance, sampling an analog signal is a timed process. A special component called a timer could be used. A timer is a device that works like a digital watch. A square-wave clock signal is counted in counter registers like the one discussed in Chapter 3. The timer can be programmed to turn on the interrupt line when it reaches a certain count and then reset itself (start over). It may be inside the CPU itself or it may be contained in peripheral devices in the microcomputer system. Timers have many automotive applications (as shown later).

Such a technique is sometimes used to trigger the output of a new number to a digital-to-analog converter at regular intervals. The microcomputer simply programs the timer for the desired amount of time by presetting the counter to some starting value other than zero. Each time the timer counts out the programmed number of pulses, it interrupts the computer. The interrupt service subroutine then gets the new binary number that has been put into memory by the microcomputer and transfers this number to the DAC data latches at the input to the DAC.

Vectored Interrupts

All of the interrupt activity is completely invisible to the program that gets interrupted. In other words, the interrupted program doesn't know it was interrupted because its execution continues without program modification with minimum delay. Interrupts allow the computer to handle two or more things *almost simultaneously*. In some systems, one interrupt line may be used by more than one device. For instance, two or more analog-to-digital converters may use the same interrupt line to indicate when either is ready. In this case, the computer doesn't know which device caused the interrupt. The computer could poll all the devices each time an interrupt occurs to see which one needs service, but as discussed, polling may waste time. A better way is to use vectored interrupts.

Vectored interrupts tell the CPU which specific device needs service, and also may implement a priority of service scheme. Vectored interrupts allow a microcomputer to handle a number of different tasks quickly.

In computer parlance, a vector is memory location that contains another address that points to another thing. It may be a specific memory location that contains the address of the first instruction of a subroutine to service an interrupt; it may be a register that contains the same type address. In this specific case, an interrupt vector is a register that peripherals use to tell the processor which device interrupted it. When a peripheral causes an interrupt, it writes a code into the interrupt vector register so that the processor can tell which device interrupted it by reading the code. The decoder for an interrupt vector usually includes circuitry that allows each device to be assigned a different interrupt priority. If two devices interrupt at the same time, the processor will service the most important one first.

The vectored interrupt enables the microcomputer to efficiently handle the peripheral devices connected to it and to service the interrupts rapidly. Interrupts allow the processor to respond to things happening in peripheral devices without having to constantly monitor the interfaces. They enable the microcomputer to handle many different tasks and to keep track of all of them. A microcomputer system designed to use interrupts is called a real-time computing system because it rapidly responds to peripherals as soon as requests occur. Such real-time systems are used in digital instrumentation and control systems.

MICROCOMPUTER APPLICATIONS IN INSTRUMENTATION AND CONTROL

There is a great variety of applications of microprocessors in automobiles. As will be explained in later chapters of this book, microprocessors find applications in engine and driveline control, instrumentation, ride control, antilocking braking and other safety devices, entertainment, heating/air conditioning control, automatic seat position control, and many other systems. In each of these applications, the microprocessor serves as the functional core of what can properly be called a special purpose microcomputer.

Although these applications are widely varied in operation, the essential configuration (or so-called architecture) has much in common for all applications. *Figure 4-21* is a simplified block diagram depicting the various components of each of the automotive systems having the applications listed above. In this block diagram, the microprocessor is denoted MPU. It is connected to the other components by means of three buses: address bus (AB), data bus (DB), and control bus (CB). Each bus consists of a set of wires over which binary electrical signals are transmitted. In a typical automotive application, the DB consists of eight wires, the AB is typically eight to 16 wires, and the control bus is a set of three or four wires.

The hardware in the microcomputer remains fixed, while the programs stored in ROM can be changed as desired to perform different applications.

The operation of each special purpose microcomputer system is controlled by a program stored in ROM. As explained earlier in this chapter, the MPU generates addresses for the ROM in sequence to obtain each instruction in corresponding sequence. The operation of each microprocessor-based automotive subsystem has a specific program that is permanently stored (electronically) in the ROM. Changes in the system operation can be achieved by replacing the ROM chip(s) with new chip(s) that contain the appropriate program for the desired operation. This feature is advantageous during the engineering development phase for any microprocessor-based system. While the hardware remains fixed, the system modifications and improvements are achieved by substituting ROM chips.

A typical automotive microprocessor-based system also incorporates some amount of RAM. This memory is used for a variety of purposes including storing temporary results, storing the stack, and storing all of the variables, not to mention all of the other activities discussed earlier in this chapter.

Figure 4-21. Architecture for Typical Automotive Computer

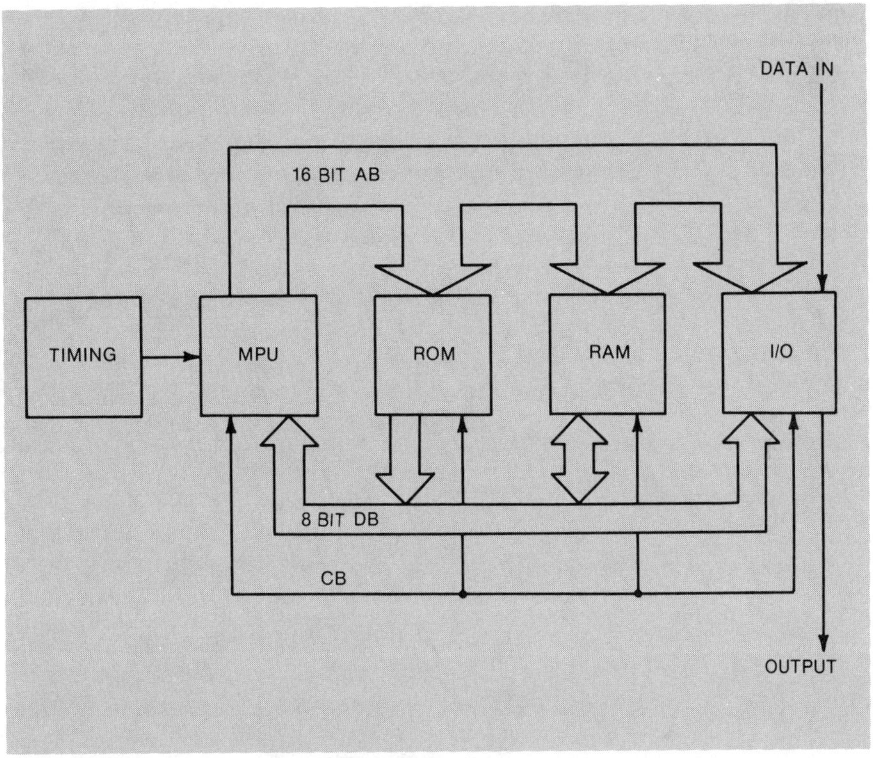

The input/output (I/O) device for any given automotive microcomputer system serves as the interface connection of the microcomputer with the particular automotive system. There are standard commercial I/O devices that are available from the manufacturers of each microprocessor and that are specifically configured to work with that processor. These I/O devices are implemented as an IC chip and are very versatile in application. A typical such I/O device has two 8-bit data ports for connecting to peripheral devices, and an 8-bit port that is connected to the data bus of the computer.

Figure 4-22 is a block diagram of a typical commercial I/O device. In this device there are two ports labeled A and B, respectively. Either of these ports can be configured to act as either input or output, depending upon the data in the data direction register. Normally the correct code for determining direction is transferred to the I/O device from the microprocessor via the system data bus.

Whenever the microprocessor is either to transfer data to the I/O device or receive data from it, a specific address is generated by the processor. This address is decoded, using standard logic, to form an electrical signal that activates the chip select inputs to the I/O.

Figure 4-22. Block Diagram of a Typical Interface Adapter

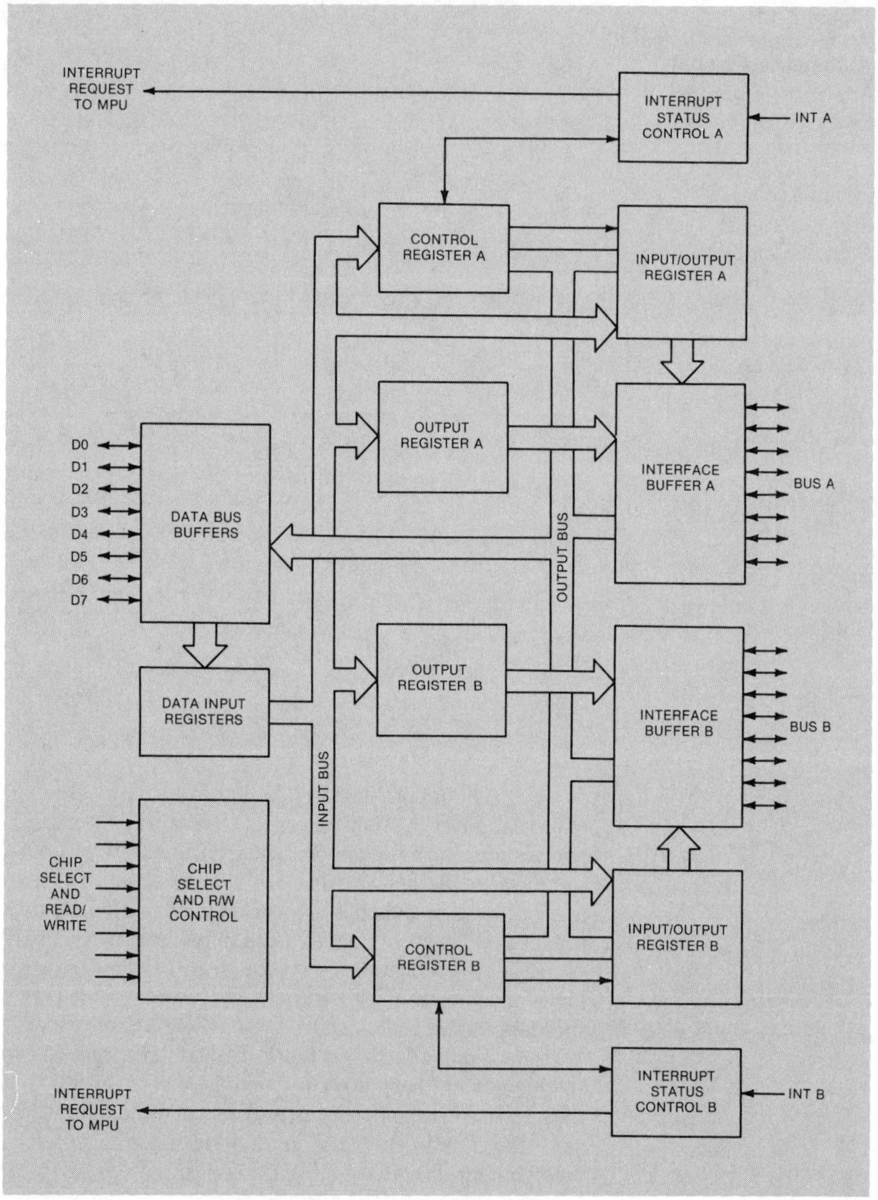

In addition, the read/write (R/W) output of the microprocessor is activated, causing data to be received (read) from a peripheral device, or transmitted (write) to a peripheral device.

This use of address lines to activate the I/O is known as memory mapped I/O. In memory mapped, I/O input and output of data is selected by reading from the I/O input address or writing to the I/O output address.

Instrumentation Applications of Microcomputers

Microcomputers can convert the nonlinear output voltage of some sensors into a linear voltage representation. The sensor output voltage is used to look up the corresponding linear value stored in a table.

In instrumentation applications of microcomputers, the signal processing operations are performed numerically under program control. The block diagram of a typical computer-based instrument is depicted in *Figure 4-23*. In this example instrument, an analog sensor provides a continuous time voltage, V_o, that is proportional to the quantity being measured. The continuous time voltage is sampled at times determined by the computer. The sampled analog voltage is then converted to digital format (typically 8 to 16 bits) using an A/D converter. The digital data is connected to port A of the I/O device of the computer to be read into memory.

The A/D converter generates a signal when the conversion from analog to digital is completed. This signal is normally termed end of conversion (EOC). The EOC signal provides an interrupt signaling the computer that data is ready.

The signal processing to be performed is expressed as a set of operations that is to be performed by the microprocessor on the data. These operations are termed the algorithm for the signal processing

Figure 4-23. Typical Automotive Instrumentation Architecture

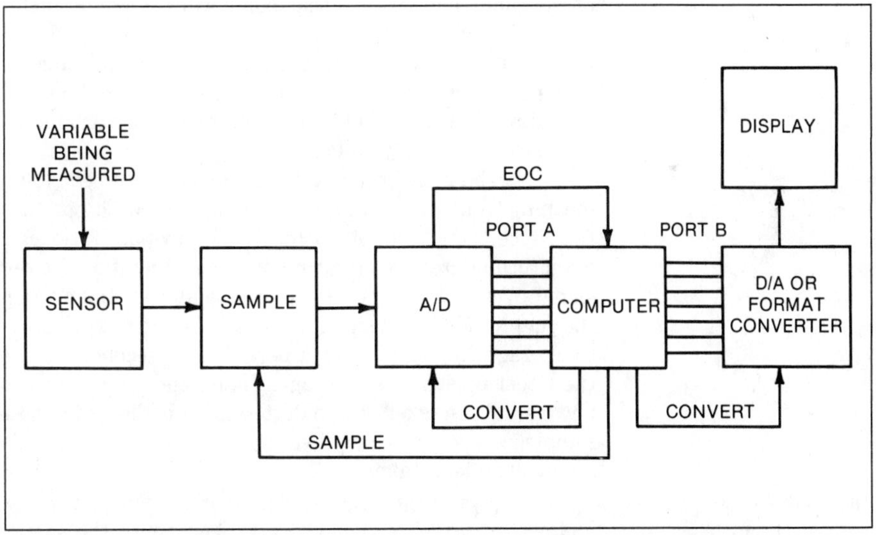

operation. The algorithm is converted to a set of specific computer operations that becomes the program for the signal processing. After the signal processing is completed, the result is ready to be sent to the display device. The digital data is sent through I/O to port B to the D/A converter. There it is converted back to sampled analog. The sampled data is "smoothed" to a suitable continuous time voltage by means of a special filter known as a reconstruction filter. The continuous time output of this filter drives the continuous time display.

In a great many applications, the display is digital (e.g., automotive speed measurement). In this case, the conversion from digital to analog is not required, and the computer output data can directly activate the digital display.

Digital Filters

Digital filters can be programmed on a microcomputer to reject specific types of signals while passing other signals.

As an example of computer-based instrumentation signal processing applications, consider the relatively straightforward task of filtering the output of a sensor. Low-pass filters pass low-frequency signals but reject high-frequency signals. High-pass filters do just the reverse; they pass high-frequency signals and reject low-frequency signals. Bandpass filters pass midrange frequencies but reject both low and high frequencies. Analog filters use resistive, capacitive, and inductive components, and sometimes operational amplifiers. Digital low-pass and bandpass filters can be programmed on a microcomputer to perform basically the same function as their analog counterparts.

A digital low-pass filter could be used, for instance, to smooth the output of an automotive fuel level sensor. The fuel level sensor produces an electrical signal that is proportional to the height of the fuel in the center of the tank. The level at that point will change as fuel is consumed, but it also will change as the car slows, accelerates, turns corners, and hits bumps. The sensor's output voltage varies wildly because of fuel slosh even though the amount of fuel in the tank changes slowly. If that voltage is sent directly to the fuel gauge, the resulting variable indication will fluctuate too rapidly to be read.

The measurement can be made more readable and more meaningful by using a low-pass filter to smooth out the signal fluctuations to reduce the effects of sloshing. The low-pass filter can be implemented in a microcomputer by programming the computer to average the sensor signal over several seconds before sending it to the display. For instance, if the fuel level sensor signal is sampled once every second and it is desirable to average the signal over a period of 60 seconds, the computer saves only the latest 60 samples, averages them, and displays the average. When a new sample is taken, the oldest sample is discarded so only the 60 latest samples are kept. A new average can be computed and displayed each time a new sample is taken.

Digital filters are performed completely through the use of software, thus their characteristics can be easily changed. Because digital filters require no extra hardware, they are low in cost.

Digital filtering (e.g., averaging) can be performed by a computer under the control of the software. Sometimes the section of code that performs the filtering task is simply called "the filter." Digital signal processing is very attractive because the same computer can be used to process several different signals. Also, since digital filters require no extra hardware, the filters can be made much more complex with relatively little increase in cost. In addition, the characteristics of the digital filter can be changed by changing the software. Changing the characteristics of an analog filter usually requires changing the hardware components. Another feature of digital filters (true for digital signal processing in general) is that they don't change with age or temperature as analog filters tend to. However, there are limitations to the use of digital filters.

The frequency range of digital filters is determined by the speed of the processor. The microcomputer must be able to sample each signal at or above the rate required by the Nyquist sampling theorem. It must also be fast enough to perform all of the signal averaging and linearization for each signal before the next sample is taken. This is an important limitation, and the system designer must be certain that the computer is not overloaded by trying to make it do too many things too quickly.

MICROCOMPUTERS IN CONTROL SYSTEMS

Computers can also be used in control applications.

Microcomputers are able to handle inputs and outputs which are either digital or converted analog signals. With the proper software, they are capable of making decisions about those signals and can react to them quickly and precisely. These features make microcomputers ideal for controlling other digital or analog systems as discussed below.

Closed-Loop Control System

Recall the basic closed-loop control system block diagram of Chapter 2. The error amplifier compares the command input with the plant output and sends the error signal to the control logic. The control logic uses the error signal to generate a plant control signal which causes the plant to react with a new output so that the error signal will be reduced toward zero. The control logic is designed so that the plant's output follows or tracks the command input. A microcomputer can replace the error amplifier and the control logic. The computer can compare command input and plant output and perform the computation required to generate a control signal.

Limit-Cycle Controller

The limit-cycle controller, discussed in Chapter 2, can readily be implemented with a microcomputer. Recall that the limit-cycle controller controls the plant output so that it falls somewhere between an upper and lower limit, preferably so that its average value is equal to the command input. The controller must read in the command input and the plant output and decide what control signal to send to the plan based on those signals alone.

Using a microcomputer, the upper and lower limit can be determined from the command input by using a lookup table similar to that discussed later in this chapter. The plant output is compared against these two limits. If the plant output is above the higher limit or below the lower limit, the microcomputer outputs the appropriate on/off signal to the plant to bring the output back between the two limits.

With proper software, a microcomputer can replace the error amplifier and control logic used in the closed-loop control system.

Recall that in Chapter 2 the concept of a feedback control system was introduced. There it was shown that a control system compares the value of some controlled variable with a desired value (or set point) for that variable. In such a control system, the difference between the desired and actual value is first obtained, then an electrical signal is generated. The resulting error signal is processed electronically, thereby generating a control signal that operates an actuator. The actuator changes the controlled system in such a way as to reduce the error. In Chapter 2, it was presumed that analog electronics were used for the control.

A feedback control system can also be implemented using digital electronics. *Figure 4-24* is a block diagram of a control system employing a computer. In this figure, there is a physical system or plant that is to be controlled. The specific variable being controlled is denoted X. For example, in an automobile, the plant might be the engine and the controlled variable might be brake torque.

Figure 4-24. Typical Digital Control System

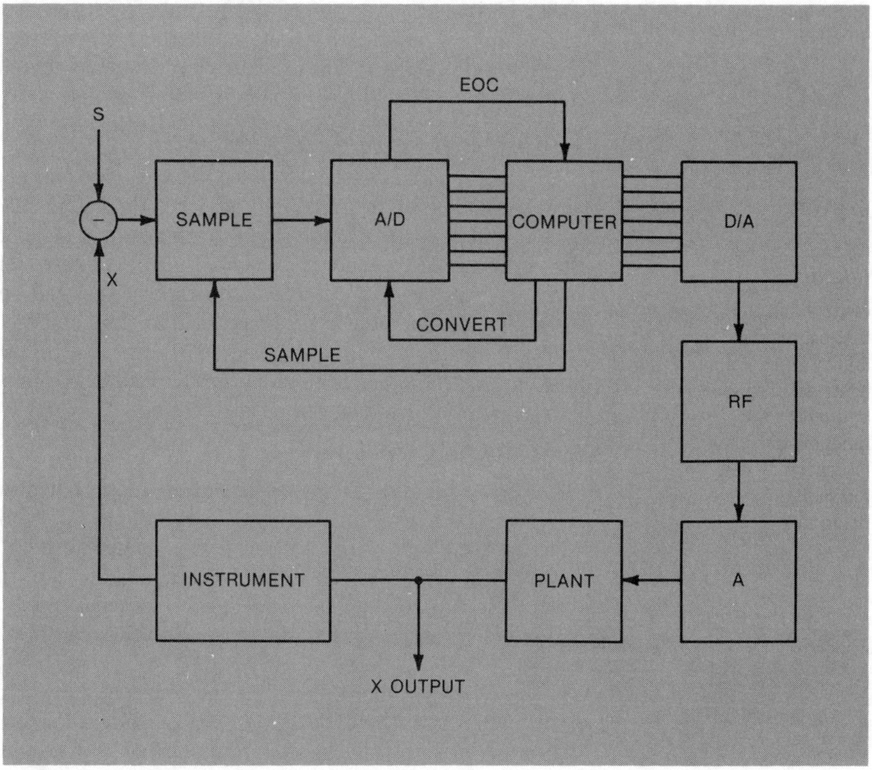

The desired value for X is the set point S. An error signal e is obtained:

$$e = S - X$$

The error signal is sampled yielding samples e_n (where n represents sample number—i.e., n - 1, 2...). In a typical digital control system, the computer generates an output y_n for each input sample.

$$\underline{y_n = y_o + Pe_n + I\,(e_n + e_{n-1} + e_{n-2})\,\Delta T + D(e_n - e_{n-1})}$$
$$\Delta T$$

where

P is the proportional gain
I is the integral gain
D is the differential gain
ΔT is the time between successive samples

The previous equation represents an example of an algorithm for the particular control strategy. The example algorithm is a form of a so-called PID (proportional-integral differential) control strategy.

After computing y_n for each input sample, a digital version of y_n is transmitted through the I/O to the D/A converter. There it is converted to analog format providing a control signal to the actuator (A) which is presumed here to be analog). The actuator controls the plant in such a way as to cause the error to be reduced toward zero. An example of the application of computer-based electronic control systems in automobiles is presented in a later chapter of this book.

Multivariable Systems

With the appropriate control scheme program, microcomputers have the ability to sample and control multiple inputs and outputs independently. This type of control is much more difficult to design when using analog circuitry.

A very important feature of microcomputer control logic is the ability to control multiple systems independently or systems with multiple inputs and outputs. The automotive applications for microcomputer control involves both of these types of so-called "multivariable" systems. For instance, the automobile engine has several inputs (such as air/fuel ratio, throttle angle, spark timing, etc.) and several outputs (torque, speed, exhaust gases, etc.). All of the outputs must be controlled simultaneously because some inputs affect more than one output. These types of controllers can be very complicated and are difficult to implement in analog fashion. The increased complexity of a multivariable microcomputer system is not much higher, nor is the cost, than for a single variable microcomputer system, presuming the microcomputer has the capacity to do the task. It only affects the task of programming the appropriate control scheme into the microcomputer. This type of control is discussed in a later chapter.

Table Lookup

One of the important functions of a microcomputer in automotive applications is table lookup. These applications include:

1. linearization of sensor data
2. multiplication
3. calibration conversion

These applications are explained in detail in later chapters where appropriate. In this chapter, we explain the basic principle using a specific example.

The concept of table lookup is illustrated in *Figure 4-25* in which a pair of variables, V_o and X, are related by the graph depicted therein. Also shown in *Figure 4-25* is a table listing certain specific values for the relationship. The functional relationship between V_o and X might, for example, be the output voltage of a nonlinear sensor V_o for measuring a quantity X. If the value for V_o is known, then the corresponding value for X can theoretically be found using the graph or the tabulated values. In the latter case, the nearest two tabulated values for V_o are located, and the corresponding values for X are read from the table. Denoting V_1 and V_2 as the nearest values and X_1, X_2 as the corresponding tabulated values, the value for X corresponding to V_o is found by linear interpolation

$$X = X_1 + (X_2 - X_1)(V_o - V_2) / (V_1 - V_2)$$

Figure 4-25. Illustration of Table Lookup and Interpolation

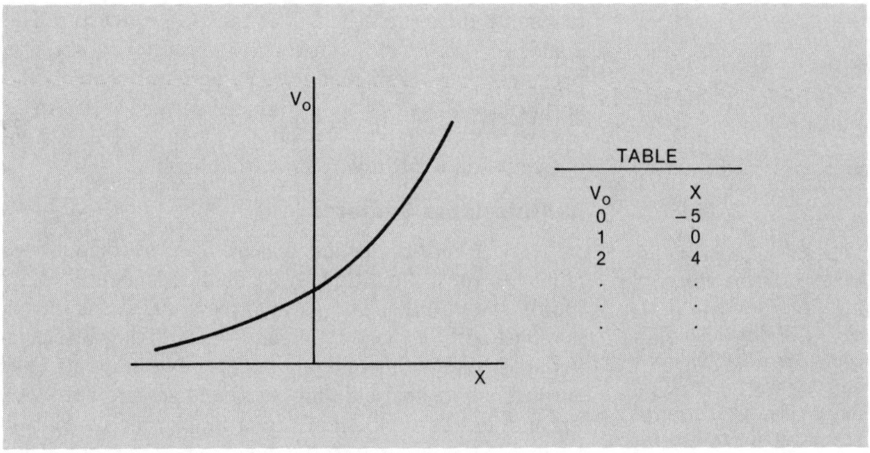

A microcomputer can perform the same operation using tabulated values for the relationship between V_o and X (i.e., $V_o(X)$ in correct mathematical notation). This method is illustrated using a specific example of the measurement of a variable X using a sensor output voltage, and variable X is assumed to be that which is illustrated in *Figure 4-24*. A microcomputer is to obtain the value for X using a table lookup operation.

The portion of the microcomputer that is involved in the table lookup process is illustrated in *Figure 4-26*. The relationship $V_o(X)$ is stored in a ROM for representative points along the curve. This data is stored using V_o values as addresses, and corresponding values of X as data. For example, consider a point V_1,X_1. The data X_1 is stored at memory location V_1 in binary format.

The operation of the table lookup is as follows. The sensor S has output voltage V_o. The computer reads the values of V_o (using an A/D converter to convert to digital format) through the input/output (I/O) device. Then the MPU under program control (program ROM) calculates the addresses for the two nearest values to V_o which are V_1 and V_2 ($V_1 < V_o < V_2$). The computer under program control, reads values X_1 and X_2 and then calculates X using the preceding formula.

Figure 4-26. Architecture Involved in Table Lookup

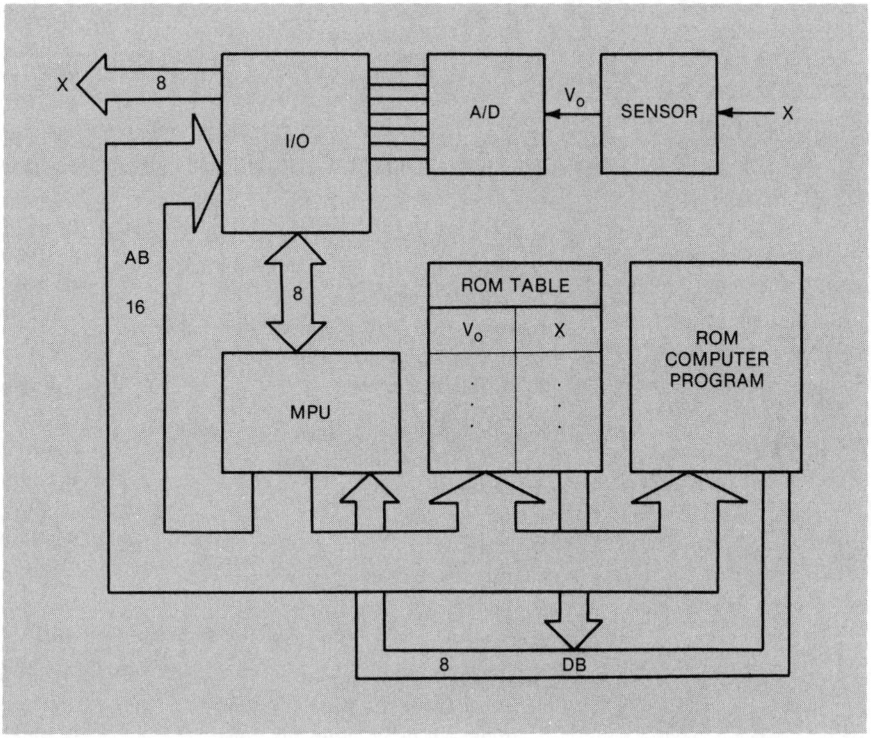

Repeated reference will be made to the table lookup function in later chapters. In particular, Chapter 7 will discuss how a typical digital engine control system frequently obtains data using table lookup.

After a chapter on sensors and actuators, this book will deal more specifically with particular microcomputer automotive instrumentation and control systems to show how these systems are used in the automobile to control the engine and drive train and many auxiliary functions.

Quiz for Chapter 4

1. The parts of a computer include
   a. CPU
   b. memory
   c. input/output
   d. all of the above.
2. What does a microcomputer use to interface with other systems?
   a. parallel interface
   b. analog to digital converter
   c. digital to analog converter
   d. all of the above
3. Which control line do peripherals use to get the computer's attention?
   a. power line
   b. read/write line
   c. interrupt line
   d. clock line
4. What is a data bus?
   a. a set of wires which carry bits to or from the processor and memory or peripherals
   b. a large yellow vehicle for carrying datas
   c. a bus carrying addresses
   d. a set of wires for control signals
5. What are computers used for in instrumentation systems?
   a. signal processing
   b. sensor, actuator, and display linearization
   c. display formatting
   d. filtering
   e. all of the above
6. According to the Nyquist sampling theorem a signal must be sampled at
   a. the highest frequency in the signal
   b. at least twice the highest frequency in the signal
   c. less than half the lowest frequency in the signal
   d. more than half the lowest frequency in the signal
7. What advantages does digital signal processing have over analog signal processing?
   a. digital is more precise
   b. digital doesn't drift with time and temperature
   c. the same digital hardware can be used in many filters
   d. all of the above
8. What advantages does analog signal processing have over digital signal processing?
   a. analog is always less expensive
   b. the same analog hardware can be used for many filters
   c. analog is sometimes less expensive
   d. high frequency signals can only be filtered with analog filters
9. What type of memory is used to permanently store programs?
   a. RAM
   b. ROM
   c. MAP
   d. RPM

10. What type of memory is used to temporarily store data and variables?
    a. RAM
    b. ROM
    c. MAP
    d. RPM

11. What distinguishes a computer from a fancy calculator?
    a. add, subtract, multiply, and divide
    b. stored program
    c. the calculators can read paper tape
    d. digital circuits

12. What part of the computer does the arithmetic and logic functions?
    a. peripherals
    b. memory
    c. CPU
    d. address bus

13. Which computer register is the main work register?
    a. program counter
    b. stack pointer
    c. condition code register
    d. accumulator

14. A short initialization program is called what kind of program?
    a. subroutine
    b. boot program
    c. main program
    d. branch

15. Which register keeps track of program steps?
    a. program counter
    b. stack pointer
    c. condition code register
    d. accumulator

16. A programmer uses what type of statements in an assembly language program?
    a. op codes
    b. mnemonics
    c. machine code

17. Most microcomputers use how many bits to address memory?
    a. 1
    b. 16
    c. 4
    d. 6

18. Most automotive microcomputers use how many bits in arithmetic?
    a. 1
    b. 6
    c. 4
    d. 8

19. Which of the following is a short program which ends with an RTS instruction?
    a. main program
    b. interrupt
    c. boot
    d. subroutine

Sensors and Actuators

ABOUT THIS CHAPTER

In this chapter, the theory and operation of two vital components of automotive control and instrumentation systems are explained: the sensor and the actuator. The sensor is an input device that gives the system information used to determine an action. The actuator is an output device in an electronic control system that performs some action in response to an electrical input.

AUTOMOTIVE CONTROL SYSTEM APPLICATIONS

In control system applications, sensors and actuators, in many cases, are the critical components for determining system performance. This is especially true for automotive control system applications. The availability of appropriate sensors and actuators dictates the design of the control system and the type of function it can perform.

Sensors and actuators play a critical role in determining automotive control system performance.

The sensors and actuators which are available to a control system designer are not always what the designer wants because the required device is not commercially available. For this reason, special signal processors or interface circuits many times must be designed to adapt to an available sensor or actuator, or the control system controller is designed in a specific way to fit available sensors or actuators. However, for automotive control systems, because of their large potential quantity, it has been worthwhile to develop a sensor for a particular application, even though it often has taken a long and expensive research project to do so.

OVERVIEW

To understand how sensors and actuators are used in a system, refer to *Figure 5-1*. As pointed out in Chapter 2, q_o is a physical quantity. The sensor converts the physical quantity, q_o, into an electrical signal, q_1, that represents the value of the physical quantity being measured. The electronic signal processor operates on q_1, the electrical signal from the sensor, and generates another electrical signal, q_2, in a form suitable to operate an actuator. If the system is an instrumentation application, then q_3 is the output action of the actuator or the readable quantity of the display. In *Figure 5-1*, we aren't concerned with whether the control system is operating in an open or closed loop. Rather, we wish to emphasize the signal flow from the sensor through some kind of processor to the display or actuator.

Figure 5-1. Instrumentation Block Diagram

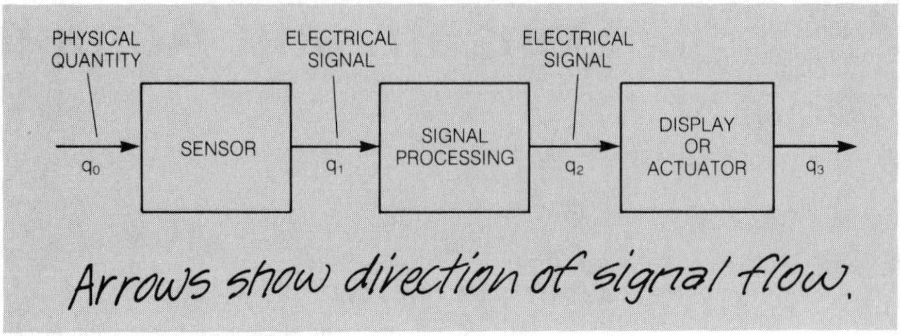

Signal flow in a monitoring system is from a sensor to a signal processor, and finally to a display or actuator.

In a control application, it is necessary to measure one or more physical quantities (to be more general we'll call them variables). The control system uses the value of these variables to determine the status of the system being controlled. The electronic control system can operate only with signals in electrical form; therefore, a sensor must be used to convert the physical variable being measured into a suitable electrical signal. Actuators usually require some form of mechanical action; therefore, the output of the signal processor is a reconversion of the electrical signal into suitable mechanical action.

VARIABLES TO BE MEASURED

Figure 5-2 shows a simplified electronic control system for an internal combustion automotive engine. The basic inputs to the engine are air and fuel and the basic outputs are the mechanical drive power and the exhaust emissions. Maximum efficiency of the conversion of fuel to drive power is desired while the exhaust emissions of burned by-products are maintained within allowable limits. The air/fuel ratio is a key control parameter. Sensors measure the physical variables and feed electrical signals through signal processors to the controller. The controller generates the electrical outputs which operate the actuators to control the engine performance.

An electronic control system for an automotive engine must deal with variables such as engine speed, various temperatures and pressures, crankshaft position, and exhaust gas oxygen concentration.

Many variables must be measured. These include:

1. coolant temperature
2. inlet air temperature
3. manifold absolute pressure
4. atmospheric absolute pressure
5. crankshaft angular position
6. engine angular speed (RPM)
7. exhaust gas oxygen concentration
8. throttle angle

At least one sensor that has acceptable performance for measuring each of these variables is presently available.

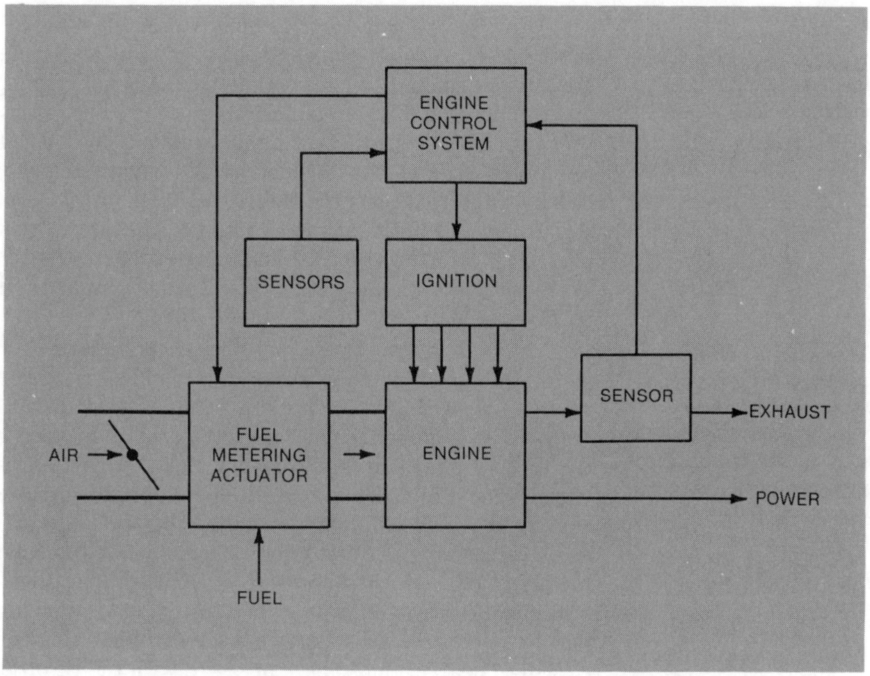

Figure 5-2. Simplified Electronic Engine Control System

There are other variables which the control system designer would like to measure directly, but a cost-effective sensor does not presently exist. These variables include:

1. engine output (brake torque)
2. in-cylinder pressure

Often the variable which the control system designer wants to measure can be obtained only indirectly by sensing a closely related variable. This will be illustrated with several automotive examples. It will be shown that it is sometimes necessary to measure several variables and perform complex mathematical operations just to obtain a measurement of a desired variable.

ANALYSIS OF INTAKE MANIFOLD PRESSURE

The air and fuel mixture enters the engine in a number of ways but usually always through the intake manifold. The intake manifold is a series of channels and passages that direct the air and fuel mixture to the cylinders. One very important engine variable associated with the intake manifold is the manifold absolute pressure (MAP). The sensor that measures this pressure is the manifold absolute pressure sensor—the MAP sensor. This sensor develops a voltage which is approximately proportional to the average value of intake manifold pressure. In Chapter 6, we'll see that the MAP sensor voltage has many applications in an engine electronic control system.

The MAP sensor output voltage is proportional to the average pressure within the intake manifold.

Figure 5-3 is a very simplified sketch of an intake manifold. In this simplified sketch, the engine is viewed as an air pump drawing air into the intake manifold. Whenever the engine is not running, no air is being pumped and the intake manifold absolute pressure is at atmospheric pressure. This is the highest intake manifold absolute pressure for an unsupercharged engine (a supercharged engine has an external air pump called a supercharger). The throttle plate shown is normally in the carburetor. When the engine is running, the air flow is impeded by the partially closed throttle plate in the carburetor. This reduces the pressure in the intake manifold so it is lower than atmospheric pressure; therefore, a partial vacuum exists in the intake.

The manifold absolute pressure varies from near atmospheric pressure when the throttle plate is fully opened to near zero pressure when the throttle plate is closed.

If the engine were a perfect air pump and if the throttle plate were tightly closed, a perfect vacuum could be created in the intake manifold. A perfect vacuum corresponds to zero absolute pressure. However, the engine is not a perfect pump and some air always leaks past the throttle plate. (In fact, some air must get past a closed throttle or the engine cannot idle.) Therefore, the intake manifold absolute pressure is slightly above absolute zero when the throttle plate is closed and the engine is running. At the other extreme, when the engine is running and the throttle plate is wide open, the manifold pressure is nearly equal to atmospheric pressure. Thus, when the engine is running, the intake manifold pressure varies from a relatively low value with the throttle plate closed, to nearly atmospheric pressure with the throttle plate wide open.

Figure 5-3. Simplified Intake System

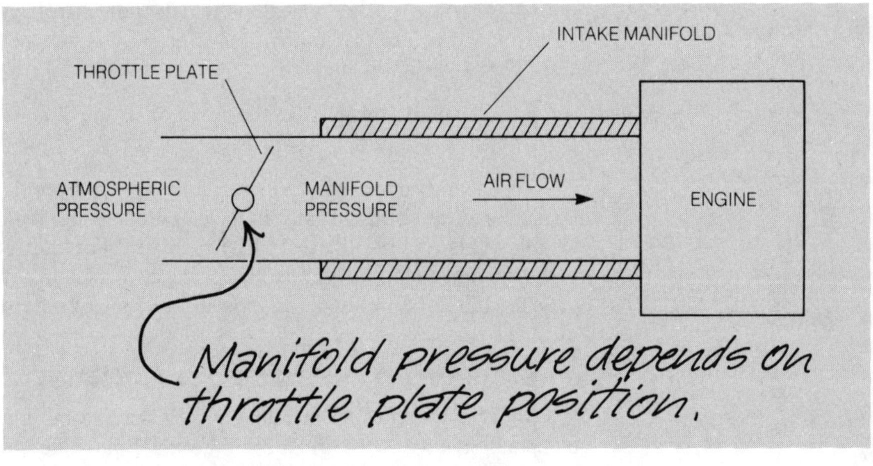

Manifold pressure fluctuates because of the pumping action of the individual cylinders. The MAP sensor filters these fluctuations so its output represents the average pressure.

The variations in intake manifold pressure as the throttle plate position is held constant also must be considered. The manifold pressure fluctuates rapidly because of the individual pumping action of the several cylinders. Each cylinder begins drawing in air when its intake valve opens and its piston begins the downward motion after top dead center (TDC). Manifold pressure decreases during this time. The drawing in of air for this cylinder ends when bottom dead center (BDC) is reached and the intake valve closes. The manifold pressure begins to increase until another cylinder begins to draw in air, then the pressure decreases again. Therefore, the manifold pressure fluctuates during the stroke of each cylinder and as pumping is switched from one cylinder to the next.

Each cylinder contributes to the pumping action every second crankshaft revolution. For an N cylinder engine, the frequency, f_p, in cycles per second, of the manifold pressure fluctuation for an engine running at a certain RPM is given by:

$$f_p = \frac{N \times RPM}{120}$$

Figure 5-4 shows manifold pressure fluctuations as well as average pressure MAP.

For a control system application, only average manifold pressure is required. The torque produced by an engine at a constant rpm is approximately proportional to the average value of MAP. The rapid fluctuations in instantaneous MAP are not of interest to the engine controller. Therefore, the manifold pressure measurement method should filter out the pressure fluctuations at frequence f_p and measure only the average pressure. One way to achieve this filtering is to connect the MAP sensor to the intake manifold through a very small diameter tube. The rapid fluctuations in pressure do not pass through this tube, but the average pressure does. The MAP sensor output voltage then corresponds only to the average manifold pressure.

MAP Sensor Concepts

Several MAP sensor configurations have been used in automotive applications. The earliest sensors were derived from aerospace instrumentation concepts, but these proved more expensive than desirable for automotive applications and have been replaced with more cost effective designs. Actually, research is continuing (and will likely continue) for lower cost and better performing MAP sensors. Several of the concepts used for sensors of manifold absolute pressure will be discussed.

It is interesting to note that none of the MAP sensors in use measure manifold pressure directly, but instead measure the displacement of a diaphragm which is deflected by manifold pressure. The details of the diaphragm displacement and the measurement of this displacement vary from one configuration to another.

Figure 5-4.
Intake Manifold
Pressure Fluctuations

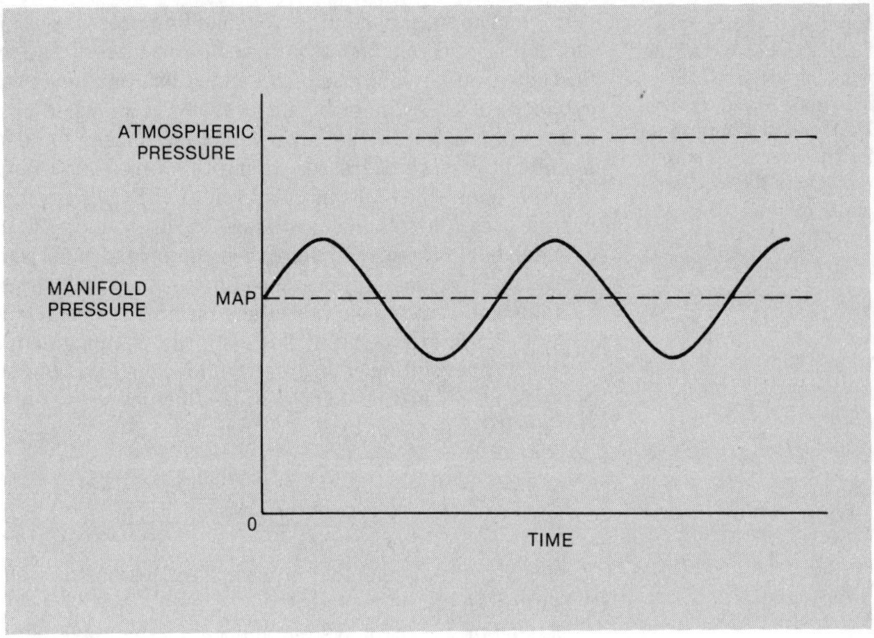

Aneroid MAP Sensor

One of the earliest MAP sensor configurations used in automotive applications is illustrated in *Figure 5-5*. This sensor actually uses a pair of diaphragms which are welded together under vacuum to form an aneroid chamber. The aneroid chamber is placed in a sealed housing which is connected by a small diameter tube to the intake manifold so that the pressure inside the sealed housing is the average manifold absolute pressure. The manifold pressure deforms the aneroid such that increasing manifold pressure compresses the aneroid. The aneroid is designed such that the displacement is almost perfectly linear with manifold pressure.

In an aneroid MAP sensor, a pair of diaphragms that respond to pressure variations are connected to the moving core in a special type of transformer. As the core moves, the output voltage of the transformer varies.

The actual measurement of aneroid displacement is done with a sensor called a linear variable differential transformer (LVDT). The LVDT has a movable core and the coupling between the iput and output transformer windings varies with core position. A 10-kHz signal is applied to the input winding. The output windings of the LVDT are balanced so that the output voltage of one winding is equal to the other with the core at its center position. However, they are connected so they cancel each other and the net output voltage is zero. As the core is displaced from this midposition by manifold pressure, the output voltage of one winding is greater than the other, so the net output voltage varies in proportion to the amount of movement of the core.

Figure 5-5.
Typical Aneroid MAP Sensor

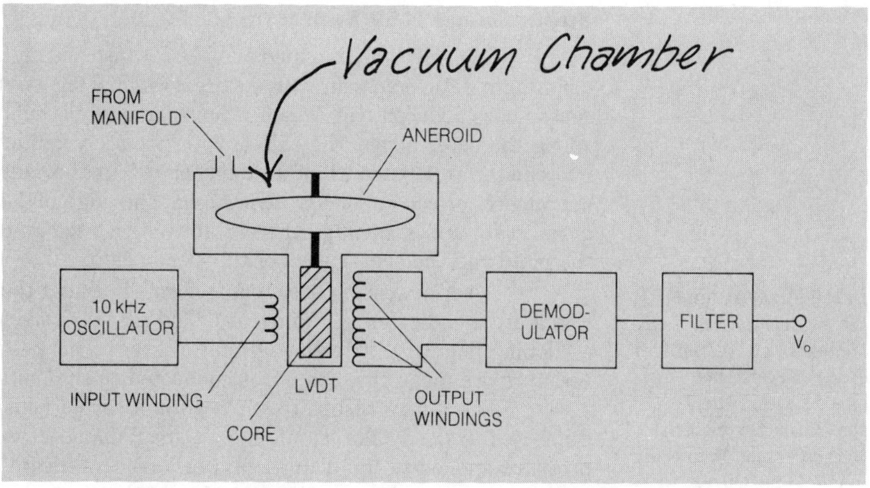

Use of the aneroid MAP sensor was discontinued in favor of less expensive sensor designs.

The electronic signal processing (demodulator and filter) produces a dc voltage which is proportional to the manifold absolute pressure, as shown in *Figure 5-6*. Unfortunately, this sensor is relatively expensive for large-scale automotive application and its use was discontinued. It was replaced with more cost-effective designs.

Figure 5-6.
V_o Versus MAP for MAP Sensor

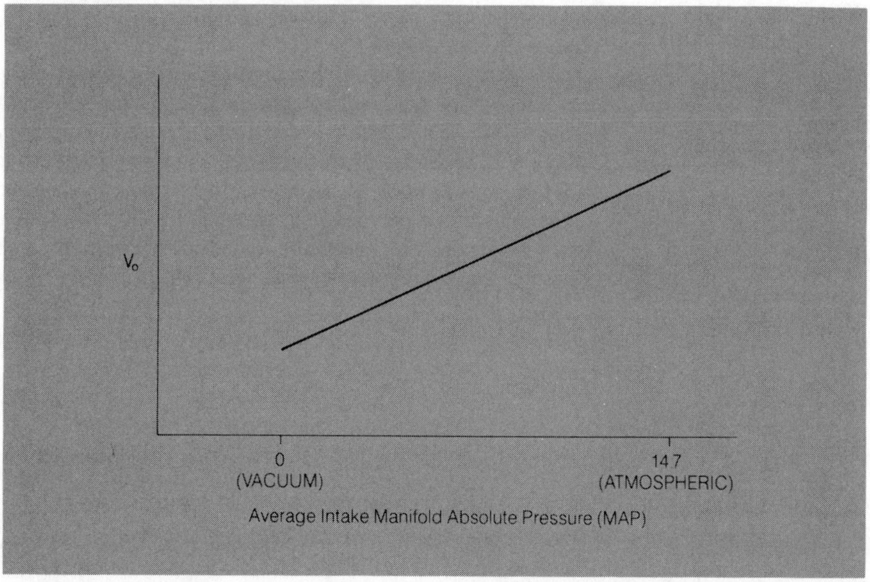

Strain Gauge MAP Sensor

One relatively inexpensive MAP sensor configuration is the silicon diaphragm diffused strain gauge sensor (SCSG) shown in *Figure 5-7*. This sensor uses a silicon chip which is approximately 3 millimeters square. Along the outer edges, the chip is approximately 250 micrometers (1 micrometer = 1 millionth of a meter) thick but the center area is only 25 micrometers thick to form a diaphragm. The edge of the chip is sealed to a pyrex plate under vacuum, thereby forming a vacuum chamber between the plate and the center area of the silicon chip.

In the strain gauge MAP sensor, manifold pressure applied to the diaphragm causes a resistance change within the semiconductor material that corresponds to the manifold pressure.

A set of sensing resistors is formed around the edge of this chamber, as indicated in *Figure 5-7*. The resistors are formed by diffusing a "doping impurity" into the silicon.[1] External connections to these resistors are made through wires connected to the metal bonding pads.

This entire assembly is placed in a sealed housing which is connected to the intake manifold by a small diameter tube. Manifold pressure applied to the diaphragm causes it to deflect. The resistance of the sensing resistors changes in proportion to the applied manifold pressure by a phenomenon which is known as piezoresistivity. Piezoresistivity occurs in certain semiconductors so that the actual resistivity (a property of the material) changes in proportion to the strain (fractional change in length).

The resistors in the strain gauge MAP sensor are connected in a Wheatstone bridge circuit. Output voltage of the circuit varies as the resistance varies in response to manifold pressure variations.

An electrical signal which is proportional to the manifold pressure is obtained by connecting the resistors in a circuit called a "Wheatstone bridge," as shown in the schematic diagram of *Figure 5-8a*. The voltage regulator holds a constant dc voltage across the bridge. The resistors diffused into the diaphragm are denoted R_1, R_2, R_3, and R_4 in *Figure 5-8a*. When there is no strain on the diaphragm, all four resistances are equal, the bridge is balanced, and the voltage between points A and B is zero. When manifold pressure changes, it causes these resistances to change in such a way that R_1 and R_3 increase by an amount which is proportional to pressure and, at the same time, R_2 and R_4 decrease by an identical amount. This unbalances the bridge and a net difference voltage is present between points A and B. The differential amplifier generates an output voltage proportional to the difference between the two input voltages, as shown in *Figure 5-8b*.

[1]*Understanding Solid State Electronics,* Engineering Staff of Texas Instruments, 1972, Chapter 7, Texas Instruments Incorporated.

Figure 5-7. Typical Silicon-Diaphragm Strain Gauge MAP Sensor

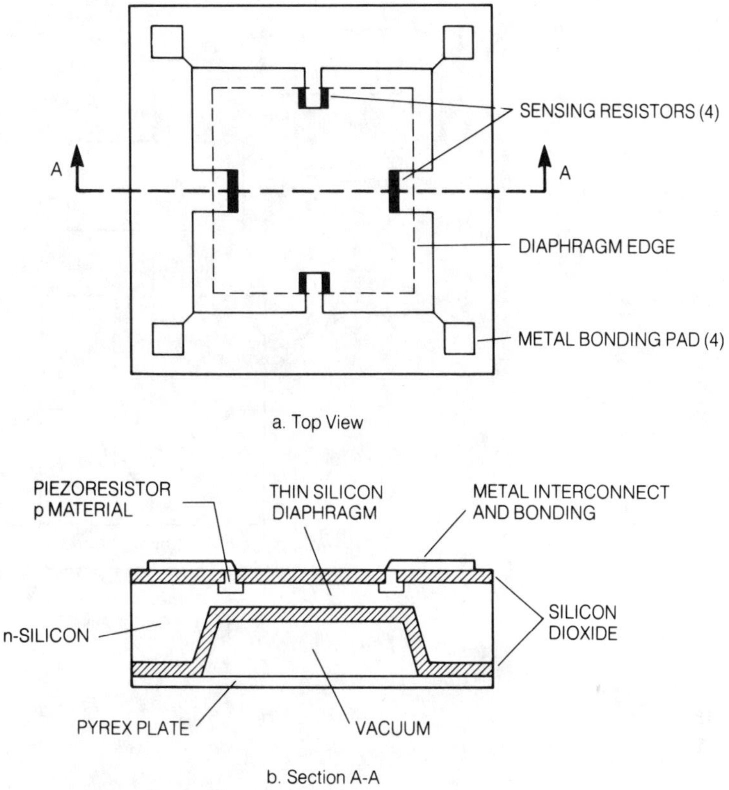

Capacitor-Capsule MAP Sensor

In the capacitor capsule MAP sensor, two flexible metal plates separated by an insulating spacer and air form a capacitor. Variations in manifold pressure vary the distance between plates. The resultant change in capacitance indicates absolute manifold pressure.

Another interesting MAP sensor configuration is the capacitor-capsule MAP sensor shown in *Figure 5-9.* A film electrode is deposited on the inside face of each of the two alumina plates and a connecting lead is extended for external connections. The plates are sealed together with an insulating hollow cylindrical spacer (i.e., washer shaped) between to form an aneroid chamber. The capacitor capsule is placed inside a sealed housing which is connected to manifold pressure by a small diameter tube. The film electrodes face one another on the inside of this aneroid and form a parallel plate capacitor. The alumina plates are flexible so that they deflect inward under the influence of manifold pressure. The deflection of these plates causes the distance between the electrodes to change in response to manifold pressure.

Figure 5-8.
Circuit Using a Strain Gauge MAP Sensor

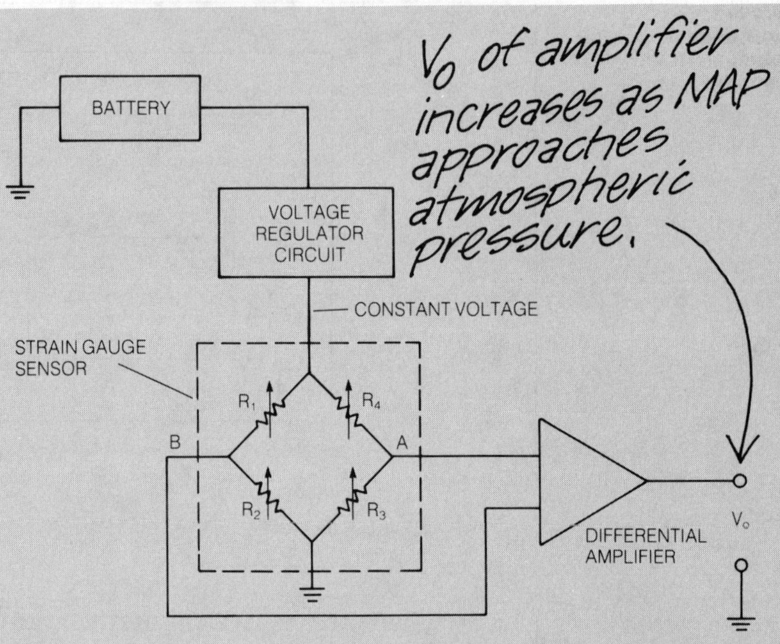

a. Circuit

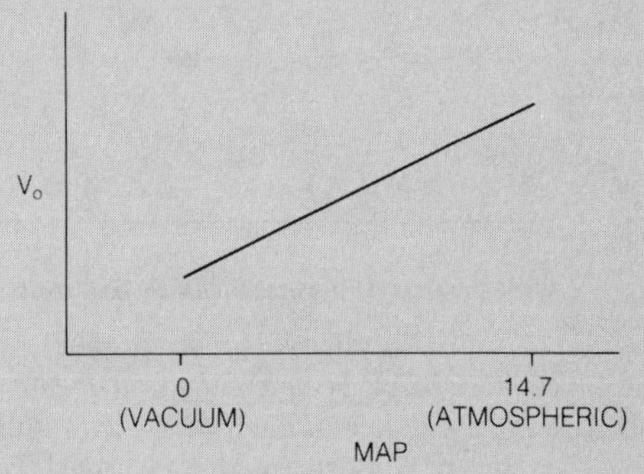

b. V_o vs MAP

Figure 5-9. Capacitor-Capsule MAP Sensor

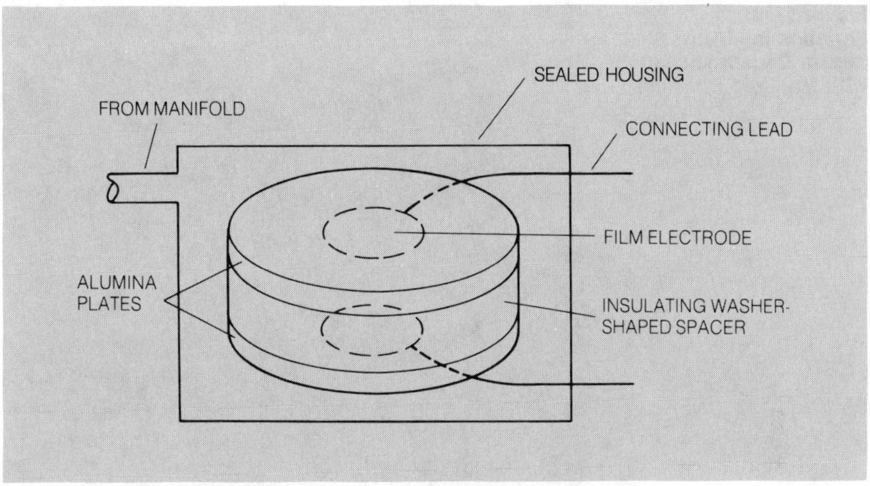

It is known from basic physics that the capacitance, C, of such a capacitor is given approximately by:

$$C = \frac{\epsilon_0 A}{d}$$

where

ϵ_0 = dielectric constant for air
A = area of film electrodes
d = distance between electrodes

The manifold pressure causes the distance, d, to decrease as pressure increases; therefore, the capacitance increases as pressure increases, as indicated in *Figure 5-10.*

The change in capacitance can be used to generate a voltage by placing the sensor in a resonant circuit. Changes in the sensor's capacitance causes corresponding changes in the output voltage.

Several methods can be used to generate a voltage in proportion to the change in capacitance so that manifold pressure can be measured. One relatively simple and inexpensive scheme involves connecting the sensor in a series resonant circuit, as shown in *Figure 5-11.* In this circuit, the inductor and capacitive sensor form a series resonant circuit whose resonant frequency, f_r, is given by:

$$f_r = \frac{1}{2\pi \sqrt{LC}}$$

where

L is inductance in henrys
C is capacitance in farads
π = 3.1416

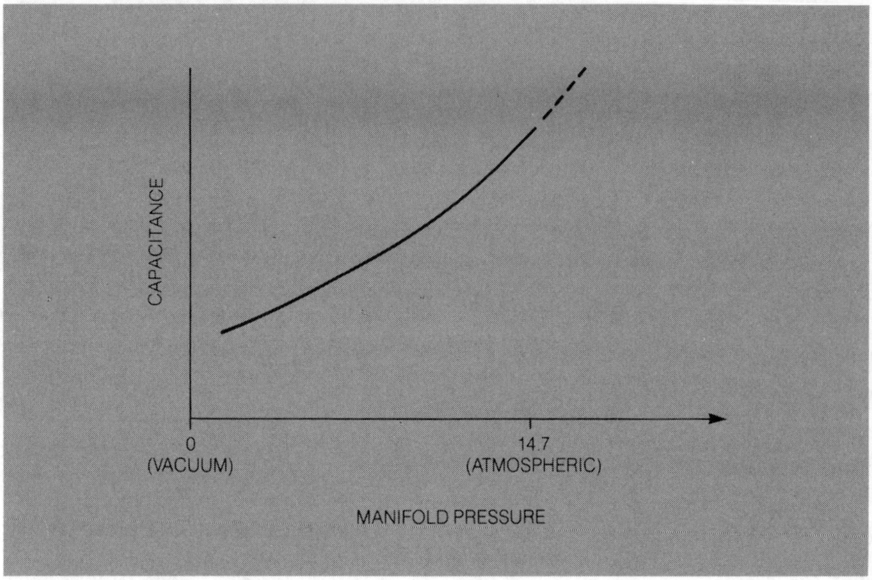

Figure 5-10. Variation in MAP Sensor Capacitance with Manifold Pressure

The oscillator frequency is tuned to the circuit's resonant frequency for atmospheric absolute manifold pressure. At resonance, the voltage across the inductor and the voltage across the capacitor are equal, but of opposite phase, and cancel each other so that the voltage across the resistor is the applied voltage. Therefore, the output, V_o, of the phase detector is zero volts because the voltage across the resistance, V_R, is in phase with the reference phase. As manifold pressure varies the capacitance in the circuit, the resonant frequency is changed. Since the oscillator frequency stays the same, the phase of the voltage across R relative to the reference phase varies sharply. The phase detector detects the change in phase and produces a voltage, V_o, which is proportional to the change in phase. Therefore, the output voltage of the phase detector is proportional to the manifold pressure.

ENGINE CRANKSHAFT ANGULAR POSITION SENSOR

Crankshaft angular position is an important variable in automotive control systems, particularly for controlling ignition timing and fuel injection timing.

Besides pressure, the position of shafts, valves, levers, etc., must be sensed for automotive control systems. Let's look at the concepts used by several sensors for important position variables. A significant variable which must be sensed in an automotive control system is crankshaft angular position. Imagine the engine as viewed from the rear, as shown in *Figure 5-12*. On the rear of the crankshaft is a large, heavy, circular steel disk called the flywheel which is connected to and rotates with the crankshaft. Let's mark a point on the flywheel, as shown in *Figure 5-12*, and draw a line through this point and the axis of rotation. Let's draw another line through the axis of rotation parallel to the horizontal center line of the engine. This line is simply for a reference line. The crankshaft angular position is the angle between the reference line and the mark on the flywheel.

Figure 5-11. Signal Processing for Capacitor-Capsule MAP Sensor

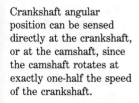

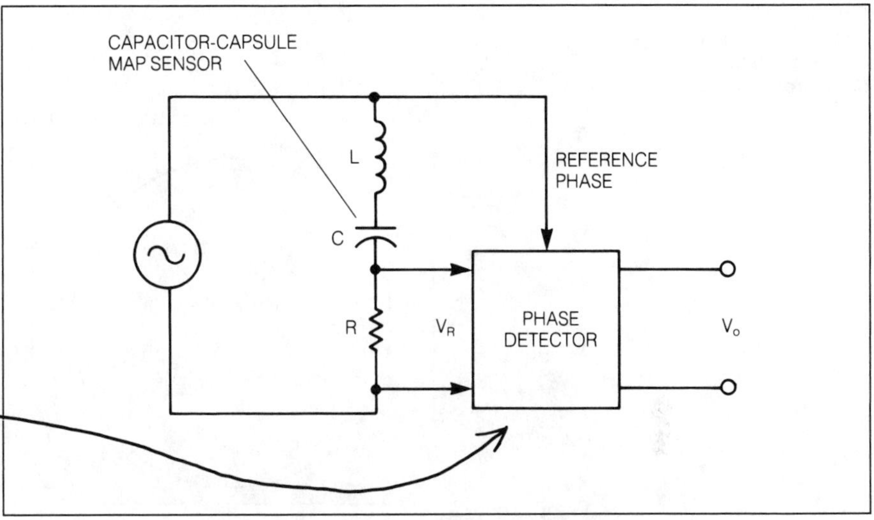

Phase detector compares phase of oscillator to reference phase.

Imagine that the flywheel is rotated so that the mark is directly on the reference line. This is an angular position of zero degrees and, for our purposes, assume that this angular position corresponds to the No. 1 cylinder at TDC (top dead center). As the crankshaft rotates, this angle increases from zero to 360° in one revolution. However, one full engine cycle from intake through exhaust requires two complete revolutions of the crankshaft. That is, one complete engine cycle corresponds to the crankshaft angular position going from zero to 720°. During each cycle, it is important to measure the crankshaft position with reference to TDC for each cylinder. This information is used by the electronic engine controller to set ignition timing and, in some cases, to adjust the fuel control system parameters.

Crankshaft angular position can be sensed directly at the crankshaft, or at the camshaft, since the camshaft rotates at exactly one-half the speed of the crankshaft.

In automobiles having electronic engine control systems, angular position can be sensed on the crankshaft directly or on the camshaft. Recall that the piston drives the crankshaft directly, while the valves and the distributor for the spark ignition are driven from the camshaft. The camshaft is driven from the crankshaft through a 1:2 reduction drive train, which can be gears, belt, or chain. Therefore, the camshaft rotational speed is one-half that of the crankshaft so the camshaft angular position goes from zero to 360° for one complete engine cycle. Either of these sensing locations have been used in one electronic control system or another. Although the crankshaft location is superior for accuracy because of torsional and gear backlash errors in the camshaft drive train, many production systems locate this sensor in the distributor where it measures camshaft position. At the present time, there appears to be a trend toward measuring crankshaft position directly. Examples of both sensor configurations for engine angular position measurement will be presented.

Figure 5-12. Engine Crankshaft Angular Position Measurement

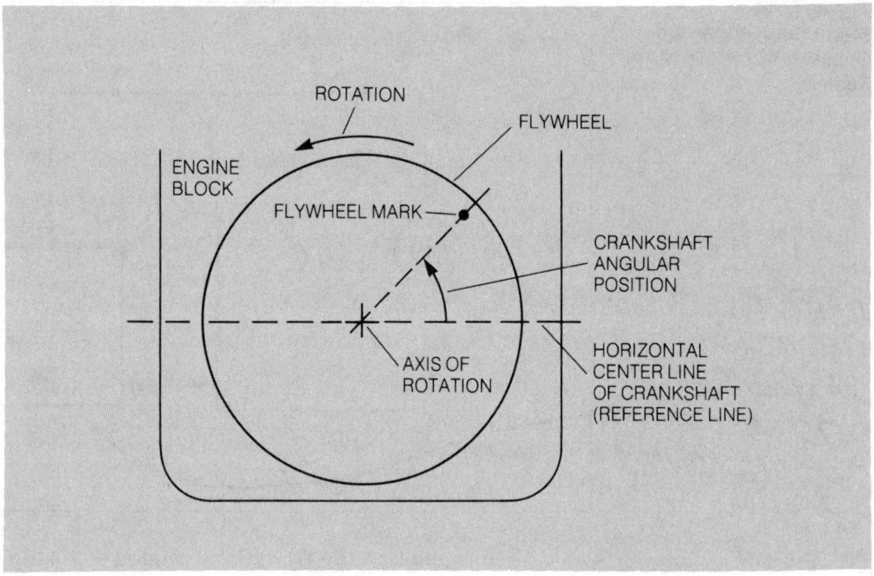

It is desirable to measure engine angular position with a noncontacting sensor to avoid mechanical wear and corresponding changes in accuracy of the measurement. The two most common methods for noncontact coupling to a rotating shaft employ magnetic fields or optics. Let's consider the concepts used for magnetically coupled sensors.

Magnetic Reluctance Position Sensor

In the magnetic reluctance position sensor, a coil wrapped around the magnet senses the changing intensity of the magnetic field as the tabs of a ferrous disk pass between the poles of the magnet.

One engine sensor configuration which measures crankshaft position directly is illustrated in *Figure 5-13*. This sensor consists of a permanent magnet with a coil of wire wound around it. A steel disk which is mounted on the crankshaft (usually in front of the engine) has tabs that pass between the pole pieces of this magnet. In *Figure 5-13*, the steel disk has four protruding tabs which are appropriate for an 8-cylinder engine. The passage of each tab corresponds to the TDC position of a cylinder on its power stroke.

This sensor is of the magnetic reluctance type and is based upon the concept of a "magnetic circuit." A magnetic circuit is a closed path through a magnetic material (i.e. iron, cobalt, nickel, or man-made magnetic material called ferrite). In the case of the sensor in *Figure 5-13*, the magnetic circuit is the closed path through the magnet material and across the gap between the pole pieces.

The magnetic field in a magnetic circuit is described by a pair of field quantities which can be compared to the voltage and current of an ordinary electric circuit. One of these quantities is called the magnetic field intensity. It exerts a force similar to the voltage of a battery.

Figure 5-13.
Magnetic Reluctance Crankshaft Position Sensor

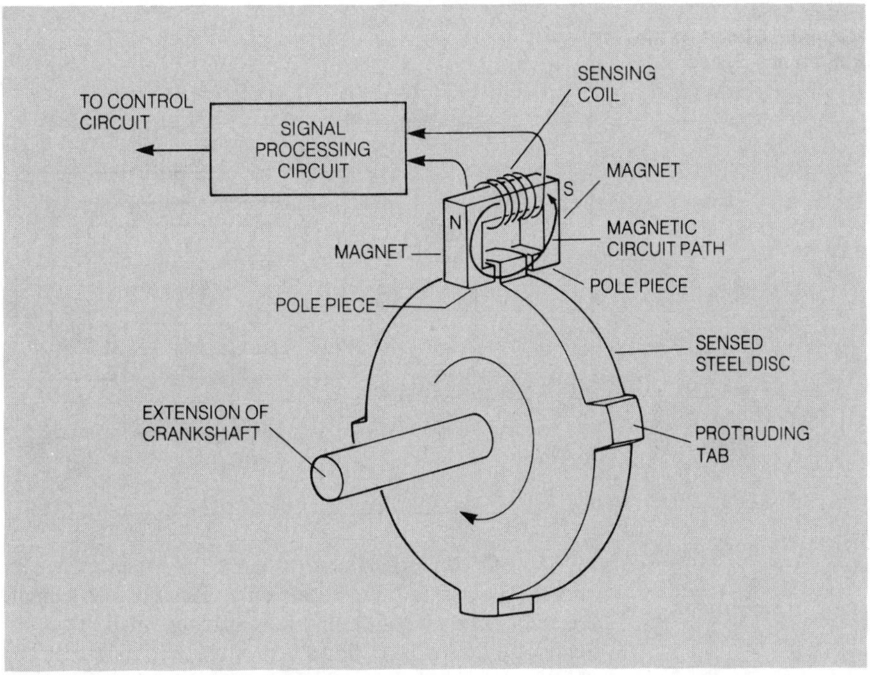

The response of the magnetic circuit to the magnetic field intensity is described by the second quantity which is called magnetic flux. A line of constant magnetic flux is a closed path through the magnetic material. The magnetic flux is similar to the current which flows when a resistor is connected across a battery forming a closed electric circuit.

The voltage generated by the magnetic reluctance position sensor is determined by the strength of the magnetic flux. When a tab on the steel disk passes through the gap, the flow of the magnetic flux changes significantly.

As we shall see, the voltage generated by the reluctance sensor is determined by the strength of this magnetic flux. The strength of the magnetic flux is, in turn, determined by the reluctance of the magnetic circuit. Reluctance is to a magnetic circuit what resistance is to an electric circuit.

The path for the magnetic flux of the reluctance sensor is illustrated in *Figure 5-14*. The reluctance of a magnetic circuit is inversely proportional to the magnetic permeability of the material along the path. The magnetic permeability of steel is roughly a few thousand times larger than air; therefore, the reluctance of steel is much lower than air. Note that when one of the tabs of the steel disk is located between the pole pieces of the magnet, a large part of the gap between the pole pieces is filled by the steel. Since the steel has a lower reluctance than air, the "flow" of magnetic flux increases to a relatively large value.

Figure 5-14. Magnetic Circuit of the Reluctance Sensor

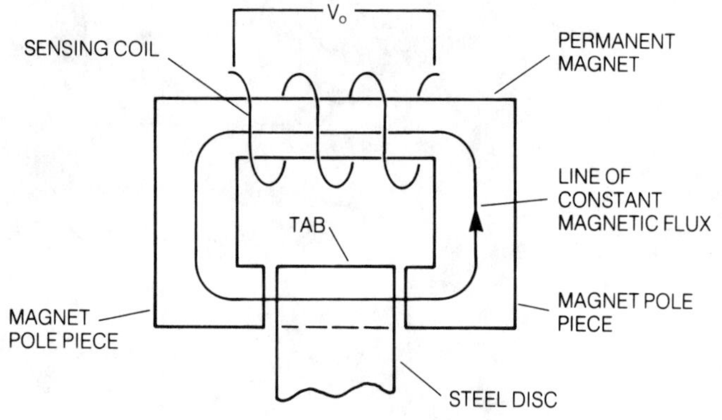

On the other hand, when a tab is not between the magnet pole pieces, the gap is filled by air only. This creates a high reluctance circuit for which the magnetic flux is relatively small. Thus, the magnitude of the magnetic flux which "flows" through the "magnetic circuit" depends upon the position of the tab which, in turn, depends on the crankshaft angular position.

The magnetic flux is least when none of the tabs is near the magnet pole pieces. Then, as a tab begins to pass through the gap, the magnetic flux increases, reaches a maximum when the tab is exactly between the pole pieces, then decreases as the tab passes out of the pole piece region. In most control systems, the position of maximum magnetic flux corresponds to TDC for one of the cylinders.

The voltage induced in the sensing coil varies with the rate of change of the magnetic flux. When the tab is centered between the poles of the magnet, the voltage is zero because the flux is not changing.

A voltage, V_o, *is induced in the sensing coil by the change in magnetic flux which is proportional to the rate of change of the magnetic flux.* Since the magnetic flux must be changing to induce a voltage in the sensing coil, its output voltage is zero whenever the engine is not running regardless of the position of the crankshaft. *This is a serious disadvantage for this type sensor because the engine timing cannot be set statically.*

As shown in *Figure 5-15*, the coil voltage, V_o, begins to increase from zero as a tab begins to pass between the pole pieces, reaches a maximum, then falls to zero when the tab is exactly between the pole pieces. (Note that although the value of magnetic flux is maximum at this point, *the rate of change of magnetic flux is zero*; therefore, the induced voltage in the sensing coil is zero.) Then it increases with the opposite polarity, reaches a maximum, and falls to zero as the tab passes out of the gap between the pole pieces. The coil voltage waveform shown in *Figure 5-15b* occurs each time a tab passes between the pole pieces. Thus, a voltage pulse having the waveform of *Figure 5-15b* occurs each time one of the cylinders reaches TDC on its power stroke. It should be noted that the number of tabs always will be half the number of cylinders for this crankshaft position sensor because it takes two crankshaft rotations for a complete engine cycle.

Figure 5-15. Output Voltage Waveform from the Magnetic Reluctance Crankshaft Position Sensor Coil

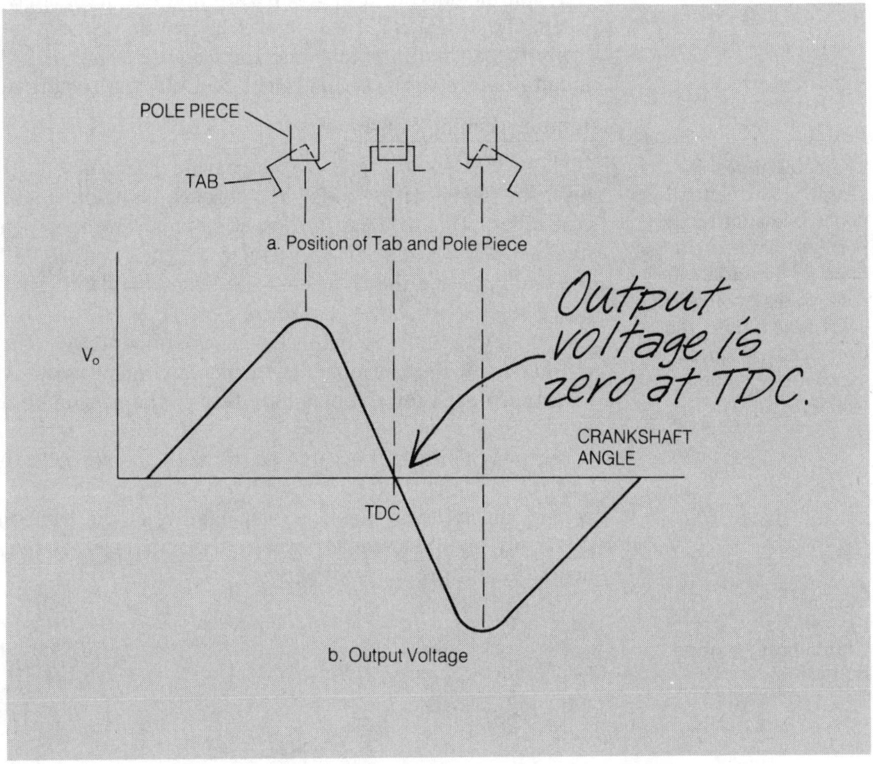

Engine Speed Sensor

Engine speed can be calculated in a number of ways. Digital circuits use counters and crankshaft sensors to calculate actual engine speed.

An engine speed sensor is needed to provide an input for the electronic controller for several functions. The position sensor discussed above can be used to measure engine speed. The reluctance sensor is used in this case as an example; however, any of the other position sensor techniques could be used as well. Refer to *Figure 5-13* and notice that the four tabs will pass through the sensing coil once for each crankshaft revolution. Therefore, if we count the pulses of voltage from the sensing coil in one minute and divide by four, we will know the engine speed in revolutions per minute (RPM).

This is easy to do with digital circuits. Precise timing circuits such as those used in digital watches can start a counter circuit which will count pulses until the timing circuit stops it. The counter can have the divide-by-4 function included in it or a separate divider circuit may be used. In many cases, the actual RPM sensor disk is mounted near the flywheel and has many more than four tabs and the counter does not actually count for a full minute before the speed is calculated, but the results are the same.

Ignition Timing Sensor

The notched position sensor uses an effect opposite that of the tab position sensor. As a notch in a rotating steel disk passes by a variable reluctance sensor, the decrease in magnetic flux generates a voltage pulse in the sensor coil.

For some types of electronic engine control, it is desirable to have a sensor for detecting a single reference point during one revolution of the crankshaft. One scheme for detecting this reference point uses the harmonic damper, a steel, disk-shaped device which is connected to the crankshaft at the end opposite the flywheel. The harmonic damper has a notch cut in its outer surface as shown in *Figure 5-16.*

A variable reluctance sensor is mounted on the engine block near the harmonic damper. The harmonic damper provides a relatively low reluctance path for the magnetic flux of the sensor because it is made of steel.

Whenever the notch aligns with the sensor axis, the reluctance of this magnetic path is increased because the permeability of air in the notch is very much lower than the permeability of the harmonic damper. This relatively high reluctance through the notch causes the magnetic flux to decrease and produces a change in V_o.

Figure 5-16. Crankshaft Position Sensor

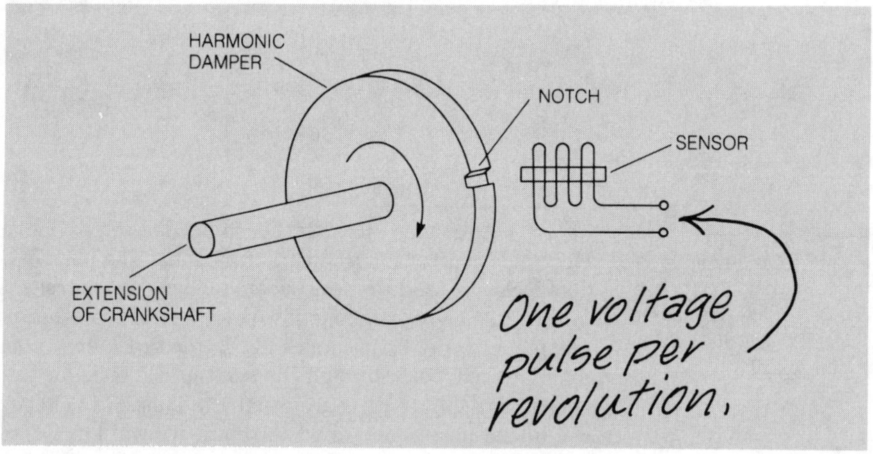

As the crankshaft rotates, the notch passes under the sensor once each engine revolution. The magnetic flux abruptly decreases, then increases as the notch passes the sensor. This generates a voltage pulse which can be used on electronic control systems to set ignition timing.

Hall-Effect Position Sensor

As mentioned previously, one of the main disadvantages of the magnetic reluctance sensor is its lack of output when the engine isn't running. A crankshaft position sensor which avoids this problem is the Hall-effect position sensor. This sensor is normally located in the distributor where it measures camshaft position rather than crankshaft position. This sensor is relatively inexpensive and requires only small modifications to a conventional distributor with ignition points to use it. In fact, with appropriate circuitry, this sensor also can be used to replace distributor ignition points.

The Hall-effect position sensor also uses magnets and a steel disk with tabs to sense crankshaft position. It usually is located in the distributor and actually senses camshaft position.

A Hall-effect position sensor is shown in *Figure 5-17*. This sensor is similar to the reluctance sensor in that it employs a steel disk having protruding tabs and a magnet for coupling the disk to the sensing element. Another similarity is that the steel disk varies the reluctance of the magnetic path as the tabs pass between the magnet pole pieces.

Figure 5-17. Hall-Effect Position Sensor

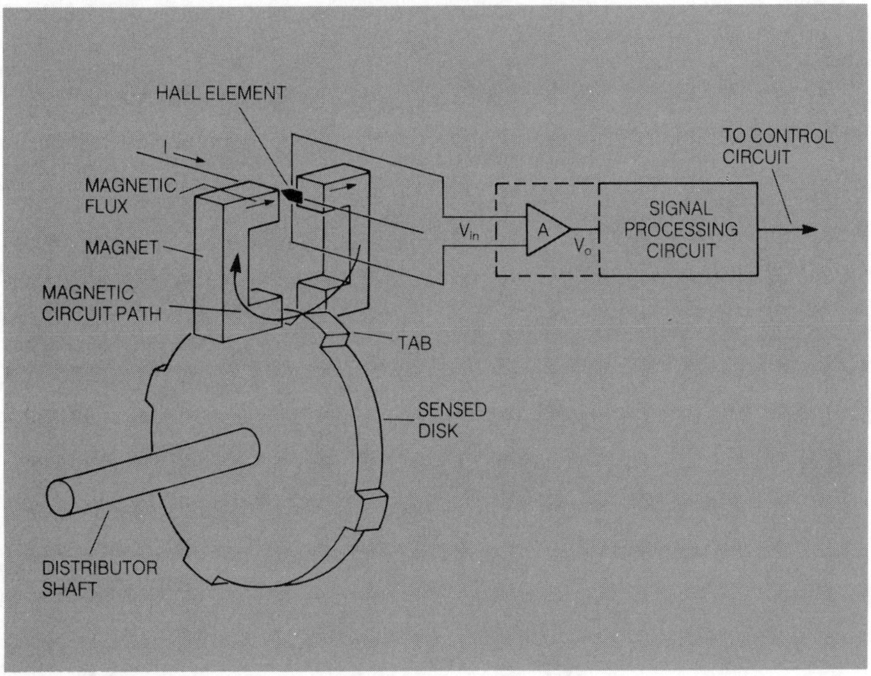

The Hall Effect

The Hall element is a small, thin, flat slab of semiconductor material. When a current, I, is passed through this slab by means of an external circuit as shown in *Figure 5-18a*, a voltage is developed across the

The Hall element is a thin slab of semiconductor material which is placed between the magnets so it can sense the magnetic flux variations as the tab passes. A constant current is passed through the semiconductor in one direction and a voltage is generated that varies with the strength of the magnetic flux.

slab perpendicular to the direction of current flow and perpendicular to the direction of magnetic flux. This voltage is proportional to both the current and magnetic flux density which flows through the slab. This effect—the generation of a voltage that is dependent on a magnetic field—is called the Hall effect.

In *Figure 5-18b*, the current, I, is represented by electrons, e, which have negative charge, flowing from left to right. The magnetic field, B, is perpendicular to the page and into the page. This is indicated by the arrows into the page of *Figure 5-18b*. Whenever an electron moves through a magnetic field, a force (called the Lorentz force) is exerted on the electron which is proportional to the electron velocity and the strength of the magnetic flux. The direction of this force is perpendicular to the direction of the magnetic flux lines and perpendicular to the direction in which the electron is moving. In *Figure 5-18b*, the Lorentz force direction is such that the electrons are deflected toward the lower sense electrode. Thus, this electrode is more negative than the upper electrode and a voltage exists between the electrodes, having the polarity shown in *Figure 5-18b*.

Figure 5-18.
The Hall Effect

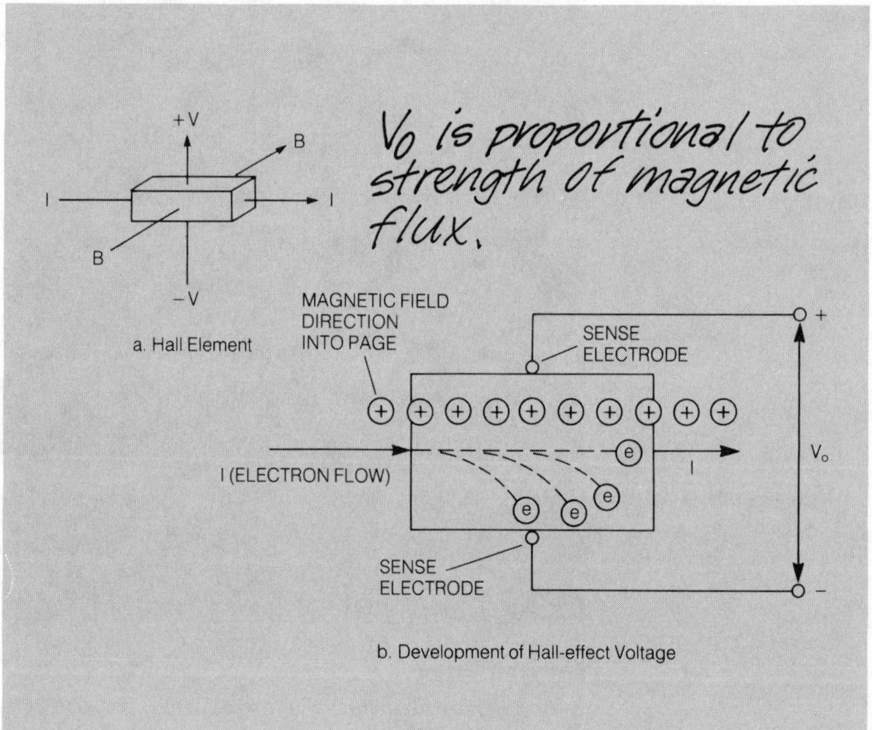

As the strength of the magnetic flux density increases, more of the electrons are deflected downward. If the current, I, is held constant, then the voltage, V_o, is proportional to the strength of the magnetic flux density. This voltage tends to be relatively weak so it is amplified, as shown in *Figure 5-17.*

Output Waveform

It was shown in the discussion of the reluctance crankshaft position sensor that the magnetic flux density for this configuration depends upon the position of the tab. Recall that the magnetic flux is largest when one of the tabs is positioned symmetrically between the magnet pole pieces and that this position normally corresponds closely to TDC of one of the cylinders.

Because the Hall-effect sensor produces the same output voltage waveform regardless of engine speed, the engine timing can be set when the engine is not running.

The voltage, V_o, waveform which is produced by the Hall element in the position sensor of *Figure 5-17* is illustrated in *Figure 5-19.* Since V_o is proportional to the magnetic flux density, it reaches maximum when any of the tabs is symmetrically located between the magnet pole pieces (i.e. corresponding to TDC of a cylinder). If the disk is driven by the camshaft, then the disk must have as many tabs as the engine has cylinders. Therefore, the disk shown would be for a 4-cylinder engine. It is important to realize that voltage output vs crankshaft angle is independent of engine speed. Thus, this sensor can be used for setting the engine timing when the engine is not running.

Figure 5-19. Waveform of Hall-Element Output Voltage for Position Sensor of Figure 5-17

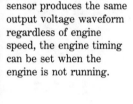

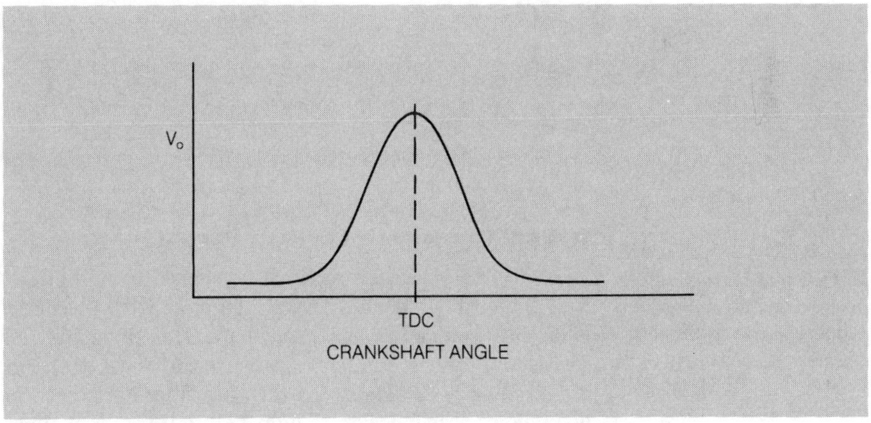

Shielded Field Sensor

Figure 5-20 shows another concept that uses the Hall-effect element in a way different from that just discussed. In this method, the Hall element is normally exposed to a magnetic field and produces an output voltage. When one of the tabs passes between the magnet and the sensor element, the low reluctance of the tab and disk provides a path for the magnetic flux which bypasses the Hall-effect sensor element. Since the sensor element is shielded from the magnetic field, the Hall-effect voltage and sensor output drops to near zero. Note in *Figure 5-20b* that the waveform is just opposite of the one in *Figure 5-19*.

Figure 5-20. Hall-Effect Position Sensor that Shields the Magnetic Circuit

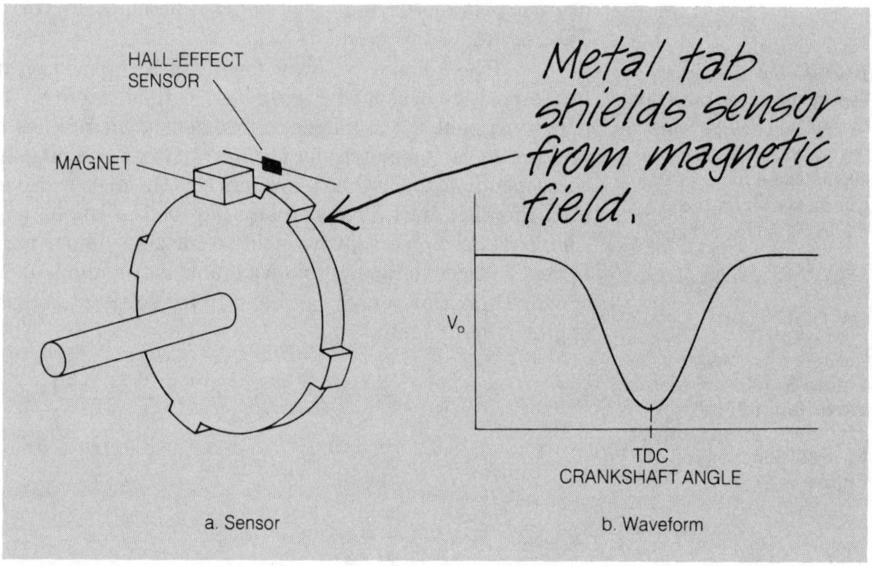

Optical Crankshaft Position Sensor

In the optical crankshaft position sensor, a disk coupled to the crankshaft has holes to pass light between the LED and the phototransistor. An output pulse is generated as each hole passes.

Shaft position can also be sensed using optical techniques. *Figure 5-21* illustrates such a system. Again, as with the magnetic system, a disk is directly coupled to the crankshaft. This time, the disk has holes in it that correspond to the number of tabs on the disks of the magnetic systems. Mounted on each side of the disk are fiber-optic light pipes. The hole in the disk allows transmission of light through the light pipes from the light-emitting diode source to the phototransistor used as a light sensor. Light would not be transmitted from source to sensor when there is no hole because the solid disk blocks the light. As shown in *Figure 5-21*, the pulse of light is detected by the phototransistor and coupled to an amplifier to obtain a satisfactory signal level. The output pulse level can very easily be standard transistor logic levels of +2.4V for the high level and +0.8V for the low level. Used as pulses, the signals provide time referenced pulses that can be signal processed easily with digital integrated circuits.

Figure 5-21.
Optical Position Sensor

Rotation of disk causes alternate blocking and transmission of light.

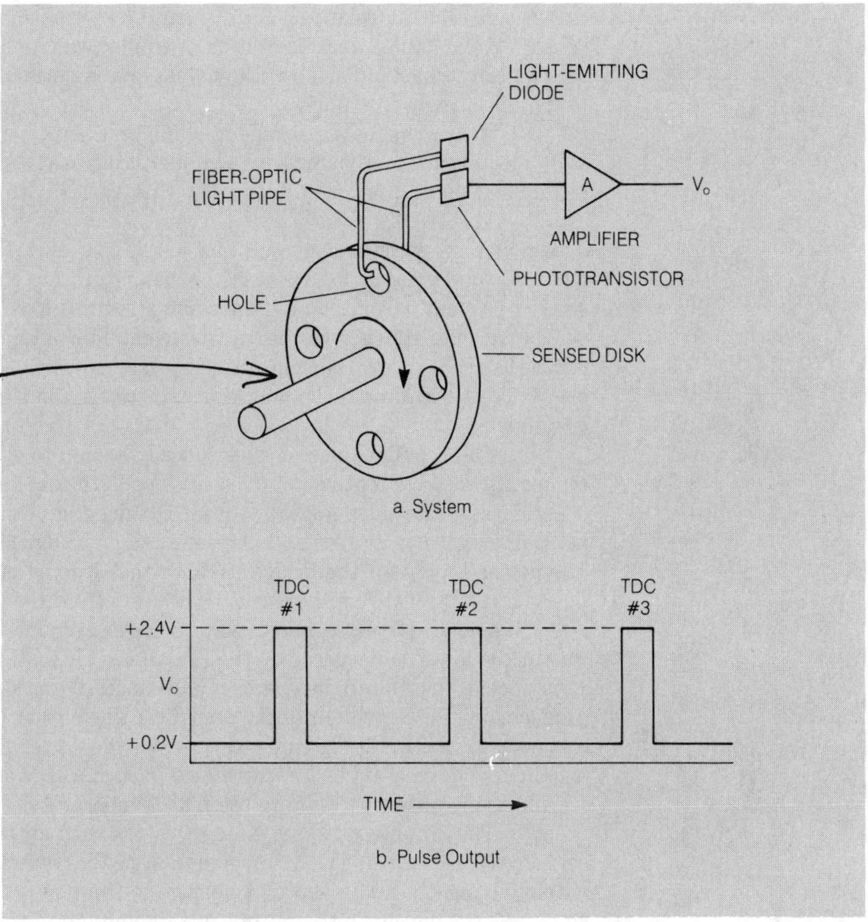

One of the problems with optical sensors is that they must be protected from dirt and oil; otherwise, they will not work properly. They have the advantage that they can sense position without the engine running and the pulse amplitude is constant with variation in speed.

AIR FLOW RATE SENSOR

Chapter 6 shows that the correct operation of an electronically controlled engine operating with constrained exhaust emission requires a measurement of the mass flow rate of air (R_{am}) into the engine. Since the advent of emission control legislation, considerable research effort has been expended to develop a relatively low-cost sensor for measuring R_{am}. For a time, there was no cost effective sensor capable of directly measuring R_{am}; instead, indirect (volumetric) measurements using multiple sensors and computer calculations (see Chapter 6) were used.

By 1984, a relatively simple and inexpensive mass airflow rate sensor (MAS) for R_{am} had been developed and was in volume production. This sensor, which is used on many GM cars, is normally mounted as part of the air cleaner assembly.

It is a ruggedly packaged, single unit sensor which includes solid-state electronic signal processing. In operation, the MAS generates a continuous signal that has a frequency that varies with R_{am}.

The MAS is a variation of a classical airflow sensor which was known as a hot wire anemometer and which was used, for example, to measure wind velocity for weather forecasting. In the MAS, the hot wire or sensing element is replaced by a hot film structure mounted on a substrate. On the air inlet side is mounted a honeycomb flow straightener that "smooths" the airflow (causing nominally laminar airflow over the film element). At the lower portion of the structure is the signal processing circuitry.

The hot film element is electrically heated to a constant temperature above that of the inlet air. The latter air temperature is sensed using a solid-state temperature sensor (explained later in this chapter). The hot film element is incoporated in a wheatstone bridge circuit (*Figure 5-22a*). The power supply for the bridge circuit comes from an amplifier. As air flows across the hot film, heat is carried away from the film by the moving air. The amount of heat carried away varies in proportion to the mass flow rate of the air. The heat lost by the film to the air tends to cause the resistance of the film to vary, which unbalances the bridge circuit, thereby producing an input voltage to the amplifier. The output of the amplifier is connected to the bridge circuit and provides the power for this circuit. The amplified voltage changes the resistance in such a way as to maintain a fixed hot film temperature relative to the inlet temperature.

The amplifier output voltage varies with air mass flow rate and serves as a measure of R_{am}. In the actual MAS system, the amplifier output voltage is connected to a voltage-to-frequency converter. The actual sensor output is the output of this voltage-to-frequency converter. The relationship between this frequency and mass flow rate is seen in *Figure 5-22b.*

This conversion of voltage to frequency is advantageous in digital engine control applications because the frequency is readily converted to digital format without requiring an A/D converter. One method of obtaining a digital output from the sensor output is shown in *Figure 5-22a.* The sensor output is connected to an electronic switch, the output of which is connected to a binary counter. The electronic switch is closed for an interval τ during which time the frequency is counted. At the end of this time interval, the binary counter contains a digital value P.

$$P = f\tau$$

where f is the sensor frequency that is a known function of mass flow rate. In actual operation, repeated measurements of frequency f are made under control of the digital engine control module (see Chapter 7).

Figure 5-22.
Mass Air Flow Center

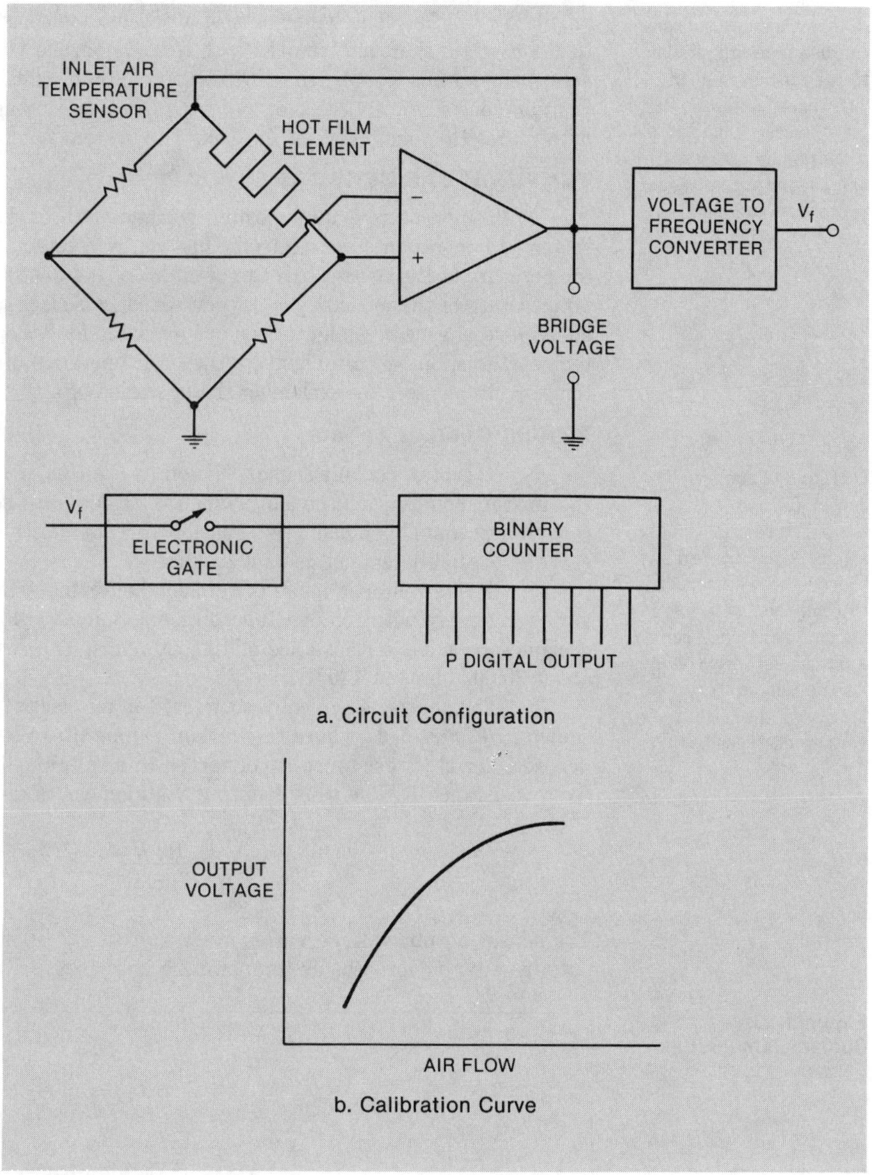

a. Circuit Configuration

b. Calibration Curve

Throttle Angle Sensor

Still another variable which must be measured for an electronic fuel control application is throttle angle or the position of the throttle plate. It is common practice to use a potentiometer to measure throttle angle. A potentiometer is a variable resistor, such as is used as a volume control for

A throttle angle sensor can use a design similar to the air-flow sensor. The throttle plate is mechanically linked to a potentiometer wiper arm and the output voltage represents the angle of the throttle plate.

an audio amplifier. The wiper arm of a potentiometer is connected directly to the throttle shaft and rotates with it. A reference voltage is applied across the potentiometer; thus, the wiper voltage, which is the throttle position sensor output voltage, indicates the throttle angle. Throttle angle determines the amount of air entering the system for mixing with the fuel.

TEMPERATURE SENSORS

Temperature is an important parameter throughout the automotive system. In operation of an electronic fuel control system it is vital to know the temperature of the coolant, the temperature of the inlet air, and the temperature of the exhaust gas oxygen sensor, a sensor to be discussed a bit later. Several sensor configurations are available for measuring these temperatures, but we can illustrate the basic operation of most of the temperature sensors by explaining the operation of a typical coolant sensor.

Typical Coolant Sensor

One kind of coolant sensor uses a temperature-sensitive semiconductor called a thermistor. The sensor is typically connected as a varying resistance across a fixed reference voltage. As the temperature increases, the output voltage decreases.

A typical coolant sensor, shown in *Figure 5-23*, consists of a thermistor mounted in a housing which is designed to be inserted in the coolant stream. This housing is typically threaded with pipe threads which seal the assembly against coolant leakage.

A thermistor is made of semiconductor material whose resistance varies inversely with temperature. For example at −40°C, a typical coolant sensor has a resistance of 100,000 ohms. The resistance decreases to about 70,000 ohms at 130°C.

The sensor is typically connected in an electrical circuit like that shown in *Figure 5-24* where the coolant temperature sensor resistance is denoted R_T. This resistance is connected to a reference voltage through a fixed resistance R. The sensor output voltage, V_T, is given by:

$$V_T = \frac{R_T V}{R + R_T}$$

The sensor output voltage varies inversely with temperature; that is, the output voltage decreases as temperature increases.

Figure 5-23. Coolant Temperature Sensor

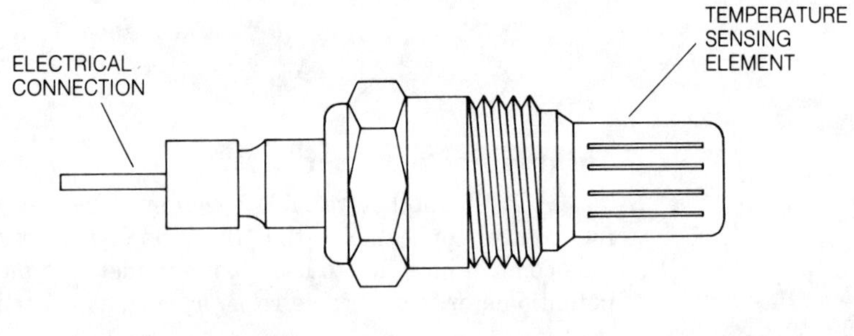

Figure 5-24.
Typical Coolant Temperature Sensor Circuit

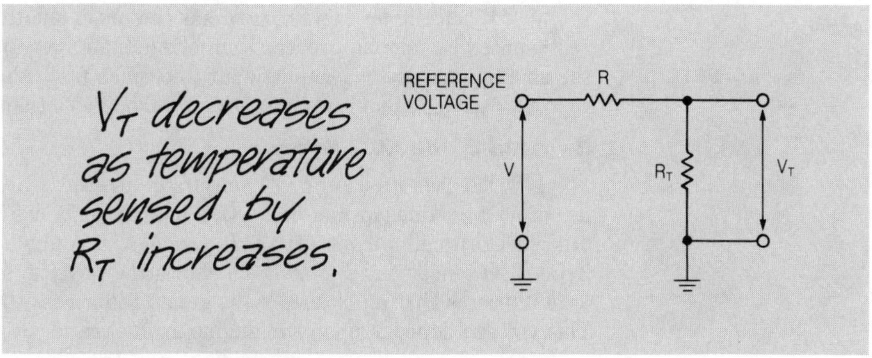

EXHAUST GAS EMISSION

It was noted at the beginning of this chapter that air and fuel are the basic inputs to an internal combustion automotive engine and that the outputs are the drive power and the exhaust emissions. It is very important to control the quantity of these exhaust emissions. Most electronic control systems use a reference point called stoichiometry in the scheme to control exhaust emissions.

Stoichiometry

Stoichiometry is the ideal air/fuel ratio at which the amount of air and the amount of fuel are a perfect match for perfect combustion. In theory, this ratio is 14.7:1.

The *air/fuel ratio* at stoichiometry is that mixture of air and fuel *in which, when ignited, all of the carbon and hydrogen would completely burn* yielding only carbon dioxide and water in the exhaust if combustion were perfect. The theoretical ratio of air mass to fuel mass for which this would occur is 14.7:1; that is, 14.7 pounds of dry air for 1 pound of gasoline.

An air/fuel ratio which exceeds stoichiometry means that more air is present than is needed for perfect combustion. In this situation, oxygen would be left in the exhaust because not all of the intake oxygen would be combined with carbon or hydrogen. A mixture with this air/fuel ratio is called a lean mixture.

Conversely, when the air/fuel ratio is less than stoichiometry, the amount of oxygen is insufficient to react with all of the carbon and hydrogen in the fuel. In this case, the exhaust gas contains unburned hydrocarbons (unburned fuel). A mixture with this air/fuel ratio is called a rich mixture.

EXHAUST GAS OXYGEN SENSOR

The amount of oxygen in the exhaust gas is used as an indirect measurement of the air/fuel ratio. As a result, one of the most significant automotive sensors in use today is the exhaust gas oxygen (EGO) sensor. This sensor is often called a lambda sensor from the Greek letter lambda (λ), which is commonly used to denote the equivalence ratio:

$$\lambda = \frac{\text{air/fuel}}{\text{air/fuel at stoichiometry}}$$

When the air-fuel mixture has too much air, the condition is represented by lambda greater than one (denoted $\lambda > 1$). Conversely, when the air-fuel mixture has too little air (too much fuel), the condition is represented by an equivalence ratio of lambda less than one ($\lambda < 1$).

Zirconia Oxide EGO Sensor

The two types of EGO sensors in use today are based upon the use of active oxides of materials. One uses zirconia oxide (ZrO_2) and the other uses titanium oxide (TiO_2). *Figure 5-25* is a photograph of a typical ZrO_2 EGO sensor and *Figure 5-26* shows the physical structure. *Figure 5-26* indicates that a voltage, V_o, is generated across the ZrO_2 material. This voltage depends upon the engine air/fuel ratio.

Figure 5-25. Zirconia Oxide (ZrO_2) EGO Sensor

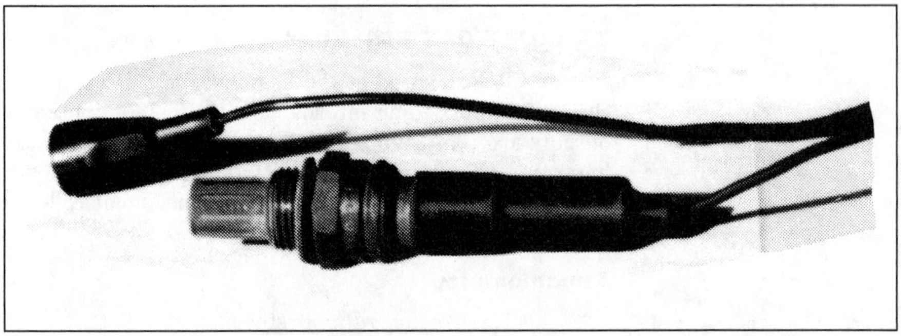

The zirconia oxide EGO sensor uses zirconia oxide sandwiched between two platinum electrodes. One electrode is exposed to exhaust gas and the other is exposed to normal air for reference.

In essence, the EGO sensor consists of a thimble-shaped section of ZrO_2 with thin platinum electrodes on the inside and outside of the ZrO_2. The inside electrode is exposed to air and the outside electrode is exposed to exhaust gas through a porous protective overcoat.

A simplified explanation of EGO sensor operation is based upon the distribution of oxygen ions. An ion is an electrically charged atom. Oxygen ions have two excess electrons and each electron has a negative charge; thus, oxygen ions are negatively charged. The ZrO_2 has a tendency to attract the oxygen ions and they accumulate on the ZrO_2 surface just inside the platinum electrodes.

Because the exhaust contains fewer oxygen ions than air, the "air" electrode becomes negative with respect to the "exhaust" electrode. The voltage developed across the electrodes depends on the number of oxygen ions present in the air/fuel mixture.

The platinum plate on the air reference side of the ZrO_2 is exposed to a much higher concentration of oxygen ions than the exhaust gas side. The air reference side becomes electrically more negative than the exhaust gas side; therefore, an electric field exists across the ZrO_2 material and a voltage, V_o, results. The polarity of this voltage is positive on the exhaust gas side and negative on the air reference side of the ZrO_2. The magnitude of this voltage depends upon the concentration of oxygen in the exhaust gas and upon the sensor temperature.

Figure 5-26.
EGO Mounting and Structure

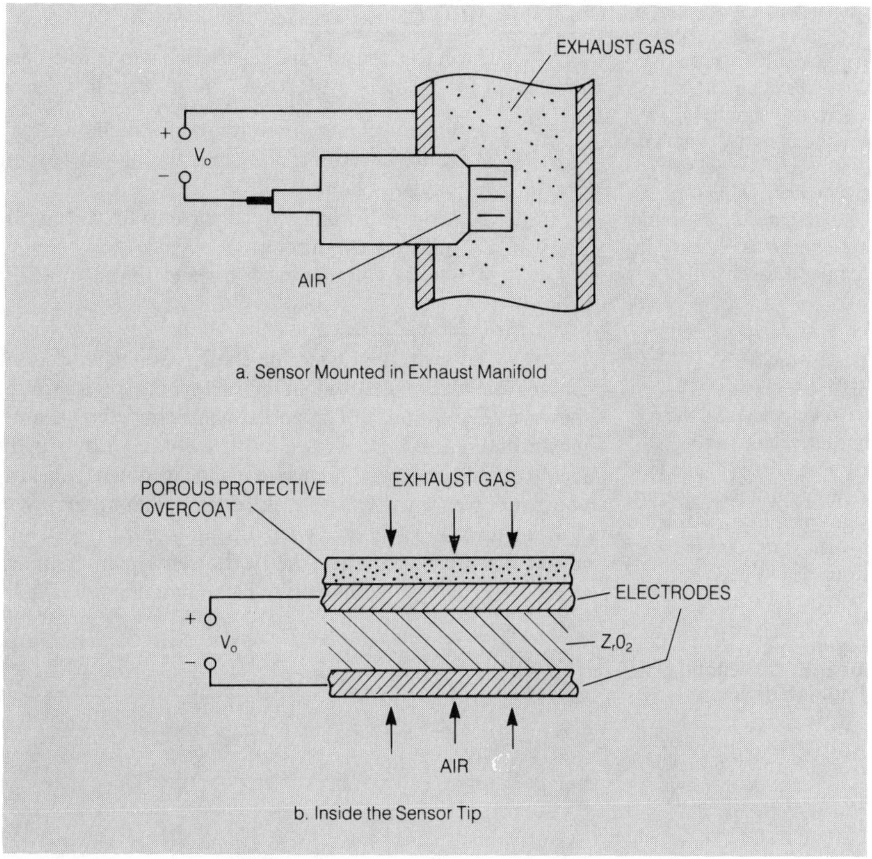

The quantity of oxygen in the exhaust gas is represented by the oxygen partial pressure. Basically, this partial pressure is that proportion of the total exhaust gas pressure (nearly at atmospheric pressure) which is due to the quantity of oxygen. The exhaust gas oxygen partial pressure for a rich mixture varies over the range of 10^{-16} to 10^{-32} of atmospheric pressure. The oxygen partial pressure for a lean mixture is roughly 10^{-2} atmosphere.

If one wishes a more detailed discussion of this very complex reaction, consult the references given below.[1,2]

[1]Young, C. T., Bode, J. D., *Characteristics of $ZrO_{2\text{-}type}$ Oxygen Sensors for Automotive Applications*, SAE Publ. 790143, 1979.

[2]Young, C. T., *Experimental Analysis of ZrO_2 Oxygen Sensor Transient Switching Behavior*, SAE paper 810380, 1980.

An *ideal* EGO sensor would have an abrupt, rapid, and significant change in output voltage as the mixture passes through stoichiometry. The output voltage would not change as exhaust gas temperature change.

Hysteresis is the difference in the switching point of the output voltage with respect to stoichiometry as a mixture passes from lean to rich, as contrasted to a mixture that passes from rich to lean.

Desirable EGO Characteristics

The EGO sensor characteristics which are desirable for the type of limit cycle fuel control system we will discuss in Chapter 6 are:

1. abrupt change in voltage at stoichiometry
2. rapid switching of output voltage in response to exhaust gas oxygen changes
3. large difference in sensor output voltage between rich and lean mixture conditions
4. stable voltages with respect to exhaust temperature

Switching Characteristics

The switching time for the EGO sensor also must be considered in control applications. An ideal characteristic for a limit-cycle controller is shown in *Figure 5-27*. The actual characteristics of a new EGO sensor are shown in *Figure 5-28*. This data was obtained by slowly varying air/fuel across stoichiometry. The arrow pointing down indicates the change in V_o as air/fuel was varied from rich to lean. The up-arrow indicates the change in V_o as air/fuel ratio was varied from lean to rich. Note that the sensor output doesn't change at exactly the same point for increasing air/fuel ratio as for decreasing air/fuel ratio. This phenomenon is called hysteresis.

Figure 5-27. Ideal EGO Switching Characteristics

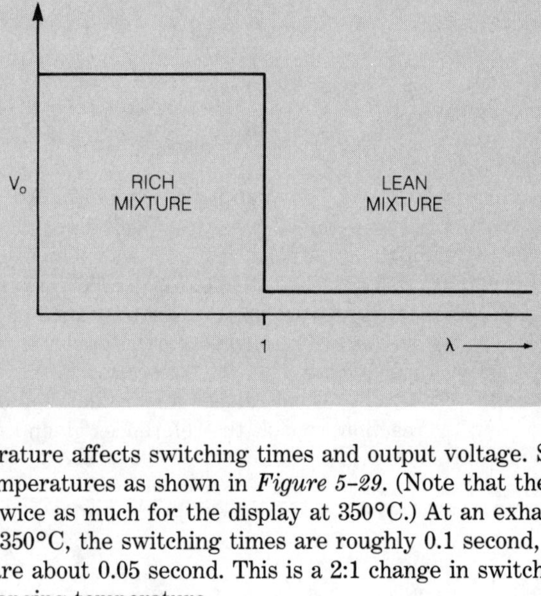

Temperature affects switching times and output voltage. Switching times at two temperatures as shown in *Figure 5-29*. (Note that the time per division is twice as much for the display at 350°C.) At an exhaust temperature of 350°C, the switching times are roughly 0.1 second, whereas at 800°C they are about 0.05 second. This is a 2:1 change in switching times due to changing temperature.

Figure 5-28. Typical EGO Sensor Characteristics

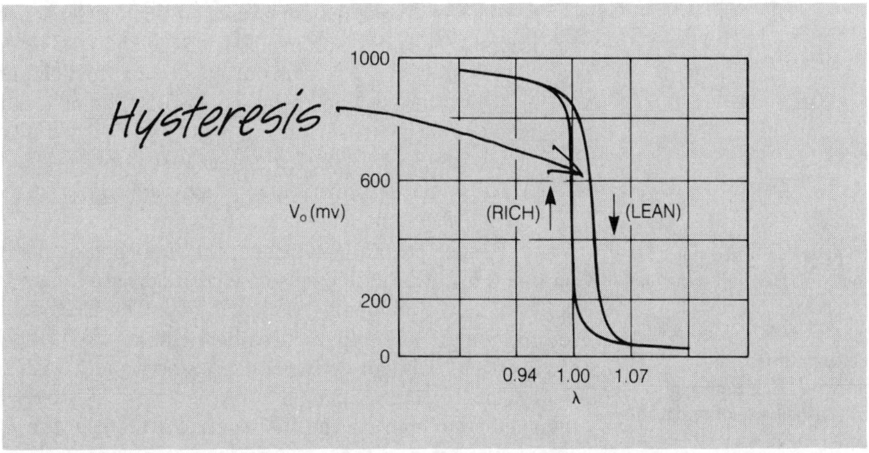

Figure 5-29. Typical Voltage Switching Characteristics of EGO

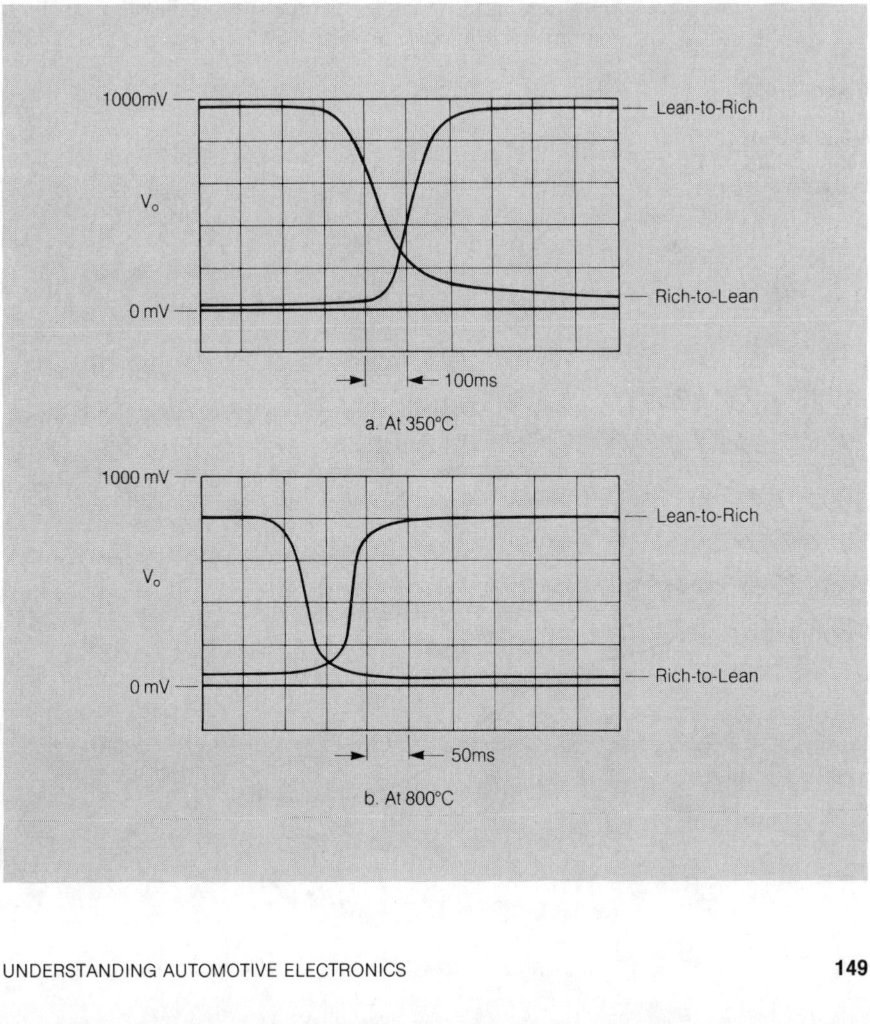

a. At 350°C

b. At 800°C

The temperature dependence of the EGO sensor output voltage is very important. The graph in *Figure 5-30* shows the temperature dependence of an EGO sensor output voltage for lean and rich mixtures and for two different load resistances—5 megohms (million ohms) and 0.83 megohm. The EGO sensor output voltage for a rich mixture is in the range from about 0.80 to 1.0 volt for an exhaust temperature range of 350 to 800°C. For a lean mixture, this voltage is roughly in the range of 0.05 to 0.07 volt for the same temperature range.

EGO sensors are not used for control when exhaust gas temperature falls below 300°C because the voltage difference between rich and lean conditions are minimal in this range.

Under certain conditions, the fuel control system explained in Chapter 6 using an EGO sensor will be operated open loop and for other conditions it will be operated closed loop. The EGO sensor should not be used for control at temperatures below about 300°C, because the difference between rich and lean voltages decreases rapidly with temperature in this region. This important property of the sensor is partly responsible for the requirement to operate the fuel control system in the open loop mode at low exhaust temperature. Closed loop operation with the EGO output voltage used as the error input cannot begin until the EGO sensor temperature exceeds about 300°C.

Figure 5-30. Typical influence of Mixture and Temperature on EGO Output Voltage

Should not be used for control in this temperature range.

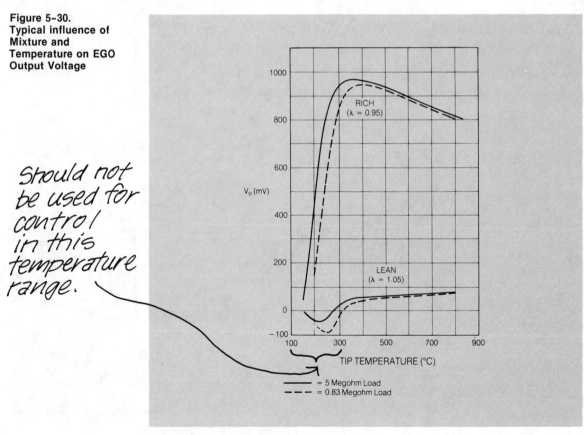

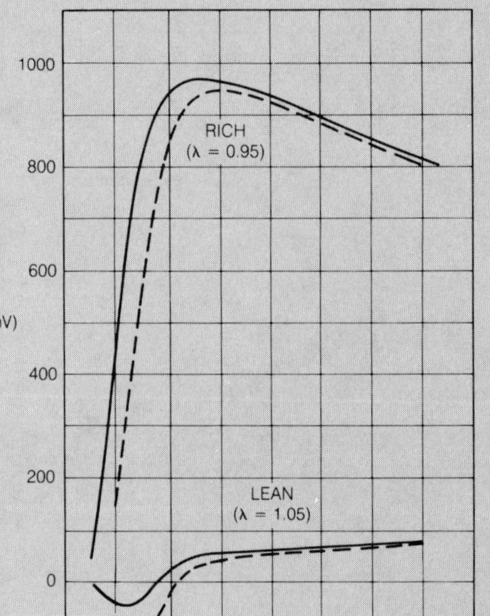

KNOCK SENSORS

For certain electronic engine control systems, it is desirable to have a sensor which can detect an engine occurrence called "knock." Although a detailed discussion of knock is beyond the scope of this book, it can be described generally as a rapid rise in cylinder pressure during combustion. It does not occur normally, but under special conditions. It occurs most commonly with high manifold pressure and excessive spark advance. It is important to detect knock and avoid excessive knock; otherwise, there will be damage to the engine.

Some engine knock sensors use rods within a magnetic field to detect the presence of knock. Others use vibration-sensitive crystals or semiconductors.

One way of controlling the knocking is to sense when knocking begins and then retard the ignition until the knocking stops. A key to the control loop for this is a knock sensor. A knock sensor using magnetostrictive techniques is shown in *Figure 5-31.* When sensing knock, the magnetostrictive rods, which are in a magnetic field, change the flux field in the coil. This change in flux produces a voltage change in the coil. Other sensors use piezoelectric crystals, or the piezoresistance of a doped silicon semiconductor. Whichever type is used, it forms a closed loop system that retards the ignition to reduce the knock detected at the cylinders. Systems using knock sensors are explained in Chapter 7. The problem of detecting knock is complicated by the presence of other vibrations and noises in the engine.

Figure 5-31. Knock Sensor

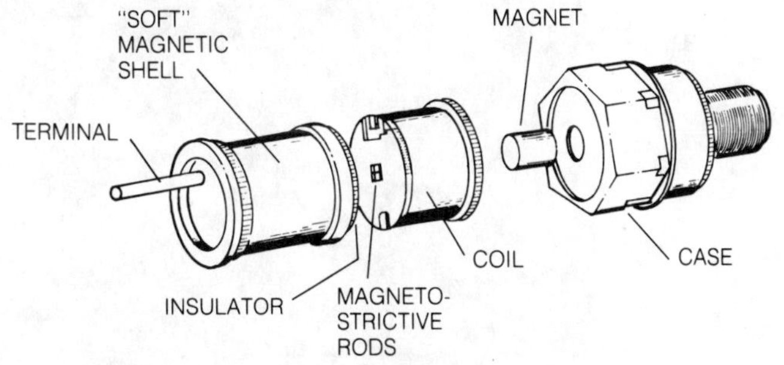

AUTOMOTIVE ENGINE CONTROL ACTUATORS

In addition to the set of sensors, the electronic engine control is critically dependent upon a set of actuators to control air/fuel ratio, ignition, and EGR. Each of these devices will be discussed separately.

FUEL METERING ACTUATOR

In engine control systems, it is necessary to maintain the air/fuel ratio at or very near 14.7:1. This is accomplished by controlling fuel flow with a fuel metering actuator. The two major classes of fuel metering actuators are the electronic carburetor and the throttle body fuel injector (TBFI). The electronic carburetor has been in production for some time, but it will probably be replaced in the future by the TBFI.

Electronic Carburetor

In an electronic carburetor, the metering rod which adjusts the fuel flow is controlled by a vacuum regulator which receives its control signals from the electronic engine controller.

The electronic carburetor is similar to a conventional carburetor except that the fuel metering rods can be electrically controlled. *Figure 5-32* is a drawing of a typical electronic carburetor. The mechanism for varying air/fuel ratios in response to an electrical command signal is provided by an electromechanical vacuum regulator and a special set of metering rods whose position is controlled by vacuum.

The vacuum regulator is an actuator which supplies a control vacuum signal ranging from zero to about 8 inches of mercury depending upon the command from the electronic controller. The vacuum regulator is designed so that the control vacuum varies inversely with the command current. This control vacuum remains constant for a given command current provided the source vacuum (manifold vacuum) exceeds the control vacuum by about one inch of mercury. *Figure 5-33* is a graph of the control vacuum versus current for a typical vacuum regulator.

Figure 5-32. Simplified Electronic Carburetor

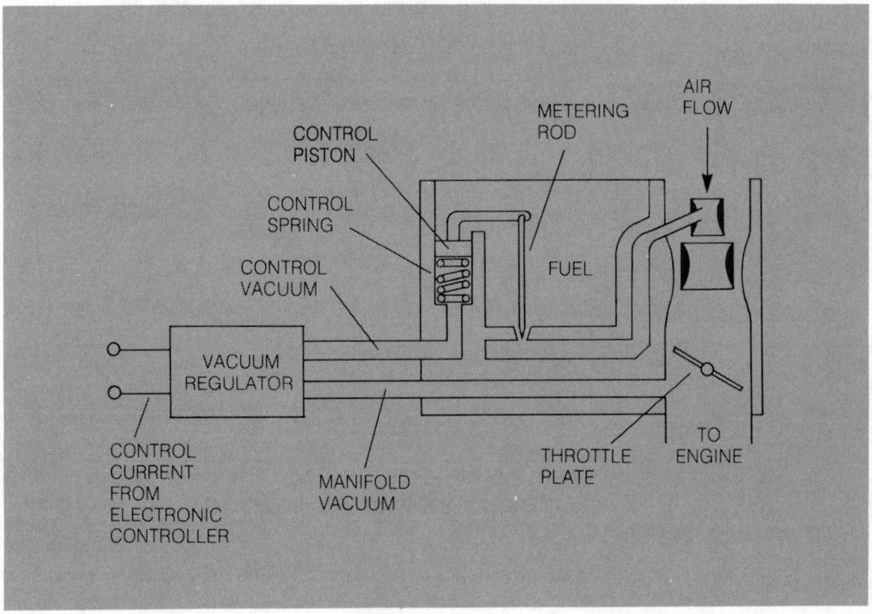

The control piston and spring in the carburetor move the metering rods between their extreme limits. The spring holds the metering rods open with no vacuum present. When control vacuum is applied, it pulls the piston against the opposing spring pressure. As the piston moves down, it pulls the metering rod down to allow less fuel to pass. As the control

Figure 5-33. Typical Vacuum Regulator Control Characteristic Curve

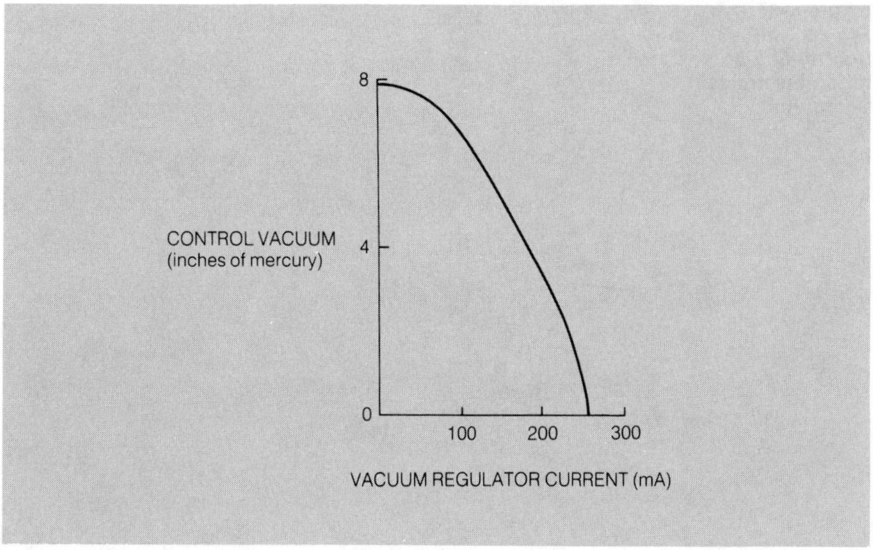

With no control vacuum, the metering rod is held open by a spring, resulting in maximum fuel flow. As control vacuum increases, the metering rod closes to reduce fuel flow.

vacuum increases, the metering rod closes more to allow a lower rate of fuel flow into the moving air stream. *Figure 5-34* is a graph of air/fuel ratio versus control vacuum for a typical electronic carburetor. Notice that the air/fuel ratio can be varied electrically from just under 14 to about 17. This is a sufficient range for electronic fuel control applications.

Fuel Injection

The other major fuel metering actuator is the electromechanical fuel injector. This device is a solenoid operated valve that passes fuel from a constant pressure source when being operated (i.e., solenoid current on) and blocks fuel when not being operated (i.e., solenoid current off).

There are two types of fuel injector configurations: the throttle body fuel injector (TBFI) and the multipoint fuel injector. Both configurations use a similar solenoid-operated fuel metering valve. In the TBFI configuration, one or more fuel injectors are mounted in a housing which is similar to a carburetor and which is located near a throttle plate. *Figure 5-35* is a picture of a typical TBFI configuration. The TBFI mixes fuel and air passing into the intake manifold very much like a carburetor does.

In the multipoint fuel injection system, there is one fuel injector for each cylinder mounted, for example, in the intake port near the intake valve. As both systems use a similar device for metering fuel, it is possible to explain the operation of both configurations by describing the operation of a fuel injector.

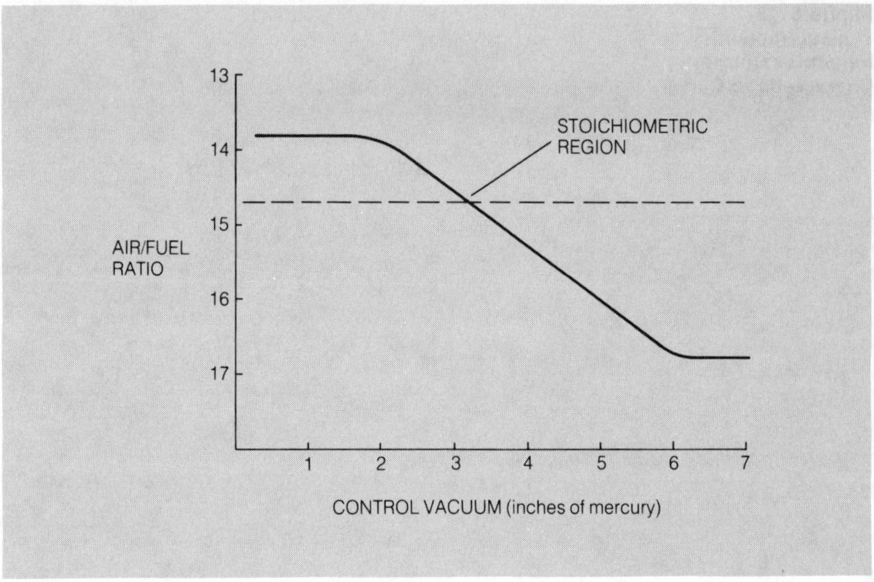

Figure 5-34. Typical Air/Fuel Ratio Control Characteristic for an Electronic Carburetor

Figure 5-36 is a schematic drawing of a fuel injector. Fuel is pumped from the tank and enters the system unregulated, but the pressure is regulated to about 10 psi by a fuel pressure regulator assembly. The pressure regulated fuel is applied to the fuel injector.

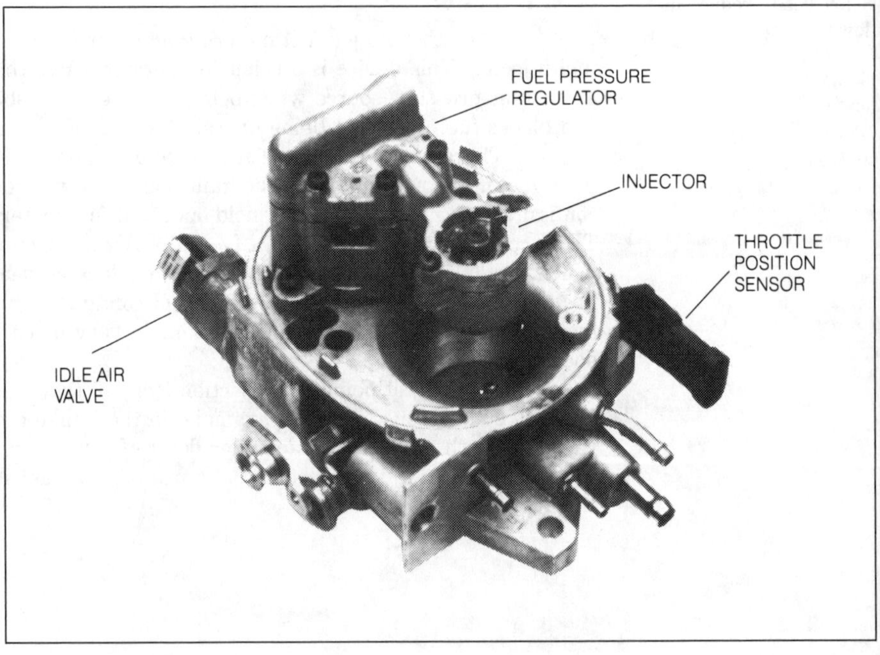

Figure 5-35. Single Bore TBFI

Figure 5-36. Throttle Body Fuel Injection (TBFI) Fuel Metering Schematic

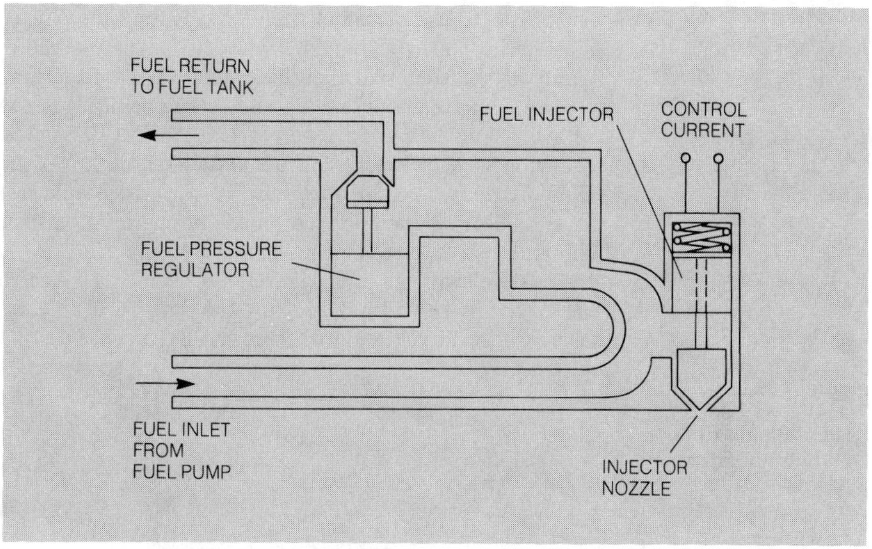

The fuel injector consists of a spray nozzle and a solenoid operated plunger. Whenever the plunger is against the nozzle, fuel is prevented from flowing. Whenever the plunger is lifted from the nozzle, fuel flows at a fixed rate through the nozzle into the air stream going to the intake manifold. Thus, the plunger acts as a fuel injection on-off valve.

A throttle body fuel injector contains a solenoid, a spring-loaded plunger, and an injector nozzle that act as an on-off valve under electrical control.

The plunger position is controlled by a solenoid and a spring. The plunger is held down tightly against the nozzle by a powerful spring when no current is applied to the solenoid. A solenoid is actually a form of electromagnet in which a magnetic field is created that is proportional to the current passing through the coil. The magnetic field in the solenoid draws the plunger away from the nozzle. Although a certain amount of time is required to open the valve, for the present discussion consider that the plunger motion is so rapid that the change in plunger position can be considered instantaneous. Hence, the solenoid, plunger, and nozzle act as an electrically switched valve. This valve is either closed or open, depending upon whether the control current is off or on, respectively.

The fuel flow rate through the nozzle is constant for a given regulated fuel pressure and nozzle geometry; therefore, the quantity of fuel injected into the air stream is proportional to the time the valve is open. The control current that operates the fuel injector is pulsed on and off, and the air/fuel ratio is proportional to the duty cycle of the pulse train from the electronic controller.

Fuel-Injector Signal

Consider an idealized fuel injector in which the injector is open when the applied voltage is on and is closed when the applied voltage is off. In this idealization, the control voltage operating the fuel injector is a binary pulse train (i.e., "on" or "off"). For a pulse train signal, the ratio of on time, t, to the period of the pulse, T, (on time plus off time) is called the duty cycle. This is shown in *Figure 5-37*. The fuel metering actuator is energized for time t to allow fuel to spray from the nozzle into the air stream going to the intake manifold. The actuator is deenergized for the remainder of the period. Therefore, a low duty cycle, as seen in *Figure 5-37a*, is used for a high air/fuel ratio (lean mixture), and a high duty cycle (*Fig. 5-37b*) is used for a low air/fuel ratio (rich mixture).

During the open loop mode of operation, a fixed duty cycle is chosen by the electronic controller to supply the basic air/fuel ratio. When the system switches to the closed loop mode, the electronic controller varies the pulse width (t) to vary the duty cycle to vary the air/fuel ratio in response to the error signal from the EGO sensor.

Figure 5-37. Pulse Mode Fuel Control Signal to Fuel Metering Actuator

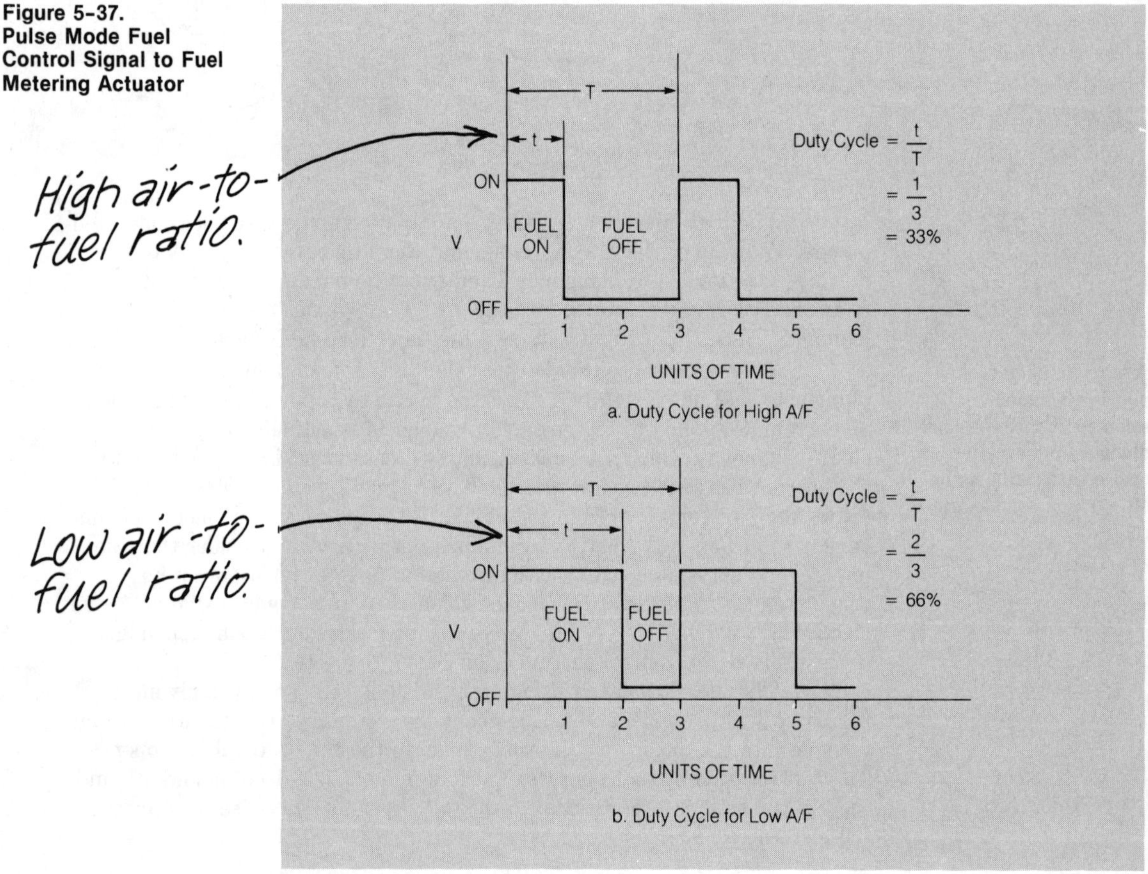

Low and High Duty Cycle

The frequency of the pulses (pulses per second) of the duty cycle signal for the actuator is determined by engine RPM. As engine speed increases, the pulse frequency increases. However, at some upper

Because the flow of fuel through the nozzle is either on or off, the air/fuel ratio must be regulated by controlling the duty cycle; that is, the ratio of injector on time to total on-and-off time.

frequency limit which is determined by the duty cycle, the controller holds the frequency at a fixed value. This is because the period (T) of the pulse signal takes less time as frequency increases; thus, the on time (t) also gets shorter in real time even if the duty cycle remains constant. It takes a certain amount of time for the solenoid valve to open and a certain amount of time for it to close. Therefore, as t gets shorter with increasing frequency and a low duty cycle, a point is reached where the on time is not long enough to open the valve. Similarly, for high frequency and a high duty cycle, the off time is not sufficient for the valve to close.

The duty cycle signal can be sent to the TBFI actuator directly from the computer or by a special purpose interface which converts a binary number into a duty cycle output.

IGNITION ACTUATOR

The combination of components that make up a complete ignition system can be viewed overall as an actuator; that is, the input electrical signals produce an action (the ignition of the air/fuel mixture).

Strictly speaking, the actuator in an ignition system should be viewed as a coil, distributor, and spark plugs in combination. Interrupting the coil primary current produces an action—ignition of the air and fuel mixture. However, many electronic ignition systems package the coil and associated electronics in a single module. With this in mind, the term actuator in ignition systems is expanded to include the associated electronic circuitry as part of the actuator.

With this viewpoint, *Figure 5-38* illustrates an electronic ignition circuit. Chapter 6 will have further discussion of ignition systems and the control of spark ignition and timing; however, a typical actual actuator circuit is shown in *Figure 5-39.* Note that the actuator receives its control pulse from an ignition timing sensor of the type discussed earlier. The basic behavior of an ignition system is explained in Chapter 1.

Figure 5-38. Ignition Actuator

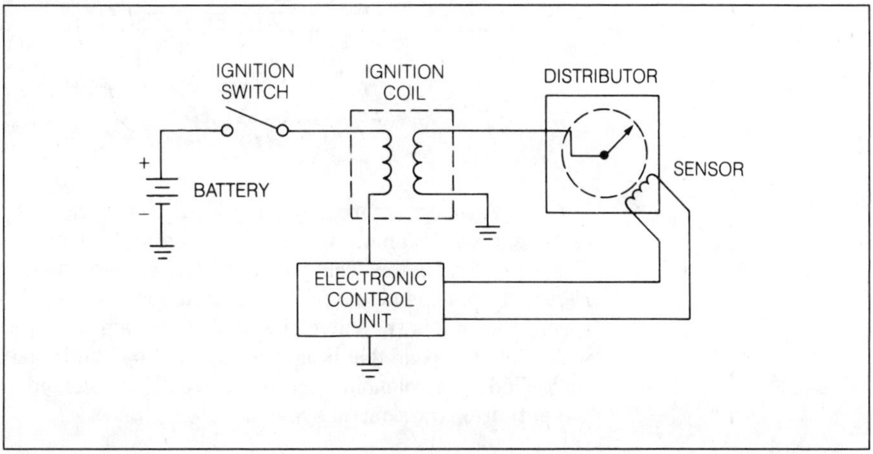

EXHAUST GAS RECIRCULATOR ACTUATOR

Another important actuator for modern emission controlled engines is the exhaust gas recirculator (EGR) actuator. EGR refers to the addition of exhaust gas to the intake charge to lower NO_x emissions. The EGR actuator is a valve which essentially connects the intake and exhaust manifolds. When the valve is open, a portion of the exhaust gas flows into the intake manifold because of the lower pressure in the intake manifold.

Figure 5-39. Electronic Control Unit

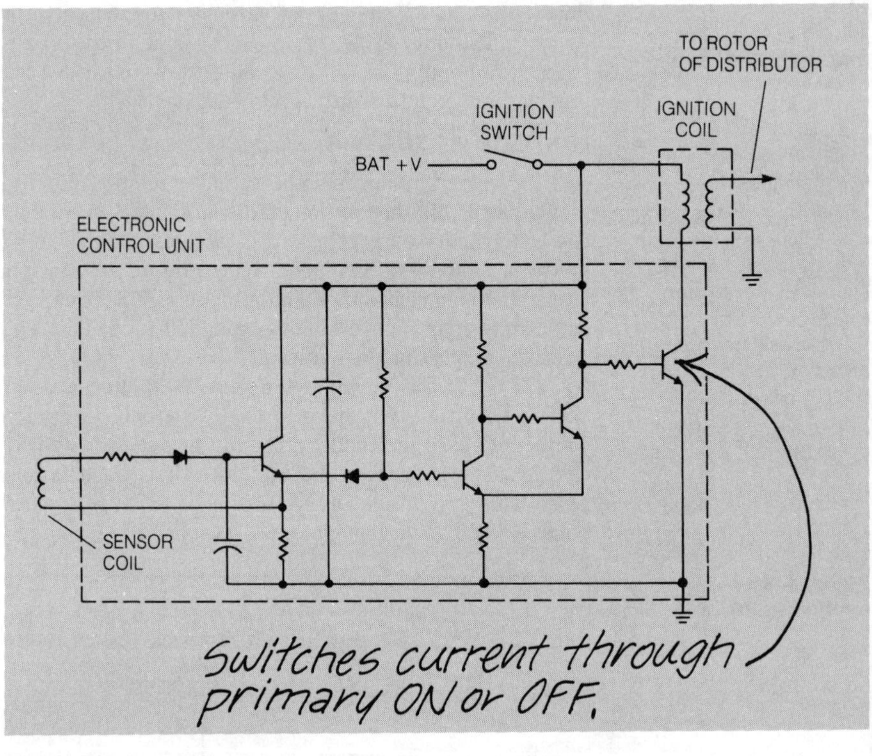

Although there are many EGR configurations, only one representative example will be discussed to explain the basic operation of this type of actuator. The example EGR actuator is shown schematically in *Figure 5-40*. This actuator is a vacuum operated diaphragm valve with a spring that holds the valve closed if no vacuum is applied. The vacuum which operates the diaphragm is supplied by the intake manifold and is controlled by a solenoid operated valve. This solenoid valve is controlled by the output of the control system.

One kind of EGR actuator consists of a vacuum operated valve with the vacuum supply controlled by a solenoid. When the EGR valve is open, exhaust gas flows into the intake manifold.

This solenoid operates essentially the same as that explained in the TBFI. Whenever the solenoid is energized (i.e., by current supplied by the control system flowing through the coil) the EGR valve is opened by the applied vacuum. Whenever the solenoid is deenergized, the vacuum is cut off from the EGR valve and the spring holds the EGR valve closed. The amount of EGR is controlled by the average time the solenoid is energized (i.e., duty cycle of the pulsed control current) as was described for the TBFI.

Figure 5-40. EGR Actuator Control

Vacuum pulls up diaphragm

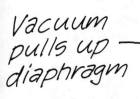

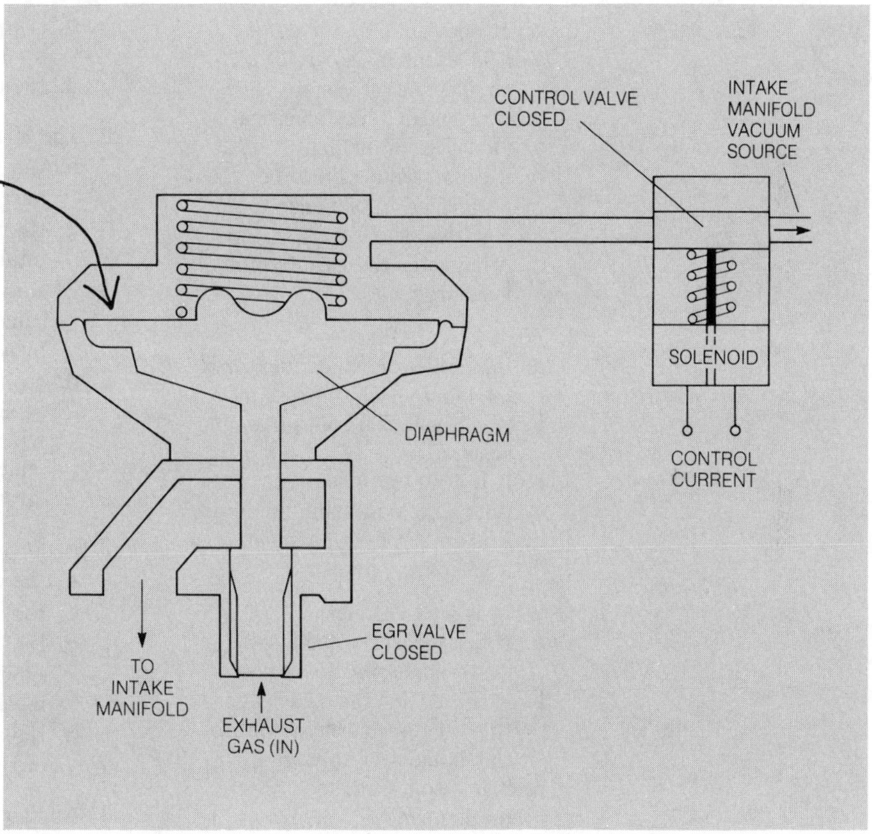

Quiz for Chapter 5

1. Which of the following operations is performed by a sensor?
   a. it selects transmission gear ratio
   b. it measures some variable
   c. it is an output device
   d. it sends signals to the driver

2. What does an actuator do?
   a. it is an input device for an engine control system
   b. it provides a mathematical model for an engine
   c. it causes an action to be performed in response to an electrical signal
   d. it indicates the results of a measurement

3. What is a MAP sensor?
   a. it is a sensor which measures manifold absolute pressure
   b. it is a vacation route planning scheme
   c. it is a measurement of fluctuations in manifold air
   d. it is an acronym for mean atmospheric pressure

4. What is an EGO sensor?
   a. it is a measure of the self-centeredness of the driver
   b. it is a device for measuring the oxygen concentration in the exhaust of an engine
   c. it is a spark advance mechanism
   d. it measures crankshaft acceleration

5. The crankshaft angular position sensor measures
   a. the angle between the connecting rods and the crankshaft
   b. the angle between a line drawn through the crankshaft axis and a mark on the flywheel and a reference line
   c. the pitch angle of the crankshaft axis
   d. the oil pressure angle

6. The Hall effect is
   a. the resonance of a long, narrow corridor
   b. the flow of air through the intake manifold
   c. zero crossing error in camshaft position measurements
   d. a phenomenon occurring in semiconductor materials in which a voltage is generated which is proportional to the strength of a magnetic field

7. A mass airflow sensor measures
   a. the density of atmospheric air
   b. the composition of air
   c. the rate at which air is flowing into an engine measured in terms of its mass
   d. the flow of exhaust out of the engine

8. An electronic carburetor is
   a. a carburetor having electronically controlled fuel metering rods
   b. a device for injecting electrons into the engine
   c. a carburetor having a mass airflow sensor
   d. a carburetor having an electronically controlled throttle

9. Throttle body fuel injection refers to
  a. inserting fuel below the throttle plate
  b. a form of fuel metering actuator
  c. unregulated fuel flow
  d. a continuous flow fuel injection system

10. A thermistor is
  a. a semiconductor temperature sensor
  b. a device for regulating engine temperature
  c. a temperature control system for the passenger compartment
  d. a new type of transistor

11. Intake manifold pressure
  a. is constant
  b. fluctuates as air is drawn into each cylinder
  c. is produced by an external pump
  d. none of the above

12. An aneroid chamber is a
  a. chamber holding high air pressure
  b. small tube connected to the intake manifold
  c. displacement sensor
  d. pair of diaphragms which are welded to form an evacuated chamber

13. Piezoresistivity is
  a. a property of certain semiconductors in which resistivity varies with strain
  b. a resistance property of insulators
  c. metal bonding pads
  d. an Italian resistor

14. The resonant frequency, f_r, of a circuit is given by
  a. $\frac{1}{2\pi\sqrt{LC}}$
  b. $2\pi\sqrt{LC}$
  c. $\frac{2\pi\sqrt{LC}}{c}$
  d. none of the above

15. Reluctance is
  a. the reciprocal of permeability
  b. a property of a magnetic circuit which is analogous to resistance in an electrical circuit
  c. a line of constant magnetic flux
  d. none of the above

16. An optical crankshaft position sensor
  a. senses crankshaft angular position
  b. operates by alternately passing or stopping a beam of light from a source to an optical detector
  c. operates in a pulsed mode
  d. all of the above

17. The resistance of a thermistor
  a. varies inversely with temperature
  b. varies directly with temperature
  c. is always 100,000 ohms
  d. none of the above

18. Duty cycle in a fuel metering actuator refers to the ratio of
  a. fuel ON time to fuel OFF time
  b. fuel OFF time to fuel ON time
  c. fuel ON time to fuel ON time plus fuel OFF time
  d. none of the above.

19. An EGO sensor is
  a. a perfectly linear sensor
  b. a sensor having two different output levels depending upon air/fuel ratio
  c. unaffected by exhaust oxygen levels
  d. unaffected by temperature

20. A potentiometer is
  a. a variable resistance circuit component
  b. sometimes used to sense airflow
  c. can be used in throttle angle sensor
  d. all of the above

The Basics of Electronic Engine Control

ABOUT THIS CHAPTER

Engine control in the vast majority of engines means regulating fuel and air intake as well as spark timing to achieve desired performance in the form of torque or power output. Until recently, control of the engine output torque and RPM was accomplished through some combination of mechanical, pneumatic, or hydraulic system. Suddenly, in the 1970s, electronic control systems were introduced.

This chapter is intended to explain, in general terms, the theory of electronic control of the automotive engine. Chapter 7 explains practical control methods and systems. The examples used to explain the major developments and principles of electronic control have been culled from the techniques used by various manufacturers and are not representative of any single automobile manufacturer.

MOTIVATION FOR ELECTRONIC ENGINE CONTROL

The motivation for electronic engine control came in part from two government requirements. The first came about as a result of legislation to regulate automobile exhaust emissions under the authority of the Environmental Protection Agency (EPA). The second was a thrust to improve the national average fuel economy by government regulation.

Exhaust Emissions

The combustion of gasoline in an engine results in exhaust gases including CO_2, H_2O, CO, oxides of nitrogen, and various hydrocarbons.

The engine exhaust consists of the products of combustion of the air and gasoline mixture. Gasoline is a mixture of chemical compounds that are called hydrocarbons. This name is derived from the chemical formation of the various gasoline compounds, each of which is a chemical union of hydrogen (H) and carbon (C). In addition, the gasoline also contains natural impurities as well as chemicals added by the refiner. All of these can produce undesirable exhaust elements.

During the combustion process, the carbon and hydrogen combine with oxygen from the air, releasing heat energy and forming various chemical compounds. If the combustion were perfect, the exhaust gases would consist only of carbon dioxide (CO_2) and water (H_2O), neither of which are considered harmful in the atmosphere. In fact, these are present in a human's breath.

Unfortunately, the combustion of the SI engine is not perfect. In addition to the CO_2 and H_2O, the exhaust contains contains amounts of carbon monoxide (CO), oxides of nitrogen (chemical unions of nitrogen and oxygen which are denoted NO_x), unburned hydrocarbons (HC), oxides of sulfur, and other compounds. Some of the exhaust constituents are considered harmful and have come under the control of the Federal Government. The exhaust emissions controlled by government standards are CO, HC, and NO_x.

Automotive exhaust emission control requirements started in the United States in 1966 when the California state regulations became effective. Since then, the federal government has imposed emission control limits for all states, and the standards became progressively more difficult to meet through the decade 1970–1980. Auto manufacturers found that the traditional engine controls could not control the engine sufficiently to meet these emission limits and maintain adequate engine performance at the same time, so they turned to electronic controls.

Fuel Economy

Everyone has some idea of what fuel economy means. It is related to the number of miles that can be driven for each gallon of gasoline consumed. It is referred to as miles per gallon (MPG) or simply "mileage." Just like it improves emission control, another important feature of electronic engine control is its ability to improve fuel economy.

Electronic engine control is used to reduce exhaust emissions and improve fuel economy, both of which have limits set by the government.

It is well recognized by layman and expert alike that the mileage of a vehicle is not unique. It depends upon size, shape, weight, and how the car is driven. The best mileage is achieved under steady cruise conditions. City driving, with many starts and stops, yields worse mileage than steady highway driving.

The government fuel economy standards are not based on just one car, but are stated in terms of the average rated miles per gallon fuel mileage for the production of all models by a manufacturer for any year. This latter requirement is known in the automotive industry by the acronym CAFE (Corporate Average Fuel Economy). It is a somewhat complex requirement and is based upon measurements of the fuel used during a prescribed, simulated standard driving cycle.

FEDERAL GOVERNMENT TEST PROCEDURES

For an understanding of both emission and CAFE requirements, it is helpful to review the standard cycle and how the emission and fuel economy measurements are made. The U.S. Federal Government has published test procedures that include several steps. The first step is to place the automobile on a chassis dynamometer, like the one shown in *Figure 6-1*.

Government test procedures use a chassis dynamometer to simulate actual driving conditions in a controlled environment.

A chassis dynamometer is a test stand that holds a vehicle. The vehicle might be a car, truck, etc. It is equipped with instruments capable of measuring the power that is delivered at the drive wheels of the vehicle under various conditions. The vehicle is held on the dynamometer so that it cannot move when power is applied to the drive wheels. The drive wheels are in contact with two large rollers. One roller is mechanically coupled to

Figure 6-1. Chassis Dynamometer

an electric generator that can vary the load on its electrical output. The other roller has instruments to measure and record the vehicle speed. The generator absorbs all mechanical power that is delivered at the drive wheels, and the horsepower is calculated from the electrical output. (Seven hundred forty-six watts of electrical output equals one horsepower.) The controls of the dynamometer can be set to simulate the correct load and inertia of the vehicle moving along a road under various conditions. The conditions are the same as if the vehicle actually were being driven.

Emission samples are collected and measured during a simulated urban trip containing a high percentage of stop-and-go driving.

The vehicle is operated according to a prescribed schedule of speed and load to simulate the specified trip. One is an urban trip and one is a highway trip. The schedules are shown in *Figure 6-2*. The 18 cycles of the urban simulated trip take 1,372 seconds and include acceleration, deceleration, stops, starts, and steady cruise such as would be encountered in a "typical" city automobile trip of 7.45 miles (12 km). The highway schedule takes 765 seconds and simulates 10.24 miles (16.5 km) of highway driving.

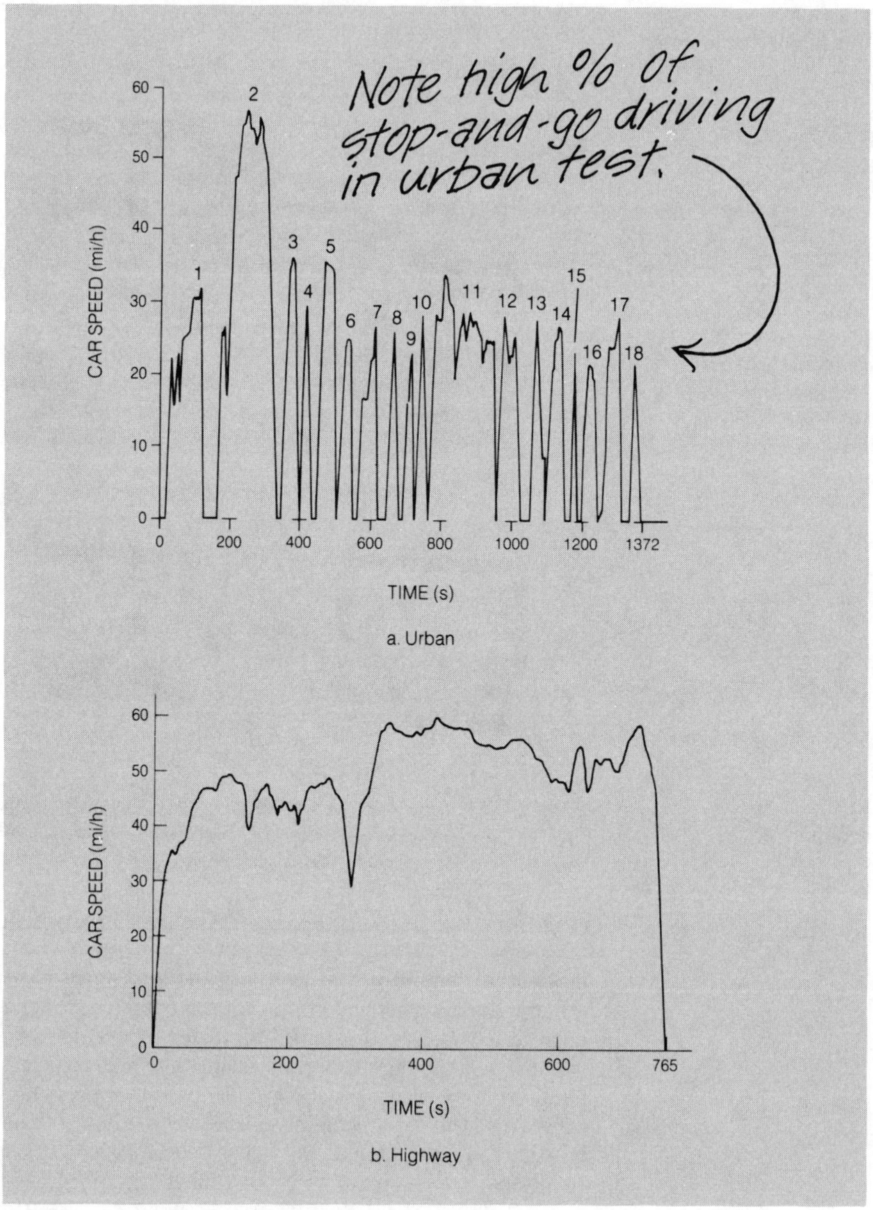

Figure 6-2. Federal Driving Schedules *(Title 40 United States Code of Federal Regulations)*

During the operation of the vehicle in the urban test, the exhaust is continuously collected and sampled. At the end of the test, the absolute mass of each of the important exhaust gases is determined. The regulations are stated in terms of the total mass of each exhaust gas divided by the total distance of the simulated trip.

Fuel consumption also is measured during the tests. Emission and MPG requirements have grown increasingly stringent since 1968.

In addition to emission measurement, each manufacturer must determine the fuel consumption in MPG for each type of vehicle and must compute the corporate average mileage for all vehicles of all types produced in a year. Fuel consumption is measured during both an urban and a highway test, and the composite fuel economy is calculated.

*Table 6-1*is a summary of the exhaust emission requirements and CAFE for representative years. It shows the emission reductions and increased fuel economy required. Because of these requirements, each manufacturer has a strong incentive to minimize exhaust emissions and maximize fuel economy for each vehicle produced.

Table 6-1. Emission and MPG Requirement

YEAR	FEDERAL $HC/CO/NO_x$	CALIFORNIA $HC/CO/NO_x$	CAFE MPG
1968	3.2/33/—	———	—
1971	2.2/23/—	———	—
1978	1.5/15/2.0	0.41/9.0/1.5	18
1979	1.5/15/2.0	0.41/9.0/1.5	19
1980	0.41/7.0/2.0	0.41/9.0/1.5	20

Meeting the Requirements

Engines using mechanical, hydraulic, or pneumatic controls do not meet government regulations, but engines using electronic engine controls can.

Unfortunately, as seen later in this chapter, meeting the government regulations causes some sacrifice in performance. Moreover, attempts to meet the *Table 6-1* standards using mechanical, electromechanical, hydraulic, or pneumatic controls like those used in the past have not been cost effective. In addition, such controls do not have the capability to reproduce functions with sufficient accuracy across a range of production vehicles, over all operating conditions and over the life of the vehicle to stay within the tolerance required by the EPA regulations. Each automaker must verify that each model produced will still meet emission requirements after traveling 50,000 miles.

The Role of Electronics

The use of digital electronic control has enabled automakers to meet the government regulations by controlling the system accurately with excellent tolerance. In addition, the system has long-term calibration stability. As an added advantage, this type of system is very flexible. Because it uses microcomputers, it can be modified through programming changes to meet a variety of different vehicle-engine combinations. Critical quantities that describe an engine can be changed easily by changing data that is stored in the system's computer memory.

Additional Cost Incentive

Dropping costs of microprocessors and other very large scale integrated circuits have made electronic engine control an increasingly attractive system for automobile manufacturers.

Besides providing control accuracy and stability, there is a cost incentive to use digital electronic control. The system components, the multifunction digital integrated circuits, are decreasing in cost, thus decreasing the system cost. During the decade of the 1970s, considerable investment was made by the semiconductor industry for the development of low cost, multifunction integrated circuits. In particular, the microprocessor and microcomputer have reached an advanced state of capability at relatively low cost. This has made the electronic digital control system for the engine as well as other on-board automobile electronic systems commercially feasible.

As pointed out in Chapter 3, as the multifunction digital integrated circuits continue to be designed with more and more functional capability through very-large-scale integrated circuits (VLSI), the costs continue to decrease. At the same time, these circuits offer improved electronic system performance in the automobile.

In summary, the electronic engine control system duplicates the function of conventional fluidic control systems, but with greater precision. It has the capability of optimizing engine performance while meeting the exhaust emission and fuel economy regulations.

CONCEPT OF AN ELECTRONIC ENGINE CONTROL SYSTEM

An electronic engine control system is an assembly of electronic and electromechanical components that continuously vary the fuel and spark settings in order to satisfy government exhaust emission and fuel economy regulations. *Figure 6–3* is a block diagram of a generalized electronic engine control system.

Figure 6-3. Generic Electronic Engine Control System

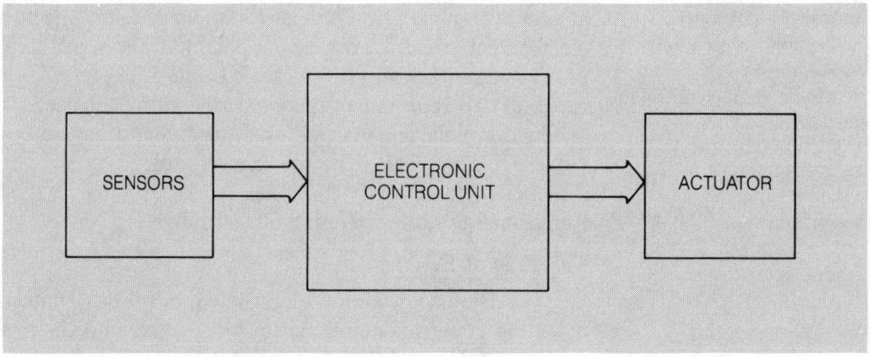

As explained in Chapter 2, a control system requires measurements of certain variables that tell the controller the state of the system being controlled. The electronic engine control system receives input electrical signals from the various sensors which measure the state of the engine. From these signals, the controller generates output electrical signals to the actuators that determine the engine calibration.

Examples of automotive engine control system sensors were discussed in Chapter 5. As mentioned, the configuration and control for an automotive engine control system is determined in part by the set of sensors that are available to measure the variables. In many cases, the sensors available for automotive use involve compromises between performance and cost. In other cases, only indirect measurements of certain variables are feasible.

Overall engine functions that are subject to electronic engine controls are air/fuel ratio, spark control, and exhaust gas recirculation.

Figure 6-4 identifies the automotive functions that surround the engine in a bit more detail. There is a fuel metering system to set the air-fuel mixture going into the engine through the intake manifold. Spark control determines when the air-fuel mixture is ignited after it is compressed in the cylinders of the engine. The power is at the drive shaft, and the gases which result from combustion flow out of the exhaust system. In the exhaust system, there is a valve to control the amount of exhaust gas being recirculated back to the input and a catalytic converter to further control emissions. This addition to the engine is explained later.

Earlier models of electronic control systems used separate controllers for each engine function. The current trend is toward a single, integrated controller that monitors multiple functions.

At one stage of development, the electronic engine control consisted of separate subsystems for fuel control, spark control, and exhaust gas recirculation. As shown in *Figure 6-4b*, it appears that the automotive engine control system is evolving toward an integrated digital system in which these subsystems are treated as separate functions of the same controller.

This chapter discusses the various electronic engine control functions separately and explains how each function is implemented by a separate control system. It then shows how these separate control systems are being integrated into one system.

DEFINITION OF GENERAL TERMS

Before proceeding with the details on engine control systems, certain definitions of terms must be clarified; first some general terms and then some specific engine performance terms.

Parameters

Design parameters such as engine size, compression ratio, etc., are fixed; therefore, they are not subject to any engine operating control.

A parameter is a numerical value of some engine dimension that is fixed by design. Examples of engine design parameters include the piston diameter (bore), the distance the piston travels on one stroke (stroke), and the length of the crankshaft lever arm (throw). The bore and stroke determine the cylinder volume and the displacement. Displacement is the total volume of air that is displaced as the engine rotates through two complete revolutions. Compression ratio is the ratio of cylinder volume at BDC to the volume at TDC. Other parameters which engine designers must specify include combustion chamber shape, camshaft cam profile, intake and exhaust valve size, and valve timing. All of these design parameters are fixed by design and are not subject to control while the engine is operating.

Figure 6-4.
Engine Functions and Control

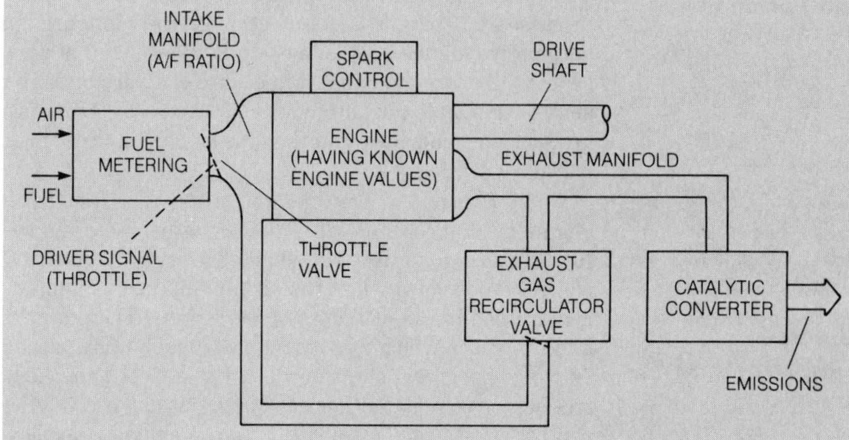

a. Overall Engine Functions

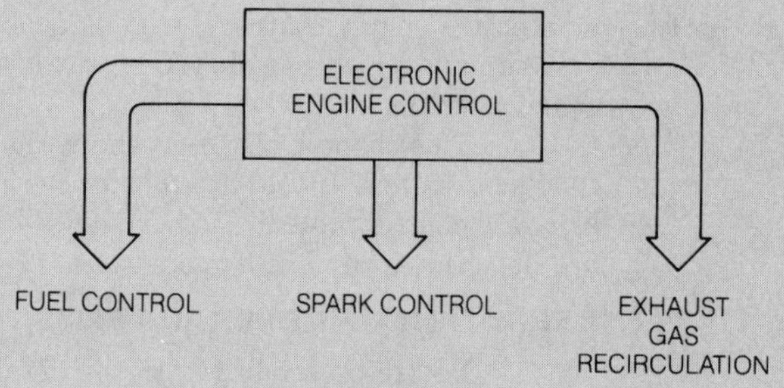

b. Major Subsystems

Variables

A variable is a quantity that changes or may be changed as the engine operates. *Figures 6-5* and *6-6* identify specific engine control variables.

Inputs to Controllers

A variable is a quantity which can be changed as the engine operates.

Figure 6-5 identifies the major physical quantities that are sensed and provided to the electronic controller as inputs. They include:

1. throttle-valve position
2. manifold absolute pressure (MAP)
3. engine temperature (coolant temperature)
4. engine speed (RPM)
5. exhaust gas recirculation valve position
6. oxygen content in exhaust gas.

Figure 6-5. Major Controller Inputs from Engine

sensors input provides value to engine control.

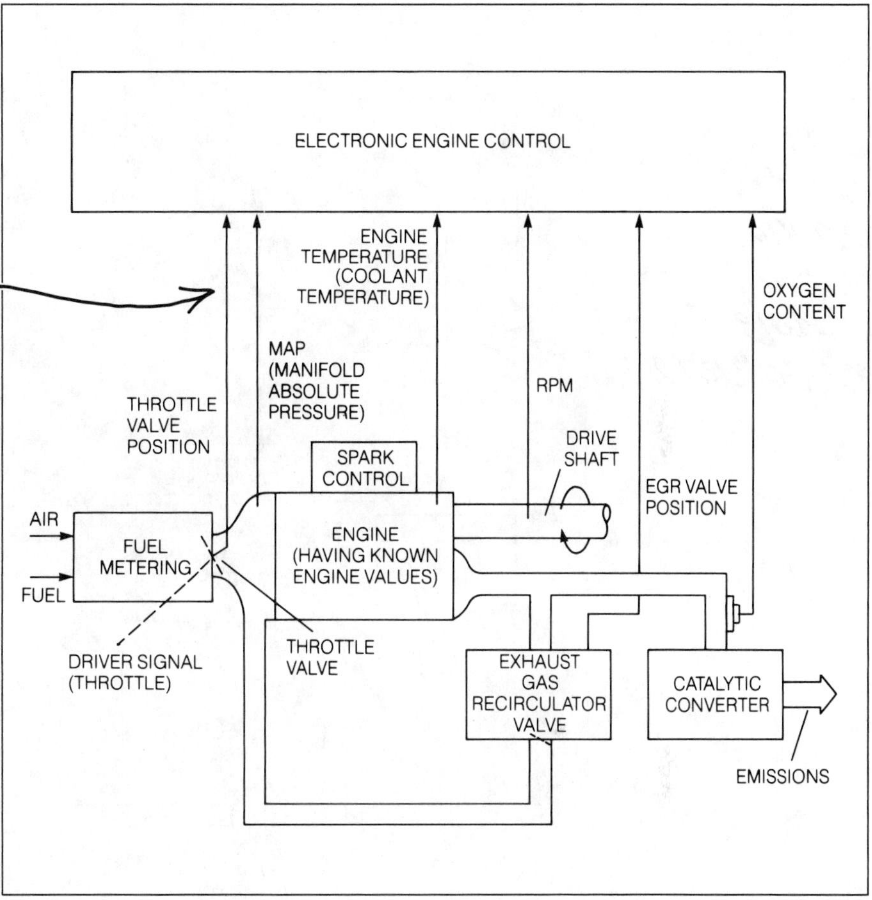

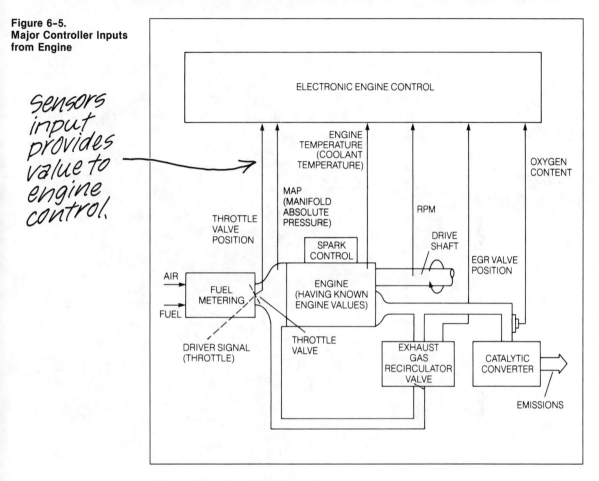

Outputs from Controllers

Figure 6-6 identifies the major physical quantities that are outputs from the controller. These include:

1. fuel metering control
2. ignition control
3. ignition timing
4. exhaust gas recirculation control

DEFINITION OF ENGINE PERFORMANCE TERMS

Common terms are used to describe an engine's performance. Here are a few.

Figure 6-6. Major Controller Outputs to Engine

Engine control provides output signals to the actuators.

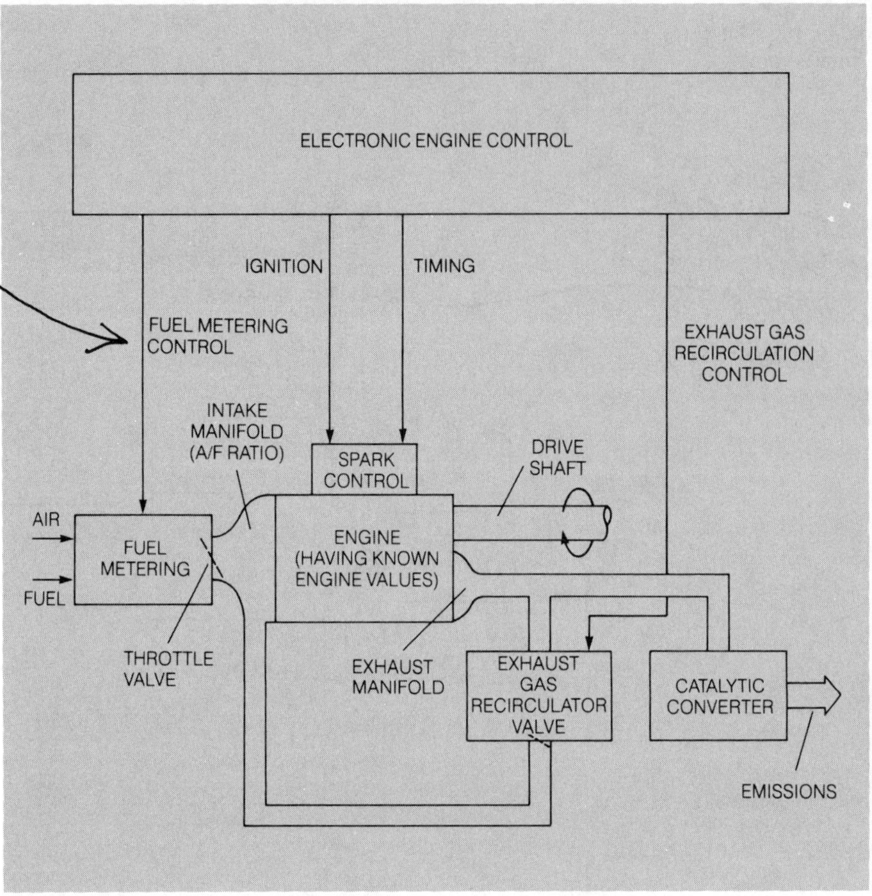

Power

The most common performance rating that has been applied to automobiles is a power rating of the engine. It normally is given in horsepower. Power is the rate at which the engine is doing useful work. It varies with engine speed and throttle angle. Power may be measured at the drive wheels or at the engine output shaft, depending upon which is desired. It is more convenient and useful to the designer of an electronic engine control system to know the output power of *only the engine*. This permits realistic comparisons of engine data as engine controls are varied. To make such measurements, an engine dynamometer is used. This dynamometer is similar to the one in *Figure 6-1* except that the engine output shaft drives the dynamometer directly instead of coupling the output through wheels and rollers.

Power is a measurement of an engine's ability to perform useful work. Brake power, which is measured with an engine dynamometer, is the actual power developed by the engine minus losses due to internal friction.

The power delivered by the engine to the dynamometer is called the brake power and is designated P_b. The brake power of an engine is *always less* than the total amount of power that is actually developed in the engine. This developed power is called the indicated power of the engine and is denoted P_i. The indicated power differs from the brake power by the loss of power in the engine due to friction between cylinder and piston, and other friction losses.

$$P_b = P_i - \text{friction losses}$$

BSFC

BSFC is a measurement of an engine's fuel economy. It is the ratio of fuel flow to the brake power output of the engine.

Fuel economy can be measured while the engine delivers power to the dynamometer. The engine is typically operated at a fixed RPM and a fixed brake power, P_b (fixed dynamometer load), and the fuel flow rate, r_f (in kilograms/hour) is measured. The fuel consumption is then given as the ratio of this fuel flow rate, r_f, to the brake power output, P_b. This fuel consumption is known as the brake specific fuel consumption, or BSFC.

$$\text{BSFC} = \frac{r_f}{P_b}$$

By improving the BSFC of the engine, the fuel economy of the vehicle in which it is installed is also improved. Electronic controls help to greatly improve BSFC.

Torque

Torque is the twisting force of an engine's crankshaft.

Engine torque is the twisting action produced on the crankshaft by the cylinder pressure pushing on the piston during the power stroke. Torque is produced whenever a force is applied to a lever. The length of the lever (the lever arm) in the engine is determined by the "throw" of the crankshaft (the offset from the crankshaft centerline of the point where the force is applied). The torque is expressed as the product of this force and the length of the lever. The units of torque are N.m (newton meters) in the metric system or ft.lb. (foot pounds) in the English system. (One ft.lb. is the torque produced by one pound acting on a lever arm one foot long.) The torque of a typical engine varies with RPM.

Volumetric Efficiency

Other measurements of engine performance include volumetric, or "breathing," efficiency and thermal efficiency.

The variation in torque with RPM is strongly influenced by the volumetric efficiency or "breathing efficiency." Volumetric efficiency actually describes how well the engine functions as an air pump, drawing air and fuel into the various cylinders. It depends upon various engine design parameters such as piston size, piston stroke, number of cylinders, etc.

Thermal Efficiency

Thermal efficiency expresses the mechanical energy that is delivered to the vehicle relative to the energy content of the fuel. In the typical SI engine, 35% of the energy that is available in the fuel is lost as heat to the coolant and lubricating oil, 40% is lost as heat and unburned fuel in exhaust gases, and another 5% is lost in engine and drivetrain friction. This means that only about 20% is available to drive the vehicle and accessories. These percentages vary with operating conditions.

Calibration

The definition of engine calibration is the setting of the air-fuel ratio and ignition timing for the engine. With the new electronic control systems, calibration is determined by the electronic engine control system.

ENGINE MAPPING

Engine mapping is a process by which measurements are made of important engine variables while the engine is operated throughout its speed and load ranges.

The development of any control system comes from knowledge of the "plant" or system to be controlled. In the case of the automobile engine, this knowledge of the plant (the engine) comes primarily from a process called engine mapping.

For engine mapping, the engine is connected to a dynamometer and operated throughout its entire speed and load range. Measurements are made of the important engine variables while varying quantities, such as the air/fuel ratio and the spark control, in a known and systematic manner. Such engine mapping is done in engine test cells that have engine dynamometers and complex instrumentation under computer control.

From this mapping, a mathematical model is developed that explains the influence of every measurable variable and parameter on engine performance. The control system designer must select a control configuration, control variables, and control strategy which will satisfy all performance requirements (including stability) as computed from this model, and which are within the other design limits such as cost, quality, and reliability. To understand a typical engine control system, let's look at the influence of control variables upon engine performance.

Effect of Air/Fuel Ratio on Performance

Figure 6-7 illustrates the variation in performance variables of torque, T, and brake power, BSFC, as well as engine emissions with variations in air/fuel ratio with fixed spark timing and a constant engine speed. Relatively low air/fuel ratio (below 14.7) is called a "rich" mixture and relatively high air/fuel ratio (above 14.7) is called a "lean" mixture.

Note from *Figure 6-7* that torque T reaches a maximum in the air/fuel ratio range of 12 to 16. The exact air/fuel ratio for which torque is maximum depends upon the engine configuration, engine speed, and ignition timing.

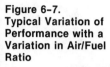

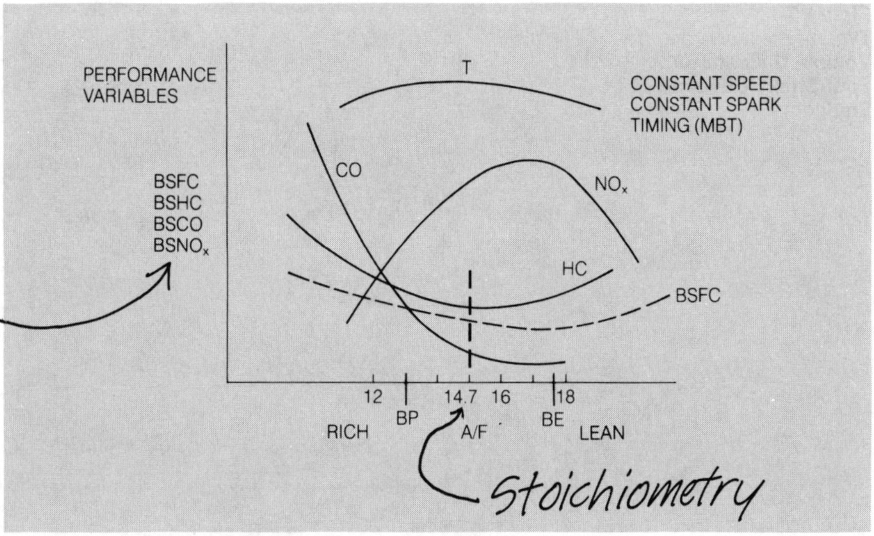

Figure 6-7. Typical Variation of Performance with a Variation in Air/Fuel Ratio

Most (but not all) values are optimized at or near Stoichiometry.

The air/fuel ratio has a significant effect on engine torque and emissions. A particular problem is that nitrous oxide emissions and engine torque are greatest near the same air/fuel ratio.

A further examination of Figure 6–7 reveals the influence of the air/fuel ratio on the emission of NO_x. In this case, however, note that the relative maximum which occurs in NO_x emissions is near the air/fuel ratio where torque is greatest. *This characteristic of the engine causes some rather challenging problems in attempting to control exhaust emission while preserving vehicle performance.*

Effect of Spark Timing on Performance

Figure 6–8 is a typical pressure-volume diagram for a four-stroke engine. Top dead center (TDC) is at B, and bottom dead center (BDC) is at A. The stroke from A to B is the compression stroke; B to C is the power stroke; C to D is the exhaust stroke, and D to A is the intake stroke. The valve openings and closures are defined by points 1 to 4. Spark occurs at 5 and the flame extinguishes at 6.

Spark timing also has a major effect on emissions and engine performance. Maximum engine torque occurs at MBT.

Spark advance is the time before TDC when the spark is initiated. It is usually expressed in number of degrees of crankshaft rotation relative to TDC. *Figure 6–9* reveals the influence of spark timing upon brake specific exhaust emissions with constant speed and constant air/fuel ratio. Note that both NO_x and HC generally increase with increased advance of spark timing. BSFC and torque are also strongly influenced by timing. *Figure 6–9* shows that maximum torque occurs at a particular advanced timing referred to as minimum advance for best timing (MBT).

Effect of Exhaust Gas Recirculation on Performance

Exhaust gas recirculation greatly reduces nitrous oxide emissions.

Up to this point in the discussion, only the traditional calibration parameters of the engine (air/fuel and spark timing) have been considered. However, by adding another calibration parameter, the undesirable exhaust gas emission of NO_x can be significantly reduced while maintaining a relatively high level of torque. This new parameter is exhaust gas

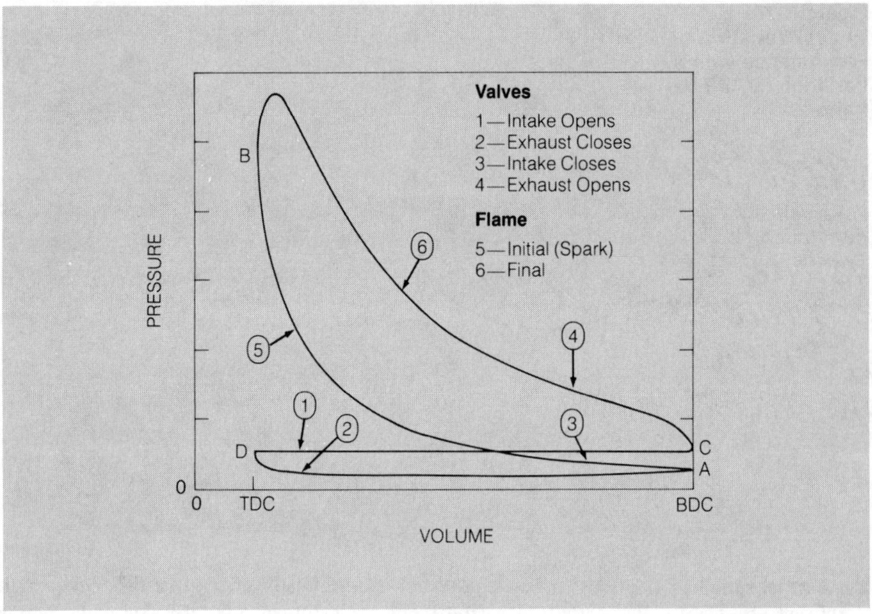

Figure 6-8. Typical Pressure-Volume Diagram for a Four-Stroke Gasoline Engine

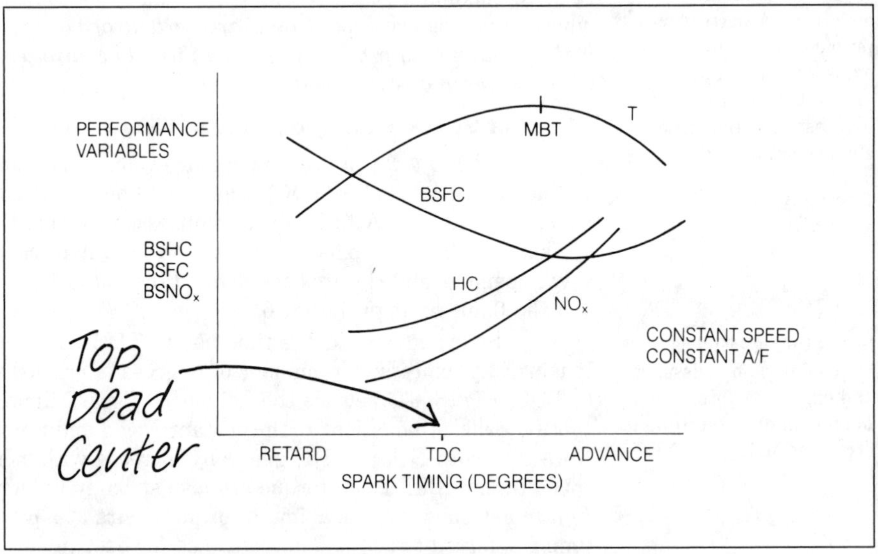

Figure 6-9. Typical Variation of Performance with Spark Timing

recirculation (EGR) and consists of recirculating a precisely controlled amount of exhaust gas into the intake. *Figure 6-4* shows that exhaust gas recirculation is a major subsystem of the overall control system. Its influence upon emissions is shown in *Figures 6-10* and *6-11* as a function of the percentage of exhaust gas in the intake. *Figure 6-10* shows the dramatic reduction in NO_x emission when plotted against air/fuel ratio, and

Figure 6–11 shows the effect on performance variables as the percent of EGR is increased. Note that the emission rate of NO_x is most strongly influenced by EGR and decreases as the percentage of EGR increases. The HC emission rate increases with increasing EGR; however, for relatively low EGR percentages, the HC rate changes only slightly.

Figure 6-10. NO_x Emission as a Function of EGR at Various Air/Fuel Ratios

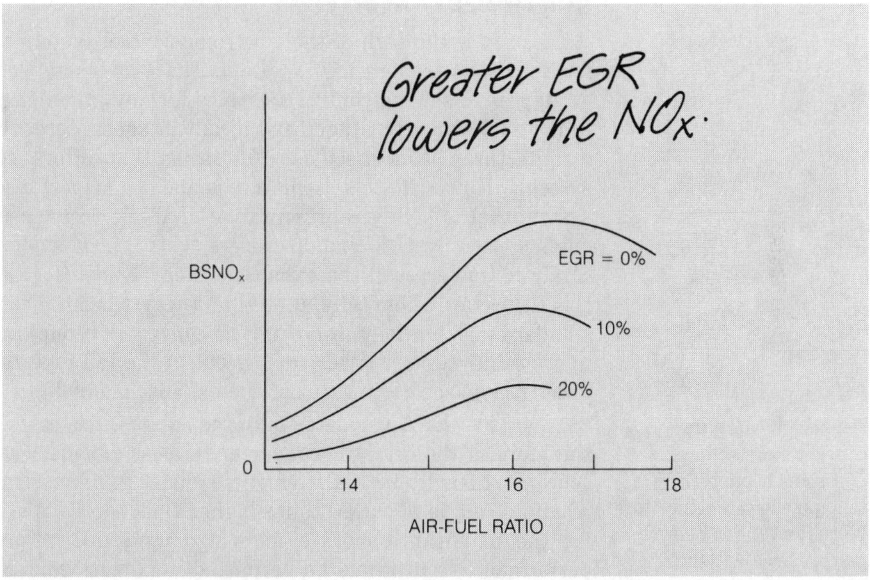

Figure 6-11. Typical Variation of Engine Performance with EGR

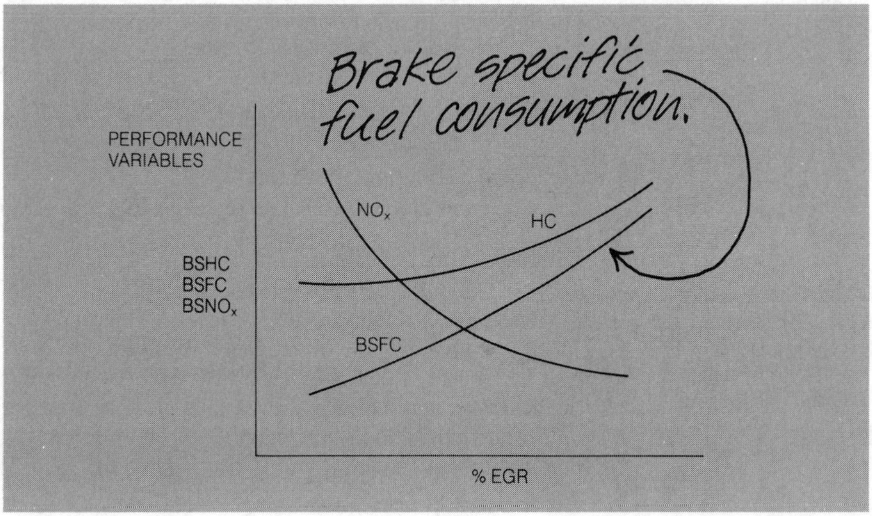

The mechanism by which EGR affects NO_x production is related to the peak combustion temperature. Roughly speaking, the NO_x generation rate increases with increasing peak combustion temperature if all other variables remain fixed. Increasing EGR tends to lower this temperature; therefore, it tends to lower NO_x generation.

CONTROL STRATEGY

It is the task of the electronic control system to set the calibration for each engine operating condition. There are many sets of possible control strategies to set the control variables for any given engine, and each tends to have its own advantages and disadvantages. Moreover, each automobile manufacturer has a specific configuration that differs from competitive systems. However, this discussion is about a typical electronic control system that is highly representative of all electronic control systems for engines used by U.S. manufacturers. This typical system is one that has a catalytic converter in the exhaust system. Exhaust gases passed through this device are chemically altered in a way which helps meet EPA standards. Essentially, the catalytic converter reduces the concentration of undesirable exhaust gases coming out of the tail pipe relative to engine-out gases (the gases coming out of the exhaust manifold).

The use of catalytic converters to reduce emissions leaving the tailpipe allows engines to be calibrated for better performance without violating emission regulations.

The EPA regulates only the exhaust gases that leave the tail pipe; therefore, if the catalytic converter reduces exhaust gas emission concentrations by 90%, the engine exhaust gas emissions at the exhaust manifold can be about 10 times higher than the EPA requirements. This has the significant benefit of allowing engine calibration to be set for better performance than would be permitted if exhaust emissions in the engine exhaust manifold had to satisfy EPA regulations. This is the type of system that is chosen for the typical electronic engine control system.

Several types of catalytic converters are available for use on an automobile. The desirable functions of a catalytic converter include:

a. oxidation of hydrocarbon emissions to carbon dioxide (CO_2) and water (H_2O)
b. oxidation of CO to CO_2
c. reduction of NO_x to nitrogen (N_2) and oxygen (O_2).

Oxidizing Catalytic Converter

The oxidizing catalytic converter increases the rate of oxidation of HC and CO to further reduce HC and CO emissions.

The oxidizing catalytic converter has been one of the most significant devices for controlling exhaust emissions since the era of emission control began. An oxidizing catalytic converter is shown in *Figure 6-12*. The purpose of the oxidizing catalyst (OC) is to increase the rate of chemical reaction, which initially takes place in the cylinder as the compressed air/fuel mixture burns, toward an exhaust gas that has a complete oxidation of HC and CO to H_2O and CO_2.

Figure 6-12. Oxidizing Catalytic Converter

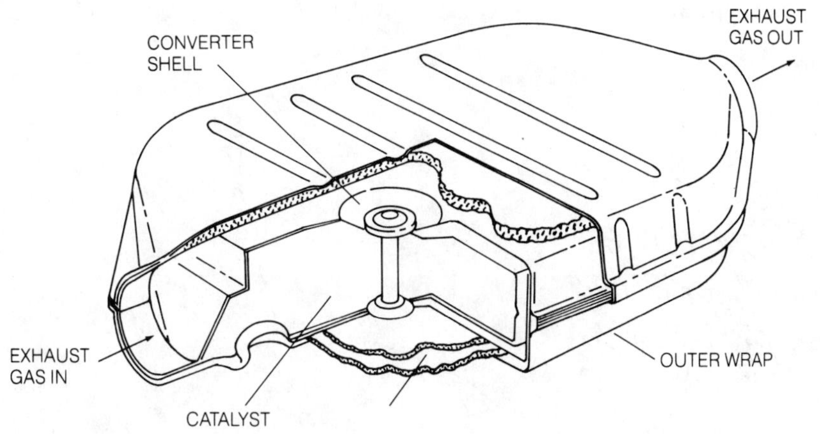

The extra oxygen required for this oxidation is often supplied by adding air to the exhaust stream from an engine driven air pump. This air, called secondary air, is normally introduced into the exhaust manifold.

The most significant measure of the performance of the OC is its conversion efficiency, n_c.

$$n_c = \frac{(M_i - M_o)}{M_i}$$

where

M_i = mass air flow rate of gas into converter,
M_o = mass flow rate of gas leaving converter which has been oxidized.

The conversion efficiency of the OC depends upon its temperature. *Figure 6-13* shows the conversion efficiency of a typical OC for both HC and CO as functions of temperature. Above about 300°C, the efficiency approaches 98% to 99% for CO and more than 95% for HC.

The Three-Way Catalyst

The three-way catalyst uses a specific chemical design to reduce all three major emissions (HC, CO, and NO_x) by approximately 90%.

Another catalytic converter configuration which is extremely important for modern emission control systems is called the three-way catalyst (TWC). It uses a specific catalyst formulation containing platinum, palladium, and rhodium to reduce NO_x and oxidize HC and CO all at the same time. It is called three way because it simultaneously reduces the concentration of all three major undesirable exhaust gases by about 90%.

Figure 6-13.
Oxidizing Catalyst Conversion Efficiency Versus Temperature

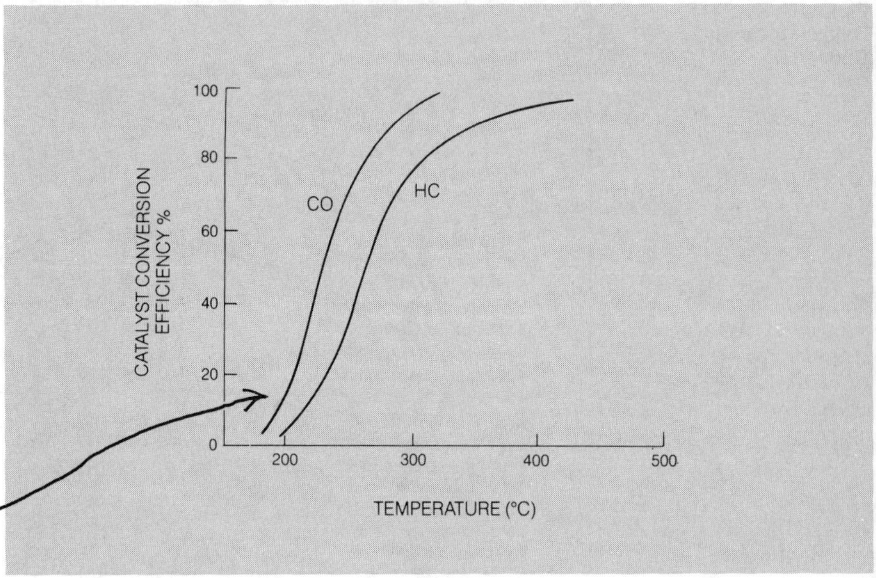

Note loss of efficiency at low operating temperatures.

The conversion efficiency of the TWC for the three exhaust gases depends mostly upon air/fuel ratio. Unfortunately, the air/fuel ratio for which NO_x conversion efficiency is highest corresponds to a very low conversion efficiency for HC and CO and vice versa. However, as shown in *Figure 6-14*, there is a very narrow range of air/fuel ratio (called the window) in which an acceptable compromise exists between NO_x and HC/CO conversion efficiencies. The conversion efficiencies within this window are sufficiently high to meet the very stringent EPA requirements established so far.

Figure 6-14.
Conversion Efficiency of TWC

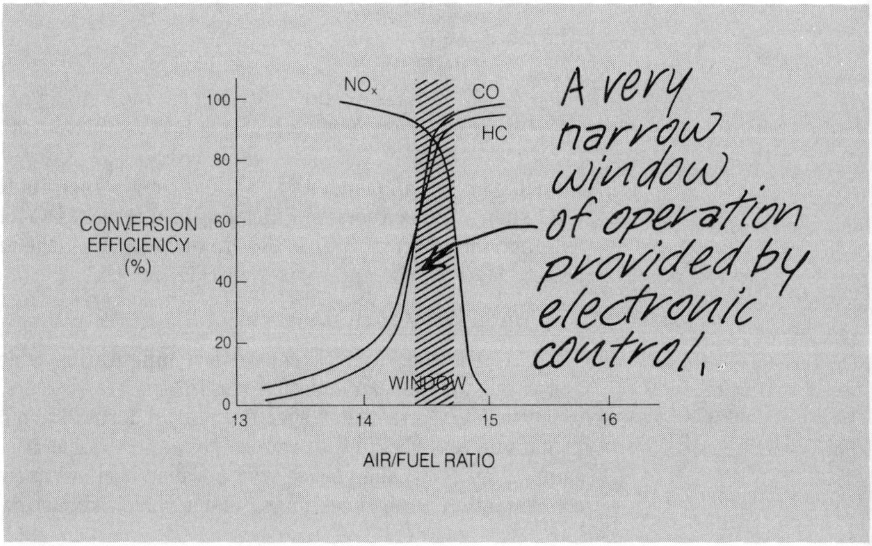

Note that this window is only about 0.1 air/fuel ratio wide (± 0.05 air/fuel ratio) and is centered at stoichiometry. Recall that stoichiometry is the air/fuel ratio that would result in complete oxidation of all carbon and hydrogen in the fuel if burning in the cylinder were perfect. For gasoline, stoichiometry corresponds to an air/fuel ratio of 14.7. This ratio and the concept of stoichiometry is extremely important in an electronic fuel controller. In fact, the primary function of most modern electronic fuel control systems is to maintain average air/fuel ratio at stoichiometry.

The three-way catalyst operates at peak efficiency when the air/fuel ratio is at or very near stoichiometry. An electronic fuel control system is required to maintain the required air/fuel ratio.

Control of average air/fuel ratio to the tolerances of the TWC window (for 50,000 miles) is beyond the capabilities of a conventional carburetor. However, as was mentioned previously, the electronic fuel control system can meet such a performance requirement. It is the primary function of the electronic engine control system. The operation of the three-way catalytic converter is adversely affected by lead. Thus, in automobiles using any catalyst, it is necessary to use lead-free fuel.

ELECTRONIC FUEL CONTROL SYSTEM

For an understanding of the configuration of an electronic fuel control system, refer to *Figure 6-15*. Remember that an electronic fuel control system requires sensors to measure the state of the engine. It also requires one or more actuators to do the actual controlling. The sensors measure exhaust gas oxygen, manifold absolute pressure, crankshaft angular position and speed, inlet air, and coolant temperatures. Actuators are energized to control the air/fuel ratio as explained in Chapter 5.

Figure 6-15. Simplified Block Diagram of Fuel Control System

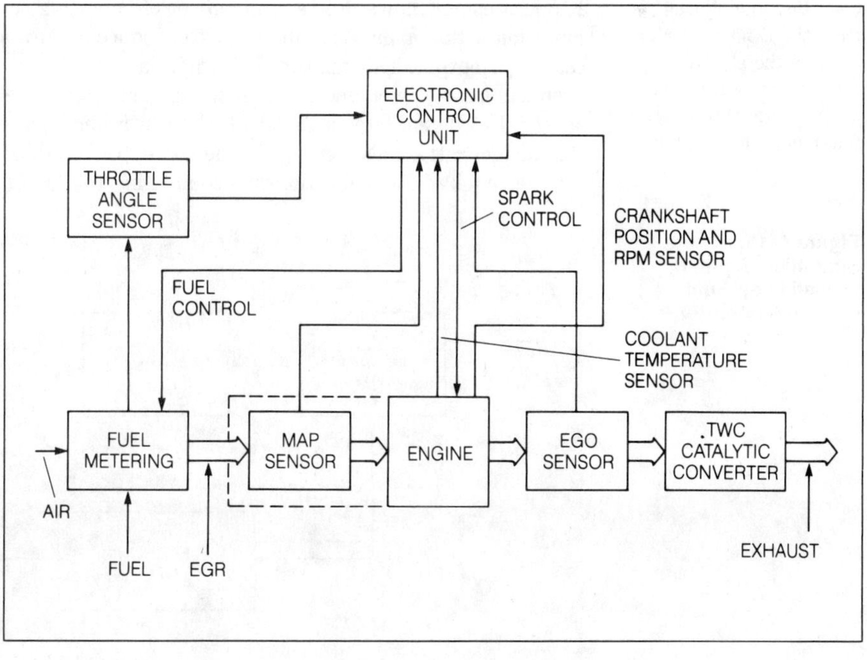

Depending on conditions, an electronic fuel system can operate in open-loop or closed-loop mode. In either mode, exhaust emissions satisfy government limits if the air/fuel ratio is held very near stoichiometry.

The primary purpose of this control system is to maintain the air/fuel ratio at or near stoichiometry. This is accomplished in two modes (during normal operation)—open loop and closed loop. The concepts of these modes are discussed in Chapter 2. Recall that an error signal is fed back from output to input in the closed-loop mode. The electronic fuel control system can operate closed loop only when certain conditions are satisfied. The open-loop mode is employed whenever these conditions are not satisfied. However, for either mode, the exhaust emissions will satisfy EPA limits if the average air/fuel ratio is held within the tolerance limits of ± 0.05 of stoichiometry.

In addition to the open-loop and closed-loop control modes, a practical fuel control system has other operating modes depending on engine conditions. These handle such conditions as starting, rapid acceleration or heavy load, sudden deceleration, idling, etc. These are covered in more detail in the next chapter.

Closed-Loop Control

The step-by-step events after engine start begin with the system operating in the open-loop mode. After a set of operating conditions are satisfied, the system is converted to closed-loop operation. However, it is easier to understand the total system operation by beginning the discussion with an explanation of closed-loop operation. The series of steps that occur in time from engine start are discussed in Chapter 7.

In the closed-loop mode of operation, the signals from the EGO sensor are used by the electronic controller to adjust the air/fuel ratio through the fuel metering actuator.

Figure 6-16 is a block diagram of a closed-loop fuel control system. It operates as follows. For any given set of operating conditions, the fuel metering actuator provides fuel flow to produce an air/fuel ratio set by the controller output. This mixture is burned in the cylinder and the combustion products leave the engine through the exhaust pipe. The exhaust gas oxygen sensor (EGO) generates a signal for the controller input that depends upon the air/fuel ratio. This signal tells the controller to adjust the fuel flow rate for the required air/fuel ratio, thus completing the loop.

Figure 6-16. Simplified Typical Closed-Loop Fuel Control System

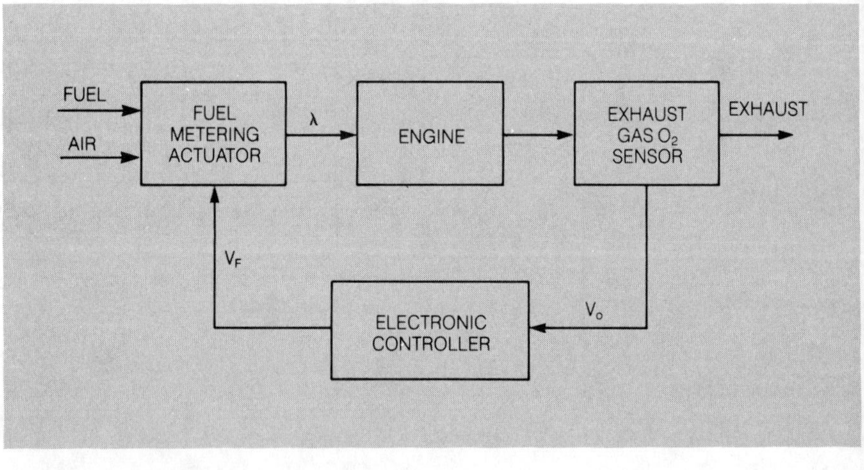

One control scheme which has been used in practice results in the air/fuel ratio cycling around the desired set point of stoichiometry. Recall from Chapter 2 that this type of control is provided by a limit-cycle controller (e.g., typical furnace controller). The important parameters for this type of control include the amplitude and frequency of excursion away from the desired stoichiometric set point. Fortunately, the engine's mechanical characteristics are such that only the time average air/fuel ratio determines its performance. The variation in air/fuel ratio during the limit cycle operation is so rapid that it has no effect upon engine performance or emissions, provided that the average air/fuel ratio remains at stoichiometry.

Fuel Metering

As shown in *Figure 6-16*, the closed-loop fuel control is based upon two critical components—the fuel metering actuator and the exhaust gas oxygen sensor. The two classes of fuel metering actuators, the electronic carburetor and the throttle body fuel injector, were discussed in Chapter 5. The electronic carburetor is essentially a conventional carburetor that has been modified to permit electrical control of the metering rods.

The actuators commonly used for electronic control of fuel metering are the throttle body fuel injector and the electronic carburetor.

The TBFI typically consists of one or two solenoid-operated fuel injectors that are mounted in a specially designed housing on the intake manifold. This class of TBFI functions similarly to a carburetor in that fuel is injected into and atomized by the moving air stream which flows into the intake manifold. (Recall that fuel is pulled from the conventional carburetor by the air stream moving through the venturi.) The calibration of the TBFI is controlled by the electronic control system.

Exhaust Gas Oxygen Concentration

The EGO sensor is used to determine the air/fuel ratio.

The second critical component, the EGO sensor, is explained also in Chapter 5. Recall that the EGO generates an output signal that depends upon the amount of oxygen in the exhaust. This oxygen level, in turn, depends upon the air/fuel ratio entering the engine. The amount of oxygen is relatively low for rich mixtures and relatively high for lean mixtures. An equivalence ratio λ (lambda) commonly used by automotive engineers is:

$$\lambda = \frac{\text{(air/fuel)}}{\text{(air/fuel at stoichiometry)}}$$

Recall that $\lambda = 1$ corresponds to stoichiometry, that $\lambda > 1$ corresponds to a lean mixture with an air/fuel ratio greater than stoichiometry, and that $\lambda < 1$ corresponds to a rich mixture where the air/fuel ratio is less than stoichiometry. (The EGO sensor is sometimes called a lambda sensor.)

Lambda is used in the block diagram of *Figure 6-16* to represent the equivalence ratio at the intake manifold. The exhaust gas oxygen concentration determines the EGO output V_o. The EGO output voltage switches (as discussed in Chapter 5) abruptly between the lean and the rich levels as the air/fuel ratio crosses stoichiometry.

In a closed-loop system, the time delay between sensing a deviation and the action to correct for the deviation must be compensated for in system design.

The operation of the control system using EGO output V_o of *Figure 6-16* is complicated somewhat because of the time delay from the time that λ changes at the input until V_o changes at the exhaust. This time delay, t_D, is the range of 0.1 to 0.2 second, depending on engine speed. It is the time that it takes the output of the system to respond to a change at the input. The electrical signal from the EGO sensor (V_o) going into the controller produces a controller output of V_F, which energizes the fuel metering actuator.

Closed-Loop Operation

One type of engine control system operates as a limit-cycle controller where the air/fuel ratio cycles up and down about the set point of stoichiometry, as shown in *Figure 6-17*. The air/fuel ratio is either increasing or decreasing; it is never constant. The increase or decrease is determined by the EGO sensor output voltage. Whenever the EGO output voltage level indicates a lean mixture, the controller causes the air/fuel ratio to decrease, that is, to change in a direction of a rich mixture. On the other hand, whenever the EGO sensor output voltage indicates a rich mixture, the controller changes air/fuel ratio in the direction of a lean mixture.

The air/fuel ratio in a closed-loop system is always increasing or decreasing in the vicinity of stoichiometry. This is in response to the EGO sensor's output, which indicates a rich or lean fuel mixture.

The simplified waveforms of V_F, λ, and V_o are shown in *Figure 6-17*. These waveforms will be used to understand the operation of the closed-loop fuel control system. The time delay t_D is used as the major division of time for the time axis in *Figure 6-17*.

Consider V_F, the output of the electronic controller. In the simplified example system, this waveform (*Figure 6-17a*) increases or decreases linearly with time, depending upon the EGO output. Beginning with $t = 0$, this voltage increases linearly with time to a maximum which occurs at t_D. Then the waveform decreases linearly, reaching its lowest level at $3t_D$. The cycle repeats continuously.

The fuel metering actuator is presumed to control fuel in such a way that the intake equivalence ratio λ increases in proportion to V_F, as shown in *Figure 6-17b*. If this were expressed as a transfer function mathematically, it would appear as:

$$\lambda - 1 = k_F V_F$$

where k_F is a constant for the fuel metering actuator. When the controller voltage equals zero ($V_F = 0$), λ equals one ($\lambda = 1$) and the input mixture is at stoichiometry. As V_F varies, λ varies. A positive V_F produces a lean mixture (i.e., $\lambda > 1$), and a negative V_F produces a rich mixture ($\lambda < 1$).

When the electronic controller output voltage is zero, the air/fuel ratio is at stoichiometry. In this example, a positive voltage from the controller produces a lean mixture, while a negative voltage produces a rich mixture.

The EGO sensor output begins at time t=0 and at a voltage level for a rich mixture, V_R. When the influence of the lean mixture (which takes place between t=0 and $2t_D$) reaches the EGO, it switches to V_L. This occurs at a time t_D after the lean mixture first occurs. The response of the output V_o is delayed in time from the input change by the time delay t_D.

The intake mixture is richer than stoichiometry between time $2t_D$ and $4t_D$. The effect of the rich mixture reaches the EGO at time $3t_D$ (i.e., at time t_D after the rich mixture occurs). The end of the rich mixture reaches the EGO at time $5t_D$ (t_D after the end of the input rich period at $4t_D$). This cycle repeats with a period of $4t_D$.

Figure 6-17. Simplified Waveforms in a Closed-Loop Fuel Control System

Controller output reflects changes in EGO sensor output.

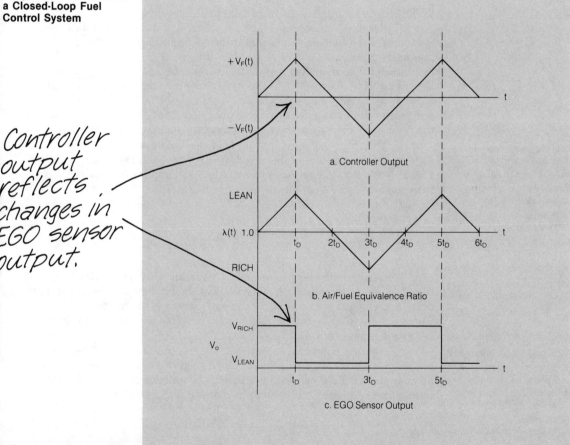

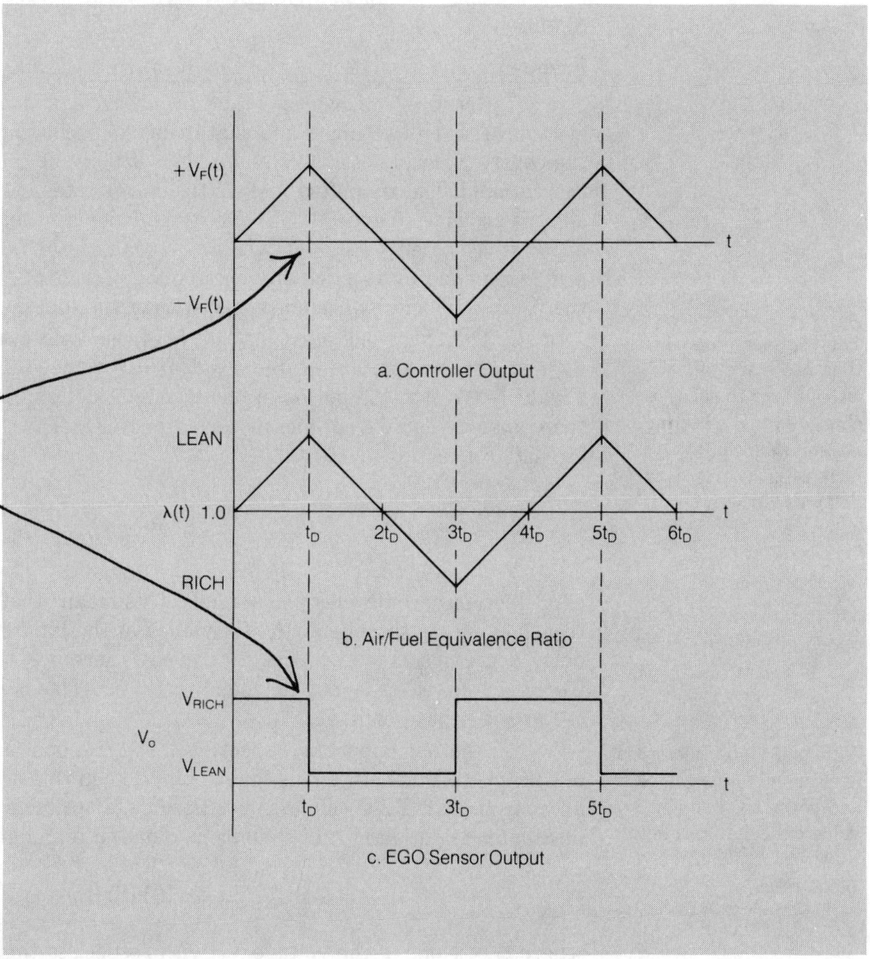

The electronic controller output waveform changes follow the EGO sensor output waveform changes. In actual practice, the changes may not be linear.

Note that the direction of the electronic controller output waveform (*Fig. 6–17a*) changes whenever the EGO sensor output (*Fig. 6–16c*) changes. The shape of the electronic controller output waveform determines the variation of λ with time. Straight line segments were used in order to simplify the explanation; however, in practice the waveform may be curved and it may not be linear with time. The controller output voltages for the two EGO sensor output states also is shown having the correct amplitude but having opposite signs. That too is for simplification because the actual controller output voltage amplitudes may not be equal. These simplifications are consistent with the simplified system block diagram, and the explanation still applies to the operation under real conditions.

Frequency and Deviation of the Fuel Controller

Recall from Chapter 2 that a limit-cycle controller controls a system between two limits and that it has an oscillatory behavior; that is, the control variable oscillates about the set point or the desired value for the variable. The simplified fuel controller operates in a limit-cycle mode and, as shown in *Figure 6–17b*, the equivalence air/fuel ratio λ oscillates about stoichiometry (i.e., average air/fuel ratio is 14.7). The two end limits are determined by the rich and lean voltage levels of the EGO sensor, by the controller, and by the characteristics of the fuel metering actuator.

The transport delay is the time necessary for the EGO sensor to sense a change in fuel metering. As engine speed increases, the transport delay decreases.

The frequency of oscillation, f_L of this limit-cycle control system is defined as the reciprocal of its period. It can be seen from the waveform in *Figure 6–17b* that the period of one complete cycle is $4t_D$ (recall that t_D is the transport delay from fuel metering to EGO). Thus, the frequency of oscillation f_L is:

$$f_L = \frac{1}{4t_D}$$

expressed in hertz (cycles per second). This means that the shorter the transport delay, the higher the frequency of the limit cycle. The transport delay decreases as engine speed increases; therefore, the limit-cycle frequency increases as engine speed increases. This is depicted in *Figure 6–18* for a typical engine.

Although the air/fuel ratio is constantly swinging up and down, the average value of deviation is held to within ± .05 of the 14.7:1 ratio.

Another important aspect of limit-cycle operation is the deviation of λ from stoichiometry. It is important to keep this deviation small because the net TWC conversion efficiency is optimum for λ = 1. The maximum deviation of λ from unity is denoted d and given by:

$$d = (k_F)\,(S)\,(t_D)$$

where S = slope of the voltage V_F with respect to time (i.e., in volt/sec.). This deviation typically corresponds to an air/fuel ratio deviation of about ±1.

It is important to realize that the air/fuel ratio oscillates between a maximum value and a minimum value. There is, however, an average value

Figure 6-18. Typical Limit-Cycle Frequency Versus RPM

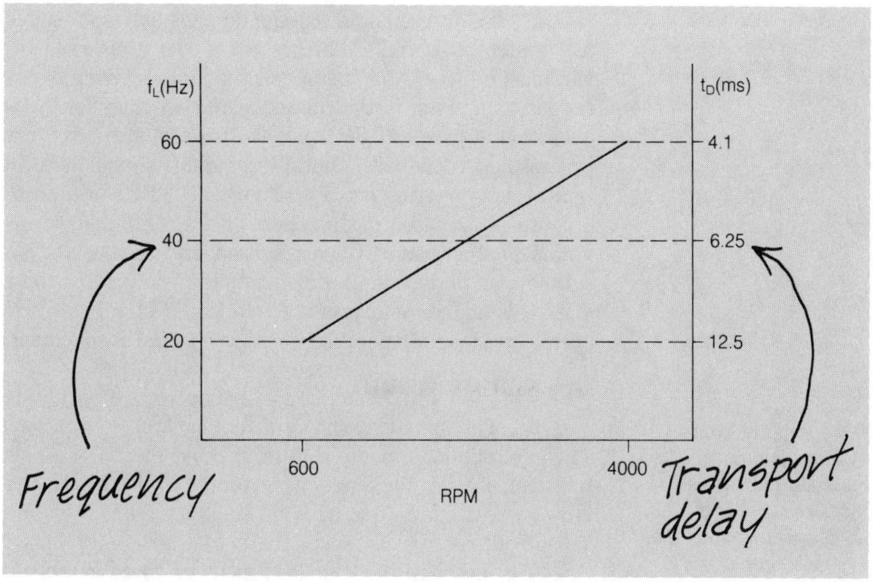

for the air/fuel ratio that is intermediate between these extremes. Although the deviation of the air/fuel ratio during this limit cycle operation is about ± 1, the *average* airfuel ratio is held to within ± 0.05 of the desired value of 14.7.

Figure 6-19 shows a typical curve of this maximum deviation versus engine speed. Note that this deviation decreases with increasing engine speed because of the corresponding decrease in t_D. The parameters of the control system are adjusted such that d at the worst case is within the required acceptable limits for the TWC used.

Figure 6-19. Typical Limit-Cycle Maximum Deviation from Set Point as Speed Varies

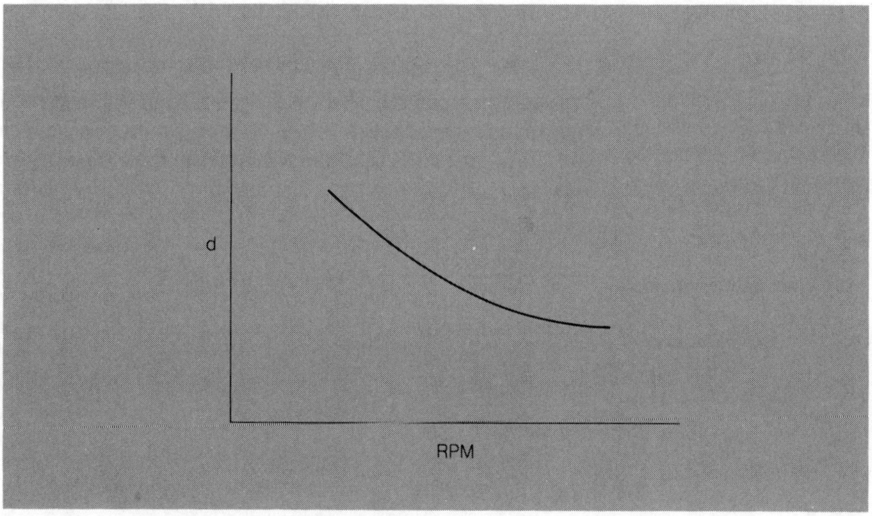

The preceding discussion applies only to a simplified idealized analog fuel control system; i.e., the system is operating with continuously changing variables between the limits, and the fuel metering is changing in an analog fashion as a result of the continuously changing V_F. In the next chapter, the operation of practical electronic fuel control systems where the main signal processing is done with digital techniques is explained. In such a system, the typical fuel metering actuator is either a TBFI or a port fuel injector, and it operates in a pulsed mode rather than a continuous analog mode. Also, variables other than EGO are sensed, and the control computer makes several calculations to determine which actuators to control and how to control them. With this understanding of a closed-loop system, it is helpful to consider the open-loop mode of operation of the simplified fuel control system.

OPEN-LOOP MODE

Open-loop fuel control systems also must maintain the air/fuel mixture at or near stoichiometry, but these systems must do it without the benefit of feedback.

The open-loop mode of fuel control must accomplish the same thing as the closed-loop mode; that is, it must maintain an air/fuel ratio very close to stoichiometry for efficient system operation with the TWC used. However, it must do it without feedback from the exhaust gas oxygen sensor output, which senses the actual air/fuel ratio.

Although the open-loop mode of operation varies somewhat from one model to the next, many features of this mode of operation are common to all models. In reading the following discussion it is important to realize that the throttle (under driver control) actually controls the flow of air into the engine. The correct fuel flow is determined by the engine control system.

Measuring Air Mass

Probably the most common open-loop fuel control system is based on a rather simple concept of measuring the air mass drawn into any cylinder. If the controller has the correct value for air mass, the correct mass of fuel to be injected for stoichiometry can be determined; that is, the ratio of air mass to fuel mass should be 14.7.

Most open-loop systems operate by estimating the amount of air taken into an engine and calculating the amount of fuel needed to maintain stoichiometry. The speed-density method is commonly used to estimate the mass flow rate of air into an engine.

A sensor for directly measuring air mass has been explained in Chapter 5. It is worthwhile to illustrate an alternate method of measuring or closely estimating the mass flow rate of air into the engine intake by measuring other quantities. It is then theoretically possible to adjust the fuel flow rate such that the ratio of the mass flow rate of air to the mass flow rate of fuel is at stoichiometry. Many of the production fuel control systems operate essentially on this principle in the open-loop mode.

Speed-Density Method

One common method of estimating mass flow rate of air into the engine is known as the speed-density method. This is based upon the concept of mass density as applied to air. As shown in *Figure 6–20a*, for a given volume of air at a temperature T and with a mass of M_a, the density, d_a, of a sample of air occupying volume V is given by:

$$d_a = \frac{M_a}{V}$$

If M_a is in kg and V is in cubic cm, d_a is in kg per cubic cm. This assumes a constant pressure to keep the air in volume V. The mass of air in a given volume depends on the temperature; therefore, the density of air depends upon its temperature. (Cooler air is more dense than relatively warmer air.) Tables of the density of air measured versus temperature are available and can be stored in the system as lookup tables (lookup tables are discussed in Chapters 4 and 7).

Figure 6-20. Volume Flow Rate

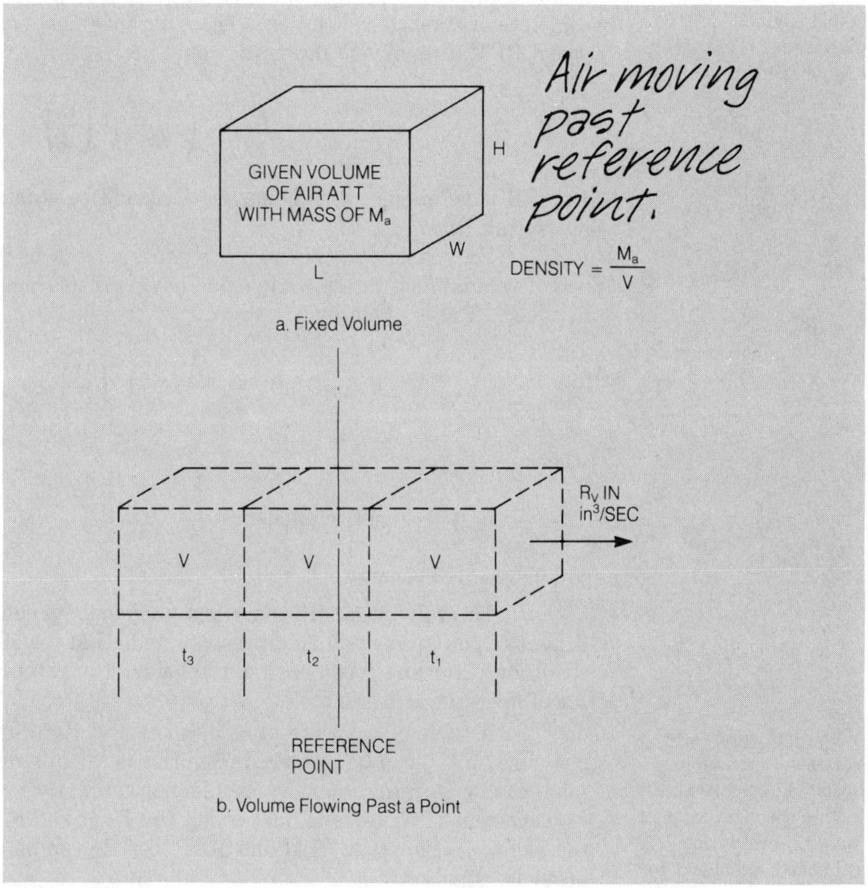

A given volume of air moving past a fixed reference point during a specific period of time is the volume flow rate.

This notion can be extended to a moving stream of air flowing through the intake of an engine, as shown in *Figure 6-20b*. V, the given volume, flows by a reference point. It takes a certain period of time, t_1, for this volume of air to flow past a given point. Other similar volumes take the same amount of time. Therefore, the volume moving in a set time is a volume flow rate. If the volume flow rate in cubic cm per second is R_V, the mass flow rate R_M in kg per second is given by the product of density and volume flow rate:

$$R_M = R_V d_a$$

A close estimate of volume flow rate can be made by considering actual engine displacement and given engine speeds.

A relatively close estimate of R_V can be made using inexpensive sensors. The engine acts like an air pump during intake. If it were a perfect pump, it would draw in a volume of air equal to its displacement, D, for each two complete crankshaft revolutions. Then, for this ideal engine running at a speed RPM, the volume flow rate would be:

$$R_V = \left(\frac{RPM}{60}\right)\left(\frac{D}{2}\right)$$

For this ideal engine, with D known, R_V could be obtained simply by measuring RPM.

Unfortunately, the engine is not a perfect air pump. In fact, the actual volume flow rate for an engine having displacement D and running at speed RPM is given by:

$$R_V = \left(\frac{RPM}{60}\right)\left(\frac{D}{2}\right) n_v$$

where

n_v = volumetric efficiency

Volumetric Efficiency

The volumetric efficiency is a number between 0 and 1 that depends upon intake manifold pressure and RPM for all engine operating conditions. For any given engine, the value of n_v can be measured for any set of operating conditions.

Volumetric efficiency varies with manifold absolute pressure and engine speed. A table of values representing volumetric efficiency for given speeds and MAP values can be stored in memory as a lookup table.

A table of values of n_v as a function of RPM and intake manifold pressure (MAP) can be prepared from this data. In a digital system, the table can be stored in memory as a lookup table. By knowing the displacement of the engine, measuring the RPM and MAP, and looking up the value of n_v for that RPM and MAP, the R_V can be computed using the previous equation.

Including EGR

Calculating R_V is relatively easy for a computer, but another factor must be taken into account. Exhaust gas recirculation requires that a certain portion of the charge into the cylinders be exhaust gas. Because of this, a portion of the displacement, D, is exhaust gas; therefore, the volume flow rate of EGR must be known. A valve-positioning sensor in the EGR valve can be calibrated to provide the flow rate.

Exhaust gas recirculation also must be considered when calculating volume flow rate. The true volume flow rate of air is calculated by subtracting the volume flow rate of EGR from the total volume flow rate.

From this information, the volume flow rate of air, R_a, can be determined by subtracting the volume flow rate of EGR (i.e., R_{EGR}) from R_V. The total cylinder air charge flow rate is given as follows:

$$R_a = R_V - R_{EGR}$$

Substituting the equation for R_V. the volume flow rate of air is:

$$R_a = \left[\left(\frac{RPM}{60} \right) \left(\frac{D}{2} \right) n_v \right] - R_{EGR}$$

Knowing R_a and the density d_a gives the mass flow rate of air R_{am} as follows:

$$R_{am} = R_a d_a$$

Knowing R_{am}, the stoichiometric mass flow rate for the fuel R_{fm} can be calculated from

$$R_{fm} = \frac{R_{am}}{14.7}$$

Analog systems continuously adjust the fuel metering actuator to set the fuel flow rate to maintain stoichiometry for the value of the volume flow rate of air. Digital systems perform the adjustment between 100 and 300 times each second.

It is the function of the fuel metering actuator to set the fuel mass flow rate at this desired value based upon the value of R_a. The control system continuously calculates R_{am} from R_a and d_a at the temperature involved, and it generates an output electrical signal to operate the fuel metering actuator to produce a stoichiometric mass fuel flow rate. For a practical engine control system, it completes such a measurement, computation, and control signal generation at least once for each cylinder firing.

ELECTRONIC IGNITION

The engine ignition system exists solely to provide an electric spark to ignite the mixture in the cylinder. In the first chapter the basics of a conventional, purely electrical ignition system were discussed. The ignition system in most modern automobiles is electronic as opposed to this conventional system.

Electronic ignition can operate as an independent system, or as a function of an integrated engine control system.

Electronic ignition has a relatively long history compared, for example, with the fuel control system. It was one of the first nonentertainment electronic systems on the automobile. Electronic ignition can either be a separate system, independent of the engine control system, or it can be incorporated as a secondary function of the engine control system.

Separate System

As a separate system, the electronic ignition system is essentially an improvement of the conventional system. One of the major differences is the replacement of the breaker points with an electronic circuit (Chapter 5). An ignition timing sensor "measures" the engine angular position, in order to calculate the position at which the spark is to occur.

Ignition Trigger Pulse

One kind of separate electronic ignition system uses a magnetic position sensor to determine timing of the spark. The pickup coil produces a high control voltage each time one of the cogs on the rotating ferromagnetic element passes by.

The sensor generates a pulse that triggers the ignition electronic circuit that in turn drives the coil primary. This circuit, when so triggered, switches off the current in the coil primary, thereby initiating the spark.

The concept of an engine position sensor used as an ignition timing sensor was introduced in Chapter 5. Another more detailed example is shown in *Figure 6–21*. Here a permanent magnet couples to a ferromagnetic element which is mounted on the distributor shaft and rotates with it. As this element rotates, the strength of the magnetic field varies, being largest when the air gap is smallest. The time-varying magnetic field induces a voltage in the coil that is proportional to the rate of change of the magnetic field, and has a waveform as illustrated in *Figure 6–22*. Each time one of the cogs on the ferromagnetic wheel passes under the coil axis, one of the sawtooth-shaped pulses is generated. This wheel has one cog for each cylinder, and the voltage pulses provide a timing pulse for calculating the spark time for the corresponding cylinder. In a sense, the rotary wheel plays a role similar to that of the cam in a conventional distributor.

Distributor

The pickup coil output is amplified by a control circuit, and the amplified and shaped signal controls an electronic switch. The switch controls current flow in the ignition coil circuit to generate a high voltage for the spark.

The remainder of the electronic ignition system is illustrated in *Figure 6–23* in block diagram form. The sensor output operates an ignition circuit (an actual circuit is shown in *Figure 5–39*) that generates a pulse at the correct time for ignition. This impulse is amplified and triggers a switching amplifier, causing it to stop conducting. This is analogous to opening the breaker points in a conventional ignition system. The remaining action of this system is identical to the conventional system. When the primary of the coil is suddenly open circuited, the collapsing magnetic field generates a high voltage in the coil secondary. As explained in Chapter 1, this secondary voltage is connected to the rotor of the distributor. The distributor shaft is connected by gears to the camshaft and rotates synchronously with the crankshaft. The distributor connects the coil high voltage alternately to the appropriate spark plug wire.

In many cases, the peak coil secondary voltage is 30,000 to 35,000 volts in order to ignite the air/fuel mixture under the engine operating conditions that must prevail to control the emissions and fuel economy and still allow for spark plug and distributor variations.

Figure 6-21. Magnetic Position Sensor

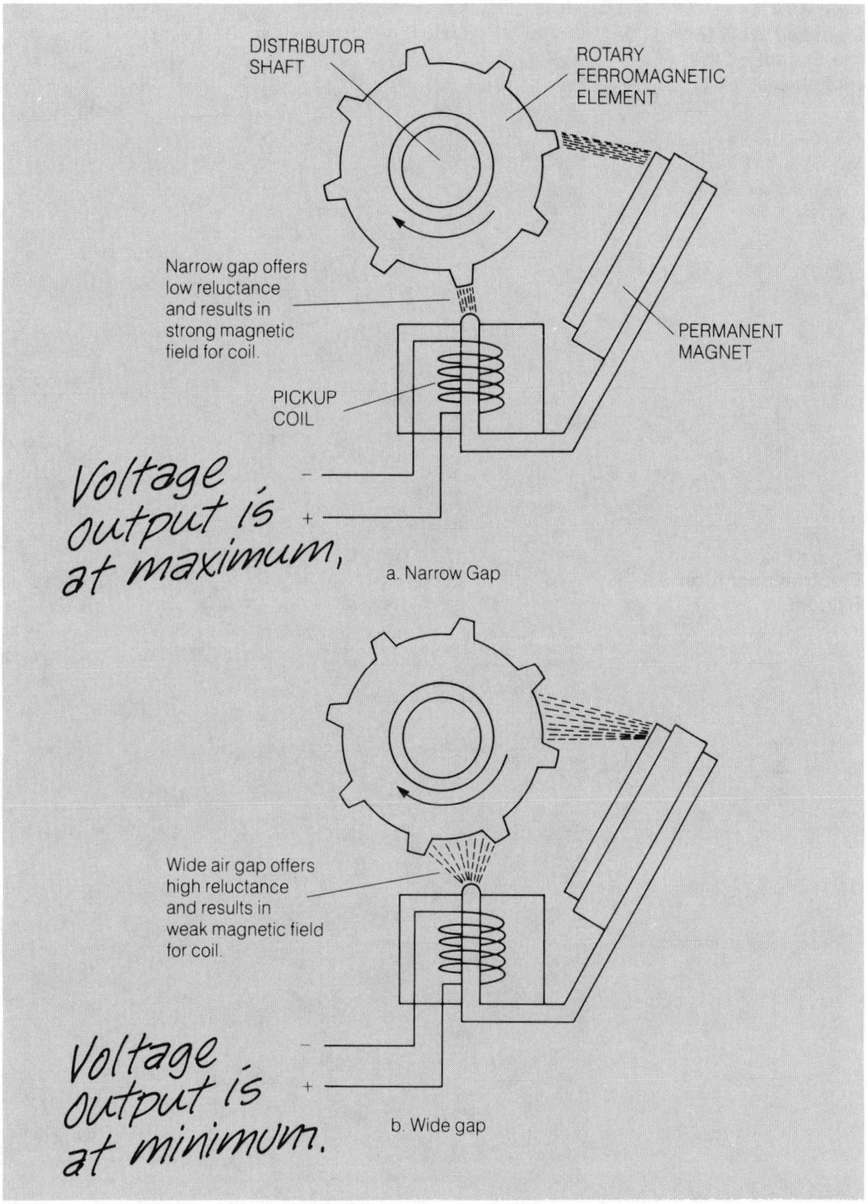
DISTRIBUTOR SHAFT
ROTARY FERROMAGNETIC ELEMENT
Narrow gap offers low reluctance and results in strong magnetic field for coil.
PERMANENT MAGNET
PICKUP COIL
−
+
Voltage output is at maximum,
a. Narrow Gap
Wide air gap offers high reluctance and results in weak magnetic field for coil.
−
+
Voltage output is at minimum.
b. Wide gap

Figure 6-22. Idealized Waveform at the Output of the Pickup Coil

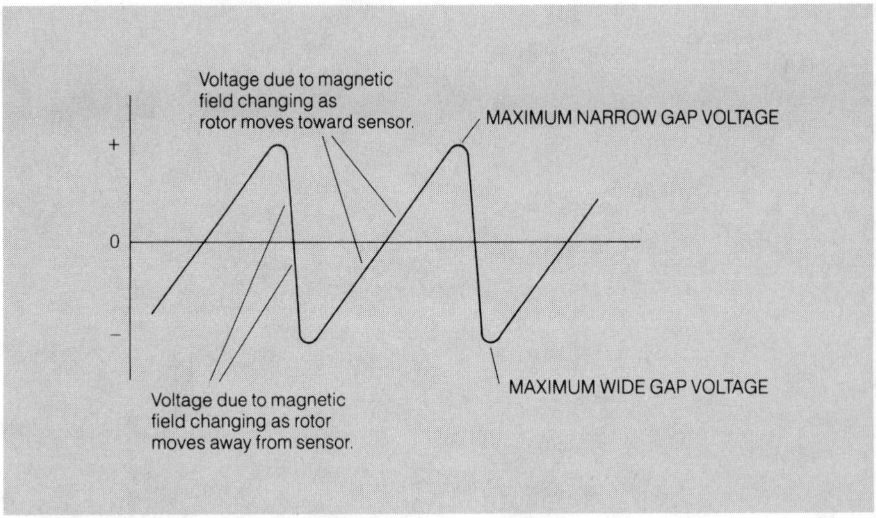

Figure 6-23. Electronic Ignition System

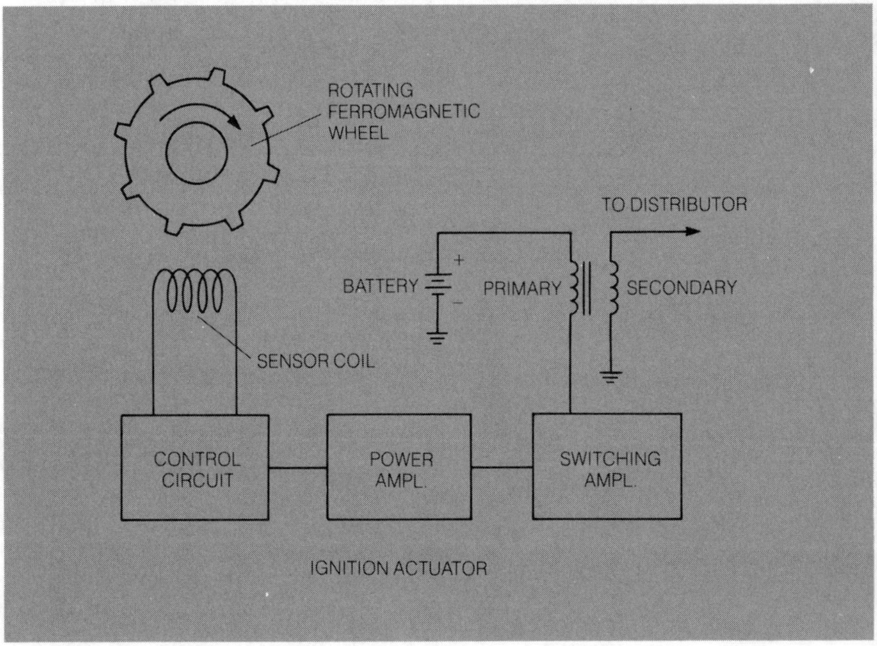

Integrated System

In a modern digital ignition system, spark advance is computed from MAP and RPM measurements.

In this and previous chapters, it is shown that the timing of the spark relative to the time the piston reaches TDC is critical, and that the spark advance markedly affects engine exhaust emissions and performance. In many of the earliest electronic ignition systems, spark advance control for changes in engine load and speed was achieved in much the same way as in a conventional system. That is, manifold vacuum and centrifugal force were employed to move the sensor coil relative to the ferromagnetic wheel by rotating a plate in the distributor upon which the sensor coil was mounted.

With a digital system controller, the spark advance can be controlled electronically. Sensors that measure MAP and engine RPM provide the inputs to the computer which calculates the spark advance needed. Then the computer generates the pulse to drive the ignition actuator circuit, or to open the coil primary itself. Such a system is discussed in the next chapter.

Quiz for Chapter 6

1. What is the primary motivation for engine controls?
   a. consumer demand for precise controls
   b. automotive industry's desire to innovate
   c. government regulations concerning emissions and fuel economy
2. What is the primary purpose of fuel control?
   a. to minimize fuel economy
   b. to eliminate exhaust emissions
   c. to optimize catalytic converter efficiency
   d. to maximize engine or torque
3. What is the primary purpose of spark timing controls?
   a. to maximize fuel economy
   b. to minimize exhaust emissions
   c. to optimize catalytic converter efficiency
   d. to optimize some aspect of engine performance (e.g., torque)
4. What does exhaust gas recirculation do?
   a. improve fuel economy
   b. reduce NO_x emission
   c. increase engine torque
   d. provide air for the catalytic converter
5. What does secondary air do?
   a. dilute the air fuel ratio
   b. help oxidize HC and CO in the exhaust manifold
   c. help oxidize NO_x and CO in the catalytic converter
   d. help reduce the production of NO_x
6. What is air fuel ratio?
   a. the mass of air in a cylinder divided by the mass of fuel
   b. the volume of air in a cylinder divided by the volume of fuel
   c. the ratio of the mass of HC to mass of NO_x
7. What electronic device is used in engine controls?
   a. AM radio
   b. catalytic converter
   c. microcomputer
8. What air/fuel ratio is desired for a 3-way catalytic converter?
   a. 12:1
   b. 17:1
   c. 14.7:1
   d. none of the above
9. What is the desired operation of a catalytic converter on HC emissions?
   a. oxidation to H_2O and CO_2
   b. reduction to H and C
   c. reaction with NO_x
   d. none of the above
10. What is the desired operation of a catalytic converter on NO_x emissions?
    a. reaction with HC
    b. oxidation to N_2 and O_2
    c. reduction to N_2 and O_2
    d. none of the above
11. What is stoichiometry?
    a. a very lean air/fuel ratio
    b. a very rich air/fuel ratio
    c. an air/fuel ratio for which complete combustion is theoretically possible
    d. none of the above

12. How is CO emission affected by air/fuel ratio?
    a. it generally decreases with increasing air/fuel ratio
    b. it increases monotonically with air/fuel ratio
    c. it is unaffected by air/fuel ratio
    d. none of the above

13. What is MBT?
    a. mean before top-center
    b. miles per brake torque
    c. mean spark advance for best torque
    d. none of the above

14. What is the function of electronic fuel control in a vehicle having a 3-way catalyst?
    a. to maximize brake specific fuel consumption
    b. to maintain the average air/fuel ratio at stoichiometry
    c. to always keep the air/fuel ratio within ± 0.05 of stoichiometry
    d. to minimize NO_x emissions

15. What is the fuel flow rate for an electronic fuel control system for a vehicle having a 3-way catalyst?
    a. $R_{fm} = R_{am}/14.7$
    b. $R_a/14.7$
    c. $R_v - R_{EGR}/14.7$
    d. none of the above

16. What is one difference between a conventional and an electronic ignition system?
    a. there are no differences
    b. the electronic system produces a lower coil secondary voltage
    c. the coil is eliminated in the electronic system
    d. distributor points are replaced by a crankshaft position sensor and electronic circuit

17. What engine quantities are measured to determine spark advance for an electronic ignition system?
    a. manifold pressure and RPM
    b. coolant temperature and mass air flow
    c. manifold position and crankshaft position
    d. none of the above

18. In an electronic fuel control system, what causes the time delay between fuel metering and the EGO sensor response?
    a. dynamic response of the electronics
    b. transport time of the air and fuel through the engine
    c. limit cycle theory
    d. none of the above

19. Brake power of an engine is:
    a. the power required to decelerate the car
    b. an electronic system for stopping the car
    c. the difference between indicated power and power losses in the engine
    d. none of the above

20. What is engine calibration?
    a. adjustment of air/fuel ratio, spark timing, and EGR
    b. instrumentation parameter setting
    c. electronic control system parameters
    d. none of the above

Digital Engine Control System

ABOUT THIS CHAPTER

The preceding chapter discussed some of the fundamental issues involved in electronic engine control. This chapter explores some practical digital control systems. There is, of course, considerable variation in the configuration and control concept from one manufacturer to another. However this chapter describes representative control systems that are not necessarily based upon the system of any given manufacturer, thereby giving the reader an understanding of the configuration and operating principles of a generic representative system. As such, the systems in this discussion are a compilation of the features used by several manufacturers. Although such control is theoretically possible using analog technology, virtually all systems in production use digital techniques; consequently, this chapter discusses only digital engine control. This chapter also discusses secondary functions (including management of secondary air that must be provided to the catalytic converter and evaporative emission control) which have not been discussed before.

DIGITAL ENGINE CONTROL FEATURES

Recall from the previous chapter that the primary purpose of the electronic engine control system is to regulate the mixture (i.e., fuel/air), the ignition timing, and EGR. Virtually all major manufacturers of cars sold in the United States (both foreign and domestic) use the three-way catalyst for meeting exhaust emission constraints. For such cars, the air/fuel is held as closely as possible to stoichiometric value of about 14.7. Ignition timing and EGR are controlled to optimize performance or fuel economy.

Figure 7-1 illustrates the primary components of an electronic engine control system. The controller includes a special purpose digital computer that computes the correct fuel flow rate and ignition timing from the data it receives from the sensors and from the driver (throttle) input. The actual fuel metering system can be an electronic carburetor, throttle body fuel injector system, or a set of individual fuel injectors that inject fuel into the port near each cylinder. The ignition system may include a distributor as described in Chapter 1, or it may involve a set of coils for firing individual spark plugs without requiring a distributor, as explained later in this chapter.

Figure 7-1.
Components of Electronically Controlled Engine

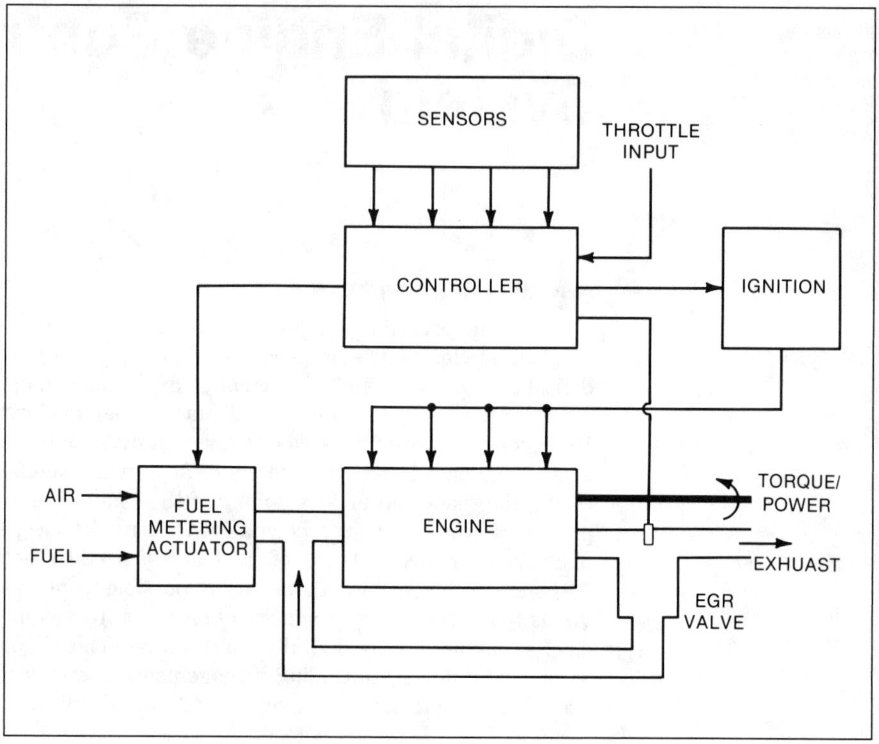

CONTROL MODES FOR FUEL CONTROL

The engine control system is responsible for controlling fuel and ignition for all possible engine operating conditions. However, there are a number of distinct categories of engine operation, each of which corresponds to a separate and distinct operating mode for the engine control system. The differences between these operating modes are sufficiently great that different software is used for each. The control system must determine the operating mode from the existing sensor data, and call the particular corresponding software routine.

Engines have different modes of operation as the operating conditions change. Seven different modes of operation commonly affect fuel control.

For a typical engine there are seven different engine operating modes that affect fuel control: *engine crank, engine warmup, open-loop control, closed-loop control, hard acceleration, deceleration,* and *idle*. The program for mode control logic determines the engine operating mode from sensor data and timers.

In the example configuration (*Figure 7-1*), fuel metering is assumed to be throttle body fuel injection (TBFI) as explained in Chapter 5. It is further assumed that the engine controller has an open-loop mode based upon the calculation of mass airflow rate using the speed-density method.

The example fuel control system requires sensors for the following variables: EGO, MAP, throttle angle, RPM inlet air, and coolant temperatures. Although any given control system might employ additional sensors, this set is assumed for the present discussion.

During engine crank and engine warm-up modes, the controller holds the air/fuel ratio to a purposely low value (rich fuel mixture).

When the ignition key is switched on initially, the mode control logic automatically selects an engine start control scheme which provides the low air/fuel ratio required for starting the engine. Once the engine RPM rises above the cranking value, the controller identifies the engine started mode and passes control to the program for the engine warm-up mode. This operating mode keeps the air/fuel ratio low to prevent engine stall during cool weather until the engine coolant temperature rises above some minimum value. The particular value for the minimum coolant temperature is specific to any given engine and, in particular, to the fuel metering system.

After warm-up, the controller switches to open loop control until accurate readings can be obtained from the EGO sensor. The controller then changes to, and remains in, closed-loop mode under ordinary driving conditions.

When the coolant temperature rises, the mode control logic directs the system to operate in the open-loop control mode until a certain time has elapsed, and the EGO sensor warms up enough to provide accurate readings. This condition is detected by monitoring the EGO sensor's output for voltage readings above a certain minimum air/fuel rich mixture voltage set point. When the sensor has indicated rich at least once, and after the engine has been in open loop for a specific time, the control mode selection logic selects the closed-loop mode for the system. The engine remains in the closed-loop mode until either the EGO sensor cools and fails to read a rich mixture for a certain length of time, or a hard acceleration or deceleration occurs. If the sensor cools, the control mode logic selects the open-loop mode again.

During conditions of hard acceleration or deceleration, the controller adjusts the air/fuel ratio as needed for those conditions. During idle periods, the controller adjusts engine speed to reduce engine roughness and stalling.

During hard acceleration or heavy engine load, the control mode selection logic chooses a scheme that provides a rich air/fuel mixture for the duration of the acceleration or heavy load. This scheme provides maximum torque but relatively poor emissions control and poor fuel economy regulation as compared with stoichiometric air/fuel. After the need for enrichment has passed, control is returned to either open loop or closed loop, depending upon the control mode logic selection conditions that exist at that time.

During periods of deceleration, the air/fuel ratio is increased to reduce emissions of HC and CO due to unburned excess fuel. When idle conditions are present, control mode logic passes system control to the idle speed control mode. In this mode, the engine speed is controlled to reduce engine roughness and stalling which might occur because the idle load has changed due to air conditioner compressor operation, alternator operation, or gearshift positioning from park/neutral to drive.

Engine Crank

During engine crank, the controller compares the value from the coolant temperature sensor with values stored in a lookup table to determine the correct air/fuel ratio at that temperature.

While the engine is being cranked, the fuel control system must provide an intake air/fuel ratio of anywhere from 2/1 to 12/1, depending on engine temperature. Low temperatures affect the carburetor's ability to atomize or mix the incoming air and fuel. At low temperatures, the fuel tends to form into large droplets in the air which don't burn as efficiently as tiny droplets. The larger fuel droplets tend to increase the apparent air/fuel ratio, because the amount of usable fuel (on the surface of the droplets) in the air is reduced; therefore, the carburetor must provide a decreased air/fuel ratio to provide the engine with a more combustible air/fuel mixture. A diagram of the system operation is shown in *Figure 7-2*. The computer reads the engine temperature through an analog-to-digital converter from a temperature sensor in the engine water coolant. A lookup table is used to determine the proper air/fuel ratio at the temperature. The air/fuel ratio is determined and controlled as in the open-loop mode, which will be discussed shortly. The main control concern is for reliable engine start, not for emission control or for fuel economy.

Figure 7-2. Engine Crank Operating Mode

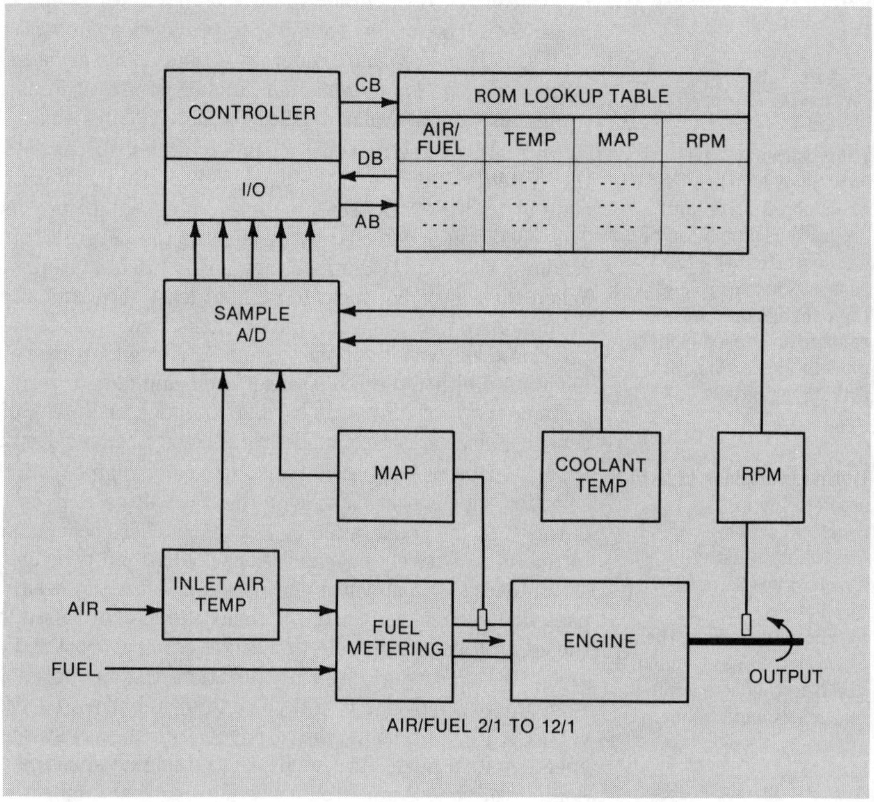

The output of the controller is a variable duty cycle pulse that meters the correct amount of fuel (i.e., that necessary to obtain the calculated air/fuel ratio). The average quantity of fuel flowing into the engine is proportional to this duty cycle.

Engine Warm-Up

The controller selects a warm-up time from a lookup table based on the temperature of the coolant. During engine warm-up the air/fuel ratio is still rich, but it is changed by the controller as the coolant temperature increases.

While the engine is warming up, an enriched air/fuel ratio is still needed to keep it running smoothly, but the required air/fuel ratio changes as the temperature increases. Therefore, the fuel control system stays in the open-loop mode, but the air/fuel ratio commands continue to be altered due to the temperature changes. The emphasis in this control mode is on rapid and smooth engine warmup. Fuel economy and emission control are still a secondary concern. A diagram of just the controller is shown in *Figure 7-3*. The controller determines the warm-up time period based on the coolant temperature when the warm-up mode was selected. Of course, the time required to reach the warmed-up condition increases as the engine initial temperature is decreased. The time allowed by the controller timer is chosen from a lookup table and is as short as possible so that the controller can begin full regulation of emissions and fuel economy as quickly as possible. In a digital control system, the timer is implemented in the computer itself.

Figure 7-3. Warm-Up Operating Mode

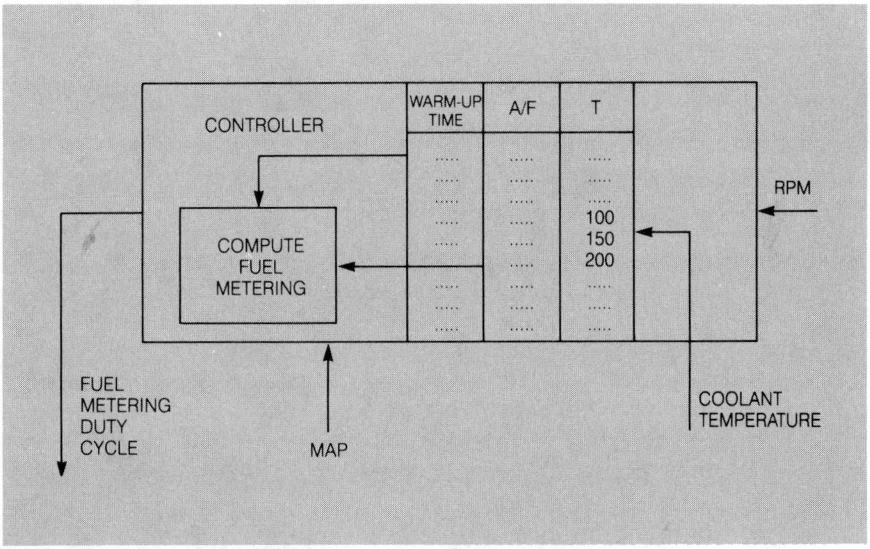

Open-Loop Control

After engine warm-up, open loop-control is used. The most popular method uses the mass density equation to calculate the amount of air entering the intake manifold.

Once the engine is warmed up and the warm timer has timed out, the fuel control system operates as an open-loop control system to more closely control emissions and fuel economy. As mentioned in Chapter 6, the open-loop fuel mass flow rate is computed from the air mass flow rate. The fuel mass flow rate is regulated so as to maintain the air/fuel ratio as close as possible to 14.7.

The most common method of computation of air mass flow rate has been the speed density equation, although there is now a trend toward using the direct measurement of mass flow rate method (explained later in this chapter). As discussed previously, this method requires knowledge of an engine's volumetric efficiency, cylinder displacement, and the intake air density. These parameters, along with engine RPM and manifold absolute pressure (MAP), are sufficient to compute the mass flow rate of air drawn through the intake manifold.

Volumetric efficiency and cylinder displacement are well known by the engine designers for a particular engine and can be tabulated in a lookup table using engine RPM as a lookup index. Intake air density can be computed from measurement of manifold pressure with the engine off (for barometric pressure) and temperature (coolant temperature). Some systems have separate sensors to measure barometric pressure and intake air temperature directly. A diagram of the control system operation is shown in *Figure 7-4*.

Figure 7-4.
Open-Loop Control

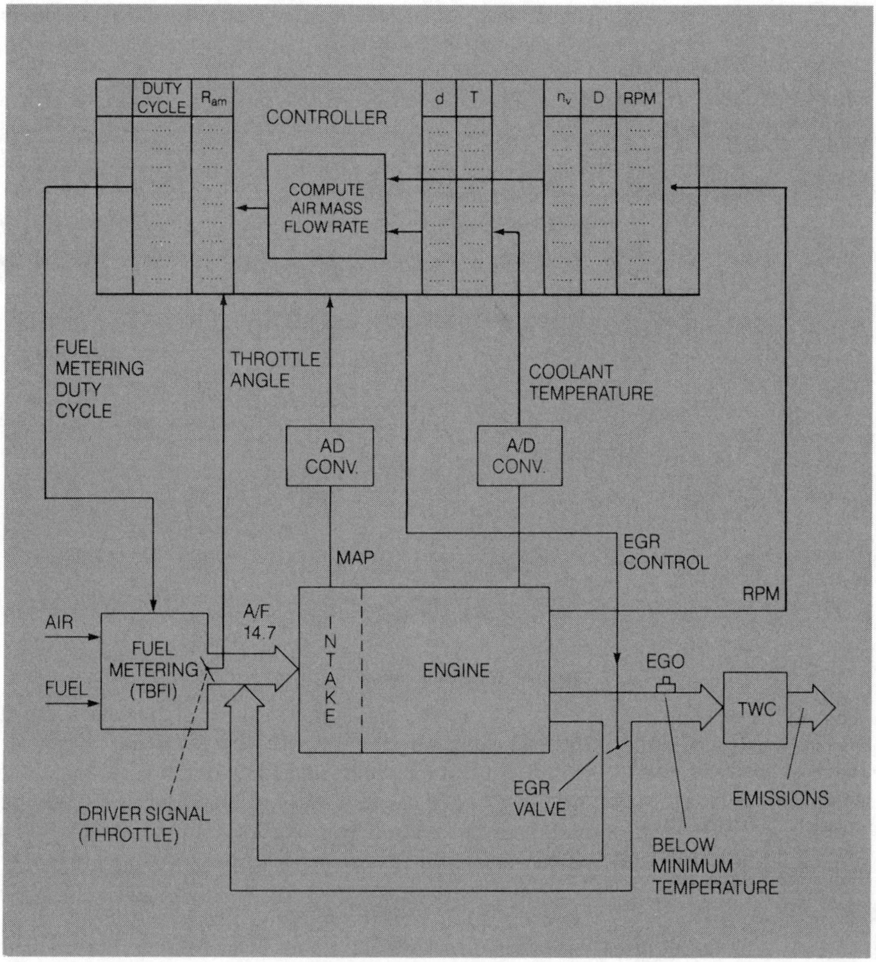

The volume flow rate for intake air is determined from engine angular speed and MAP measurements.

The air volume flow rate is computed as a function of RPM. This value is adjusted to account for MAP and air density at the ambient air temperature. The resulting value is an estimate of air mass flow rate, which is then corrected for EGR mass and is used in another lookup table to determine the appropriate duty cycle for fuel metering to provide the proper air/fuel ratio.

Basically there are two ways to compute the TBFI duty cycle from the mass density equations that were given in Chapter 6. The most direct way is to program the computer to perform all of the multiplications and division indicated in the air mass equations and then compute EGR mass using a similar equation. The EGR mass is then subtracted from the air mass and the result is used to compute the fuel mass and corresponding TBFI duty cycle. This might require 5 or 6 multiplications, 2 or 3 divisions, and a few additions or subtractions. Multiplication and division in a microcomputer require 15 to 30 microseconds, and addition and subtraction require 2 or 3 microseconds. After each operation is performed, the computer must check for overflow or underflow and make corrections when necessary. These computations can stretch the total air/fuel ratio computation time to several milliseconds. The computation time is very critical because a new air/fuel ratio computation must be made every 20 to 50 milliseconds, (depending upon engine RPM), and the computer has other jobs to do besides just computing air/fuel ratio.

To reduce the amount of computation time necessary for complete mass density equations, lookup tables are often used. However, direct computation of the equations also are used in some engine control systems.

To reduce computation time, lookup tables like those shown in the example of *Figure 7-4* are sometimes used to eliminate some of the multiplications and divisions. Lookup tables also reduce the overflow detection and correction problems. Input values that would normally cause overflow to occur in the direct computation approach automatically return overflow corrected values from the lookup table. Both methods, direct computation and lookup tables, are used to some extent in virtually every current production engine control system.

As before, MAP and coolant temperature are read into the computer through A/D converters. The MAP and coolant temperature are analog signals, while the RPM is determined from ignition timing pulses. EGR is usually controlled by the computer, so the amount of EGR is already known. In systems where EGR is not under computer control, the amount of EGR can be determined by measuring the amount of opening in the EGR valve with a sensor similar to a throttle position sensor (proportional EGR), or by measuring the duty cycle in a pulsed EGR system.

The use of lookup tables for determination of mass airflow rate R_{am} is illustrated in *Figure 7-5*. This figure shows a simplified block diagram of that portion of the engine controller that is involved in the table lookup process. The value of the speed density product R_{am} (i.e., see Chapter 6) where:

$$R_{am} = R_a d_a = \text{mass flow rate for air}$$

$$R_a = \left(\frac{RPM}{60}\right)\left(\frac{D}{2}\right) n_v - R_{EGR}$$

$$= \text{volume flow rate for air}$$

is stored in memory for values of RPM, MAP, inlet air temperature (T_i), and EGR. Also depicted in this figure is a ROM table memory for storing: the desired result of computation (this is analogous to storing a multiplication table); the main ROM, which stores the system programs; a RAM for storing temporary results, etc.; an I/O device; address bus AB;

data bus (DB); and the read/write (R/W) control. The correct mass flow rate is computed for a relatively large number of representative operating conditions over the entire range of operating conditions for the engine.

Figure 7-5. Use of Lookup Table

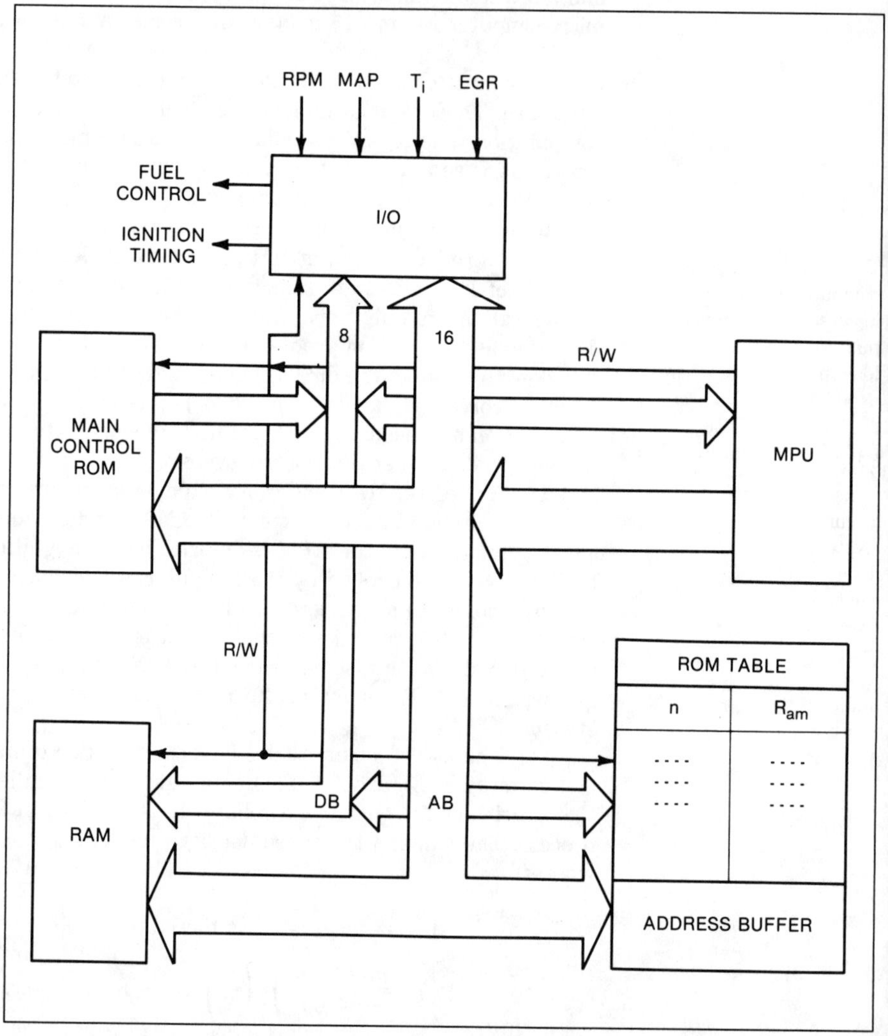

During normal operation, the engine control system obtains the values for MAP, RPM, inlet air temperature, and EGR. Then, under program control, the engine control computer determines the address of the nearest stored R_{am} data corresponding to this operating condition. The associated address is issued over the address bus AB, and the correct R_{am} value is read from the memory.

In some cases it might be desirable to determine values for R_{am} that are intermediate between a pair of stored values. A method of linear interpolation can be used to obtain these values. For example, data might be stored for RPM values R_1 and R_2. The actual RPM (R) is between these values. The correct air mass role R_{am} can be computed using the equation:

$$R_{am} = \left(\frac{R_{am}(1) - R_{am}(2)}{R_1 - R_2} \right) (R - R_2) + R_{am}(2)$$

where

$R_{am}(1)$ = air mass rate at R_1
$R_{am}(2)$ = air mass rate at R_2

A similar procedure can be followed to interpolate between values stored based upon MAP, T_i, or EGR.

When the coolant temperature sensor indicates that the engine is warm and the EGO sensor is providing accurate signals, the system changes to closed-loop control. The controller acts as a limit cycle controller, varying fuel metering in response to the lean or rich indication from the EGO sensor.

Closed-Loop Control

Closed-loop fuel control (*Figure 7-6*) is selected when the engine is warm and the exhaust gas oxygen sensor has exceeded its minimum operating temperature. The intake air/fuel ratio is controlled in a closed loop by measuring the EGO at the exhaust manifold, and altering the input fuel flow rate with a TBFI fuel metering actuator to correct for a rich or lean mixture indication. The EGO signal is a digital signal with two states (see Chapter 6). A high level indicates a rich mixture, and a low level indicates a lean mixture. The signal is amplified and fed into a digital input port on the computer. The computer determines on which side of stoichiometry the air/fuel ratio is based on the state of the EGO signal. The full fuel control system operates as a limit cycle, closed-loop control system.

The controller continuously adjusts the output signal to the TBFI in order to maintain stoichiometric air/fuel by varying the duty cycle. Whenever the EGO sensor detects a rich mixture, the duty cycle of the output controller is reduced, thereby increasing the leanness of the air/fuel mixture. Eventually the mixture will become sufficiently lean that the EGO sensor will generate a "lean mixture signal." At this point the controller will begin to increase the duty cycle, thereby moving the mixture toward rich. The controller continuously switches from rich to lean to rich, maintaining the average mixture of stoichiometry.

Variations in engine transport delay with RPM are corrected by reducing the cycle frequency and ramp rate with decreasing RPM. The long intake to exhaust transport delay time at very low RPM tends to cause the air/fuel ratio to swing wildly between very rich and very lean conditions. Slowing the duty cycle ramp rate tends to reduce the amplitude of the swing by allowing the EGO sensor more time to react to input air/fuel ratio changes at low RPM. This keeps the average intake air/fuel ratio within acceptable limits.

Figure 7-6.
Closed-Loop Control

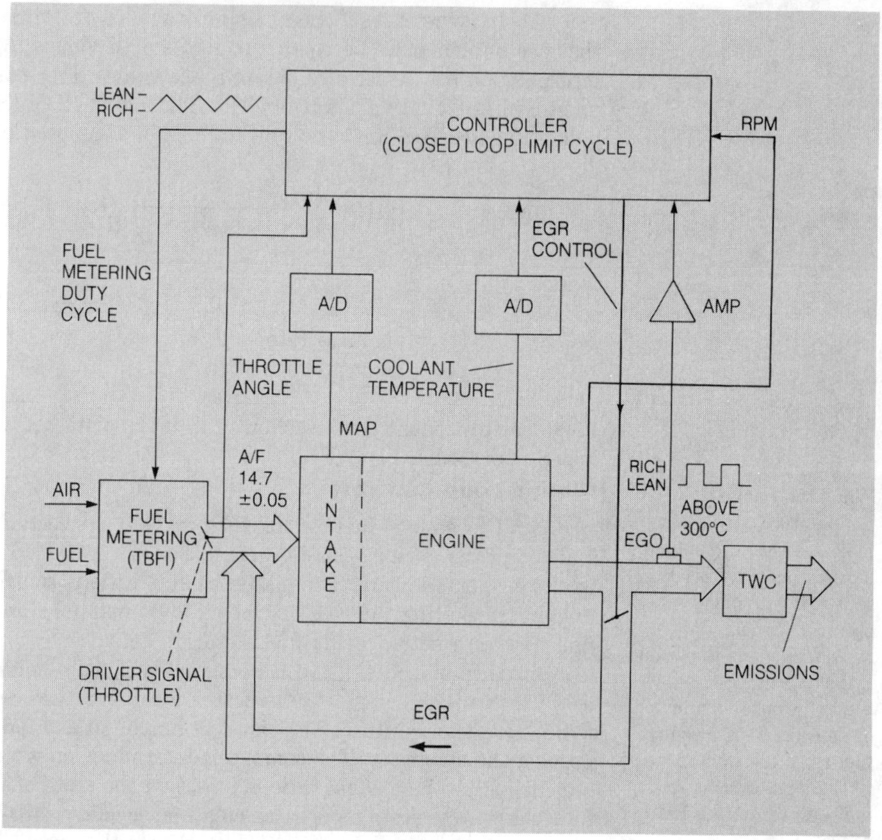

Acceleration Enrichment

The mixture is enriched to maximize torque during very heavy load (e.g., wide open throttle.)

During periods of heavy engine load such as during hard acceleration, fuel control is adjusted to provide an enriched air/fuel ratio to maximize engine torque and neglect fuel economy and emissions. This condition of enrichment is permitted within the regulations of the EPA as it is only a temporary condition. It is well recognized that hard acceleration is occasionally required for maneuvering in certain situations and is, in fact, related at times to safety.

The computer detects this condition by reading the throttle angle sensor voltage or from the MAP sensor. High intake manifold pressure or throttle angle corresponds to heavy engine load. In some vehicles a switch is provided to detect wide open throttle. The fuel system controller responds by increasing the duty cycle of the fuel metering signal for the duration of the heavy load. This enrichment enables the engine to operate with a torque greater than that allowed when emissions and fuel economy are controlled. Enrichment of the air/fuel ratio of about 12:1 is sometimes used.

Deceleration Enleanment and Idle Speed Control

Fuel flow is reduced during deceleration with closed throttle.

During periods of light engine load and high RPM such as during coast or hard deceleration, the engine requires a very lean/fuel ratio to reduce excess emissions of HC and CO. Deceleration is indicated by a sudden decrease in MAP and throttle angle. When these conditions are detected by the control computer, it computes a decrease in the duty cycle of the fuel metering signal. The fuel may even be turned off completely for very heavy deceleration.

Idle Speed Control

When the throttle angle reaches its closed position and engine RPM falls below a preset value, the controller switches to idle speed control. A stepping motor opens a valve, allowing a limited amount of air to bypass the closed throttle plate.

Idle speed control is used by some manufacturers to prevent engine stall during idle. The goal is to allow the engine to idle at as low an RPM as possible, yet keep the engine from running rough and stalling when power takeoff accessories, such as air conditioning compressors and alternators, turn on.

The control mode selection logic switches to idle speed control when the throttle angle reaches its zero (completely closed) position and engine RPMs fall below a minimum value, and when the vehicle is stationary. Idle speed is controlled by using an electronically controlled throttle bypass valve (*Figure 7-7*) which allows air to flow around the throttle plate and produces the same effect as if the throttle had been slightly opened.

Figure 7-7.
Idle Air Control

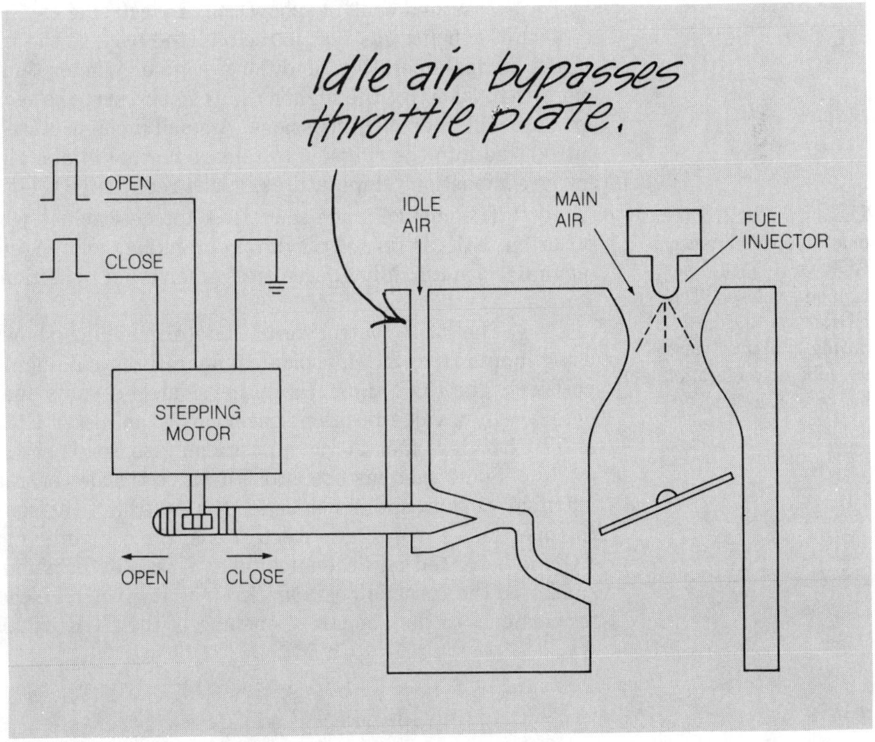

There are various schemes for operating a valve to introduce bypass air for idle control. Perhaps the simplest scheme uses a solenoid to open or close a valve in the air bypass passage. By varying the duty cycle of the valve from fully closed to fully open, it is possible to control the average flow rate of the bypass air. In an alternate scheme, the valve opens or closes by a fixed amount each time a pulse is received from the computer. The computer can open the valve all the way by pulsing the open control input a certain number of times. The same number of pulses on the close control input will completely close the valve.

Idle speed is detected by the RPM sensor, and the speed is adjusted to maintain the idle RPM constant. The computer receives digital on-off status inputs from several power takeoff devices attached to the engine, such as the air-conditioner clutch switch, park-neutral switch, and the battery charge indicator. These inputs indicate the load that is applied to the engine during idle.

When the engine is not idling, the idle speed control valve is completely closed so that the throttle plate has total control of intake air. During periods of deceleration enleanment, the idle speed valve may be opened to provide extra air to increase the air/fuel ratio in order to reduce HC emissions.

EGR CONTROL

A second control subsystem of electronic engine control is the control of exhaust gas that is recirculated back to the intake manifold. Under normal operating conditions, engine cylinder temperatures can reach more than 3000°F. The higher the temperature, the more chance the exhaust will have NO_x emissions. A small amount of exhaust gas is introduced into the cylinder to replace normal intake air. This results in lower combustion temperatures, which reduces NO_x emissions.

The engine controller also must determine when EGR valve should be opened or closed. The EGR valve is closed during cranking, warm-up, idling, acceleration, or heavy engine load.

The control mode selection logic determines when EGR is turned off or on. EGR is turned off during cranking, cold engine temperature (engine warm-up), idling, acceleration, or other conditions demanding high torque.

The EGR control signal is determined, as shown in *Figure 7–8*, by using inputs from RPM, coolant temperature, and engine load (throttle position). The EGR signal can either control a valve opening, which is detected by a valve position sensor, or it can meter EGR in the same way as TBFI meters fuel. A valve positioning sensor is shown in *Figure 7–8*.

Some systems use an EGR valve that is controlled directly by manifold vacuum and is not under the control of the computer. To perform the open-loop air/fuel ratio calculations, the computer must know how much EGR is being fed into the air intake. This is determined by using a sensor similar to the throttle position sensor that gives an electrical signal which is proportional to the amount of opening of the EGR valve.

Figure 7-8.
EGR Control

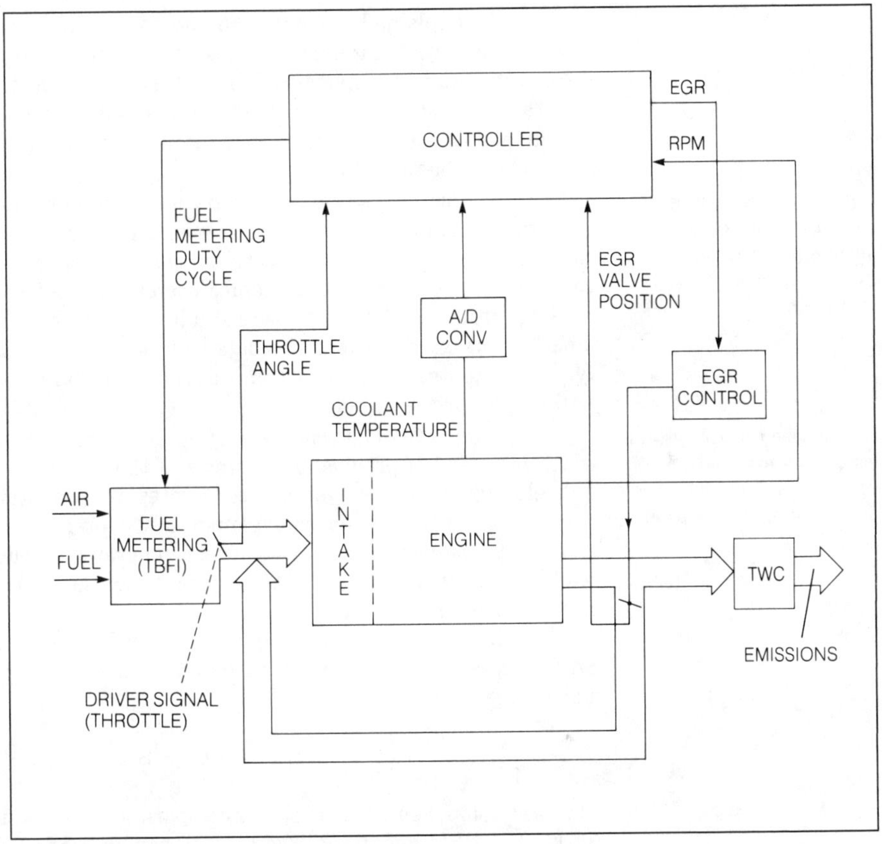

ELECTRONIC IGNITION CONTROL

As we have seen in Chapter 1, an engine must be provided with fuel and air in correct proportions, and the means to ignite this mixture in the form of an electric spark. The traditional ignition system includes spark plugs, a distributor, and a high voltage ignition coil. The distributor sequentially connects the coil to the correct spark plug. In addition, it causes the coil to generate a spark by interrupting the primary current (ignition points) in the desired coil, thereby generating the required spark. The time of occurrence of this spark (i.e., the ignition timing) in relation of the piston to TDC influences the torque generated.

In engines that are not constrained by exhaust emission regulations, it is possible to vary mixture and ignition timing as functions of RPM and manifold pressure to maximize performance (i.e., maximize torque or horsepower). For example, the ignition timing can be chosen to produce the best possible engine torque of any given operating condition. This optimum ignition timing is known for any given engine configuration from studies of engine performance as measured on an engine dynamometer.

As explained in Chapter 6 and earlier in this chapter the strategy for satisfying exhaust emission requirements requires the use of the 3-way catalytic converter. For such systems, the mixture is maintained at stoichiometry. It is possible within the constraint of stoichiometric air/fuel ratio to vary ignition timing to maximize performance or fuel economy.

Ignition timing can be adjusted to maximum engine performance within emission constraints.

The variables that influence the optimum spark timing at any operating condition include RPM, manifold pressure, barometric pressure, and coolant temperature. The correct ignition timing for each value of these variables is stored in a lookup table. The engine control system obtains readings from the various sensors and generates an address to the lookup table (ROM). After reading the data from the lookup tables, the control system computes the correct spark advance. An output signal is generated at the appropriate time to activate spark.

The engine control system calculates spark advance from several variables, including MAP and RPM.

Figure 7–9 is a schematic of an electronic spark control system which is typical of productions systems of the late 1970s or early 1980s. This electronic ignition system incorporates a distributor in which is mounted a position sensor as explained in Chapter 5. At a specific crankshaft angular position, this sensor generates an output pulse that is read by the control system. At the same time, the control system obtains readings from the various sensors.

In a typical electronic ignition control system, the spark advance, SA (in degrees before TDC), is made up of several components that are added together:

$$SA = SA_S + SA_P + SA_T$$

The first component, SA_S is the basic spark advance which is a tabulated function of RPM and MAP. The control system reads RPM and MAP, and calculates the address in ROM of the SA_S that corresponds to these values. Typically the advance of RPM from idle to about 1200 RPM is relatively slow. Then, from about 1200 to about 2300 RPM, the RPM advance is relatively quick. Beyond 2300 RPM, the increase in RPM is again relatively slow. Each engine configuration has its own spark advance characteristic, which is normally a compromise between a number of conflicting factors (the details of which are beyond the scope of this book).

The second component, SA_P, is the contribution to spark advance due to barometric pressure. This value is obtained from ROM lookup tables.

Figure 7-9.
Early Electronic Ignition System

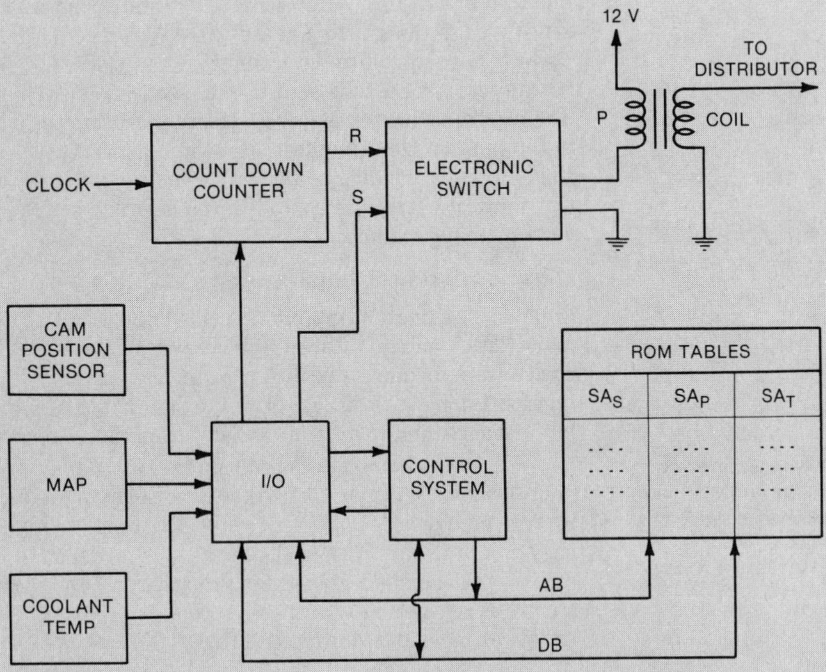

9a. Block Diagram

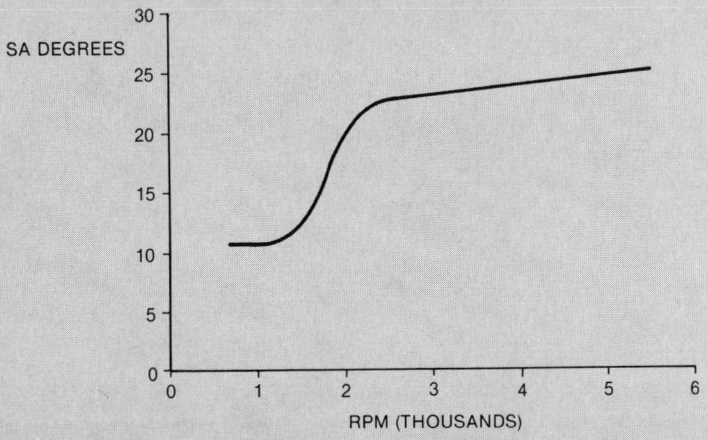

9b. Typical SA Curve Versus RPM

The final components, SA_T, is the contribution to spark advance due to temperature. After computing total spark advance, a binary value is sent through the I/O to a preset count-down counter. The counter counts down to zero at a rate determined by the clock, CK. When the counter reaches zero, a pulse is sent to the electronic switch, causing it to open. The electronic switch is closed, thereby causing primary current to build up in the ignition coil. Opening this switch generates the high voltage spark in the secondary winding of the coil. The spark voltage is sent to the distributor, where it is routed to the desired spark plug to fire the corresponding cylinder.

Closed-Loop Ignition Timing

The ignition system described above is an "open-loop" system. The major disadvantage of open-loop control is that it cannot automatically compensate for mechanical changes in the system. Closed-loop control of ignition timing is desirable from the standpoint of improving engine performance, and maintaining that performance in spite of system changes.

For best performance spark is advanced until excessive knock occurs.

One scheme for closed-loop ignition timing is based upon the improvement in performance that is achieved by advancing the ignition timing relative to TDC. For a given RPM and manifold pressure, the variation in torque with spark advance is as depicted in *Figure 7-10.* One can see that advancing the spark relative to TDC increases the torque until a point is reached at which best torque is produced. This spark advance is known as mean-best-torque or MBT.

Figure 7-10. Torque Versus SA for Typical Engine

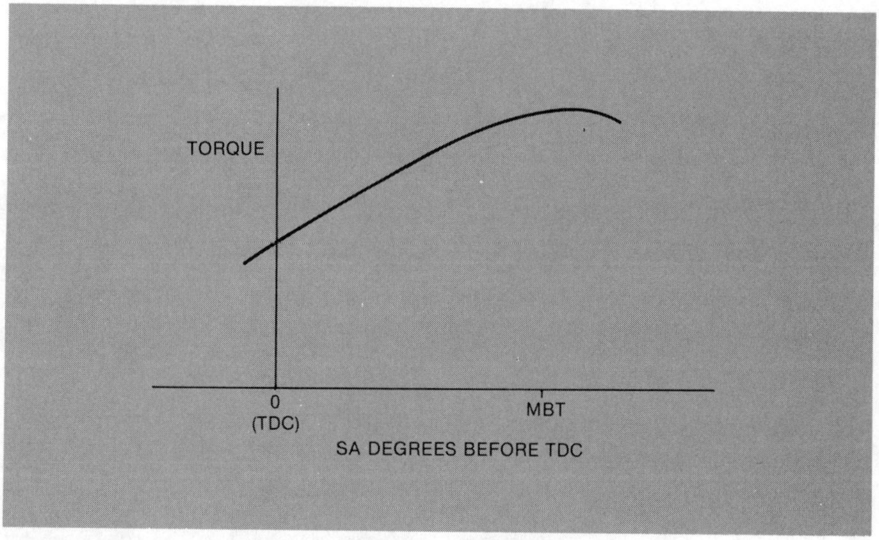

When the spark is advanced too far, an abnormal combustion phenomenon occurs that is known as *knocking.* At the present time, knocking is not a fully understood phenomenon, although much is known about it. It is characterized by an abnormally rapid rise in cylinder pressure during combustion, followed by very rapid oscillations in cylinder pressure. The frequency of these oscillations is specific to a given engine configuration and is typically in the range of a few kilohertz. *Figure 7-11* is a graph of a typical cylinder pressure versus time under knocking conditions. A relatively low level of knock is arguably beneficial to performance, excessive knock is unquestionably damaging to the engine and must be avoided.

Figure 7-11. Cylinder Pressure (Knocking Condition)

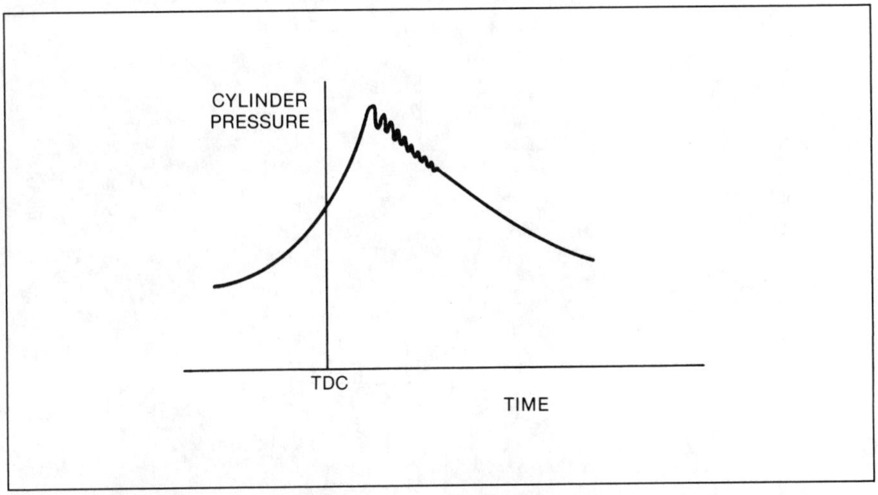

One control strategy for spark under closed-loop control is to advance the spark timing until the knock level becomes unacceptable. At this point, the control system reduces the spark advance (retarded spark) until acceptable levels of knock are achieved. Of course, a spark advance control scheme based upon limiting the levels of knocking requires a knock sensor such as that explained in Chapter 5. This sensor responds to the acoustical energy in the spectrum of the rapid cylinder pressure oscillations, as shown in *Figure 7-11.*

Figure *7-12* is a schematic of instrumentation for measuring knock intensity. Output voltage V_K of the knock sensor is proportional to the acoustical energy in the engine block at the sensor mounting point. This voltage is sent to a narrow bandpass filter that is tuned to the knock frequency. The filter output voltage is proportional to the amplitude of the knock oscillations, and is thus a "knock signal." The envelope voltage of these oscillations, V_d, is obtained with a detector circuit. This voltage is sent to the controller where it is compared with a level corresponding to knock intensity threshold. Whenever the knock level is less than the threshold, the spark is advanced. Whenever it exceeds the threshold, the spark is retarded.

Figure 7-12. Instrumentation and Waveforms for Ignition Control

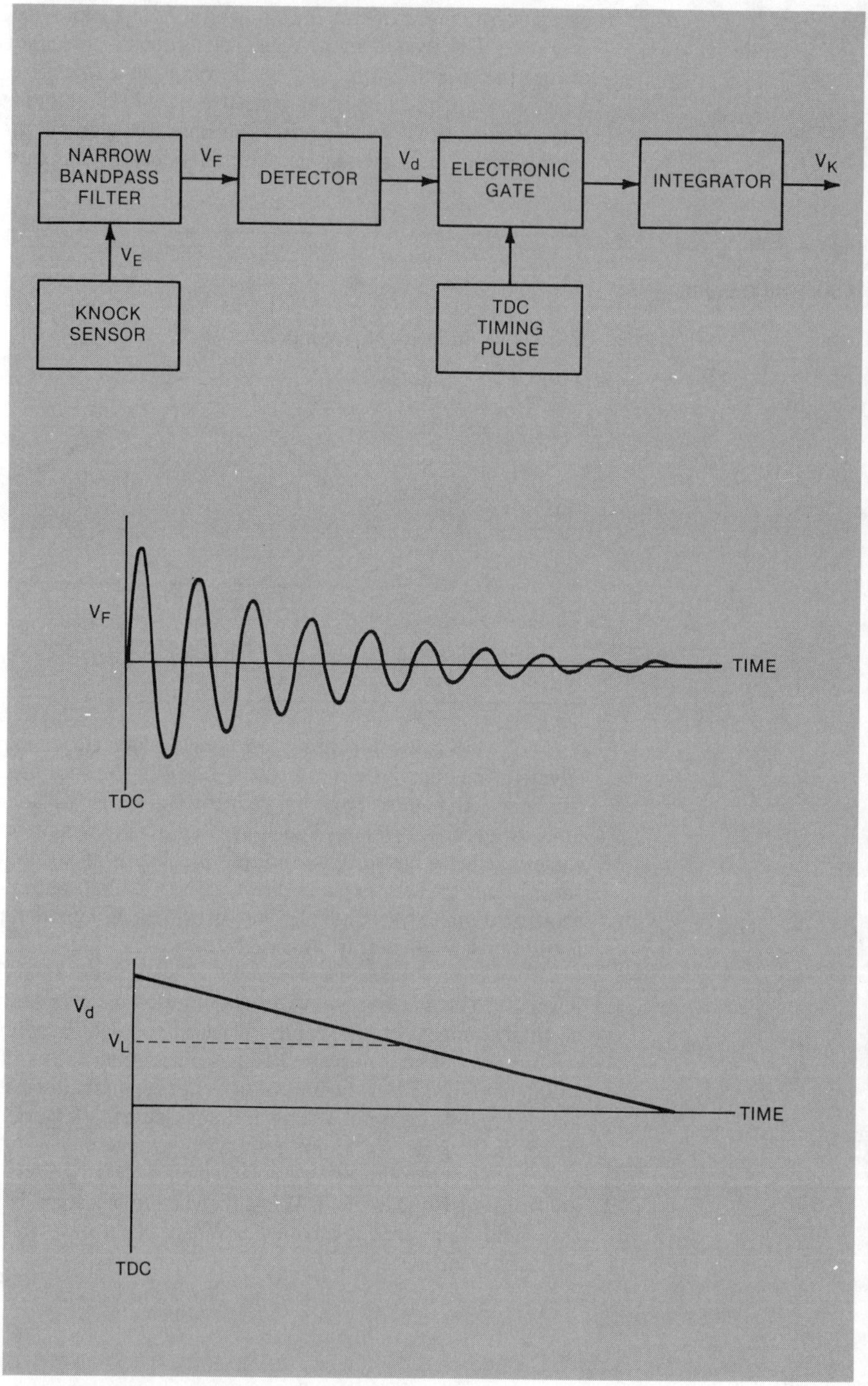

Figure 7-12. Cont.

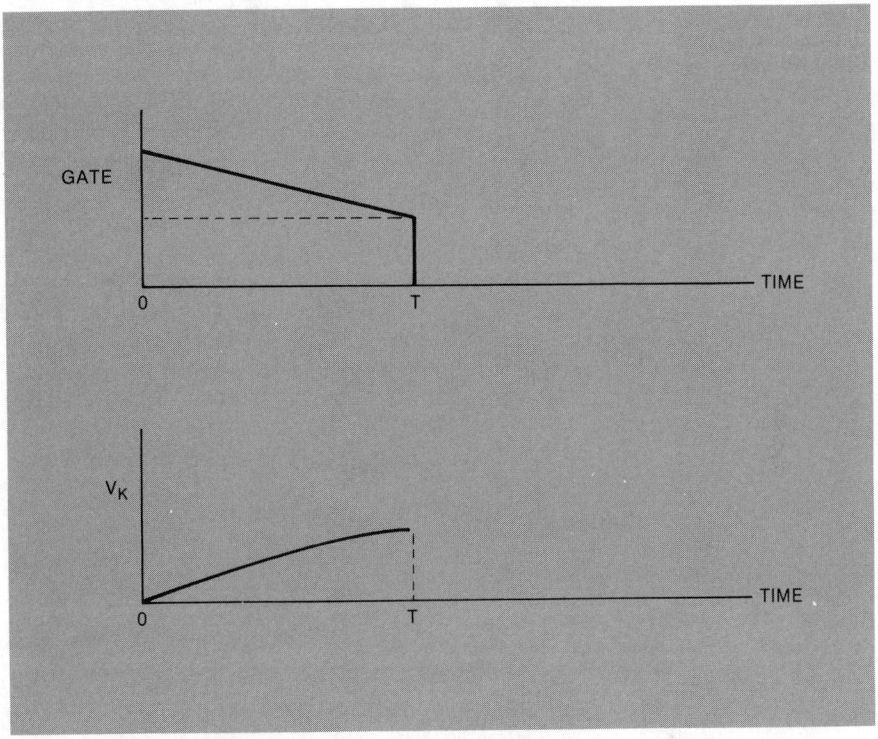

Following the detector in the circuit of *Figure 7-12* is an electronic gate that examines the knock sensor output at the time for which the knock amplitude is largest (i.e., shortly after TDC). The gate is, in essence, an electronic switch that is normally open, but is closed for a short interval (i.e., from 0 to T) following TDC. It is during this interval that the knock signal is largest in relationship to engine noise. The probability of successfully detecting the knock signal is greatest during this interval. Similarly, the possibility of mistaking engine noise for true knock signal is smallest during this interval.

The final stage in the knock measuring instrumentation is integration with respect to time; this can be accomplished using an operational amplifier. For example, the circuit of *Figure 7-13* could be used to integrate the gate output. The electronic gate actually controls switches S_1 and S_2. The output voltage V_K at the end of the gate interval T is given by:

$$V_K = -(1/RC) \int_0^T V_d(t)dt$$

This voltage increases sharply (negative), reaching a maximum amplitude at the end of the gate interval, as shown in *Figure 7-13*, provided that knock occurs. However, if there is no knock, V_K remains near zero.

Figure 7-13. Example Integrator Circuit Diagram

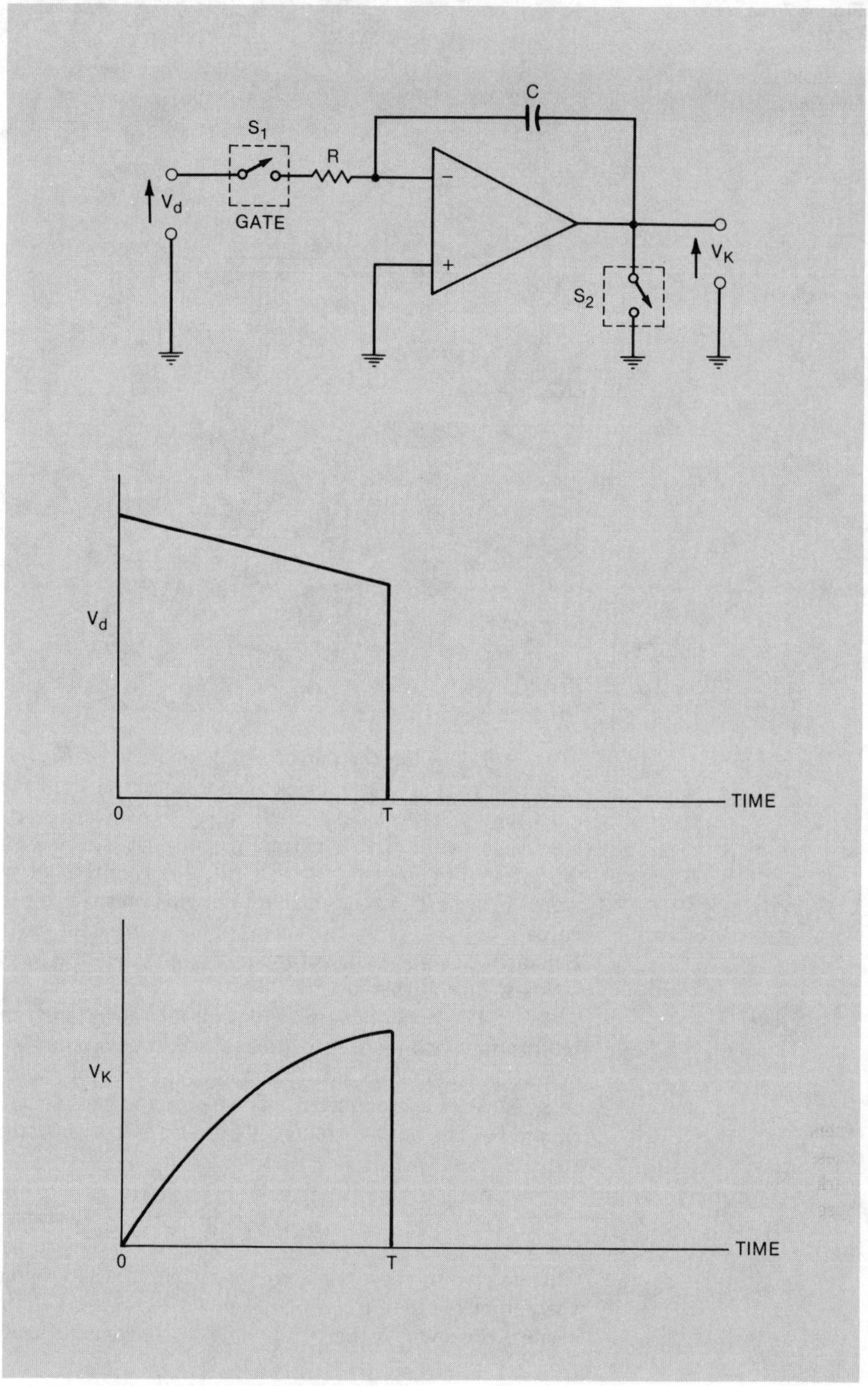

The acoustical knock signal is compared with a threshold level corresponding to unacceptable knock.

The level of knock intensity is indicated by voltage $V_K(T)$ at the end of the gate interval. The spark control system compares this voltage with a threshold voltage to determine whether knock has or has not occurred (*Figure 7-14*). The comparator output voltage is binary valued, depending upon the relative amplitude of $V_K(T)$ and the threshold voltage. Whenever $V_K(T)$ is less than the threshold voltage, the comparator output is low, indicating no knock. Whenever $V_K(T)$ is greater than the threshold value, the comparator output is high indicating knock.

Figure 7-14. Knock Level Detector Circuit

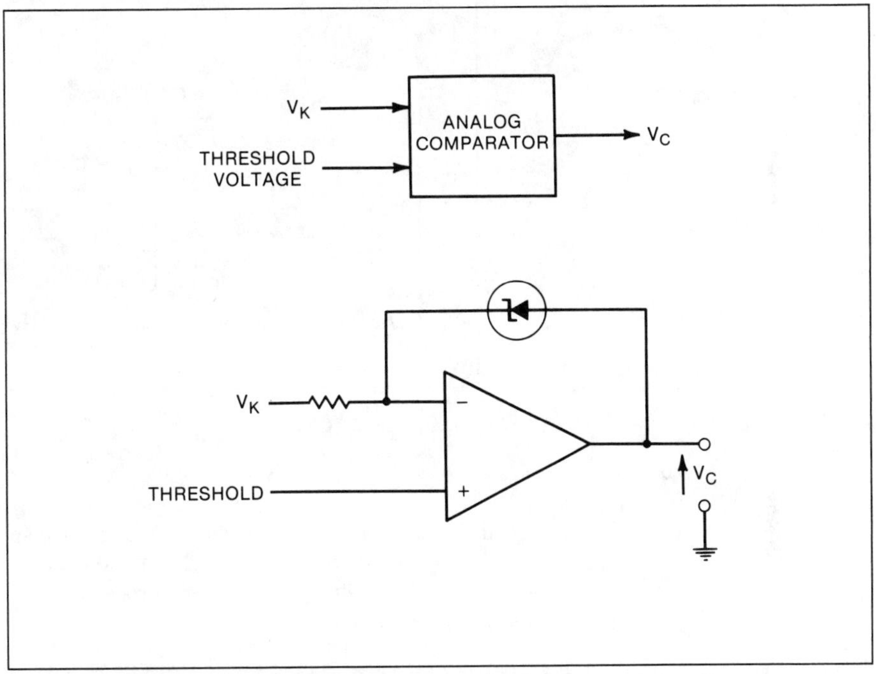

Although the above scheme for knock detection has shown a constant threshold, there are some production applications that have a variable threshold. The threshold in such cases increases with RPM, because the competing noises in the engine increase with RPM.

Spark Advance Correction Scheme

Whenever knock is excessive, a closed-loop spark advance system causes spark to retard.

Although the details of spark advance control vary from manufacturer to manufacturer, there are generally two classes of correction that are used—fast correction and slow correction. In the fast correction scheme, the spark advance is decreased for the next engine cycle by a fixed amount (typically from 5° to 10°) whenever knock is detected. Then the spark advance is advanced in one-degree increments every 5 to 20 crankshaft revolutions.

The fast correction ensures that minimum time is spent under heavy knocking conditions. Further, this scheme compensates for hysteresis (i.e., for one degree of spark advance to cause knocking, more than one degree must be removed to eliminate knocking). The fast correction scheme is depicted in *Figure 7-15*.

Figure 7-15. Fast Correction Spark Advance

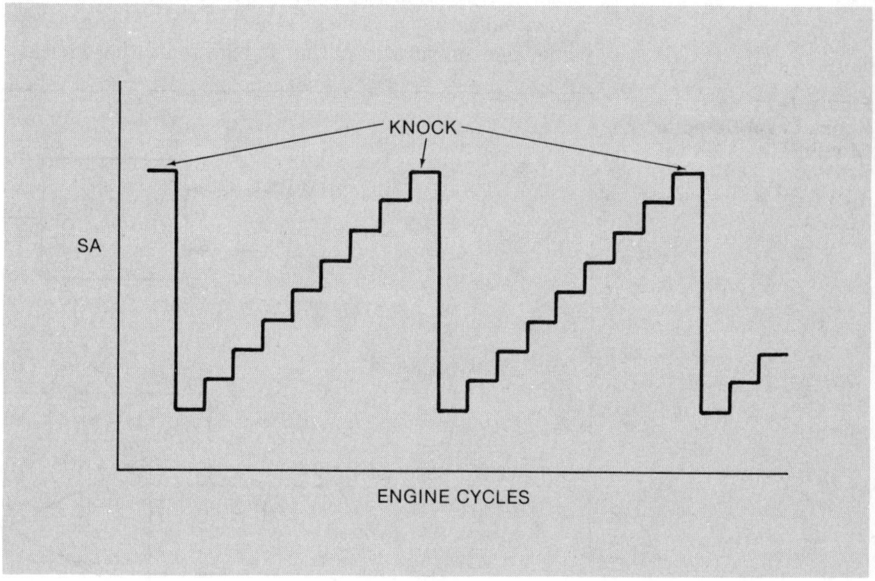

In the slow correction scheme (*Figure 7-26*) spark advance is decreased by one (or more) degree each time knock is detected, until no knocking is detected. The spark advance proceeds in one-degree increments after many engine cycles.

Figure 7-16. Slow Correction Spark Advance

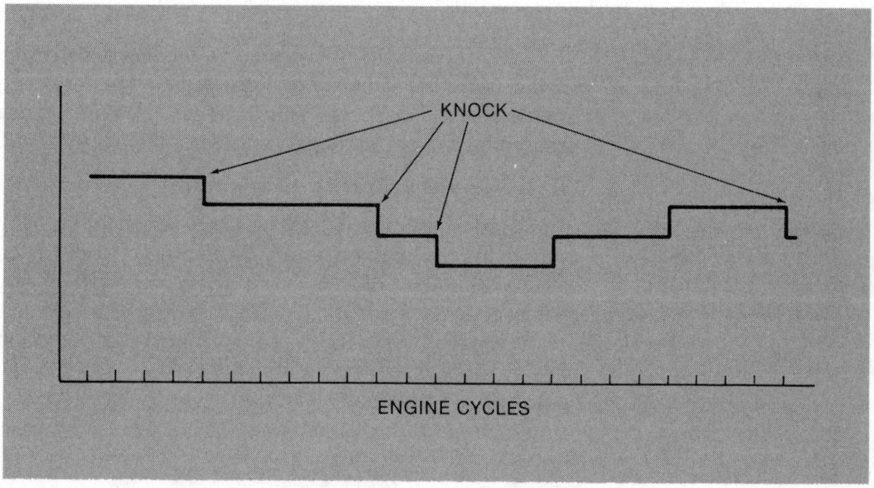

The slow correction scheme is more of an adaptive closed-loop control than is the fast correction scheme. It is primarily employed to compensate for relatively slow changes in engine condition or fuel quality (i.e., octane rating).

INTEGRATED ENGINE CONTROL SYSTEM

Each control subsystem for fuel control, spark control, and EGR has been discussed separately. However, as indicated in *Figure 6–5* and *6–6* in Chapter 6, a fully integrated electronic engine control system can include these subsystems and provide additional functions. (Usually the flexibility of the digital control system allows such expansion quite easily because the computer program can be changed to accomplish the expanded function.) Several of these additional functions are discussed below.

Secondary Air Management

Secondary air management is used to improve performance of the catalytic converter. During engine warm-up, secondary air is routed to the exhaust manifold to speed warm-up of the converter.

Secondary air management is used to improve the performance of the catalytic converter by providing extra oxygen rich air to either the converter itself, or to the exhaust manifold. The catalyst temperature must be above about 200°C to efficiently oxidize HC and CO and reduce NO_x. During engine warm-up when the catalytic converter is cold, HC and CO are oxidized in the exhaust manifold by routing secondary air to the manifold. This creates extra heat to speed warm-up of the converter and EGO sensor, enabling the fuel controller to go to the closed-loop mode more quickly.

The converter can be damaged if too much heat is applied to it. This can occur if large amounts of HC and CO are oxidized in the manifold during periods of heavy loads which call for fuel enrichment, or during severe deceleration. In such cases, the secondary air is directed to the air cleaner where it has no effect on exhaust temperatures.

After warm-up, the main use of secondary air is to provide an oxygen rich atmosphere in the second chamber of the three-way catalyst, dual chamber converter system. In a dual chamber converter, the first chamber contains rhodium, palladium, and platinum to reduce NO_x and to oxidize HC and CO. The second chamber contains only platinum and palladium. The extra oxygen from the secondary air improves the converter's ability to oxidize HC and CO in the second converter chamber.

The computer controls secondary air by using two solenoid-operated valves that route air to the air cleaner, exhaust manifold, or directly to the converter.

The computer program for the control mode selection logic can be modified to include the conditions for controlling secondary air. The computer controls secondary air by using two solenoid valves similar to the EGR valve. One valve switches air flow to the air cleaner or to the exhaust system. The other valve switches air flow to the exhaust manifold or to the converter. The air routing is based on engine coolant temperature and air/fuel ratio. The control system diagram for secondary air is shown in *Figure 7–17*.

Figure 7-17.
Secondary Air

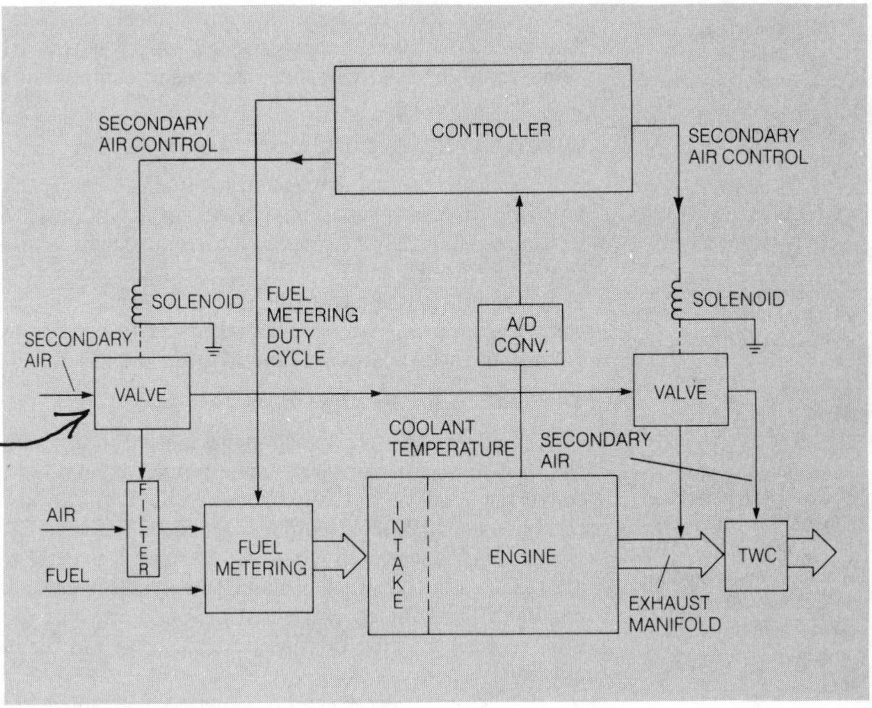

Secondary air either to intake, exhaust, or converter.

Evaporative Emissions Canister Purge

During engine off conditions, the fuel stored in the carburetor tends to evaporate into the atmosphere. To reduce these HC emissions, they are collected by a charcoal filter in a canister. The collected fuel is released into the carburetor through a solenoid valve controlled by the computer. This is done during closed-loop operation to reduce fuel calculation complications in the open-loop mode.

Torque Converter Lock-Up Control

Automatic transmissions use a hydraulic or fluid coupling to transmit engine power to the wheels. Because of slip, the fluid coupling is less efficient than the nonslip coupling of a pressure plate manual clutch used with a manual transmission. Thus, fuel economy is usually lower with an automatic transmission than with a standard transmission. This problem has been partially remedied by placing a clutch similar to a standard pressure-plate clutch inside the torque converter of the automatic transmission, and engaging it during periods of steady cruise. This enables the automatic transmission to provide fuel economy near that of a manual transmission and still retain the automatic shifting convenience.

When the engine controller detects periods of steady cruise, it can energize a solenoid-operated lock-up clutch in the automatic transmission torque converter to increase fuel economy at cruise speeds.

Here is a good example of the ease of adding a function to the electronic engine control system. The torque converter locking clutch is activated by a lock-up solenoid controlled by the engine control system computer. The computer determines when a period of steady cruise exists from throttle position and vehicle speed changes. It pulls in the locking clutch and keeps it engaged until it senses conditions that call for disengagement.

Automatic System Adjustment

A digital control system can actually "learn" from previous performances.

Another important feature of microcomputer engine control systems is their ability to be programmed to learn from their past experiences. Many control systems use this feature to enable the computer to learn new lookup table values for computing open-loop air/fuel ratio. While the computer is in the closed-loop mode, the computer checks its open-loop calculated air/fuel ratios and compares them with the closed-loop average limit cycle values. If they match closely, nothing is learned and the open-loop lookup tables are unchanged. If the difference is large, the system controller corrects the lookup tables so that the open-loop values more closely match the closed-loop values. This updated open-loop lookup table is stored in memory (RAM), which is always powered directly by the car battery so that the new values are not lost while the ignition key is turned off. The next time the engine is started, the new lookup table values will be used in the open-loop mode and will provide more accurate control of the air/fuel ratio. This feature is very important because it allows the system controller to adjust to long-term changes in engine and fuel system conditions. This feature can be applied in individual subsystem control systems, or in the fully integrated control system. If not available initially, it may be added to the system by modifying its control program.

System Diagnosis

Another important feature of microcomputer engine control systems is their ability to diagnose failures in their control systems and alert the operator. Sensor and actuator failures or misadjustments can be easily detected by the computer. For instance, the computer will detect a malfunctioning MAP sensor if the sensor's output goes above or below certain specified limits, or fails to change for long periods of time. A prime example is the automatic adjustment system just discussed. If the open-loop calculations consistently come up wrong, the engine control computer may determine that one of the many sensors used in the open-loop calculations has failed.

Abnormal responses from sensors or actuators can be detected by microcomputer engine control systems. The system can switch to an alternate means of engine control, and alert the driver by means of a dashboard indicator.

If the computer detects the loss of a primary control sensor or actuator, it may choose to operate in a different mode until the problem is repaired. The operator is notified of a failure by blinking lights or some other indicator on the dashboard. Because of the flexibility of the microcomputer engine control system, additional diagnostic programs might be added to accommodate different engine models that contain more or less sensors. Keeping the system totally integrated gives the microcomputer controller access to more sensor inputs so they can be checked. Chapter 10 discusses system diagnosis more fully.

SUMMARY OF CONTROL MODES

Now that a typical electronic engine control system has been discussed, let's summarize what happens in an integrated system operating in the various modes.

Engine Crank (Start)

Table 7-1 summarizes the engine operation in the engine crank (starting) mode. Primary control concern is for reliable engine start.

Table 7-1. Engine Crank

1. Engine RPM at cranking speed
2. Engine coolant at low temperature
3. A/F ratio low
4. Spark retarded
5. EGR off
6. Secondary air to exhaust manifold
7. Fuel economy not closely controlled
8. Emissions not closely controlled

Engine Warm-Up

Table 7-2 summarizes the engine operations while the engine is warming up. The engine temperature is rising to its normal operating value. Primary control concern is for rapid and smooth engine warm-up.

Table 7-2. Engine Warm-Up

1. Engine RPM above cranking speed at command of driver
2. Engine coolant temperature rises to minimum threshold
3. A/F ratio low
4. Spark timing set by controller
5. EGR off
6. Secondary air to exhaust manifold
7. Fuel economy not closely controlled
8. Emissions not closely controlled

Open-Loop Control

Table 7–3 summarizes the engine operations when the engine is being controlled with an open-loop system. This is before the EGO sensor has reached the correct temperature for closed-loop operation. Fuel economy and emissions are closely controlled.

Table 7–3. Open-Loop Control

1. Engine RPM at command driver
2. Engine temperature above warm-up threshold
3. A/F ratio controlled by an open-loop system to 14.7
4. EGO sensor temperature less than minimum threshold
5. Spark timing set by controller
6. EGR controlled
7. Secondary air to catalytic converter
8. Fuel economy controlled
9. Emissions controlled

Closed-Loop Control

For the closest control of emissions and fuel economy under various driving conditions, the electronic engine control system is in a closed loop. *Table 7–4* summarizes the engine operation. Fuel economy and emissions are controlled very tightly.

Table 7–4. Closed-Loop Control

1. Engine RPM at command of driver
2. Engine temperature in normal range (above warm-up threshold)
3. Average A/F ratio controlled to 14.7 ± 0.05
4. EGO sensor's temperature above minimum threshold detected by a sensor output voltage indicating a rich mixture of air and fuel for a minimum amount of time
5. System returns to open loop if EGO sensor cools below minimum threshold or fails to indicate rich mixture for given length of time
6. EGR controlled
7. Secondary air to catalytic converter
8. Fuel economy tightly controlled
9. Emissions tightly controlled

Hard Acceleration

When the engine must be accelerated quickly or if the engine is under heavy load, it is in a special mode summarized by *Table 7-5.* The engine controller is primarily concerned with providing maximum performance.

Table 7-5. Hard Acceleration

1. Driver asking for sharp increase in RPM or in engine power, demanding maximum torque
2. Engine temperature in normal range
3. A/F ratio rich mixture
4. EGO not in loop
5. EGR off
6. Secondary air to intake
7. Relatively poor fuel economy
8. Relatively poor emissions control

Deceleration and Idle

Slowing down, stopping, and idling are combined in another special mode. The engine operation is summarized in *Table 7-6.* The engine controller is primarily concerned with reducing excess emissions during deceleration, and keeping idle fuel consumption at a minimum.

Table 7-6. Deceleration and Idle

1. RPM decreasing rapidly due to driver command or else held constant at idle
2. Engine temperature in normal range
3. A/F ratio lean mixture
4. Special mode in deceleration to reduce emissions
5. Special mode in idle to keep RPM constant at idle as load varies due to air conditioner, automatic transmission engagement, etc.
6. EGR on
7. Secondary air to intake
8. Good fuel economy during deceleration
9. Poor fuel economy during idle, but fuel consumption kept to minimum possible

IMPROVEMENTS IN ELECTRONIC ENGINE CONTROL

Although major improvements have been made in electronic engine control, the fuel strategy continues to maintain stoichiometry.

The digital engine control system, which has been described above, represents the state of technology as introduced in about 1979-1980. A number of improvements have subsequently been introduced and, of course, the technology continues to be improved. However, the basic control strategy for fuel metering continues to be based upon the three-way catalytic converter and upon stoichiometric air/fuel ratio. It is worthwhile to review some of the technological improvements that have occurred in digital engine control.

Integrated Engine Control System

One of the developments that has occurred since the introduction of digital engine control technology is the integration of the various functions into a single control unit. Whereas the earlier systems in many cases had separate control systems for fuel and ignition control, the trend is toward integrated control. This trend has been made possible, in part, by improvements in digital hardware and in computational algorithms and software. For example, one of the hardware improvements which has been achieved is the operation of the MPU at higher clock frequencies. This higher frequency results in a reduction of the time for any given MPU computation. Moreover, since the control of fuel and ignition requires, in some cases, data from the same sensor set, it is advantageous to have a single integrated system for fuel and ignition timing control.

Direct measurement of mass airflow rate is an improvement over indirect measurements.

Another major improvement in digital engine control technology occurred due to the development of a cost-effective mass airflow sensor (see Chapter 5). A mass airflow sensor (MAS) generates an output that is directly proportional to the air mass flow rate R_{am}, whereas in the earlier technology, R_{am} had to be computed from indirect measurements of MAP, RPM, T_i, and EGR using the speed density method (Chapter 6). The complex computation of R_{am} is no longer required.

One of the disadvantages of the MAS is the need to maintain a carefully controlled surface condition, as explained in Chapter 5. The thermal transport characteristics of the hot surface depend upon the condition of that surface. The possibility of accumulating deposits requires some care in the use of the MAS. For example, the GM film MAS requires heating the film to relatively high temperatures to remove oxides and hydrocarbons. This heating occurs whenever the control system is shut down. For a short time after the engine is switched off, a special circuit passes a relatively high current through a heater that removes all oxides and preserves a known surface condition. In this way, the calibration of the MAS is maintained.

By model year 1987, control systems based upon MAS were introduced by several manufacturers. The success of this technology is likely to spur widespread use of MAS.

Oxygen Sensor Improvements

Improvements have also been made in the exhaust gas oxygen sensor which remains today as the primary sensor for closed-loop operation in cars equipped with the three-way catalyst. As explained in Chapter 5, the signal from the oxygen sensor is not useful for closed-loop control until the sensor has reached a temperature of about 300°C. Typically, the temperature of the sensor is too low during the starting and engine warm-up phase, but it can also be too low during relatively long periods of deceleration. It is desirable to return to closed-loop operation in as short a time as possible. In this case, the oxygen sensor must reach its minimum operating temperatures in the shortest possible time.

An exhaust gas oxygen sensor has recently been developed that incorporates an electric heating element inside the sensor, as shown in *Figure 7-18*. The heat current is automatically switched on and off, depending upon the engine operating condition. The regions in which heating is applied are determined by the engine control system as derived from engine RPM and MAP sensors.

Figure 7-18. Heated Gas Oxygen Sensor

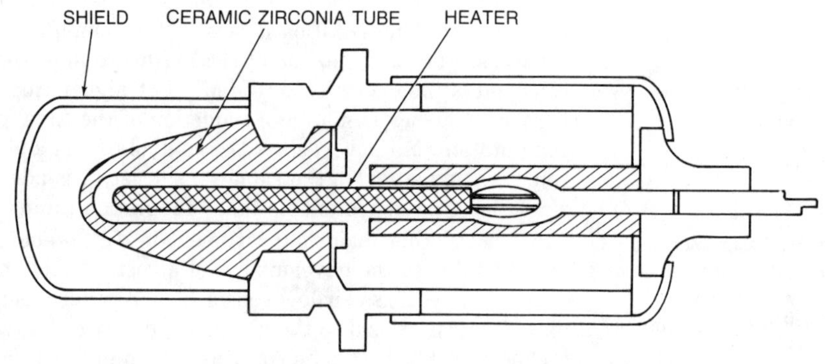

Fuel Injection Improvements

Significant improvements have been made in fuel injection technology in recent years.

In Chapters 5 and 6, both the electronically controlled carburetor and throttle body fuel injection were described as fuel metering devices, and there has been increasing use of multipoint fuel injection in which fuel injection is provided for each cylinder. In many systems in the past, all injectors were simultaneously activated for every crankshaft revolution. Typically two injections of fuel were taken into the cylinder. Currently, fuel is often being injected individually and sequentially into the intake port near each cylinder, with injection timing being computed by the control system using information from a crankshaft position sensor.

Alternatively, group injection also is often being used now on certain V-6 engines. In this system the cylinders are divided into two groups. The timing for a representative V-6 engine is shown in *Figure 7-19*. The sequential or group fuel injection is preferred for improved performance. However, such a scheme requires relatively precise measurement of crankshaft angular position and identification of individual cylinder TDC position.

Figure 7-19.
Group Injection Timing for V-6 Engine

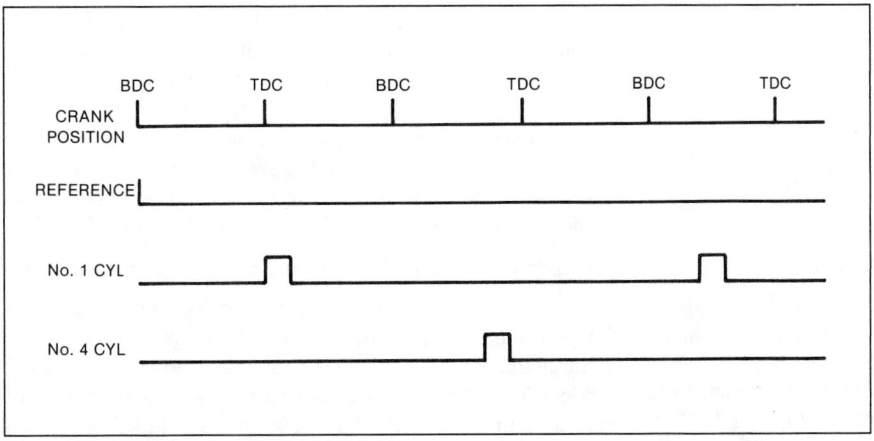

Direct Ignition

A direct ignition system eliminates the need for a distributor.

Still another improvement in electronic engine control is direct ignition. In this system, there is no distributor. Rather, there is one ignition coil for each cylinder or one for each pair of cylinders. The electronic control system generates a trigger pulse to the driver (power) transistor for each coil at the desired spark time for the corresponding cylinder. *Figure 7-20* is a schematic for a direct ignition system in which there is a separate coil for each cylinder.

Figure 7-20.
Distributorless Ignition System

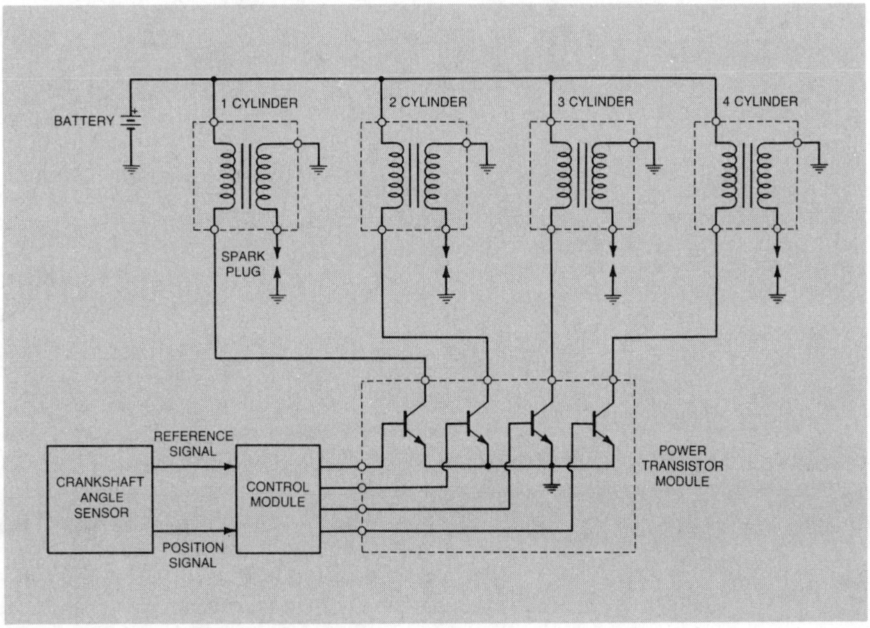

There are generally three advantages for a direct ignition system compared to one employing a distributor. One advantage is the relatively short time required to build primary current to full strength compared to a conventional coil. Consequently, the coil can be "charged" to full energy over a wide range of RPM (e.g., up to 9000 RPM for one high performance engine). The second advantage is that there is no mechanical wear such as is associated with distributor systems. The third advantage is that space in the camshaft area is free from the encumbrance of the distributor.

Improvement in Measurement of Crankshaft Angular Position

Sequential timed fuel injection requires precise measurements of crankshaft or camshaft position.

Sequential fuel injection and direct ignition require improvement in the measurement of crankshaft angular position relative to earlier methods. In the earlier electronic engine control systems, this measurement was often accomplished using a magnetic sensor and a ferromagnetic (steel) disk connected to the front end of the crankshaft (Chapter 5).

A number of alternative sensor configurations have been developed that have greater angular resolution than is normally possible with the ferromagnetic sensor. One interesting example sensor uses a photoelectric sensor and a disk with multiple slots, such as depicted in *Figure 7-21.* This particular sensor has 360 slots uniformly spaced around its circumference, yielding 1° resolution in crankshaft measurement.

Figure 7-21. Improved Crankshaft Angle Sensor

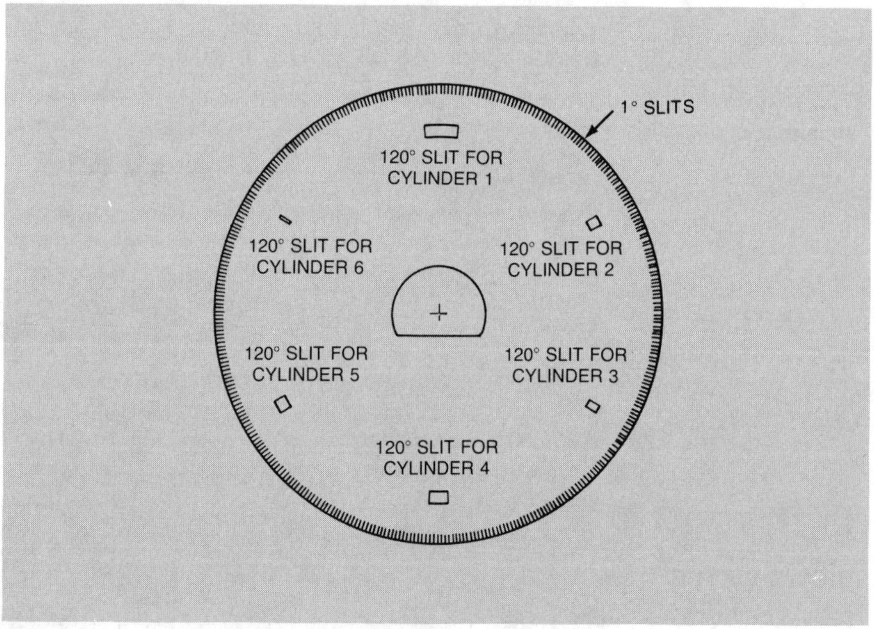

The sensor depicted in *Figure 7-21* is used on a 6-cylinder 4-stroke/cycle engine. The crankshaft angular position associated with any given cylinder is identified by the position of 6 additional slots. These latter slots are of unequal angular width, thereby facilitating the identification of the position of each cylinder. Of course, an additional sensor on the cam shaft is required if the specific stroke is to be identified for each cylinder.

Fuel Injector Driver Circuitry

Still another improvement in electronic engine control systems is in the area of the driver electronics for fuel injectors. The discussion of fuel injectors in Chapter 5 has been simplified considerably for clarity. There the concept of a simple current pulse waveform (i.e., on or off) has been assumed for the injector current. The actual current and voltage for an injector may be very complex, owing to the electrical and mechanical characteristics of the injector.

A fuel injector is essentially a solenoid-operated valve.

A fuel injector is (in essence) a solenoid-operated valve. The valve opens or closes permitting or blocking fuel flow to the engine. The valve is switched by the solenoid (*Figure 7-22*) which is a form of electromagnet. A coil is wound around a hollow ferromagnetic core into which a movable ferromagnetic rod is placed as shown in *Figure 7-22*. Whenever a current, I, passes through the coil, a magnetic field is established which applies a force to the movable rod. If the magnetic force is sufficiently great to overcome the spring force holding the rod down, the rod moves up. However, as the rod moves up, the magnetic force of attraction increases sharply, causing a further motion upward. The rod accelerates upward stopping only when a mechanical limit stop is reached. In this sense, a solenoid acts like an electromechanical switch.

Figure 7-22. Schematic Drawing of Solenoid

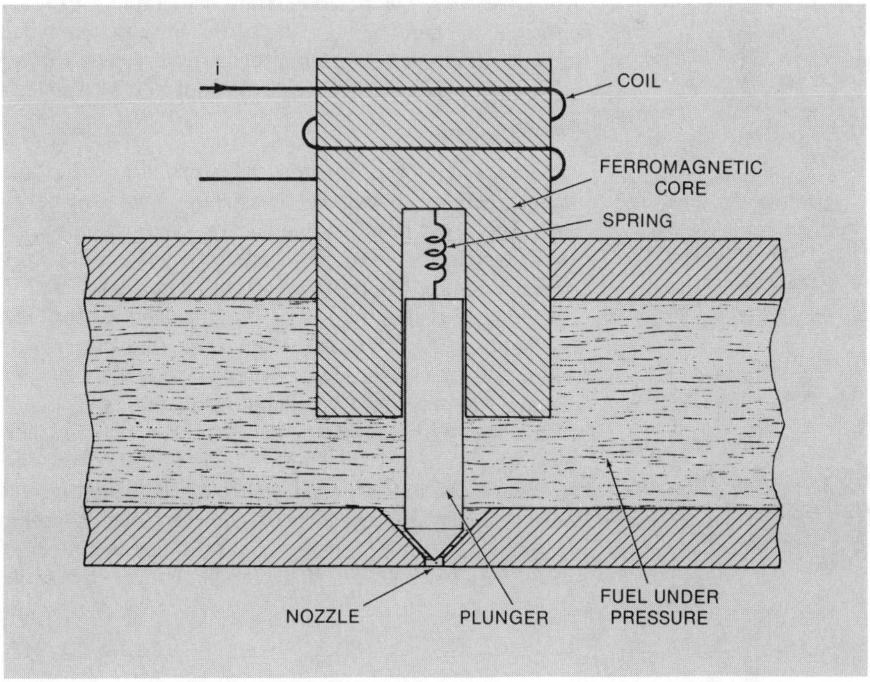

In a fuel injector, the movable rod is held down against the stop covering the aperture. Fuel is thereby blocked from flowing from the pressurized fuel chamber into the aperture. When the movable rod is switched upward, the aperture is exposed and fuel (under pressure) sprays through this aperture.

In the discussion of fuel injector current in Chapter 5, it was assumed that the current waveform can switch abruptly from zero current to a current level sufficient to open the valve. In fact, the solenoid is an inductor that has the property that current flowing through it cannot be changed instantaneously.

The voltage across an inductor is proportional to the derivative of current with respect to time. Stated mathematically we have:

$$V = L\frac{di}{dt}$$

In essence, this equation states that an infinite voltage is required to instantaneously switch a solenoid "on." In practice, this limitation is circumvented (partially) by incorporating "ballast resistors" in series with the solenoid, as shown in *Figure 7-23a*. Unfortunately, ballast resistors introduce heat loss which is wasteful.

In recent years, an alternative driver circuit has been developed that requires no ballast resistors and yet which permits rapid switching of solenoid current. *Figure 7-23b* depicts this circuit. The waveform is shown in *Figure 7-24*. The drive current rises rapidly to I_{max} level, which is sufficient to open the injector, and then the current falls to I_{min}. The current continues to switch alternately between the two levels, which is sufficient to hold the solenoid open but not waste electric power.

CPU Backup

A digital engine control system requires a backup so that the vehicle will continue to operate in the event of a failure of the main engine controller.

Still another important feature of any digital engine control system is the capability to switch to a backup mode that permits operation of the car in the event of an engine control-system failure. For example, in one particular electronic control system, whenever the system diagnosis detects a sensor failure, the control system switches to an alternate calculation method that avoids the use of the impaired sensor. This example system uses sequential multiport fuel injection that incorporates a mass airflow sensor. Whenever there is a failed mass airflow sensor, the control system changes the program for calculating injector pulse width to a fail-safe mode in which only two injector pulse widths are generated. The choice among these two pulse widths is based upon a signal from the throttle switch. There are also fail-safe modes that can be called up in case of failure in coolant temperature, knock, ECG, or pressure sensors.

In addition to sensor fail-safe modes, there is (in the example system) a CPU backup. This system actually carries a separate CPU of

Figure 7-23. Fuel Injector Driver Circuitry

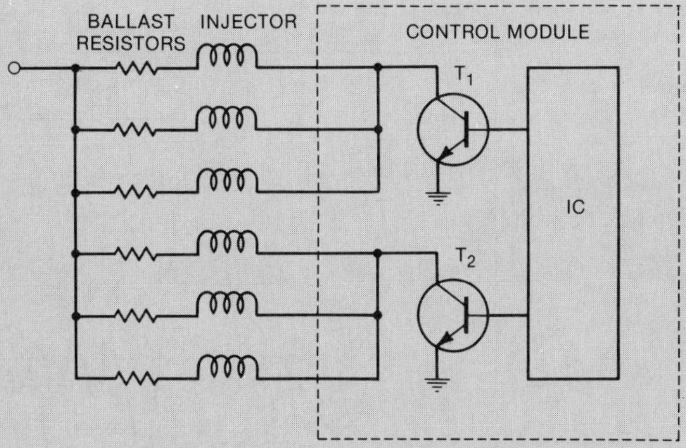

a. Conventional

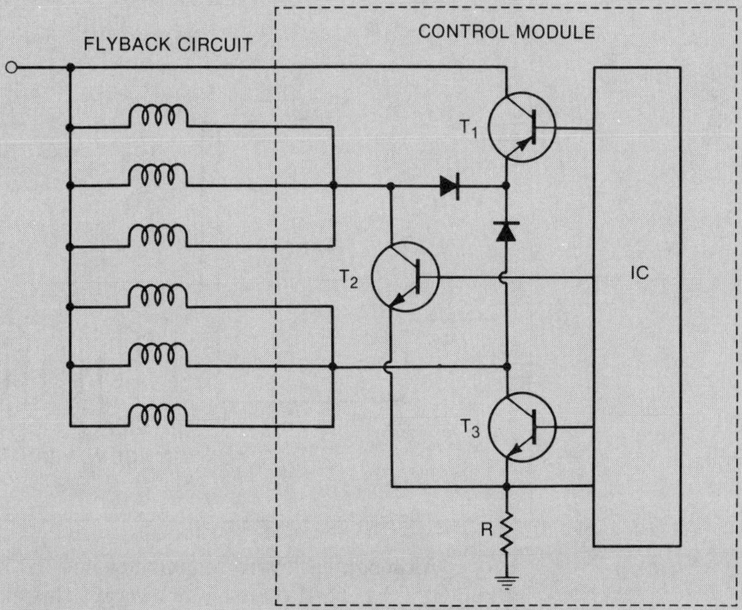

b. Improved

reduced complexity compared to the main CPU. The backup CPU has limited functions, but these are sufficient for "limp-in" engine operation. The backup CPU has 1K bytes of ROM and 20 I/O ports, compared with 16K bytes of ROM and 46 ports for the main CPU. *Figure 7-25* is a block diagram of the entire system.

Figure 7-24. Injector Current Waveforms

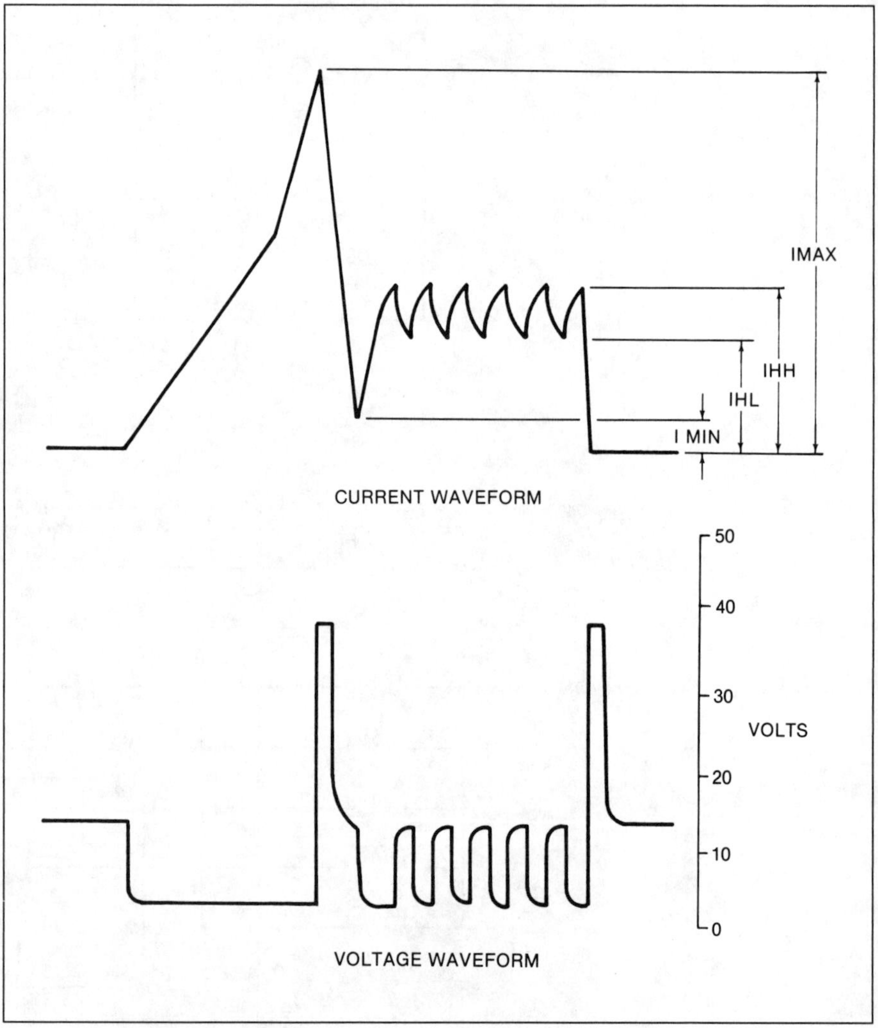

Although hardware redundancy such as is incorporated in the backup CPU has been common on aircraft, this extra hardware has heretofore been rare in automobiles where cost constraints are severe. However, in the future there is likely to be a trend toward hardware redundancy because the cost of electronic systems continually decreases and the demand for automotive reliability by the customer increases.

Figure 7-25.
Backup System for CPU

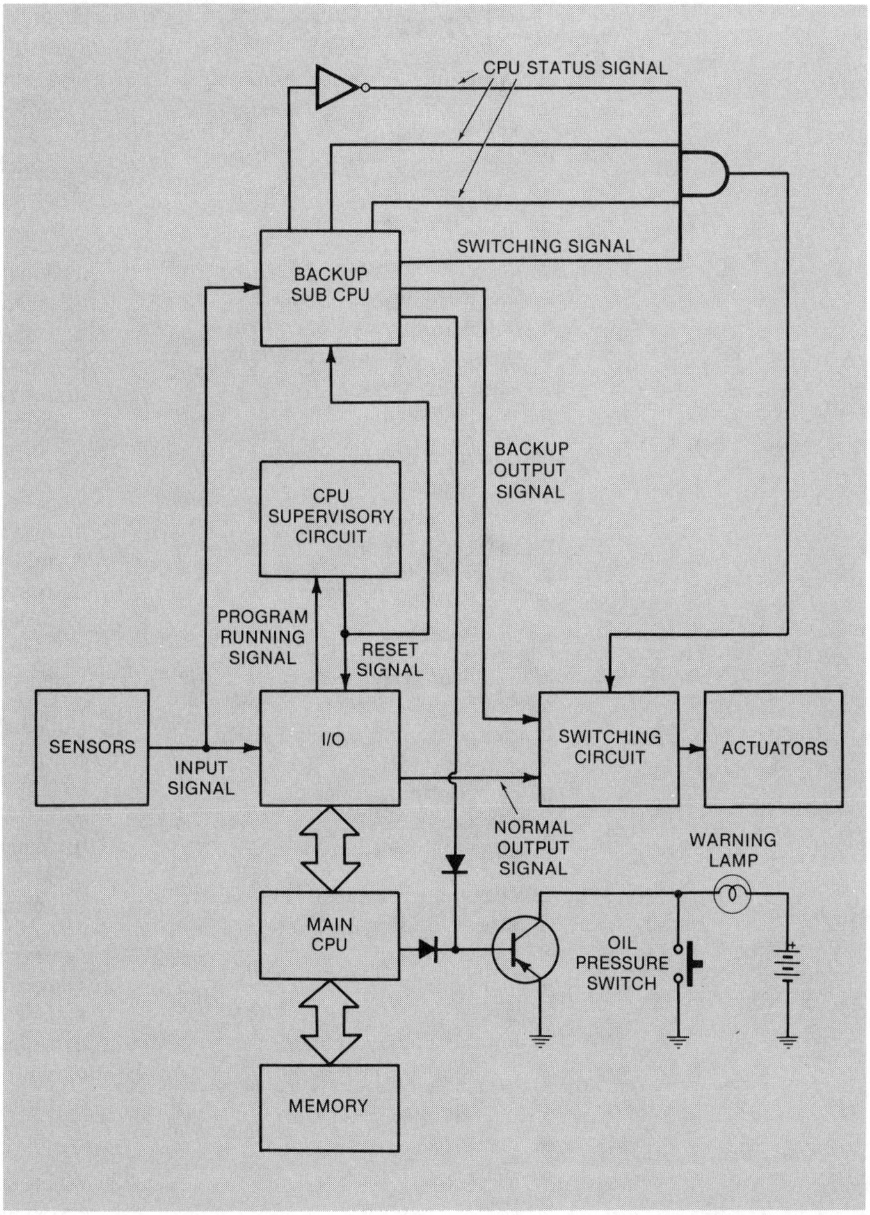

Quiz for Chapter 7

1. A typical fuel control system may include the following components
   a. MAS sensor
   b. fuel injector.
   c. EGO sensor
   d. all of the above
2. A fuel control system
   a. has many operating modes
   b. is never operated open loop
   c. does not control air/fuel during warm-up
   d. none of the above
3. During hard deceleration the engine requires
   a. very rich mixture
   b. very lean mixture
   c. stoichiometric mixture
   d. none of the above
4. Electronic control system for ignition can perform
   a. timing for maximum torque
   b. correct timing calculation with respect to RPM
   c. correct timing calculation with respect to MAP
   d. all of the above
5. The controller discussed in this chapter is what type of controller?
   a. analog
   b. digital
   c. both analog and digital
6. A low air/fuel ratio is what type of fuel mixture?
   a. lean
   b. rich
   c. poor
   d. fat
7. Open- and closed-loop fuel control systems control air/fuel ratio near which of the following?
   a. rich
   b. lean
   c. stoichiometry
   d. rich and lean
8. Acceleration enrichment is used for what purpose?
   a. reduce fuel consumption
   b. reduce exhaust emissions
   c. provide maximum torque
   d. provide minimum fuel economy
9. Idle speed control is used for what reason?
   a. maximum idle speed
   b. minimum idle fuel consumption
   c. deceleration enleanment
   d. maintaining desired idle speeds
10. Under closed-loop ignition timing control spark advance is limited by
    a. the distributor rotation
    b. knock
    c. MBT
    d. coolant temperature limits
11. Secondary air management system is used
    a. to control EGR
    b. to avoid knock
    c. with low octane fuels
    d. to improve performance of the catalytic converter
12. When knock is detected in a closed-loop ignition system, spark timing is
    a. initially advanced then retarded slowly
    b. always advanced to BDC
    c. retarded then advanced
    d. none of the above

13. Secondary functions of a digital engine control system may include
   a. evaporative emissions canister purge
   b. torque converter lockup
   c. secondary air management
   d. all of the above

14. In a direct electronic ignition control system
   a. the distributor is not required
   b. spark plugs are not needed
   c. the coil is not needed
   d. none of the above

Vehicle Motion Control

ABOUT THIS CHAPTER

Electronic controls can automate some driver functions that were previously performed manually.

The previous chapter discussed the application of digital electronics to engine control. This chapter discusses the application of electronics to cruise control, tire slip control, engine speed control, ride control, and antilock braking.

TYPICAL CRUISE CONTROL SYSTEM

A cruise control is a closed-loop system that uses feedback of vehicle speed to adjust throttle position.

The purpose of the cruise control system is to maintain a constant vehicle speed on the highway without driver input (i.e., no foot on the gas pedal). The driver selects the desired speed and activates the cruise control by means of switches. The essential features of a typical cruise control are shown in *Figure 8-1*. The electronic control system has two inputs—the command speed signal that indicates the desired speed, and the feedback speed signal that indicates the actual vehicle speed. The electronic control system detects the difference between the two inputs (the error) and produces a throttle control signal that is sent to the throttle actuator. The throttle actuator sets the engine throttle position which alters the engine speed to correct for the vehicle speed error detected by the control electronics. The vehicle speed is detected by the speed sensor and is converted to an electrical voltage proportional to vehicle speed. The control system is operating closed-loop because the speed signal is fed back to the control electronics to be compared to the command signal.

Cruise Controller Operation

Cruise controllers adjust speed by increasing or decreasing throttle angle in response to feedback that indicates whether actual speed is above or below the desired speed. Time lags in vehicle response must be taken into account in controller design.

Cruise controllers regulate vehicle speed by adjusting the engine throttle angle to increase or decrease the engine drive force, depending on whether the speed is below or above the command value. The controller has to take into account the time lag between its newly commanded drive force and the resulting final speed. The vehicle speed can become unstable and oscillate (vary up and down) if the controller tries to correct speed errors too quickly.

Figure 8-1. Block Diagram of Cruise Control

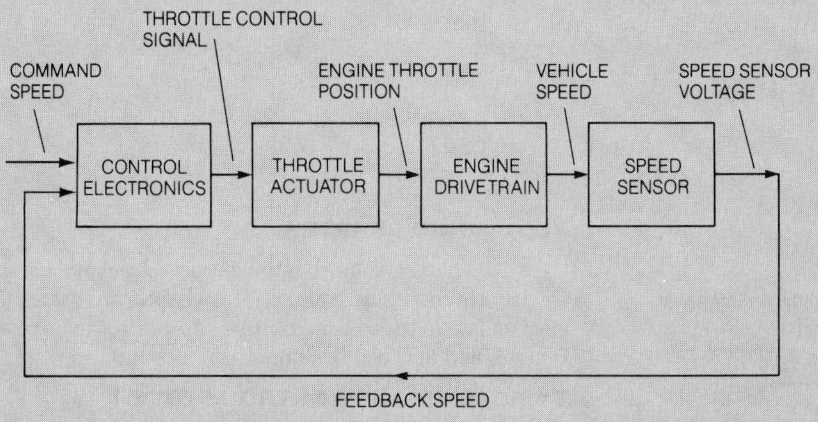

Most speed controllers use proportional-integral (PI) control. The control signal is the sum of two signals, one that is proportional to the error signal and one whose ramp rate is proportional to the error signal.

Most vehicle speed controllers use a type of control electronics known as proportional-integral control, or PI control (*Figure 8-2*). One of the major drawbacks of using proportional control alone is the size of the steady-state error allowed by proportional control systems (see Chapter 2). The final error depends on the proportional gain constant. To reduce the final error to a very small difference requires a large control effort or gain.

In a PI control system, the control signal is actually the sum of two signals. The proportional gain block K_p in *Figure 8-2* provides a control signal that is proportional to the error signal, e. The other block, the integrator block, generates an output that is proportional to the integral of the error. Integration is a concept from calculus. For those readers not familiar with this subject, the integrator can be understood qualitatively for the special case of a constant error signal. In this case, the integrator output voltage increases or decreases linearly with time (i.e., slopes up or down) depending upon whether e is positive or negative, respectively. The gains K_p and K_I are chosen so that the system has quick response, high accuracy, and no instability or oscillations.

The integral control is used in addition to proportional control to help drive the steady state error to zero. It does this by effectively adding up the error as time goes by. The integral control block always drives the final error toward zero. The time required to drive the error to zero is determined by the integral control gain.

Performance Curves

The performance of such PI systems can be described by plotting the vehicle speed (velocity) response of the system of *Figure 8-2* against time when a new command speed is required. The system cannot respond instantaneously. Rather, the system has a specific response time.

Figure 8-2. Block Diagram of Cruise Controller Using PI Control

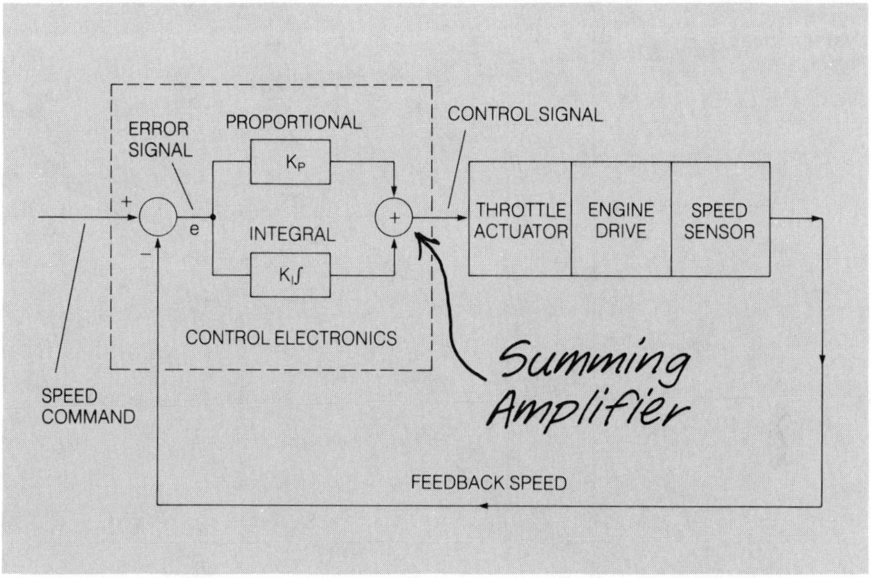

The response time is specified by the time constant of the system measured to the point where the speed is 63% of what its final value will be. The time constant varies with the parameters of the complete system. However, a major controlling parameter is the damping coefficient.

Speed Response Curves

When a new speed is requested, the time required for the vehicle to reach that speed is affected by the control system's damping coefficient.

Systems that have an overdamped response are sluggish. Systems that are underdamped provide quick response, but oscillate. Critically and optimally damped systems come closer to an ideal response.

The curves seen in *Figure 8-3* are plots for systems with different damping coefficients. Curve 1 is the speed response of a system that is overdamped. The speed of the system rises sluggishly and takes a long time to reach the command velocity. It has a time constant determined by point A. Curve 4 is the speed response of a system that is underdamped. The speed curve rises quickly, but overshoots the commanded speed and then oscillates around the commanded speed until it finally settles down. The frequency of the oscillations is called the system's natural frequency. The time constant is determined by point D.

Curves 2 and 3 are systems that have damping coefficients that make critically damped or optimally damped systems. The critically damped system rises smoothly to the command speed with no overshoot and in a minimum amount of time. The optimally damped system rises quickly and overshoots a little, but settles quickly to the commanded velocity. This system is called optimally damped because the vehicle speed follows the command speed more closely than it does for any of the other systems.

Figure 8-3. System Speed Performance

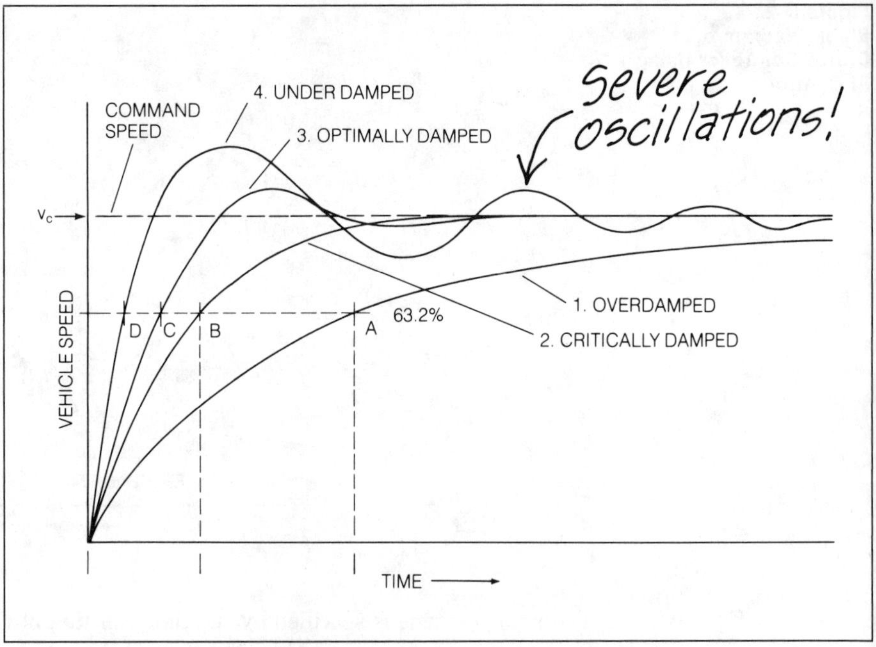

Designers usually strive for an optimally damped control system, but engine power limits and other practical limitations may force the designer to choose a different response.

Usually a control system designer attempts to balance the proportional and integral control gains so that the system is optimally damped. However, because of system characteristics, it is impossible, impractical, and/or inefficient in many cases to achieve the optimal time response; so, another response is chosen. The control system should make the engine drive force react quickly and accurately to the command speed, but should not overtax the engine in the process. Therefore, the system designer chooses the control electronics that provide the following system qualities:

1. quick response
2. relative stability
3. small steady-state error
4. optimization of the control effort required.

Digital Cruise Control

The explanation of the operation of cruise control thus far has been based upon continuous time or analog electronics. However, cruise control is now mostly implemented digitally using a microprocessor-based computer. For such a system, proportional and integral control computations are performed numerically in the computer. A block diagram for a typical digital cruise control is shown in *Figure 8-4*. The vehicle speed sensor (described later in this chapter) is digital. When the car reaches the desired speed, S_d, the driver activates the speed set switch. At this time, the output of the vehicle speed sensor is transferred to a storage register.

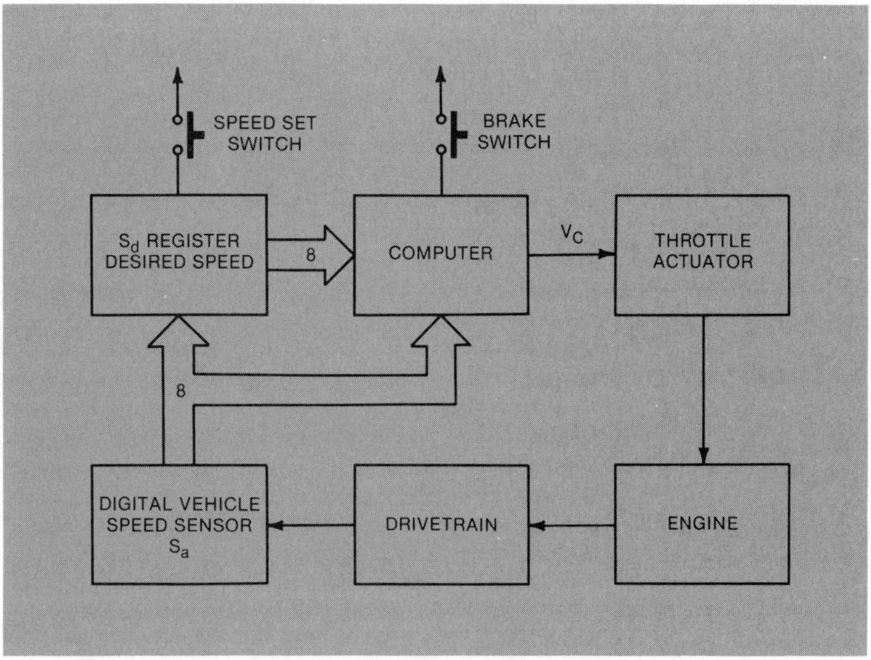

Figure 8-4. Digital Cruise Control System

The computer continuously reads the actual vehicle speed, S_a, and generates an error, e_n, at the sample time, t_n (n is an integer).

$$e_n = S_d - S_a \qquad \text{at time } t_n$$

A control signal, d, is computed which has the form:[1]

$$d = K_P e_n + K_I \sum_{m=1}^{M} e_{n-m}$$

This control signal is actually the duty cycle of a square wave (v_c) which is applied to the throttle actuator (as explained later). The throttle opening increases or decreases as d increases or decreases.

The operation of the cruise control system can be further understood by examining the vehicle speed sensor and the actuator in detail. *Figure 8-5* is a sketch of one type of sensor which is suitable for vehicle speed measurement.

In a typical vehicle speed measurement system, the vehicle speed information is mechanically coupled to the speed sensor by a flexible cable coming from the driveshaft, which rotates at an angular speed proportional

[1]Note that the latter symbol means to sum the M previously calculated errors to the present error.

to vehicle speed. A speed sensor driven by this cable generates a pulsed electrical signal (*Figure 8-6*) that is processed by the computer to obtain a digital measurement of speed.

Figure 8-5. Digital Speed Sensor

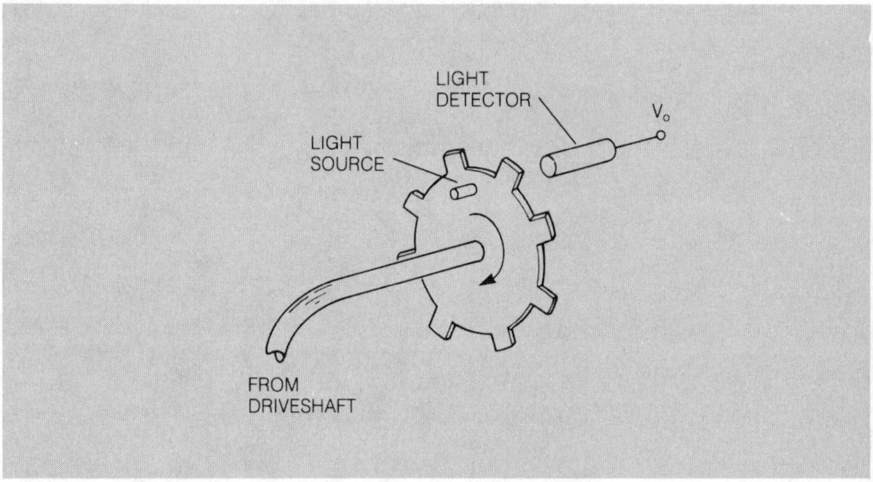

Figure 8-6. Digital Speed Signal

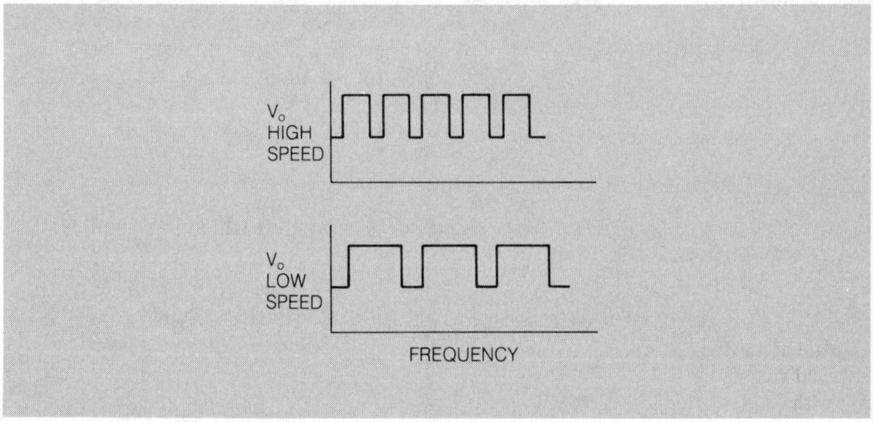

The flexible cable drives a slotted disk that rotates between a light source and a light detector. The placement of the source, disk, and detector is such that the slotted disk interrupts or passes the light from source to detector, depending upon whether a slot is in the line of sight from source to detector. The light detector produces an output voltage whenever a pulse of light from the light source passes through a slot to the detector. The number of pulses generated per second is proportional to the number of slots in the disk and the vehicle speed.

$$f = NSK$$

where

f = frequency in pulses per second
N = number of slots in the sensor disk
S = vehicle speed
K = proportionality constant which accounts for differential gear ratio and wheel size

The output pulses are passed through a sample gate to a digital counter (*Figure 8-7*). The sample gate is an electronic switch that either passes the pulses to the counter or does not pass them. The time interval during which the gate is open is precisely controlled by the computer. The digital counter counts the number of pulses from the light detector during time t that the gate is open. The number of pulses that are counted by the digital counter is given by:

$$P = tNSK$$

That is, the number P is proportional to vehicle speed S.

Figure 8-7. Digital Speed Measurement System

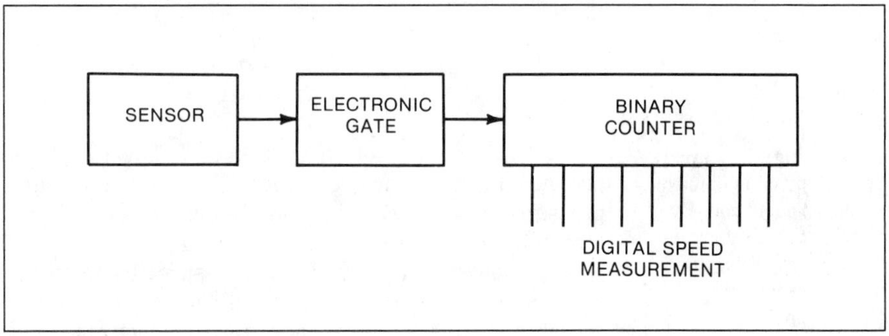

Throttle Actuator

Throttle actuators use manifold vacuum to pull a piston that is mechanically linked to the throttle. The amount of vacuum provided is controlled by a solenoid valve that is turned on and off rapidly.

An actuator which is important to the cruise control system that was not covered in Chapter 5 is the throttle actuator. In all of the discussions thus far, it is assumed that the throttle is being activated by the vehicle driver who is outside the electronic control system. With cruise control, however, throttle actuation is a part of the electronic control system.

Many cruise control throttle actuators (*Figure 8-8*) use a type of pneumatic piston arrangement that is driven from the intake manifold vacuum. The piston connecting rod is attached to the throttle lever. There is also a spring attached to the lever. If there is no force applied by the piston, the spring pulls the throttle closed. When an actuator input signal energizes the electromagnet in the control solenoid, the pressure control valve is pulled down and changes the actuator cylinder pressure by providing a path to manifold pressure. Manifold pressure is lower than atmospheric pressure, so the actuator cylinder pressure quickly drops, causing the piston to pull against the throttle lever to open the throttle.

Figure 8-8.
Vacuum Operated Throttle Actuator

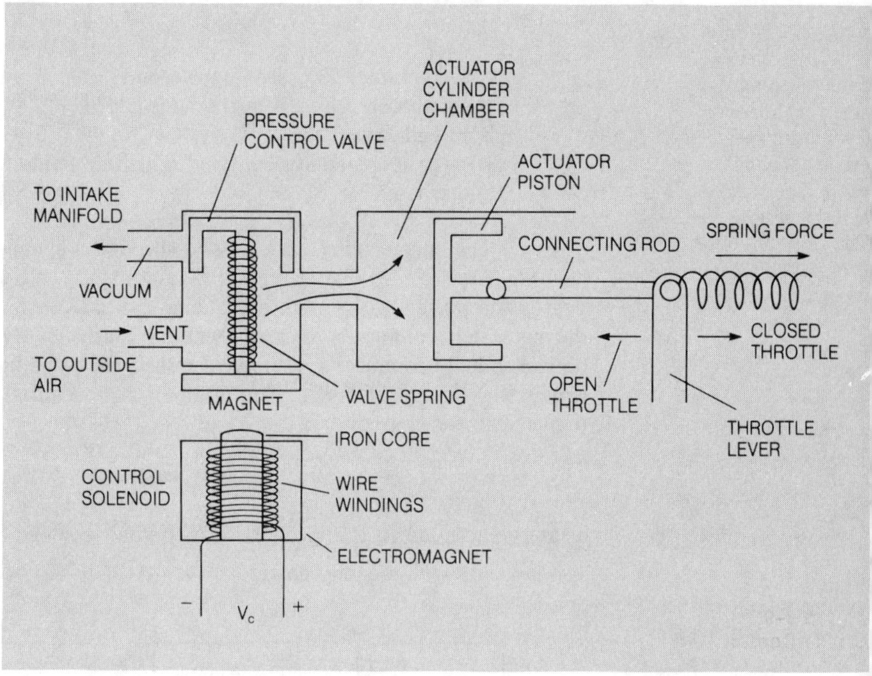

A switching, duty cycle type of signal is applied to the solenoid coil. By varying the duty cycle, the amount of vacuum, and corresponding throttle angle, is varied.

The force exerted by the piston is varied by changing the average pressure in the cylinder chamber. This is done by rapidly switching the pressure control valve between the outside air port, which provides atmospheric pressure, and the manifold pressure port, the pressure of which is lower than atmospheric pressure. The actuator control signal V_c, is a variable duty cycle type of signal like that discussed for the fuel injector actuator. A high V_c signal energizes the electromagnet; a low V_c signal deenergizes the electromagnet. Switching back and forth between the two pressure sources causes the average pressure in the chamber to be somewhere between the low manifold pressure and outside atmospheric pressure. This average pressure and, consequently, the piston force are proportional to the duty cycle of the valve control signal V_c.

This type of duty cycle controlled throttle actuator is ideally suited for use in digital control systems. If used in an analog control system, the analog control signal must first be converted to a duty cycle control signal. The same frequency response considerations apply to the throttle actuator as to the speed sensor. In fact, with both in the closed-loop control system, each contributes to the total system phase shift and gain.

CRUISE CONTROL ELECTRONICS

The preceding discussion has explained the operating principles of a cruise control system for both analog (continuous time) and digital (discrete time) systems. At this point, it is instructive to consider the electronics that implement these system concepts.

In an analog cruise control system, an error amplifier compares actual speed and desired (command) speed. The error signal output is fed to a proportional amplifier and an integral amplifier. The resultant outputs are combined by a summing amplifier.

An example of electronics for a cruise control system that is basically analog is shown in *Figure 8-9*. Notice that the system uses four operational amplifiers (op amps) and that each op amp is used for a specific purpose. Op amp 1 is used as an error amplifier. The output of op amp 1 is proportional to the difference between the command speed and the actual speed. The error signal is then used as an input to op amp 2 and op amp 3. Op amp 2 is a proportional amplifier with a gain of $K_p = -R_2/R_1$. Notice that R_1 is variable so that the proportional gain can be adjusted. Op amp 3 is an integral amplifier or integrator with a gain of $K_I = -1/R_3C_1$. Resistor R_3 is variable to permit adjustment of the gain. The op amp causes a current to flow into capacitor C_1which is equal to the current flowing into R_3. The voltage across R_3 is the error amplifier output voltage, V_e. The current in R_3 is found from Ohm's law to be:

$$I = \frac{V_e}{R_3}$$

which is identical to the current flowing into the capacitor. If the error signal V_e is constant, the current I will be constant and the voltage across the capacitor will steadily change at a rate proportional to the current flow.

Figure 8-9. Cruise Control Electronics (Analog)

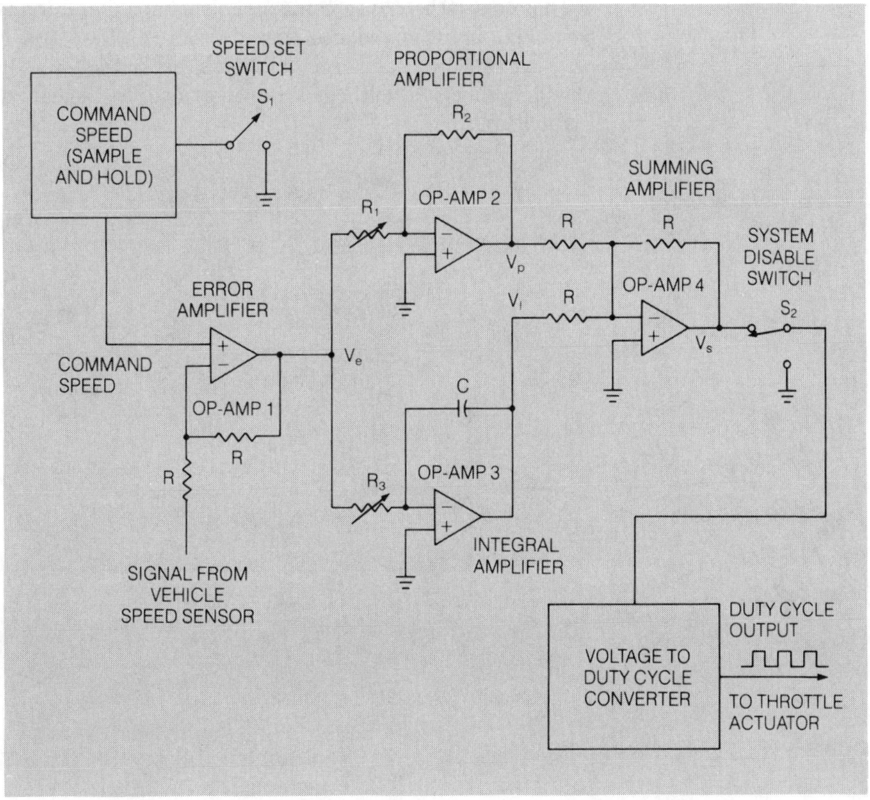

The output of the integral amplifier V_I increases or decreases with time depending upon whether V_e is above or below zero volts. The voltage V_I is steady or unchanging only when the error is exactly zero; this is why the integral gain block in the diagram in *Figure 8-9* can reduce the system's steady-state error to zero. Even a small error causes V_I to change to correct for the error.

The outputs of the proportional and integral amplifiers are added together using a summing amplifier, op amp 4. The summing amplifier adds voltages V_p and V_I and inverts the resulting sum. The inversion is necessary because both the proportional and integral amplifiers invert their input signals while providing amplification. Inverting the sum restores the correct sense or polarity to the control signal.

Because the output of the summing amplifier is an analog signal, it must be converted into a duty cycle signal to pulse the throttle actuator.

The summing amplifier op amp produces an analog voltage, V_S, that must be converted to a duty cycle signal before it can drive the throttle actuator. A voltage-to-duty cycle converter is used whose output directly drives the throttle actuator solenoid.

Shown in *Figure 8-9* are two switches, S_1 and S_2. Switch S_1 is operated by the driver to set the desired speed. It signals the sample-and-hold electronics (*Figure 8-10*) to sample the present vehicle speed and hold that value. Voltage V_1, representing the vehicle speed at which the driver wishes to set the cruise controller, is sampled and it charges capacitor C. A very high input impedance amplifier detects the voltage on the capacitor without causing the charge on the capacitor to "leak" off. The output from this amplifier is a voltage, V_s, proportional to the command speed to the error amplifier.

Figure 8-10. Typical Sample-and-Hold Circuit

Sensor voltage (V_1) represents vehicle speed.

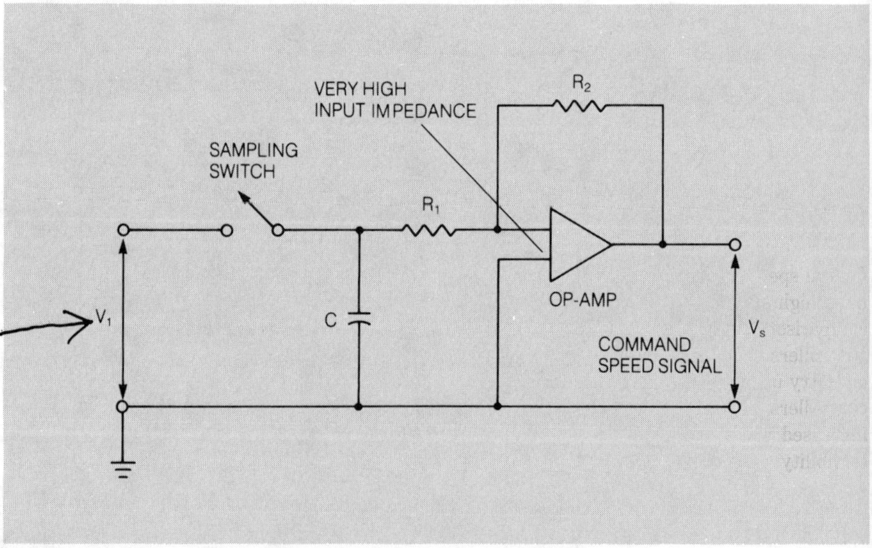

Switch S_2 is used to disable the speed controller by interrupting the control signal to the throttle actuator. Switch S_2 disables the system whenever the ignition is turned off, the controller is turned off, or when the brake pedal is pressed. The controller is switched on when the driver presses the speed set switch S_1.

For safety reasons, the brake turnoff is performed two ways. As just mentioned, pressing the brake pedal turns off or disables the electronic control. The brake pedal also mechanically opens a separate valve that is located in a hose connected to the throttle actuator cylinder. When the valve is opened by depression of the brake pedal, it allows outside air to flow into the throttle actuator cylinder so that the throttle plate instantly snaps closed. The valve is shut off whenever the brake pedal is in its inactive position. This ensures a fast and complete shut down of the speed control system whenever the driver presses the brake pedal.

Digital Speed Control

Digital speed controllers store command speed sensor pulses directly, and convert these values to binary codes. The codes are compared mathematically to produce the error signal used by the proportional gain and integrator gain logic.

As was mentioned earlier, the speed controller can be implemented using digital logic instead of analog circuitry. At the beginning of the chapter, a microprocessor-based cruise control scheme was explained. However, it is possible to implement a digital cruise control without using a microprocessor. *Figure 8–11* is a block diagram of a representative example digital cruise control.

When digital circuitry is used, the input speed command and the actual vehicle speed are stored directly as numbers. The actual speed signal is sampled periodically, while the command speed signal is sampled only when the driver sets a new speed. The pulses coming from the speed sensor are counted in a given time period and converted to a digital number code representing the speed. The digital numbers are subtracted from each other to get a difference, and a number representing the error is processed over two paths just as in the analog controller. The one path uses a lookup table which provides a number that represents the proportional gain for the system. The other path integrates the error numbers over time and provides a number that represents the integral gain. An adder sums these numbers and a duty cycle generator provides the timed on-off pulses to the throttle actuator.

Digital speed controllers have high stability in comparison to analog controllers. VSLI circuitry used in digital controllers provides increased programming flexibility.

A significant advantage that the digital circuitry has over analog circuitry is that the data or information contained in the system in digital codes does not change with severe temperature and humidity changes. Therefore, digital systems have much more stability over these extremes.

Due to the advances made in LSI and VLSI technology, the digital controller can be a single integrated circuit contained in one package. Alternatively, the microcomputer that is providing the electronic engine control could, in principle, be used to also provide the speed control. This demonstrates another distinct advantage of digital systems—additional functions can be added to a programmable digital system just by changing the program. This saves expensive control hardware.

Figure 8-11. Digital Vehicle Speed Controller

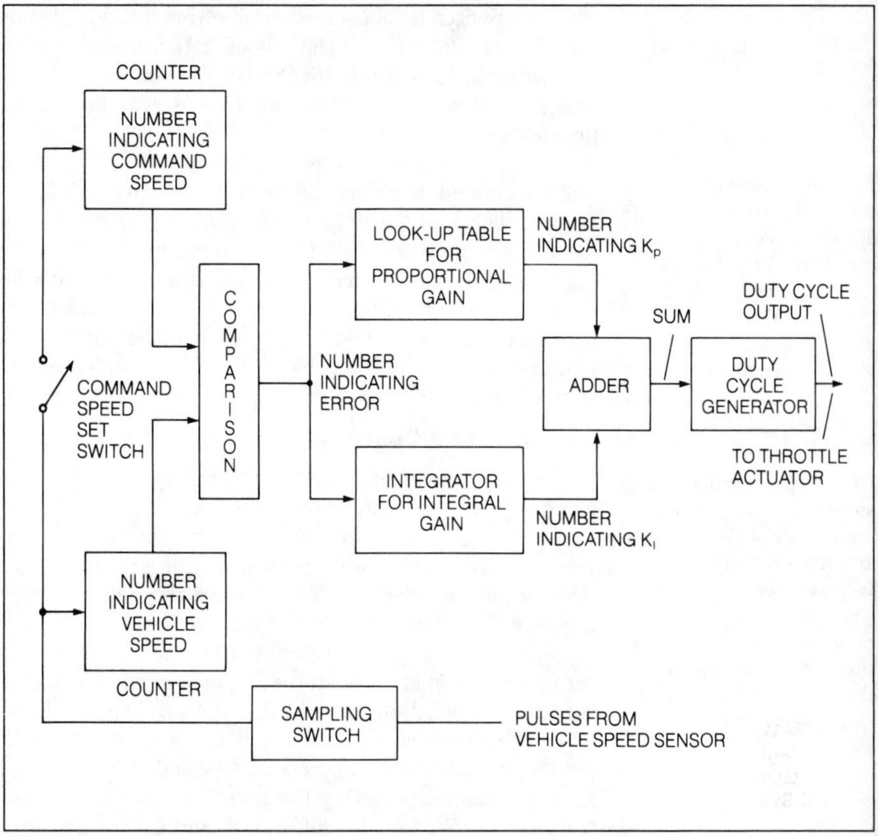

ENGINE GOVERNOR

Engine governors limit maximum engine speeds to prevent damage to engine parts.

Another application of a speed controller is the engine governor. An engine governor controls and limits engine speed below some maximum limit without regard to vehicle speed. An engine governor is used mostly on heavy duty trucks and construction vehicles to prevent excessively high engine speed which can damage engine bearings and severely strain certain engine parts. Mechanical governors have been used in the past to control and limit engine speed.

The electronic engine governor controls and limits engine speed by adjusting the engine throttle (for an SI engine) with an actuator similar to the cruise control throttle actuator discussed earlier. Engine RPM is measured by the same type of sensor as is used to measure vehicle speed; in this case, however, it may be mounted on the distributor shaft or the crankshaft rather than the driveshaft.

The engine governor control electronics closely matches that of the cruise control system of *Figure 8-9* except for some significant differences. One of these is that engine speed may be allowed to vary through a range below a certain maximum limit. When the maximum limit is reached, the engine speed is held constant at or below the maximum limit. Another difference is that now only the engine speed is being controlled; therefore, the mass M and the friction C will be much less than that for the complete vehicle involved in the cruise control system.

Anticipation

Engine governor control electronics utilize an additional signal called lead term. The lead term signal is used to predict future RPM by monitoring the rate of change in engine speed.

Since the engine speed is allowed to vary below the maximum limit, the governor must be able to detect how fast the engine speed is accelerating so that the speed does not overshoot the limit before the governor control takes effect. To understand how this is done, examine the block diagram of *Figure 8-12.* The same proportional gain, K_p, and integral gain, K_I, are included in the engine governor block diagram as for the cruise control. However, now there is an additional block for gain K_d. The extra control block adds an extra signal to the PI control signal in order to take control of the throttle a little bit before the engine speed rises past the preset limit. The new control block is called a lead term because it anticipates or predicts the engine speed at some time in the future. It makes this prediction based on the *rate of change* of the engine RPM. For those readers familiar with calculus, this rate of change is obtained by calculating the derivative with respect to time of the RPM signal. If the engine RPM is rising rapidly, the lead-term control block adds a signal which takes control earlier than if engine RPM is rising slowly. This allows enough time for the system to respond, so that the throttle angle is reduced before engine speed becomes excessive.

Figure 8-12. Block Diagram of Engine Governor Control System

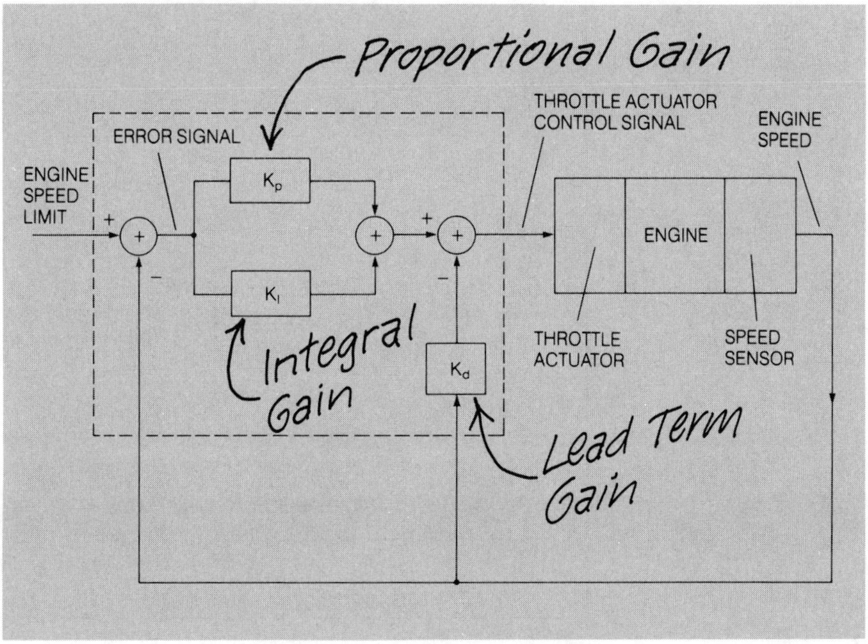

Lead term action purposely leads the system response to successfully predict the proper throttle angle.

As shown in *Figure 8-12*, the engine speed is used as the input to the lead term. When the engine speed increases rapidly, the lead term reduces the engine throttle position in proportion to the rate of engine speed rise. This makes the engine feel a little bit sluggish, because the effect of a quick accelerator depression, which normally produces a rapid increase in engine speed and fast acceleration, is reduced by the lead term. The amount of sluggishness is determined by the lead term gain, K_d. A large K_d causes a very sluggish response, while a small K_d allows a crisper response.

Governor Control Electronics

An analog governor control circuit uses a lead term op amp to provide a gain constant with phase shift. Since the lead term amp inverts its signal, a second op amp corrects the inversion.

The control circuit for the engine speed governor is almost identical to the vehicle speed control schematic of *Figure 8-12*. The one difference is the inclusion of the lead-term circuitry. *Figure 8-13* shows the additional electronics for a lead term and how they fit into the circuitry of *Figure 8-9*. Another input is added to the summing amplifier to accept the lead-term signal in addition to the proportional and integral signals. The lead amplifier provides a gain constant $K_d = C_1R_1$. The lead amplifier is an inverting amplifier, so another inverting amplifier is placed immediately before the lead circuit to correct the sign change.

Figure 8-13. Lead Term Circuit for Governor Control

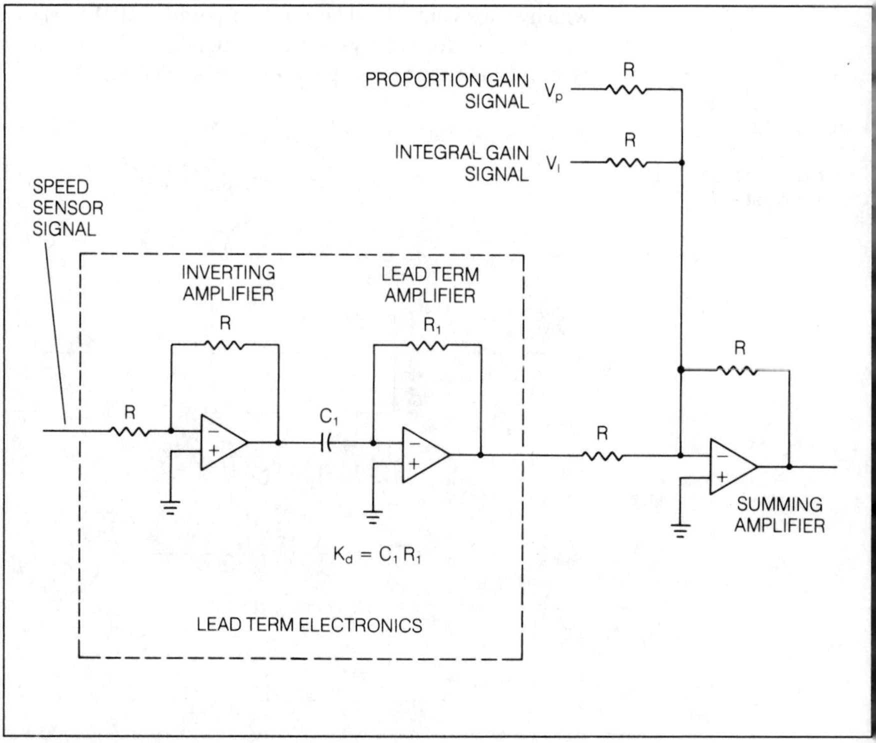

The system seen in *Figure 8–12* is the analog circuit version of an engine governor. If the control is accomplished digitally, a program for the integrated control system that differentiates the RPM signal (i.e., calculates the derivative of RPM) must be added to, or a separate digital circuit, which is called a differentiator, must be substituted in the system to accomplish what the lead circuitry does in the analog system.

TIRE-SLIP CONTROLLER

The force that moves a car forward is actually a reaction to the torque that is applied to the driving wheel axles. This force actually is produced at the point of contact of the tire and the road and depends upon friction between the tire and the road. If there were no friction at this point, the tires would simply spin and the car would stand still.

There are circumstances in which the friction between tire and road is reduced or disappears, such as when driving on wet or icy roads. A tire-slip controller is an electronic system that first detects the tendency of a tire to slip in reduced friction situations, and then regulates the engine torque to prevent a slip.

Tire-slip controllers detect tire slip by monitoring the speed relation between the driving wheels and the vehicle speed.

Figure 8–14 is a sketch of a tire running on a road surface. The torque produced by the engine is converted to a force F which drives the vehicle in the direction shown. As long as F is developed, the vehicle moves forward just as much as the wheel turns on the surface. However, if F can no longer be maintained by the friction between the tire and the surface, the tire slips on the surface and the vehicle forward motion is slowed or stopped. The wheel spins on the surface, resulting in wheel speed that is much greater than vehicle speed.

Figure 8–14. Tire Running on a Surface

Slip occurs due to loss of friction.

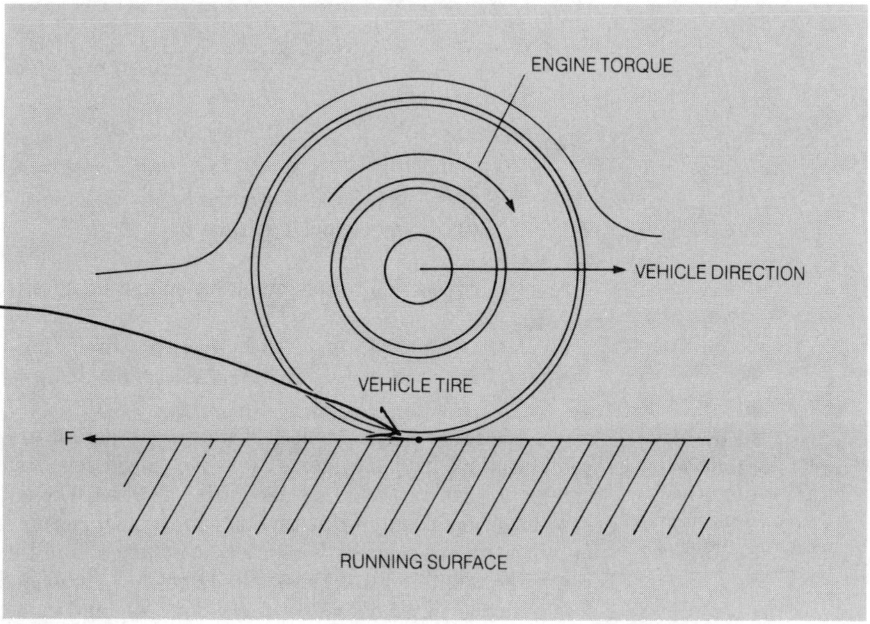

One relatively straightforward tire-slip controller concept is based upon measuring vehicle speed S and tire speed S_T:

$$S_T = \pi aR/30$$

where

a = tire radius
R = tire RPM

Slip is characterized by tire speed exceeding vehicle speed:

$$S_T - S > 0$$

Unfortunately, no cost effective sensor has been found for measuring vehicle speed which doesn't involve measuring a wheel speed. Consequently, this relatively simple concept for measuring slip hasn't been found to be practically feasible.

On the other hand, an alternate scheme for detecting tire slip is based upon measuring changes in wheel speed. The change in wheel speed, which can occur without tire slip, is limited by the inertia of the car. However, the wheel speed can change very quickly in tire-slip situations. That is to say, the tire angular acceleration is much higher in a slip situation than when there is no slip.

The angular acceleration of the tire, A, is the rate of change of tire speed, which can be obtained by measuring wheel speed at two closely spaced instants:

$$A = \frac{(S_T(1) - S_T(2))}{(t_1 - t_2)} = \text{rate of change of wheel speed}$$

where

$S_T(1)$ = wheel speed at time t_1
$S_T(2)$ = wheel speed at time t_2

Tire slip corresponds to this acceleration exceeding a threshold value A_T:

$$A > A_T \rightarrow \text{slip}$$
$$A < A_T \rightarrow \text{no slip}$$

One theme for tire slip control senses sudden angular acceleration of the driven wheel such as occurs during tire slip.

Figure 8–15 is a block diagram of a digital tire-slip controller configuration. In this system, the wheel speed sensor is presumed to be similar to that described earlier in this chapter. The output of this sensor is sent to binary counter 1 at time t_1 and to binary counter 2 at time t_2. The output of these counters is digitally subtracted, and this difference compared (digitally) to a threshold value (A_T). As long as the difference is less than the threshold value, there is no slip and no action is taken by the controller. Whenever the difference exceeds the threshold, an output is generated that stops the fuel from going to the engine. The torque produced by the engine is thereby reduced, and tire slip is eliminated.

Figure 8-15. Digital Tire-Slip Control System

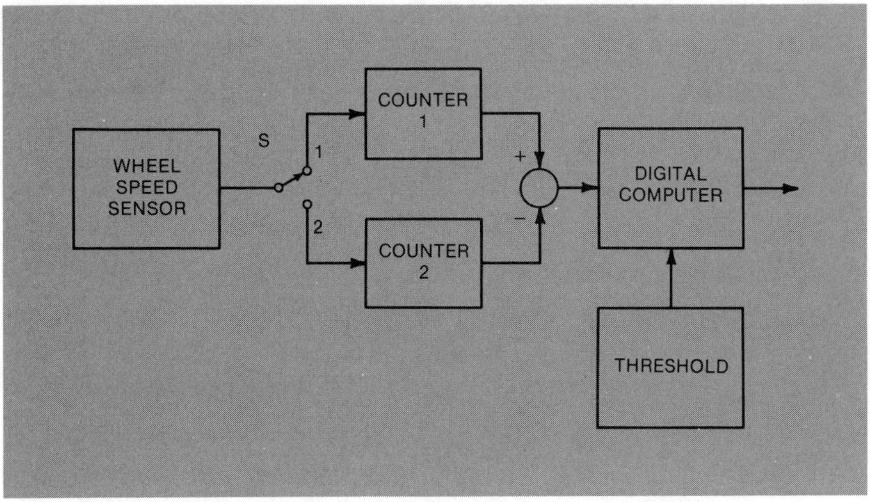

Experimental versions of the tire-slip controller have been built and tested. However, as of the present time, no such system is commercially available.

ANTILOCK BRAKING SYSTEM

Antilock braking system prevents wheel lock during heavy breaking on wet or icy surfaces.

Another very important application of electronics to vehicle motion control is the antilock braking system (ABS). This system functions to prevent wheels from locking when the brakes are applied in a relatively low wheel/road friction situation, such as on wet or icy roads.

If the brakes are applied with sufficient force (panic braking) one or more of the wheels may "lock" (i.e., cease rotating) and the tire "skids" over the road surface. In a severe skid, there is usually a loss of steering control over the vehicle. Severe loss of steering control in a panic braking situation can result in collision, and is clearly an undesirable condition.

An ideal ABS system would measure wheel skid by measuring the difference between wheel speed and vehicle speed (as in the case of tire-slip controller). However, as in the case of the tire-slip controller, no cost effective sensor for vehicle speed has been developed that operates independently of wheel speed.

On the other hand, a number of commercially viable ABS systems have been developed that are based upon measurements of wheel deceleration. Wheel deceleration can be measured using a scheme similar to that depicted in *Figure 8-15*. Wheel speeds at two closely spaced instants are measured and subtracted. Whenever the earlier wheel speed exceeds the later by a threshold value, a skid condition is detected.

In a skid condition, the ABS system generates an electrical signal that lowers the brake pressure by an amount which is sufficient to eliminate brake lock. There are many schemes that have been produced and sold. *Figure 8-16* is a schematic drawing of one such system. In this figure, the modulators are the devices that lower the brake pressure.

Figure 8-16. Antilock Braking System

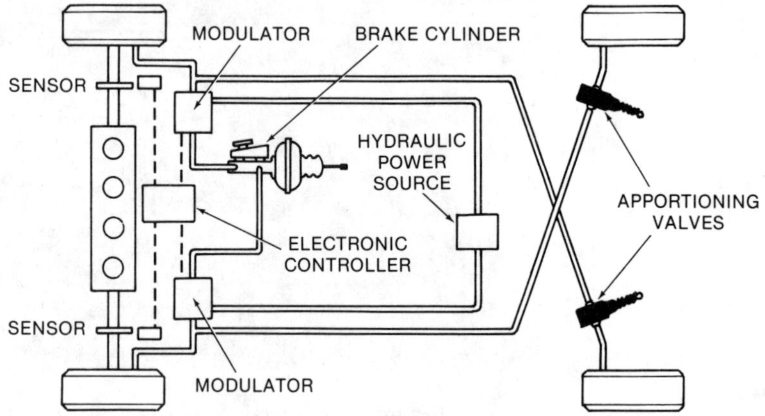

The antilock braking system has become quite common in Europe and will undoubtedly increase in popularity in the United States as more experience is gained in its use.

ELECTRONIC RIDE CONTROL

An electronic ride control system modifies suspension system parameters to alter the "ride."

One of the most exciting new applications of electronics to automotive motion control is in the area of vehicle ride control. Before the advent of adaptive ride control, a car was designed to have one specific ride characteristic. Typically, passenger cars had a "soft" suspension in which the car body tended to remain level when driving over a rough road because of the relatively compliant suspension system. This relatively soft suspension tended to be a compromise with respect to handling qualities. A sports car, for example, typically has very "firm" suspension to provide good handling in driving through curves.

Electronic ride control has the potential to continuously change the suspension system parameters to match driving conditions. In most electronic ride control systems, the shock absorber characteristics are varied so as to be able to change the ride. In a typical system, the driver selects "firm" or automatic suspension control by means of a switch. In the firm mode the system sets the shock absorber for a firm suspension. In automatic mode, the shock absorber is changed continuously depending upon the driving conditions; during normal steady cruise on a nominally straight road, the system adjusts for "soft" suspension and during hard cornering, braking, or acceleration, the system adjusts for firm suspension.

Sensors

A ride control system senses lateral and longitudinal acceleration to calculate the desired shock absorber rate.

In the example ride control system, three variables must be measured: (1) lateral acceleration (A_L) during cornering, (2) deceleration, and (3) acceleration. The lateral acceleration is approximately given by the expression:

$$A_L = kS^2\Theta$$

where

S = vehicle speed
Θ = steering angle

A vehicle speed sensor has already been described. The steering angle can be measured by measuring the rotation of the steering wheel. This is done by using photocells, a light source, and a disk with multiple holes. There are many configurations that are suitable for the disk, such as the simple pattern of *Figure 8-17* which is presented here only by way of illustration.

Figure 8-17. Wheel Position Sensor Disk

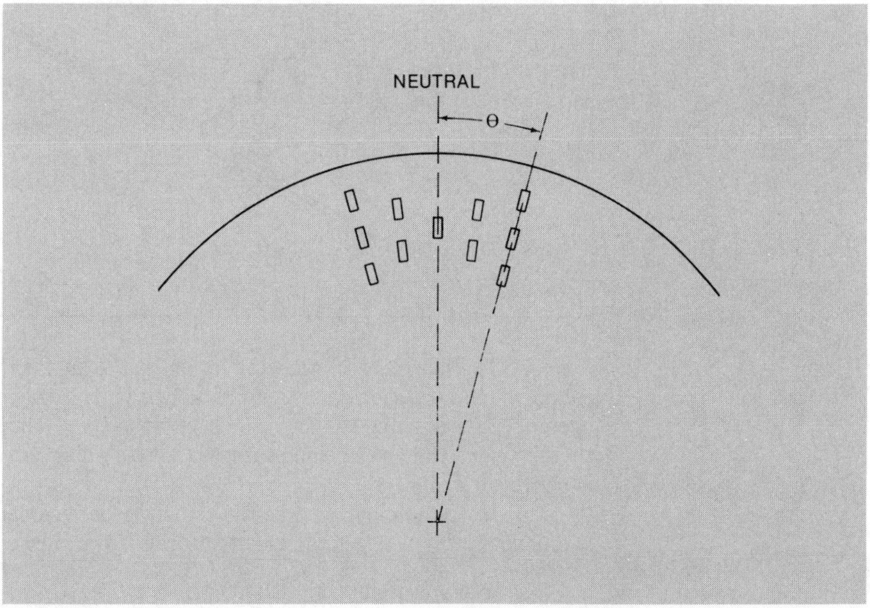

The vehicle deceleration is proportional to braking force. In the example electronic ride control, braking force is measured by measuring brake-line pressure.

Vehicle acceleration can be estimated from throttle angle and manifold pressure. Sensors for these variables are typically already on the car for electronic engine control purposes. Representative examples of such sensors have already been explained in Chapter 5.

The ride control actuator is a special, adjustable shock absorber. In general, a shock absorber consists of a piston in an oil-filled cylinder, such as is depicted in *Figure 8–18.* The piston has small holes through which the oil flows. As the piston moves in the cylinder, a force opposes the motion which is due to the motion of the oil through the holes. The oil is incompressible and must pass through the holes to make room for the piston motion. Usually, the force increases with increasing piston speed and decreases with increasing hole size.

Figure 8–18. Adjustable Shock Absorber Sketch

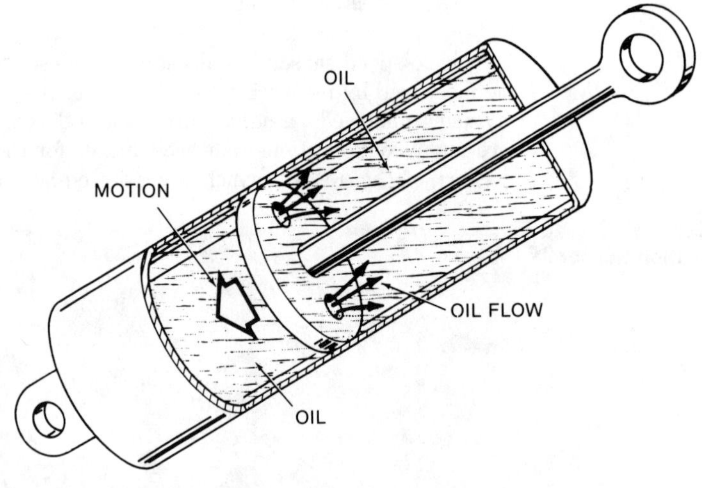

The ride control actuator incorporates an electrically operated rotary valve through which the oil must pass. By varying the valve opening, it is possible to vary the shock absorber "damping" force and thereby vary the suspension stiffness. A block diagram for the ride control is shown in *Figure 8–19.*

In the automatic mode, the computer obtains data from the sensors and momentarily changes the shock absorber to firm ride whenever:

brake pressure >	400 psi
vehicle speed >	83 mph
engine MAP >	8 psi boost
throttle >	90% of wide open throttle
lateral acceleration >	.35 g

Figure 8-19. Digital Ride Control System

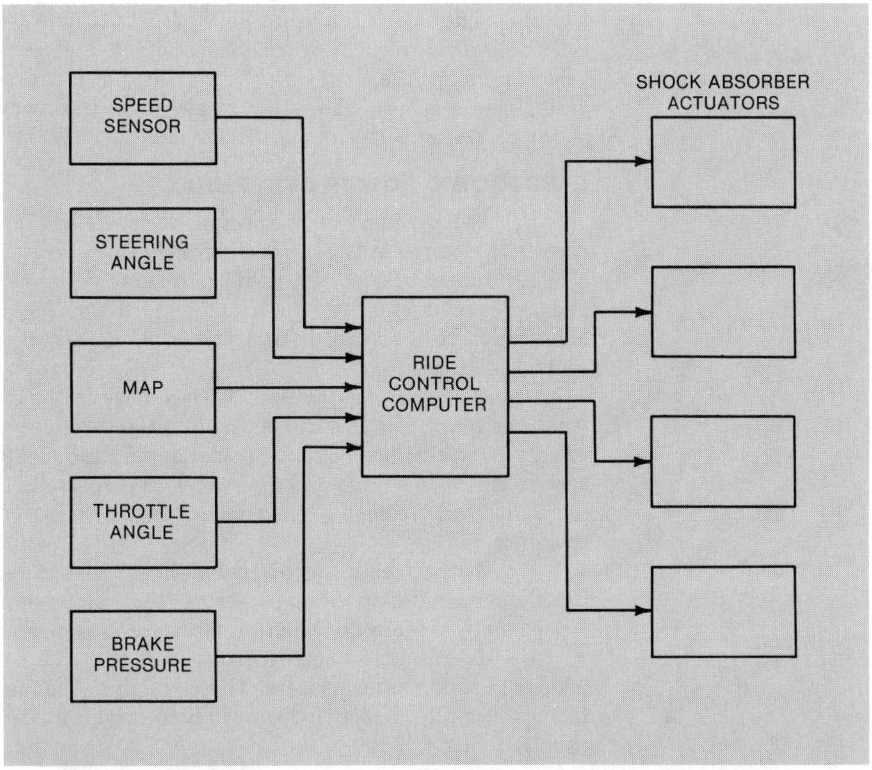

Figure 8-20. Influence of Lateral Acceleration on Ride

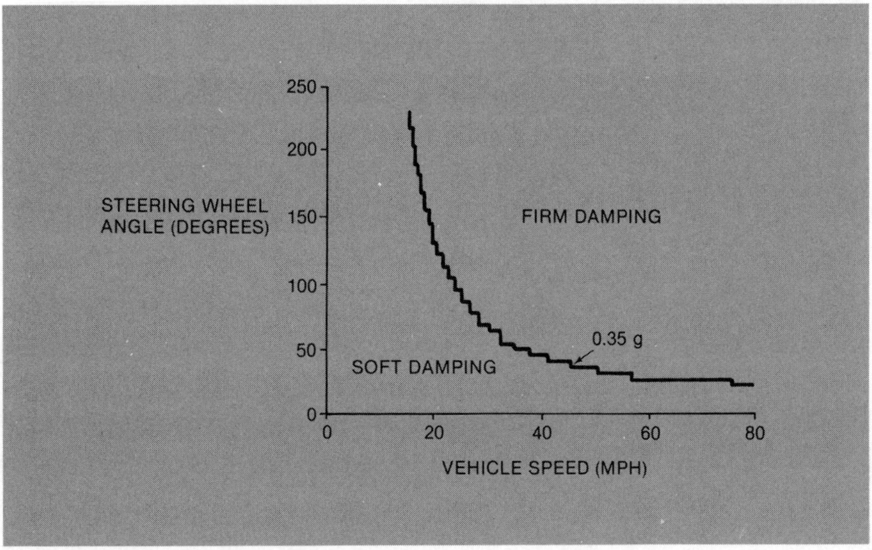

Figure 8–20 is a graph showing lateral acceleration influence on ride. Electronic ride control has many potential advantages for optimizing vehicle performance. It is capable of giving small cars some of the large car "ride," and it can give large cars, which have traditionally had soft ride, better cornering performance than would otherwise be possible.

ELECTRONIC POWER STEERING

Another important aspect of electronic motion control is the advent of electronically controlled, electrically activated power steering. The advantages of such a system are relative energy efficiency compared to hydraulic power steering, and adaptability to varying driving conditions. In addition, there is a trend to incorporate all-wheel steering in electronically controlled steering.

At low speeds the front wheels move in the direction of the turn, while the rear wheels rotate opposite to the turn direction. The motion greatly facilitates maneuvering (especially for parallel parking). At higher speeds the front wheels and the rear wheels rotate in the direction of the turn. This will result in precise and abrupt maneuvering such as lane changing.

The control of the 4-wheel electronic/electric power steering will be based upon vehicle speed and steering wheel direction measurements; consequently, senors are required for these variables.

Electronic, 4-wheel steering is presently in early stages of introduction on passenger cars. There will likely be many developments in this emerging technology which will be reported in various automotive journals.

Quiz for Chapter 8

1. A typical cruise control system senses the difference between
   - **a.** vehicle speed and tire speed
   - **b.** set speed and actual vehicle speed
   - **c.** engine angular speed and wheel speed
   - **d.** none of the above

2. A cruise control system controls vehicle speed using
   - **a.** a feedback carburetor
   - **b.** a distributorless ignition system
   - **c.** a throttle actuator
   - **d.** a MAS sensor

3. One of the major drawbacks to a proportional controller is
   - **a.** steady-state error
   - **b.** integral of the error
   - **c.** gain error
   - **d.** all of the above

4. A critically damped system has a response to a step input which
   - **a.** has overshoot
   - **b.** rises smoothly to the final value with no overshoot
   - **c.** can only be achieved with a proportional control system
   - **d.** is the slowest of all possible responses

5. A digital cruise control system
   - **a.** operates on samples of the error signal
   - **b.** computes a control signal numerically
   - **c.** obtains a digital measurement of vehicle speed
   - **d.** all of the above

6. In the example digital cruise control system of this chapter the vehicle speed sensor
   - **a.** counts pulses of light at a frequency which is proportional to vehicle speed
   - **b.** generates an analog signal
   - **c.** measures crankshaft rotation speed directly
   - **d.** none of the above

7. One advantage of digital motion control system is
   - **a.** the ability to work with analog signals
   - **b.** the stability of operation with respect to environmental extremes
   - **c.** the exclusive ability to generate integrals of the error signal
   - **d.** all of the above

8. An engine governor system incorporating a lead term predicts future engine RPM by
   - **a.** using an integral of the error
   - **b.** determining the rate of change of RPM
   - **c.** amplifying the proportional error
   - **d.** eliminating the lead term

9. A practical tire-slip controller is based upon measurement of
   - **a.** wheel speed
   - **b.** vehicle speed
   - **c.** both of the above
   - **d.** neither of the above

10. An ideal antilock braking system measures skid by
    a. measuring the difference between wheel speed and vehicle speed
    b. differentiating vehicle speed with respect to time
    c. measuring crankshaft angular speed
    d. none of the above

11. The example digital ride control system of this chapter incorporates
    a. a special electrically adjustable shock absorber
    b. a measurement of steering angle
    c. a measurement of vehicle speed and brake line pressure
    d. all of the above

Automotive Instrumentation

ABOUT THIS CHAPTER

Automotive instrumentation includes the equipment and devices that measure engine and other vehicle variables and display their status to the driver. From about the late 1920s until the late 1950s, the standard automotive instrumentation included the speedometer, oil pressure gauge, coolant temperature gauge, battery charging rate gauge, and fuel quantity gauge. Strictly speaking, only the latter two are electrical instruments. In fact, this electrical instrumentation was generally regarded as a minor part of the automotive electrical system. However by the late 1950s, the gauges for oil pressure, coolant temperature, and battery charging rate were replaced by warning lights that were turned on only if specified limits were exceeded. This was done primarily to reduce vehicle cost and because of the presumption that many people did not read the gauges.

Low cost solid-state electronics, including microprocessors, display devices, and some sensors, have brought about major changes in automotive instrumentation.

Automotive instrumentation was not really electronic until the 1970s. At that time, the availability of relatively low-cost, solid-state electronics brought about a major change in automotive instrumentation as the use of low-cost electronics has increased with each new model year. Some of the electronic instrumentation presently available is described in this chapter.

MODERN AUTOMOTIVE INSTRUMENTATION

The evolution of instrumentation in automobiles has been influenced by electronic technological advances in much the same way as the engine control system, which has already been discussed. Of particular importance has been the advent of the microprocessor, solid-state display devices, and solid-state sensors. In order to put these developments into perspective, recall the general block diagram for instrumentation, which is repeated here in *Figure 9-1.*

Figure 9-1. General Instrumentation Block Diagram

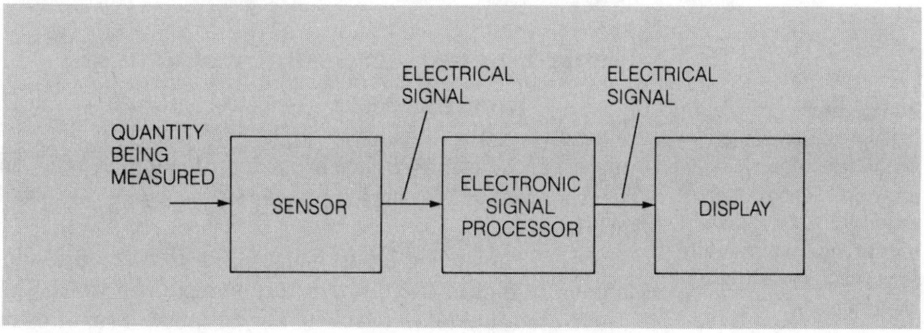

In electronic instrumentation, a sensor is required to convert any nonelectrical signal to an equivalent voltage or current. Then, electronic signal processing is performed on the sensor output to produce an electrical signal that is capable of driving the display device. The display device is either an electromechanical device or an electro-optical device that can be read by the vehicle driver. If a quantity is to be measured that is already in electrical form, e.g., the battery charging current, this signal can be used directly and no sensor is required.

In some modern automotive instrumentation, a microcomputer performs all of the signal processing operations for several measurements. A block diagram for such an instrumentation system is shown in *Figure 9-2*.

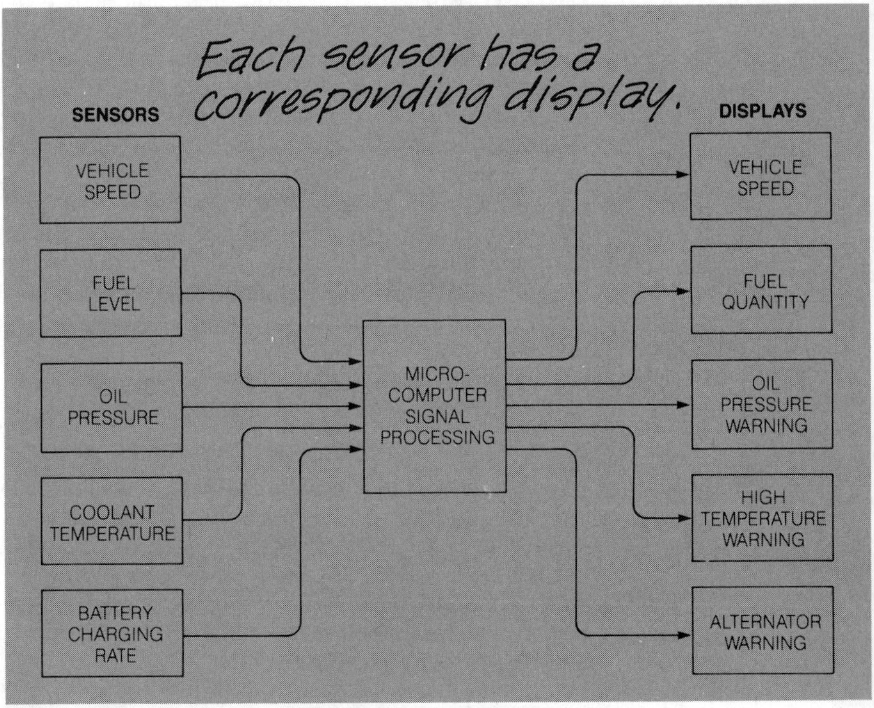

Figure 9-2. Microcomputer-Based Signal Processing System

INPUT AND OUTPUT SIGNAL CONVERSION

Most sensors provide an analog output, while computers require digital inputs. A/D converters convert analog signals to digital codes appropriate for signal processing by the computer.

With reference to *Figure 9-2*, it can be seen that the system inputs are either analog or digital. It should be emphasized that any single input can be either digital or analog, depending upon the technology used for the sensor. The choice presented in *Figure 9-2* has been made arbitrarily.

The analog inputs must all be converted to digital format using an analog to digital (A/D) converter as explained in Chapter 4, and as illustrated in *Figure 9-3*. The digital inputs are, of course, already in the desired format. The conversion process requires an amount of time that depends primarily upon the A/D converter. After the conversion is complete, the digital output generated by the A/D converter is the closest possible approximation to the equivalent analog voltage, using an 8-bit binary number. The A/D converter then signals the computer by changing the logic state on a separate lead (labeled "conversion complete" in *Figure 9–3*) that is connected to the computer. (Also, recall the use of interrupts for this purpose as discussed in Chapter 4.) The output voltage of each analog sensor for which the computer performs signal processing must be converted in this way. Once the conversion is complete, the digital output is transferred into a register in the computer.

Figure 9–3. Analog-to-Digital Conversion

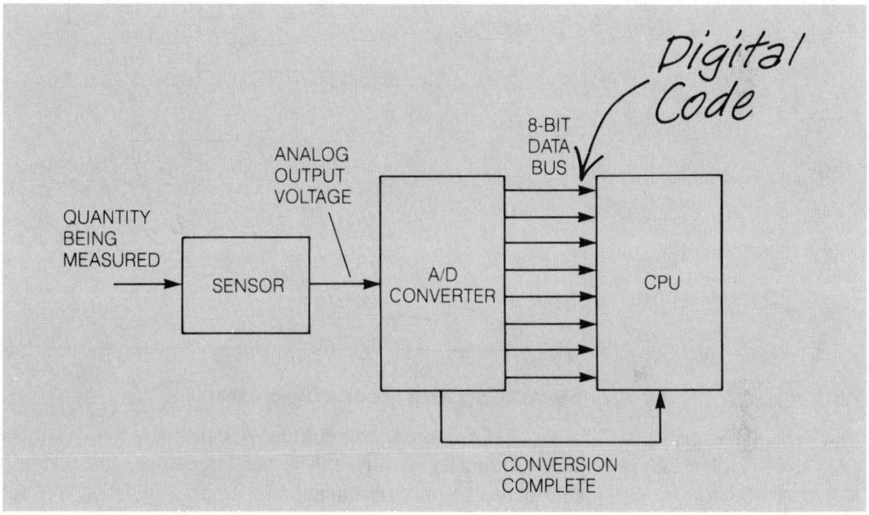

The results of the signal processing (i.e., the computer output) are produced in a digital format. In most automotive applications, it is an 8-bit binary number. If the output is to drive a digital display, this output can be used directly. However, if an analog display is used, the binary number must be converted to the appropriate analog signal by using a digital-to-analog (D/A) converter (see Chapter 4 for an explanation of D/A converter).

When an analog output signal is required to drive an analog display, a D/A converter is used. The DAC generates a voltage that is proportional to the binary number that the computer sends to the converter.

Figure 9–4 illustrates a typical D/A converter used to transform digital computer output to an analog signal. The eight digital output leads transfer the results of the signal processing to a D/A converter. When the transfer is complete, the computer signals the D/A converter to start converting. The D/A output generates a voltage that is proportional to the binary number in the computer output. A capacitor is often connected across the D/A output to store the analog output between samples. The sampling of the sensor output, A/D conversion, digital signal processing, and D/A conversion all take place during the time slot allotted for the measurement of the variable in a sampling time sequence to be discussed shortly.

Figure 9-4. Digital-to-Analog Conversion

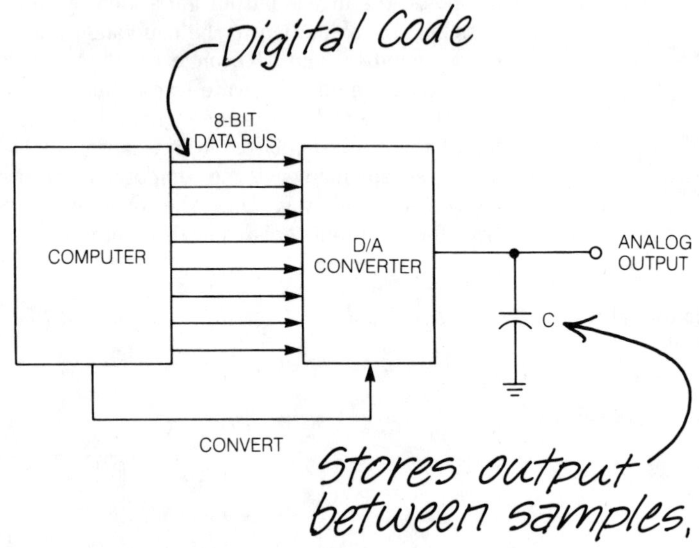

Switching and Reconfiguration

The computer monitors each sensor individually, and provides output signals to its display component before going on to another sensor.

Of course, the computer can only deal with the measurement of a single quantity at any one time. Therefore, the computer input must be connected to only one sensor at a time, and the computer output must be connected only to the corresponding display. The computer performs any necessary signal processing on that sensor signal, and then it generates an output signal to the appropriate display device.

In *Figure 9-5* the various sensor outputs and display inputs are connected to a pair of multiposition rotary switches—one for the input and one for the output of the computer. The switches are functionally connected such that they rotate together. Whenever the input switch connects the computer input to the appropriate sensor for measuring some quantity, the output switch connects the computer output to the corresponding display or warning device. Thus, with the switches in a specific position, the automotive instrumentation system corresponds to the block diagram shown in *Figure 9-1*. The switching process can be understood with reference to *Figure 9-5* which depicts a functionally equivalent block diagram for the system.

Figure 9-5.
Input/Output Switching Scheme for Sampling

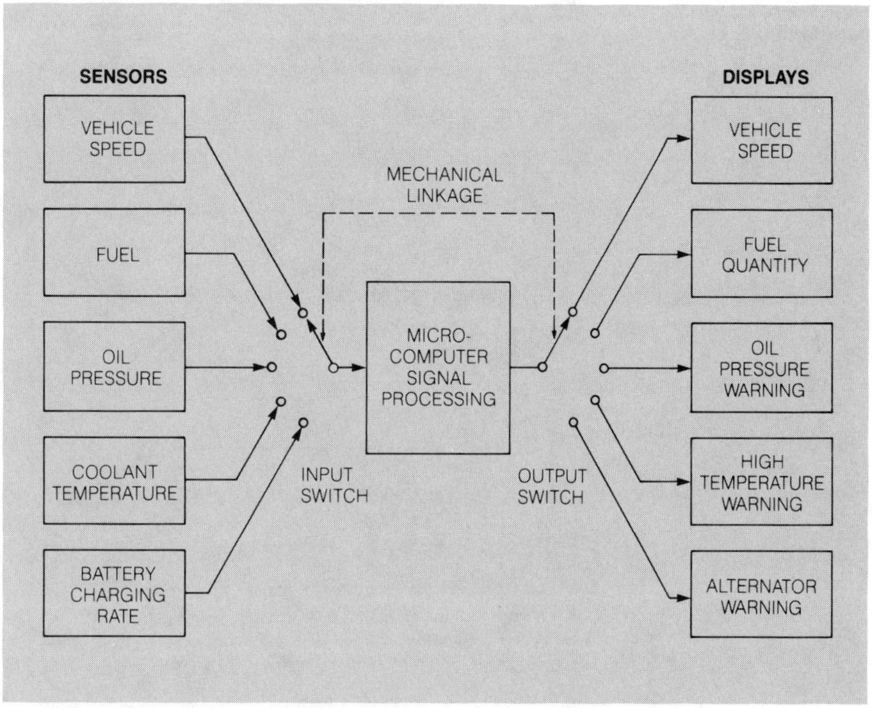

The switching of sensor and display inputs is performed with solid-state switches known as multiplexers and output switching by demultiplexers.

The computer can control the input and output switching operation. However, instead of a mechanical switch as shown in *Figure 9-5*, the actual switching is done by means of a solid-state electronic switching device called a multiplexer, or MUX (*Figure 9-6*), that selects one of several inputs for each output. The MUX has data select inputs that the computer activates to select the desired input signal. Similarly, the output switching (which is often called demultiplexing or DEMUX) is performed with a MUX connected in reverse, as shown in *Figure 9-7*. The MUX and DEMUX selection is controlled by the computer. Note that in *Figures 9-6* and *9-7*, each bit of the digital code is multiplexed and demultiplexed.

SAMPLING

Only one variable can be sampled by the computer at a time. The other variables must wait a set period of time before being sampled again by the computer.

The measurement of any quantity takes place only when the input and output switches (MUX and DEMUX) actually connect the corresponding sensor and display to the computer. However, there are several variables to be measured and displayed, but only one variable can be accommodated at any given instant. Once a quantity has been measured, it must wait until the other variables have been measured before it is measured again. This process of measuring a quantity intermittently is called sampling, and the time between successive samples of the same quantity is called the sample period, as explained in an earlier chapter.

Figure 9-6. Data Multiplexer

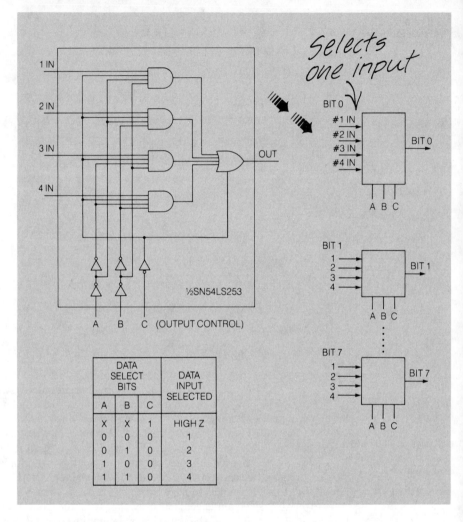

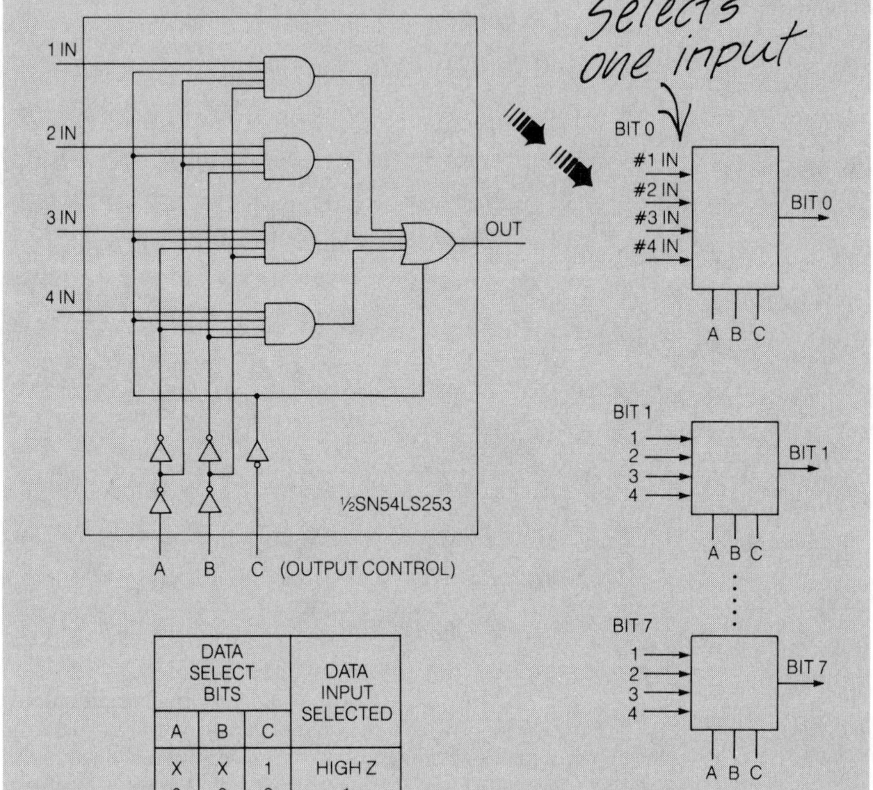

DATA SELECT BITS			DATA INPUT SELECTED
A	B	C	
X	X	1	HIGH Z
0	0	0	1
0	1	0	2
1	0	0	3
1	1	0	4

One possible scheme for measuring several variables by this process is to sample each quantity sequentially, giving each measurement a fixed timeslot, t, out of the total sample period, T, as illustrated in *Figure 9-8.* This method is satisfactory as long as the sample period is small compared to the time in which any quantity changes appreciably. Certain quantities, such as coolant temperature and fuel quantity, change very slowly with time. For such variables, a sample period of a few seconds or longer is often adequate.

Figure 9-7.
Data Demultiplexer

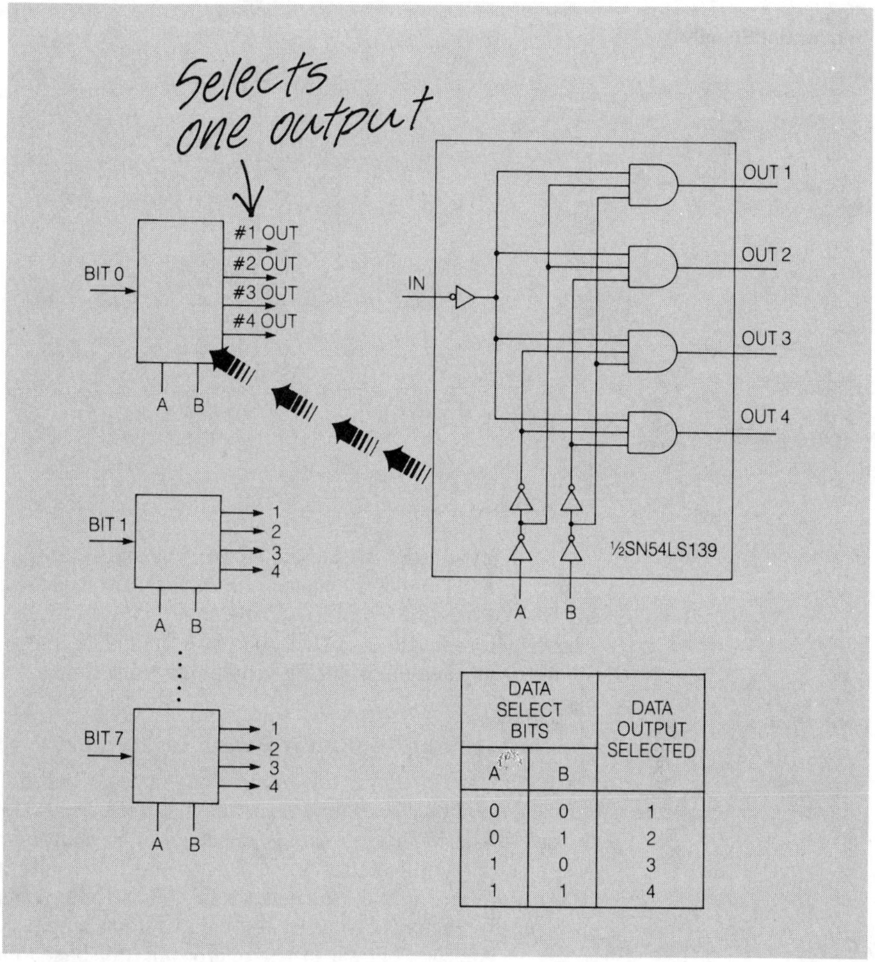

DATA SELECT BITS		DATA OUTPUT SELECTED
A	B	
0	0	1
0	1	2
1	0	3
1	1	4

Some variables, such as speed and battery charge, change much faster than others. To effectively monitor these differences the computer uses different sampling times.

On the other hand, variables such as vehicle speed, battery charge, and fuel consumption rate change relatively quickly and require a much shorter sample period, perhaps every second or even tenths of a second. To accommodate the various rates of change of the automotive variables being measured, the sample period varies from one quantity to another. The most rapidly changing quantities are sampled with a very short sample period, whereas those that change slowly are sampled with a long sample period.

Figure 9-8.
Sequential Sampling

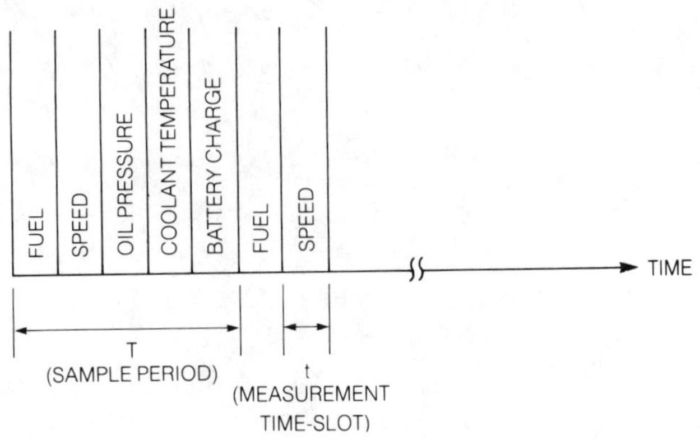

In addition to sample period, the time slot allotted for each quantity must be long enough to complete the measurement and any A/D or D/A conversion required. The computer program is designed with all of these factors in mind so that adequate time slots and sample periods are allowed for each variable. The computer then simply follows the program schedule.

Advantages of Computer-Based Instrumentation

One of the big advantages of computer-based instrumentation is its great flexibility. To change from the instrumentation for one vehicle or one model to another requires only a change of computer program. This change can often be implemented by replacing one ROM with another. Remember that the program is permanently stored in a ROM (read-only memory) that is typically packaged in a single plug-in IC package.

Another benefit of the microcomputer-based electronic automotive instrumentation is its improved performance compared to the conventional instrumentation. In the electronic instrumentation, measurement errors are much smaller than for the conventional instrumentation. For example, the conventional fuel gauge system has errors which are associated with variations in the:

1. mechanical characteristics of the tank
2. sender unit
3. instrument voltage regulator
4. indicator (galvanometer)

Computer-based intrumentation is more accurate than conventional instrumentation. And due to the computer's program they are more easily changed.

The electronic instrumentation system completely eliminates the error that results from imperfect voltage regulation. Generally speaking, the electronic fuel quantity measurement maintains calibration over essentially the entire range of automotive electrical system conditions. Moreover, it significantly improves the indicator accuracy by replacing the electromechanical galvanometer indicator with an all-electronic digital display.

While the impact of these improvements varies with the vehicle and fuel level, a typical electronic system has about 44% less error at half-a-tank than a conventional system. It is worthwhile to illustrate these benefits with the specific example of fuel quantity measurement.

FUEL QUANTITY MEASUREMENT

During a measurement of fuel quantity, the MUX switch connects the computer input to the fuel quantity sensor, as shown in *Figure 9-9*. This sensor output is converted and then sent to the computer for signal processing.

Figure 9-9. Fuel Quantity Measurement

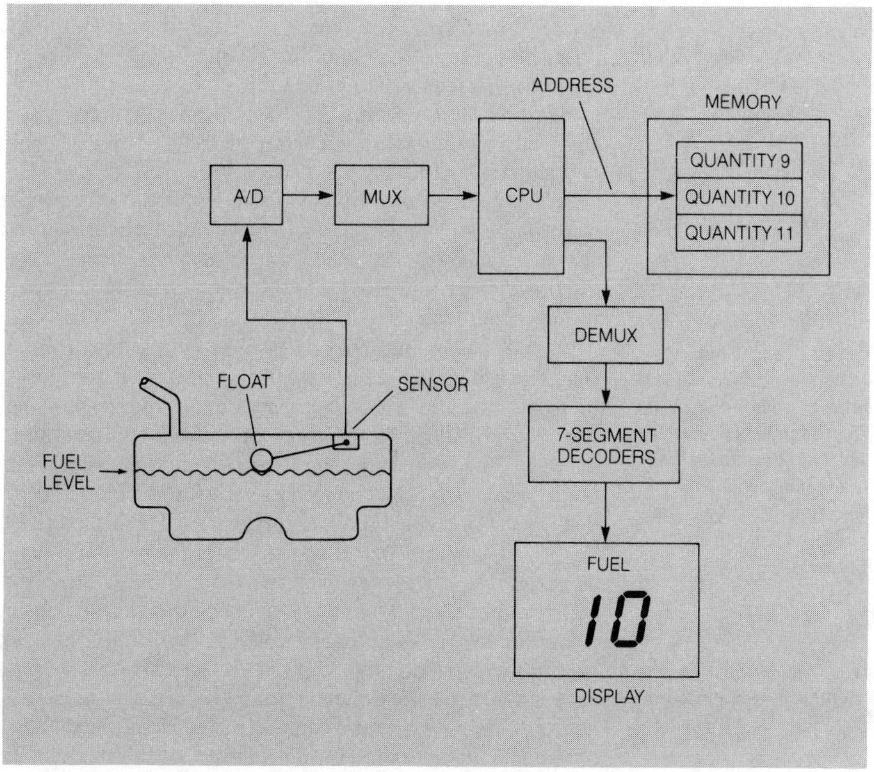

Several fuel quantity sensor configurations are available. *Figure 9-10* illustrates the type of sensor to be described.

Figure 9-10.
Fuel Quantity Sensor

Voltage level represents fuel level.

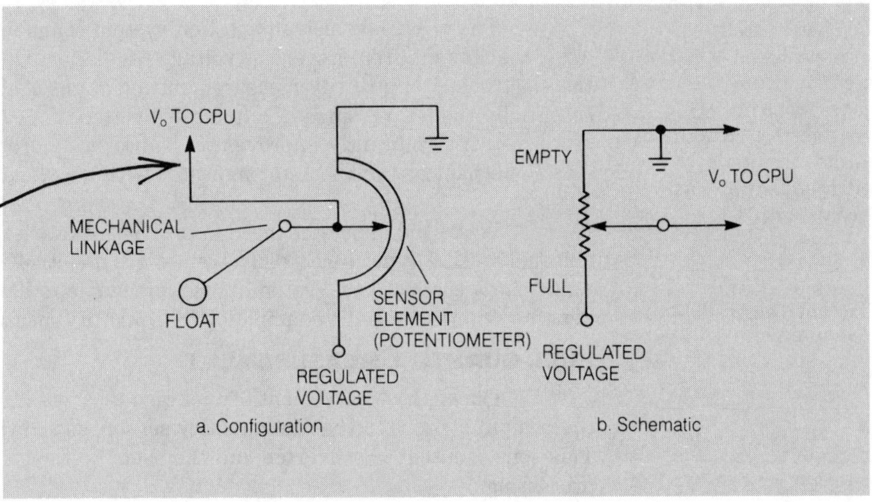

Some fuel quantity sensors use a float within the fuel tank; the float is mechanically linked to a potentiometer which operates as a voltage divider.

Normally, the sensor is mounted so that the float remains laterally near the center of the tank for all fuel levels. A constant current passes through the sensor potentiometer, since it is connected directly across the regulated voltage source. The potentiometer is used as a voltage divider so that the voltage at the wiper arm is related to the float position, which is determined by fuel level.

The sensor output voltage is not directly proportional to fuel quantity in gallons because of the complex shape of the fuel tank. The computer memory contains the relationship between sensor voltage (in binary number equivalent) and fuel quantity for the particular fuel tank used on the vehicle.

The fuel sensor output voltage is converted into a binary code by an ADC. The computer compares this code to codes stored in a lookup table that correspond to actual fuel quantities for the specific fuel tank.

The computer reads the binary number from the A/D converter that corresponds to sensor voltage and uses it to address a particular memory location. Another binary number corresponding to the actual fuel quantity in gallons for that sensor voltage is stored in that memory location. The computer then uses the number from memory to generate the appropriate display voltage; i.e., either analog or digital, depending upon display type, and sends that signal via DEMUX to the display.

The computer compensates for fuel slosh by averaging float sensor readings over a period of time.

Computer-based signal processing can also compensate for fuel slosh. As the car moves over the road, the fuel sloshes about and the float bobs up and down around the average position which corresponds to the correct level for a stationary vehicle. The computer compensates for slosh by computing a running average. It does this by storing several samples over a few seconds and computing the arithmetic average of the sensor output. The oldest samples are continually discarded as new samples are obtained. The averaged output is used as the memory address as described above. It should be noted that this is a form of digital filtering.

COOLANT TEMPERATURE MEASUREMENT

Another important automotive parameter that is measured by the instrumentation is the coolant temperature. The measurement of this quantity is different from that of fuel quantity because usually it is not important for the driver to know the actual temperature at all times. For safe operation of the engine, the driver only needs to know that the coolant temperature is less than a critical value. A block diagram of the measuring system is shown in *Figure 9-11*.

Figure 9-11. Coolant Temperature Measurement

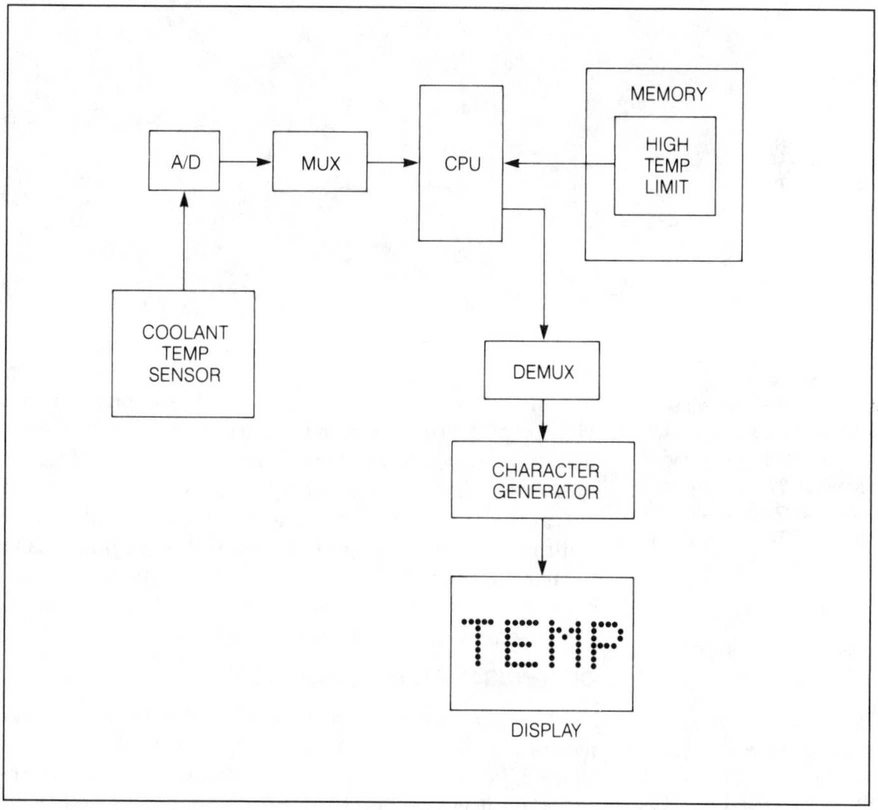

The coolant temperature sensor used in most cars is a solid-state sensor called a thermistor. Recall that this type of sensor was discussed in Chapter 5 where it was shown that the resistance of this sensor decreases with increasing temperature. *Figure 9-12* shows the circuit connection and a sketch of a typical sensor output voltage versus temperature curve.

Figure 9-12. Coolant Temperature Sensor

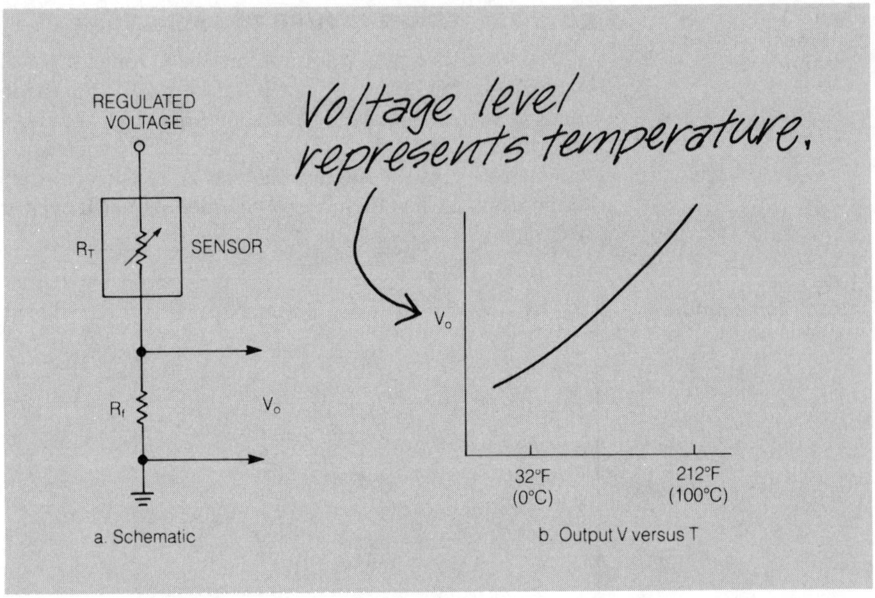

To measure coolant temperature, the sensor output from a thermistor is converted into a digital signal and compared to a maximum safe value stored in memory. If the maximum value is exceeded, the computer generates a signal to trigger a temperature warning lamp.

The sensor output voltage is sampled during the appropriate time slot and is converted to a binary number equivalent by the A/D converter. The computer compares this binary number to the one stored in memory that corresponds to the high temperature limit. If the coolant temperature exceeds the limit, an output signal is generated that activates the warning indicator. If the limit is not exceeded, the output signal is not generated and the warning message is not activated. A proportional display of actual temperature can be used if the memory contains a cross reference table between sensor output voltage and the corresponding temperature, similar to that described for the fuel quantity table.

OIL PRESSURE MEASUREMENT

Oil pressure warning systems use a variable resistance sensor as part of a voltage divider. This arrangement provides a varying voltage that corresponds to changes in oil pressure.

Whenever the oil pressure exceeds allowable limits, a warning message is displayed to the driver. This function is similar in many respects to the high coolant temperature warning function. In the case of oil pressure, it is important for the driver to know whenever the oil pressure falls below a lower limit. It is also possible for the oil pressure to go above an allowable upper limit; however, many manufacturers do not include high oil pressure warning in the instrumentation.

An oil pressure warning system is illustrated in *Figure 9-13*. This system uses a variable resistance oil pressure sensor such as seen in *Figure 9-14*. A voltage is developed across a series fixed resistance that is proportional to oil pressure.

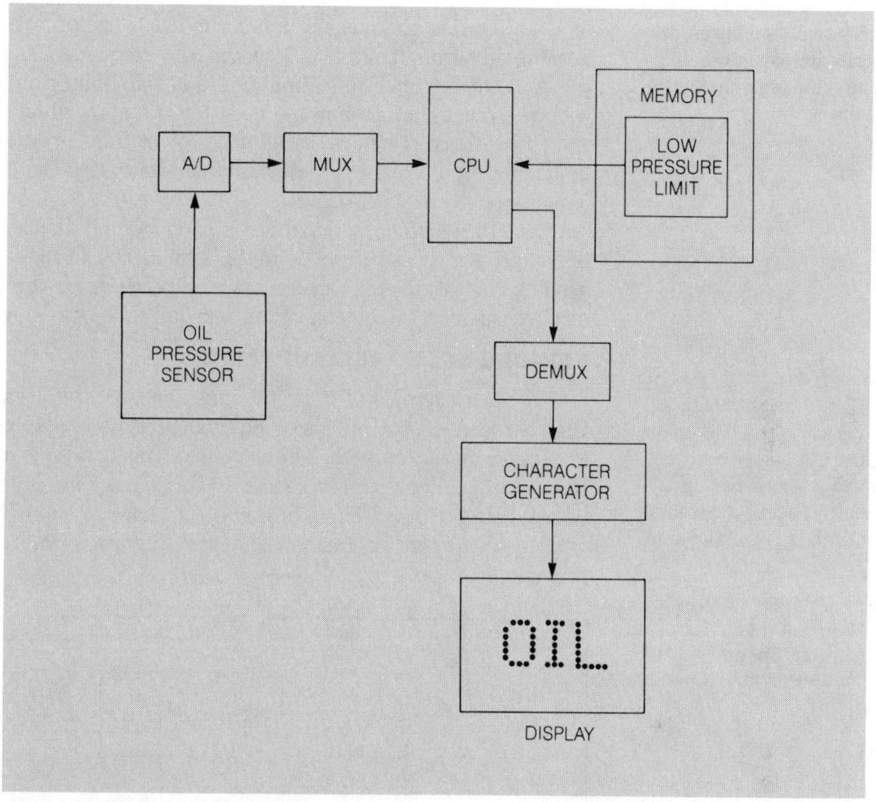

Figure 9-13. Oil Pressure Measurement

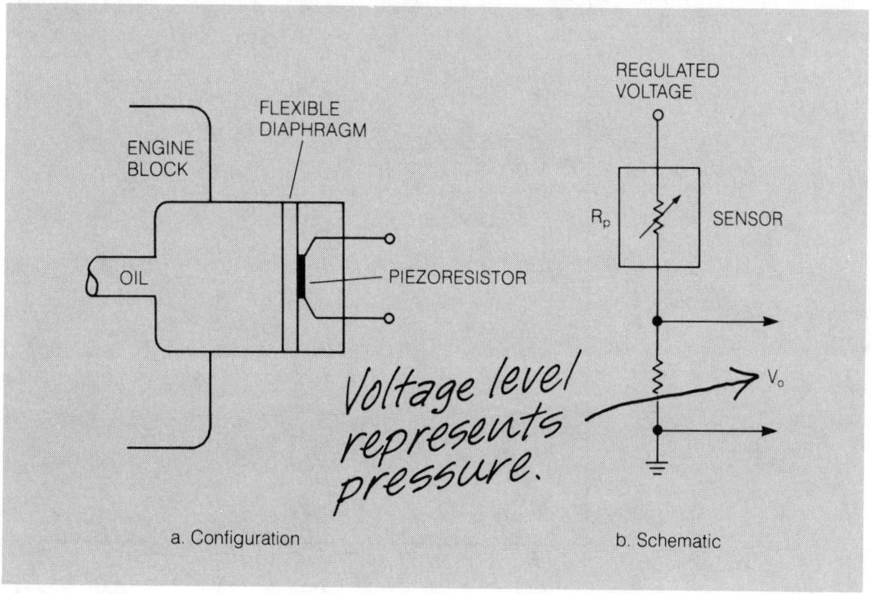

Figure 9-14. Oil Pressure Sensor

Continuous oil pressure measurements are possible using an analog sensor.

During the measurement time slot, the oil pressure sensor voltage is sampled through the MUX switch and converted to a binary number in the A/D converter. The computer reads this binary number and compares it with the binary number in memory for the allowed oil pressure limits. If the oil pressure is below the allowed lower limit or above the allowed upper limit, an output signal is generated that activates the oil pressure warning light through the DEMUX.

It is also possible to use a proportional display of actual oil pressure, if a cross-reference table, similar to the fuel quantity table, is used. A digital display can be driven directly from the computer. An analog display, such as the electric gauge, requires a D/A converter.

VEHICLE SPEED MEASUREMENT

Digital measurement of vehicle speed is possible using a binary counter and a sensor having an output signal frequency which is proportional to speed.

An example of a digital speed sensor has already been described in Chapter 8. A sensor of this or equivalent type is assumed to be used for car speed measurements. The output of this sensor is a binary number, P, that is proportional to car speed S. This binary number is contained in a binary counter (see Chapter 8). A block diagram of the instrumentation for vehicle speed measurement is shown in *Figure 9–15*. This system is presumed to use a digital speed sensor.

Figure 9–15. Vehicle Speed Measurement

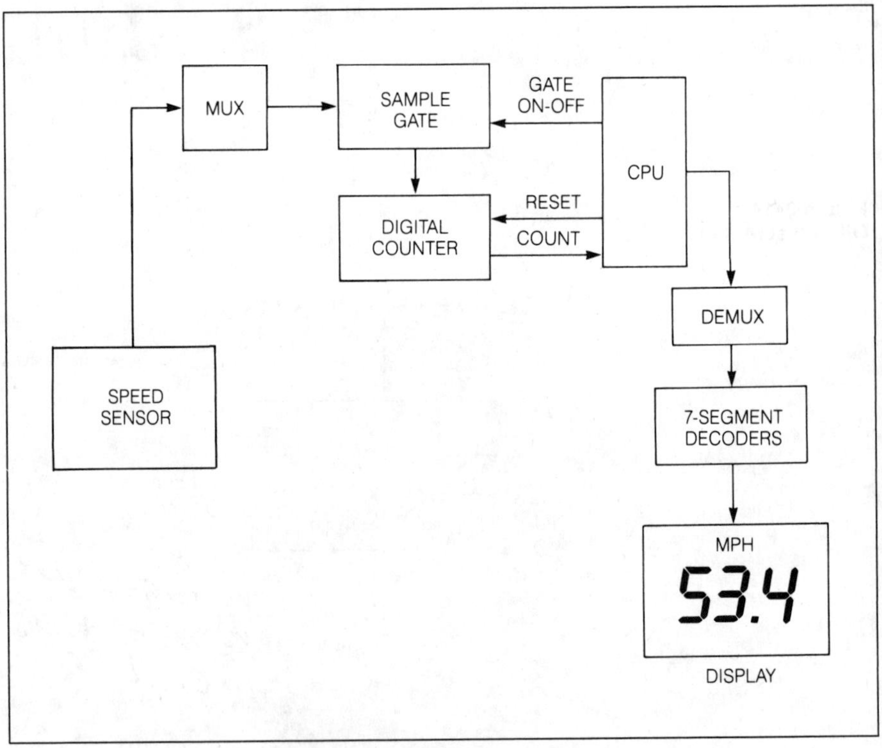

The computer reads the number P, then resets the counter to zero to prepare it for the next count. After performing computations and filtering, the computer generates a signal for the display to indicate the vehicle speed. A digital display can be directly driven by the computer. Either MPH or KM/H may be selected. If an analog display is used, a D/A converter must drive the display. Both MPH and KM/H usually are calibrated on an analog scale.

DISPLAY DEVICES

One of the most important components of any measuring instrument is the display device. In automotive instrumentation, the display device must present the results of the measurement to the driver in a form that is easy to read and understand. The first automotive electronic displays were electromechanical devices. The speedometer, ammeter, and fuel quantity gauge were originally electromechanical devices. Then automotive manufacturers began using warning lamps instead of gauges to cut cost. A warning lamp can be considered as a type of electro-optical display.

Electromechanical and simple electro-optical displays are being replaced by sophisticated electronic displays that provide the driver with numeric or alphabetic information.

Recent developments in solid-state technology in the field called optoelectronics have led to much more sophisticated electro-optical display devices that are capable of indicating alphanumeric data. This means that both numeric and alphabetic information can be used to display the results of measurements of automotive variables or parameters. This capability allows messages in English or other languages to be given to the driver. The input for these devices is an electronic digital signal which makes these devices compatible with computer-based instrumentation, whereas electromechanical displays require a D/A converter.

Automobile manufacturers have considered many different types of electronic displays for automotive instrumentation, but only four have been seriously considered—light-emitting diode (LED), liquid-crystal display (LCD), vacuum-fluorescent (VF), and the cathode ray tube (CRT). It now appears that the VF display will be the predominant type of instrumentation for at least the near future. Each of these types is discussed briefly to explain their uses in automotive applications.

LED

LEDs are solid-state devices that emit light when current is passed through the diode. LEDs are difficult to view in bright sunlight.

The light-emitting diode is a semiconductor diode that is constructed in a manner and of a material so that light is emitted when an electrical current is passed through it. The semiconductor material most often used for an LED that emits red light is gallium arsenide phosphide. Light is emitted at the diode's PN junction when the positive carriers combine with the negative carriers at the junction. The diode is constructed so that the light generated at the junction can escape from the diode and be seen.

An LED display is normally made of small dots or rectangular segments arranged so that numbers and letters can be formed when selected dots or segments are turned on. The LED display was the first display used in electronic digital watches.

A single LED is not well suited for automotive display use because of its low brightness. Although it can be seen easily in darkness, it is difficult-to-impossible to see in bright sunlight. It also requires more electrical power than an LCD display; however, its power requirements are not great enough to be a problem for automotive use.

LCD

LCDs use a liquid that possess the ability to rotate the polarization of polarized light. LCD displays have low power requirements.

The LCD display is commonly used in electronic digital watch displays because of its extremely low electrical power and relatively low voltage requirements.

The heart of an LCD is a special liquid which is called a twisted nematic liquid crystal. This liquid has the capability of rotating the polarization of linearly polarized light. Linearly polarized light has all of the vibrations of the optical waves in the same direction. Light from the sun and from most artificial light sources is not polarized, and the waves vibrate randomly in many directions.

Nonpolarized light can be polarized by passing the light through a polarizing material. To illustrate, think of a picket fence with narrow gaps between the pickets. If a rope is passed between two of the pickets and its end is whipped up and down, the ripples in the rope will pass through the fence. The ripples represent light waves and the picket fence represents a polarizing material. If you whip the rope in any other direction other than vertically, the ripples will not pass through.

Now visualize another picket fenced turned 90° so the pickets are horizontal. Place this fence behind the vertical picket fence. This arrangement is called a cross-polarizer. if the rope is now whipped in any direction, no ripples will pass through both fences. Similarly, if a cross-polarizer is used for light, no light will pass through this structure.

The configuration of an LCD can be understood from the schematic drawings of *Figure 9-16*. The liquid crystal is sandwiched between a pair of glass plates that have transparent, electrically conductive coatings. The transparent conductor is deposited on the front glass plate in the form of the character, or segment of a character, which is to be displayed. Next, a layer of dielectric (insulating) material is coated on the glass plate to produce the desired alignment of the liquid crystal molecules. The polarization of the molecules is vertical at the front, and they gradually rotate through the liquid crystal structure until the molecules at the back are horizontally polarized. Thus, the molecules of the liquid crystal rotate 90° from the front plate to the back plate so their polarization matches that of the front and back polarizers with no voltage applied.

Figure 9-16. Typical LCD Construction

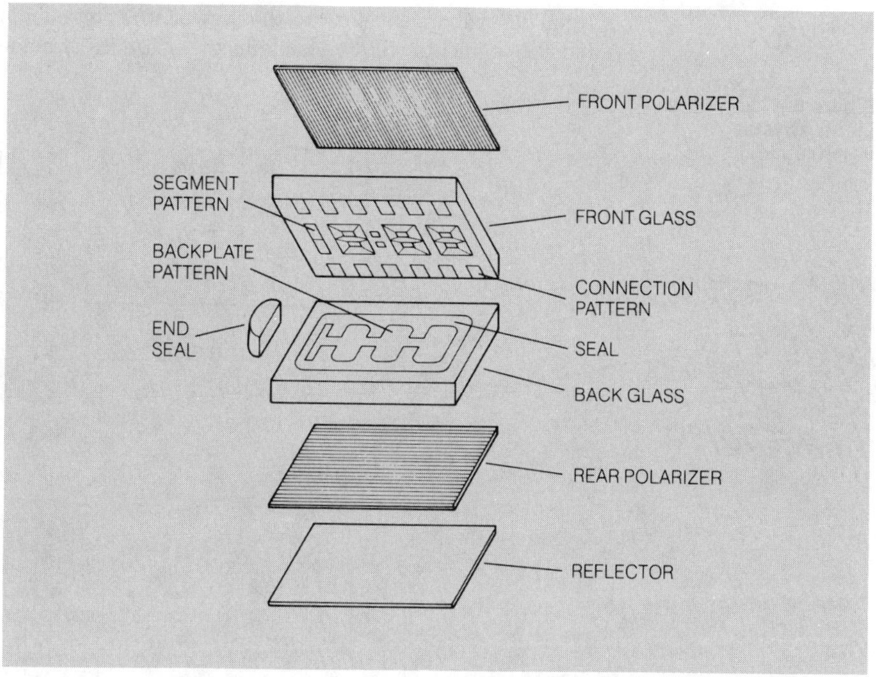

When current is not being applied to an LCD display, light entering the crystal is polarized by the front polarizer, rotated, passed through the rear polarizer and then reflected off the reflector. The reflected light causes the segment to appear blank.

When a voltage is applied to a display segment, the crystal's molecules change and do not rotate the polarized light. Since the light cannot align with the rear polarizer, it is not reflected, and the segment appears dark.

The operation of the LCD in the absence of applied voltage can be understood with reference to *Figure 9-17a*. Ambient light enters through the front polarizer so that the light entering the front plate is vertically polarized. As it passes through the liquid crystal, the light polarization is changed by the orientation of the molecules. When the light reaches the back of the crystal, its polarization has been rotated 90° so that it is horizontally polarized. The light is reflected from the reflector at the rear. It passes back through the liquid crystal structure, the polarization again being rotated, and passes out of the front polarizer. Thus, a viewer sees reflected ambient light.

The effect of an applied voltage to the transmission of light through this device can be understood from *Figure 9-17b*. A voltage applied to any of the segments of the display causes the liquid crystal molecules under those segments only to be aligned in a straight line rather than twisted. In this case, the light that enters the liquid crystal in the vicinity of the segments passes through the crystal structure without the polarization being rotated. Since the light has been vertically polarized by the front vertical polarizing plate, the light is blocked by the horizontal polarizer so it cannot reach the reflector. Thus, light that enters the cell in the vicinity of energized segments is not returned to the front face. These segments will appear dark to the viewer, the surrounding area will be light, and the segments will be visible in the presence of ambient light.

Figure 9-17. Liquid Crystal Polarization

Only pass light in a specific direction.

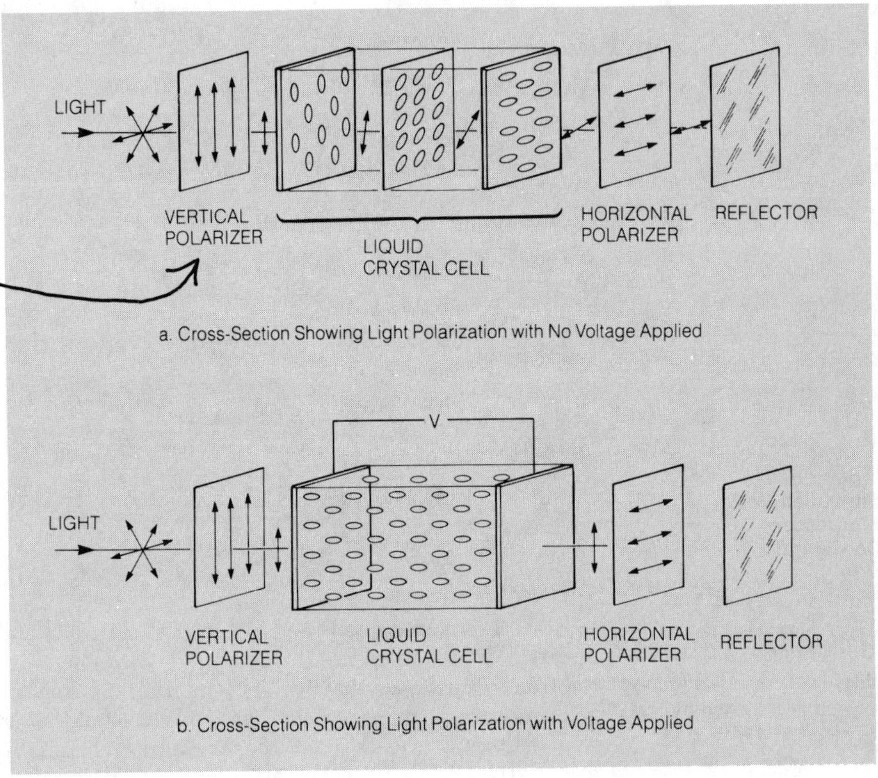

The LCD is an excellent display device because of its low power requirement and relatively low cost. However, a big disadvantage of the LCD for automotive application is the need for an external light source for viewing in the dark. Its characteristic is just the opposite of the LED; that is, the LCD is readable in the daytime, but not at night. For night driving, the display must be illuminated by small lamps inside the display. Another disadvantage is that the display does not work well at the low temperatures that are encountered during winter driving in some areas. These characteristics of the LCD have limited its use in automotive instrumentation.

VFD

VFDs use a phosphor material that emits light when bombarded by electrons. VFDs provide readability over a wide range of conditions.

One of the most common automotive display devices in use today is the vacuum-fluorescent display (VFD). This device generates light in much the same way as a television picture tube does; that is, a phosphor material emits light when it is bombarded by energetic electrons. The display uses a filament coated with material that generates "free" electrons when the filament is heated. The electrons are accelerated toward the anode by a relatively high voltage. When these high speed electrons strike the phosphor material on the anode, the phosphor material emits light. Most VF displays have a phosphor material that emits a blue-green light which provides good readability in the wide range of ambient light conditions that are present in an automobile.

The numeric characters are formed by shaping the anode segments in the form of a standard 7-segment character. The basic structure of a typical VFD is depicted in *Figure 9-18.* The filament is a special type of resistance wire and is heated by passing an electrical current through it. The coating on the heated filament produces free electrons that are accelerated by the electric field produced by a voltage on the accelerating grid. This grid consists of a fine wire mesh that allows the electrons to pass through. The electrons pass through because they are attracted to the anode which has a higher voltage than the grid. The high voltage is applied only to the anode of the segments needed to form the character to be displayed. The instrumentation computer selects the set of segments that are to emit light for any given message.

Figure 9-18. Simplified Vacuum-Fluorescent Display Configuration

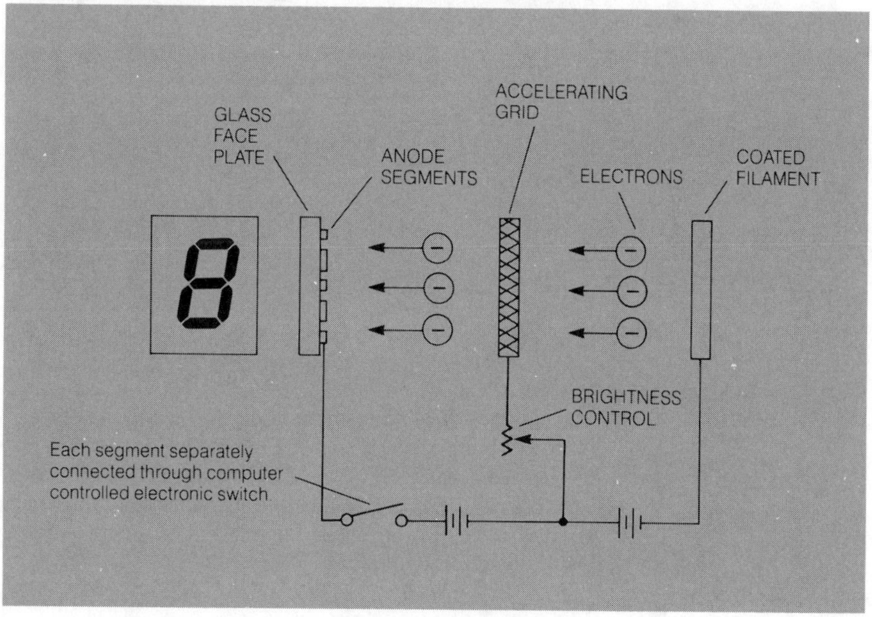

VFD brightness can be controlled by varying the voltage on the accelerator grid. As the accelerator grid voltage increases, the electrons strike the phosphor with greater intensity, resulting in an increased light output.

Since the ambient light in an automobile varies between sunlight and darkness, it is desirable to adjust the brightness of the display in accordance with the ambient light. The brightness is controlled by varying the voltage on the accelerating grid. The higher the voltage, the greater the energy of the electrons striking the phosphor, and the brighter the light. *Figure 9-19* shows the brightness characteristics for a typical VFD device. A brightness of 200 fl (foot lamberts) might be selected on a bright sunny day, whereas the brightness might only be 20 fl at night. The brightness can be set manually by the driver, or automatically. In the latter case, a photoresistor is used to vary the grid voltage in accordance with the amount of ambient light. A photoresistor is a device whose resistance varies in proportion to the amount of light striking it.

Figure 9-19. Brightness Control Range for Vacuum-Fluorescent Display

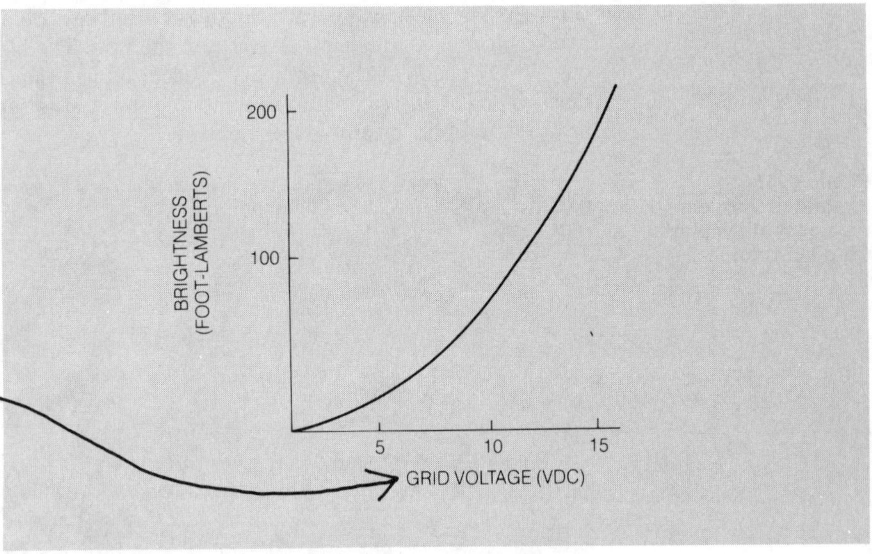

The VFD display is likely to be the most widely used for some time. It operates with relatively low power and operates over a wide temperature range. The most serious drawback for automotive application is its susceptibility to failure due to vibration and mechanical shock. However, this problem can be reduced by mounting the display on a shock absorbing isolation mount.

CRT

The display devices which have been discussed to this point have one rather serious limitation. The characters that can be displayed are limited to those symbols that can be approximated by the segments that can be illuminated. Furthermore, illuminated warning messages such as the "Check Engine" or "Oil Pressure" are *fixed* messages that are either displayed or not, depending upon the engine conditions. The primary disadvantage of such ad-hoc display devices is the limited flexibility of the displayed messages.

The cathode ray tube (CRT) is similar to a TV picture tube and has great potential for automotive display applications.

The display device that has the greatest flexibility for displaying messages or pictorial information is the cathode ray tube (CRT). The CRT that is perhaps most familiar to the reader is the TV picture tube. However, the CRT is also the display device most commonly used in personal computers.

The CRT is being used increasingly for display purposes in the aerospace industry where it is used to display aircraft altitude information (sometimes pictorially), aircraft engine or airframe parameters, navigational data, and warning messages. Clearly the CRT has great potential for automotive instrumentation display.

It has, however, certain disadvantages compared to solid-state or electromechanical display devices. For example, its size and shape make it complicated to locate in the instrument panel, where it can most easily be read by the driver. In addition, the CRT requires circuitry for its operation that is not required by a solid-state digital display. Furthermore, the CRT is more expensive than a typical solid-state or vacuum-fluorescent display. The cost incurred for a CRT is essentially independent of the complexity of displayed messages, whereas the cost of alternate solid-state or vacuum-fluorescent displays increases somewhat with complexity of the messages. Thus, the cost of the CRT only becomes comparable with vacuum-fluorescent displays as message complexity increases.

Although there have been numerous experimental and a few commercially successful automotive CRT display systems, the future of this application is uncertain. However, it is worthwhile to describe the technology to give the reader some insight into the varied, potential automotive instrumentation application. While it is beyond the scope of this book to explain the CRT and its associated electronic circuits, a relatively simple overview of the CRT as a display device should be sufficient to explain corresponding automotive applications.

Figure 9-20 is a sketch of a typical CRT. It is an evacuated glass tube that has a nominally flat surface that is coated with a phosphorescent material. This surface is the "surface" or "face" on which the displayed messages appear. At the rear is a somewhat complex structure called an "electron gun." This device generates a stream of electrons that is accelerated toward the screen and brought to convergence at a spot on the screen. A system of coils in the form of electromagnets causes this convergence of electrons (or beam) and is referred to as the "magnetic focusing" system. The focused stream of electrons is called the "beam."

Figure 9-20. Illustration of CRT and Associated Circuitry

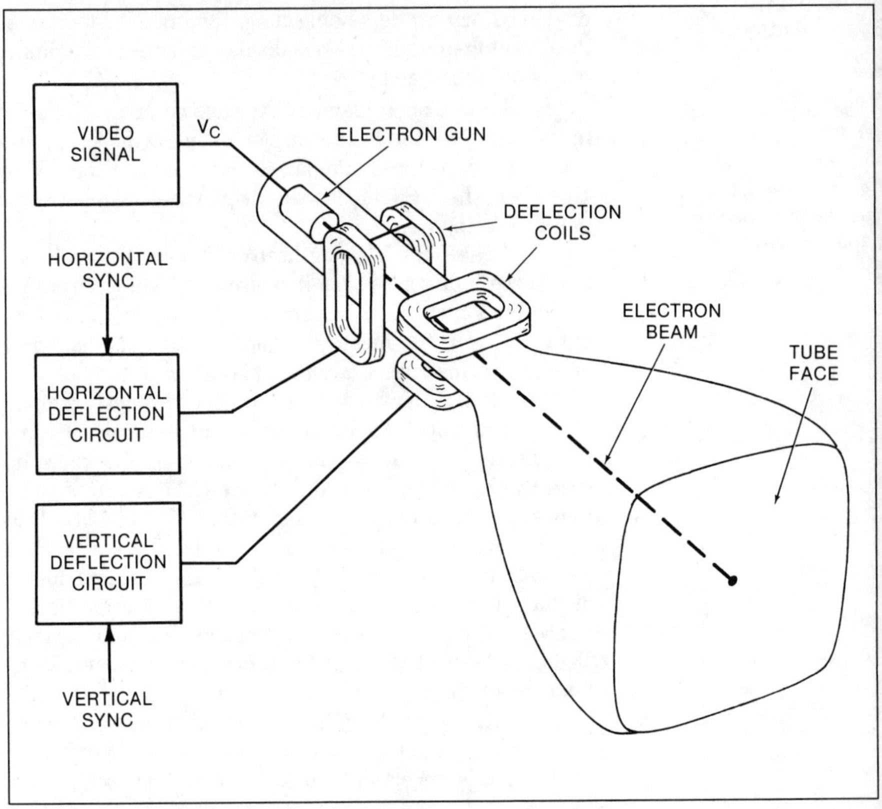

The electron beam generates a spot of light at the point on the screen. The intensity of the light is proportional to the electron beam current. This current is controlled by the voltage (V_c), which is called the video signal, on an electrode that is located near the electron gun.

In the majority of applications (including TV), the electron beam is scanned in a pattern known as a "raster" by means of specially located electromagnets (*Figure 9-20*). The magnetic fields created by the scanning coils deflect the beam horizontally and vertically. The amount of deflection is proportional to the current flowing through the respective coils. The raster pattern traced by the beam is illustrated on the face of the CRT in *Figure 9-21*.

Figure 9-21. Raster Pattern

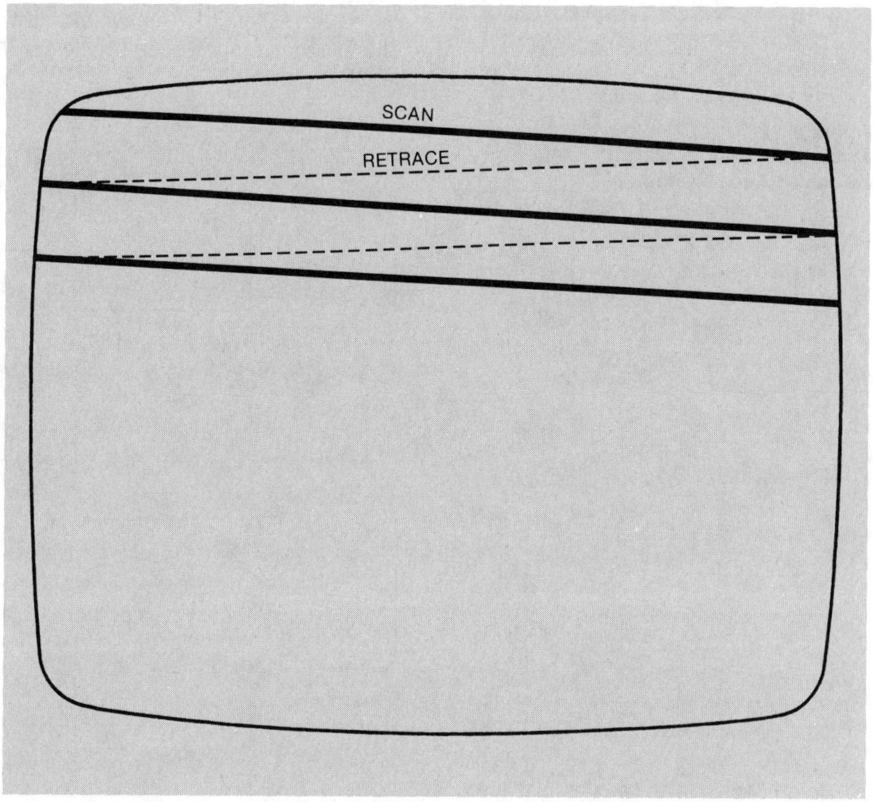

The scanning motion is done in synchronism with the source of information being displayed. At the end of each horizontal scan line, a synchronizing pulse (called horizontal sync) causes the beam to deflect rapidly to the left and then to begin scanning at a constant rate to the right. A similar synchronizing pulse is generated at a time when the beam is at the bottom of the CRT. This pulse (called vertical sync) causes the beam to deflect rapidly to the top of the CRT face and then to begin scanning downward at a uniform speed.

The information (or picture) displayed on the face of the CRT is controlled by the voltage V_c as a function of time relative to the horizontal and vertical sync pulses. Thus, to generate a message on an automotive CRT display, a specific voltage pattern for V_c must be generated in timed relationship to the sync pulses. This voltage is typically referred to as the *video voltage*.

n automotive ıstrumentation pplications a CRT ısplay is driven by a pecial electronics system alled the CRT controller.

In a typical CRT display device, the video voltage and sync pulses are generated in a special circuit called the CRT controller. A simplified block diagram for a system incorporating a CRT display with the associated CRT controller is depicted in *Figure 9-22.* At the left of this figure are shown the sensors and instrumentation computer (MPU based) which have the same function as the corresponding components of the system in *Figure 9-2*. The output of the instrumentation computer controls the CRT display, working through the CRT controller.

Figure 9-22.
Automotive CRT Instrumentation System

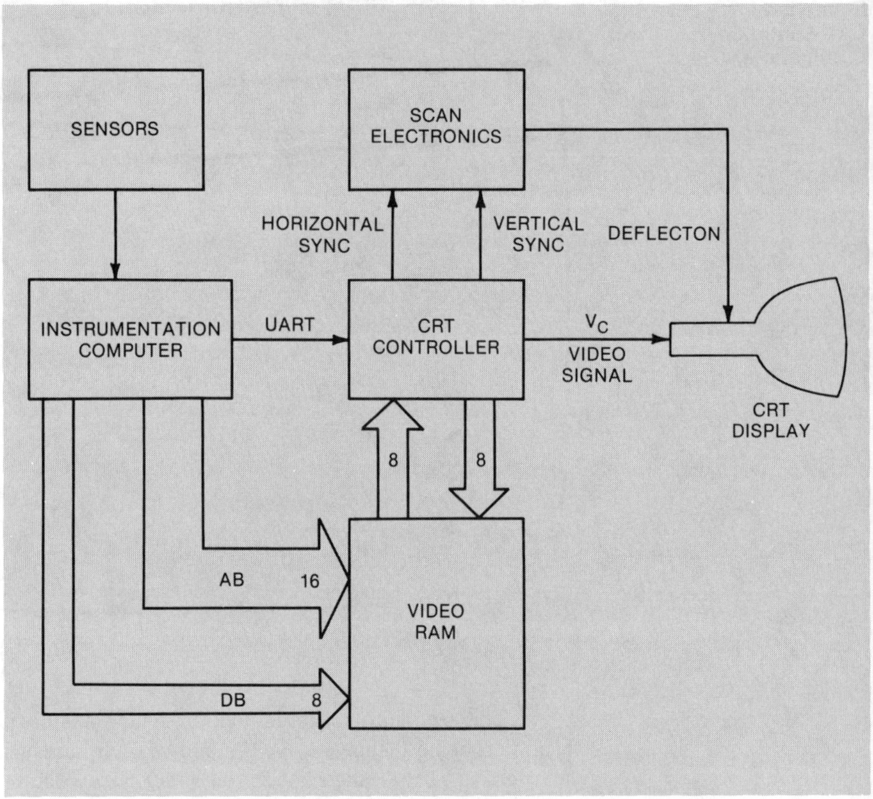

The instrumentation computer communicates with the CRT controller via address and data buses (DB and AB), and via a serial link along a line labeled UART (universal asynchronous receiver/transmitter). The data which is sent over the DB is stored in a special memory called video RAM. This memory stores digital data that is to be displayed in alphanumeric or pictorial patterns on the CRT screen. The CRT controller obtains data from the video RAM and converts it to the relevant video signal (V_c). At the same time, the CRT controller generates the horizontal and vertical sync necessary to operate the raster scan in synchronism with the video signal.

The video controller in the example system (*Figure 9-23*) itself incorporates a microprocessor (MPU) for controlling the CRT display. The video signals that are required to operate the CRT, i.e., V_c (video), H_s

(horizontal sync), V_s (vertical sync), are typically generated in a special purpose integrated circuit, which in the present example is denoted video generator.

Figure 9-23. CRT Controller Configuration

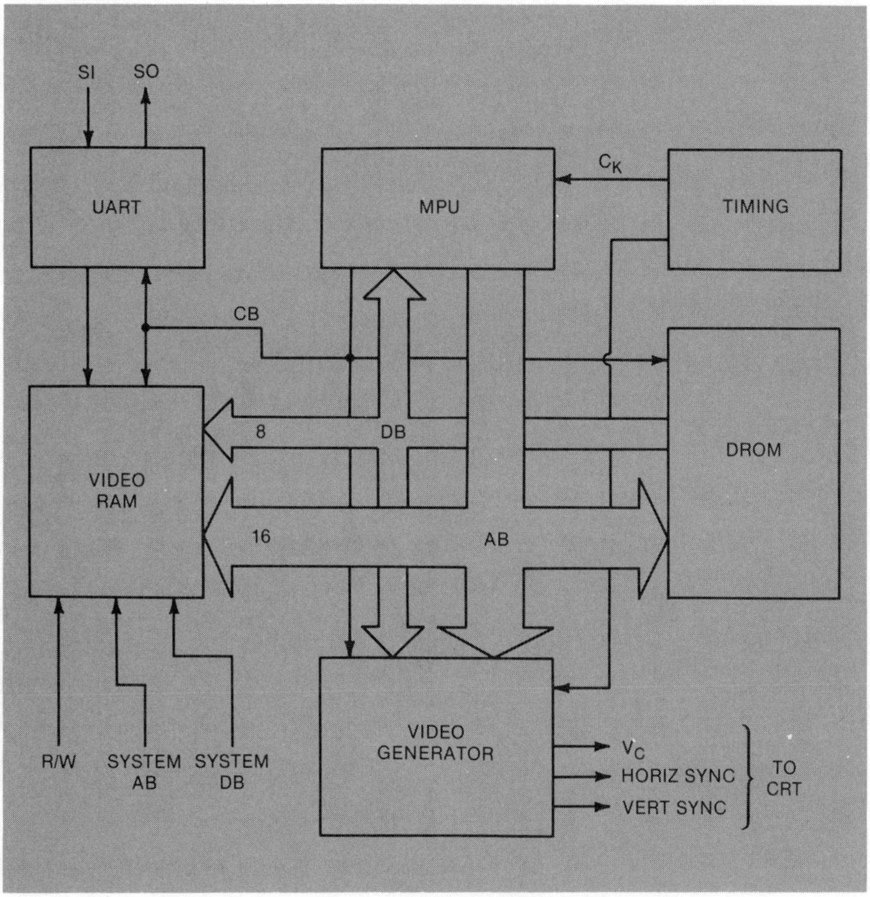

The data to be displayed is stored in the video RAM via the system buses under control of the instrumentation computer. The operation of the MPU is controlled by programs stored in a display ROM (i.e., DROM). This ROM might also store data which is required to generate particular characters. The various components of the CRT controller are internally connected by means of data and address buses similar to those used in the instrumentation computer.

The operation of the CRT controller is under control of the instrumentation computer. This computer transfers data that is to be displayed to the video RAM, and signals the CRT controller via the UART link. During the display time, the MPU operates under control of programs stored in the DROM. These programs cause the MPU to transfer data from the video RAM to the Video IC (chip) in the correct sequence for display.

The details of the transfer of data to the Video IC and the corresponding generation of video signals vary from system to system. In the hypothetical system seen in *Figure 9-22*, the display on the CRT screen consists of a sequence of data arranged in 256 rows vertically by 256 horizontally. Here the display is to generate characters F and P (see *Figure 9-24*). The dots are generated by switching on the electron beam at the desired location. The beam is switched by pulsing the video voltage at the time relative to H_s and V_s at which a dot is to appear. The resolution of the display is one dot, which is often termed a "pixel" (i.e., picture element).

Figure 9-24. Display of Characters F and P

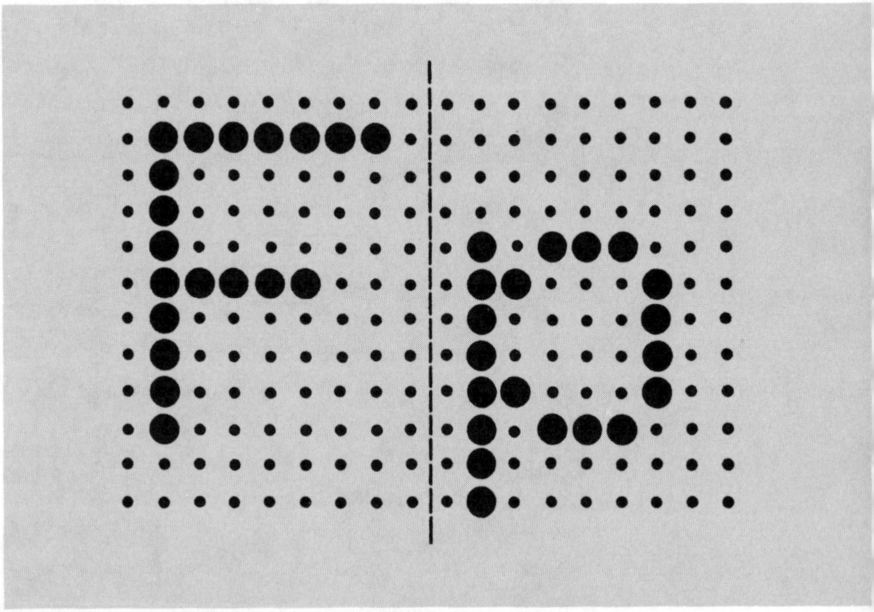

A typical CRT uses a raster scan method and generates dots on the screen by means of suitably timed "video" signals.

A scheme for generating the suitable video signals for such a display is shown (greatly simplified) in the block diagram of *Figure 9-25*. During the horizontal retrace time when the electron beam is moving rapidly from right to left, the MPU (under program control) determines which data pattern is to be displayed during the next scanning line. The MPU maintains an internal record of the current active line on the CRT by counting vertical sync pulses. The actual bit pattern associated with the character being displayed along the active line on the CRT is loaded into the shift register. This data comes in eight separated 8-bit bytes from video RAM. Then during the scanning of the active line the bit pattern is shifted out one bit at a time by a pulse signal, H_{ck}, at a frequency that is 256 times that of the horizontal sync frequency.

Figure 9-25.
Video Signal Generation

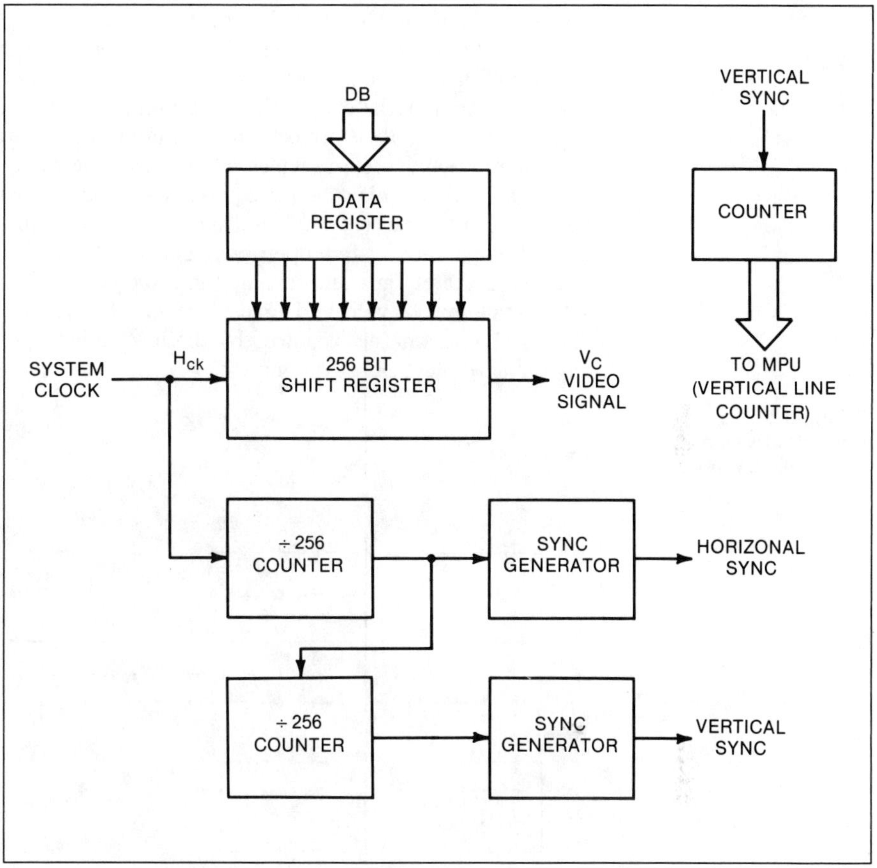

Each bit location in the shift register corresponds to a pixel location on the CRT screen. A "one" stored at any shift register location corresponds to a bright spot on the CRT. Thus, by placing a suitable pattern in the shift register for a particular line, it is possible to display complex alphanumeric or pictorial data on the CRT.

The enormous flexibility of the CRT display offers the potential for a very sophisticated automotive instrumentation system. In addition to displaying the normal variables and parameters which have traditionally been available to the driver, the CRT can display engine data for diagnostic purposes (see Chapter 10), vehicle comfort control system parameters, and entertainment system variables. The data required for such displays can, for example, be transmitted via a UART link between the various onboard electronics systems.

There are several reasons for using the serial UART link for transmitting data between the various systems rather than tying the internal data buses together. For example, it is desirable to protect any given system from a failure in another. A defect affecting the data bus of the comfort system could adversely affect the engine control system. In addition, each internal data bus tends to be busy handling internal "traffic." Moreover, the transfer of data to the instrumentation computer can take place at relatively low data rates (for the diagnostic application outlined above).

Figure 9–26 is a block diagram of an integrated vehicle instrumentation system in which all onboard electronic systems are coupled by a UART link. This system requires a keyboard (KB) or similar input device for operator control. The driver can, for example, select to display the entertainment system operation. This display mode permits the driver to select radio or tape and to tune the radio to the desired station and to set the volume. In vehicle diagnostic mode, the CRT can be configured to display the parameters required by the mechanic to perform a diagnosis of any onboard electronic system.

Figure 9-26. Integrated Vehicle Electronic Systems

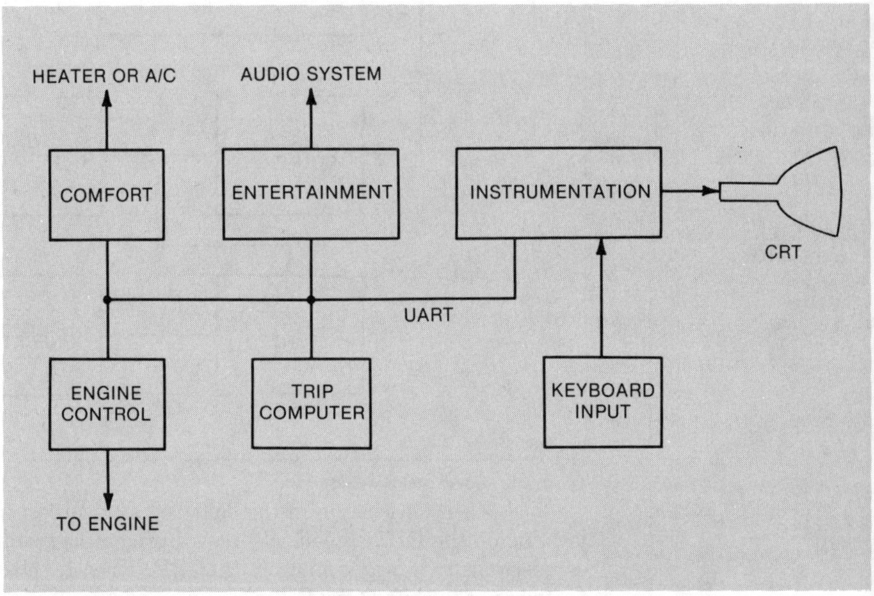

Automotive instrumentation based upon a CRT display has enormous potential. However, the relatively high cost of such a system compared to standard solid-state electromechanical devices is severely limiting the application of this advanced technology. It is likely that the CRT systems will appear in only the most expensive models for the foreseeable future.

TRIP INFORMATION COMPUTER

One of the most popular electronic instruments for automobiles is the trip information system. This system has a number of interesting functions and can display many useful pieces of information, including:

1. present fuel economy
2. average fuel economy

3. average speed
4. present vehicle location (relative to total trip distance)
5. total elapsed trip time
6. fuel remaining
7. miles to empty fuel tank
8. estimated time of arrival
9. time of day
10. engine RPM
11. engine temperature
12. average fuel cost per mile

Trip information computers analyze fuel flow, vehicle speed, and fuel tank quantities, and then calculate information such as miles to empty, average fuel economy, and estimated arrival times.

Additional functions can be performed which no doubt will be part of future developments. However, we will discuss a representative system having features which are common to most available systems.

A block diagram of this system is shown in *Figure 9-27.* Not shown in the block diagram are MUX, DEMUX, and A/D converter components which are normally part of a computer-based instrument. This system can be implemented as a set of special functions of the main automotive instrumentation system, or it can be a stand-alone system employing its own computer.

Figure 9-27. Trip Information System

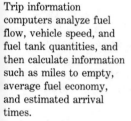

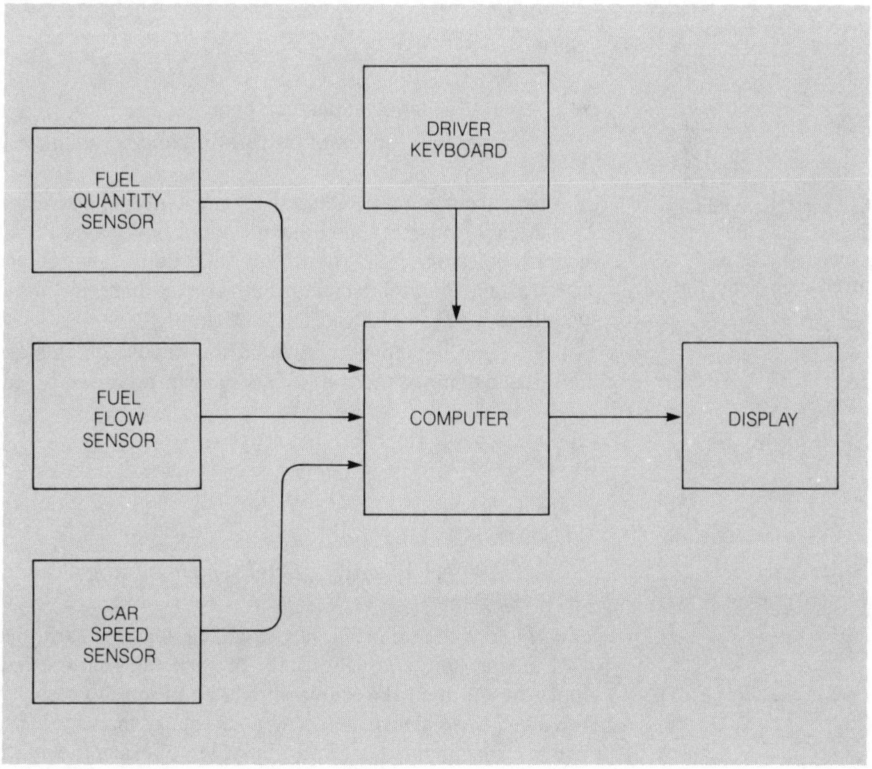

The vehicle inputs to this system come from the three sensors that measure the:

1. quantity of fuel remaining in the tank
2. instantaneous fuel flow rate
3. vehicle speed

Other inputs which are obtained by the computer from other parts of the control system are:

1. odometer mileage
2. time-of-day clock in the computer

The driver enters inputs to the system through the keyboard. At the beginning of a trip, the driver initializes the system and enters the total trip distance and fuel cost. At any time during the trip, the driver can use the keyboard to ask for information to be displayed.

The system computes a particular trip parameter from the input data. For example, fuel economy in miles per gallon (MPG) can be found by computing:

$$MPG = S/F$$

where

S = speed in miles per hour
F = fuel consumption rate in gallons per hour

As operating conditions change, the values provided by a trip information computer may also change.

Of course, this computation varies markedly as operating conditions vary. At a steady cruising speed along a level highway with a constant wind, fuel economy is constant. If the driver then depresses the accelerator (e.g., to pass traffic), the fuel consumption rate temporarily increases faster than speed and MPG is reduced for that time.

Another inportant trip parameter which this system can display is the miles to empty fuel tank, D. This can be found by calculating:

$$D = MPG \times Q$$

where

Q = the quantity of fuel remaining in gallons

Since D depends on MPG, it also changes as operating conditions change (e.g., during heavy acceleration). In such cases, the calculation of miles to empty based upon the above simple equation is grossly incorrect. However, this calculation gives a correct estimate of the miles to empty for steady cruise along a highway in which operating conditions are constant.

Still another pair of parameters which can be calculated and displayed by this system are distance to destination, D_d, and estimated time of arrival, ETA. These can be found by computing:

$$D_d = D_T - D_P$$

$$ETA = T_1 + \frac{D_d}{S}$$

where

D_T = trip distance (entered by the driver)
D_P = present position (in miles traveled since start)
S = present vehicle speed
T_1 = start time

The computer can calculate the present position, D_P by subtracting the start mileage, D1 (from the odometer reading when the trip computer was initialized by the driver), from the present odometer mileage.

The average fuel cost per mile C can be found by calculating:

$$C = (D_P/MPG) \times \text{fuel cost per gallon}$$

There are many other useful and interesting operations that can be performed by the variety of available systems. Actually, the number of such functions that can be performed is limited primarily by cost and by the availability of sensors to measure the required variables.

AUTOMOTIVE DIAGNOSTICS

The instrumentation computer can also be used as a diagnostic aid, during vehicle manufacturing, operation, or repair.

In certain automobile models, the instrumentation computer can perform the important function of diagnosis of the electronic engine control system. This diagnosis takes place at several different levels. One level is used during manufacturing to test the system, and another level is used by mechanics or interested car owners to diagnose engine control system problems. Some levels operate continuously and others are available only upon request from the keyboard.

In the continuous monitor mode, the diagnosis takes place under computer control. The computer activates connections to the vehicle sensors and looks for an open- or short-circuited sensor. If such a condition is detected, a failure warning message is given to the driver on the alphanumeric display or by turning on a labeled warning light. A detailed discussion of automotive diagnostics appears in Chapter 10.

Quiz for Chapter 9

1. What is the primary purpose of automotive instrumentation?
   a. to indicate to the driver the value of certain critical variables and parameters
   b. to extend engine life
   c. to control engine operation
   d. entertainment of passengers

2. What are the three functional components of electronic instrumentation?
   a. sensor, MAP, display
   b. sensor, signal processing, error amplifier
   c. display, sensor, signal processing
   d. none of the above

3. What is the function of a multiplexer in computer-based instrumentation?
   a. it measures several variables simultaneously
   b. it converts sensor analog signals to digital format
   c. it sequentially switches a set of sensor outputs to the instrumentation computer input

4. What is sampling?
   a. a signal processing algorithm
   b. a selective display method
   c. a method of measuring a continuously varying quantity at discrete time instants
   d. the rate of change of battery voltage

5. What is an A/D converter?
   a. a device which changes a continuously varying quantity to a digital format
   b. an 8-bit binary counter
   c. an analog-to-decimal converter
   d. a fluid coupling in the transmission

6. What type of sensor is commonly used for fuel quantity measurement?
   a. a thermistor
   b. a strain gauge
   c. a potentiometer whose movable arm is connected to a float
   d. a piezoelectric sensor

7. How is coolant temperature measured?
   a. with a mercury bulb thermometer
   b. with a strain gauge
   c. with a thermistor as a sensor
   d. with a galvanometer

8. A digital vehicle speed sensor incorporates:
   a. a variable frequency pulse generator and digital counter
   b. a variable resistor
   c. a variable capacitance
   d. none of the above

9. What is the predominant type of automotive digital display?
   a. light-emitting diode
   b. galvanometer
   c. vacuum-fluorescent
   d. liquid crystal

10. What sensor input variables are used in a typical "Trip Computer" system?
a. manifold pressure and engine speed
b. RPM, barometric pressure, and fuel quantity remaining
c. MPG and fuel consumption
d. car speed, fuel flow rate, fuel quantity remaining in tank

11. A CRT display device uses
a. a cathode ray tube scanned in a raster pattern
b. a vacuum-fluorescent tube
c. an incandescent light source
d. none of the above

12. In the digital video signal generator used with a CRT display
a. each bit in the shift register corresponds to a pixel location
b. each pixel on the screen corresponds to a specific video voltage level
c. scanning of the CRT by the electron beam is from right to left and from bottom to top
d. all of the above are true

13. The term MUX refers to
a. an electronic switch which selects one of a set of inputs per an input code
b. a digital output device
c. a time slot
d. none of the above

14. A D/A converter
a. is a disk access device
b. converts the digital output of an instrumentation computer to analog form
c. stores analog data
d. enters digital data in a computer.

15. In electronic instrumentation, fuel quantity is displayed by
a. an ammeter
b. a potentiometer
c. a digital display
d. none of the above

16. The term LED refers to
a. level-equalizing detector
b. light-emitting diode
c. liquid crystal display
d. none of the above

17. An LCD display uses
a. a nematic liquid
b. an incandescent lamp
c. large electrical power
d. a picket fence

18. Light is produced in a VFD by
a. ionic bombardment of a filament
b. ambient temperature
c. bombardment of a phosphor material by energetic electrons
d. chemical action

19. Fuel economy is calculated in a trip computer by:
a. SF
b. F/S
c. S/F
d. none of the above

Diagnostics

From the earliest days of the commercial sale of the automobile, it has been obvious that maintenance is required to keep automobiles operating properly. Of course, automobile dealerships have provided this service for years, as have independent repair shops and service stations. But until the early 1970s, a great deal of the routine maintenance and repair was done by car owners themselves, using inexpensive tools and equipment. However, The Clean Air Act impacted not only the emissions produced by automobiles, but also the complexity of the engine control systems and, as a result, the complexity of automobile maintenance and repair. Car owners can no longer, as a matter of course, do their own maintenance and repairs.

The development of electronic engine control has increased the complexity of diagnosis and maintenance.

The change from the traditional fluidic/pneumatic engine controls to the microprocessor-based electronic engine controls was a direct result of the need to control automobile emissions, and has been chronicled throughout this book. However, little has been said thus far about the diagnostic problems involved in electronically controlled engines. This type of diagnostics requires a fundamentally different approach than that for traditionally controlled engines because it requires more sophisticated equipment than is required for diagnostics in pre-emission control manufactured automobiles. In fact, the best diagnostic methods use special purpose computers which are themselves microprocessor based. However, before launching into a discussion of electronic control system diagnostics, there are two nonmicroprocessor diagnostic instruments that are still used in garages and repair shops that should be discussed—the timing light and the engine analyzer.

TIMING LIGHT

The timing light (*Figure 10-1*) is used to measure and set ignition timing. It is a special stroboscopic light source that generates very short duration light pulses, the timing of which coincides with ignition pulses. The timing of these pulses is obtained from a special probe connected to a spark-plug wire. *Figure 10-2* is a block diagram of a typical timing light.

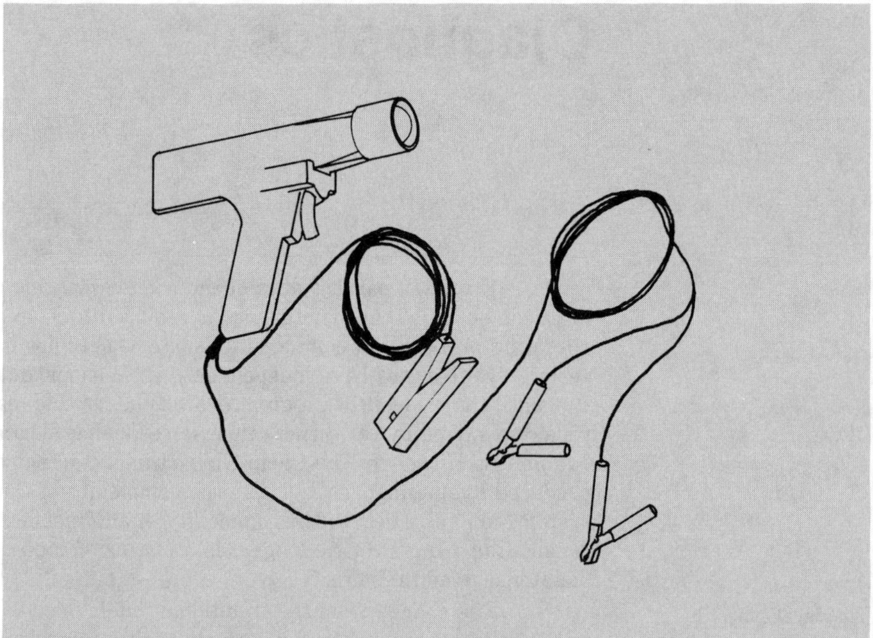

Figure 10-1. Typical Engine Timing Light

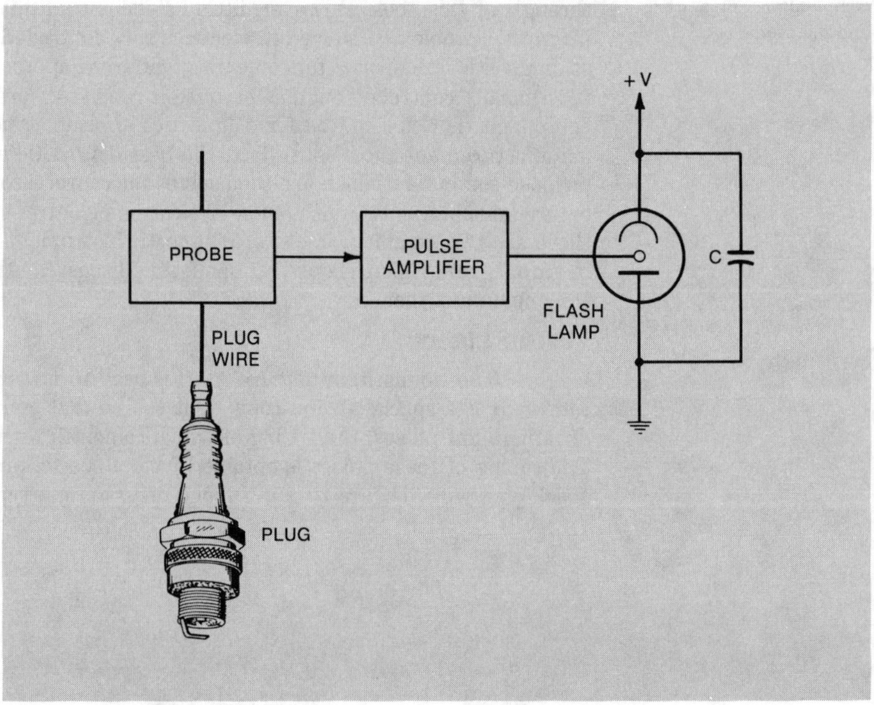

Figure 10-2. Timing Light Block Diagram

The probe generates a very short duration voltage pulse each time the spark plug fires. The pulse is amplified and then operates a trigger electrode on a flash lamp which is a gas discharge tube. When triggered, a current pulse flows through the flashlamp generating a short burst of light.

In timing the ignition, the light from the flash lamp is directed at the pulley on the front end of the crankshaft. Adjacent to the pulley is a pointer, such as seen in *Figure 10-3.* On the pulley are several marks. The relationship between the pointer and these marks corresponds to specific crankshaft angular position relative to top dead center (TDC). The relationship of the pointer and crankshaft pulley marks at the time of ignition can be seen by viewing the pulley using the light from the flash lamp. When the ignition timing is correct, the pointer will align with the correct pulley mark.

Figure 10-3. Timing Marks

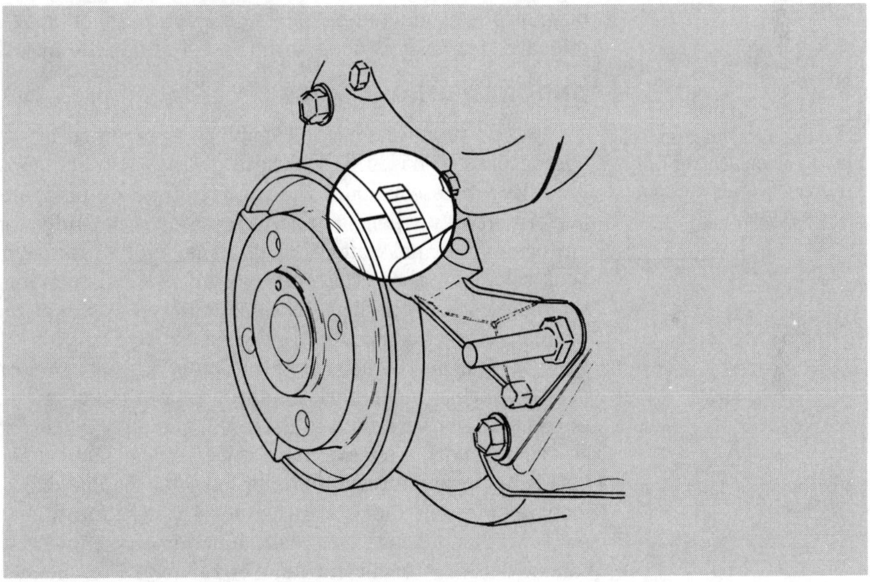

ENGINE ANALYZER

The timing light and traditional engine analyzer are not enough for diagnosis of engine problems.

The engine analyzer is an instrument that has existed for many years and continues to be used in garages for several tuneup tasks. It provides, for example, a means for optimally setting the gap for ignition points (in cars that still have them of course) by measuring the so-called "dwell." Dwell is essentially the fractional duration that the ignition points are closed. However, an engine analyzer's role in diagnosing cars that have digital engine control systems is markedly different than its role in the diagnosis of cars that have analog or mechanical control systems. For example, ignition points have virtually been eliminated in digitally controlled cars. Nevertheless, the concept of dwell is still applicable, only today it represents the amount of time current flows through the coil primary circuit before this circuit is interrupted (see Chapter 7). In addition, in certain cases ignition timing can be measured by measuring the relative strength (peak voltage) of ignition pulses. Although the engine analyzer continues to be a useful instrument, it is not adequate for diagnosing problems in electronically controlled systems.

While it is true that both the timing light and the engine analyzer will continue to be used as there are million of cars still on the roads whose engines are controlled either by analog or mechanical systems, it is probable that the use of these two diagnostic instruments will be phased out within ten years.

ELECTRONIC CONTROL SYSTEM DIAGNOSTICS

Diagnosis of problems in digital electronic engine control systems are done partly onboard the vehicle and partly offboard. The onboard diagnosis is conducted by the engine control system (ECS) itself; the offboard diagnosis is done with the aid of outside instrumentation.

ONBOARD DIAGNOSTICS

Existing microprocessor-based engine control systems incorporate some self-diagnosis.

Limited diagnostic capability is provided in any modern microprocessor-based ECS. These diagnostic functions are performed by the microprocessor under the control of stored programs, and are performed only when the microprocessor is not fully committed to performing normal control calculations. While it is beyond the scope of this book to review the actual software involved in such diagnostic operations, the diagnostic procedures that are followed and explanations of onboard diagnostic functions can be reviewed.

During the normal operation of the car, there are intermittent periods during which various electrical and electronic components are tested. Whenever a fault is detected, the data is stored in memory in accordance with a specific fault code. At the same time, the controller generates or activates a warning lamp (or similar display) on the instrument panel indicating that service is required.

The onboard diagnostic functions have one major limitation—they cannot detect intermittent failures reliably. For the system to detect and isolate a failure, the failure must be nonreversible. In most onboard diagnostics, the electronic control module stores trouble codes that are automatically cleared by the microprocessor after a set number of engine cycles have occurred without a fault reappearing.

The onboard diagnostic capabilities can be manually activated by causing the engine controller to enter a diagnostic mode. The method for accomplishing this task varies from car to car. For example, in certain fuel injected Cadillac cars, the diagnostic mode is entered by first switching on the ignition, then simultaneously depressing the OFF and WARMER buttons on the climate control system.

The use of onboard diagnostics can easily be illustrated by outlining typical procedures and using the Cadillac system as an example system. Although display of the fault codes varies from car to car, in each case the codes must be readable as a numeric code. A typical method involves flashing the "check engine" light. The mechanic enters the display mode and then counts the number of times that this light is flashed, in two digit groups. For example, a fault code 24 would be given by 2 flashes then 4 flashes. After a short time interval the next code would similarly be flashed in two digit sequence. Cadillac uses the environmental controller to display a two-digit code. *Figure 10-4* is a drawing of a Cadillac environmental system displaying code 88. This particular code is used to check that all display segments are working correctly and is the first display shown when the diagnostic mode is entered.

Figure 10-4. Drawing of Fault Code Display

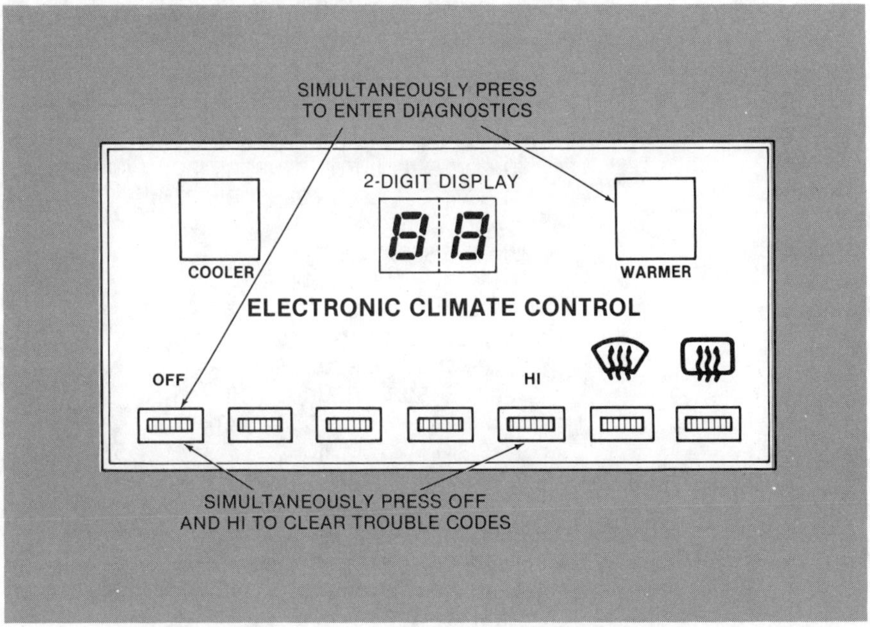

A 2-digit fault code is assigned to each failure.

After verifying that all display segments are working, the fault codes for all component failures are displayed in sequence, beginning with the lowest and proceeding to the highest. The mechanic notes the fault codes that are displayed, and using a reference manual, identifies the failed components. *Table 10-1* is a summary of the Cadillac fault codes. After all fault codes have been displayed, the number 70 appears on the climate control head, and the engine control system awaits further action by the mechanic.

Table 10-1. Summary of Fault Codes

CIRCUIT AFFECTED	2-DIGIT FAULT CODE
NO DISTRIBUTOR SIGNAL	12
EGO SENSOR NOT READY	13
COOLANT SENSOR CIRCUIT (SHORT)	14
COOLANT SENSOR (OPEN)	15
GENERATOR VOLTAGE OUT OF RANGE	16
CRANK SIGNAL (SHORT)	17
CRANK SIGNAL (OPEN)	18
FUEL PUMP CIRCUIT (SHORT)	19
FUEL PUMP CIRCUIT (OPEN)	20
THROTTLE POSITION SENSOR CIRCUIT (SHORT)	21
THROTTLE POSITION SENSOR (OPEN)	22
IGNITION/BYPASS	23
ENGINE SPEED SENSOR	24
THROTTLE SWITCH (SHORT)	26
THROTTLE SWITCH (OPEN)	27
IDLE SPEED CONTROL	30
MAP SENSOR CIRCUIT (SHORT)	31
MAP SENSOR CIRCUIT (OPEN)	32
MAP/BARO SENSOR CORRELATION	33
MAP SIGNAL TOO HIGH	34
BARO SENSOR CIRCUIT (SHORT)	35
BARO SENSOR CIRCUIT (OPEN)	36
MANIFOLD AIR TEMP (SHORT)	37
MANIFOLD AIR TEMP (OPEN)	38
LEAN EXHAUST SIGNAL	44
RICH EXHAUST SIGNAL	45
PROM ERROR INDICATOR	51
TRANSMISSION NOT IN DRIVE	60
SET AND RESUME CIRCUITS ENGAGED SIMULTANEOUSLY	61
CAR SPEED EXCEEDS MAX. LIMIT	62
CAR AND SET SPEED TOLERANCE EXCEEDED	63
CAR ACCELERATION EXCEEDS MAX. LIMIT	64
SYSTEM READY FOR FURTHER TESTS	70
CRUISE CONTROL BRAKE CIRCUIT TEST	71
THROTTLE SWITCH CIRCUIT TEST	72
DRIVE (ADL) CIRCUIT TEST	73
REVERSE CIRCUIT TEST	74
CRUISE ON/OFF CIRCUIT TEST	75
"SET/COAST" CIRCUIT TEST	76
"RESUME/ACCELERATION" CIRCUIT TEST	77
"INSTANT/AVERAGE" CIRCUIT TEST	78
"RESET" CIRCUIT TEST	79
AIR COND CLUTCH CIRCUIT TEST	80

DISPLAY CHECK	88
SYSTEM READY TO DISPLAY ENGINE DATA	90
ALL DIAGNOSTICS COMPLETE	00

A 2-digit fault code is assigned to each failure.

Typically the "check engine" light on the instrument panel is illuminated whenever any fault occurs. For codes 12 through 38 and 51, this warning light goes out automatically if the malfunction clears. However, the control module stores the code associated with the detected failure until the diagnostic system is manually cleared, or until 20 engine cycles occur with no malfunction. For codes 44 and 45, the "check engine" light will not go out until cleared from memory by the mechanic. For codes 60 through 68, there is no activation of the "check engine" light.

Whenever a defect occurs (as indicated by a fault code), the mechanic must follow a specific procedure to isolate the particular problem. These procedures are outlined for the mechanic in charts in the shop manuals. An example procedure will be illustrated here by following the steps necessary to respond to the specific fault code 13, which indicates that the oxygen sensor (i.e., O_2 or EGO) sensor is not ready. Recall from the discussion in Chapter 5 that the O_2 sensor switches between approximately 0 and 1 volt as the mixture switches between the extreme conditions of lean and rich. Recall also that this voltage swing requires that the O_2 sensor must be at a temperature above 200°C. Fault code 13 means that the O_2 sensor will not swing above or below its cold voltage of approximately .5 volt, and that the electronic control system will not go into closed-loop operation (see Chapters 6 and 7),

Possible causes for fault code 13 include:

O_2 sensor is not functioning correctly
defective connections or leads
the control unit is not processing the O_2 signal

Further investigation is required to attempt to isolate the specific problem.

To check the operation of the O_2 sensor, the average value of its output voltage is measured using the electronic engine control system (the procedure for which is explained later in this chapter). The desired voltage is displayed on the climate control head in multiples of 1/100 volt. That is to say, "00" corresponds to 0 volts and "99" corresponds to .99 volts, etc.

Using this voltage, the mechanic follows a procedure outlined in *Figures 10-5, 10-6,* and *10-7.* If this voltage is less than .37 volt or greater than .57 volt, the mechanic is asked to investigate the wiring harness for defects.

Figure 10-5.
DFI Oxygen Sensor Circuit

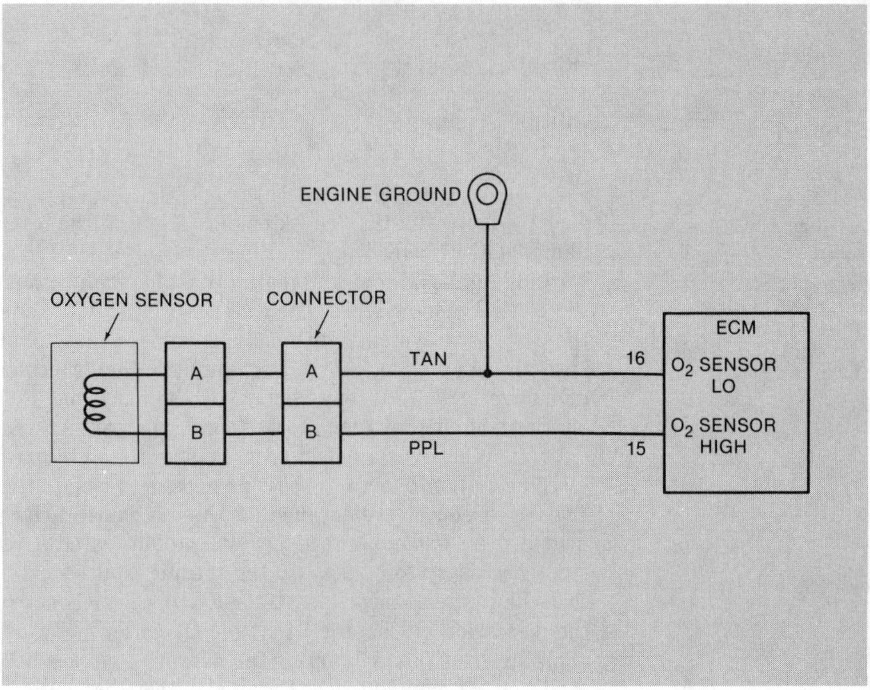

If the O_2 sensor voltage is between .37 volt and .57 volt, tests are performed to determine whether the O_2 sensor or the control unit is faulty. The mechanic must jumper the O_2 sensor leads together at the input to the control unit, simulating a sensor short circuit, and must read the sensor voltage value using the climate control display. If this voltage is less than .05 volt, the control unit is functioning correctly and the O_2 sensor must be investigated for defects. If the indicated sensor voltage is greater than .05 volt, the control unit is faulty and should be replaced.

When diagnosing a problem the mechanic might wish to clear a fault code from the electronic control memory. A good reason to do this, for example, would be to test whether a failure is "hard" or intermittent. To clear trouble codes (with the system in diagnostic mode), the mechanic simultaneously pushes the "OFF" and "HI" buttons on the climate control head until "00" is displayed. After all fault codes are cleared, code 70 will appear.

Figure 10-6.
DFI Code 13: Oxygen Sensor Not Ready

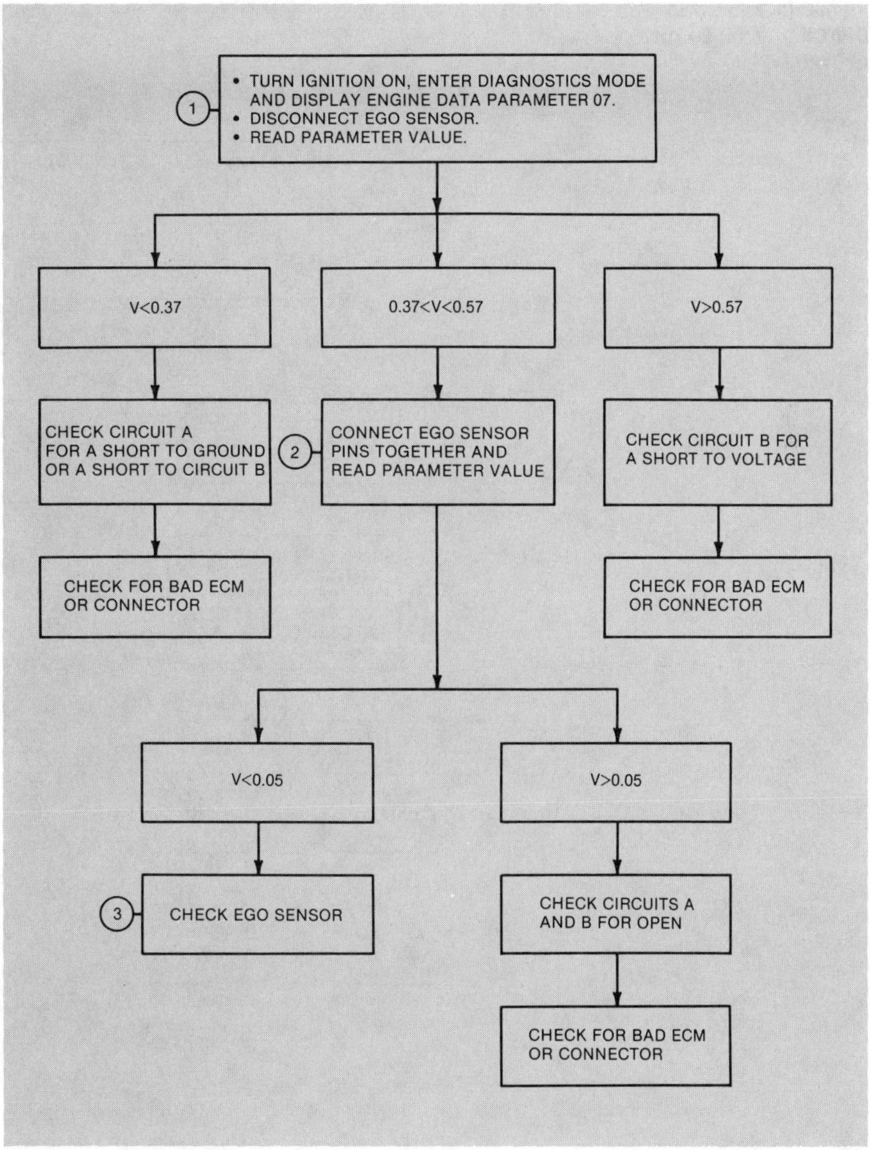

Figure 10-7.
DFI Chart # 14: Oxygen Sensor Test

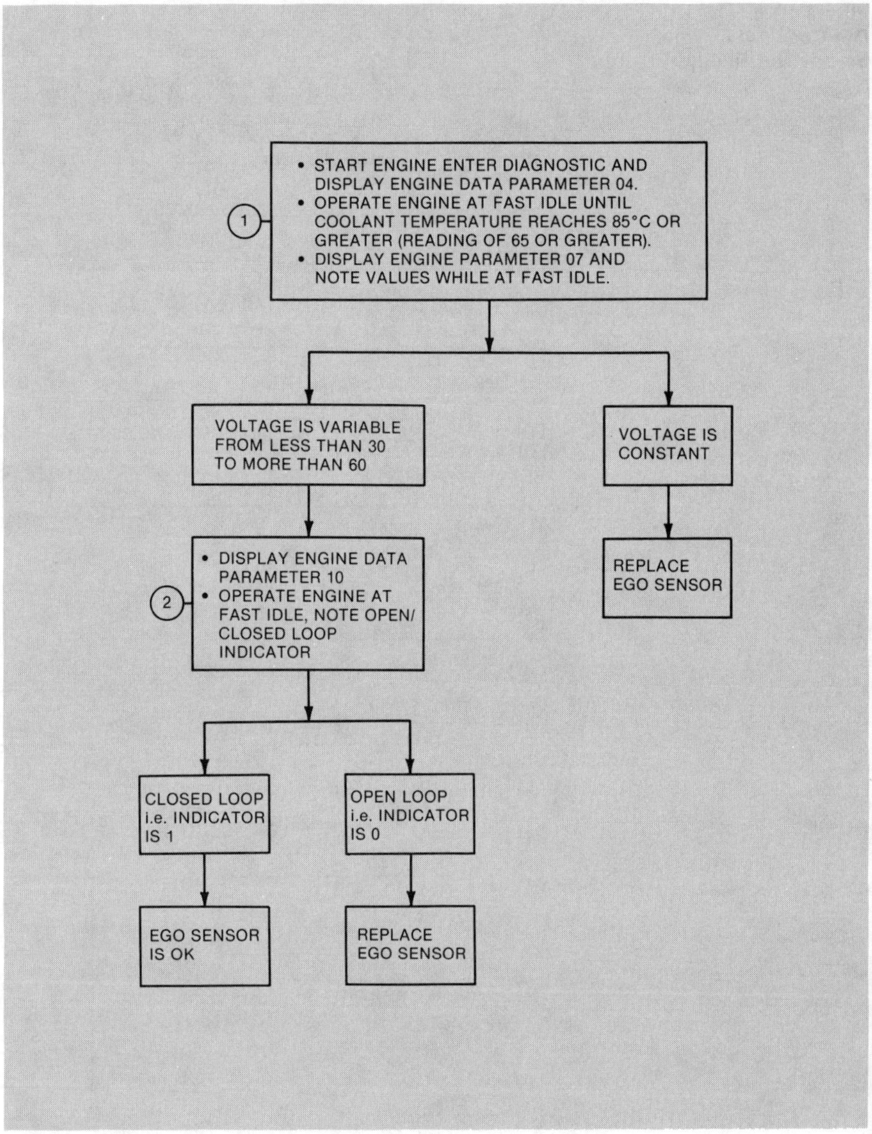

On-board diagnosis also examines the status of several switches.

Code 70 represents a decision point in the diagnostic procedure. At this point, the mechanic has several choices including:

switch tests
engine data display
output cycling tests
cylinder select tests
exit from diagnostic mode

Each of the above procedures provides an important diagnostic capability to the mechanic.

The switch tests involve fault codes 71–80 and provide checks on the switches indicated in *Figure 10-8*. To begin the switch tests, the mechanic must depress and release the brake pedal. If there is no brake switch failure, then the code advances to 71. If the display doesn't advance, then the control unit is not processing the brake switch signal and further diagnosis is required. For such a failure, the mechanic locates the specific chart (such as seen in *Figures 10-9* and *10-10*) for diagnosis of the particular switch failure and follows the procedure outlined. The detailed tests performed by the mechanic are continuity checks that are performed with a test light.

Figure 10-8. Switch Test Series

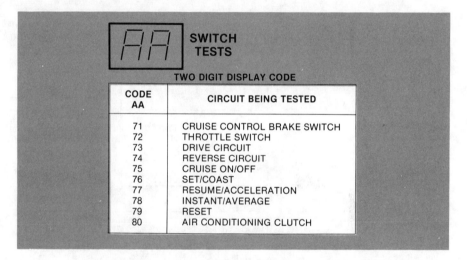

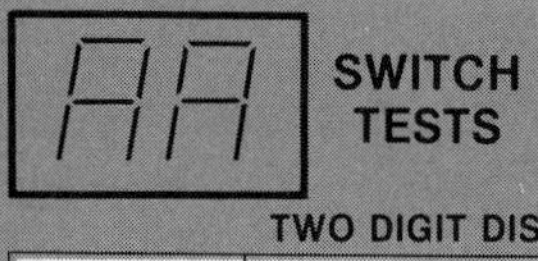

CODE AA	CIRCUIT BEING TESTED
71	CRUISE CONTROL BRAKE SWITCH
72	THROTTLE SWITCH
73	DRIVE CIRCUIT
74	REVERSE CIRCUIT
75	CRUISE ON/OFF
76	SET/COAST
77	RESUME/ACCELERATION
78	INSTANT/AVERAGE
79	RESET
80	AIR CONDITIONING CLUTCH

Similar procedures are followed for each switch test in the sequence. This procedure sequence is as follows:

With code 71 displayed, depress and release brake pedal. For normal operation, the display advances to 72.

With 72 displayed, depress the throttle from idle position to wide open position. The control unit tests the throttle switch, and advances the display to 73 for normal operation.

With 73 displayed, the transmission selector is moved to drive and then neutral. This operation tests the drive switch, and the display advances to 74 for normal operation.

With 74 displayed, the transmission selector is moved to reverse and then to park. This tests the reverse switch operation, and the display advances to 75 for normal operation.

Figure 10-9. DFI Cruise Control Brake Circuit

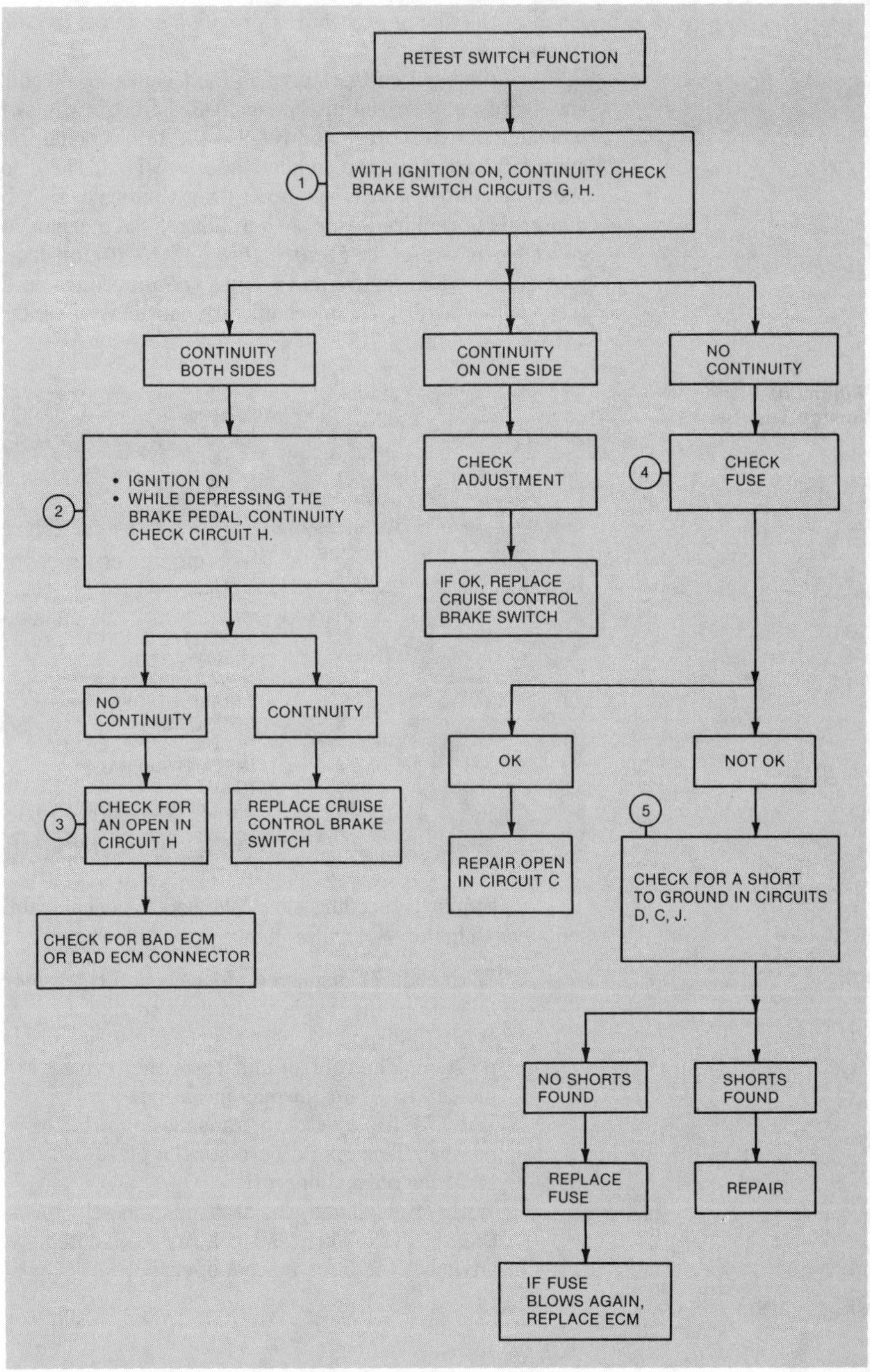

Figure 10-10. DFI Code 71L Cruise Control Brake Circuit

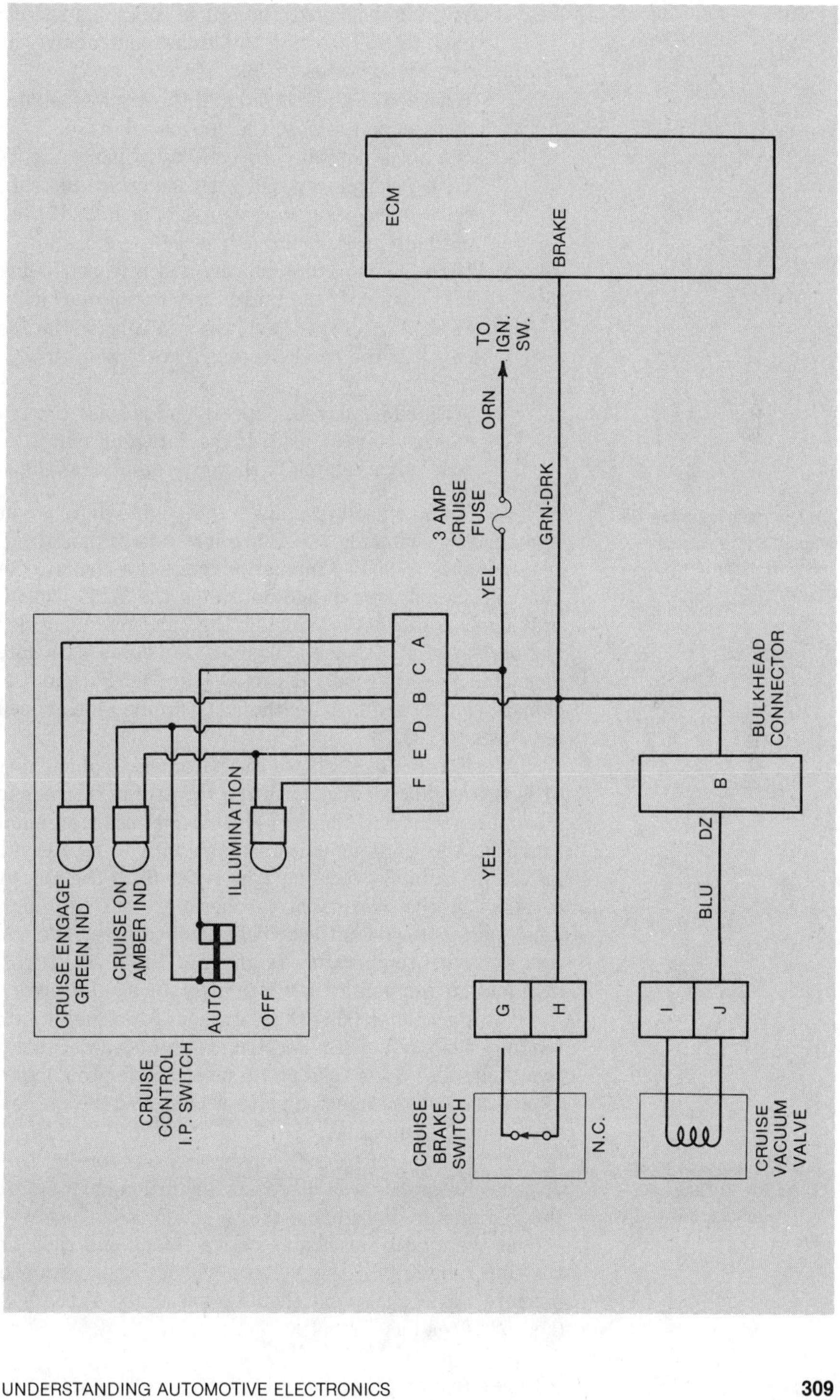

With 75 displayed, the cruise control is switched from OFF to ON and back to OFF testing the cruise control switch. For normal operation, the display advances to 76.

With code 76 displayed and the cruise instrument panel switch on, depress and release the set/coast button. If the button (switch) is operating normally, the display advances to 77.

With 77 displayed and with the cruise instrument on, depress and release the resume/acceleration switch. If the switch is operating normally, the display advances to 78.

With 78 displayed, depress and release the instant/average button on the MPG panel. If the button is working normally, the code advances to 79.

With 79 displayed, depress and release the reset button on the MPH panel. If the reset button is working normally, the code will advance to 80.

With 80 displayed, depress and release the rear defogger button on the climate control head. If the defogger switch is working normally, the code advances to 70, thereby completing the switch tests.

A few vehicles have the capability to measure certain parameters.

With code 70 displayed, the engine data can be displayed in sequence by switching the cruise instrument panel "off." The code should then advance to 90. To further advance the display, the mechanic must depress the instant/average button on the MPG panel (to return to the previously displayed parameter, the mechanic must depress the reset button on the MPG panel). To exit the engine parameter display mode, the mechanic simultaneously depresses the "OFF" and "HI" buttons on the climate control head. After the last parameter has been displayed, the code advances to "95."

Figure 10-11 shows the parameter values in sequence. parameter 01 is the angular deflection of the throttle in degrees from idle position. Parameter 02 is the manifold absolute pressure in kilopascals (kPa). The range for this parameter is 14 to 99, with 14 representing about the maximum manifold vacuum. Parameter 02 is the absolute atmospheric pressure in kPa. Normal atmospheric pressure is roughly 90–100 kPa at sea level. parameter 04 is the coolant temperature. The conversion from this code to actual temperature is given in *Table 10–2*. Parameter 05 is the manifold air temperature, which uses the same conversion as parameter 04.

Parameter 06 is the duration of the fuel injector pulse in msec. In reading this number, the mechanic assumes a decimal point between the two digits (i.e., 16 is read at 1.6 msec). Refer to Chapters 5, 6, and 7 for an explanation of the injector pulse widths and the influence of these pulse widths on fuel mixture.

Measurements of average O_2 sensor voltage are useful for diagnosis of this sensor.

Parameter 07 is the average value for the O_2 sensor output voltage. Reference was made earlier in this chapter to the diagnostic use of this parameter. Recall that the O_2 sensor switches between about 0 and 1 volt as the mixture oscillates between lean and rich. The displayed value is the time average for this voltage which varies with the duty cycle of the mixture. A decimal point should be assumed at the left of the two digits (i.e., 52 is read as .52 volt).

Figure 10-11.
Engine Data Display

ENGINE DATA

PARAMETER NUMBER	PARAMETER	NORMAL RANGE
01	THROTTLE POSITION	0-31
02	MANIFOLD PRESSURE	14-99
03	BAROMETRIC PRESSURE	14-99
04	COOLANT TEMPREATURE	0-99
05	MANIFOLD AIR TEMPERATURE	9-99
06	INJECTOR PULSE DURATION	0-9.9
07	EGO SENSOR VOLTAGE	0-0.99
08	SPARK ADVANCE (DEGREES)	0-52

Parameter 08 is the spark advance in degrees before TDC. This value should agree with that obtained using a timing light or engine analyzer.

Parameter 09 is the number of ignition cycles that have occurred since a trouble code was set in memory. If 20 such cycles have occurred without a fault, this counter is set to zero and all trouble codes are cleared.

Parameter 10 is a logical (binary) variable that indicates whether the engine control system is operating in open or closed loop. A value 1 corresponds to closed loop, which means that data from the O_2 sensor is fed back to the controller to be used in setting injector pulse duration. Zero for this variable indicates open-loop operation as explained in Chapters 6 and 7.

Parameter 11 is the battery voltage minus 10. A decimal point is assumed between the digits. Thus 2.3 is read as 12.3 volts.

After completion of parameter data values, the climate control display will advance to 95. The remaining codes are specific to certain Cadillac models and are not germane to the present discussion.

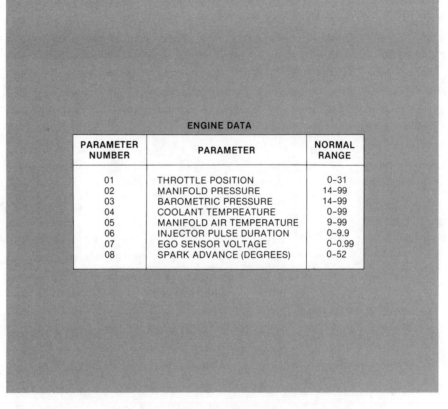

Table 10-2. Temperature Conversion Table

COOLANT TEMPERATURE CONVERSION

CODE	°F
0	−40
8	−12
12	+1
16	15
21	32
25	46
30	64
35	81
40	98
45	115
50	133
52	140
54	147
56	153
58	160
60	167
62	174
64	181
66	188
68	195
70	202
72	209
73	212
75	219

Once the mechanic has read all of the fault codes, he/she proceeds with the diagnosis using the shop manual in the same manner as explained for the Cadillac example. For each fault code there is a procedure that is followed that attempts to isolate the specific components that have failed. Obviously the process of diagnosing a problem can be lengthy and can involve many steps. However, without the aid of the onboard diagnostic capability of the electronic control system, such diagnosis would take much more time and might, in certain cases, be impossible.

OFFBOARD DIAGNOSIS

An alternative to the onboard diagnostics is available in the form of a service bay diagnostic system. This system uses a computer that has a greater diagnostic capability than the vehicle-based system, because its computer is typically much larger and has only a single task to perform—that of diagnosing problems in engine control systems.

Special purpose digital computers are coming into use in service bay diagnosis systems.

An example of a service bay diagnostic system is General Motors CAMS (Computerized Automotive Maintenance System). The GM-CAMS uses an IBM PC/AT computer which has considerable computational capability. Its memory includes 640K bytes of RAM, 1.2 million bytes on 5.75 inch diskette drive, and 20 million bytes on a fixed disk drive. This system is capable of detecting, analyzing, and isolating faults in late model GM vehicles that are equipped with digital engine control system. This system is commonly called the technicians' terminal.

The technicians' terminal is mounted on a rugged portable cart (*Figure 10-12*) suitable for use in the garage. It connects to the vehicle through the assembly line data link (ALDL). The data required to perform diagnostics is obtained by the terminal through this link. The terminal has a color CRT monitor (similar to that of a typical home computer) that displays the data and procedures. It has a touch-sensitive screen for technician input to the system. The terminal features a keyboard for data entry, printer for hard copy output, and a modem for a telephone link to a network that collects and routes GM-CAMS information.

Figure 10-12. GM-CAMS Computer

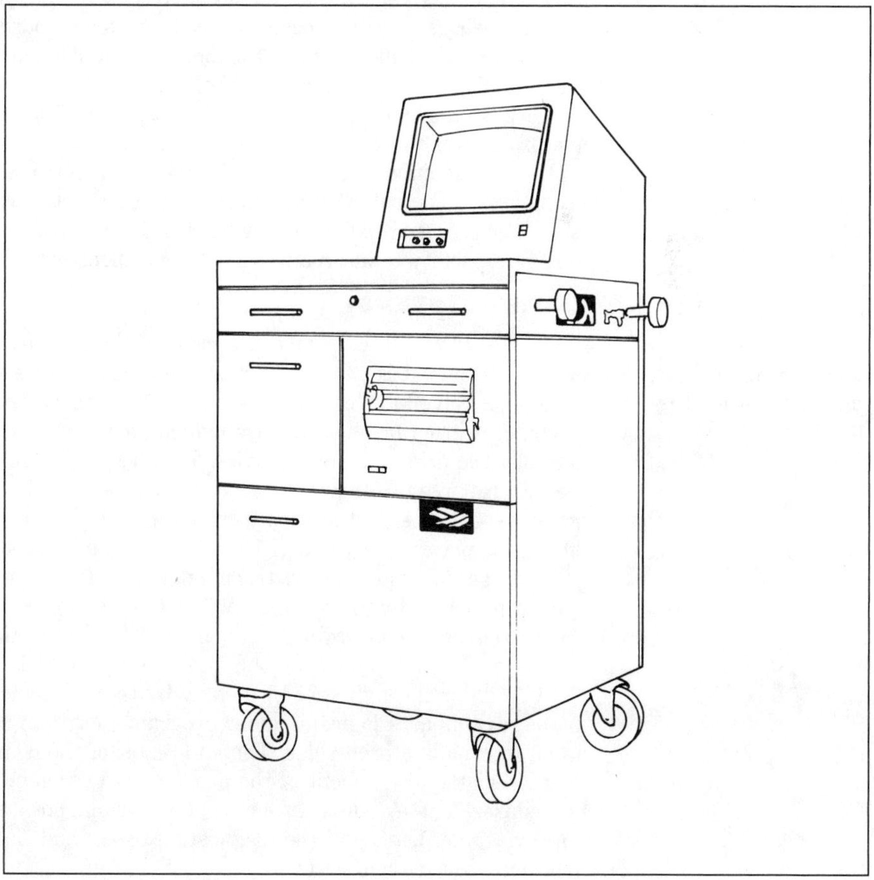

The GM system also features a main frame computer system at the General Motors Information Center (GMIC) that contains a master data base which includes the most recent information relating to repair of applicable GM cars. This information as well as computer software updates are relayed throughout the network. Mechanics can also obtain diagnostic assistance by calling the GM-CAMS Customer Support Center.

When using the GM-CAMS, the mechanic enters the vehicle identification number (VIN) via the terminal, and the computer responds by displaying a "menu" in which several choices are presented. To select a particular choice the technician touches the portion of the display associated with that choice. Next the computer displays an additional menu of further choices; this continues until the mechanic has located the desired choice.

The service bay diagnostic system can be readily updated with new service bulletins.

Among the many capabilities of the technicians' terminal is its ability to store and display the diagnostic charts which appear in the shop manual. Whenever a fault is located, the appropriate chart(s) are automatically displayed for the mechanic. This capability greatly increases the efficiency of the diagnostic process. In addition, the GM-CAMS computer can store all of the data that is associated with the diagnostic procedures for several vehicles and then locate, virtually instantaneously, and display each specific procedure as required. Furthermore, updates and the most recent service bulletins are brought into the mechanics' terminal over the phone network, so that mechanics lose no time trying to find the most recent data and procedures for diagnosing vehicular electronic systems.

In addition to storing and displaying shop manual data and procedures, a computer-based garage diagnostic system can automate the diagnostic process itself. In achieving this objective, the technicians' terminal has the capability to incorporate what is commonly called an expert system.

EXPERT SYSTEMS

An expert system is a form of artificial intelligence which has great potential for automotive diagnosis.

Although it is beyond the scope of the present book to explain expert systems, it is perhaps worthwhile to introduce some of the major concepts involved in this rapidly developing technology. An expert system is a computer program that employs human knowledge to solve problems normally requiring human expertise. The theory of expert systems is part of the general area of computer science known as artificial intelligence (AI). The major benefit of expert system technology is the consistent, uniform, and efficient application of the decision criteria or problem-solving strategies.

The diagnosis of electronic engine control systems by an expert system proceeds by following a set of rules that embody steps similar to the diagnostic charts in the shop manual. The diagnostic system receives data from the electronic control System (e.g., via ALDL connector in the GM-CAMs) or through keyboard entry by the mechanic. The system processes this data logically under program control in accordance with the set of internally stored rules. The end result of the computer-aided diagnosis is an assessment of the problem and recommended repair procedures. The use of an expert system for diagnosis can significantly improve the efficiency of the diagnostic process and can thereby reduce maintenance time and costs.

An expert system takes information from experts and converts this to a set of logical rules.

The development of an expert system requires a computer specialist who is known in AI parlance as a "knowledge engineer." The knowledge engineer must acquire the requisite knowledge and expertise for the expert system by interviewing the recognized experts in the field. In the case of automotive electronic engine control systems the experts include the design engineers as well as the test engineers and the mechanics and technicians involved in the development of the control system. In addition, expertise is developed by the mechanics who routinely repair the system in the field. The expertise of this latter group can be incorporated as evolutionary improvements in the expert system. The various stages of acquisition of knowledge (obtained from the experts) is outlined in *Figure 10-13.* It can be seen from this figure that several iterations are required to complete the knowledge acquisition. Thus the process of interviewing experts is a continuing process.

Figure 10-13. Stages of Knowledge Acquisition

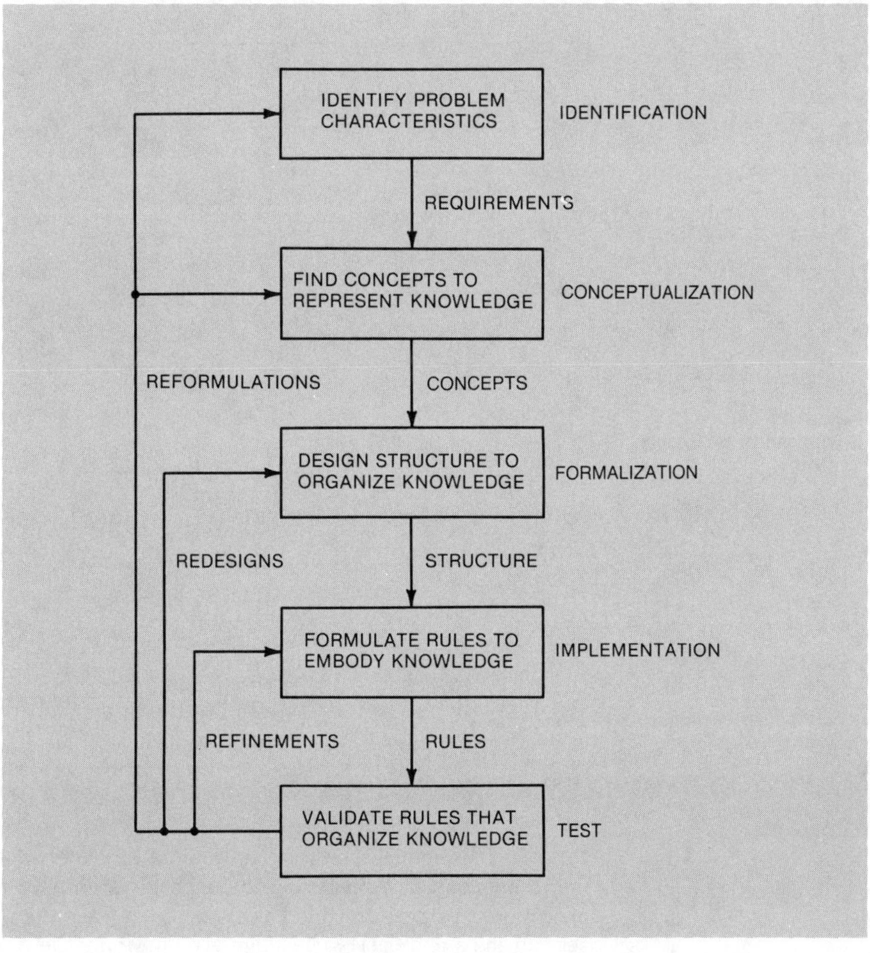

Not to be overlooked in the development of an expert system, is the personal relationship between the experts and the knowledge engineer. The experts must be fully willing to cooperate and to explain their expertise to the knowledge engineer if a successful expert system is to be developed. The personalities of the knowledge engineer and experts can become a factor in the development of an expert system.

Figure 10-14 represents the environment in which an expert system evolves. Of course, a digital computer of sufficient capacity is required for the development work. A summary of expert system development tools which are applicable for a main frame computer is presented in *Table 10-3.*

Table 10-3. Expert System Developing Tools for Main Frame

NAME	COMPANY	MACHINE
Ops5	Carnegie Mellon University	VAX
S.1	Teknowledge	VAX
		Xerox 1198
Loops	Xerox	Xerox 1108
Kee	Intelligenetics	Xerox 1198
		Symbolics
Art	Inference	Symbolics

Figure 10-14. Environment of Expert System

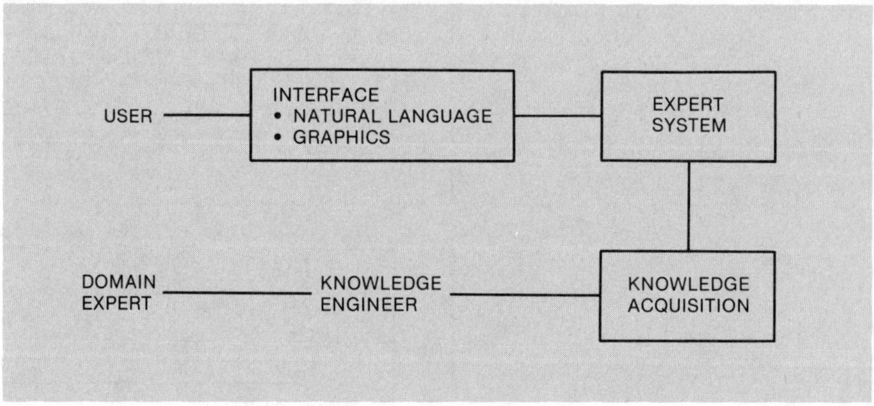

It is common practice to think of an expert system as having two major portions. The portion of the expert system in which the logical operations are performed is known as the *inference engine*. The various relationships and basic knowledge are known as the *knowledge base*.

The general diagnostic field to which an expert system is applicable is one in which the procedures used by the recognized experts can be expressed in a set of rules or logical relationships. The automotive diagnosis area is clearly such a field. The diagnostic charts which outline repair procedure (as outlined earlier in this chapter) represent good examples of such rules.

To clarify some of the ideas embodied in an expert system, consider the following example of the diagnosis of an automotive repair problem. This particular problem involves failure of the car engine to start. It is presumed in this example that the range of defects is very limited. Although this example is not very practical, it does illustrate some of the principles involved in an expert system.

A typical export system formulates expertise in IF-THEN rules.

The fundamental concept underlying this example is the idea of condition-action pairs that are in the form of IF-THEN rules. These rules embody knowledge that is presumed to have come from human experts (e.g., experienced mechanics or automotive engineers).

The expert system of this example consists of three components: (1) a rule base of IF-THEN rules; (2) a data base of facts; and (3) a controlling mechanism.

Each rule of the rule base is of the form of "if condition A is true, then action B should be taken or performed." The IF portion contains conditions that must be satisfied if the rule is to be applicable. The THEN portion states the action to be performed whenever the rule is activated (fired).

The data base contains all of the facts or information that are known to be true about the problem being diagnosed. The rules from the rule base are compared with the knowledge base to ascertain which are the applicable rules. When a rule is fired, its actions normally modify the facts within the data base.

The controlling mechanism of this expert system determines which actions are to be taken, and when they are to be performed. The operation follows 4 basic steps:

Compare the rules to the data base to determine which rules have the "IF" portion satisfied and can be executed. This group is known as the conflict set in AI parlance. A conflict set is a type of set, i.e., as in set theory.

If the conflict set contains more than one rule, resolve the conflict by selecting the highest priority rule. If there are no rules in the conflict set-stop, **stop** the procedure.

Execute the selected rule by performing the actions specified in the THEN portion, and then modify the data base as required.

Return to step 1 and repeat the process until there are no rules in the conflict set.

In the present simplified example, it is presumed that the rule base is given in *Figure 10–15* for diagnosing a problem starting a car. Rules R2 through R7 draw conclusions about the suspected problem and rule R1 identifies problem areas that should be investigated. It is implicitly assumed that the actions specified in the THEN portion include "add this fact to the data base." In addition, some of the specified actions have an associated fractional number. These values represent the confidence of the expert who is responsible for the rule that the given action is true for the specified condition.

Figure 10-15. Simple Automobile Diagnostic Rule Base

R1: IF starter turns engine but it fails to start
THEN suspect no fuel reaches engine OR
suspect there is no spark OR
suspect too much fuel is reaching engine

R2: IF suspect no fuel reaches engine AND
gas gauge works AND
gas gauge is on empty
THEN gas tank is empty (0.95)

R3: IF suspect no fuel reaches engine AND
gas gauge is not on empty AND
temperature is less than 32 degrees Fahrenheit
THEN fuel line is frozen (0.75)

R4: IF suspect no fuel reaches engine AND
can smell gas
THEN break in fuel line (0.65)

R5: IF suspect no fuel reaches engine AND
gas gauge is not on empty AND
do not smell gas
THEN water in gas tank (0.5) OR
gas gauge broken (0.6)

R6: IF suspect too much fuel is reaching engine AND
can smell gas
THEN mixture is too rich (0.7)

R7: IF suspect there is no spark AND
gas gauge not on empty AND
(weather is damp OR weather is rainy)
THEN spark plug wires are wet (0.6)

Further suppose that the facts known to be true are as shown in *Figure 10-16*. The controlling mechanism follows Step 1 above and discovers that only R1 is in the conflict set. This rule is executed, deriving the additional facts in performing Steps 2 and 3:

suspect there is no spark
suspect too much fuel is reaching the engine

At Step 4, the system returns to Step 1 and learns that the conflict set includes R1, R4, and R6. Since R1 has been executed, it is dropped from the conflict set. In this simplified example, assume that the conflict is resolved by selecting the lowest numbered rule (i.e., R4 in this case). Rule

R4 yields the additional facts after completing Steps 2 and 3 that there is a break in fuel line (.65). The value .65 refers to the confidence level of this conclusion.

Figure 10-16. Starting Data Base of Known Facts

gas gauge works
starter turns engine but it fails to start
gas gauge is not on empty
can smell gas

The procedure is repeated with the resulting conflict set R6. After executing R6, the system returns to Step 1, and finding no applicable rules, it stops. The final fact set is shown in *Figure 10-17.* Note that this diagnostic procedure has found two potential diagnoses: break in fuel line (confidence level .65), and mixture too rich (confidence level .70).

Figure 10-17. Final Resulting Data Base of Known Facts

gas gauge works
starter turns engine but it fails to start
gas gauge is not on empty
can smell gas
suspect no fuel reaching engine
suspect there is no spark
suspect too much fuel is reaching engine
break in fuel line (0.65)
mixture too rich (0.7)

The previous example is intended merely to illustrate the application of artificial intelligence to automotive diagnosis and repair.

To perform diagnosis on a specific car using an expert system the mechanic identifies all of the relevant features to the mechanics' terminal including, of course, the engine type. After connecting the data link from the electronic control system to the terminal, the diagnosis can begin. The terminal can ask the mechanic to perform specific tasks that are required to perform the diagnosis, including, for example, starting or stopping the engine as required.

The mechanic uses the expert system interactively in diagnosing problems.

The expert system is an interactive program and, as such, has many interesting features. For example, when the expert system requests the mechanic to perform some specific task, the mechanic can ask the expert system why should I do this, or why do you ask this question? The expert system then explains the motivation for the task, much the way a human expert would do if he/she were there guiding the mechanic. An expert system is frequently formulated on rules-of-thumb that have been acquired through years of experience by human experts. It often benefits the mechanic in his/her task to have requests for tasks explained in terms of both of these rules and the experience base that has led to the development of the expert system.

The general science of expert systems is so broad that it cannot possibly be covered in the present book. The interested reader can contact any good engineering library for further material in this exciting area. In addition, the Society of Automotive Engineers has many interesting publications covering the application of expert systems to automotive diagnosis.

From time to time, automotive maintenance problems will occur which are outside the scope of the expertise incorporated in the expert system. In this case, an automotive diagnostic system needs to be supplemented by direct contact of the mechanic with human experts. The GM-CAMS system, for example, has incorporated this feature into its customer support center.

The vehicle offboard diagnostic systems (whether they are expert systems or not) continue to be developed and refined as experience is gained with the various systems, as the diagnostic data base expands and as additional software is written. The evolution of such diagnostic systems is leading in the direction of fully automated, rapid, and efficient diagnoses of problems in cars equipped with modern digital control systems.

Quiz for Chapter 10

1. In a microprocessor based digital electronic engine control system diagnosis
   a. is not really required
   b. can be accomplished with a voltmeter
   c. can be accomplished with a multimeter
   d. is best accomplished with a computer based system

2. A timing light is useful for
   a. locating timing marks in the dark
   b. adjusting ignition timing
   c. checking dwell
   d. reading the clock on the instrument panel in the dark

3. An engine analyzer has been used to
   a. set ignition points in cars equipped with them
   b. measuring intake fuel flow rate
   c. setting the choke
   d. none of the above

4. In modern engines incorporating computer-based control systems diagnosis is performed
   a. is performed with a timing light only
   b. with a timing light and voltmeter
   c. in the digital control system
   d. none of the above

5. Diagnosis of intermittent failures
   a. is routinely accomplished with the onboard diagnostic capability of the engine control system
   b. is readily found using standard service bay equipment
   c. is accomplished by displaying fault codes to the driver at the time of the failure
   d. none of the above

6. A fault code is
   a. a numerical indication of failure in certain specific engine components
   b. is displayed to the mechanic during diagnostic mode
   c. is registered in memory whenever a failure in a component occurs
   d. all of the above

7. Failures can be detected by a computer based control system in the following components:
   a. O_2 sensor
   b. MAP sensor
   c. brake switch on cars equipped with cruise control
   d. all of the above and more

8. An expert system is
   a. a computer program which incorporates human knowledge to solve problems normally solved by humans
   b. an organization of automotive engineers
   c. a digital computer
   d. none of the above

9. An expert system is applicable to automotive diagnosis because
   a. automobiles are designed by experts
   b. the diagnostic procedures used can be expressed in a set of rules or logical relationships
   c. modern automobiles incorporate complex digital computers
   d. all of the above

10. In addition to displaying fault codes the example onboard diagnostic system explained in this chapter can
    a. tell the mechanic where to locate the faulty component on the engine
    b. measure certain engine parameters
    c. detect failures in the catalytic converter
    d. all of the above

Future Automotive Electronic Systems

ABOUT THIS CHAPTER

Up to this point, this book has been discussing automotive electronic technology of the recent past or present. This chapter speculates about the future of automotive electronic systems. Some concepts are only in the laboratory stage and may not, at the time of this writing, have had any vehicle testing at all. Some of the system concepts have been or are currently being tested experimentally. Some are operating on a limited basis in automobiles. Some of the concepts that were included in the corresponding chapters of the previous editions of this book are now in production automobiles.

Whether or not any of the concepts discussed here ever reaches a production phase will depend largely upon its technical feasibility and marketability. Some will simply be too costly to have sufficient customer appeal and will be abandoned by the major automobile manufacturers.

On the other hand, one or more of these ideas may become a major market success and be included in many models of automobiles. Some of these systems may even prove to be a significant selling point for one of the large automobile manufacturers.

The following is a summary of the major electronic systems that have been considered and that may be considered for future automotive application. For convenience, these ideas are separated into the following categories:

1. engine and drivetrain
2. safety
3. instrumentation

ENGINE AND DRIVETRAIN

The first edition of this book described electronic engine control technology that had been developed up to about the 1981 model-year cars. Considerable technical innovations have evolved in the interval from 1981 through 1987. Some of these technological developments include:

1. knock control
2. linear solenoid idle speed control
3. sequential fuel injection
4. distributorless ignition

5. self diagnosis for fail-safe operation
6. back up MPU
7. crankshaft angular position measurement for ignition timing
8. direct mass airflow sensor

Although these technological changes have improved the performance and reliability of the electronically controlled engine, the fundamental control strategy for fuel metering has not changed. The fuel metering strategy has been and will probably continue to be (at least for the short term) to provide a stoichiometric mixture to the engine. This strategy will remain intact as long as a three-way catalytic converter is used to reduce undesirable tailpipe output exhaust gas emissions. However, within the constraint of stoichiometric mixture control strategy, there will be some technological improvements in engine control. These improvements will occur in mechanical and electrical components as well as in software which is optimized for performance and efficiency.

In the area of mechanical components there is research being done in the area of variable parameter intake structures. New mechanisms and electromechanic actuators are being developed that will permit:

1. induction systems with variable geometry
2. variable valve timing
3. variable nozzle turbo chargers
4. throttle actuators

The performance and efficiency of any engine are markedly influenced by the intake system. The intake system configuration directly affects the volumetric efficiency of the engine, which is a measure of engine performance as an air pump. The design of an intake system in the past has involved many compromises and trade-offs which were made to enable high volumetric efficiency over the entire engine operating range. Variable geometry is achieved through the use of new electromechanical mechanisms or actuators which can change the shape and dimensions of intake system components.

One such system is illustrated in *Figure 11-1* for an experimental V-6 engine. This system has two separate intake systems, each of which has a throttle valve. In a traditional engine, the intake manifold is "tuned" to achieve maximum torque at a particular rpm.

The system of *Figure 11-1* which is known as *V*ariable *I*mpedance *A*spiration *S*ystem has two separate intake pipes leading from a plenum chamber to the cylinder banks, with a butterfly valve connecting the two sides. By suitably opening and closing this valve, the effective dimensions of the intake pipes are changed, thereby "tuning" the intake. *Figure 11-1b* shows the relative torque output for open and closed valve. Note the improved torque at low rpm.

Figure 11-1. Configuration of Variable Geometry Intake System

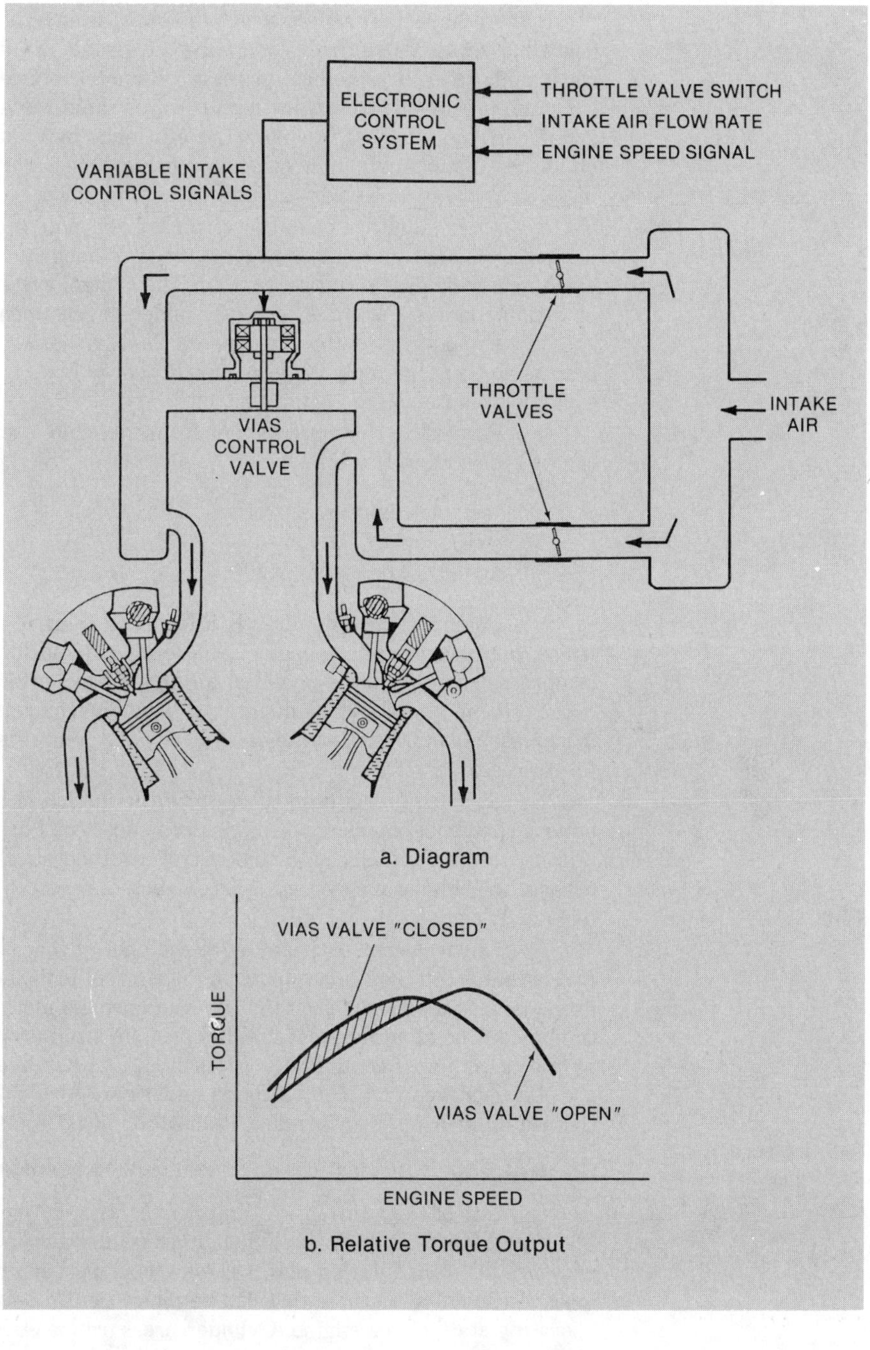

An important aspect of volumetric efficiency is the valve timing (see Chapter 1). Valve timing and valve lift profile are designed with many constraints to ensure the best possible volumetric efficiency over a wide range of engine operations. In the future, variable valve timing will provide significant improvement in volumetric efficiency by reducing the constraints on valve timing. Again, new electromechanical mechanisms will play an important role in achieving variable valve timing.

Variable intake components offer great potential for engine performance improvement. However, these components must be controlled by the engine's digital control system. The control system for optimal use of variable intake system is currently under development and is, of course, equally as important as the components themselves. in addition, there is an increasing trend to apply modern control theory (e.g., adaptive, learning systems) to automotive engine control.

Perhaps in the more distant future, technological improvements can be expected in the areas of:

variable compression ratio
swirl control
fuel atomization control

Compression ratio directly affects the thermal efficiency and, hence, performance of the engine. It also affects knocking. A variable compression ratio has the potential for significant performance improvement when controlled suitably. The development of actuator mechanisms and control strategies for variable compression are important future research areas.

Swirl is a term used to describe the motion of intake gases as they enter the combustion chamber. Swirl influences combustion speed and, thereby, thermal efficiency. Swirl control can theoretically be achieved by using a variable intake system. There is active research currently being done in this area.

Efficient combustion of all of the energy that is available in the fuel is influenced by fuel atomization. When fuel is mixed with air, the droplets should be sized such that air and gasoline molecules can readily be combined. The atomization of fuel to optimum sized droplets is influenced by the fuel injector configuration. Research into new fuel injectors that can provide improved fuel atomization is underway. Also being researched is the use of ultrasonics to increase atomization after injection has occurred.

Control Based upon Cylinder Pressure Measurements

One of the more interesting new control concepts currently under investigation is based upon cylinder pressure measurements. Cylinder pressure developed during power stroke has long been recognized as the most fundamental variable that can be monitored to determine the operating state of the engine. Cylinder pressure measurements provide realtime combustion process feedback which can be used for control of engine variables of individual cylinders.

Figure 11-2 is a block diagram of an engine control system that obtains the required feedback signal from a cylinder pressure sensor. An example of fuel control strategy using cylinder pressure is based upon the relationship between air/fuel and the cyclic fluctuation in cylinder pressure. *Figure 11-3* is a graph of the fluctuation in peak cylinder pressure as a function of air/fuel ratio. This fluctuation remains relatively low for air/fuel ratios of approximately 13 to 20. For leaner mixtures, the random fluctuations in cylinder pressure increase. Such fluctuations are equivalent to "rough" engine operation and are undesirable. In the example fuel control strategy, the air/fuel ratio is maintained near 20 and is reduced whenever the measured cycle fluctuation in cylinder pressure exceeds a threshold value.

Figure 11-2. Block Diagram of Engine Control System Based upon Cylinder Pressure in Measurements

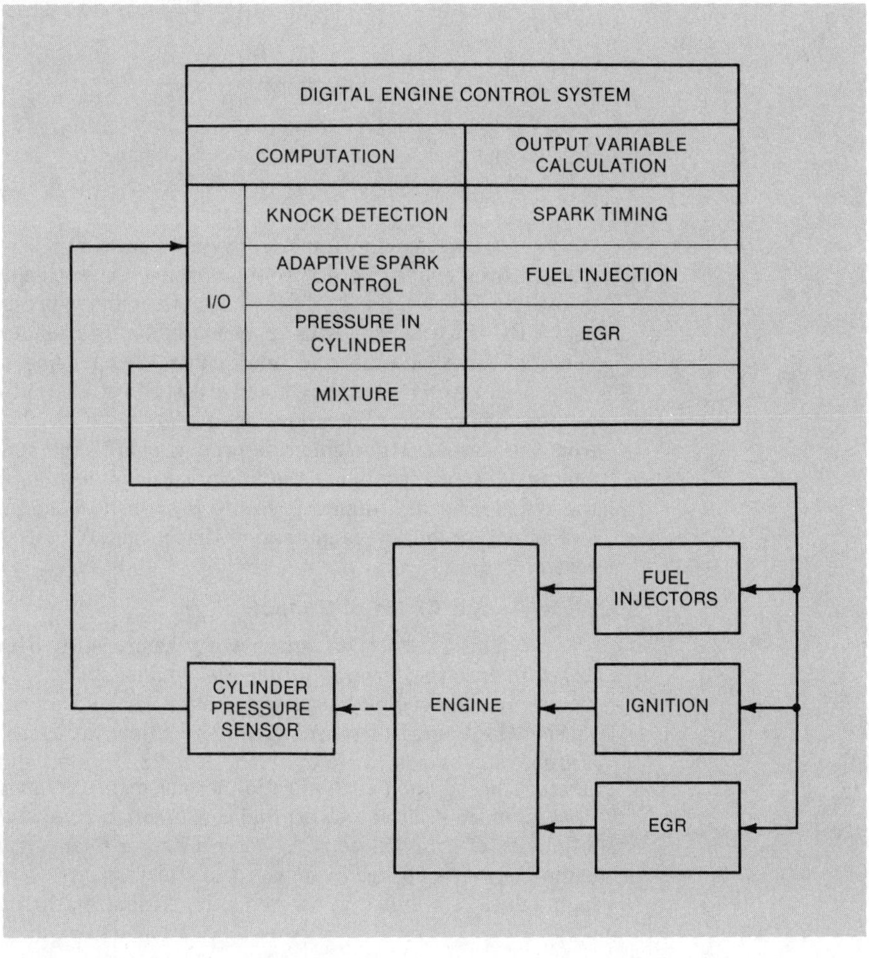

Figure 11-3. Variation in Cylinder Pressure with Air/Fuel

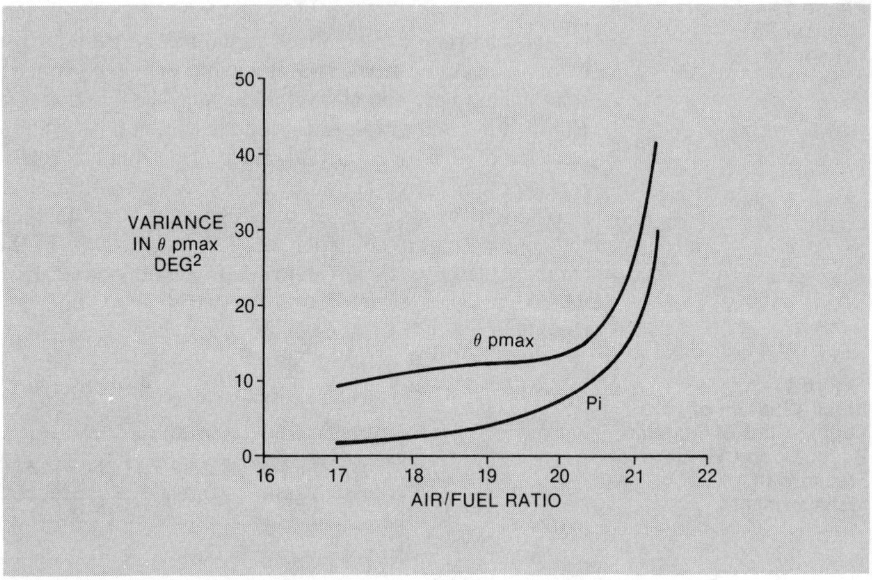

A corresponding spark-advance control strategy can be similarly derived from cylinder pressure measurements. In Chapter 7, a scheme for measuring knock intensity from the rapid cylinder pressure fluctuations near TDC is explained. Thus, a measurement of cylinder pressure has the potential to provide fuel and spark control from a single sensor.

An experimental cylinder pressure sensor that uses a piezoelectric element has recently been developed (*Figure 11-4a*). The output voltage from the piezoelectric element is proportional to the applied pressure. *Figure 11-4b* is a sketch of the mounting configuration for this sensor in the cylinder head. Cylinder pressure is applied to the piezoelectric element, and an output voltage is generated that is suitable for closed-loop engine control.

Wide Range Air/Fuel Sensor

There is another sensor which has recently been developed that may influence the trend of future fuel control systems. This sensor is mounted in the engine exhaust pipe similarly to the presently used O_2 sensor. However, this sensor generates an output that varies linearly with air/fuel ratio over a range of about 12 to 22. The importance of a control strategy based upon air/fuel ratio measurements is illustrated in *Figure 11-5* in which relative power, fuel consumption rate, and NO_x emissions as a function of equivalence ratio λ (see Chapter 6) are depicted. Note that engine power is reduced compared to stoichiometry ($\lambda = 1$) for relatively high values of λ, but that the reduction is smaller than the reduction in

Figure 11-4. Cylinder Pressure Sensor

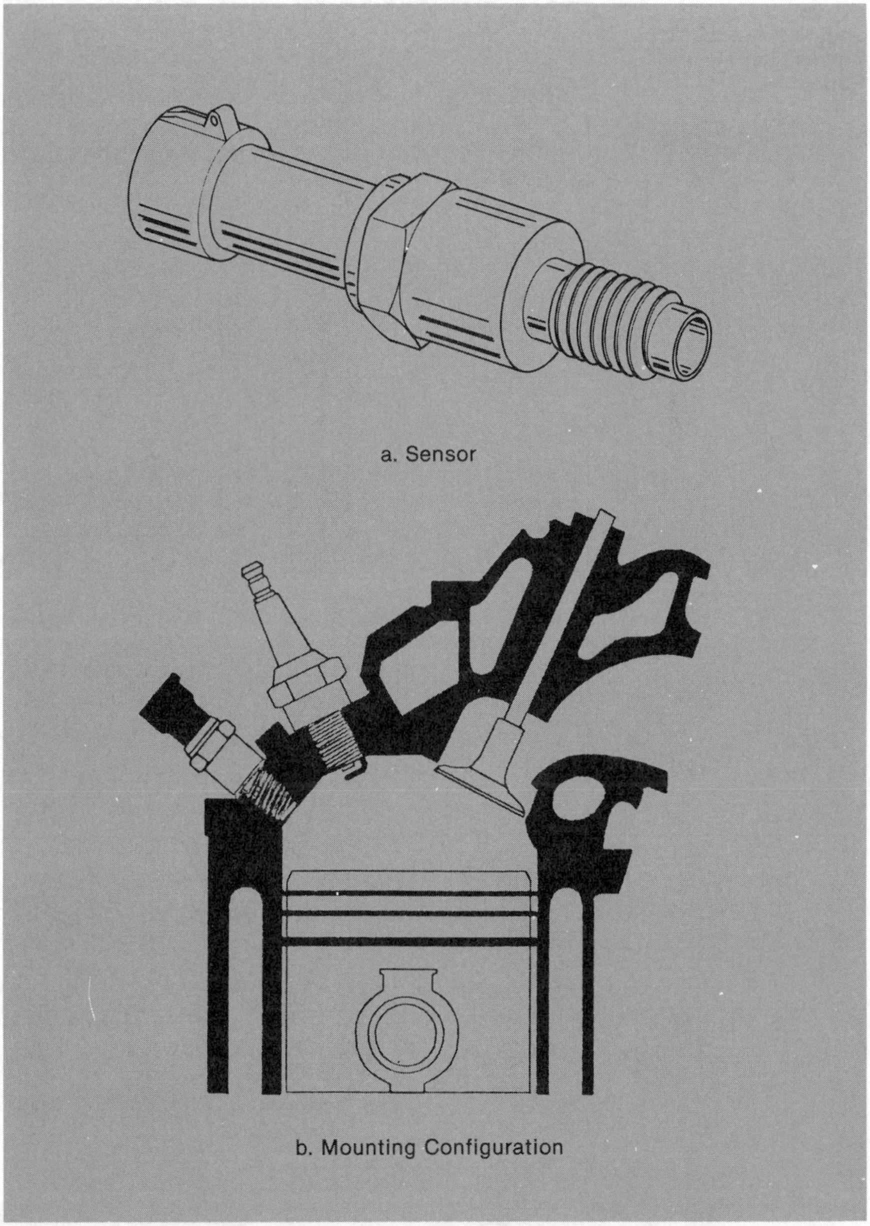

NO_x emission. The fuel consumption rate is minimum for $\lambda \approx 1.5$. In contrast, these variables are shown versus the output of a standard O_2 sensor.

Figure 11-5. Engine Performance Versus Equivalence Ratio

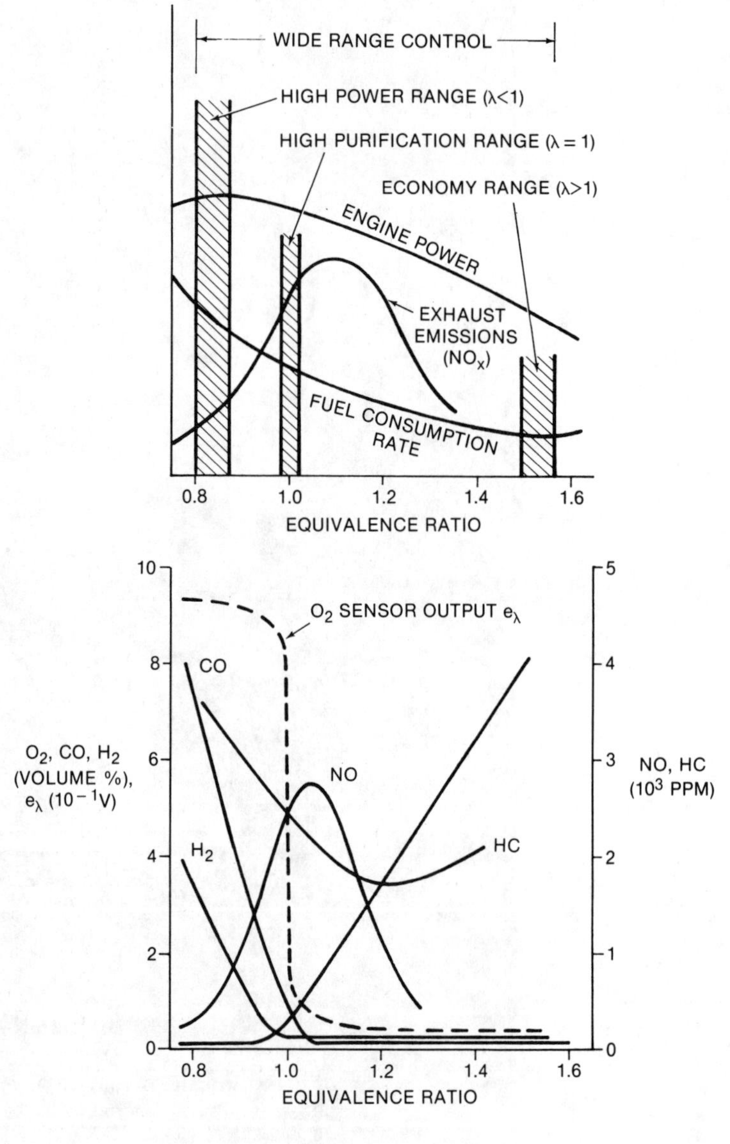

The sensor configuration is shown in *Figure 11-6*. This sensor uses Yttria (Y_2O_3) stabilized Zirconia (ZrO_2) as a diffusion element which is preheated to a desired operating temperature.

Figure 11-6. Linear Air/Fuel Sensor Configuration

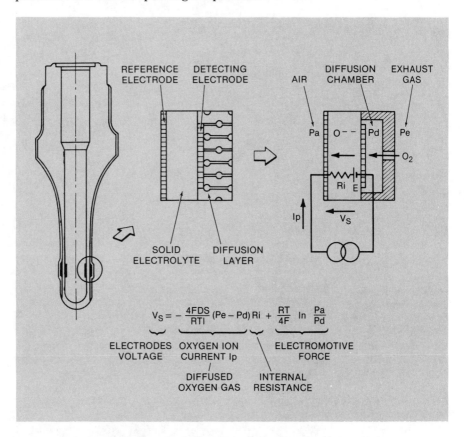

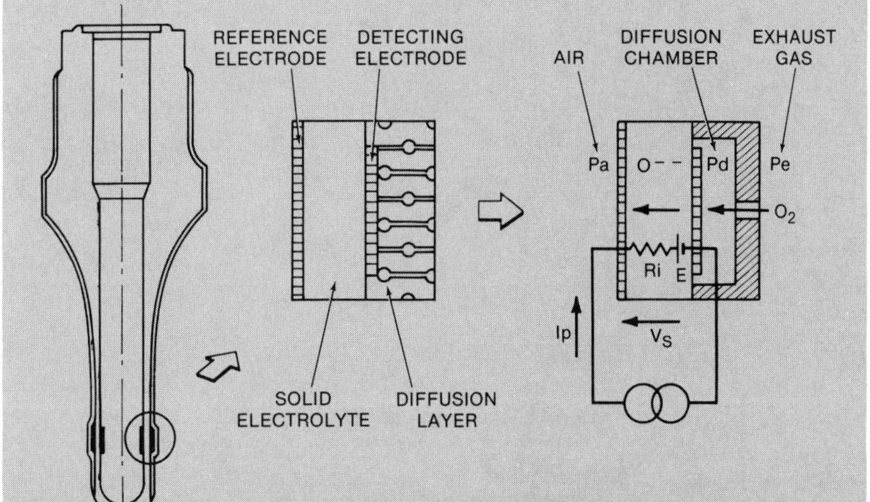

$$V_S = -\frac{4FDS}{RTl}(Pe - Pd)Ri + \frac{RT}{4F}\ln\frac{Pa}{Pd}$$

In actual operation, a voltage, V_s, is applied across this element, and a current, I_p, flows. The theory of operation is beyond the scope of this book, though it is based upon the diffusion of various ions through the element. Nevertheless, current I_p varies linearly with λ, as shown in *Figure 11-7*. A measurement of the current (which is straightforward) yields a measurement of λ.

Whether this sensor concept will be broadly applied in engine control is yet to be determined. However, the control strategy based upon measurements has the benefit of providing emission control without requiring a three-way catalytic converter, and at the same time achieving relatively good fuel economy.

Figure 11-7. Functional Operation of Lambda Sensor

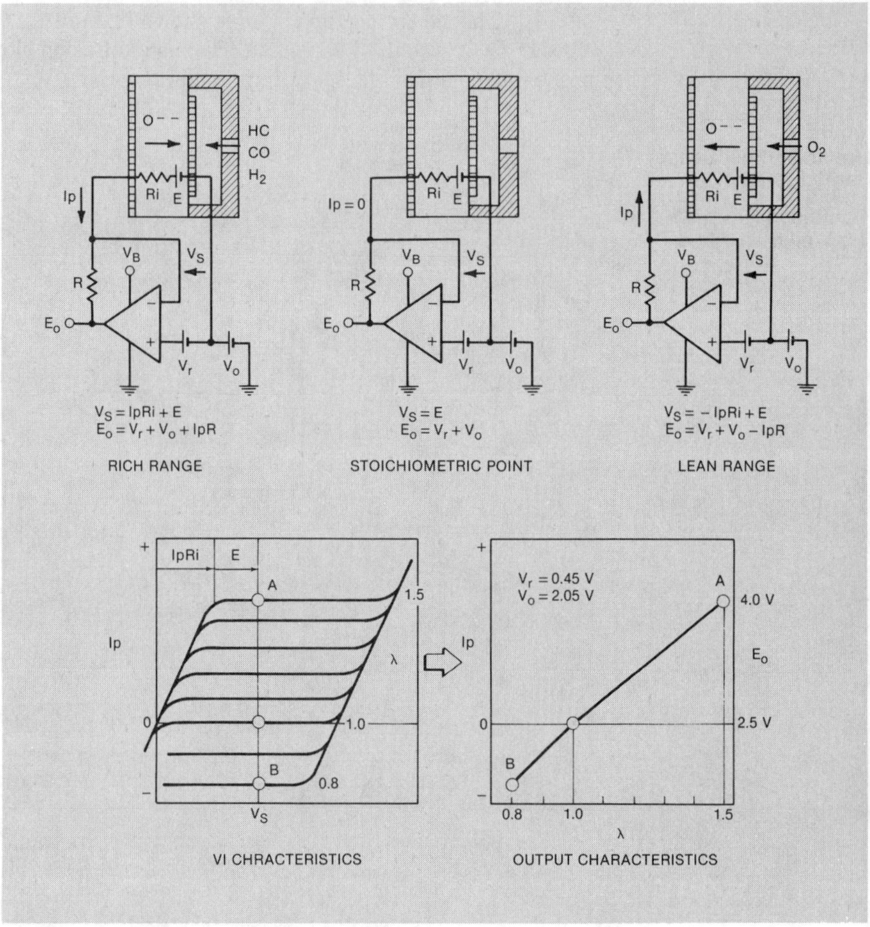

Transmission Control

Electronic control of an automotive transmission could provide maximum performance by matching engine controls and transmission gear ratios.

The automatic transmission is another important part of the drivetrain that must be controlled. Traditionally, the automatic transmission control system has been hydraulic and pneumatic. However, there are some potential benefits to the electronic control of the automatic transmission.

The engine and transmission work together as a unit to provide the variable torque needed to move the car. If the transmission were under control of the electronic engine control system, then optimum performance for the entire drivetrain could be obtained by coordinating the engine controls and transmission gear ratio. Various experimental programs for electronic control or shifting of the automatic transmission have been tried; at this time, however, there is no widespread use of this technology.

Continuously Variable Transmission

The continuously variable transmission (CVT) is an alternative to the present automatic transmission. It is being developed presently and will likely see considerable commercial use in production cars. The principle of the CVT is shown in *Figure 11-8.*

Figure 11-8. Continuously Variable Transmission (CVT)

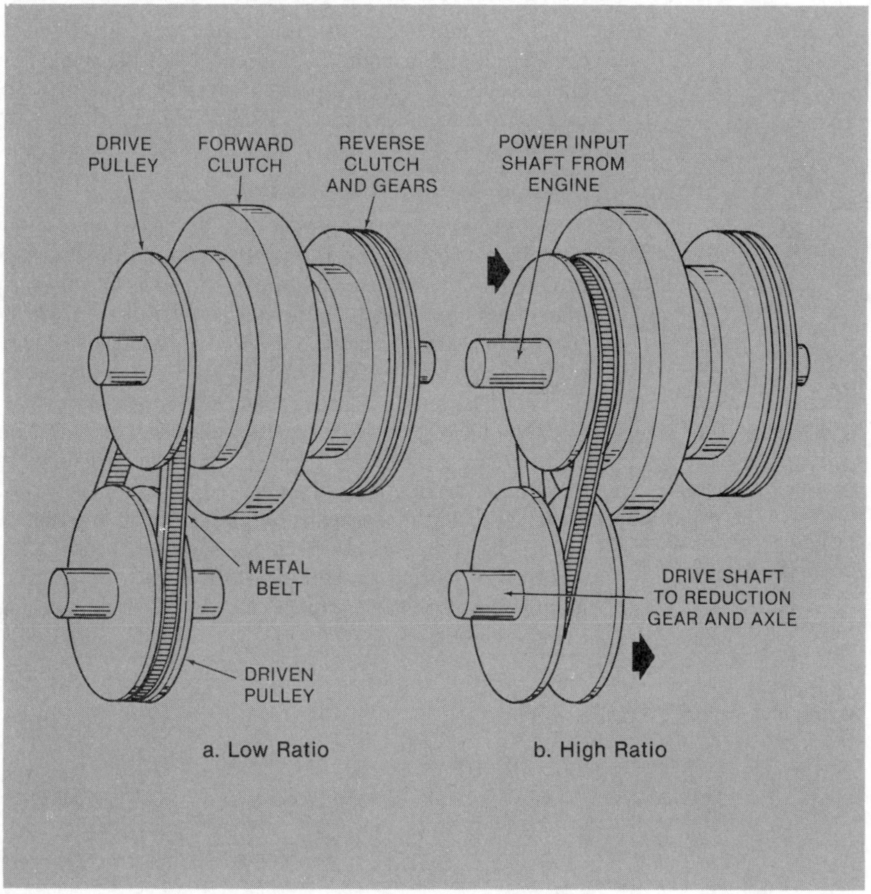

Power is transmitted from the driving shaft to the driven shaft by a belt that couples a pair of split pulleys. The effective gear ratio is the ratio of pulley radii at the contact point of the belt. These radii vary inversely with the spacings of the split pulleys. These spacings are controlled by a pair of hydraulic cylinders that push the left hand half of each pulley in or out.

The control strategy for a CVT is relatively complicated and involves measuring vehicle speed and load torque. Considerable research effort has been and will continue to be expended to develop a suitable control system, the technology of which will, undoubtedly, be digital electronic controls.

AUTOMOTIVE SAFETY RELATED ELECTRONIC SYSTEMS

A number of interesting concepts pertaining to safety have been considered and brought to different levels of development. Some of these have been initiated by proposed government regulation. A few of these are presented here, although the likelihood of production application is very uncertain.

Vehicle Occupant Protection

One safety concept widely discussed in the news media and strongly pushed by the U.S. government is the "airbag." The airbag is for protection of the occupants of a car in collisions that usually cause severe injury and death, such as the head-on collision in which the occupants are thrown forward against the dashboard, windshield, and protruding objects, particularly the steering wheel.

Air bags are flexible, inflatable bags that are used in the event of a collision to minimize injuries to the vehicle's occupants. Air bags are inflated under electronic control.

The airbag concept takes advantage of the very short time interval from the instant the vehicle hits something until the car occupants start moving forward relative to the car interior. For example, in a car traveling at 60 mph striking a fixed object (e.g., a tree), there is a time interval of about 50 to 100 milliseconds (a millisecond is one-thousandth of a second) before the occupants start moving forward toward the instrument panel or windshield. During this time, a flexible bag similar to a large balloon inflates between the occupants and the dash or steering wheel, as shown in the sketch of *Figure 11-9.*

Figure 11-9. Airbag Illustration

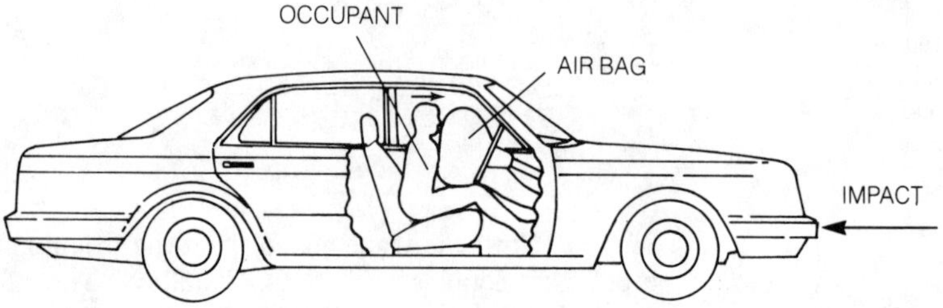

The airbag absorbs the energy of the forward motion of the occupants and prevents contact between them and the rigid portion of the car interior. In fact, tests with dummies, which closely simulate the human bodies and their motion in a car, have shown that the occupants can survive a relatively high speed head-on collision with minimal injury if an airbag is optimally deployed.

The block diagram for a hypothetical electronic airbag system is shown in *Figure 11-10.* In this scheme, the airbag is folded and placed in a small container in the dashboard (or in the steering column). Compressed gas, (or an explosive charge) which is used to inflate the airbag is in another container that is connected to the airbag. The two devices are isolated by a solenoid-operated valve, which is normally tightly closed to prevent leakage of the compressed gas into the airbag.

Figure 11-10. Airbag Control System

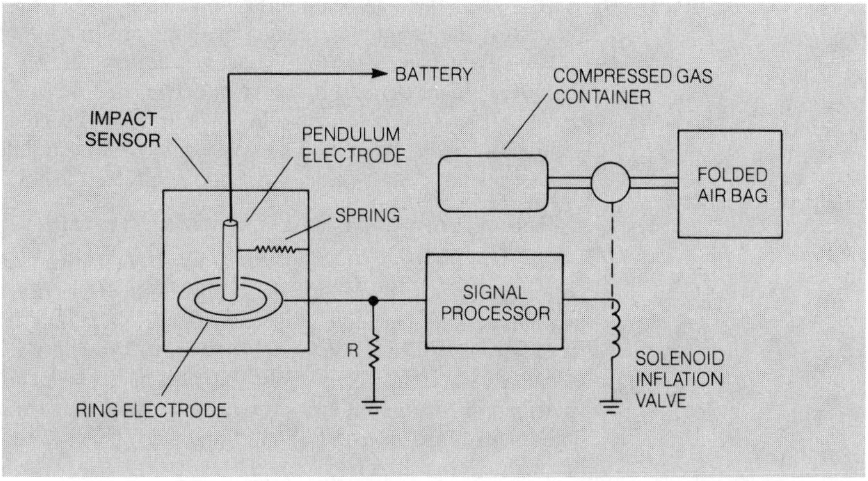

In the event of a collision, an impact sensor sends a signal to a processing circuit opening a valve-operated solenoid. The solenoid allows compressed gas to flow from a tank into the air bag.

The occurrence of a severe impact (e.g., head-on collision) is detected by means of an impact sensor. Normally this impact sensor would be mounted near the front of the vehicle where it would provide earliest possible detection of a head-on collision. In the hypothetical system in *Figure 11-10*, this sensor consists of a pendulum and ring electrode switch. The pendulum is held in an open-circuit position by a relatively strong spring. Normal motion of the car, including rapid acceleration and hard braking, will not move the pendulum enough to make contact with the ring. However, rapid deceleration due to an impact causes the pendulum to swing over to contact the ring, thereby closing the switch. The closed switch sends an electric signal to the electronic signal processor. The signal from the impact sensor is processed (possibly e.g., using a second sensor for detecting false alarms), and the electrical signal, which operates the solenoid valve to inflate the airbag is generated.

There have been numerous technical problems in developing the airbag system. However, the airbag has been tested and has actually been placed in some production vehicles. There has been considerable debate about the merits of airbags for occupant protection, particularly in relation to passive restraints, and automakers have been cautious about their installation. However, airbags have begun to be installed on a limited basis. For example,

Mercedes offers driver-side airbags as standard equipment in all of its cars, beginning with the 1987 model year, Porsche offers driver- and passenger-side airbags as standard on its *944 Turbo*, and Ford, Volvo, and BMW are offering driver-side airbags on some models as either standard or optional equipment. In 1988, Chrysler will offer driver-side airbags as standard equipment in several of its models, and GM will offer them as an option on one model. By 1990, the majority of Chrysler cars and possibly half of Ford cars will be equipped with driver-side airbags as long as the federal government will extend to 1994 the airbag incentive issued by the National Highway Traffic Safety Administration. This incentive, which is due to expire in 1990, would allow the passenger side to be equipped with manual seatbelts.

A major nontechnical issue affecting use of the airbag in production vehicles is the liability for airbag malfunction. In spite of highly developed technology, it is impossible to construct any system that makes no errors. If the airbag should inflate by error under normal driving conditions, it could *cause* an accident. If it should fail to inflate as expected in a collision, occupants may be injured. The question of who would be liable for such events has not been resolved and partly affects the future of this system.

Collision Avoidance Radar Warning System

Another interesting safety related electronic system having potential for future automotive application is the anticollision warning system. An on-board low-power radar system can be used as a sensor for an electronic collision avoidance system to provide warning of a potential collision with an object lying in the path of the vehicle. As early as 1976, at least one experimental system was developed that could accurately detect objects up to distances of about 100 yards. This system gave very few false alarms in actual highway tests.

Collision avoidance radar systems use low-power radar to sense objects and provide warnings of possible collisions.

For an anticollision warning application, the radar antenna should be mounted on the front of the car and it should project a relatively narrow beam forward. Ideally, the antenna for such a system should be in as flat a package as possible, and should project a beam that has a width of about 2° to 3° horizontally and about 4° to 5°vertically. Large objects such as signs can reflect the radar beam, particularly on curves, and trigger a false alarm. If the beam is scanned horizontally for a few degrees, say 2.5° either side of center, false alarms from roadside objects can be reduced.

In order to test whether a detected object is in the same lane as the radar-equipped car traveling around a curve, the radius of the curve must be measured. This can be estimated closely from the front wheel steering angle for an unbanked curve. Given the scanning angle of the radar beam and the curve radius, a computer can quickly perform the calculations to determine whether or not a reflecting object is in the same lane as the protected car.

For the collision warning system, better results can be obtained if the radar transmitter is operated in a pulsed mode rather than in a continuous wave mode. In this mode, the transmitter is switched on for a very short time, then it is switched off. During the off time, the receiver is set to receive a reflected signal. If a reflecting object is in the path of the transmitted microwave pulse, a corresponding pulse will be reflected to the receiver. The round trip time, t, from transmitter to object and back to receiver is proportional to the range, R, to the object, as illustrated in *Figure 11-11.*

$$t = \frac{2R}{c}$$

where

c = speed of light (186,000 miles per second)

The radar system has the capability of accurately measuring this time to determine the range to the object.

Figure 11-11. Range to Object for Anticollision Warning System

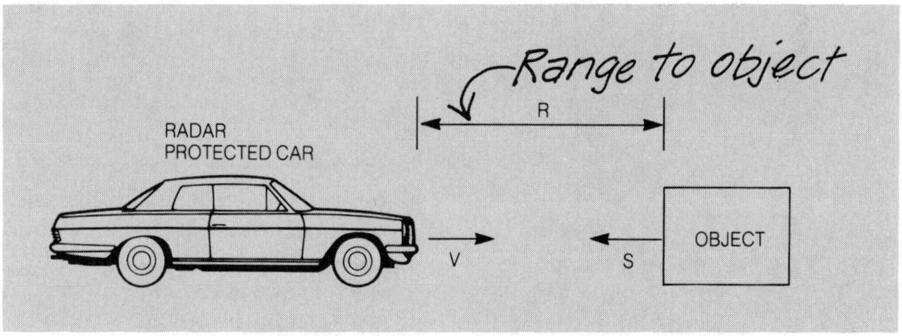

It is possible to measure the vehicle speed, V, by measuring the Doppler frequency shift of the pulsed signal reflected by the ground. (The Doppler frequency shift is proportional to the speed of the moving object. The Doppler shift is what causes the pitch of the whistle of a moving train to change as it passes.) This reflection can be discriminated from the object reflection because the ground reflection is at a low angle and a short, fixed range.

A collision avoidance system compares the time needed for a microwave signal to be reflected from an object to the time needed for a signal to be reflected from the ground. By comparing these times with vehicle speed data, the computer can calculate a "time to impact" value, and sound an alarm if necessary.

The reflection from an object will have a pulse shape which is very nearly identical to that of the transmitted pulse. As noted, the radar system can detect this object reflection and find R to determine the distance from the vehicle to the object. In addition, the relative speed-of-closure between the car and the object can be calculated by adding the vehicle speed, V, from the ground reflected pulses and the speed of the object, S, which can be determined from the change in range of the object's reflection pulses. A block diagram of an experimental collision warning system is shown in *Figure 11-12.* In this system, the range, R, to the object and the closing speed, V + S, are measured.

The computer can perform a number of calculations on this data. For example, the computer can calculate the time-to-collision, T. Whenever this time is less than a preset value, a visual and audible warning is generated. The system could also be programmed to release the throttle and apply the brakes, if automatic control were desired.

Figure 11-12. Block Diagram of Collision Avoidance Warning System

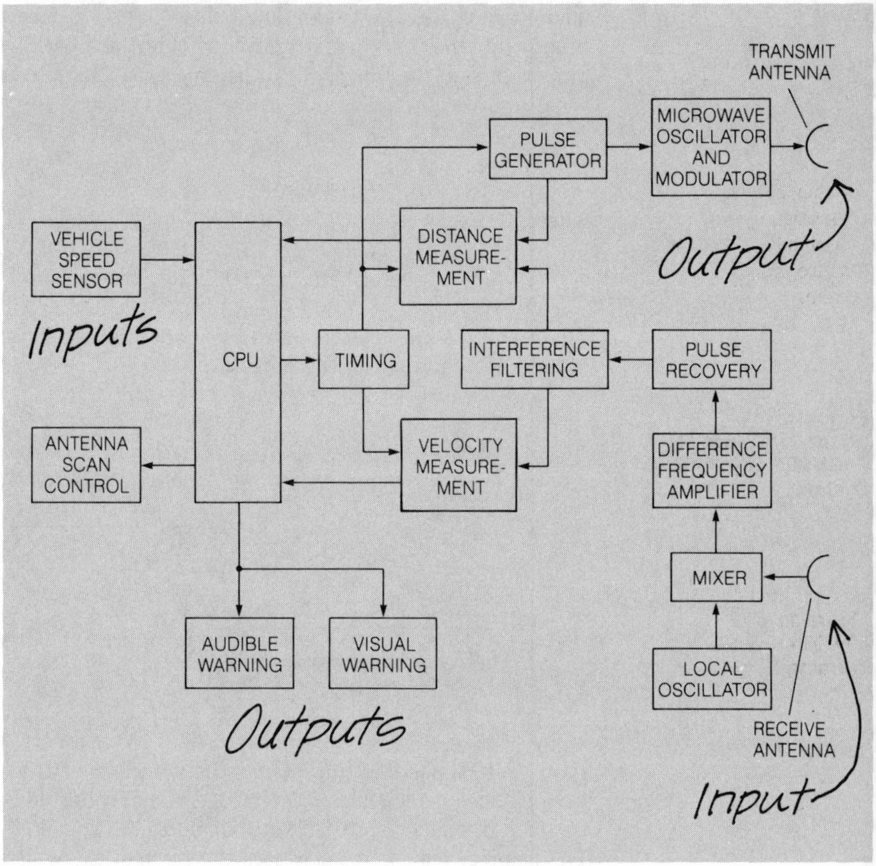

If the object is traveling at the same speed as the radar-equipped car and in the same direction, S = −V, and T is infinite. That is, a collision would never occur. If the object is stationary, S = O and the time to collision is:

$$T = \frac{R}{V}$$

Note that this system can give the vehicle speed which is applicable for antilock braking systems. If the object is another moving car approaching the radar-equipped car head-on, the closing speed is the sum of the two car speeds. In this case, the time to closure is:

$$T = \frac{R}{(V + S)}$$

This concept already has been considerably refined from its earliest inception. However, there are still some technical problems that must be overcome before this system is ready for production use.

Nevertheless, the performance of the experimental systems that already have been tested is impressive. It will be interesting to watch this technology improve and to see which, if any, of the present system configurations becomes commercially available.

Low Tire Pressure Warning System

Another potential application of electronics to automotive safety is a low tire pressure warning system.

Another interesting electronic system that may be used on future automobiles is a warning system for low tire pressure that works while the car is in motion. A potentially dangerous situation could be avoided if the driver could be alerted to the fact that a tire has low pressure, particularly if it happens while driving. For example, if a tire develops a leak, the driver could be warned in sufficient time to stop the car before control becomes difficult.

There are several pressure sensor concepts that could be used. A block diagram of a hypothetical system is shown in *Figure 11-13*. In this scheme, a tire pressure sensor, S, continually measures the tire pressure. The signal from the sensor mounted on the rolling tire is coupled by a link to the electronic signal processor. Whenever the pressure drops below a critical limit, a warning signal is sent to a display on the instrument panel to indicate which tire has the low pressure.

Figure 11-13. Low Tire Pressure Warning System

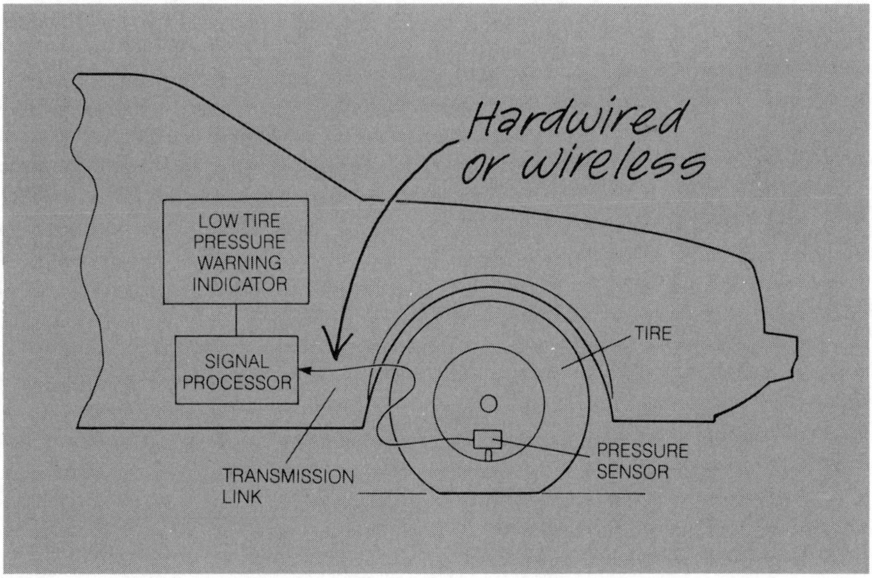

A low tire pressure warning system utilizes a tire mounted pressure sensor. The pressure sensor signals a loss in tire pressure, either by wiring to the axle through slip rings, or radio transmission from a transmitter mounted in the valve stem.

The difficult part of this system is the link from the tire pressure sensor mounted on the rotating tire to the signal processor mounted on the body. Several concepts theoretically have the potential to provide this link. For example, slip rings, which are similar to the brushes on a dc motor, could be used. However, this would require a major modification to the wheel-axle assembly and does not appear to be an acceptable choice at the present time.

Another concept for providing this link is to use a small radio transmitter mounted on the tire. By using modern solid-state electronic technology, a low-power transmitter could be constructed. The transmitter could be located in a modified tire valve cap and could transmit to a receiver in the wheel well. The distance from the transmitter to the receiver would be only about one foot, so only very low power would be required.

One problem with this method is that electrical power for the transmitter would have to be provided by a self-contained battery. However, the transmitter need only operate for a few seconds and only when the tire pressure falls below a critical level. Therefore, a tiny battery could theoretically provide enough power.

The scheme is illustrated schematically for a single tire in *Figure 11-14*. The sensor switch is usually held open by normal tire pressure on a diaphragm mechanically connected to the switch. Low tire pressure allows the spring-loaded switch to close, thereby switching on the microtransmitter. The receiver, which is directly powered by the car battery, receives the transmitted signal and passes it to the signal processor, also directly powered by the car battery. The signal processor then activates a warning lamp for the driver, and it remains on until the driver resets the warning system by operating a switch on the instrument panel.

Figure 11-14. Low Pressure Sensor Concept

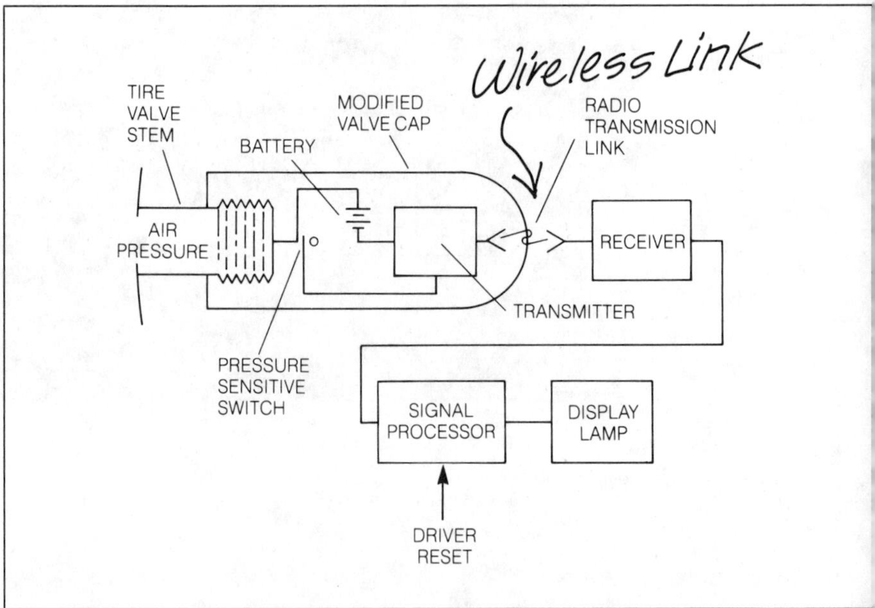

One reason for using a signal processing unit is the relatively short life of the transmitter battery. The transmitter will remain on until the low pressure condition is corrected or until the battery runs down. By using a signal processor, the low pressure status can be stored in memory so the warning will still be given even if the transmitter quits operating. The need for this feature could arise if the pressure dropped while the car was parked. By storing the status, the system would warn the driver as soon as the ignition was turned on.

Many other concepts have been proposed for providing a low tire pressure warning system. The future of such a system will be limited largely by its cost and/or reliability.

AUTOMOTIVE INSTRUMENTATION

The reduced cost of VLSI and microprocessor electronics are resulting in advanced instrumentation and the use of voice synthesis in warning systems.

It is very likely that some interesting advances in automotive instrumentation will be forthcoming, such as functions that are not presently available, new display forms including audible messages by synthesized speech, and interactive communication between the driver and the instrumentation. These advances will come about partly because of increased capability at reduced cost for modern solid-state circuits, particularly microprocessors and microcomputers.

One of the important functions which an all electronic instrumentation system can have in future automobiles is continuous diagnosis of other onboard electronic systems. In particular, the future computer-based electronics instrumentation may perform diagnostic tests on the electronic engine control system. This instrumentation system might display major system faults and even recommend repair actions.

Another function that might be improved in the instrumentation system is the trip computer function. The system probably will be highly interactive; that is, the driver will communicate with the computer through a keyboard or maybe even by voice.

The full capabilities of such a system are limited more by human imagination and cost than technology. Most of the technology for the systems discussed is available now and can be packaged small enough for automotive use. However, in a highly competitive industry where the use of every screw is analyzed for cost-effectiveness, the cost of these systems still limits their use in production vehicles.

HEADS UP DISPLAY

In the first edition of this book, it was speculated that CRT display would appear in production cars. This has, in fact, occurred, and there is a description of the CRT display in Chapter 9. It was also speculated that the CRT might be used in conjunction with a heads up display (HUD). Although HUD has not yet appeared in production cars, there is increasing likelihood that it will appear in the near future as part of the display for instrumentation on a car.

The CRT when combined with a partially reflective mirror, results in a HUD. Information is displayed on the CRT in the form of a reversed image. The image is reflected by the mirror, and viewed normally by the driver.

There is no clear sign, however, that the basic display source will be a CRT. In fact, any light-emitting display device can be used with HUD. Nevertheless, it is convenient to describe HUD presuming that the display source is a CRT, keeping in mind that many other display sources can be substituted for the CRT. *Figure 11–15* illustrates the concept of a HUD.

In this scheme, the information that is to be displayed appears on a CRT which is mounted as shown. A partially reflecting mirror is positioned above the instrument panel in the driver's line-of-sight of the road. In normal driving, the driver looks through this mirror at the road. Information to be displayed appears on the face of the CRT upside down, and the image is reflected by the partially reflecting mirror to the driver right side up. He can read this data from the HUD without moving his head from the position for viewing the road. The brightness of this display would have to be adjusted so that it is compatible with ambient light. The brightness of this data image should never be so great that it inhibits the driver's view of the road, but it must be bright enough to be visible in all ambient lighting conditions. Fortunately, the CRT brightness can be automatically controlled by electronic circuits to accommodate a wide range of light levels.

Figure 11-15. HUD Display

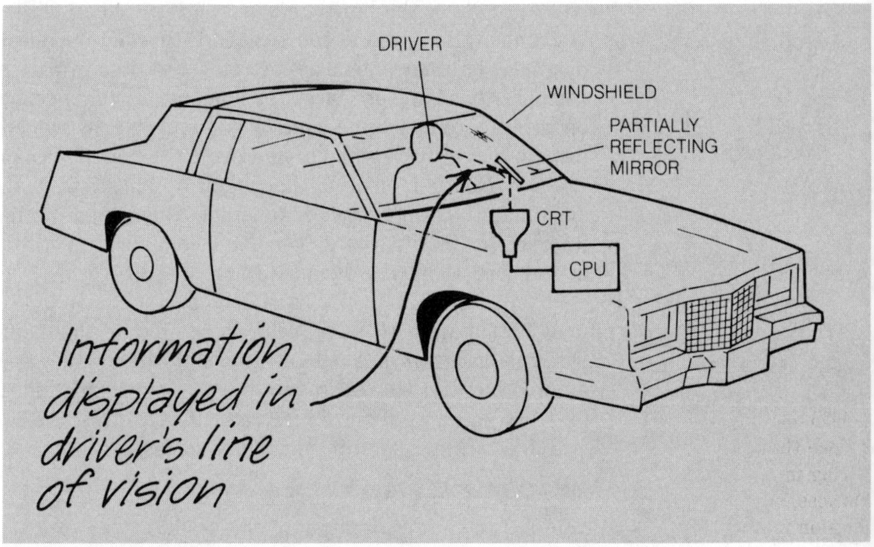

Speech Synthesis

One really exciting new display device, audible display by synthesized speech, has great potential for future automotive electronic instrumentation. Important safety or trip-related messages could be given audibly so the driver doesn't have to look away from the road. In addition to its normal function of generating visual display outputs, the computer generates an electrical waveform which is approximately the same as a human voice speaking the appropriate message. The voice quality of some types of speech synthesis is often quite natural and closely similar to human speech.

Speech synthesizers use phoneme synthesis, a method of imitating basic sounds used to build speech. Computers rely on an inventory of phonemes to build the words for various automotive warning messages.

There are several major categories of speech synthesis that have been studied experimentally. Of these, the phoneme synthesis is probably the most sophisticated. A phoneme is a basic sound that is used to build speech. By having an inventory of these sounds in computer memory and by having the capability to generate each phoneme sound, virtually any word can be constructed by the computer in a manner similar to the way the human voice does. Of course, the electrical signal produced by the computer is converted to sound by a loudspeaker.

Synthesized speech is already being used to automatically provide data over the phone from computer-based systems. It seems very likely that the voice synthesis display will shortly become available in some production cars. Some auto experts believe that use of this display method will become widespread before 1990.

MULTIPLEXING IN AUTOMOBILES

One of the high-cost items in building and servicing vehicles is the electrical wiring. Wires of varying length and diameter form the interconnection link between each electrical/electronic component in the vehicle. Virtually the entire electrical wiring for a car is made up in the form of a complex, expensive cable assembly called a "harness." Building and installing the harness requires manual assembly and is time consuming. The increased use of electrical and electronic devices has significantly increased the number of wires in the harness.

Sensor Multiplexing

The use of microprocessors for computer engine control, instrumentation computers, etc., offers the possibility of significantly reducing the complexity of the harness. For example, consider the engine control system. In the present configuration, each sensor and actuator has a separate wire connection to the CPU. However, each sensor only communicates periodically with the computer for a short time interval during sampling.

Sensor multiplexing can reduce the necessary wiring in an electrical harness, by using time division multiplexing.

It is possible to connect all the sensors to the CPU with only a single wire (with ground return, of course). This wire, which can be called a data bus, provides the communication link between all of the sensors and the CPU. Each sensor would have exclusive use of this bus to send data (i.e., measurement of the associated engine variable/parameter) during its time slot. A separate time slot would be provided for each sensor.

This process of selectively assigning the data bus exclusively to a specific sensor during its time slot is called time division multiplexing (or sometimes just multiplexing—MUX). Recall that multiplexing was discussed as a data selector for the CPU input and output in a digital instrumentation system.

To understand the operation of time division multiplexing of the data bus, refer to the system block diagram in *Figure 11-16.* The CPU controls the use of the data bus by signaling each sensor through a transmitter/receiver (T/R) unit. Whenever the CPU requires data from any sensor, it sends a coded message on the bus which is connected to all T/R units. However, the message consists of a sequence of binary voltage pulses that are coded for the particular T/R unit. A T/R unit responds only to one particular sequence of pulses which can be thought of as the address for that unit.

Figure 11-16. Sensor Multiplexing Block Diagram

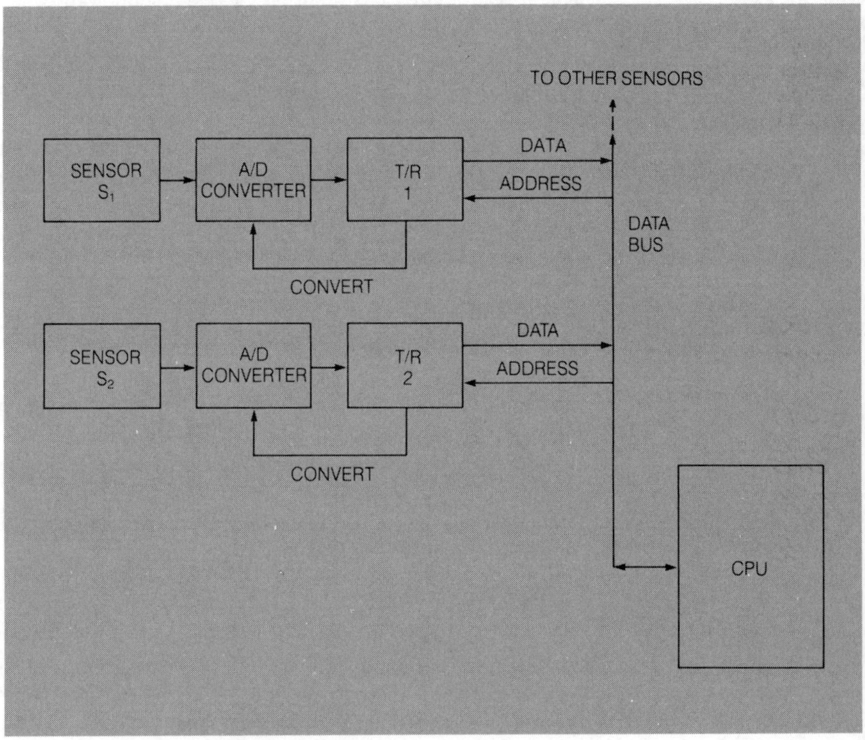

Each sensor in a multiplexed system sends its individual data over a common bus. The computer identifies the sensor by signaling each sensor with a unique address.

Whenever a T/R unit receives data corresponding to its address, it activates an analog-to-digital converter. The sensor's analog output at this instant is converted to a digital binary number as already discussed. This number and the T/R unit's address is included so that the CPU can identify the source of the data. Thus, the CPU interrogates a particular sensor and then receives the measurement data from the sensor on the data bus. The CPU then sends out the address of the next T/R unit whose sensor is to be sampled.

Control Signal Multiplexing

It also is possible to multiplex control signals to control switching of electrical power. Electrical power must be switched to lights, electric motors, solenoids, and other devices.

The system for multiplexing electrical power control signals around the vehicle requires two buses—one carrying battery power and one carrying control signals. *Figure 11-17* is a block diagram of such a multiplexing system. In a system of this type, a remote switch applies battery power to the component when activated by receiver module, RM. The receiver module is activated by a command from the CPU that is transmitted along the control signal bus.

Figure 11-17. Control Signal Multiplexing Block Diagram

Receiver module activates its related component or subsystem.

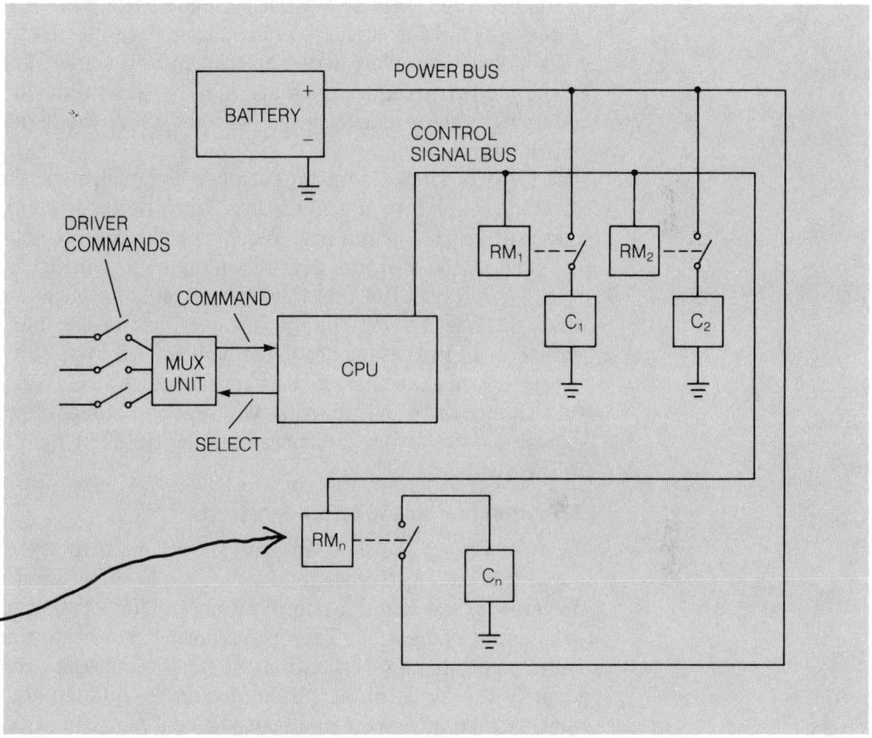

A multiplexed system can also control switching of electrical power for lights, motors, and similar devices. Each RM would switch power to the appropriate device in response to a CPU command.

This control signal bus operates very much like the sensor data bus described in the multiplexed engine control system. The particular component to be switched is initially selected by switches operated by the driver. (Of course, these switches can be multiplexed at the input of the CPU.) The CPU sends an RM address as a sequence of binary pulses along the control signal bus. Each receiver module responds only to one particular address. Whenever the CPU is to turn a given component on or off, it transmits the coded address and command to the corresponding RM. When the RM receives its particular code, it operates the corresponding switch, either applying battery power or removing battery power, depending upon the command transmitted by the CPU.

Fiber Optics

Signal buses using fiber optics would transmit data and control signals in the form of light pulses along thin fiber cables. Such systems would be relatively immune from noise interference.

It is possible, maybe even desirable, to use an optical fiber for the signal bus. For such a system, the address voltage pulses from the CPU are converted to corresponding pulses of light that are transmitted over an optical fiber. An optical fiber, which is also known as a light pipe, consists of a thin transparent cylinder of light conducting glass about the size of a human hair. Light will follow the "light pipe" along its entire path, even around corners, just as electricity follows the path of wire. A big advantage of the optical fiber signal bus for automotive use is that external electrical noise doesn't interfere with the transmitted signal. The high voltage pulses in the ignition circuit, which are a major potential source of interference in automotive electronic systems, will not affect the signals traveling on the optical signal bus.

For such a system, each component has an RM that has an optical detector coupled to the signal bus. Each detector receives the light pulses that are sent along the bus. Whenever the correct sequence (i.e., address) is received at the RM, the corresponding switch is either closed or opened.

A variety of multiplexing systems have been experimentally studied. It seems very likely that one form or another of multiplex system will be used in the near future whenever the cost of a multiplex system becomes less than that of the harness which it is to replace. It is possible that the move to multiplexing will occur in stages. For example, one experimental system incorporates a multiplex system for switches located in the door only.

Automotive Navigation Systems

One of the more interesting potential future developments in the application of electronics to automobiles is the area of navigation. Every driver who has taken a trip to an unfamiliar location understands the problem of navigation. The driver must first obtain maps having sufficient detail to locate the destination. Along the trip the driver must be able to identify the car location in relationship to the map and make decisions at various road intersections about the route continuation.

There has been considerable research done into the development of an electronic automatic navigation system which may someday lead to the widespread commercial sale of such a system. *Figure 11-18* is a block diagram showing the major components of a generic automatic navigation system. The display portion of a research system is typically a CRT. This display depicts one of many maps which are stored in memory.

Ideally the display device should have the capability of displaying maps with various levels of magnification. As the car approaches its destination, the map detail should increase until the driver can locate his/her position within an accuracy of about 1/2 block.

Figure 11-18.
Generic Automotive Navigation System Block Diagram

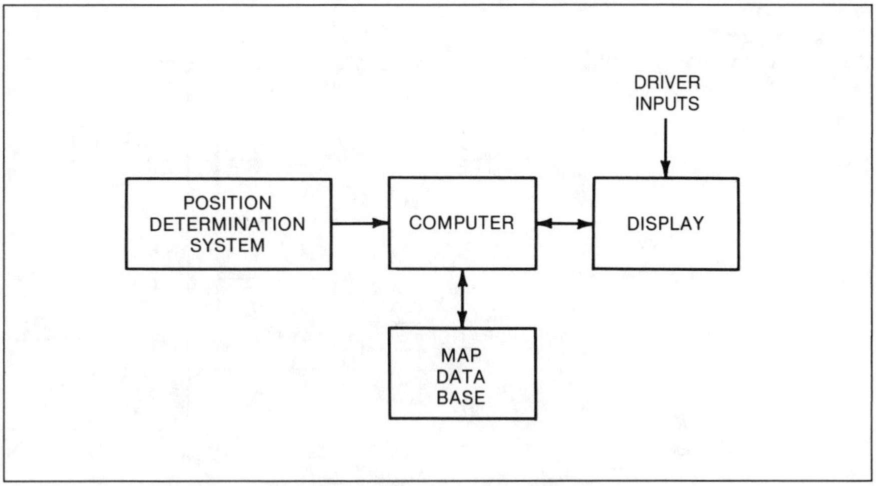

The map data base must be capable of storing sufficient data to construct a map of an entire region. For example, data could be stored on floppy disks (one for each region of the country) which are read into computer RAM as desired for a particular trip. Alternatively, a CD (compact disc) record player could be used for large scale data storage. In this case, the CD player would be part of the entertainment system. If the vehicle electronic system is integrated, the CD player can function as a large scale memory for onboard navigation data.

The computer portion of the generic navigation system obtains signals from position sensors and calculates the correct vehicle position in relationship to the map coordinates. The computer also controls the map display, accounting for magnification (called for by driver), and displaying the vehicle position superposed on the map. The correct vehicle position might, for example, be shown as a flashing bright spot.

Navigation Sensors

The most critical and costly component in the generic navigation system is the position determining system (i.e., position sensor). Among the concepts presently being considered for automotive navigation are (1) inertial navigation, (2) radio navigation, (3) signpost navigation, and (4) dead reckoning navigation. Each of these has relative advantages in terms of cost and performance.

An inertial navigation sensor has been developed for aircraft navigation, but it is relatively expensive. The aircraft inertial navigation sensor consists of 3 gyros, 3 accelerometers, and control electronics for gyros and accelerometers. *Figure 11-19* is a block diagram of a typical navigation system using inertial navigation.

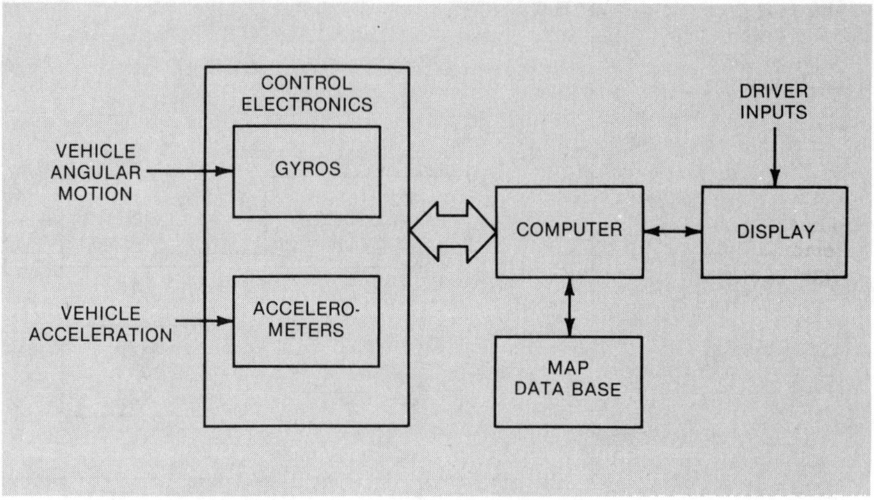

Figure 11-19. Block Diagram for Automotive Inertial Navigation System

An inertial navigation system locates the vehicle position relative to a known starting point by integrating acceleration twice with respect to time. For example, along the x direction, vehicle position at time t is x(t):

$$x(t) = x_o + \int_o^t \int_o^\tau a(\gamma)d\gamma dt$$

where

x_o = initial x position
a = acceleration along x direction

A similar integration is performed along the two orthogonal directions.

An inertial navigation system has position errors due to (1) initial gyro alignment errors, (2) uncompensated gyro drift, and (3) accelerometer errors. A typical high quality commercial navigation system (e.g., Carousel IV) has a position error of about 3000 feet for each hour of flight. Position errors generated at this rate in an automotive environment implies a trip of no more than 1/2 hour before the error exceeds the 1/2 block limit. This error in combination with its relatively high cost (about $120,000) renders the inertial navigation system unfeasible for automotive use for the foreseeable future.

Radio Navigation

A radio-based automotive navigation system uses either land-based or satellite-based transmitters and automotive receivers for position location. Land-based transmitter systems that are potentially applicable include (1) Decca, (2) Loran-C, (3) VOR, and (4) Omega. The only satellite-based system that is potentially applicable is the Global Positioning Satellite (GPS). The land-based systems are primarily intended for aircraft or ship navigation and have somewhat limited coverage. For example,

Loran-C has no coverage for large portions of Southwest United States. Nevertheless, research is being done on the applicability of these land-based systems to automotive navigation.

The GPS, when fully operational, will have 18 orbiting satellites, of which there will be a minimum of four within line-of-sight of any location on earth. This is sufficient for position location. *Figure 11-20* is a block diagram of a GPS-based automotive navigation system.

Figure 11-20. Automotive GPS Navigation System

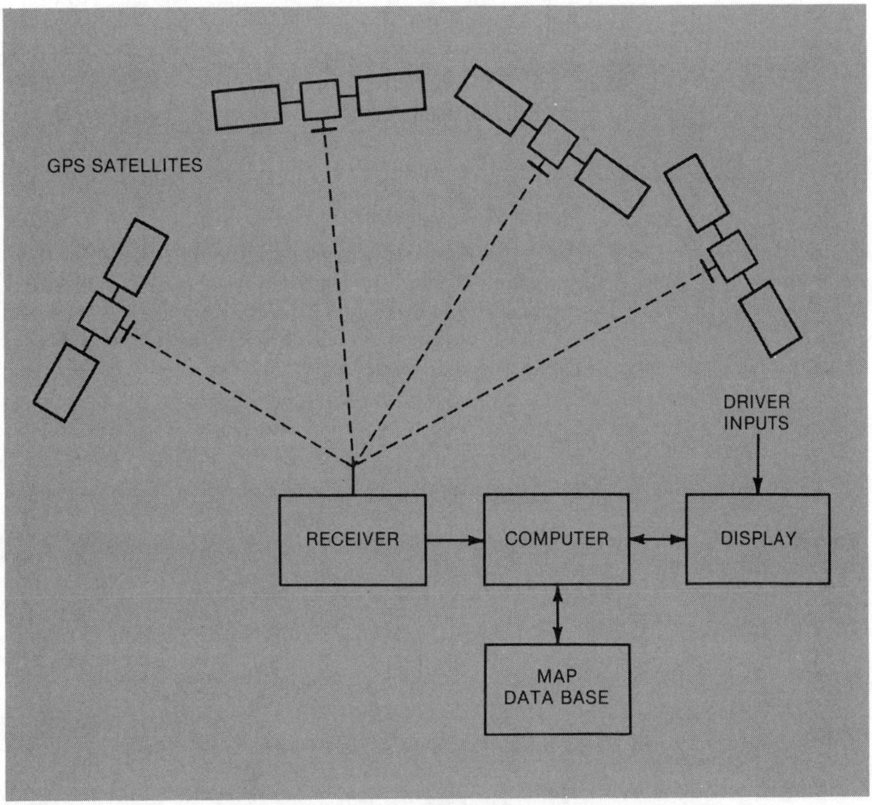

In final operational service, there will be two classes of user service available for GPS—the Precise Positioning Service (PPS), which is available only to the military, and the Standard Position Service (SPS), which is available for automotive navigation. Each satellite transmits clock pulses. The distance to any satellite is known by the relationship

$$R_i = Ct_i \qquad i = 1,2,3,4$$

where

R_i = distance to any satellite
C = speed of light
t_i = propagation time from satellite to car

Position is determined (in three dimensions and time) by solving four equations involving the range to four satellites. In SPS service, an accuracy of 100 meters is quoted. In experiments, absolute accuracies of 30 meters have been achieved.

There are a number of problems associated with GPS-based navigation systems, including cost, time-to-fix position, and propagation considerations. The cost of experimental receivers is well beyond the feasible range for widespread automotive use. However, produced in sufficient quantities, the receiver cost could be brought under $1,000 per unit. The time-to-fix position is on the order of two to three minutes, which is inconvenient but possibly acceptable. In addition, it is necessary to maintain a direct line of sight. This can be a problem in areas of tall buildings or in mountainous terrain. Nevertheless, the GPS is potentially viable for future automotive navigation and has many advocates.

Signpost Navigation

In signpost navigation, a number of information stations (signposts) are located throughout the road network. In one scheme, the signpost continuously transmits data on its geographic location. The onboard navigation system converts this data to map coordinates which are displayed.

Figure 11-21 is a block diagram of a typical signpost navigation system. This system requires an augmented data base to convert the transmitted data to map coordinates. This system has the capability to provide position to an accuracy of a few meters.

Figure 11-21. Signpost Navigation System

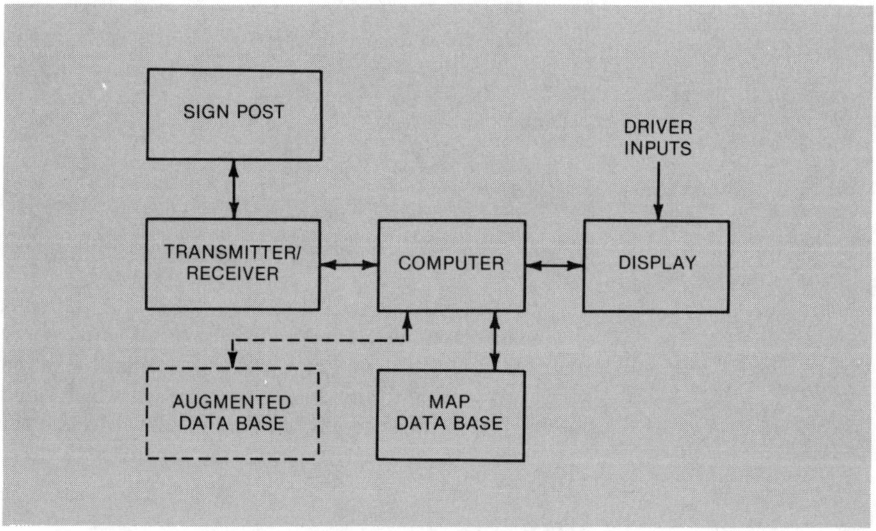

There are drawbacks, however, to the signpost system including (1) inability to determine position between signposts, (2) inability to show a turn until the next signpost is reached, (3) the need for signposts at every intersection, and (4) requirement for large number of codes. Thus, in spite of the high accuracy of this system, it inherently requires a huge investment in transmitters.

Dead Reckoning Navigation

Dead reckoning navigation is a method of determining present position from a known earlier position and information about vehicle motion. *Figure 11-22* is a block diagram for such a system. The sensor components of this system include a heading sensor and a wheel speed sensor. The use of heading and speed information is illustrated in *Figure 11-23*. Experimental systems have used a form of magnetic compass, known as a flux gate, to measure heading. Wheel speed sensors have already been explained in Chapter 8. Although this system is conceptually simple, it suffers from poor accuracy. It is estimated that position error of about 1/2 block would accrue for trips of less than 6 miles.

Figure 11-22. Dead Reckoning Navigation System

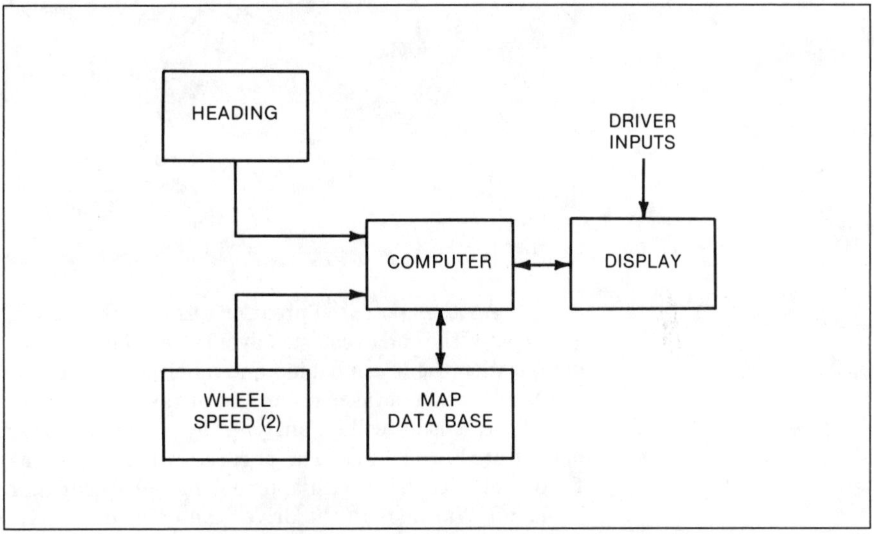

At the present time it is too early to speculate with confidence which, if any, of the automotive navigation systems will appear on future cars. Majority opinion among some experts favors the GPS-based system. It should be interesting to follow the technical development of automotive navigation systems in the future.

Figure 11–23.
Dead Reckoning
Navigation Computation

$$\overline{P}_1 = \overline{P}_o + (D_1 \sin H_1 \cdot D_1 \cos H_1)$$
$$\overline{P}_2 = \overline{P}_1 + (D_2 \sin H_2 \cdot D_2 \cos H_2)$$

WHERE
$\overline{P}$ = POSITION
D = DISTANCE TRAVELED
H = HEADING

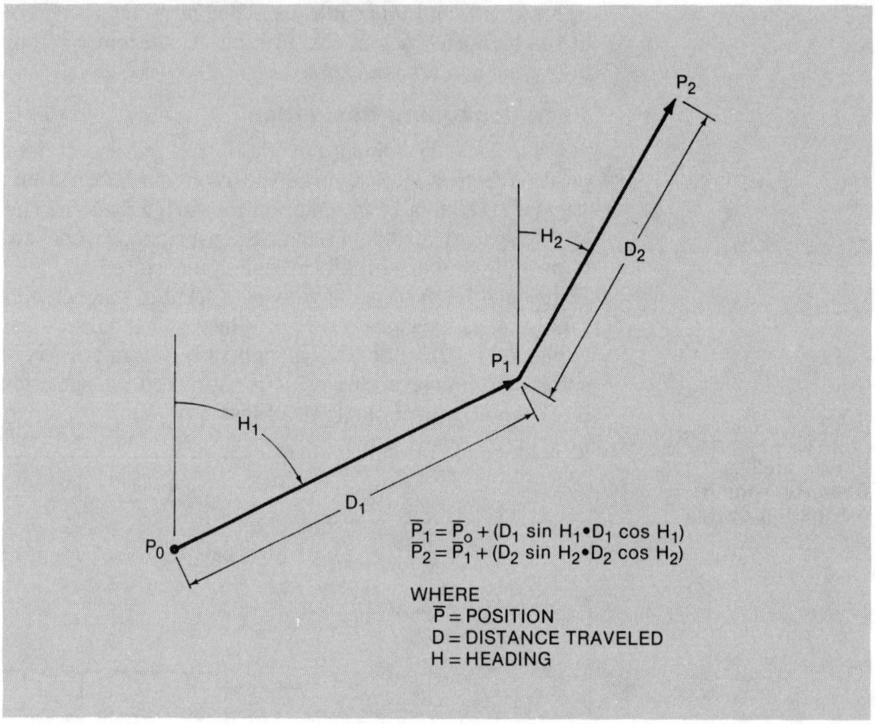

Another potential area for future technological development is an extension of the radar collision-avoidance scheme. In at least one proposed configuration the areas behind and on either side of the vehicle are scanned by a combination of laser radar and ultrasonic sensing system. The data from these sensors will be analyzed by a computer running some very sophisticated algorithms. The purpose of these systems is to warn drivers of a potential collision with approaching vehicles (e.g., before lane changes are made). Warnings to the driver can be made by synthesized voice or visual HUD display.

Still another potential technical development in automotive electronics involves the application of artificial intelligence to voice recognition. In such a system the driver can activate electronic functions by simply speaking to the car. A microphone will pick up his speech, recognize what is spoken, and take action accordingly. Such a system has the advantage that the driver can enter commands or data without looking away from the road while keeping both hands safely on the steering wheel.

Another interesting technical development which is likely to occur in the future involves the use of electronically controlled window transparency. Using advanced electrochromic material it is possible to reduce window transparency on very bright sunny days or to increase transparency on darker days. This has the advantage of reducing glare and improving the heat load on the air conditioning system within the vehicle.

Quiz for Chapter 11

1. Engine performance may be improved in the future by
   a. "tuning" the intake manifold
   b. use of variable compression ratio
   c. variable value timing
   d. all of the above
2. One potential engine control strategy based upon a feedback signal from cylinder pressure may incorporate
   a. a piezoelectric cylinder pressure sensor
   b. a new MAP sensor
   c. an exhaust air/fuel sensor
   d. none of the above
3. An air bag is
   a. a mechanism for occupant protection in a car
   b. a container for use in case of airsickness
   c. an impact sensor
   d. all of the above
4. One concept for automotive collision avoidance involves
   a. braking rapidly in dangerous situations
   b. measuring the round-trip time of a radar pulse from protected car to collision object
   c. aircraft surveillance of highways
   d. wheel speed sensors
5. Doppler shift has potential automotive application for
   a. measuring the speed of passing trains
   b. automatic gear changing
   c. measuring vehicle speed over the road
   d. none of the above
6. The major problem associated with a practical low tire pressure sensor is
   a. developing a means of getting the electrical signal from the rotating sensor to the car body
   b. developing a sensor which can measure relative pressure
   c. absolute pressure calibration
   d. measuring tire pressure when the vehicle is stopped
7. A CRT has potential automotive application for
   a. controlling vehicle motion
   b. recording vehicle transient motion
   c. monitoring entertainment systems
   d. displaying information to the driver
8. The term HUD refers to
   a. housing and urban development
   b. heads up display
   c. heads up driver
   d. none of the above
9. Speech synthesis is
   a. a system which automatically recognizes human speech
   b. an automatic check-book balancing system
   c. a visual display of speech waveforms
   d. a means of electronically generating human speech

10. An optical fiber is
- **a.** a tiny beam of light
- **b.** an optical waveguide which is often called a light pipe
- **c.** an optical switch
- **d.** none of the above

11. An inertial navigation system incorporates the following sensors
- **a.** radio receivers
- **b.** doppler radar
- **c.** gyros and accelerometers
- **d.** none of the above

Glossary

A/F: See Air/Fuel Ratio.

Accumulator: The basic work register of a computer.

Actuator: A device which performs an action in response to an electrical signal.

A/D (also ADC): Analog-to-digital converter; a device which proportional to the analog voltage level input.

Analog Circuits: Electronic circuits which amplify, reduce or otherwise alter a voltage signal which is a smooth or continuous copy of some physical quantity.

Assembly Language: An abbreviated computer language which humans can use to program computers. Assembly language eventually is converted to machine language so that a computer can understand it.

BDC: Bottom dead center; the extreme lowest position of the piston during its stroke.

Bit: A binary digit; the smallest piece of data a computer can manipulate.

Block Diagram: A system diagram which shows all of the major parts and their interconnections.

BSCO: Brake specific CO; the ratio of the rate at which carbon monoxide leaves the exhaust pipe to the brake horsepower.

BSFC: Brake specific fuel consumption; the ratio of the rate at which fuel is flowing into an engine to the brake horsepower being generated.

BSHC: Brake specific HC; the ratio of the rate at which hydrocarbons leave the exhaust pipe to the brake horsepower.

$BSNO_x$: Brake specific NO_x; the ratio of the rate at which oxides of nitrogen leave the exhaust pipe to the brake horsepower.

Byte: 8 bits dealt with together.

CAFE: Corporate-Average-Fuel-Economy. The government mandated fuel economy which is averaged over the production for a year for any given manufacturer.

Capacitor: An electronic device which stores charge.

Catalyst: A material which speeds up or stimulates a chemical reaction.

Catalytic Converter: A device which enhances certain chemical reactions which help to reduce the levels of undesirable exhaust gases.

Closed-Loop Fuel Control: A mode where input air/fuel ratio is controlled by metering fuel response to the rich-lean indications from an exhaust gas oxygen sensor.

CO: Carbon monoxide; an undesirable chemical combustion product due to imperfect combustion.

Combinational Logic: Logic circuits whose outputs depend only on the present logic inputs.

Combustion: The burning of the fuel-air mixture in the cylinder.

Comparator, Analog: An electronic device which compares the voltages applied to its inputs.

Compression Ratio: The ratio of the cylinder volume at BDC to the volume at TDC.

Control Variable: The plant inputs and outputs which a control system manipulates and measures to properly control it.

Conversion Efficiency (Catalytic Converter): The efficiency with which undesirable exhaust gases are reduced to acceptable levels or are converted to desirable gases.

CPU: Central processing unit; the calculator portion of a computer.

Cutoff: A transistor operating mode where very little current flows between the collector and emitter.

D/A (also DAC): Digital-to-analog converter; a device which produces a voltage which is proportional to the digit input number.

Damping Coefficient: A parameter which affects a system's time response by making it more or less sluggish.

DEMUX: Demultiplexer; a type of electronic switch uses to select one of several output lines.

Diesel: A class of internal combustion engine in which combustion is initiated by the high temperature of the compressed air in the cylinder rather than an electrical spark.

Digital Circuits: Electronic circuits whose outputs can change only at specific instances and between a limited number of different voltages.

Diode: A semiconductor device which acts like a current check valve.

Display: A device which indicates in human readable form the result of measurement of some variable.

Drivetrain: The combination of mechanisms connecting the engine to the driving wheels including transmission, driveshaft, and differential.

Dwell: The time that current flows through the primary circuit of the ignition coil for each spark generation.

Dynamometer: A device for loading the engine and measuring engine performance.

EGO: Exhaust gas oxygen; the concentration of oxygen in the exhaust of an engine. An EGO sensor is used in closed-loop fuel control systems to indicate rich or lean A/F.

EGR: Exhaust gas recirculation; a procedure in which a portion of exhaust is introduced into the intake of an engine.

Electronic Carburetor: A fuel metering actuator in which the air/fuel ratio is controlled by continual variations of the metering rod position in response to an electronic control signal.

Engine Calibration: The values for air/fuel, spark advance and EGR at any operating condition.

Engine Crankshaft Position: The angular position of the crankshaft relative to a reference point.

Engine Mapping: A procedure of experimentally determining the performance of an engine at selected operating points and recording the results.

Equivalence Ratio: Actual air/fuel ratio divided by the air/fuel ratio at stoichiometry.

Evaporative Emissions: Evaporated fuel from the carburetor or fuel system which mixes with the surrounding air.

Foot-Pound: A unit of torque corresponding to a force of one pound acting on a one foot level arm.

Frequency Response: A graph of a system's response to different frequency input signals.

Gain: The ratio of a system's output magnitude to its input magnitude.

HC: Hydrocarbon chemicals, such as gasoline, formed by the union of carbon and hydrogen.

Ignition Timing: The time of occurrence of ignition measured in degrees of crankshaft rotation relative to TDC.

Inductor: A magnetic device which stores energy in a magnetic field produced by current flowing in it.

Instrumentation: Apparatus (often electronic) which is used for measurement or control, and for display of measurements or conditions.

Integral Amplifier: A control system component whose voltage output changes at a rate proportional to its input voltage.

Integrated Circuit: A semiconductor device which contains many circuit functions on a single chip.

Interrupts: An efficient method of quickly requesting a computer's attention to a particular external event.

Lead Term: A control system component which anticipates future inputs based on the current signal trend.

Limit Cycle: A mode of control system operation in which the controlled variable cycles between extreme limits with the average near the desired value.

Linear Region: A transistor operating mode where the collector current is proportional to the base current.

Logic Circuits: Digital electronic circuits which perform logical operations such as NOT, AND, OR, and combinations of these.

Lookup Table: A table in computer memory which is used to convert an important value into a related value from the table.

MAP: Manifold absolute pressure; the absolute pressure in the intake manifold of an engine.

Mathematical Model: A mathematical equation which can be used to numerically compute a system's response to a particular input.

Microcomputer: A small computer which uses an integrated circuit which contains a central processing unit and other control electronics.

MUX: Multiplexer; a type of electronic switch used to select one of several input lines.

NO_x: The various oxides of nitrogen.

Op Code: A number which a computer recognizes as an instruction.

Open-Loop Fuel Control: A mode where engine input air/fuel ratio is controlled by measuring the mass of input air and adding the proper mass of fuel to obtain a 14.7 to 1 ratio.

Operational Amplifier: A standard analog building block with two inputs, one output and a very high voltage gain.

Optimal Damping: The damping which produces the very best time response.

Peripheral: An external input-output device which is connected to a computer.

Phase Shift: A measure of the delay in degrees between the time a signal enters a system and the time it shows up at the output as a fraction of a full cycle of 360°.

Plant: A system which is to be controlled.

Proportional Amplifier: A control system component which produces a control output proportional to its input.

Qualitative Analysis: A study which reveals how a system works.

Quantitative Analysis: A study which determines how well a system performs.

RAM: Random access memory; read/write memory.

Random Error: A measurement error which is neither predictable nor correctable, but has some statitical nature to it.

ROM: Read only memory; permanent memory used to store permanent programs.

RPM: Revolutions per minute; the angular speed of rotation of the crankshaft of an engine or other rotating shaft.

Sample and Hold: The act of measuring a voltage at a particular time and storing that voltage until a new sample is taken.

Sampling: The act of periodically collecting or providing information about a particular process.

Semiconductor: A material which is neither a good conductor nor a good insulator.

Sensor: An energy conversion device which measures some physical quantity and converts it to an electrical quantity.

Sequential Logic: Logic circuits whose output depends on the particular sequence of the input logic signals.

SI Engine: Abbreviation for spark ignited, gasoline fueled, piston type, internal combustion engine.

Signal Processing: The alteration of an electrical signal by electronic circuitry; used to reduce the effects of systematic and random errors.

Skid: A condition in which the tires are sliding over the road surface rather than rolling; usually associated with braking.

Slip: The ratio of the angular speed of the driving element to the angular speed of the driven element of a torque converter; also, the condition in which a driven tire loses traction so that the driving torque does not produce vehicle motion.

Software: The computer program instructions used to tell a computer what to do.

Spark Advance: The number of degrees of crankshaft rotation before TDC where the spark plug is fired. (See ignition timing.)

Spark Timing: The process of firing the spark plugs at the proper moment to ignite the combustible mixture in the engine cylinders.

Stoichiometry: The air/fuel ratio for perfect combustion; it enables exactly all of the fuel to burn using exactly all of the oxygen in the air.

System: A collection of interacting parts.

Systematic Error: A measurement error in an instrumentation system which is predictable and correctable.

TBFI: Throttle-body-fuel-injector; a fuel metering actuator in which the air/fuel ratio is controlled by injecting precisely controlled spurts of fuel into the air stream entering the intake manifold.

TDC: Top dead center; the extreme highest point of the piston during its stroke.

Throttle Angle: The angle between the throttle plate and a reference line; engine speed increases as the angle increases.

Torque Converter: A form of fluid coupling used in an automatic transmission which acts like a torque amplifier.

Torque: The twisting force of the crankshaft or other driving shaft.

Transfer Function: A mathematical equation which, when graphed, produces a system's frequency response plot.

Transistor: An active semiconductor device which operates like a current valve.

Transport Delay: The time required for a given mass of fuel and air to travel from the intake manifold through the engine to the EGO sensor in the exhaust manifold.

Volumetric Efficiency: The pumping efficiency of the engine as air is drawn into the cylinders.

Answers to Quizzes

Chapter 1

1. c
2. a
3. b
4. d
5. b
6. b
7. c
8. b
9. a
10. a
11. a
12. d

Chapter 2

1. e
2. b
3. b
4. a
5. b
6. c
7. b
8. d
9. d
10. d

Chapter 3

1. a
2. c
3. b
4. a
5. c
6. b
7. d
8. e
9. b
10. d
11. b
12. d
13. b
14. a
15. d
16. c
17. b
18. d
19. c
20. a

Chapter 4

1. d
2. d
3. c
4. a
5. e
6. b
7. d
8. c
9. b
10. a
11. b
12. c
13. d
14. b
15. a
16. b
17. b
18. d
19. d

Chapter 5

1. a
2. c
3. a
4. b
5. b
6. d
7. c
8. a
9. b
10. a
11. b
12. d
13. a
14. a
15. b
16. d
17. a
18. c
19. b
20. d

Chapter 6

1. c
2. c
3. d
4. b
5. b
6. a
7. c
8. c
9. a
10. c
11. c
12. a
13. c
14. c
15. a
16. d
17. a
18. b
19. c
20. a

Chapter 7

1. d
2. a
3. b
4. d
5. b
6. b
7. c
8. c
9. d
10. b
11. d
12. c
13. d
14. a

Chapter 8

1. b
2. c
3. a
4. b
5. d
6. a
7. b
8. b
9. a
10. a
11. d

Chapter 9

1. a
2. c
3. c
4. c
5. a
6. c
7. c
8. a
9. c
10. d
11. a
12. a
13. a
14. b
15. c
16. b
17. a
18. c
19. c

Chapter 10

1. d
2. b
3. d
4. c
5. d
6. d
7. d
8. a
9. b
10. b

Chapter 11

1. d
2. a
3. a
4. b
5. c
6. a
7. d
8. b
9. d
10. b
11. c

Index